THE WHOLE HORSE CATALOG

STEVEN D. PRICE, EDITORIAL DIRECTOR
BARBARA BURN, DAVID A. SPECTOR and GAIL RENTSCH
ILLUSTRATIONS by WERNER RENTSCH

SIMON AND SCHUSTER   NEW YORK

Published by Simon and Schuster
A Division of Gulf & Western Corporation
Simon & Schuster Building
Rockefeller Center
1230 Avenue of the Americas
New York, New York 10020

Designed by Werner Rentsch
Manufactured in the United States of America

2 3 4 5 6 7 8 9 10

Library of Congress Cataloging in Publication Data

Main entry under title:

The Whole horse catalog.

Includes index.

1. Horses.　2. Horsemanship.　I. Price, Steven D.
SF285.W63　1977　　　636.1　　　77-15468
ISBN 0-671-22636-3
ISBN 0-671-22692-4 Pbk.

CONTENTS

INTRODUCTION vii

1. SELECTING A HORSE 1
Colors and Markings 1
Where to Look 4
Assessing Individual Horses 6
The Purchase 9
Insurance 10
Joint Ownership 10
Breed Associations 10

2. STABLING 16
What Kind of Horse-Keeping
  Arrangement is Right? 16
The Remuda 17
Field Keeping 17
Sheds and Free-Access Shelters 18
Stables 19
Rings and Arenas 35
Fencing 37

3. STABLE MANAGEMENT 40
Basic Care 40
Feeding 42
Exercising 50
Bedding 51
Grooming 53
Horseshoeing 60

4. HORSE HEALTH 65
Soundness in Horses 65
Routine Preventive Care 67
EIA and the Coggins Test Controversy 82
The Horse in Trouble: Problems
  and Treatments 84
Special Medical Problems 105
  Gelding 105
  Breeding a Mare 107
  Raising a Foal 110

5. TACK 112
Bits 112
Bridles 119
Supplements to the Bit 124
Saddles 127
  English Saddles 128
  Western Saddles 133
  Packsaddle 138
Supplements to the Saddle 139
Halters 144

Harness 146
Saddle Pads 148
Blankets 149
Tack for Specialized Training 150
Protective Equipment 152

6. APPAREL 155
The History of Apparel for Horsemen 155
Boots 157
Pants 164
Shirts 170
Vests 171
Coats 172
Gloves 175
Hats 177
Sticks 180
Spurs 182
Miscellaneous Accessories 183
Special Notes on Buying
   Riding Apparel 185
Dress Requirements 186

7. EQUESTRIAN ACTIVITIES 189
Horse Shows 189
Dressage 198
Rodeos 201
Polo 202
Combined Training 205
Fox Hunting 207
Driving 211
Gymkhanas 211
Distance Riding 217
Horse Transportation 218

8. EQUESTRIAN VACATIONS 224
The United States and Canada 224
Dude Ranching and Pack Tripping 225
Riding Resorts 226
Summer Camps 226
International 229

9. ORGANIZATIONS 236
Magazines 236
Equine Humane Movements 237
Future Farmers of America 238
Pony Clubs 238
Intercollegiate Horse Show
   Association 239
Catalogs 241

INDEX 244

INTRODUCTION

Half a century ago as the internal-combustion engine gave a new meaning to the word "horsepower," most people predicted that the horse would go the way of the dinosaur and the dodo. Progress, they called it, as they watched automobiles, trucks, and tractors push beasts of burden and transportation off roads and fields. But that did not happen. Although the equine population was indeed reduced, it was by no means eliminated as a vital aspect of national life.

Recently, equestrian activities have begun to stage a renascence. Like tennis ten years ago and skiing a decade before, horse-related sports are coming into full flower. Public and private stables and clubs, horseback resorts, and backyard barns are springing up all over the United States and Canada. So is attendance at shows, rodeos, and other spectator events. The result is staggering. More than ten million pleasure horses are the beneficiaries, as are manufacturers and retailers of equestrian products and services to the tune of a nine-billion-dollar-a-year industry. Although it's impossible to determine the precise number of human participants, it must be at least several million, and it's growing steadily. Every year another crop of horse-crazy youngsters comes along, joined by their seniors who are also discovering the excitement and satisfaction of the equestrian world.

All horsemen and horsewomen, whether occasional riders or full-time professionals, share an urge to know as much as they can about equestrian products, services, and organizations. Toward that end, they're inveterate and voracious readers. Tack-shop catalogs and manufacturers' brochures are well-thumbed fixtures in homes and barns. Advertisements and product analyses are major features in magazines, while almost every newspaper's classified section contains columns of horses, tack, and trailers for sale.

One purpose of *The Whole Horse Catalog* is to present the wide range of products, services, organizations, and events available to owners, trainers, riders, drivers, and spectators. In that regard, this book is not very different from a complete catalog or magazine. But another, and we think more important, goal is to lead you through the maze of what's available by explaining what can be of best use and interest for your own purposes. For example, tack-shop catalogs and counters display dozens of kinds of snaffle bits, yet they don't go into the items' relative merits and applicability. On the other hand, hoof picks are rather self-explanatory, but you'll need to know how to use one properly. *The Whole Horse Catalog* covers these subjects, and many more.

Each chapter contains general textual material, followed by discussions and descriptions of products or services. To include all the hundreds of thousands of horse-related items was an impossibility, but we tried to mention those which seem most useful, accessible, and interesting or, with regard to particular value, well worth seeking out. We obtained the information by writing and talking to producers and retailers and by making our own observations (helped in many instances by expert consultants). We neither sought nor received any promotional consideration; any logos or advertisements that appear are for decorative purposes only or to accompany our independently determined references. The balance of the material is essays on a variety of subjects by several contributors. Then too, none of us—and we hope, none of you—could resist the anecdotes, quotations, and trivia scattered throughout.

As originally envisioned, *The Catalog* was going to say everything about everything horsey. That naive yet optimistic approach has been somewhat altered. We omitted material on equestrian techniques (i.e., how to ride or drive) and on racing, since such sizable subjects are better left to specialists. We also left out decorative items like glassware, stationery, and bumper stickers; you can find such things on your own quite easily.

There are at least twenty thousand tack shops and outlets in the United States and Canada. To list all was out of the question. We do, however, refer to many that do substantial mail-order business and/or provide specialized products. Far from intending to slight others, we strongly recommend that you regard your local tack shop as the primary place to find and purchase your needs.

That brings us to prices. What with runaway (or at least galloping) inflation, prices vary from area to area, and they rise with every flip of the calendar. We mention approximate prices and/or ranges; manufacturers and retailers are the ultimate source of what an item or service will cost.

A way in which we hope this book will be of special value is to point out the interdisciplinary uses of equestrian gear. At a time when Western horses are schooled in dressage and when open jumpers compete in hackamores, all trainers and riders can profit from equipment once considered the exclusive property of "those other" styles. Read, inspect, evaluate, and experiment—just as we did and continue to do. We'd like to hear from you about products, services, and organizations you've come across. Write to Brigadore Press, c/o Simon and Schuster, 1230 Avenue of the Americas, Rockefeller Center, New York, N.Y. 10020, and perhaps we can include your findings in future editions of *The Whole Horse Catalog.*

The idea for this book popped up in September, 1975. On the way home from a local tack shop, its catalog jutting out of a package, I stopped off at a bookstore. A table there was laden with oversized paperback source books which had been published in the wake and manner of *The Whole Earth Catalog.* "Hmm," I mused. "If there are arts catalogs, crafts catalogs, and even a *Catalogue of Catalogues,* why not a horse catalog?"

Bill Steinkraus was the most likely person to sound out about the project. In addition to his involvement with the U.S. Equestrian Team, Bill had recently become a senior editor at Simon and Schuster. His reaction smacked of a good news/bad news joke. Yes, such a source book was a fine idea. No, the undertaking would be too complicated for S and S to produce. Why didn't I find some other people with whom to package the book?

David A. Spector, who has the good sense to hold down a day job as a partner in an important brokerage house, also writes books and articles about horses. He had told me that he'd like to become involved with *The Catalog* if it ever got out of the starting gate— and did he ever! Dave's business expertise was essential in the formation of Brigadore Press.* His experience in owning show horses highly qualified him to do the section on activities, while Dave's friendship with many noted members of the equestrian community brought forth others to consult and write for the book.

Barbara Burn, an editor at The Viking Press, once introduced herself as "someone who as a child outfitted a shed in her parents' backyard as a stable for the horse they never bought her." Indefatigably enthusiastic about riding and the resident expert on the packaging of books, Barbara opted for the chapters on apparel and equine health, the latter since her husband is a veterinarian.

Gail Rentsch, publicity manager of Macmillan Publishing Company, has a farm in upstate New York where three horses reside. She was the likely choice to write on stabling, stable management, and tack.

Werner Rentsch, noted equestrian artist, agreed to supply the pasture's visual dimension.

I assumed the role of a "Whinny the Pooh-Bah," Lord High Everything Else, designated to tell the world about selecting a horse, fox hunting, and taking horseback vacations.

We did our homework and presented a proposal to Simon and Schuster. Bill Steinkraus responded to our periodic inquiries about its progress with considerable patience. Yes, his editorial colleagues liked the idea (we suspected that we had a friend in editor-in-chief Michael Korda, whose office looks like the annex of a saddlery shop). So did the sales people. No, the production people hadn't yet vetted our design and layout figures. Keep going, Bill urged; and we did.

We sent out letters of inquiry to manufacturers and retailers, to tack shops and magazine publishers. No breeder, trainer, veterinarian, blacksmith, or any other horse person we encountered was safe from having his or her brain hoof-picked for information and further leads. Much to our surprise and gratitude, unsolicited suggestions came in as news of the project circulated. Letters and phone calls put us on to people and articles, some in unlikely places but all helpful. The more we read, talked, and listened, the more we found, not only in our primary areas of responsibility but also in others, so that editorial meetings became horsey show-and-tell and swapping sessions.

When Simon and Schuster finally made an offer, it was only for the text and illustrations; the publisher had decided to produce the book itself. Our response was unbridled glee. *The Catalog* had become too massive a project for us to want to be saddled with the packaging load. S and S made Brigadore an offer, and after a bit of publishing horse tradin', *The Whole Horse Catalog* was accepted at full board.

* Brigadore, by the way, was Sir Guyon's horse in Spenser's *The Faerie Queene.* The word means "golden bridle," the animal was stoned by the character Braggadochio, and both aspects seemed eminently appropriate.

ACKNOWLEDGMENTS

William C. Steinkraus, founder of the feast, receives Brigadore's cheers, an enthusiasm equal to the acclamation he received in the show ring throughout his illustrious career.

Alexander Mackay-Smith, International Editor of *The Chronicle of the Horse* and former master of foxhounds, shared his encyclopedic knowledge with avuncular counsel and fraternal generosity.

Marilyn Mackay-Smith, who as "Gamecock" has had her fine photographs published in many equestrian books and magazines. Their presence here graces *The Whole Horse Catalog*.

Michael Cody and Anthony D'Ambrosio, Jr., good friends of the Brigadore team, were sources of invaluable practical information on horse selection, care, and competition.

Charles Kauffman, of H. Kauffman and Sons, who knows the world about catalogs, helped us with ours.

Jerry Trapani, a fine farrier and the owner of an upcoming dressage prospect named Busman's Holiday, provided us with helpful advice about shoeing horses and some good looks at the horse from the feet up.

Emil P. Dolensek, D.V.M., Chief Veterinarian at the Bronx Zoo and Honorary Veterinarian for the New York City Police Department, helpfully vetted the health chapter and gave a lot of moral support.

Carlos Marban of Sunnyfield Farm in Bedford, New York, a fine horseman in every sense of the word—trainer, rider, and teacher extraordinaire—gave us encouragement and advice.

Rita Rottkamp, teacher, neighbor, and horse owner, lent us books and a lot of good stories.

Bill Decker, the only editor in New York City with a lariat in his office desk, a tack room in his city apartment, and working experience on several ranches and polo fields, gave us invaluable tips about tack, apparel, and riding and roping techniques.

Hank Vogel of E. Vogel, master bootmakers, answered a lot of pertinent and impertinent questions with patience and good advice.

Mary Dee English, who breaks and trains her own dressage horses, is an equestrian artist and the contributor of the charming and instructive essay on "Painting Your Own Horse."

Catherine McWilliams, instructor at Bear Ridge Riding Club in Pleasantville, New York, has been successfully involved with dressage, combined training, hunter exhibition, and the Pony Club. We appreciate all her assistance.

Fred A. Brill, of the Hamilton Travel Service, provided much material on equestrian vacations.

Reid Graham, who comes from a noted polo family, played for the University of Virginia and is now a law student. His family home is a mallet stroke away from the Ox Ridge Hunt Club.

Sarijane "Sassy" Stanton, who admits to being over 25, has been entangled with horses for many years. Her best to date was the famed hunter Circuit Breaker, whom she wishes she hadn't sold.

William P. Brayton, horseman, valued friend and teacher, has that incurable disease known as horse fever, and he managed to infect some very grateful people.

Dean Peters, a Quarter Horse man, can curse his horse and scratch it behind the ear at the same time, but that's probably to be expected from a guy who's tasted a first-timer's piggin' string.

Allegro, an old Palomino who has put up with dummies and eager children with a saintly patience and good humor, discovered in his later years that elementary jumping and even an occasional two-track while jogging along the trails are okay.

William G. Robertson, owner of Winter's Gone Ranch in Humble, Texas, was a member of the U.S. Equestrian Team in the early 1960s. Bill is now a leading professional, and he and his wife, Patty, ship horses hundreds of thousands of miles every year to compete on various show circuits.

Robert Heath, international horseman, musician, and television commentator, is Secretary of the American Driving Society.

Michael Korda, Gypsy da Silva, and their Simon and Schuster colleagues saw this project through from its foaling to the starting gate.

And finally, everyone who offered information, advice, and encouragement. We regret, as well as delight, to say that there were far too many for us to be able to name all of them individually.

STEVEN D. PRICE
Editorial Director
Brigadore Press, Inc.

1 SELECTING A HORSE

The process of selecting a horse should be simplicity itself. You determine what kind you want, take a look at what's available, and then choose the best animal you can find. Although this process seems easy on paper, unfortunately horses aren't found on paper. They're obtained from breeders, race tracks, dealers, and private owners under a variety of conditions. Moreover, animals come in all kinds of shapes and sizes, ages and conditions, genders and temperaments. Cost, too, must be taken into account.

No one goes into the business of selecting a horse completely blind,* at least to the extent of not having any idea why he wants an animal. You will know ahead of time whether you plan to do pleasure riding, ranch work, or distance riding. Perhaps you're interested in driving, combined training, or some other form of competition, and if so, you'll already have some idea in what classes you'd like to show—such as hunter/jumper, saddle seat, or Western stock seat. Whatever the case, your choice of activity has both pointed you toward certain breeds and types (e.g., Thoroughbreds, Trakeheners, or Hanoverians for dressage) and eliminated others (a Hackney is as unlikely for three-day eventing as a Clydesdale would be for cutting cattle).

But since there's such a wide range of horses suitable for so many equestrian purposes, your first step in deciding what kind to look for would be to gather some information. Start with what you already learned as a participant and spectator; then talk to owners and, in the case of competition horses, exhibitors.

With regard to printed matter, breed registries and associations will supply material ranging from professionally prepared brochures to handwritten letters (depending on the organization's size and financial resources). Keep in mind that registries and associations are in the business of singing their animals' praises. Most emphasize versatility, from excellence in the show ring to a flair for differential calculus, so read these publications critically.

General books tend to go into a breed's history and present activities in greater detail and with a little less hype. You might also want to check into books recommended in this *Catalog*'s chapters on specific equestrian sports to see what kind of horses are recommended.

COLORS AND MARKINGS

In the course of your research and observation, you'll come across a veritable Joseph's coat of equine hues and markings. Some colorations define particular breeds or types, while others can be found in many breeds.

COLORS

albino A pure white coat, genetically a result of a mutation. (As with mice and other species, equine albinos have blue or pink eyes).

appaloosa Characterized by a large light-colored patch (or blanket) on the hindquarters on which are darker markings. A *leopard* appaloosa is light gray with dots of one or two darker colors all over the body—something of an equine Dalmatian.

bay A brown coat with black mane and tail.

black A solid black coat with or without white markings.

brown A coat that is darker than chestnut. (If there is any doubt in distinguishing color, as between, for example, chestnut and brown or brown and black, the color of hairs on the horse's muzzle controls.)

buckskin A tan to light-brown coat with a black stripe along the spine.

chestnut A reddish-brown coat with mane and tail of the same color. A *liver* chestnut has a lighter mane and tail.

dun A tan to light-brown coat; a buckskin without the dorsal stripe.

gray A mixture of black and white hairs. A *dapple* gray has mottled markings of a darker shade.

palomino A coat of yellow with a white mane and tail over a black skin. The most prized palominos, such as Roy Rogers' Trigger, approximate the color of a newly minted gold coin.

pinto (or *paint*) A coat with patches of white and another color. *Piebald* describes a black-and-white combination; *skewbald* is brown and white. Another distinction is *overo* (a darker coat with white patches), as opposed to *tobiano* (white with colored patches).

---

* Some people have selected completely blind horses, but we'll show you how to minimize that possibility.

roan A coat composed of white and colored (any but black) hairs. *Strawberry roan* is a combination of chestnut and white; *blue roan* is dark gray and white; and *bay roan* is dark brown and white.

sorrel A Western term for chestnut.

white Properly, the word is "albino." It is also something of a shorthand word for light gray, as in describing a piebald as a horse with a black-and-white-patched coat.

MARKINGS

This denotes certain white patterns, most often on blacks, browns, bays, and chestnuts.

bald A facial patch covering one or both eyes.

blaze A marking starting on the forehead and extending down the muzzle.

girth mark A spot behind the foreleg.

saddle mark A spot behind the withers.

snip An isolated spot near the nostril.

sock A marking from hoof to fetlock.

star A mark on the forehead.

stocking A marking from hoof extending to the knee.

stripe A narrow band extending the length of the face.

further information: The Color of Horses by Ben K. Green (Northland) opinionated and often plumb wrong, is always lively. Doc Green was a Texas veterinarian who did a considerable amount of research into coloration and conformation. A colorful, crusty man, Green wrote several books about buying and selling horses full of anecdotes about the shady side of horse tradin'. Although they're out of print, search out *Horse Tradin', More Horse Tradin', Wild Cow Tales,* and *Village Horse Doctor* at libraries and secondhand-book stores. All were published by Knopf.

OTHER FACTORS

Now we move to more general factors in selecting a horse. Much of this category relates to personal considerations in terms of what you'll need in the way of an animal.

SIZE.

A small child on a horse 16+ hands high or a tall adult on a pony will feel as awkward as they look. Horses and ponies to be used under saddle would be well matched to their riders. In the case of youngsters, our British cousins start them off on ponies. Then as the kids grow, they are moved up to horses.

Draft (or cold-blooded)

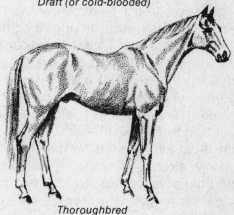

Thoroughbred

Morgan

Grade pony

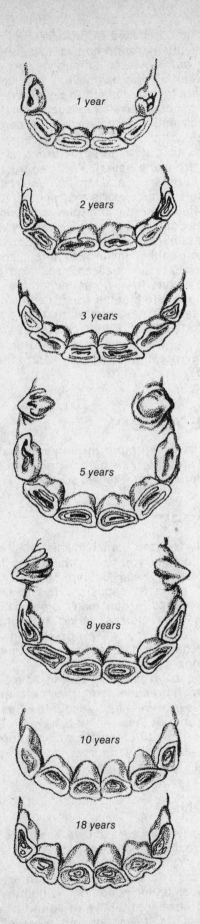

1 year

2 years

3 years

5 years

8 years

10 years

18 years

GENDER.

A horse's sex (or lack thereof) directly affects its temperament and, accordingly, its performance. Stallions (also known as studs) are characteristically testy, the reason why female riders and drivers have traditionally been barred from showing them in certain classes. Mares can be equally difficult when they go into heat (every twenty-one days is the cycle), and if there's a stallion, the mutual urge to go tandem can prove overpowering.

Geldings are males that have been altered—an operation that produces equine equanimity. Most colts are gelded almost as a matter of course just because people tend to want horses with stable temperaments. Of course, if you're planning to breed your horse, it will need its faculties unimpaired, and a stallion's bloodlines will be a strong factor in the decision to cut or not to cut. (See page 105 for more information on the gelding procedure.)

AGE.

One of the great rewarding joys of the horse world is to "bring along"—to break and school—a young horse. On the other hand, unless you have the time, facilities, and know-how, an older animal will be a better choice. As with other species, age brings with it a certain maturity of temperament (unless the animal has been mistreated or is a congenital rogue). A horse that's too old, however, has its future behind it, and you shouldn't consider asking one over the age of twenty to perform strenuous tasks.

Unless valid registration papers accompany a horse, the way to determine age is by examining teeth. The following chart and illustrations show how to do it.

Age	Characteristics of Teeth
2½ years	Permanent central incisors appear.
3½ years	Permanent second incisors appear.
4½ years	Permanent third incisors appear; canine teeth (in males and some females) appear.
6 years	Cups (indentations) in central incisors disappear.
7 years	Cups of second incisors disappear.
8 years	Cups of third incisors disappear.
9–10 years	Tops of central incisors appear rectangular.
11–12 years	Tops of central incisors appear oval.
13–14 years	Tops of central incisors appear triangular.
15 years	A groove ("Galvayne's groove") appears in the third incisor.
17 years	The groove extends halfway down the third incisor.
20 years	The groove extends the length of the third incisor.

5 years   7 years   20 years

"Bishoping" (probably named after an unscrupulous horse trader) is the process of altering teeth to try to make a horse look younger. The equivalent of turning back a car's odometer, bishoping can involve the use of a hot iron or drill to recreate incisor cups or to stain the cups (often using apple juice and peels) to obtain an appropriate color.

EXPERIENCE.

Age is just one small factor in this area, since an older horse hasn't necessarily had the training and opportunity to perform to qualify it as "experienced." Again, some people will want to bring a green horse along, but others will want to buy a "made" animal.

If the latter is your goal, especially for a competition horse, you can check blue-ribbon lists or observe the animal in action during a polo match, calf-roping event, or driving trial. Then approach the horse's owner with an offer. You should realize, of course, that you'll be paying top dollar for a top horse, and the purchase price will include what his owner could make in the future with the animal as well as the time and expense invested in the horse's training.

A horse's experience can also work against him in another discipline, even though the animal comes with ribbons, pedigree, and letters of recommendation that would impress a Rhodes Scholarship committee. Just a few case histories will make this point clear. One horse was purchased from the show ring to be used as a pleasure horse. The several months required to teach the animal to negotiate unlevel terrain weren't much of a pleasure. Another, trained as a cow pony, had been taught never to cross a fence. When sent East and asked to jump even a low fence, the horse refused. And refused again, almost requiring a lobotomy to overcome his basic training. Moral: You can lead a horse to a new activity, but he may take a while—if not forever—to respond.

A Note About Experts. Now that you're about to go out in search of a horse, it's time to spend a few moments assessing your own capabilities in that area. Although it's one thing to be able to distinguish a hock from a hip, relying on limited knowledge is quite another. That is, unless in all candor you feel thoroughly confident about your knowledge of horseflesh (based on experience), you'd do well to enlist the services of an expert. That person might be a riding instructor, a stable manager, another kind of professional, or anyone else who's been around horses for a long time. An expert is *not,* however, someone who rides only once a week or who has never had a horse of his own to care for. In addition to an experienced eye, the expert should have a realistic understanding of your needs and a complete degree of objectivity (the latter criterion means no incentive to persuade you to buy a horse in order to receive a kickback from the seller). With regard to money, some experts may accompany you as a favor, while others some experts may accompany you as a favor, while others will require a fee. In the case of a professional's judgment, it's money well spent.

A necessary expert is a veterinarian—a doctor who is thoroughly familiar with horses and not one who specializes in small animals. You can learn the name of one from horse owners in your area, and as you talk to him, be sure to explain how you plan to use your purchase so that the vet can examine it in that light. If the vet doesn't accompany you when you scour the highways for horses, he'll look at any possible prospects soon after you locate them.

WHERE TO LOOK

Armed with background information and accompanied by an expert, it's time to go out in search of a horse. Here are the likeliest sources.

BREEDERS.

Organizations listed earlier in this chapter will be delighted to refer you to members who have animals for sale. These people also advertise in equestrian journals, especially those devoted to particular breeds. Since many breeders are also exhibitors, their horses range from top show horses to "culls" (culls are non-show-quality animals). Breeders tend to have young animals—foals and yearlings.

Speaking of yearlings, yearling sales are auctions to which breeders bring their colts and fillies. We've all seen newspaper accounts of astronomical sums some of these animals have brought, but it's also possible to pick up a well-conformed and otherwise attractive youngster for less than what Secretariat's get-set fetches.

AUCTIONS.

If yearling sales are auto shows, livestock auctions are used-car lots, and they tend to be classic examples of "You pays your money and you takes your chance." Horses sold at auction are seldom salable under better conditions, whether because they aren't terribly attractive or sound or because their owners don't want to put more effort into their disposition. However, more than a handful of equine nuggets have been located in this fashion.

One that appealed to Rodney Jenkins and Bernie Traurig turned out to be hell on wheels to load into a trailer after he was purchased. Never losing his bad temper, Sloopy went on to international stardom on the United States Equestrian Team. More often than not, however, auction horses are candidates less for the Olympics than for dog food.

Auctions seldom allow much opportunity for testing a horse, but that procedure is essential anywhere and especially here. Show up early to look over the lot. If any strike your fancy, arrange to try them out, if only by trotting once around the parking lot. (A few bucks slipped to an auction's stable hand will facilitate matters.) If you continue to like what you see, and your expert agrees, make a bid. Return privileges depend on the auction's policy. Usually there's none, unless you can subsequently produce a vet's certificate saying the purchase is diseased or unsound.

RACETRACKS AND TRAINING CENTERS.

Many Thoroughbreds and Standardbreds have been reclaimed from racing and gone on to successful careers in other disciplines. The best method to explore this source is through a trainer. He'll know what animals are for sale, and he may also be candid about their injuries and other problems (since it's possible to race horses at many tracks and in the cheapest of company, animals for sale in this way are usually beset by all sorts of wind, leg, and other disabilities). Racers also need to be acclimated to civilian life, as in the case of one man who started buying Thoroughbreds off the track to turn them into hunters and jumpers. Without realizing that racehorses are trained to break from the starting gate when they hear the bell, he installed a telephone in one of his barns. At the first phone call, the barn's occupants, in a response that would have made Pavlov grin from ear to ear, crashed through their doors and hightailed it across the countryside.

DEALERS.

Dealers specialize in buying and selling horses. They either own the animals or act as brokers for those who do. You'll find their names in magazine advertisements and telephone directories, as well as by inquiry at public and private stables, tack shops, and feed stores, and at rodeos, horse shows, and other events.

A telephone call in advance will set up an appointment and will also alert a dealer to your requirements. Tell him about your past and present equestrian career, future hopes, and more mundane matters such as what you can afford to spend. Even if the dealer doesn't have a likely prospect in his barn, he may be able to get one on consignment or refer you elsewhere (he'll receive a finder's fee in the event a sale is made).

Horse dealers don't always enjoy the world's best reputations. Their daily bread comes from turning over a supply of merchandise, so be prepared for a hard-sell approach. Restrain your enthusiasm, heed your expert, and generally conduct yourself in a businesslike manner.

PRIVATE SALES.

Hundreds of thousands of horses change hands every year through nonprofessional deals. Sources include conversations with veterinarians, blacksmiths, and feed dealers (who may be familiar with an animal's condition, temperament, and abilities). Other ways to learn of available animals are newspaper and magazine advertisements and signs on stable or tack-shop bulletin boards. We've all seen them: "OWNER GOING TO COLLEGE," "HORSE SADLY OUTGROWN," or "MOVING TO ANOTHER CITY." But the fact that you might be buying from a nonprofessional shouldn't mean that you can be unprofessional. Don't be led on by a low price without the same kind of assessment you'd give to a prospect being sold by a dealer.

A Note About Gift Horses: What if Uncle Charley wants to give the kids a Christmas present in the form of a real live horse, or those nice people down the road are willing to give away their family's equine pet? The offer may be tempting, but look such gift horses in the mouth as well as all over. An animal that isn't suitable will be a liability, not an asset, no matter how little it costs. In the case of Uncle Charley, let him read this book: perhaps a piece of tack or a scholarship for riding lessons would be a better present. Your neighbors should understand enough about horses to accept a firm but polite "No, thank you" as a response if their animal isn't what you're looking for.

Gift horses are sometimes available from urban and county police departments. Mounted units occasionally give away retired animals, and a letter to the departments will put you on their lists. Police horses are put up for adoption when they're about twenty years old, and if your facility is approved, you'll be the recipient of a well-schooled, savvy animal not suitable for hard work but excellent for safe pleasure riding.

~~~~~~~~~~~~~~~~~~~~~~~~~~~~~~~~~

Shakespeare on the "perfect" horse:

Round-hoof'd, short-jointed, fetlocks shag and long,
Broad breast, full eye, small head, and nostril wide,
High crest, short ears, straight legs and passing
*   strong,*
Thin mane, thick tail, broad buttock, tender
*   hide:*
Look, what a horse should have he did not lack,
Save a proud rider on so proud a back.
Venus and Adonis.
~~~~~~~~~~~~~~~~~~~~~~~~~~~~~~~~~

ASSESSING INDIVIDUAL HORSES

The way to judge specific candidates is in terms of conformation, temperament, movement, and condition.

CONFORMATION.

This word describes how an individual horse compares with certain ideal physical standards that characterize a particular breed or type. The process is more than a beauty contest; in the course of seeing how an animal is "put together," you'll be able to estimate how its features (and combinations of features) will influence its performance. Although precise points vary from breed to breed, all well-conformed horses share certain attributes.

- The *head* should be well formed, with responsive eyes and ears. Although a Roman nose (convex between eyes and nostrils) is a feature of mustangs and several draft breeds, some people deem it a mark of stupidity. Wide nostrils permit unimpeded breathing. A horse with an extended upper lip is said to have a "parrot mouth," an extended lower lip is a "salmon mouth," and neither is terribly attractive. A rogue or sluggard is somehow betrayed by its expression, so look for an overall impression of alertness and intelligence.
- Since the *neck* is used for balance, one too long or too short will impair optimum performance at extended gaits or in jumping. A "ewe neck," one wider at the poll than at the withers, forces a horse to carry its head at an awkward angle and makes collection difficult.
- Among parts of the *forequarters,* the shoulder is a most important factor. A sloping, powerful shoulder is the mark of a good galloper; a straighter one (less than 45 degrees) is preferred for Western and harness horses. Well-defined, prominent withers allow a suitable length of shoulder muscles. If the withers are too low, keeping a saddle in place will be difficult. If they are too high, fitting a saddle will be a problem, and the horse may be prone to sores. A large chest and rib cage in proportion to the animal's size provide room for healthy lungs and a "big" heart.
- *Hindquarters* should be rounded and well muscled. Long backs afford more comfortable rides under saddle, but short backs are the mark of greater power. In either case, the coupling (the space between the last rib and the point of hip) should be short. A swayback, usually a sign of age, interferes with fluid movement and makes a saddle difficult to fit.
- *Legs* should be tapered and free of blemishes. Forearms and gaskins should be wide, and cannons and hocks should be solid. Pasterns absorb shock, so they should be neither too straight nor too sloping (as a rule of thumb, pasterns should be at the same angle as the shoulder).
- Good *feet* are extremely important, since they bear the brunt of any kind of performance. The soles of forefeet should be round and flat, while those of hind feet should be slightly elliptical. The outsides of the hooves should be smooth and resilient, firm enough to retain shoes.

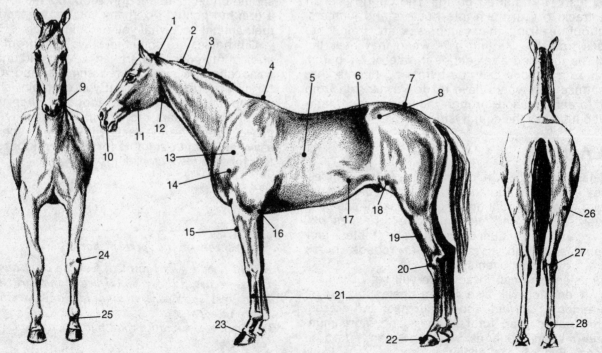

1. poll 2. mane 3. crest 4. withers 5. ribs 6. loin 7. croup 8. point of hip 9. nostril 10. muzzle 11. cheek 12. throatlatch 13. shoulder 14. point of shoulder 15. forearm 16. point of elbow 17. flank 18. stifle 19. gaskin 20. hock 21. cannon 22. hoof 23. coronet 24. knee 25. pastern 26. thigh 27. point of hock 28. fetlock

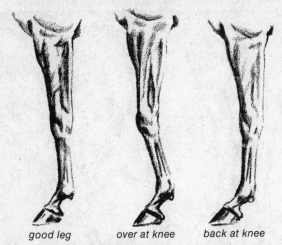

good leg   *over at knee*   *back at knee*

How individual features stand in relation to others is of equal importance. For example, when the horse is viewed from the front or rear, its legs should be well set apart so that the animal is standing squarely. "Cow" hocks bend toward each other, "sickle" hocks bend apart, and neither permit a horse to carry weight to best advantage. Standing "over at the knee" is preferable to "back at the knee," yet a horse whose legs hang down well is best of all. Good proportion is most highly prized, with no feature standing out as a glaring fault.

A NOTE ABOUT CONFORMATION.

This side of the Platonic ideal of the horse, perfectly conformed animals are few and far between. Most have at least one imperfection, if not an outright deformity, and many are collections of conformation faults.

When asked when conformation faults become rejectable disabilities, several big-league riders and trainers were agreed: only when they affect performance. Then too, it's a matter of degree. One sickle hock, a bit of a Roman nose, or pigeon toes or paddle feet aren't a ground on which to dismiss a horse completely, except perhaps for model-conformation classes. There's no hard-and-fast formula—there are just rules of reason and good sense. To complicate matters, the experts referred to horses that had overcome faults and problems, going on to great success. Forego, the great racehorse, has the legs of a Joe Namath, yet emulating the football player, the animal has achieved the equine equivalent of Super Bowl fame. Several open jumpers and Olympic show-jumping mounts aren't much to look at, but they get the job done.

There's a considerable difference between assessing a green horse and assessing one that's already performing. Untried prospects are unknown quantities, so textbook conformation considerations become important indications toward future success. On the other hand, one trainer pointed out that "I'll look at any horse that's been winning consistently, even if it has three legs and the heaves." The statement may be a bit extreme, but

the implication is clear: overcoming handicaps is always a possibility.

Further information:
The Anatomy of a Horse by Robert F. Way and
   Donald G. Lee (Lippincott)
Horse Conformation by Ben K. Green (Northland)
The Points of the Horse by M. Horace Hayes (Arco)

TEMPERAMENT.

Start evaluating this factor as soon as the horse is led into view. How does it react to contact with humans and its surroundings? Any biting, kicking, shying? Does the animal stand quietly yet alertly while its conformation is being assessed, appearing like neither a candidate for a straitjacket nor a basket case? Experienced horsemen can cope with tough customers, while other people want a more mannerly animal.

Check the horse's stall to look for cribbing (biting on wooden fixtures), kicking, and other indication of an unhappy lodger. Cribbing may be a consequence of boredom, but it can also be the sign of a horse with serious respiratory problems.

MOVEMENT.

A horse in action provides a way to learn about its attitude as well as its athletic ability. Watch how it goes in hand. Does it move easily and in a workmanlike fashion? As it trots, look to see whether it interferes (bumping forelegs or hind legs) or forges (striking a foreleg with a hind leg).

As the seller tacks up and mounts the horse, watch to see how the animal responds to the process. As you ask the seller to work the horse at all gaits and in both directions, confer with your expert. Does the horse move freely and respond to simple aids? Then as you climb into the saddle, confirm your preliminary reactions. Depending on the animal's training, how does it respond to your aids? Do you like its gaits? Any doubts can be resolved by your expert companion, who should be willing to try out the horse while you observe and heed his reactions.

Special requirements mandate specialized testing. A horse to be used for jumping should be tried over a few fences, while draft and driving candidates need to be assessed in harness. Don't expect the world from a green horse, but also don't settle for any animal that shows no aptitude for what you want.
A Note on Testing a Horse.

One expert reminded us to mention that the testing process should include an opportunity for a horse to demonstrate what it doesn't know as well as any temperament flaws. The expert suggested beginning the test by riding passively, or "like a dummy." "I look to see whether the horse will wait for my cues or whether it will start meandering around," he said. "Then I'll give it conflicting cues to see whether it becomes confused. In the course of testing, I'll ask someone to throw a

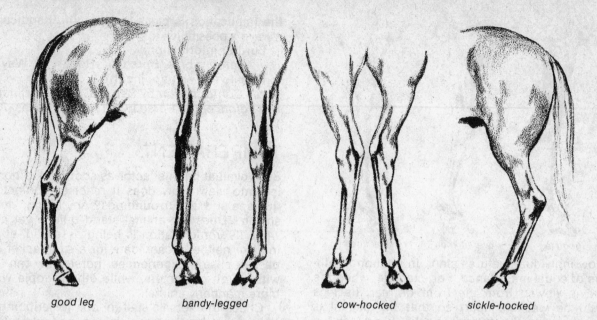

good leg   bandy-legged   cow-hocked   sickle-hocked

wad of newspaper or a towel in the horse's path—I hope it won't spook or buck me off, but I'd rather learn about such problems before I buy an animal. I'll also give a horse the chance to run away and to rub me off against a tree.''

CONDITION.

The best judge of a horse's condition is a veterinarian, but a layman can spot certain signs of an unhealthy animal. Obvious medical problems include runny eyes, a runny nose, and heaving flanks, although a certain amount of the last can be expected from a physically unfit horse after unaccustomed exercise. Sores and subdermal lumps may indicate the presence of secondary infections.

Particular attention should be paid to scars for several reasons. First of all, they are unsightly, but more important, they can indicate that the animal is a fighter. Scars on the lower leg may be the result of the firing process used to cure tendon problems. Sometimes firing can be successful, but often it's a process that must be repeated throughout the horse's working career.

A healthy, "blooming" coat is one sign of a healthy horse. Adding small doses of arsenic to a thin animal's diet was (perhaps it still is) an old horse trader's trick; the chemical would cause the horse to "flesh out," at least temporarily—but once deprived of the arsenic, it would return to a scarecrow state. Horse dealers and auctioneers, who have never enjoyed reputations for great honesty, still include among their numbers people

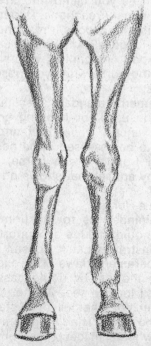
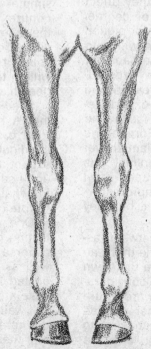
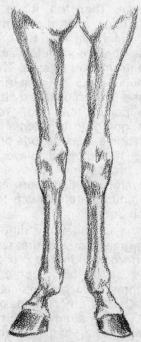

knock-kneed   pigeon-toed   base-narrowed

who will resort to tricks to make their wares more attractive than would normally be the case. Tranquilizers will turn a congenital rogue into a veritable Emily Post, at least until the drug wears off (that is, after the sale has been concluded). We're not saying that all dealers and auctioneers are unscrupulous—merely that the professional services of a veterinarian are an essential element in the selection process.

~~~~~~~~~~~~~~~~~~~~~~~~~~~~

Modern civilization started out as a horseless society, even though horses had been on earth for millions of years, evolving right alongside Homo sapiens. *Babylonia, for all its sophistication and wisdom, had no horses, and Egypt managed to build its pyramids without any help from equines.*

Even the Arabs didn't use horses until after the beginning of the Christian era. It wasn't until the barbaric tribes of Persia invaded the plains of Mesopotamia on horseback and drove out the inhabitants that civilized Babylonians became aware of the advantages of using "asses from the east."

~~~~~~~~~~~~~~~~~~~~~~~~~~~~

THE PURCHASE

Congratulations—you've finally located a suitable horse. Now comes another part of horse tradin', and that's to agree on a price. Even though the seller may say that the asking price is firm, it wouldn't hurt to try to bargain, and you might find yourself saving a bit of money. All the factors you've been considering will determine the actual price, as well as how eager the owner or dealer is to sell the animal. As something of a guideline, the minimum going rate for grades is $200, a Thoroughbred bought off the track may fetch ten times that figure, and proved competition horses command from five thousand to several hundred thousand dollars.

As in any substantial purchase, a sales contract is a good idea. It needn't be chock-full of legalese—just a clear statement of who's giving what to whom and when. The agreement can be in the form of a letter, as the following example illustrates:

Dear (buyer): (date)
I hereby sell you my 8-year-old Quarter Horse gelding "Big Charlie" (registration papers attached). You agree to pay the total purchase price of $1,800.00 as follows:

$400. today, receipt of which I acknowledge, and $1,400. within three days after your veterinarian has certified the horse to be sound and free of disease. If the vet doesn't certify the horse, I'll refund the $400.

The purchase price also includes the saddle and bridle you took with you today, as well as my vanning the horse to your stable. If you don't buy the horse, you'll return the tack in good condition or else forfeit the $400.

Your signature below shows your agreement to these terms.

Sincerely,
(seller)

AGREED:

_____
(buyer)

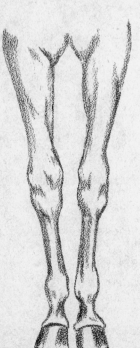

too close at the ground

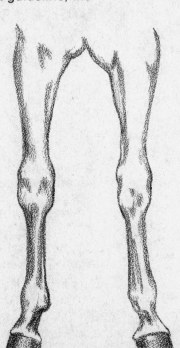

too wide at the ground

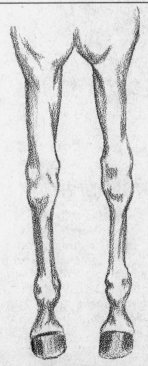

bow-kneed

Some sellers will agree to a trial period during which a prospective purchaser can determine the horse's suitability more thoroughly. Many dealers, however, are reluctant to entrust their animals into the hands of novices. Trial periods are a matter of negotiation, and if one is obtained, it should be spelled out in the contract. Here's some sample language:

You have one week from today to determine whether the horse is satisfactory exclusive of veterinary considerations. If you want to return the horse, you'll forfeit $200. and return the saddle and bridle in good condition. You'll also pay for the cost of returning the horse to me.

The reason why the buyer, not the seller, should select a veterinarian is obvious. The buyer also pays for the doctor's services, which should include a Coggins test.

INSURANCE

You should also consider insuring your new purchase. Horses can be insured against death and debilitating injuries. (While you're at it, you might think about taking a floater against tack and stable equipment's being stolen.) Annual premiums are approximately 5 percent of the animal's value. Owners may estimate the value, but when the figure goes above $50,000, the insurance company will make an independent evaluation. And not just expensive horses are insured; one broker does a sizable business with owners of backyard animals. There are also special packages for sales and boarding stables, training and breeding farms, and horse-show coverage.

Four leading equine insurance agencies are these:

Kohler Bloodstock Agency, Inc.
Middleburg, Virginia 22117

Paoli Insurance Agency, Inc.
11 South Valley Road
Paoli, Pennsylvania 19301

Poquessing Insurance Corp.
7346 Frankford Avenue
Philadelphia, Pennsylvania 19136

Rhulen Agency
Monticello, New York 12701

JOINT OWNERSHIP

Perhaps you can't afford to own a horse by yourself, or one of your friends has persuaded you to become partner in an animal he or she already has. Such an arrangement can be perfectly satisfactory, but only if you and the other person have a realistic understanding of what it entails.

An important consideration is how you both plan to use the horse. One person's wanting to compete the horse in dressage while the other wants an animal for distance riding will create problems. Similarly, before the purchase is made, the breed or type, size, and amount of training should be a matter of mutual agreement or at least compromise. Another series of questions to be dealt with in advance is who does and pays for what. For example, who gets to ride the animal when (don't forget that the animal will need rest periods too)? Who will do the feeding, grooming, and mucking out, if performing such chores yourselves is necessary? What if (perish the thought, but recognize the possibility) that one of you is responsible in a situation in which the horse is fatally injured or must be put down? We suggest that you and your prospective partner discuss all possible costs, schedules, and contingencies. Then too, consider the mechanics of someone's wanting out of the arrangement, such as in the event of moving away or merely losing interest. Decide whether one partner will buy out the other or whether the horse will be placed for sale.

Once you've pondered and resolved these and any other contingencies that come to mind, set them down on paper. Many lovely friendships have disintegrated faster than a plastic hoof pick over "But I never agreed to that" reactions.

Another joint-ownership situation involves a "silent partner" who foots all or part of the finances in order to participate in a horse's show career. You may not be good enough to campaign a horse from the saddle or driver's seat, yet you can go into partnership with an exhibitor. Typically, you'd pay all the bills and be entitled to any trophies and prizes, although your rider or driver colleague might be expected to pay entry fees and/or transportation to and from events. Decide who contributes how much, and get it in writing.

BREED ASSOCIATIONS

The following list of associations begins with the major American breeds:

AMERICAN SADDLE HORSE.

primary use: Three- or Five-Gaited show horses or fine harness driving.
further information:
American Saddle Horse Breeders Association
929 South 4th Street
Louisville, Kentucky 40203

American Saddlebred Pleasure Horse Association
801 South Court Street
Scott City, Kansas 67871

The Horse America Made by Louis Taylor
(Harper & Row)
Saddle Seat Equitation by Helen Crabtree
(Doubleday)

APPALOOSA.

primary use: Western riding.
further information:
Appaloosa Horse Club, Inc.,
P.O. Box 8403
Moscow, Idaho 83843

Appaloosa Horse by Bill and Dona Richardson (Wilshire)

ARABIAN.

primary use: Western and English riding.
further information:
Arabian Horse Registry of America, Inc.
7801 East Belleview Avenue
Englewood, Colorado 80110

International Arabian Horse Association
P.O. Box 4502
Burbank, California 91503

Arabian Horse by Reginald S. Summerhays (Wilshire)

MORGAN.

primary use: English and Western riding; driving.
further information:
American Morgan Horse Association
P.O. Box 29, West Lake Moraine Road
Hamilton, New York 13346

The Morgan Horse by Jeanne Mellin (Stephen Greene Press)

PALOMINO.

primary use: Western riding.
further information:
Palomino Horse Association, Inc.
P.O. Box 324
Jefferson City, Missouri 65101

Palomino Horse Breeders of America
P.O. Box 249
Mineral Wells, Texas 76067

PINTO (also known as *Paint*).

primary use: Western riding.
further information:
American Paint Horse Association
P.O. Box 12487
Fort Worth, Texas 76116

The Pinto Horse Association of America, Inc.
910 West Washington Avenue
San Diego, California 92103

QUARTER HORSE.

primary use: Western riding and racing.
further information:
American Quarter Horse Association
P.O. Box 200
Amarillo, Texas 79168

National Quarter Horse Registry, Inc.
Raywood, Texas 77582

America's Quarter Horses by Paul Laune (Arco)

The Complete Book of the Quarter Horse by Nelson C. Nye (Arco)

STANDARDBRED.

primary use: Harness racing.
further information:
U.S. Trotting Association
750 Michigan Avenue
Columbus, Ohio 43215

The Complete Book of Harness Racing by Philip A. Pines (Grosset & Dunlap)

TENNESSEE WALKING HORSE.

primary use: Pleasure riding and showing.
further information:
Tennessee Walking Horse Breeders and Exhibitors Association
P.O. Box 286
Lewisburg, Tennessee 37091

THOROUGHBRED.

primary use: flat and steeplechase racing; dressage and combined training; English riding.
further information:
The Jockey Club
300 Park Avenue
New York, New York 10022

For information about *draft and driving horses:*

BELGIAN.

primary use: draft.
further information:
Belgian Draft Horse Corporation of America
P.O. Box 335
Wabash, Indiana 46992

CLEVELAND BAY.

primary use: driving.
further information:
Cleveland Bay Society of America
Berryville, Virginia 22611

CLYDESDALE.

primary use: draft.
further information:
Clydesdale Breeders Association of the United
    States
Batavia, Iowa 52533

PERCHERON.

primary use: draft.
further information:
Percheron Horse Association of America
Route 1
Belmont, Ohio 43718

SHIRE.

primary use: draft.
further information:
American Shire Horse Association
P.O. Box 19
Pingree, Idaho 83262

SUFFOLK.

primary use: draft.
further information:
American Suffolk Horse Association
672 Polk Boulevard
Des Moines, Iowa 50312

See *The Gentle Giants* by Stanley Jepson (Arco)
for more information about draft breeds.

Among the most popular breeds of ponies:

CONNEMARA.

primary use: English riding.
further information:
American Connemara Pony Society
HoshieKon Farm
Goshen, Connecticut 06756

HACKNEY.

primary use: fine-harness driving.
further information:
American Hackney Horse Society
P.O. Box 174
Pittsfield, Illinois 62363

PONY OF THE AMERICAS.

primary use: Western riding.
further information: Pony of the Americas Club
Box 1447
Mason City, Iowa 50401

SHETLAND.

primary use: English and Western riding.
further information:
American Shetland Pony Registry
P.O. Box 435
Fowler, Indiana 47944

WELSH MOUNTAIN.

primary use: English riding and driving.
further information:
Welsh Pony Society of America
Drawer A
White Post, Virginia 22663

More exotic breeds have been either imported or
maintained for contemporary use. Lesser known,
they require a word or two of identification:

ALBINO.

Pure-white coats mark this breed, primarily used
    for Western riding.
further information:
American Albino Association, Inc.
Box 79
Crabtree, Oregon 97335

APPALOOSA PONY.

This diminutive Appaloosa is used primarily for
    Western riding.
further information:
National Appaloosa Pony, Inc.
P.O. Box 206
Gaston, Indiana 47342

ANDALUSIAN.

Originating in southern Spain, Andalusians are
    best known in connection with classical
    dressage.
further information:
American Andalusian Horse Association
P.O. Box 809
Warrenton, Virginia 22186

Andalusian Horse Registry of the Americas
P.O. Box 1290
Silver City, New Mexico 88061

BASHKIR.

Short and sturdy, with a curly-haired coat, the
    breed is used for pleasure riding.
further information:
American Bashkir Curly Registry
Box 453
Ely, Nevada 89301

BAY.

This is a color designation: horses with brown coats and black manes and tails.

further information:
American Bay Horse Association
Box 884F
Wheeling, Illinois 60090

American Bay Horse Registry
5310 Highway 66
Ashland, Oregon 97520

BUCKSKIN.

This is a color designation, referring to a tan or light brown coat.

further information:
American Buckskin Registry Association
P.O. Box 1125
Anderson, California 96007

International Buckskin Horse Association
P.O. Box 357
St. John, Indiana 46373

CHICKASAW.

This breed, descended from Spanish horses brought to the New World, is used primarily for pleasure riding.

further information:
Chickasaw Horse Association
Love Valley
Statesville, North Carolina 28677

GALICENO.

A small-sized breed with a natural running walk, the Galiceno originated in northwestern Spain.

further information:
Galiceno Horse Breeders Association, Inc.
111 East Elm Street
Tyler, Texas 75701

GOTLAND.

Originally from Sweden, this breed is compact and sturdy.

further information:
American Gotland Horse Association
R.R. 2, Box 181
Elkland, Missouri 65644

HORSE OF THE AMERICAS.

This category refers basically to mustangs and other feral types.

further information:
Horse of the Americas Registry
248 North Main
Porterville, California 93257

INDIAN HORSE.

This category encompasses Western-based horses.

further information:
American Indian Horse Registry, Inc.
Rocking LJK Ranch
Route 9, Box 127
Apache Junction, Arizona 85220

LIPIZZANER.

The stars of Vienna's Spanish Riding School, this breed is used primarily for classical dressage.

further information:
Royal International Lipizzaner Club of America
Route 7
Columbia, Tennessee 38401

MISSOURI FOX TROTTING HORSE.

This breed is characterized by its ambling trot.

further information:
Missouri Fox Trotting Horse Breed Association, Inc.
P.O. Box 637
Ava, Missouri 65608

MUSTANG.

These are the feral horses of the Western American states.

further information:
American Mustang Association
P.O. Box 388
Yucaipa, California 92399

PASO FINO.

This breed, originally from Puerto Rico, is known for its lateral four-beat gait.

further information:
American Paso Fino Horse Association, Inc.
525 William Penn Plaza, Room 3018
Pittsburgh, Pennsylvania 15219

PERUVIAN PASO.

This breed is characterized by its lateral gait, similar to the singlefoot or rack.

further information: American Association of Owners and Breeders of Peruvian Paso Horses
P.O. Box 2035
California City, California 94505

RACKING HORSE.

These are horses trained to execute the rack gait.

further information:
Racking Horse Breeders of America
Helena, Alabama 35080

RANGERBRED.

Similar to mustangs, these are among America's feral horses.
further information:
Colorado Ranger Horse Association
7023 Eden Mill Road
Woodbine, Maryland 21797

SPANISH BARB.

These are descendants of the light Arabian-type horse of north Africa.
further information: Spanish-Barb Breeders Association
P.O. Box 7479
Colorado Springs, Colorado 80907

SPANISH MUSTANG.

The Spanish mustang traces its ancestry to the horses brought to the Southwest by Spanish explorers and settlers.
further information:
The Spanish Mustang Registry, Inc.
Route 2, Box 80
Marshall, Texas 75670

TRAKEHNER.

This German breed is used primarily for dressage and driving.
further information:
American Trakehner Association
P.O. Box 268
Norman, Oklahoma 73069

Trakehner Breed Association and Registry of America, Inc.
Route 1, Box 177
Petersburg, Virginia 23803

TROTTINGBRED.

Similar to Standardbreds, these horses are used in harness racing.
further information:
National Trotting and Pacing Association
575 Broadway
Hanover, Pennsylvania 17331

TROTTING BRED PONY.

A Shetland–Standardbred cross, these ponies are used for harness racing.
further information:
New Jersey Trotting Breed Pony Registry
P.O. Box 202
Newton, New Jersey 07860

WALKING PONY.

This breed is the pony version of the Tennessee Walking Horse.
further information:
American Walking Pony Association
Route 5, Box 88
Upper River Road
Macon, Georgia 31201

Crossbreds exist in almost every possible combination. Most have been created for specific purposes or characteristics, such as the Irish hunter, a Thoroughbred–draft cross produced to provide a speedy yet sturdy type to hunt over the Emerald Isle's rugged terrain. Temperament can also be a reason: an infusion of "cold blood" (the larger draft-type breeds) into "hot-blood" breeds such as Thoroughbreds and Arabs will produce a more tractable offspring. Many of these horses are excellent for driving and dressage.

In addition to the following organizations, you might contact "purebred" registries to inquire about their breeds' crosses; "ethnic purity" notwithstanding, many breeders like to experiment by crossing their horses with other breeds.

CROSSBRED PONY (any cross of two pony breeds or types).

further information:
American Crossbred Pony Registry
P.O. Box 202
Newton, New Jersey 07860

HALF-ARABIAN
ANGLO-ARAB.

further information:
Half-Arabian Registry and Anglo-Arab Registry
International Arabian Horse Association
224 East Olive Avenue
Burbank, California 91503

HALF QUARTER HORSE.

further information:
Original Half Quarter Horse Registry
c/o Ina Knight, Secretary
Hubbard, Oregon 97032

HALF SADDLEBRED.

further information:
The Half Saddlebred Registry of America
660 Poplar Street
Coshocton, Ohio 43812

HALF-THOROUGHBRED.

further information:
American Remount Association
P.O. Box 1066
Perris, California 92370

MORAB (Morgan-Arabian).

further information:
Morab Horse Registry of America
P.O. Box 143
Clovis, California 93612

PART-BLOODED (Light-breed cross).

further information:
American Part-Blooded Horse Registry
4120 Southeast River Drive
Portland, Oregon 97222

PERUVIAN PASO HALF-BLOOD.

further information:
Peruvian Paso Half-Blood Association
43058 North 42nd Street West
Lancaster, California 93534

ASSES AND MULES.

"Ass," "donkey," and "burro" are different names for the same animal, *Equus asinus*. A mule is a hybrid offspring of an ass and a horse: a jackass and a mare (female horse) will produce a mule, while a stallion and a jenny (she-ass) will produce a hinny. Both mules and hinnies are sterile. Depending on the size of the animal, asses and mules can be used for riding and/or as beasts of burden.

American Council of Spotted Asses
Box 21
Fishtail, Montana 59028

American Donkey and Mule Society, Inc.
2410 Executive Drive
Indianapolis, Indiana 46241

Standard Jack & Jennet Registry of America
300 Todds Road
Lexington, Kentucky 40511

A Note About Registries: A registration certificate is valuable for two reasons. It is required for competing in certain show classes (see the *American Horse Shows Association Rule Book* for details), and it is essential to attract breeders who want their stock to obtain or maintain particular pedigrees.

Nevertheless, as the preceding list indicates, almost any equine can qualify for admission to at least one registry. Some organizations, like The Jockey Club, the U.S. Trotting Association, and the Appaloosa Horse Club, rigorously set and enforce strict qualifications. At the other end of the spectrum, however, there are groups that eagerly welcome any animal whose color, talents, or vague ancestry meet rather loose standards. Then, too, there are competing organizations, each claiming to be "the" registry.

Moral: there are registries and there are registries. Some are useful and valuable, while others are about as exclusive and organized as rush hour on the subway. A bit of investigation goes a long way in determining whether a certificate from a specific registry will enhance a horse's value.

Basuto, Haflinger, New Forest, Cob, Knabstrup, East Bulgarian, Dóle, Vladimir Heavy Draft . . . these are but a few of the dozens of other breeds and types that exist throughout the world. Even though you may never encounter them, if you'd like to expand your equine horizons, read "Horses" by Kate Reddick (Ridge Press–Bantam) and "The Encyclopedia of the Horse" edited by Hope and Jackson (The Viking Press).

GRADES.

The "mutts" of the equine world, grade horses and ponies, have so few (if any) distinctive characteristics that it's impossible to predict temperament or performance. There are a lot of grades around—take a look at any riding academy, dude ranch, or summer-camp stable. Some grades are agreeable mounts, some are not, and that's about all we can say about grades.

FURTHER READING

Among books on the general subject of "horse keeping" that contain information on selection, the following are all highly recommended:

A Horse Around the House by Patricia Jacobson and Marcia Hayes (Arco).
A Horse Of Your Own by M. A. Stoneridge (Doubleday).
Horse Selection and Care for Beginners by George H. Conn (Wilshire).
Horses: Their Selection, Care and Handling by Margaret Cabell Self (Arco).
Invitation to Riding by Sheila Wall Hundt (Simon and Schuster).
A Practical Guide to Owning Your Own Horse by Steven D. Price (Wilshire).
So Your Kids Want a Pony by Joanna Forbes (The Stephen Greene Press).

2 STABLING

Most horses do very well pastured the year around with only a minimal structure for protection against wind and flies. Others need large and heated stalls. Between a remuda—a band of cow horses left loose to graze overnight—and a stable with crystal chandeliers and carpeted alleyways, however, are numerous methods for adequate horse-keeping. The remuda is practically a relic of our past, now found only in a few sparsely populated areas where hobbled horses aren't likely to go grazing through prize suburban petunia beds. At the other end of the spectrum, the befountained architectural complexes that are being featured these days in the "house and garden" sections of horse magazines are not appropriate for most backyard horses either. Obviously, the choice of stabling depends on the kind of horse or horses you have, the number you will want to keep, the type of work you will ask your horse(s) to do, and your finances.

WHAT KIND OF HORSE-KEEPING ARRANGEMENT IS RIGHT?

- You have one or two horses you enjoy saddling up and taking over the trails. But other commitments, such as a job or school or a busy household to manage, prevent you from taking long, strenuous rides or even from tacking up as often as you would like. We recommend a pasture as your best horse-keeping solution. You probably have access to a pasture, either part of your own backyard or one rented from a neighbor. The area should be large enough for the horses to move about freely and graze, and there should also be trees, brush, or even a rock outcropping for shade and protection from the summer flies and winter winds.

- You own one or more horses kept out the year around, but unfortunately the pasture has no natural protection from the elements. You also need a place to confine your horse on the morning of a planned ride and to protect its feed from wind and rain. We recommend a three-sided or open-door free-access shed as a solution.

- You own one or two horses and rent space at the local stable; and as often as you've dreamed of caring for the horse yourself, it is not possible. We recommend you read this section and the one on Stable Management with special care.* Ask questions in your stable, and if the answers are not to your liking, look around for another. Remember, if you have a horse you will have to spend some money to keep it properly, and a bargain is rarely a good deal. There's an old horse saying, "I've spent weeks training my horse to go without food, and now that I've got him trained to do it, the s.o.b. ups and dies on me."

- You have just acquired a trail horse and you anticipate spending more and more time schooling the animal and yourself. Perhaps you can also foresee having more than one horse to care for and your access to additional land is severely limited. You have looked over the old toolshed out back and decided for any number of reasons (the structure is unsound, the ground too damp, it's needed for other storage) that it is unsuitable. Now is a good time to consider building a small stable.

- You have one or more horses in a pasture with access to a shed, but you've improved your horsemanship to a point where you're ready to travel to some shows. Suddenly the long winter coat that begins growing as early as late August—and right in the middle of the show season—is most undesirable. You want to eliminate your horse's hay belly by cutting back on the grass it eats. You need a better grooming and tack area. The farrier, in order to shoe properly, needs to watch the horse as it stands on firm, level ground in a well-lighted area. You need access to electricity to use clippers. You want to blanket your clipped horse to protect it from drafts. You want to condition your horse in the ring and turn it out into the paddock for short, regulated periods. And you've sworn that the last stone bruise on your show prospect's withers received from rolling on hard ground was absolutely the last one. It will come as no surprise to hear that we recommend you give up the shed in favor of a stable.

- You are an experienced horseman with a few good broodmares and a desire to invest more energy and money in breeding, showing, and selling. In all likelihood, your goals have outgrown your existing facilities and you need to make additions. You know your limitations and have figured out just how large an operation your resources, the operation's potential, and local zoning regulations will allow. If you go all the way, you can build a stabling complex that includes broodmare barns, a stallion barn, foaling stalls, living quarters for the help, a barren-mare shed, a stud yard or barn, an isolation

* Unfortunately, as of this writing, there are few laws governing standards for commercial stables; anyone can open a stable and run it pretty much the way he wants. Several people in California are attempting to write a state law to impose standards on commercial stables—so far, unsuccessfully. There is a strict law in Maryland which tackles the problem. If you are interested in learning more about this, see page 237.

barn, offices, lounges, pastures (several), paddocks (many), and everything else such a massive operation requires (for example, its own waste-removal system, advertising and public relations, offices, accommodations for trainers and grooms, one or more tracks, or arenas, etc., etc.). On a less grandiose scale, you can also run a breeding farm in one barn with provisions for a stud stall, a breeding area, foaling stalls, a special pasture for the weanlings, and extra stalls for mares waiting to be covered.

- You are an experienced horse manager who wants to open a commercial stable. Obviously, you have given careful thought to what the market and your finances will bear. Your plans probably include a stable complex with roomy box stalls (some for boarding animals, some for schooling animals), a grooming area, a large tack room, an indoor arena, outdoor rings, trails for hacking, paddocks, offices, lounges, bleachers for audiences at your shows, parking facilities, and everything that goes along with establishing an attractive, profitable stable. If your plans are less ambitious, a stable with straight tie stalls situated near public riding trails—city or county ordinances permitting, of course—may be adequate. You will also need an outdoor ring for giving lessons and testing green riders before sending them off on their own.

THE REMUDA

The band of saddle horses used by cowboys working on open land is known as the remuda on the Southern ranges and in Texas and cavvy, from the Spanish word *caballada,* in the northwest ranges. The size of a remuda depends on the number of cowboys working; usually each cowboy has from nine to twelve horses in his personal string. Customarily two wranglers are assigned to a "horse block." It is their duty to get up early, saddle up their night horses which have been hobbled or staked nearby, find the remuda, and bring it in. The horses are driven into a corral made of rope, and the seasoned individuals move to the outside as the younger horses mill around in the center. The foreman does the roping as each cowboy calls out the name of the horse he wants for that day. The horses tend to stay calm during all this, since with so many horses in each cowboy's string, most of them are released more often than they are ridden.

FIELD KEEPING

Individual horses of hardy breeds may be pastured the year around in most climates. It is a low-cost, easy-maintenance solution to keeping a horse that's worked infrequently, especially during the winter months. The pasture should be large enough to prevent the horse from overgrazing it or from easily reinfesting itself with parasites. (A full discussion of what makes a good pasture begins on page 45.) What the novice horseman needs to be aware of is that a field-kept horse has a few basic but essential needs: fresh, available water and minerals; shelter from wind and flies; a dry, soft area to bed down; and food. Pasturing a horse the year around is certainly closest to a natural situation, and for most horses it is the healthiest one as well.

The advantages of pasture-keeping a horse are that the animal will develop a warm winter coat as protection from severe temperatures; it will not suffer the changes in temperature experienced by those horses taken from a warm barn and worked outside in cold weather; it will be receiving natural nutrients and minerals from the grasses; it will be getting some regular exercise; it will be less prone to the leg and foot problems associated with various stable floorings; and it is less likely to become bored and develop such stable vices as cribbing, weaving, or windsucking.

But there are also disadvantages to pasturing a horse the year around. Because the horse acclimates so well to its environment, in winter it will have grown a long, unattractive, and difficult-to-clean woolly coat, causing it to lather up quickly when worked on all but the coldest of days; the horse may be difficult to catch and manage if it is permitted to run wild with only minimal handling; the horse will not be in condition to do anything more than the lightest of work unless it is ridden (or lunged) and grained regularly; it will be subject to bruises, sores, or cuts caused by rolling on stones or being bitten by the "boss horse" for an infraction of the rules. Some horses' extreme temperaments, be they the meek or the bully, do not permit satisfactory pasturing with others: the meek will be chased away from the food, while the bully will become too fat from eating everyone else's portion. Horses fed from the ground, a common procedure with pasture-kept horses, run the risk of ingesting dirt and developing sand colic or becoming reinfested with parasites.

Horses turned out to pasture require anywhere from 1½ to 3 or more acres per animal. The size depends on the quality of the grasses and the amount of supplemental feed you are willing to buy. And unless the pasture is well cared for, you should expect to have to add some food to your horse's diet, at least during certain seasons of the year.

Horse owners who grain more than one horse in a pasture usually hang out a separate grain manger for each animal, situating them far enough apart so that one bully cannot dominate them all. Other horsemen prefer to build open stalls—which are like straight stalls but divided by single planks or pipes rather than walls. This arrangement forces each horse to enter a stall where it can eat its grain and hay without intimidation. Horsemen are always devising new feeding techniques. Some of the ideas are so ingenious they quickly spread and become the accepted way. Others are just strange. One farmer we know pastured five horses in a small area which they shared with a Volkswagen that needed only a few windows, a set of wheels, an engine and a new body to run perfectly again. But the old car earned its keep. When feeding time came, the farmer dumped the grain into the bucket seats and the horses stuck their heads through the car windows to eat. For some curious reason, this method has not caught on in other parts of the country.

Pastured horses that are not grained regularly are usually given hay, at least part of the year. If a number of horses are pastured together, a covered hay bunk made of wood slats and a peaked roof is a good apparatus. The most common type is V-shaped with the point of the bunk raised off the ground. The openwork slats keep the bunk clean and allow hay dust to fall to the ground as the animals pull the hay through. The eaves of the roof extend for at least a foot beyond the bunk for added protection against rain. These eaves are rarely less than 6 feet high at their lowest point. In drier climates, such a roof may not be necessary and hay may simply be loaded into uncovered bunks. For a smaller herd, hay nets may be preferable. While nylon nets are now stronger and longer-lasting than their cotton prototypes, they do tend to shred after a few months of being chewed and exposed to the weather. They are, however, easy to handle, fill, and hook onto a fence post.

Unless your pasture has a proper supply of all the minerals a horse needs (and few pastures do), mineral or salt blocks should be available at all times. Since these blocks will ''melt'' in the rain, many horsemen prefer to simply put one or two blocks in the bottom of the hay bunk. Some mineral blocks are made with a small hole molded into the bottom and are designed to be balanced atop a pipe driven into the ground. This works until the block is nearly used up. Then you (and the horses) are faced with a piece of metal sticking up from the ground—a potential source of danger. Setting it inside an old rubber tire provides better visibility and some protection from being kicked about.

If an adequate and constant supply of fresh water is unavailable in the pasture, you will have to provide one. For a few horses, simply putting out a water container to be filled daily and drained regularly is sufficient. For years, old bathtubs with rounded edges have served as troughs. To clean them out daily, one need only pull the drainage plug, wipe out any accumulated organic matter, and refill. Most horsemen prefer to use automatic water containers of the kind that is designed to release fresh water when the horse activates it by sticking its nose against the valve. For larger herds this device can save a lot of work. Steel or concrete tanks are often set into a fence line; if the fencing, however, is electric (or worse still, barbed wire), select another spot. The trough should be about 30 to 36 inches high; you can figure out the size needed by calculating one linear foot per five horses. The automatic tank should be equipped with a float valve, a cleanout drain, and, in colder climates, an electric thermostat to prevent freezing. Over the years, the manufacturers of automatic water troughs have developed and improved them until they are now nearly foolproof.

All water troughs should be situated on ground that has good natural drainage. In lush pastures, put the trough on a bed of stones or gravel extended for about 10 feet beyond the trough. Keep in mind that all the horses will be visiting the trough at least twice daily, so the gravel may help to prevent the surrounding area from turning into a mudhole. Where pastures are dry for a good part of the year, a mudhole may be just what is wanted; the mud makes an excellent treatment for dry and cracked hooves. Paint the trough white. It will look neater during the day—but more important, it will be more visible to you and the horses at night.

Rope hay rack—about $7
Plastic hay racks—about $5.50
Tubular-steel rack, 36×7×14 inches—about $25
Hay/grain metal feeders—about $32
Enclosed metal hay/grain feeder—about $60
Welded-steel horse feeder (5-foot diameter; feeds twelve horses)—about $250.00

SHEDS AND FREE-ACCESS SHELTERS

In pastures where natural shelter is unavailable, a shed is a good addition. It has a number of distinct advantages and few of the disadvantages commonly associated with stables. Only the simplest of structures is needed: an old toolshed, for instance, can easily be converted into an outdoor stall. The stall area should be at least 10 feet square for each animal—large enough to turn around in comfortably and safely, with space for the feedbox and water basin, if fresh water is not always available in the pasture. We suggest that you figure on approximately 144 square feet per horse—the equivalent of a 12×12-foot stall. The shed may have only three walls, or it can have four walls with an open doorway at least 4 feet wide and 8 feet high. The shed should be large enough to accommodate *all* the horses, and we recommend a three-sided shed for more than one or two animals. Invariably, all will head for the opening at the same time, and if the doorway is one horse width too narrow, you can count on a dispute and possible injuries.

When picking a site for the shed, look for the highest point in the pasture—which will usually be the driest spot as well. Take into account whether it will be accessible to you when it comes time to feed and water. Depending on the region in which you live, face the opening of the shed toward the mildest prevailing winds—in the Northeast, that means south; in the South, that means northeast.

Free-access shelter

The shed floor should have excellent drainage and never be damp or, even worse, wet. The base of some sheds is first covered with 6 to 8 inches of gravel, then covered with dirt or with a heavy bedding material such as tobacco stems or wood chips. (A light bedding will blow away in the first breeze.) Some horse owners prefer to store the hay and bedding in the end of the shed that faces inclement weather. Separated from the horses by a sturdy partition, the hay not only is accessible at feed time but will insulate the shed as well.

A shed provides several benefits to the horse owner as well as to the horse. For one thing, it affords a covered, protected area in which to feed hay and grain. And for another, while the advantage of protecting the feed from the elements is readily apparent, the saving from avoiding waste is often worth the price of shed lumber. One design we've seen has hay racks that run along the back wall but only halfway along the two side walls. The designer of this shed knew his horses. He anticipated the likelihood that if he built the hay racks toward the front of the shed the horses would bunch up at the entrance instead of moving inside to the back wall. This same horseman spread compacted gravel over the shed floor for about 15 to 20 feet beyond the entrance. This extra gravel kept the highly trafficked area in front of the shed dry.

Sheds are particularly useful for tying or simply enclosing a horse. The times this is desired may include the morning of a planned ride, the day the farrier is due, the night a sick animal needs nursing, or the weeks a foal is being weaned from its dam.

STABLES

A stable arrangement may vary from a simple structure organized to house one or two horses to a large, elaborate structure with indoor ring facilities designed for more than a hundred. Obviously the style chosen will depend on the horse owner's needs and finances. Many available plans for horse barns are adaptable to various regions and climates, but all share common principles of sta-

ble design. All stable buildings satisfy three basic needs of the horse owner: they confine the horse, they control its environment, and they provide storage areas for feed and tack. Some stables, however, cope with these needs better than others.

Automatic Water Trough. This automatic waterer won't freeze or break. Made of galvanized steel, it is weather-resistant and fully insulated and has a heating unit that is thermostatically controlled. It can easily water two horses at one time and will fit nicely in a fence line between two separate paddocks. From Ritchie Industries, Conrad, Iowa 50621.

WHERE TO BUILD A STABLE

It is worth considering a site that is relatively flat, since the less the grading that needs to be done, the lower the cost. However, site selection depends on several other considerations as well, and you may have to concede one aspect to find the best overall site. A low, level piece of ground will not drain as regularly as higher ground, while cold and frequent winds may make a hilltop site less than ideal. A stable should be accessible to delivery of construction materials and, more important, for later regular deliveries of feed and bedding. If the stable will not contain living quarters, it should be close enough to the house for someone to sense when there is trouble. On the other hand, since flies and horses have a relationship that is difficult to discourage, a barn built too close to the house will make commuting an easy matter for these insects.

Zoning regulations may be a major factor in the choice of the site or may not affect you at all. It obviously depends on the laws in your county or township and on what you are planning to build. We can't go into the many zoning regulations, since they are often set on a local level, and each may require different variances from its neighbor—and invariably does. So we caution the potential horse-keeper to check with his county agent to be certain the zoning laws permit keeping "livestock" (a horse), and if they do, what regulations you must follow. Often zoning boards require that a stable be so many feet from boundary lines and be equipped with approved "sanitation facilities" (meaning manure removal). By all means, do your homework. It is expensive to build a stable; it is more expensive to build or renovate a stable and then tear it down for noncompliance with existing zoning laws.

Portable and Permanent Horse Stalls. This stall is made of welded square tubular steel. It comes 10×12 feet square and 7 feet high with 4-foot-high wood panels. Each panel opens 90 degrees for cleaning. The sliding front gate features a safety latch. Available from Scranton Manufacturing Co., Scranton, Iowa 51462.

BUILDING A STABLE

Where to begin? We suggest you first look around at other stables in your areas to see what they look like and how they are built. Inquire to find out who built them. Chances are the stables you are looking at were constructed either by a company that specializes in prefabricated buildings or by local talent using standard stable plans. There is also the possibility that some were custom-designed. We suggest you be most cautious about getting involved with this type of structure. Unless you know a great deal about horse management and can recognize a genuine improvement upon traditional techniques, as opposed to a newfangled approach that sounds great in theory but fails dismally when put to the test, we recommend you let someone else experiment with his money, not with yours.

After inspecting your neighbors' accommodations, take another good look at your site. If it is near an existing building, such as a toolshed or even a garage, it may be worthwhile attaching the new stable to this building. It may cut your building costs, since you need not worry about insulating the connecting wall.

We know of one young woman who had several broodmares and a young stallion she was particularly fond of. Circumstances forced her to move from a large farm into a small house on one acre of land. She boarded out most of her mares but kept one prize dam, her filly, and the stallion—all on the single acre surrounding her house. She bought a prefabricated two-car garage, or at least the shell of one, and built two large stalls inside, one for the mare and one for the filly. Her reason for choosing a garage was a good one. When she put her house up for sale, as she intended to do in the not-too-distant future, it would be a simple matter to convert the stable back into a garage, something more desirable in that community than a horse barn would be. The remainder of the space in the garage/stable was used to store tack, feed, bedding, and other horse necessities. Two paddocks, neither on a particularly grand scale, were situated on either side of the stable. But the cleverest stabling arrangement was for the stallion which was installed in a large box stall in the house's basement garage, next to the family laundry room. The stallion quickly learned to look forward to the sound of the washing machine, since it usually meant company and sometimes even a carrot. The area just behind the house was his paddock, which he seemed delighted to share with the children of the house. We should make it clear that all three horses were exercised regularly— often by lunging in the small area that was the front lawn. The flower beds may have suffered, but the horses didn't.

MATERIALS

Choosing building materials involves considering cost, durability, amount of maintenance needed, fire resistance, and attractiveness. The most commonly used materials are wood, plywood, metal, masonry (concrete, brick, cinder block, pumice block or stone), and plastic. Wood-sided buildings

Building a stable in which to house your horse is solving only part of your horse-keeping problems. Horses in the wild travel light; domesticated horses that are asked to perform specialized tasks need accoutrements. And the new horse owner about to build a small stable or convert an existing structure needs to go through a mental checklist before setting a plan to paper—not to mention a signature to a builder's contract. These questions must be asked and be reasonably answered:

- Is there an area nearby for pasturing or exercising a horse, either in a ring or on public or private trails?
- Does my plan include storage areas for feed, hay, bedding, tack, assorted stable supplies, manure?
- Is the location accessible to deliveries of supplies?
- Is the site well drained the year around?
- Is the design compatible with that of surrounding buildings, or will mine be an eyesore?
- Is there flexibility in the design for future expansion or conversion to another use in case I must move and sell my property?
- Is there access to electricity and water hookups?
- Do the materials being used minimize the risk of fire?
- Is the environment controllable (i.e., have I planned for proper ventilation)?
- Will the structure be easy to clean and maintain?
- Does my plan meet zoning regulations?

are most people's favorite. Wood is attractive and is a naturally good insulator. But a quality wood is probably the most expensive material available today, with the cost of lumber per board foot climbing regularly. Wood also requires annual maintenance which must be calculated into the general cost of the building. Treated plywood, while not as aesthetically pleasing as planking, is also somewhat expensive. However, it has several attractive properties: it is very strong, it will not warp, it will not split, it will not shrink; it requires less maintenance than board lumber; and it can be stained.

Steel buildings are somewhat cheaper than wooden ones, and they require practically no upkeep. They are, however, cold in winter and hot in summer and so require extra insulation. Many people do not like the look of steel-sided stables and arenas. Such siding reminds them of a factory, with machines and computer printouts littering the inside. For some commercial stables, this image may be closer to the truth than we care to admit; but we prefer to think of horses in a more natural-looking setting. One alternative to the all-steel barn is a steel structure with a composition or plastic exterior. While this may not look much better than a steel structure, it insulates better. Masonry, either concrete, cinder block, brick or stone, is less commonly used today. While the materials may be equivalent in price range with the other materials discussed here—and possibly even lower—the cost of labor is an important and most expensive factor. Added to the costs of masonry must be included the cost of digging a poured foundation or concrete slab. Masonry stables, while sturdy and requiring little maintenance, are often damp and cold.

An important factor in the selection of stable materials is how fireproof they will be. It is worth considering using fireproof materials when you are planning a new stable and especially when you

are converting an old existing structure into a stable. Obviously, steel and concrete-block exteriors are impregnable and will contain a fire, preventing it from spreading. Fire-conscious horsemen store hay and bedding in a separate fireproof room or shed. One large stable stores hay in an open nook separated from the stalls by a heavy steel overhead door programmed to shut tight (much like an automatic garage door) as soon as the fire-detection system relays a signal. Fire starting in the hay area would thus be contained, while a conflagration elsewhere would starve from lack of fuel.

Umbaugh Pole Building Co., Inc., offers excellent standard designs for almost any stable need. The company's brochure covers only a cross-section of over forty-five basic designs and numerous options. Umbaugh buildings are built only by Umbaugh construction crews, and the company has field representatives in all areas of the country to help work out the best plan and determine the best location. Umbaugh has also created fireproof stables which will confine a bedding fire to a single stall until it has burned itself out, dissipate the smoke from such a fire, and greatly reduce risk of fire from such causes as lightning, faulty wiring, and carelessness.

Umbaugh Pole Building Co., Inc., P.O. Box 71, Ravenna, Ohio 44266.

A FIRE-PREVENTION CHECKLIST FOR YOUR STABLE.*

Until you can answer yes to each of the following questions, there is room for improvement in your own stable fire-prevention program.

Are your barn and stable yard free of debris such as loose piles of hay, scrap lumber, and oily rags? Loosely piled hay burns more quickly than hay that is in bales.

Is your gas pump located at least 25 to 50 feet away from the barn?

Is your hay stored away from your barn in a separate area, with the minimum required hay and bedding material brought in to the stable a couple of times a week?

Do you have several fire extinguishers properly hung in the barn, and are persons who frequent your stable trained in their use?

Are farm machinery and automobiles kept in a separate garage away from the stable? Gasoline leaks on loose hay are a frequent cause of stable fires.

Are NO SMOKING signs posted and enforced in your barn?

Is your barn wiring in conduit so that rodents cannot chew through it?

Do you have periodic inspections of your wiring and lighting by a local fire-inspection officer?

Are the lights in your stable (and especially those in the stalls) in heavy wire or glass cages so that they cannot be broken?

Is the roof of your stable an unburnable tin or asphalt? If your roof is wood, has it been treated with a chemical to retard burning?

Do you personally make sure that the hay you buy is well cured in order to prevent any spontaneous combustion?

Is manure taken outside of the barn immediately after being picked up? Piles of manure invite spontaneous combustion.

Have you rehearsed fire drills with those who use the barn? Have you worked out the quickest way to clear animals from the building?

Is the grass around your barn kept closely mowed during dry seasons as a precaution against grass fires?

Are portable space heaters operated only when someone is present to watch them?

Is your barn free of any gasoline or kerosene lighting sources?

Are combustible fluids, insecticides, and small amounts of gasoline properly stored in tight containers in minimum quantities?

Are all lightning rods, antennas, and wire fences attached to your barn properly grounded?

Are alleyways in front of stalls kept free of debris and open at all times to give easy access to each stall and to the exits?

Until this century, almost all barns stored hay in a loft, where it helped to insulate the building. Today, asbestos-covered insulation materials are preferred, with the hay stored away from the stalls. Another material finding popularity among stable designers is fiber glass, used most often to replace conventional glass windows. Fiber glass has a higher resistance to heat than regular glass, and it will not explode during a fire as glass will. Its durability is important in maintaining an airtight, fire-retentive environment, so that fire fighters can have added time to get a blaze under control.

There are a number of fire-detection systems available. While somewhat expensive to install, they will quickly prove their value if you are confronted by fire. Certain ones are designed to detect smoke, even at the first stages of a smoldering fire, while others are designed to react to heat above 135 degrees. Fire-fighting systems work on the same principle and activate an automatic sprinkler installed in the ceiling.

Even if your stable does not have such a system, it should not be without at least one easily accessible fire extinguisher that is checked monthly to make sure it is working properly. It's always a good idea to hang several extinguishers around the stable, especially near where hay is stored.

"Stop Stable Fires" posters listing twelve rules for preventing fire measure 17×11 inches and are available for 50 cents each from The American Horse Council, 1700 K Street, N.W., Suite 300, Washington, D.C. 20006.

TYPES OF BUILDINGS

The pole building is the most popular type of construction for building stables and particularly arenas. It eliminates the need for vertical support beams in the center of the building and, most welcome in this day of rising costs, eliminates the need for a poured foundation and the expensive digging such a foundation requires. The pole building is supported by wooden posts sunk 4 feet below ground level and fixed into concrete. Posts are spaced at 16-foot intervals. Trusses instead of beams support the roof. Boards treated to prevent rotting are nailed to the support posts at ground level. Usually the topsoil surrounding the building is graded up against the "foundation" boards for insulation. The outside of the building can then be finished in metal (usually steel) or wood (often rough-cut lumber pretreated against fire). The pole building is ideal for arenas as well as large stables. For an arena, the structure is simply finished with kickboards around the lower inside of the building. For stables in colder climates, the shell is insulated and then finished with heavy oak lumber for the stall area and paneling or wallboard in the tack room.

* Copyright © 1973 *Practical Horseman* magazine. Reprinted with permission.

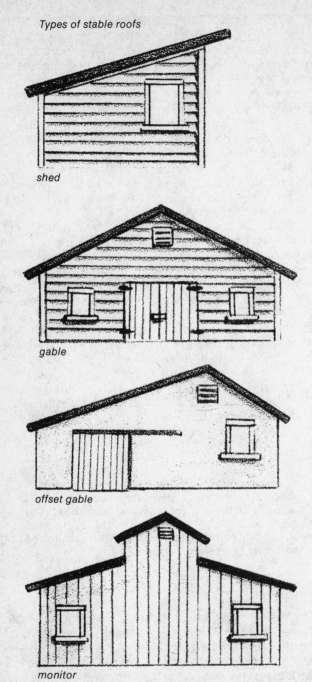

Types of stable roofs

shed

gable

offset gable

monitor

If you're planning to build a stable or arena, shop around for a builder by contacting some of the following companies:

Cal-Mor Livestock Equipment, Inc.
28095 Front Street
Rancho, California 92390

Crow Scales, Inc.
P.O. Box 7429
Waco, Texas 76710

Leach's Custom Corrals
19130 Walnut Dr.
Rowland Heights, California 91748

Lear Siegler, Inc.
Cuckler Division
P.O. Box 346
Monticello, Iowa 52310

Lester's Inc.
Lester Prairie, Minnesota 55354

OK Corrals & Equipment
25852 Springbrook Avenue
P.O. Box 184
Saugus, California 91350

People's Building & Supply Co.
761 North Main Street
Hubbard, Ohio 44425

Bill Ryan Enterprises
P.O. Box 205
Putnam, Connecticut 06260

T. C. Ranch Co.
2700 Pomona Boulevard
Pomona, California 91768

Star Building Systems
Box 94910
Oklahoma City, Oklahoma 73109

Umbaugh Pole Building Company
P.O. Box 71
Ravenna, Ohio 44266

V.I.P. Builders, Inc.
201 East Street
Southampton, Massachusetts 01073

Barns and stables may be classified by their roofs. The shed roof is recommended for small stables and for freestanding open-sided buildings in the pasture. This design also works best when an addition is attached to an existing building. The gable roof is a popular design which offers flexible layout possibilities. The monitor roof has been adopted by many of the large stall manufacturers. In milder climates, stables are made from several prefabricated stalls placed side by side in two facing rows with each row covered by a long shed roof. The alleyway formed between these two sheltered rows is capped by a short gable roof that overhangs each of the shed roofs. Together, these three roofs form an attractive and efficient structure. Often the spaces under the gables are kept open for access to air and light.

For further information, you can order a book, "Horse Handbook: Housing and Equipment," published by Midwest Plan Service, Iowa State University, Ames, Iowa 50010 ($2.00). The U.S. Department of Agriculture puts out a number of horse-barn plans, and all can be ordered by mail from the Superintendent of Documents, U.S. Government Printing Office, Washington, D.C. 20102.
- Three-stall barn: Misc. Publication No. 1224, Cooperative Farm Building Plan Exchange No. 6107, 1972, one sheet, 5 cents.
- 1½-story horse barn: Misc. Publication No. 1102, Cooperative Farm Building Plan Exchange No. 6024, 1968, paper, 5 cents.
- 8-stall horse barn: Misc. Publication No. 1098, Cooperative Farm Building Plan Exchange No. 6010, 1969, paper, 5 cents.
- 17-stall horse barn: Misc. Publication No. 1695, Cooperative Farm Building Plan Exchange No. 6011, 1968, paper, 5 cents.

● **88-horse barn:** Misc. Publication No. 1310, Cooperative Farm Building Plan Exchange No. 6148, 1975, paper, 25 cents.

Working drawings may be obtained from the extension agricultural engineer at your state university. If you don't know its location, send your request to Agricultural Engineer, Extension Service, U.S. Department of Agriculture, Washington, D.C. 20250, and it will be forwarded to the correct university.

"Western Horseman" runs a monthly feature called "Stable Plans for a Western Horseman." Most of the articles are geared to the two- to six-horse owner and are well worth reading. Each December issue of the magazine carries an index to that year's articles.

ENVIRONMENT

A stable creates an artificial environment for horses. Taking a horse out of the cold also removes it from such natural elements as sun, water, fresh air, soft ground to lie on, and well-drained ground to stand upon. In the stable the horse is forced to rely upon you for all its needs. So consideration must be given to each seemingly minor equine requirement.

POLE BUILDINGS by PEOPLES

Pole Buildings for large horse farms and backyard herds of two to four. There are many designs to choose from, and Peoples is ready to cater to special needs. Peoples Pole Building Co., 761 North Main Street, Hubbard, Ohio 44425.

TEMPERATURE AND HUMIDITY

Horses do better in a controlled temperature and a controlled humidity. In such an environment their metabolism is more stable, and they will therefore, make more efficient use of their feed and water.

The ideal temperature for most horses is somewhere between 45 and 75 degrees Fahrenheit, with 55 degrees best and for a newborn foal between 75 and 80 degrees.

The ideal humidity for horses is somewhere between 50 and 75 percent, with 60-percent humidity best. The average 1,000-pound horse breathes 2.1 gallons of moisture into the air each day. So, quickly figuring out the numbers, if the stable holds 40 horses, you come out with 84 gallons of moisture *per day.* If the moisture has no place to go, you end up with a damp, moldy, smelly stable and horses that will continually suffer from respiratory ailments, stiffness, and mushrooms growing

in stall corners. During the mild seasons of the year, simply opening the stable doors will usually draw the moisture out. But during the nontemperate times of the year, when the snow threatens to cover the windows or the blazing sun threatens to burn everything it touches, open doorways are no longer a solution. Good ventilation must be designed into the original stable plans. High ceilings, vents, or windows that open encourage the air to circulate freely. Occasionally, efficient ventilation must be helped along by strategically placed fans and blowers. Needless to say, the larger the stable and the more horses there are in an area, the better the ventilation system must be.

While many large horse barns have built-in fans, few have heaters for the stall areas. Even in the coldest of climates (where, by the way, few commercial horse farms are found), removal of excess heat is usually more of a problem than excessive cold. Good insulation and even warm blankets—sometimes as many as three piled one on top of another—will keep a horse warm enough. And since horses do give off heat, their collective B.t.u.s will make a difference inside the stable. We noted in one barn during a particular cold spell when the temperature failed to rise above zero that the temperature in the area surrounded by six stalls failed to drop below 26 degrees. The horses survived quite well with only blankets.

Farnam makes a cupola ventilator that provides 215 square inches of ventilating area. It is made of aluminum covered with baked enamel, and the joints are stainless steel. Available with or without weather vane: about $41 without.

LIGHT

There are some needs a horse has that a stable manager cannot replace artificially. Horses must be allowed some access to sunlight, for instance—an important source of Vitamin D. Obviously, a light bulb will not do the job, nor will a window or skylight replace the sun. But windows, skylights and artificial lights are important to a horse's well-being.* Horses like to see what is going on about them. A window in each box stall lets in natural daylight and allows the horse to look outside. But in many new stable designs such an arrangement is impractical or simply too expensive. Windows are often replaced with translucent Filon or fiberglass panels built into the structure in the form of skylights or strips under the eaves of the roof. These attractive translucent panels let in a soft, diffused light that is bright but not glaring. If the stable is lit by natural light during the day, then artificial light is needed only at night. A recessed

---

* Some stables that specialize in showing breeds supposed to exhibit "fire" and "spirit" will keep their horses in darkened stalls so that when they are brought out into the sunlight their eyes seem to flash. Actually, these poor animals are simply dazzled by the sudden bright light.

or protected light bulb in each stall is recommended, with brighter fluorescent fixtures for alleyways and tack and feed rooms. If the stable or arena ceilings are high, fluorescent lights can be replaced by mercury-vapor lights, several times brighter than fluorescent lights. They do cost more to install initially, but they are more efficient. Because they are so bright, fewer fixtures need be installed, thus reducing electricity bills. Ceilings should be at least 16 feet high for mercury-vapor lights to diffuse evenly.

FLOORING

Most stable designers pay a great deal of attention to flooring, especially the flooring beneath the stalls. To say that each horseman has an opinion about which type of flooring is best is to understate the case. And to do less than stress the importance of good flooring also drastically understates the case. In its natural environment, a horse will not stand in one place for hours at a time, especially in conditions that are less than ideal. So for flooring to be good it must have certain basic characteristics: it should have some "give" to reduce strain on the horse's tendons or feet, it should be absorbent, easy to clean, nonslippery, non-odor-retentive, and free of dampness. The flooring materials most commonly found under stalls are dirt, concrete, wood, clay, sand, asphalt, and brick. And not one of these materials is perfect.

Dirt, so it would seem at first thought, is the one material that most closely resembles the footing in a pasture and therefore the best flooring choice. True, it is highly absorbent, nonslippery, and easy on a horse's legs. But such flooring is not always the ideal solution. Although it is porous, soil does not dry out quickly and can retain dampness and odor. It is easily pawed and must be replaced often. Dirt floors are also difficult to muck out and in cold climates may freeze hard.

Concrete is increasing in popularity. Most horse owners appreciate its good qualities and feel they can bury the disadvantages under a thick layer of bedding. What is good about concrete? It is hard-wearing, easy to clean (especially if poured at a slight inclination to encourage drainage), rodent-proof, and difficult for a horse to damage. Concrete's disadvantages are that it is nonporous, cold, and nonelastic, the last meaning it can be particularly hard on a horse's legs.

Wood should be at least two inches thick, preferably rough oak. Once common for stall flooring, wood is now avoided by most modern stables. We suspect the primary reason is that good oak planking is prohibitively expensive. Also, its disadvantages as flooring outweigh the good points. What are they? The good news is that wood is springy and easy on a horse's legs, it keeps the stall warmer in cold weather, and most important, the horse will not have to stand on a cold surface, which can cause stiffness of muscles and joints. But there is bad news too. Wood tends to become slippery when wet; it is difficult to clean and disinfect; it retains odors; and it must be checked often for signs of wear, then replaced immediately with treated planks.

Clay is easy on the horse's legs, and if it covers a base of crushed stone, it can be highly absorbent. Its major drawbacks are that it does not hold up well under constant pawing, thus needing replacement every few years, and it can remain damp for longer than is desirable.

Sand is highly absorbent and makes a soft surface for the legs. However, it does have a number of disadvantages most horsemen find difficult to overcome. Sand has a drying effect on the hooves, and it is not unusual for hoof walls to become cracked or split. Occasionally the sand will work its way behind the walls of the foot, where it can cause severe problems. Sand is also easily pushed about by the horse and must be raked flat daily.

Asphalt is inexpensive to lay, relatively porous, and easy to clean. While it has slightly more give and therefore is not as hard on a horse's legs as concrete, it also does not hold up as long and must be replaced after several years of wear. In hot weather asphalt can become sticky; when cold it may become brittle and crack.

Brick, we must admit, looks terrific around a stable. But we have seen few recently renovated or newly built stables make use of it. For one thing, brick is incredibly expensive to lay, mostly because labor is so costly. Aside from that, brick does not have many advantages to offer the horse-owner and, in fact, is usually uneven to walk on, slippery when wet, and difficult to clean and disinfect.

ELECTRICITY AND WATER

Both electricity and running water are necessities. Where to put them is something each horseman must weigh against costs and climate. We can see no reason why electricity should not be available to every area of the stable, and we recommend that it be generously allocated in the basic plans. Conduit (BX cable) wiring is a must; all electric wires are threaded through metal or hard-rubber pipes so that they are virtually impervious to rodents' gnawing teeth. The stable should have its own fuse box to prevent overloading of circuits. Wiring for stalls should be run behind the walls or in the ceiling—out of reach of horses' teeth or inquisitive lips. Light switches and fixtures also should be out of reach or protected by bulb guards. Most horses will not disturb the light bulb in their stall, but occasionally a frisky or shying head will hit the fixture. We know of one young, impish colt that would grab at the light bulb with its teeth, pulling until the bulb and its guard were totally wrecked. Now its stall is the only one in the stable without a light. If anyone asks why, the horse's owner will gladly explain how his horse eats light bulbs for breakfast.

In the planning of a stable, it is often difficult to

anticipate exactly how much electricity you will eventually want to use. Possible needs may include electric heaters, electric clippers, an electric burner for cooking mashes, a heater cable or thermostat for the hydrants, a vacuum groomer, heat lamps for foals or sick animals, plus any number of added luxuries such as a radio or a refrigerator. True, you needn't have all these energy-consumers, but it is a good idea to wire as if you (or a future owner) might. Overloaded wiring is stupid, and extension cords are the playthings of fools. Statistics show that faulty wiring is the single largest cause of fire, and simple precautions and intelligent planning will help to keep that risk to a minimum. Of course, the decision about how to wire may be completely determined by the electric company and/or local building codes. If you run electricity into your stable, you may be required to follow their dictates with no alternatives available. So before you attempt to do the wiring yourself (something only an experienced electrician should do), check local building regulations.

Easily accessible water is essential to every stable. If you live in a region where freezing is not a problem and water is plentiful, we recommend you have water tapped into several parts of the stable. Obviously, the first requirement is to water the horses. Automatic waterers are a good solution. There are many kinds available, some with thermostats for those climates where temperatures go well below freezing. However, we know one cavalry remount veteran who scorns automatic waterers. He prefers to water his horse from a bucket three times a day in order to know exactly how much water is consumed. If the amount increases or decreases appreciably, he'll find out why. It's not surprising that because of such careful observation, his horses are rarely sick. Still, we recommend you provide a constant supply of clean water to each stall. If you choose one of the automatic troughs, make sure there is provision for turning it on and off easily, a necessity for those times (before worming, for instance) when you need to deprive the horse of water. Other logical places for faucets include the tack room, the grooming area, the feed room and the stable yard. The tack room is an excellent place for a sink or simply a hydrant and drain for cleaning saddles and bridles. A faucet in the grooming area is useful for filling a wash bucket or for attaching a hose or spray to rinse the horse down. There should of course be a drain in the floor to carry off the waste water. Water on tap in the feed room helps to clean out feed buckets, mix boiling mashes, and generally keep the room clean. Plan also on installing an outside faucet either in the stable yard or near the paddock. It will quickly change from a luxury to a how-did-we-ever-do-without-it necessity for general bathing of horses in warm weather, for hosing lame legs, for cleaning equipment, and for running water into nearby paddocks.

All water pipes leading to the stable should be buried 3 feet underground, or more in climates where the frost line is deeper. Try to avoid having the pipes laid underneath driveways where heavy trucks will be delivering feed and bedding. The weight of these trucks may be enough to snap the pipes and necessitate some expensive repairs. All drains should lead directly to a dry well or to a leach field made from perforated pipes. Zoning laws may require a separate septic system for sinks or that the waste water hook into the local waste-disposal system. Here, again, is where a quick trip to your local county agent's office can save much later grief and wasted money.

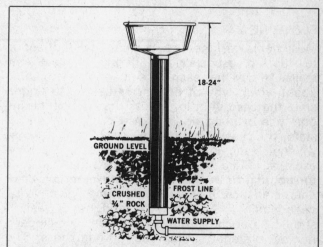

Water Witch. An automatic waterer that remains frostless without electricity or propane. The valve mechanism is located at the base of the column below the frost line. When the horse has finished drinking, an automatic drain-off feature slowly removes water from the basin before it can freeze. From Farnam for about $50.

ORGANIZING THE STABLE

Assuming you've decided on the best type of structure for your needs, you must then design an interior. We remember being asked as children to design a house on paper, and while we had vociferous convictions about where things should go, we discovered that turning the ideal into the pragmatic was more difficult than anticipated. The novice stable manager should take another tour of neighborhood facilities. Check out what others have done; interview them about what they like and dislike about their setups. With tactful prodding most horsemen are willing to admit their stable problems as they proudly point out the good features. Sources for plans are listed on page 23; we suggest you look into several of them and follow up on any ideas our listing may suggest to you.

Probably the most commonly visualized type of stabling is a long, single-floor structure with side-by-side stalls. Each stall door opens out into a stable yard, an alleyway created by the roof overhang, or directly into individual runs or a communal paddock.

There is also an arrangement that provides for a

number of stalls situated side by side along opposite stable walls. These two rows of stalls are separated by a wide alleyway which, depending upon the width, can be used for tying, grooming, saddling up, and even cooling out hot animals. This setup allows the horses to see one another if wire or openwork pipe or wood is used on the top part of the stalls. An alternative layout that benefits the bigger stables (it can be found in the barns at Belmont racetrack) is the "Island" design. It features two rows of side-by-side stalls that back each other. The stall doors open into an aisle which completely encircles the island. This outside aisleway can be used for cooling out a horse and, if the ceilings are high enough, for exercising it during bad weather. It does use up space other designs would allocate to more stalls or a larger tack room, but if you don't give a hoot about things like square-foot ratios and maximum efficiency quotients, this design may appeal to you.

We were particularly impressed with Mary Jean Vasiloff's stable arrangement in Old Lyme, Connecticut. Mrs. Vasiloff, who breeds Morgans, reached a point several years ago at which her horse population had outgrown the existing facilities. She chose an Agway pole barn with translucent fiber-glass panels inserted under the eaves of the roof. This material lets the natural daylight in, thus reducing the need for artificial lighting during the day. The stalls, which Mrs. Vasiloff built herself, line opposite sides of the building, with two stallion stalls in the corners of a third wall. The front of each stall is made of heavy-gauge wire with wooden supports. This open mesh permits Mrs. Vasiloff to glance into every stall and spot any horse that may be down and in trouble. The nicest feature of the stable, however, is the center—a big dirt-floored "ring" area large enough for schooling a horse when the weather is bad. However, Mrs. Vasiloff usually turns the foals and weanlings loose to play in the center. She does this regularly, first tying the mares in their stalls and then opening each door so that the foals can venture out into the communal ring. There, free to wander about, they play with each other and with the many visitors to the farm. After such a foalhood, gentling the Vasiloff horses is never a problem.

STALLS

Most box stalls are 12 feet square. A stall 10 feet square is often sufficient for medium-sized horses, while that size would be most generous for ponies. On the other hand, broodmare stalls are usually 16 feet square, and stallion stalls generally 14 feet square. If your horse has access to a roomy paddock, then a minimal stall is fine. The area need only be large enough for the animal to turn around comfortably, to lie down with ease, and to get up again without danger of becoming cast. (Casting occurs when a horse, rolling on its back, gets caught up against a stall wall and is unable to get its legs underneath its body.) Until only a few decades ago, most horses in this country were used

for transportation. Few of them rated box stalls at the end of the day. Nor did these horses need individual paddocks. They worked hard six days a week and got all the exercise they could use. What they needed was a quiet place to rest, eat their feed, and drink water. And what they returned home to each night was usually a straight stall, 8 to 10 feet long and 5 to 6 feet wide. These horses were tied into the stall by a stout rope attached to a halter. This arrangement allowed them to eat and even lie down, but restrained them from turning or backing out the open end of the stall. Nowadays, the straight stall is used in commercial stables, but rarely in private barns. Most commercial stables will provide boarders with box stalls and will keep their own schooling or hacking horses tied in straight stalls. Actually, the type of stall in which one keeps a horse is often determined more by fad and desire for status than by reason. If your horse is worked infrequently, then perhaps it should not be stabled at all but rather turned out to pasture. Or, if that is not possible, the horse should have regular access to a paddock. If, on the other hand, your horse is worked every day, then a tie stall may be appropriate. Large, roomy stalls are nice to look at, and they are more comfortable for most horses. But they do have some disadvantages worth acknowledging: box stalls are more difficult to clean than straight stalls; they permit the horse the freedom to develop such bad habits as stall-walking and weaving; and they may encourage the animal to expend energy unnecessarily instead of learning to stand quietly. Of course, many of these problems arise not from the stall size but from the boredom level of the animal. If a horse is not given enough exercise and lacks interesting things to see, hear, or smell, then those and other vices can be found in straight-, box-, or ballroom-housed animals.

For portable or ready-to-assemble stalls:

Farnam Companies, Inc.
2230 East Magnolia Street
P.O. Box 21447
Phoenix, Arizona 85036

HorsEquip, Inc.
P.O. Box 12291
Omaha, Nebraska 68112

Manson Industries, Inc.
Huntoon Street and Auburn Road
Topeka, Kansas 66604

Port-A-Stall
P.O. Box 447
Mesa, Arizona 85201

Horses are herd animals, happiest when they can see their stablemates. It is not uncommon for horses stabled next to each other to become devoted buddies, pairing off together in the pasture and whinnying when separated. Stalls are usually designed to allow the horses to see one another.

Stalls should be solid, light, well ventilated and draft-free. Most 8-foot-high stalls use 4-foot-high walls made of 2-inch-thick hardwood lumber (oak has been found to be the sturdiest of the woods) that has been treated with a creosote-type substance to discourage chewing. The top of the stall is often encircled by about 4 feet of vertical metal piping or wood slats (spaced about 4 inches apart), or 2-inch wire mesh. Metal is stronger and will last longer. Almost any building-supply outlet will sell piping (½-inch iron piping is good), and you can easily do your own assembling. If construction is not your forte, however, we have listed a number of builders on page 23 who will do the job.

Wood used for stalls should be treated with a nontoxic preservative to prevent it from rotting or splintering. Some horsemen install metal strips along the wooden ledges surrounding the grillwork to discourage chewing. If a horse is particularly unruly or a confirmed masticator, an electrified wire strung around the inside of the stall will usually keep it standing center stage.

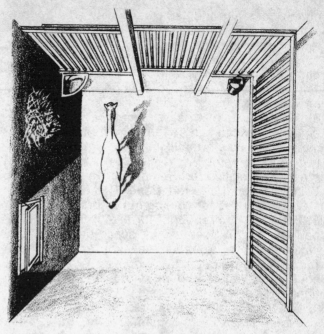

A Good Stall

TYING A HORSE

A log-and-rope arrangement is a proven method for tying a horse in its stall. It permits the horse enough rope to lie down comfortably while preventing the animal from becoming tangled in the rope's slack. One end of the rope is attached to the horse's halter. The other end is passed through an eye hook or through a hole drilled into the edge of the feed trough at about two-thirds the height of the horse at the withers. The rope should be about 3½ feet long, the length between the top of the manger and the floor. A doughnut-shaped wooden ball, hung from the bottom of the rope, is held in place by a simple knot. The ball acts as a weight, holding the rope taut at all times, taking up slack when the horse lowers its head and giving it sufficient length when the animal lies down. You can understand the value of this method when you hear a story, as we did, about a young horse incorrectly tied in its stall that got caught in the loose rope, panicked, and broke its neck. The cavalry always tied its horses (except those of the officers, who had box stalls for their mounts) into straight stalls. Instead of a wood ball, the cavalry used a variation on the hangman's knot which, when properly tied, was heavy enough to weigh down the rope but could not bruise the horse if the end swung into a knee.

Stall doors are normally made of solid wood, part wood and part grillwork, or (occasionally), all grillwork. Be it of a Dutch, swinging, or sliding design, it must be strong, yet balanced for easy opening. The Dutch door, able to be opened in separate halves, is the type of stable doorway most people think of first. In those sections of the country where stall doors can lead directly to a paddock or run, it is at once a door and, when the bottom section is latched closed, a window to the world outside. Dutch doors are less efficient for stable interiors, where many horsemen find it awkward to have a door open into an aisle trafficked by other horses. Nor is it pleasant when a horse can easily reach over the top of its door to nip any equine or human passerby (a bad habit that, unfortunately, can quickly develop). A Dutch door left open as a window encourages a horse to lean over and against the bottom door. Weeks of such weighty leaning is bound to bend almost any hinge or, at the least, alter the balance of the bottom door as it swings. A heavy-duty screen installed inside the frame of a regular one-piece door is a better solution. The screen is usually about 4½ feet high and is set about 2 feet off the ground, a height that can vary according to individual animals. Few horses can lean over the top or stretch out to nip at unsuspecting passersby, but they can have access to additional fresh air and a good view of the stable.

Doors that swing open should always be hung to swing out, never into the stall. Besides a strong lock, the door should have a separate hook to hold the opened door from swinging closed or into an entryway and blocking the area. Few of the newer stables make use of the full-size swinging door, preferring a sliding door made of 2-inch hardwood with open grillwork at the top. The sliding door, when properly hung from a top track, easily slides back against the outer wall of the stall and can be opened full width or less if desired.

Door latches should be accessible from the inside as well as from the outside of the stall. Now, obviously, you know enough not to lock yourself into the stall. But we can't remember an occasion

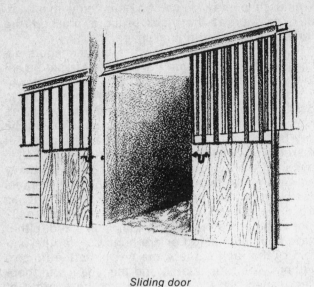

Sliding door

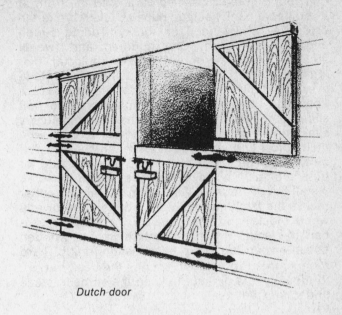

Dutch door

when a visiting youngster didn't find it wonderful fun to lock the stall door when we were inside.

Door latches must be horseproof—something easier said than achieved, since many horses are Houdinis about opening locks. It is difficult to judge what kind of latch is really horseproof. The horse that picks locks is usually spending hours and hours researching the problem and using that scientific method known as trial and error. Some horses get to be pretty good at it. For those individuals, and you will quickly discover which ones they are, we recommend that you use two locks on the stall door—one at normal height and the other at floor level where it can be fastened with your foot.

Several types of locks that are sold for horse barns are perfectly fine. But remember, it does not pay to scrimp when it comes to buying hardware for a stall. Heavy-gauge steel is a must; a light-

weight material will inevitably prove true the maxim that cost is what cost does. Even the most mild-mannered animal will lean against its door, kick to tell you that it's feeding time, or rub its backside during the shedding season. Good locks and hinges will hold up without difficulty, but thin ones will snap at an inopportune moment.

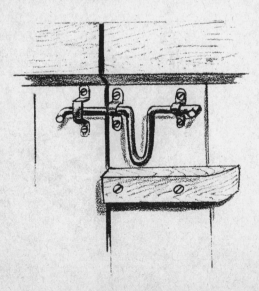

Protected stall latch

WOOD, A TASTY SUBJECT FOR HORSES

A test of eight different kinds of woods was conducted by the North Central Forest Experiment Station of the Forest Service of the U.S. Department of Agriculture and the School of Agriculture of Southern Illinois University at Carbondale to discover what woods were most durable and safe for horse stalls. Yellow poplar, elm, ash, red oak, beech, soft maple, hickory, and southern yellow pine were assessed. After seven years of testing, it was found that although none of the untreated parts decayed, the southern pine panels splintered and shelled more than the hardwoods but did not split or warp. Minor splitting occurred in soft maple and pine panels. Elm did not wear smoothly where horses' necks rubbed the door parts, while the hickory, beech, oak, and ash were rubbed smooth. Kicking and chewing damage was most obvious in the softest woods (southern yellow pine, yellow poplar, soft maple, and elm), while red oak, beech, and hickory were the least damaged.

There is one basic latch style—a simple and strong latch (see illustration) which we recommend, but with some reservations. We know of one young horse cross-tied parallel to the front of its stall that panicked and pulled back. It broke the cross ties and landed on the protruding 1-inch edge of the latch. One hundred and twenty stitches later, the horses' owner replaced that latch with one that had no protruding edges. However, we should point out that despite rare exceptions, the horse latch is efficient. When the bolt slides into the clamp, the shaft automatically slides down to hold it securely in place. Even with methodical and vigorous kicking and shaking, the bolt cannot be knocked loose. That is not true for other bolt-action locks. We recommend that you install the horse latch with an improvement: either recess the latch into the wall and the door, or add wood blocks above and below the latch (essentially replacing the metal protrusion with wooden ones), or cap the sharp edges with strips of hard rubber. This last solution sounds the best, but unfortunately it is difficult to keep the strips in place under constant use.

> **Stall screens. Round-corner or yoke style. A screen measuring 54×37 inches is about $35, 52×63 inches about $48, and the 52×45-inch yoke style about $50.**

Inside the stall is one place where decorating should be nonexistent. The interior of the stall must be free of any jutting edges and furnished with only the bare necessities. Basically, the horse requires only a feed manger and a water basin. For some horsemen even a hay rack is optional equipment.

The food manger should be hung in a corner, preferably one that is convenient for you to reach when filling it. A hole large enough to accommodate a scoop of grain cut into the stall wall directly above the feed basin saves time and labor. Most feed containers are large enough to hold from 16 to 20 quarts of grain. Pony feed boxes are somewhat smaller, in scale with their users' size. If you are planning to build your own manger, the dimensions are approximately 12 by 24 by 8 inches deep. While earlier mangers were made of either wood or galvanized iron, neither material is popular now. Wood was always difficult to clean, tended to splinter, and was easily chewed by the impatient horse thinking that feeding time was close. Galvanized iron basins were heavy and therefore difficult to lift out to clean. Even less desirable, the iron had hard edges that often caused severe cuts. Almost all horsemen appreciate the advantages of hard-plastic or heavy-rubber feed mangers. Nearly indestructible, they have a smooth, nonabsorbent surface that is easily wiped clean. The biggest single advantage, however, is that while these containers are almost impossible to kick apart, they will yield to pressure without causing any harm to the horse. We highly recommend these materials for feed mangers, water buckets, and any other containers you need

around the stable. Hard-rubber water buckets that are misshapen by ice can be pounded with a hammer; as soon as the block of ice is crushed, the bucket regains its original shape.

Before World War II, most stable managers adhered to the theory that the manger should be set low so that the horse had to bend its neck downward to eat simulating the posture necessary in pasture. These same people hung the hay racks up high so that the horse could reach up to pull at the hay but not risk catching its legs in the rack if it reared or kicked. The theory of furnishing a stall is quite different today. The grain box is normally hung at about two-thirds the height of the horse. For most horses that is between 38 and 42 inches from the ground, and for ponies from 28 to 32 inches high. Hay racks, on the other hand, either have been eliminated or are hung so that the bottom of the rack is the same height as the horse's withers. The rationale behind this change in theories, especially when it comes to the feeding of hay, is this: when the horse must reach up to pull down its hay, it will also pull down hay dust. This dust can easily lead to respiratory problems and eye infections. For this reason, many horsemen prefer to simply put the hay directly on the floor. Others object to that method, claiming it increases the chances for parasite reinfestation, as well as being wasteful. These horsemen, who have returned to the hay rack or hay net, hang it lower than did their predecessors. They use rubber, fiber, or plastic instead of metal or wood. These new materials ensure that if a horse does kick the rack, he will be less likely to be hurt.

Hay racks or nets should be large enough to hold between 25 and 30 pounds of hay for the average-size horse (between 10 and 15 pounds for ponies).

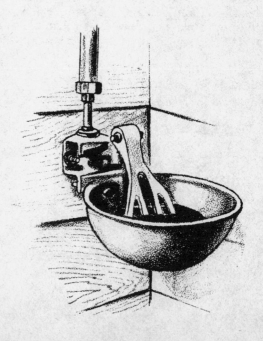

Automatic waterer

The other piece of equipment that is essential to every stall is the water trough. It may be a pail, preferably one that holds about 3 gallons, hanging at about the same height as the grain feeder. This bucket should be easily removable for at least twice-daily cleaning and refilling. Invariably, or at least it just seems that way, many horses will dump their hay into the water bucket, making it more difficult to clean out. Planning where to put the stall equipment should be determined with your convenience in mind. But sometimes you will have to accede to the horse's occasionally pointed likes and dislikes. We know of one animal that consistently dropped a load of manure into its water bucket. The solution was, of course, quite simple. After cleaning out the bucket for the third day in a row, the owner realized the only way to win this decorating disagreement was to give in. He moved the water bucket to the other side of the stall, and it has remained free of manure ever since. It's harder to make such adjustments with automatic water containers, but that is only a minor disadvantage when you consider all the good points such equipment has. True, it is more expensive to install, but it also guarantees that clean water will always be available. And since horses require about 12 gallons of water per day, you can readily see that the automatic waterer provides a huge saving in labor. In some stable designs, one automatic water container is installed in between two stalls to service two horses. This arrangement can nearly halve installation costs. The only problem is to be certain you have compatible animals. If one tends to be bossy or possessive and the other meek and acquiescent, a shared water trough will not work. Also, be aware that when two horses share a common feed utensil, they are more likely to transmit harmful bacteria.

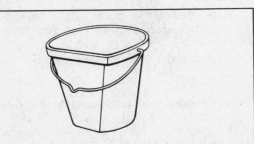

Water bucket made of high-density polyethylene plastic hangs against any flat surface. Full 18-quart capacity. About $8.

Ideally, a horse's drinking water should not be colder than 40 degrees Fahrenheit or warmer than 75 degrees. Water that is above or below that range may cause digestive problems or simply fail to cool the horse's body in the summer or heat it in the winter. In parts of the country where the temperature rarely goes below freezing, automatic water containers are ideal. For colder climates, you will need a heating unit for the pipe that leads directly to the container. In climates with fairly severe winters and cold periods that last

for several months, automatic waterers need to be chosen with special care or they may prove themselves more of an inconvenience than a help.

A piece of equipment you may want to add to the stall is a container for holding a salt and/or mineral block. (The necessity for regular access to minerals and their availability in a variety of forms are discussed in the following chapter.) If you provide minerals in the form of a block, there is a holder made for that purpose. An alternative is to set it on a small raised platform directly beneath the feedbox or, as one old horseman we know prefers, you can put a large chunk into the feedbox. This latter method requires the horse to eat slowly, pushing the block around to reach all the grain. The mineral blocks, of course, can be eliminated entirely if you add the proper minerals to each day's feed.

Cross-ties complete a well-furnished stall. They are handy for tying the horse while you muck out the night's bedding or for brushing it when the grooming area is already in use. When you want to deny the horse water, tying it away from the automatic waterer may be preferable to turning off the faucet and thus depriving a number of other horses. (This might be necessary to do after a horse returns from a heavy workout and, although cooled out, should be prevented from gulping water for about an hour.) Cross ties are easy to install. All you need is two No. 0 screw eyes and two strong beams on opposite walls. The screw eyes should be placed at about the same height as the horse's head. We recommend using a stout cord or rope for the ties themselves—something that is strong but will, with exceptional pulling or with the stroke of a penknife, break loose. Chain is stronger than rope, but we've seen too many horses panic and so tighten the chain that it could not be unhooked before the horse had done a great deal of damage to itself. Quick thinking, a rope, and a ready penknife would have saved the situation.

ALLEYWAYS

Unless your stable is so designed that each stall opens out into a paddock, there will be an alleyway in front of the stalls. This aisle should be a minimum of 8 feet wide to allow swinging doors (which are, you remember, 4 feet wide) to open without blocking the passageway and to allow the horse to be turned around with ease. We know of one old converted stable with an aisle only 4 feet wide. When a door to a stall is opened, guests must stand aside. None of the horses can be turned around in the aisle, and as they are led past the other stalls, there is invariably much squealing and kicking. Leading a belligerent horse down such an alleyway can make even an experienced horseman apprehensive.

Aisles that are wider than 8 feet may be necessary in those stables where tractors deliver feed and pick up manure. Aisles that are wider still can be used for exercising or cooling out the horses. (At some point an aisle may be classified as a center ring, but we will refrain from committing ourselves to deciding when.) In the aisle, directly outside each stall, should be hooks for hanging halters and lead ropes. It may seem a convenience, but it is also an essential safety precaution ensuring that each horse has a halter and lead rope always available. For in case of fire, the tack room, however close by, will be too far away for you to quickly find the headgear needed to lead the horse from danger. Try not to put the halter near the grillwork of the stall; it is an easy game for a horse to pull the halter into the stall and then treat the leather as if it were chewing gum. Although horses rarely get sick from this game, you may when you make an unexpected payment to your tack shop.

Halter or bridle hook; cast iron coated in nylon. About $5.

With the addition of cross ties, alleyways can be used for grooming and washing a horse. In a small stable, that is an efficient use of the space. In a larger stable, tying a horse in the aisle will probably block the flow of traffic.

The flooring in the aisle can be the same as that used in the stalls. Because the area is put to more diverse uses, however, you may find you have different requirements for its flooring. It is not uncommon for a stable to use concrete or asphalt, or even indoor/outdoor carpeting over concrete, for the alleyways or even in the tack, feed, and grooming rooms. Basically, the floor in the aisle must be skidproof, easy to sweep clean, and fireproof.

FEED ROOM

The feed room of a small stable needn't be particularly large, but it must be separated from the stall area by a sturdy partition and a horseproof lock. Horses are naturally grazing animals; in the wild they spend their time carefully clipping each blade of grass slowly and systematically. A horse's natural inclination is to eat as much as it can get, and when confronted with 100 pounds of grain, it will eat itself literally to death or, at least, to lameness (founder). Ideally, the feed room must have a solid rat- and mouse-proof flooring (concrete is best and easiest to clean). The room should also be accessible to delivery areas.

Many small stables find that aluminum or hard-plastic garbage cans with tightly locking lids are excellent for storing feed. We find that one large-size (about 30 gallons) can will hold 100 pounds of corn, while two cans are needed to hold 100 pounds of crimped oats. One horse owner, while reconverting an old barn into a stable for his mare

and her foal, found the old grain-storage bin still intact. It was made of beautifully antiqued wood perforated along the bottom with a series of equally antique mouseholes. Determined to restore the grain bin, he discovered upon inquiry that the local newspaper was delighted to sell used tin plates, sheets about 24×30 inches, for very little money. He bought enough of the sheet metal to line the grain bin completely. We know of another horseman who acquired an old dairy barn equipped with an all-metal cooler that had been used to store cans of milk. The barn was easily converted to accommodate horses, but the milk room was left intact. It was found that the milk cooler would hold as many as six 100-pound bags of grain safely out of reach of rodents. Some horse owners with limited space prefer to store their grain in large wooden boxes kept in a combination feed and tack area. If it is accessible to horses, stand the box against a wall where it will be impossible for even the most determined animal to kick it over.

Larger stables store their feed in special metal grain bins designed for that purpose. These bins are often built on the roof of the stable, connecting to the feed room by a chute that empties into a container or feed cart. Although an excellent arrangement for the larger stable that has the equipment to load the feed and unload it into the storage bin, it is totally inefficient for a smaller stable. In fact, it is unwise to attempt to store large quantities of feed that will not be used quickly. For even though buying feed in large quantities seems economical, it is anything but when the feed begins to mold.

Hay and bedding to be stored in the feed room require extra space. It is usually more economical to buy hay and bedding during a particular season—either during harvest time or, in the case of sawdust, during the mill's busiest period—and you may want to store a year's worth in the feed room. Most stables, however, simply do not have the space and order their hay in smaller batches.

Utility Scale with pounds divided into eighths; weighs up to 60 pounds. About $11.
Hanging scale, capacity 20 pounds, graduated in ounces. About $14.

HAYLOFT

Some stable designs include a loft for hay storage; others provide for a separate floor. This latter arrangement worked well for centuries. In old walled cities in Bavaria, for instance, are houses over nine hundred years old that were originally designed with the ground floor for the livestock, the two middle floors for the family, and the top floor for hay. They knew that hay insulated the building to keep it warm in winter and cool in summer. But hay also has another inherent quality that is important to keep in mind: it is highly flammable. Many stable designers opt for safety, storing hay away from the stall areas in a fireproof room or even in a separate structure.

TACK ROOM

More horses require more tack and, therefore, a larger tack room. Tack should be kept out of the stall area in a well-lighted room tightly closed against stable dust. In a one-or two-stall stable, a small area away from the horses' reach or from the direct line of traffic is satisfactory.

Tack trunk. The perfect solution for the small stable that does not have a separate tack room. This trunk holds up to four English saddles or one Western saddle as well as bridles, halters, and grooming aids. Rodent- and dustproof. About $135.

Tack rooms can be as large as requirements and finances dictate. For some stables, it serves not only as a storage room for saddles and blankets but as a workroom (and a social area for swapping horse tales). It is not uncommon to find a couch, a refrigerator, a bar, and a wall decorated with ribbons or photographs in this room.

The tack room needs to be large enough to accommodate a rack for each saddle and bridle.

Racks are necessary for several reasons: they help maintain the shape of the saddle; they organize the equipment so that it is accessible; they keep it off the floor where it might otherwise be dumped to become damp, dusty, mouse-trodden and generally unusable. Racks are sold at tack shops, and

Infrared heaters can be used in the tack room, to eliminate mildew and dampness; in foaling stalls, where they can give quick warmth for the newly dropped foal; for the horse needing therapeutic heat treatments; and for slicking up coats before a show. The Merco heat tube is guaranteed against burnout for three years and against explosion for the life of the tube. Merco Products, Inc., 1298 Bethel Drive, Eugene, Oregon 97402

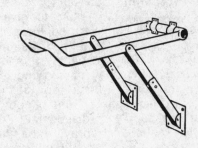

Folding Western-Saddle Rack. Rustproof enameled-steel rack attaches to any wall and will support up to 250 pounds. When not in use, it folds out of the way; especially useful in trailers and tight storage areas. About $14.50.

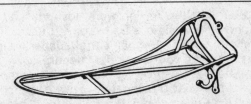

English-Saddle Bracket. Made of iron covered with brightly colored plastic for a smooth, non-rust surface over a strong brace. About $14.

you can also make your own quite easily and inexpensively. A clean 20-gallon oil drum bought from a local gas station and bolted to a tack-room wall is an excellent size for holding the saddle's shape (and for storing such equipment as spurs, ropes, and extra bits in the opening beneath). A small coffee can or cat-food can mounted on a wall is a good shape for holding bridles and halters, and you need only raid the kitchen garbage to find one.

GROOMING AREA

It is a good idea to situate the tack room near the grooming area. This spot can, again, be a separate room or simply part of the aisle outside the stalls. The grooming area should have firm, nonskid flooring, a high ceiling, drainage, electrical outlets for grooming equipment, and a storage shelf or cabinet for grooming supplies and the first-aid kit. One stable included a 10×12-foot wash room painted with marine enamel to protect the wood. The poured cement floor was scored to prevent slipping and sloped toward a drain in the center of the room. As soon as the horse had been washed and hosed down, it was moved directly under a small radiant heater that hung from the ceiling. Capable of heating the area within its range to about 70 degrees, it would quickly dry the wet horse, even when the temperature was below freezing.

TOOL STORAGE

Every stable needs certain tools for maintaining the building. A separate room isn't necessary for these supplies, yet you will have to give some thought to where they will be stored. First, let's list the items: a broom; a 4- or 5-tined manure fork (with several extra for company); a shovel; a wheelbarrow, cart or basket for carrying the manure to the manure pit; a basic tool kit that will include a screwdriver, pliers, wire clipper, hammer, and nails; a supply of disinfectant such as lime; and a fly repellent for spraying the stable in summer. Many horsemen hang forks and shovels from hooks in one corner of the feed or tack room. The only requirement is that the tools be out of the way of the horses, so that a horse standing on cross ties, for instance, cannot accidentally back into a manure fork propped against the wall.

MANURE DISPOSAL

To pit, to pile, to raise mushrooms, that is the question. Mushroom growers love it, and avid gardeners appreciate a free supply, but few horse owners know how to deal with it successfully. We are talking, of course, about manure. One 1,000-pound-horse will produce 10 tons (yes, *tons*) of manure per year. Fortunately, only 20 percent of horse manure is urine; the rest is dry. (Hog manure, for instance, is about 40 percent urine.) Horse manure can, therefore, be handled with forks as a solid rather than with shovels as a liquid. Even if you have only one or two horses, the

accumulation of manure can become a growing and unending problem. Large stables find it economical to install automatic gutter cleaners for carrying the manure through the barn and into a dump truck, a manure spreader, or a manure pit. Such equipment, while expensive to install, saves on labor. One or two people can quickly go through each stall and shovel the day's manure onto the gutter cleaners, usually located in an alleyway off the stall or along a wall behind the stall. Some stables prefer to fork the manure into the alley, where a scraper and power loader drives through and cleans up the area.

For the small stable, however, such equipment is incredibly costly. The alternatives are to arrange for daily removal of the waste, to dig a manure pit, or simply to make a pile. If you live in a strictly zoned area (regulated as to how many birdhouses permitted per tree), then consult local experts about waste storage. If you are permitted to store waste on your property, you should apply certain standards to the area as well. A manure pile or pit has certain requirements. It should be accessible to the stalls for easy filling each day. It should also be accessible to the trucks that regularly cart it away. And, since manure piles are rarely pleasing to the eye, it should be kept out of sight and out of smell. Remember that manure attracts flies, that it has a bad odor as it composts, that it is filled with the parasites eliminated by the horse (the best reason why it should never be located within a pasture or corral), that it may smoke as it composts, and that its ammonia content may be damaging to foundations. The last two points are sound reasons for locating the manure pile a distance from the stable walls. The least objectional method for dealing with manure is to dig a pit about 4 feet square and 4 feet deep. This pit can be covered with a perforated top that will keep the pit out of sight, and prevent children and other animals from falling through, but will also allow the fumes caused by the composting process to escape. Some horsemen prefer to build a concrete platform that slopes slightly to one side to encourage drainage. Manure piled on the platform for storage is scraped off with a tractor plow when enough has accumulated.

Large Stable Facilities

Another book can be written about how to organize facilities for the large breeding or training stable. We will simply outline what some of those needs are and offer suggestions about where to get more information. Even if you do not intend to build a stabling complex in your backyard, you may find some ideas that can easily adapt to your small stabling needs.

The largest breeding farms will often have separate areas (either barns, sheds, or simply pastures) for broodmares about to foal, for mares waiting to be covered by a stallion, for weanlings of various ages, for stallions, for breeding, for isolation. Broodmare barns are normally built close to living quarters (or vice versa) and often provide a place for the attendant groom to keep watch during the foaling season. A stall for a large, blooded animal (usually the only kind of horse to merit such a setup) is 16 feet square. It is well lighted and usually includes a heat lamp for the newly born foal. Soon after the foal is born, the mare and her youngster are turned out to pasture with other broodmares and their young. When the weather is too severe for the foals, they will be brought in at night (however, rarely is a large and profitable breeding complex situated in a region where the climate normally requires such additional housing).

Stallion barns in the large establishments are based on two theories: one says that the stallions ought to be kept away and upwind from the broodmares; the second theory says that stallions are herd animals that like to see other horses, even if only at a distance. Some breeders find that allowing a stud to run in pasture with two or three mares in foal keeps him quiet and content. What is obvious to anyone who keeps a stallion (something we believe should not be done unless you have both an animal with particularly good qualities that you intend to use for breeding and the facilities to keep him properly) is that extra attention must be given to his facilities. A stud stall should be fairly large—most breeders prefer a stall about 14 feet square—with its own paddock. The paddock fence should be strong and a minimum of 6 feet high, and double fence should separate nearby stallion paddocks. Many local zoning laws have restrictions against keeping stallions or may require that you obtain a special permit after passing an inspection of your facilities. And if your stallion manages to break out of his paddock to cover your neighbor's mares, don't expect to collect stud fees, no matter how valuable your horse. Do, however, expect a visit from the local police and your neighbor's attorney. The saying "Good fences make good neighbors" still holds true.

Some breeding establishments have a separate barn, shed, or other area for the actual breeding. Normally it is a roofed area about 24 feet square and may include a stall for prepping the mare (for such things as bandaging her tail, hobbling her legs, or padding her hind feet), a small stall for restraining her foal, and often a breeding rail over which the mare may first be teased. This breeding shed, usually located near the stallion barn, may even be a part of that barn.

Large establishments will also maintain a separate barn for isolating sick animals or for keeping newly arriving horses for a short quarantine period. This isolation barn should have its own watering and feeding equipment and its own waste-removal system. Manure and waste bedding from it should not be added to the regular pit if that pit is anywhere near the other barns.

Rings and Arenas

Commercial suburban and urban stables usually provide their boarders with the use of outdoor and indoor ring facilities. Some horsemen are finding it beneficial to join with others to build cooperative facilities. The type of ring that will be built is often determined by the type of riding most of the people using the facility will be doing. A jumping arena for a large horse show is usually 150×300 feet with straight sides of 200 feet. Many commercial establishments function quite well with rings only 125×250 feet. If the stable is quite small, then 80×150 feet may be sufficient.

Rings' three basic shapes are each adapted for a specialized kind of work: rectangular, rectangular with rounded edges, and oval. Rectangular "rings" are preferred by dressage riders, who will use the corners for teaching the horse to bend correctly. The rounded-ends "ring" is preferred by horsemen who jump their animals (and many stable managers are finding it an easier shape for their tractors to disk). Oval "rings" that can be banked along the sides are preferred by horsemen who work their horses with buggies and other wheeled vehicles.

For both indoor and outdoor rings, good footing is the single essential ingredient for success. And good footing depends, as do so many other things, on what kind of work you are asking your horse to perform. If you are interested in jumping, then you will want a ring with a fairly deep and soft surface to help cushion the horse's legs. If, however, you are interested in speed events, such as barrel racing or rodeo eventing, a firmer surface would be more desirable. For work that requires high collection and a high-stepping gait, you will want a springier surface that is neither too deep nor too hard. Footing in a ring also depends on drainage, and it is essential that the ring be located in a high area that is naturally dry. Many arenas' bases are stone, covered by gravel and then clay. On this surface are laid any number of materials for the desired footing: manure mixed with sand; tanbark or soil about 6 to 8 inches deep; shavings or sawdust mixed with soil; 18 to 24 inches of sand; or shredded rubber. Rings also require regular maintenence. They should be gone over with a chain harrow before each show and in between major events or each morning before regular workouts. They should be watered or coated with a thin layer of oil to keep down dust. Surfaces mixed with soil are dustier than others, and the amount of watering needed will vary accordingly. It is usually necessary to redo the surface of a ring each year. A dirt-based outdoor ring should be disced under. To prevent the ground from freezing in winter, rock salt or calcium chloride may be added to the composition.

The horse owner throughout history has always held a position of social esteem. In the European languages, for example, cavalier *in English,* chevalier *in French,* caballero *in Spanish,* Ritter *in German—all designations for aristocrats— originally simply meant "horseman."*

The huge, air-supported "tennis" bubble shown here has housed the indoor ring of the Bear Ridge Riding Club in Pleasantville, New York, for the past four years. The structure measures 300 feet long by 140 feet wide and 45 feet high. It is made of a flexible plastic material supported by slightly increased air pressure that works on the balloon principle. Fortunately, unlike a balloon, it does not burst if punctured but merely sags. Horses enter through an air lock, a specially devised automatic double-door system. Spectators use an airtight revolving door. Three separate schooling rings can be accommodated at the same time, or the entire space can be used for a horse show. Since the covering material is translucent, the arena need be lighted only at night. A provision for heating the space in the winter is not used by this club, because it is prohibitively expensive and consumes vast amounts of fuel oil. The bubble has several drawbacks. It can be extremely cold in winter. When snow collects on the roof it often cascades off the rounded sides with a loud roar that spooks many of the horses. It has also been reported that under certain conditions, indoor fog blankets the activities.

Outdoor rings should be enclosed by painted fencing that is sturdy and solid-looking, of wood plank or even of pipe. Either fencing will discourage a horse from bursting through, and it will not harm the animal when you intentionally turn it into the rails for schooling purposes. With regard to gates, if the ring is occasionally used as a paddock, then a horseproof latch is essential. A good ring, however, should be used only for working. It is more convenient to install a gate latch that can easily be opened by the rider while on horseback.

Many Western pleasure-riding classes, of course, require the rider to do just that.

Pole-constructed indoor arenas are often finished with a rim of lumber about 4 feet high. This resilient kickboard protects the horse in case it kicks out or cuts too close to the edge of the inner wall. It also encloses the steel beams that would otherwise protrude into the ring. Many stable managers wrap the exposed steel beams with a quilted material (much like the kind used by professional moving men) to protect the riders from injury if they are accidentally thrown against the beam.

Cavalletti
by Catherine McWilliams

Cavalletti are an extremely valuable aid in the training of horses and riders. In addition to their use in improving the horse's way of going on the flat, they are especially helpful in training over jumps. The cavalletti, or ground rails, are wooden poles raised from 4 to 20 inches off the ground. They are spaced in various patterns that require the horse to step over them in its normal gaits of walk, trot, and canter.

Many riders use ordinary jumping rails laid flat on the ground as cavalletti. These lack many of the advantages of properly built cavalletti. In addition, they could cause an accident by rolling under a horse's foot.

The most useful cavalletto consists of one rail supported by an attached X-shaped frame at either end. If the X is constructed so that one pair of legs is longer than the other, the resulting cavalletti can be set up at three different heights.

Aside from the obvious advantage of a choice of three heights, cavalletti of this type are easily portable and can be stacked one upon another to make a jump of any desired height and spread.

In schooling, cavalletti can largely replace the traditional standards and poles, as they require less space to store, fewer materials to construct, and less effort to set up and adjust.

The most common application of cavalletti is in the regulation of the horse's stride at the trot. Three to six cavalletti, placed in a straight line 4½ to 5½ feet apart, accommodate the stride of most horses. Experimenting will determine the exact distance for each horse. In its effort to step over the rails and place its feet on the ground between them, the horse's concentration and way of moving are both improved.

Placing cavalletti before a fence will make the jump easy for the horse, as its speed, length of stride, and straightness are all determined by the ground rails. The distance between the fence and the closest cavalletto should be twice the distance between adjacent cavalletti.

A thorough treatise on the use of cavalletti for training dressage horses as well as jumpers is *Cavalletti* by Reiner Klemke, J. A. Allen & Co., London.

~~~~~~~~~~~~~~~~~~~~~~~~~~~~~~~~

Some Famous Horses Of Myth and History

Bavieca. El Cid's horse, which survived its master by two and one-half years. The horse was buried in front of a monastery in Valencia, Spain, where two elm trees were planted to mark the grave.

Bucephalus. Alexander the Great's Horse. The emperor was the only person who could ride the horse, which, according to history, always knelt down when Alexander mounted.

Copenhagen. The mount of the Duke of Wellington during the Napoleonic Wars.

Incitatus. The horse prized by the Roman emperor Caligula, who had the animal named a priest and consul. (Some people say that that was the first time an entire horse was a politician.)

Lamri. King Arthur's mare.

Marengo. Napoleon's favorite horse, the white Arabian stallion that he rode at Waterloo.

Traveller. Robert E. Lee's horse.

White Surrey. Richard III's horse, for which he cried, according to the Shakespearean play, "A horse! A horse! My kingdom for a horse!"

~~~~~~~~~~~~~~~~~~~~~~~~~~~~~~~~

FENCING

Fences work two ways. They are necessary for keeping your horses in. They are also necessary for keeping your neighbors out. The latter problem may not seem an important one unless you live in a residential section where children and dogs are attracted, like flies, to horses. Then you must consider them seriously. For the law says that if an accident occurs on your property, you are responsible. And if negligence can be proved (for example, if an electric wire is lying loose and shocks a child, causing him to fall and hurt himself), then insurance may not protect you from loss.

Every horse magazine and book includes a photograph of a farm or ranch crisscrossed by a grid of white lines. This beautiful white-painted post-and-board fencing means horses. Always beautiful and strong (and we recommend it highly), it has also become terribly expensive to install and maintain and is now often used for small pastures. It is ideal for outdoor rings, for paddocks, and for fencing a highly visible front stretch of a pasture. For the back part of that pasture, however, or even for alternative fencing for the front, there are several kinds that are effective. The following chart includes several fencing materials, with the advantages and disadvantages of each listed.

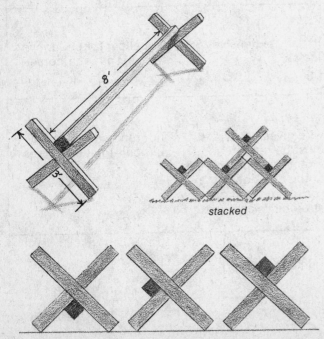

stacked

Cavalletti

Fences			
Types	Advantages	Disadvantages	Suggestions
Chain-Link (all-metal links, 2–4-inch gauge. Supported by metal vertical and horizontal pipe)	highly effective; recommended for stud paddocks; excellent for keeping out small people and dogs and for keeping in foals; low maintenance	expensive; may stretch when horse leans against it	use for difficult-to-keep horses or in highly developed residential areas
Post-and-Board (2×4-inch cedar or locust posts; 2-inch hardwood lumber; 2, 3, or 4 boards)	good-looking; increases value of property; safe for horses	expensive; requires preservative or painting; can be chewed or kicked apart; horse can loosen posts by constant pushing against boards (as he leans to eat grass on other side); not long-lasting.	to keep horse away from fence, run an electric wire along inside of top board; mow a strip of grass around the border of the paddock; place boards on inside of posts except at corners; paint boards with a chewing preventive or nail metal strips along the top of the board
Post-and-Rail (2×4-inch cedar or locust posts; 4-inch-diameter poles)	good-looking; safe for horses; need not be painted	expensive, although less than boards; same disadvantages as boards	
Pipe (prejobbed sections; rustproof metal; posts sunk into concrete)	strong; safe; maintenance-free; long-lasting	initially expensive to install	excellent for paddocks and for difficult horses
Wire-Mesh (wood or metal posts and horizontal bracing; 2–4-inch mesh)	inexpensive; will keep small animals out	wire gives easily and must be restretched often; must be braced at top and bottom to prevent curling or stretching; can rust	not recommended for difficult-to-keep horses
Rubber-Rail (wood or metal posts)	safe for horses; excellent for training rings; low maintenance	initially expensive	

Fences			
Types	Advantages	Disadvantages	Suggestions
Electric Wire (wood or metal posts; 2- or 3-strand 10–12-gauge wire; 115-volt pulsating current)	inexpensive; good for fence-training young horses	difficult to see; not recommended for populated areas; wire stretches easily and can be broken by deer and other animals; electric flow can be easily shorted by high-growing weeds or fallen branches; must be accessible to power or battery; must be maintained; not particularly attractive	good when used with board fence; recommend medium-light-gauge wire that will break in an emergency; tie white strips of cloth to wire to increase visibility; attach gate handle to the dead end of wire so that you aren't handling a live end when the gate is open
Barbed-Wire (wood or metal fence posts)	inexpensive	barbed wire can tear horses up so severely that they must be destroyed; it stretches; it is difficult to handle in installing or restretching	not recommended
Rosa Multiflora (living hedge fully grown can be 10–15 feet wide, 8–10 feet high)	attractive	requires good soil and climate; takes up some space from the pasture; takes three years to reach fence size; should be pruned and fertilized annually for good growth	

~~~~~~~~~~~~~~~~~~~~~~~~~~~~~~~~~~~

"Martha Carleton, a student at Michigan State University, has filed a paternity suit in Walled Lake, Mich., District Court against the Colonial Acres Hunt Club in South Lyon, Mich., charging that Martha's mare was unwillingly forced into a romantic affair by a stallion and as a result the mare gave birth to a colt. Martha seeks damages under an 1867 law holding stable owners responsible for such equine dalliance."

The Boston Globe
November 1976

~~~~~~~~~~~~~~~~~~~~~~~~~~~~~~~~~~~

3 STABLE MANAGEMENT

Good stable management doesn't come out of a book. True, you can outline all the procedures that are necessary for seeing that horses are well cared for, and we intend to some degree to do that here. But the best stable manager we know combines years of experience, ever-observent senses, and pure common sense to manage his horses, and they are rarely sick or troubled with such ailments as lameness, colic, heaves, or thrush. This old horseman knows even before he opens the stable door whether one of his horses is in trouble—if its nose is running, or if it is becoming constipated and in need of some bran. How does he do it? It's not something that can be explained—it's a talent either you have or you don't. It is a talent for observation, for empathizing with the animals, and for being deeply concerned for their well-being. Obviously it is not a talent that is easily taught, but nonetheless it is one that people who care for horses should concentrate on developing.

There are two essential reasons for being concerned about good management: for the safety of the horse and the safety of the horseman. A stable manager must apply his intellect to anticipate what a horse will do under any number of situations and even to anticipate the impossible (which, to every horseman's surprise, inevitably happens). In any stable there is always one animal that, when brought into the established routine, quickly finds the flaws in that routine and makes the most experienced horseman sigh in disbelief. Stating the obvious, a horse is a big animal, outweighing most horsemen by some 800 pounds. Fortunately, no one has told the horse about this. But because the horse doesn't know its own size, it is also capable of getting itself into trouble. Being a genetically flighty animal, it will normally attempt to sprint away when confronted with the unusual. Running in the face of danger has done wonders for the preservation of the species; however, when that instinct meets up with modern stabling, it can be a dangerous trait. So the contemporary stable must be analyzed and made as free as is possible of any faults potentially harmful to the horse or the horseman. For example, we know of one older and wiser gelding who had never heard live band music before, a fact that the owner did not hold against it. But one spring, the town fathers organized a parade and chose the road in front of the stable to gather the band and start them off on the right foot. The drums rolled, the cymbals crashed, the band marched off and that normally quiet old gelding quivered, reared, and bucked. And, its kicking found the one weakness in its stall—the latch on the swinging stall door. The latch, it seems, was put on with ¾-inch screws instead of bolts, and while the screws looked sturdy, one well-motivated kick proved they weren't. Even more frightened than before, the horse ran up and down the stable aisle exciting all the other horses. The owner, who only moments before had thought he had the stable well organized and safe, was confronted with a crazed horse needing to be gentled and led to safety.

Accidents or health problems caused by poor management are more common than one might think, and one minute of carelessness can easily make a valuable horse worthless and a much-loved pet into food for the dogs. Horsemen tell stories that prove beyond doubt (or logic, for that matter) that it is invariably the refined, well-bred horse that pulls a stifle en route to the stable yard while its coarser, less well-put-together counterpart will trip over the door ledge, for instance, and go down in a spectacular and terrifying spill, only to gallop off with never a pulled ligament to show for his clumsiness. We know of several coarse perfect glue-factory candidates pastured in an area surrounded on three sides by downed barbed-wire fencing. The fourth side of the pasture has no fencing, but the ground is littered with every conceivable obstacle. With open mouths we would watch these horses trot and gallop through the center of this minefield, tangle in the loose wire, and blithely kick themselves free. We can only guess that there is special attention from above for animals asked to endure such hardships. The purpose of this story is not, by any means, to encourage sloppiness in caring for horses; it is intended to assert that even though there are occasionally some horses that can survive anything, it is never your own animal.

BASIC CARE

Whether your horse is the star of the National Horse Show or a green-broke grade pastured outside the year around, it has certain basic needs you will have to see to. And failure to fulfill any of these basic needs almost certainly will end in equine health problems or even in the horse's death.

The first concern for any horse is a clean, adequate supply of water. Nothing, short of a shotgun, will kill a horse quicker than lack of water. Few people deny the substance to their horses intentionally, but occasionally water is absent through negligence. Automatic waterers, even though they have been improved over the years and are now generally reliable, can clog, freeze, or simply break. Therefore, it is a basic rule of horse care that the waterer be inspected daily. Neglect of the automatic waterer for just two or three days could be fatal. If you rely on a pond, stream, or spring-fed trough for your horse's water supply, it too should be inspected daily. Besides its possibly freezing, or unexpectedly drying up at the source, there is always the possibility that a small animal could drown in the water supply and contaminate it. The automatic water troughs inside the stalls also need to be checked for cleanliness. Some horses periodically drop their feces into the trough and then refuse to drink the polluted water. When traveling from one area to another, be sure to check to see that your horse is drinking its regular amount. Often a horse will refuse water that tastes unfamiliar, as can happen when chlorinated or fluoridated water is introduced or withdrawn. We know of one old gelding that would go without water for almost two days when first brought in from summer pasture. Used to drinking from a clear, spring-fed pond, the old fellow had developed the taste buds of a gourmet, and he made it quite clear that the metallic-tasting water from the faucet just would not do. His owners learned to anticipate the problem and now add a small amount of molasses to the water bucket, reducing the amount each day until no molasses is needed.

The second most important need every horse has is adequate feed. Again, few horse owners intentionally deny feed to their animals. Malnutrition is usually due to ignorance (for example, the pasture that seemed so green may in fact have been depleted of any nutritional grasses or legumes). The malnourished horse has a low resistance to disease and is more likely to die from a respiratory ailment than from lack of bulk food. Even stall-housed horses fed daily rations may be malnourished, so it is essential that the horse owner remain alert to the possibility. Check and clean out the feed manger daily and note when the horse is off its feed, an important sign that it is sick. Also inspect the horse's feces. If you notice a quantity of grain in the manure, call the vet to check the horse's teeth. There are terrible stories about the person (we can't call him a horseman) who, in order to economize on feed, adds sawdust for bulk. Bulk it may be, but good horse care it sure isn't.

Most feeding problems stem from overfeeding rather than underfeeding. In this country of plenty, we sometimes blindly follow the unstated concept "More is better." Often we overfeed ourselves but the effects on our health of the extra weight may not show up for forty or fifty years. However, a horse that is overfed, either with too much or with too rich a feed, can let us know immediately by going lame (founder). It is important to recognize the symptoms and to anticipate the problem by checking your horse's condition daily and asking, and taking, the advice of your veterinarian.

All horses need a certain amount of exercise. The necessary amount, like food requirements, depends on the individual animal. However, it is unusual to find privately owned horses that are over-exercised. Usually it is the other way around. Horses need exercise to keep their systems functioning properly, to keep up and develop muscle tone, and to stay in good spirits. (Horses rarely develop depression as we know it in humans; they do, however, develop bad habits—vices—that once learned are rarely forgotten.)

There are certain basic rules that every horseman learns and follows closely. And just a moment's deviation from these rules can often cause severe problems. For example, an experienced horseman knows that putting a lathered horse into its stall invites such problems as colic, founder, or respiratory ailments. Lathered or hot horses should not, for the same reason, be permitted to drink until they are sufficiently cooled out. A good horseman will also see that the horse is not asked to abruptly begin hard work without a short period of warm-up. (One old horseman refers to this warm-up as "getting the farts out.") Inexperienced horsemen will, in their enthusiasm, occasionally ask their horse to do more than it is conditioned to do. This is a serious fault and can lead to many problems. Some horses when pushed beyond their capability—and a horse's capability often depends on its conditioning—may lose their will (sense of self, heart, call it what you want).

Experienced horsemen will also groom their animals daily. During this ritual—and properly done, it becomes just that—the horseman will remove all obvious clumps of dirt from the horse's coat, taking particular care to see that the part of the back where a saddle will sit and that part of the belly where the girth fits is altogether clean and free of sores or bruises. During the daily brushing, he will be on the lookout for cuts or bruises that need first-aid attention and for heat in the legs, indicating fever, checking at the same time for running eyes or nose and whether the eye has a bright and alert look instead of a dull and cloudy one (a sign of some disorder). While cleaning the horse's feet, he will also check to see that the shoes fit firmly and that the hoof is adequately trimmed, the frog firm and pliant, and the hoofs without cracks or splits.

~~~~~~

"Medicine for an Ill-Tempered Horse"

"The Birtwick horse-balls . . . were made up of patience and gentleness, firmness and petting; one pound of each to be mixed with a pint of common-sense, and given to the horse each day."

Anna Sewell
Black Beauty

~~~~~~

SAVE MONEY AROUND THE STABLE

- Use the best-quality feeds; it's cheapest in the long run.
- Feed three times a day; your horse will waste less and get more out of each feed.
- Buy hay in bulk and as much feed as you can keep free of rodents or mold.
- Store grains in rodentproof covered containers.
- Watch the feeding ration; analyze your horse's condition and adjust quantities as needed.
- Weigh all feeds; each delivery bulks differently.
- Feed ½ teaspoon table salt per feed instead of using salt bricks.
- Clean and repair tack regularly.
- Attend to all injuries immediately; this may save a vet call later.
- Turn horses out regularly; this saves on bedding.
- Use a salt-and-water mixture instead of commercial body brace.
- Buy bedding in quantity. It may be even cheaper bought loose instead of baled.
- Old Turkish towels can be used under bandages for soaking legs.
- A bar of saddle soap will last longer if cut in half before use.
- Trace-clip your horse in winter to save on blankets.
- Worm horses regularly for better health and utilization of the feed.
- Check teeth routinely.
- Use burlap feed bags for grooming cloth or as a poor man's cooler.
- Use plastic feed sacks for household garbage; it's cheaper than buying commercial bags sold for that purpose.
- Use inexpensive thermal blankets as a cooler.
- Old bed pads can be used as extra saddle pads or in place of quilted leg wraps.
- Plastic bags from the kitchen can be used over sweat bandages or poultices.
- Check with a local farrier's school for shoeing at the cost of materials only.
- Check for local colleges that give courses in training. They will often train a young horse without charge.
- Lease your horse, if it qualifies, to a reputable equitation school for the winter months.
- Check with local schools of veterinary medicine; often students will perform castrations, for example, at less than half the usual charge.
- Sweeten the taste of the manger by sprinkling it once a month with charcoal.

FEEDING

Although any feeding program is part of stable management, the subject is so large and yet so often given short shrift that we debated whether it should be given a section of its own under the general heading of "Animal Health." We concluded, however, that it is, after all, part of what most horsemen mean when they talk about "stable management," even if it can also be described as "preventive medicine." Many ailments result from poor nutrition, and since digestive problems are not uncommon in equines, every horse owner must determine his animal's needs and fulfill them as satisfactorily as possible.

The daily food, or ration, given a horse must satisfy many requirements, summed up briefly as palatability, quantity, and quality. A horse that won't or can't eat its food, even though it contains all the appropriate nutrients, won't benefit from it. The animal may suffer from too little food, or too much, or from improperly scheduled feedings. And of course, if the quality of the food is substandard, the animal will not receive the nourishment needed to remain healthy. All of these aspects of horse nutrition are interrelated, and a working knowledge of the animal's digestive system will be a good first step in arriving at a sensible, effective feeding program.

Horses are by nature grazing animals, eating fresh grass on a relatively constant basis throughout the day. Their stomachs are relatively small (about 4 gallons in capacity) and cannot handle the daily ration all at once, as can the stomachs of many other animals. Their digestive tract, therefore, must continuously empty the stomach even as the horse eats, processing the food materials through its long (about 100 feet) series of intestinal organs until the waste is eliminated. This is why knowledgeable horsemen feed stabled horses two to three times daily. A side benefit of such multiple feedings is that it helps prevent boredom and attendant stable vices.

Many horses will do well on good pasture grass. Some, ponies, for example, are best maintained on hay alone, provided they are not heavily worked and the hay is of high quality. But because fields are often overworked and depleted of nutrients, the average horse needs concentrated feed in the form of grains and even supplementary vitamins and minerals. The pelleted feeds manufactured and sold as "complete foods" are, for the most part, nutritionally complete, but for horses that cannot forage, hay or grass is necessary to relieve boredom and to keep the animal from feeling hungry.* Also, a horse receiving only one or two feedings of concentrated food a day will tend to bolt its food, losing much of the nutritional value in the process. Therefore, it is always preferable to give

---

* Sixteen pounds of good hay, for example, will provide 6 to 7 pounds of digestible nutrients, appropriate for a 1,000-pound animal worked two to three hours a day, whereas 10 to 12 pounds of oats will provide the same quantity of the nutrients. But the bulk of hay, its 14 pounds of dry material, will help keep the horse contented and full, which the lesser quantity of oats cannot accomplish.

some of the hay ration first to take the edge off an appetite. Even better is water, if the animal does not have constant access to it, ahead of or directly after the hay. This is to prevent the horse from gulping water after eating grain, which can cause the grains to swell up in stomach and produce digestive upset.

Horses do not vomit the way humans do; instead, they may choke or cough up food that is still in the esophagus. (It will come out the nose rather than the mouth because of the way in which the pharynx—the tube connecting mouth and esophagus—works as a safety valve.)* Because of the peculiar nature of equine digestion, therefore, ailments such as colic (a catchall word indicating a stomachache but with many different causes and effects) are both common and difficult to cure; so prevention is the name of the game. Proper schedules and amounts of food are essential considerations, but perhaps the most important of all is that of quality.

Food begins to lose what nutritive value it has the moment it is harvested. Careless purchasing and storage can increase deterioration and even make foods harmful. Drying is the most common way of retaining nutrients in horse feed. To prevent loss of quality, dry foods must be stored in cool, dark, well-ventilated areas that are free of pests. If grains have been crushed, however, their storage life is shortened. Saving money by buying such feed in larger quantities than can be used up in a month is risky, for it will soon turn moldy and worthless. Hay is at its best when green, leafy, and harvested when relatively young. If stored when wet, it will become moldy and perhaps combustible; on the other hand, if too dry, it may become brittle and dusty. Most of the large feed companies are reliable about producing quality feeds, but problems may arise in distributors' handling, so should always check any feed before accepting it. One usually reliable feed supplier we know sold us some oats with stones mixed in—no disaster for cows, but a real threat to horses. Hay, whether from your own field or from a local supplier, should also be checked carefully for presence of mold, dust, or dirt. Once hay has entered your barn, it must be kept well ventilated, free from contamination by rodents and other pests, and protected from exposure to moisture or the elements. At feeding time, check the food again. Each flake of hay should be shaken as it is removed from the bale so that all dusty particles are blown away before they can do damage to a horse's eyes or respiratory tract. Dusty hay can sometimes be improved by sprinkling with water (use a coffee can with a perforated bottom). Foods such as carrots, potatoes, grass, and clover should, of course, be clean, fresh, of good general quality, and washed free of poisonous contaminants like insecticides. They should not be broken up so small that horses will be tempted to swallow the chunks without chewing.

* Horses that do vomit stomach contents, which is rare but not unknown, are showing very serious symptoms, usually of a rupture or acute dilatation, and death may be imminent.

NUTRITION IN HORSES

Before we discuss in detail the various types of feed available for horses, let's look at the animal's nutritional requirements in order to design a well-balanced ration. Requirements depend on the horse's size, age, use, and general condition, and some horses can vary considerably as individuals—"easy" or "hard" keepers—but research has shown that all horses need certain nutrients in a particular balance. The following chart, based on data furnished by the National Research Council, is a good guide. Please keep in mind that the figures given are minimums—many horses will need more than these amounts. Your veterinarian will be the best source of advice for your animal, so feel free to ask his help in establishing the best feeding program.

"A horse soldier took the utmost care of his charger. As long as the war lasted, he looked upon him as his fellow-helper in all emergencies, and fed him carefully with hay and corn. When the war was over, he only allowed the horse hay and chaff to eat, made him carry heavy loads of wood, and subjected him to slavish drudgery and ill treatment. When war was again proclaimed, the soldier clad himself in his military trappings and heavy coat of armour. When he mounted his charger, the horse fell down under the weight. No longer equal to the burden, the horse said to his master 'You must now go to war on foot. You have transformed me from a horse to an ass, and how can you expect that I can return again at a moment's notice from an ass to a horse?'"

Aesop's Fables

The basic components of food digested and used by all animals are protein, carbohydrate, fat, vitamins, minerals, and water, and some understanding of the relative properties is basic to good horse management.

Proteins, complex organic compounds made up chiefly of amino acids, are used primarily to build and repair tissue. Most foods contain protein in one form or another, but some are richer than others; grains, protein-rich pellets or food supplements, and good young hay (alfalfa, which is a legume rather than a grass, is higher in protein than timothy, for instance) contain more protein than fresh, succulent foods such as carrots and potatoes. As important as protein is, however, we tend to overrate it, taking in more than we can use, with excess protein not required for cell building utilized as energy (a fairly expensive way of providing it). Most mature horses, regardless of how much they are worked, need only 10 to 12 percent of their ration in crude protein; young horses and pregnant and lactating mares will need more. Too much protein can cause real problems, the most common being laminitis (or founder). Protein deficiency is also dangerous, resulting in poor growth,

MINIMUM NUTRITIONAL REQUIREMENTS FOR HORSES					
Type of Horse	Crude Protein (in grams and % of daily ration)	Energy (calories)	Vitamin A	Calcium (International Units)	Phosphorus
Mature animal at rest					
900 lbs.	505 gr (10%)	13,860	10,000	16,000	12,000
1100 lbs.	597 gr (10%)	16,390	12,500	20,000	15,000
Mature animal at light work					
900 lbs.	672 gr (10%)	18,360	10,000	16,000	12,000
1100 lbs.	803 gr (10%)	21,890	12,500	20,000	15,000
Mature animal at moderate work					
900 lbs.	871 gr (10%)	23,800	10,000	17,200	13,000
1100 lbs.	1,047 gr (10%)	28,690	12,500	21,200	16,000
Mares in last 90 days of pregnancy					
900 lbs.	613 gr (11.5%)	14,880	20,000	19,500	15,000
1100 lbs.	725 gr (11.5%)	17,350	25,000	24,000	18,000
Lactating mares					
900 lbs.	1,181 gr (13.3%)	24,390	20,000	42,000	35,600
1100 lbs.	1,317 gr (13.1%)	27,620	25,000	47,000	38,600
Foals (3 months) 1100 lbs. mature	834 gr (19%)	12,070	4,400	30,500	19,100
Weanlings (6 mos.) 1100 lbs. mature	800 gr (14.3%)*	15,400	9,000	46,000	28,700
Yearlings 1100 lbs. mature	750 gr (12.3%)	16,810	11,000	26,000	17,400
18-month animals 1100 lbs. mature	700 gr (11.3%)	17,160	16,000	23,000	16,000

* Experts believe that rations for foals should include at least 18% protein until the animal has reached 6 to 8 months; 16% to 2 years; 14% to 3 years; and 10–12% thereafter.

loss of weight, lack of stamina, poor hoof and hair-coat development, irregular estrous cycles, and poor milk production in mares.

Carbohydrates, such as cellulose starch or sugar, furnish the horse with heat and energy. The source of the carbohydrates is not important as long as the energy level remains the same when sources are changed. Carbohydrates make up about three-fourths of the dry matter in plants, the horse's chief source of food. The more exercise a horse is given, the more energy it will need—up to twice the energy needed to be maintained at rest. The usual way to increase energy is to feed more grain and less roughage, since grain is concentrated and takes less time to consume. Growing grass, fresh or dried, is richer in energy than the more fibrous mature grass or hay and is somewhat easier to digest; young animals and those worked strenuously must therefore have their carbohydrates low in fiber. Roughage, however, is important, for its bulk keeps the intestinal tract active, and should not be overlooked or omitted from the ration.

It has been found that horses can tolerate relatively high levels of fat in their diet—even as high as 10 percent of the daily ration when an increase in energy is required. (Fat yields more than twice as much energy as carbohydrates.) Fat may also increase the palatability of food for some horses, and it is believed to aid in the conditioning of the animal's skin and hair coat. Grains, such as corn and oats, are good sources of fat.

Vitamins, normally present in good grain and hay, are readily lost with poor harvesting and storage, and because vitamins do play a significant role in all body functions, supplements may be necessary. Vitamin A is particularly important. Deficiency may result in reproductive failure, nerve degeneration, night blindness, respiratory infections, and poor hair coat and hoof development. Green pasture grass is the best source of carotene, which is readily converted by the horse into Vitamin A. Hay kept under ideal conditions will retain its vitamin A constituent for six to 12 months, but it is quickly destroyed by oxygen and light. The vitamin A requirement for horses has been established at 1,000 to 2,000 International Units daily for every 100 pounds of body weight—the higher figure for pregnant and lactating mares. Ten times this amount can be toxic, however, so don't assume that more is necessarily better (the symptoms of toxicity are similar to those for vitamin A deficiency). Vitamin D, sometimes known as the sunshine vitamin, has an important role in the conversion of calcium and phosphorus to use in the body, necessary for good bone formation. It is produced in the skin by the solar rays. Horses without access to the outdoors can get their vitamin D from sun-cured forage or vitamin supplements; 200 to 500 I.U. daily for every 100 pounds of body weight is the recommended amount. Vitamin E seems to be good for young, rapidly growing horses, and it may (or may not) play a part in reproduction. Although its exact requirements are not known, 20 I.U. per 100 pounds is recommended. Vitamin C (ascorbic acid) may help wounds to heal and prevent nasal hemorrhage; the recommended dosage is 100 milligrams per 100 pounds daily. Both vitamins E and C are found in good feeds and in good-quality hay. Vitamin K, which preserves the clotting power in the blood, is synthesized in the gut, and supplements are not necessary. The vitamin B complex, which includes thiamine (B_1), riboflavin (B_2), niacin, pantothenic acid, and cobalamin (B_{12}) are necessary for good appetite, growth, and reproduction. Varying amounts of each are thought to be necessary (20 mg thiamine, 1.5 mg of riboflavin, .5 mg of niacin, 2 mg of pantothenic acid per 100 pounds body weight); but since all the B vitamins must work together and the exact requirements are not known, one can be safe by simply adding 1 percent brewer's yeast to the daily grain ration or checking the ingredient list on pelleted foods.

Minerals are inorganic elements, which, like vitamins, are needed in small amounts even though their exact requirements and uses are not fully known. The minerals of primary concern for horses are sodium, chlorine, calcium, and phosphorus. Sodium chloride, better known as common table salt, helps transfer nutrients to the cells and remove waste materials; hence the need for constant access to a salt block or the daily addition of salt to the feed. Most horses need about 3 ounces of salt a day; deficiency produces poor appetite, rough coat, reduced growth in young animals, and decreased milk production in mares. Calcium and phosphorus together are the major components of bone and tooth, and a deficiency of them may result in unsoundness and may retard conception in mares. In the adult animal, bone contains three parts calcium to one part phosphorus; in the young growing horse, their ratio is about equal. Most roughage is relatively high in calcium and low in phosphorus, which can be found in grains. Other minerals are needed in smaller quantities (trace minerals); these include iodine (for the thyroid gland, which controls metabolism), iron and copper (to form hemoglobin for the blood to supply oxygen to the cells), cobalt

(important in food digestion and in synthesizing B vitamins), and sulfur, (an essential part of most proteins and certain vitamins). Manganese, magnesium, selenium, and potassium are also required by all horses in small amounts. These can be supplied in mineral supplements or in blocks similar to (and perhaps attached to) the salt blocks in a stall or paddock.

Water is the cheapest and perhaps most important constituent of all diets. The body of a mature horse is composed of about 80 percent water, and fluids must be supplied on a constant basis. Fresh grass contains a good deal of water, but horses consume at least 5 gallons and as much as 15 gallons daily (an average of ½ gallon for each pound of dry food), and it must be supplied separately from food. Ordinary drinking water (cool, clean, and fresh) can perform miracles; it dissolves nutrients and carries them throughout the body via the circulatory system, picking up waste materials and eliminating them through the urine. Water also acts as a temperature control; when the horse is overheated, evaporation will cool it while watery tissues will absorb heat in cold weather. Horses deprived of water for some time can become intoxicated by it; therefore horses worked strenuously should be cooled before being allowed free access to water.

TYPES OF FOOD

A well-balanced ration of hay or grass, grains or concentrated foods, and water should provide all the nutritional requirements, with occasional or regular supplements if the foodstuff is of relatively poor quality. The following descriptions of the major sources of nutrients for horses will enable you to determine the best proportions and types of food to fit your horse's own needs.

Pasture grass of high quality is the most natural and one of the best foods for a horse. Major horse farms have fine pastures that are well fertilized, drained, and kept free of weeds. Some horses will do well on pasture alone, and even horses that are confined most of the time should be allowed short periods on grass; not only is young, growing grass high in nutrition, but the horse will have a chance to relax and to exercise at will. Horsemen can save a good deal of money as well, since hay and grain rations can be cut back if a horse is getting sufficient nutrition from forage. Don't, however, suddenly turn a hay-fed horse out to graze for long periods. Rich grasses can easily founder a horse. Herbage should not be allowed to grow too high or be clipped too short; high mature grass is less nutritious, and overgrazed land may breed parasites. For that reason, both pasture rotation and fertilization are recommended. Legumes, such as alfalfa and clover, and grasses, such as timothy and Kentucky bluegrass, are both excellent pasture feeds. Some grasses may have a laxative effect at certain times of the year, probably when animals are turned out after a period of confinement and the diet is suddenly richer. This is troublesome for heavily worked horses, but excellent for broodmares and young horses. Temporary pastures of young, growing oats, rye, wheat, or barley can provide a welcome change when the regular pastures are dormant. Cattle can improve horse pastures by fertilizing the soil and keeping the grass cropped, allowing the horse to consume the easily digestible and more nutritious young grass.

Everyone knows that hay is for horses. Although it isn't a horse's only fuel, it is the most important of the harvested roughage that horses eat throughout the temperate zones of the world, especially where growing grass is not available the year around. Absolute requirements have not been established for hay, but the intake of about 1 to 1¼ percent of the horse's body weight daily seems desirable for horses that are worked. Mature, idle horses can be maintained on good-quality hay alone, though broodmares or growing or heavily worked animals will need supplementary grain to provide sufficient proteins and vitamins. The quality of hay is directly influenced by the way in which it is harvested. Grasses should be cut when the head is just beginning to show, and when cured, the heads of timothy should be about 1½ inches long; alfalfa should be cut at the bud to early bloom stage. Rapid curing is essential if the nutrients are to be preserved; dust and mold are signs of badly cured hay and may be harmful to horses. Good hay can be provided on a free-choice basis (as much as horses will eat); distended "hay bellies" are caused by overly mature hay, not by overconsumption.

As with forage there are two basic kinds of hay—legume and grass. Each type has its own qualities, and mixtures are often fed. Even in dried form legumes are richer in protein, calcium, and vitamins A and D, though they are not rich in phosphorus. The important legumes used for forage are alfalfa, red clover, and other clovers; grasses include timothy, prairie grass, bromegrass, orchard grass, Bermuda grass and Kentucky bluegrass.

Many people believe that alfalfa, the most widely grown tame hay in the United States, should be limited in use, with not more than 1 pound per day allowed for every 100 pounds of body weight. Most problems from feeding alfalfa, however, are the result of putting horses on it too suddenly, and two weeks of gradual conversion from timothy to alfalfa, for instance, should prevent any difficulties. Increased urine production, due to increased excretion of nitrogen, is common with alfalfa and not harmful.

~~~~~~~~~~~~~~~~~~~~~~~~~~~~~

"In enclosing a pasture for mares and sucklings care must be taken to place the bottom rail or plank close to the ground; otherwise the foal is likely to be down by the fence and get up on the opposite side, much to the frantic dismay of all concerned."

Peggy Jett Pittenger
The Back-Yard Foal
Arco Publishing Co., 1965

~~~~~~~~~~~~~~~~~~~~~~~~~~~~~

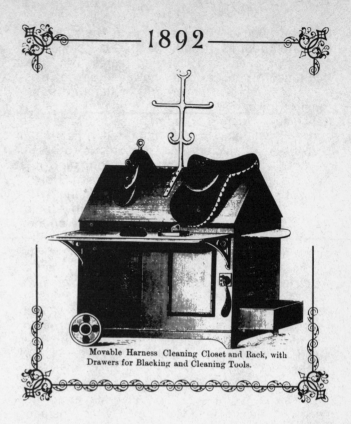

—1892—

Movable Harness Cleaning Closet and Rack, with Drawers for Blacking and Cleaning Tools.

Red clover, often grown in combination with timothy, is second only to alfalfa in food value, containing about two-thirds as much digestible protein. It does furnish more total digestible nutrients than alfalfa, however, and thus exceeds it slightly in net energy.

Timothy is the most important hay grass in the country, especially in the Northern states. It is usually freer of dust and mold than legume hay and is standard roughage for mature horses, whose need for protein, calcium, and vitamins is not so high as that of broodmares and growing horses. Wheat grasses, buffalo grass, and bluestem are leading native grasses used for hay in the Western states, though their value depends on climate and soil, the best (those equal to timothy) being grown on mountain meadows and upland prairies. Bermuda grass is the most important pasture grass of the South, but will not grow in a severe climate. It is about equal to timothy in value. Horsemen in the Central states find that orchard grass (grown in partial shade and often seeded with red clover), bromegrass (which is very palatable), and others are good, especially when mixed with legumes for higher nutritional value. Kentucky bluegrass is probably the best hay of all, being high in protein (up to 20 percent) and retaining it when cut before it heads out in the spring.

Corn silage and straw are also considered roughage suitable for horses, though most horsemen dismiss straw (the mature stems and leaves of any forage plant) as suitable only for bedding because of its lack of nutritional and digestive qualities. Corn and other fodder can be substituted for timothy if they are of good quality. Silage can be used only if it is perfectly free of decay and mold, for horses are far more susceptible to poisoning than cattle or sheep. Silage should not be the only roughage, but it may replace one-third to one-half the hay ration. Other roughages include low-grade milling by-products such as oat hulls, ground corncobs, and cottonseed hulls, but these are not particularly suitable—or palatable—to horses.

Concentrated foods are low in fiber (18 percent or less) but high in nutrients. This category includes grains and high-grade by-products such as hominy feed, wheat bran, cottonseed and linseed meal, and corn-gluten feed, with protein content up to 16 percent (a substance with more than 16 percent is considered a protein supplement). In concentrates, unlike most roughages, the nutrients are stored in large amounts as the plants mature, usually in the form of seeds.

Oats, the most widely used grain, are the standard by which other grains are judged. Although oats are not necessarily the richest grain, they are one of the safest, since because of their hulls they form a relatively loose, digestible mass in the stomach, unlike heavier corn and barley, which tend to pack. Oats weigh about 32 pounds or more per bushel and may be purchased whole, crimped, or crushed—the last two preferred for animals that tend to bolt their grain or for those with poor or developing teeth. New or mushy oats should never be fed to horses, for they may cause colic.

Wheat bran, the outer coating of the wheat kernel, is twice as bulky as oats, is richer in phosphorus and niacin, and has a better-quality protein than corn, although some experts believe it has been overrated as a food for horses since it is low in calcium and vitamins A and D. Nevertheless, because it is bulky and mildly laxative, as well as palatable, it mixes well with oats (two parts oats to one part bran) for feeding hard-working, hard-fed animals on their idle days to prevent tying up from an overproduction of lactic acid (a description of the ailment azoturia follows). Bran is also an excellent additive to the rations of breeding stock and foals. Constipation can be relieved if bran is fed wet; it is more laxative in this state than when dry and mixed with other feed. Pour hot water over the bran and let it stand for approximately a half hour before feeding. Wet mash should be given at night preferably before a day of rest. A mash made of 1 pound of bran mixed with warm water, 2 tablespoons of salt, and a cup of mineral oil may also be used to relieve colic.

Sorghum grains are popular in some areas, but the protein is not of good quality. The small seeds must be crushed or rolled to permit easy chewing and mixed with bran, barley, or oats if they are to be fully digested. Other meals such as soybean or linseed meal are so high in protein that they are considered protein supplements rather than basal concentrates. Also very heavy, they must be mixed with bulkier grains to avoid packing up in the stomach. It's not a good idea to feed them in quantities of more than a pound a day, and they should be incorporated gradually into the ration to avoid digestive upset. Young horses should not be

fed linseed meal, since it is higher in fiber and lower in quality and digestibility than soy meal.

RECOMMENDED DAILY RATIONS

Mature horse at light work (1 to 3 hours daily):
½ pound grain mix and 1¼ to 1½ pounds hay (or pasture equivalent) per hundred pounds of body weight. (A good ration for a pleasure or show horse might be, for a 1,000-pound animal, 5 pounds oats or mixture of 4 parts oats to 1 part corn or barley and 12 to 15 pounds hay.)

Mature horse at moderate work (3 to 5 hours daily):
1 pound grain mix and 1 to 1¼ pounds hay per hundred pounds of body weight

Mature horse at heavy work (5 to 8 hours daily):
1¼ to 1½ pounds grain mix and 1 pound of hay for every hundred pounds of body weight

Stallions
breeding: 1 to 1½ pounds alfalfa; 1¼ pounds grain mix per hundred pounds of body weight
idle: ¾ to 1½ pounds alfalfa and ¾ pound grain per hundred pounds of body weight

Broodmares
early pregnancy: ½ to 1 pound grain and ¾ to 1½ pound hay per hundred pounds of body weight
late pregnancy: 1 to 1½ pounds grain and ¾ to 1½ pounds hay
lactating: 1½ to 2 pounds grain and 1 to 1¾ pounds alfalfa

Suckling foals:
½ to ¾ pound grain mix per hundred pounds of body weight

Weanlings:
1 to 1½ pounds grain and 1½ to 2 pounds hay per hundred pounds of body weight

Yearlings:
½ to 1½ pounds grain and ½ to ¾ pounds hay per hundred pounds of body weight

A good grain mix for breeding stock is 35 percent rolled barley, 30 percent rolled oats, 10 percent rolled corn, 10 percent linseed or soybean meal, 7 percent molasses, 6 percent calf manna or bran, 1 percent iodized salt, 1 percent bone meal.

Linseed meal is sometimes used as a supplement to improve hair coat, but the addition to the feed of polyunsaturated fat (corn or other vegetable oil) in small (2-ounce) doses can be more effective. Moreover, it does not adversely affect the protein supply by adding more than you want to the grain ration. Molasses is a useful supplement to grain because it is highly palatable, has a slightly laxative effect, and will bind together any dusty particles in grain. Succulent, fresh foods, such as root vegetables (carrots, potatoes) or apples, traditional treats for horses, provide some vitamins (though not many) and are highly palatable.

Most of the large feed companies produce prepared horse feeds, usually called "sweet feed," which are combinations of oats, corn and molasses fortified with alfalfa, linseed, salt, vitamins, and minerals. These feeds will often be accepted by fussy horses and are easier on the owners, since they need no preparation and take up less storage space. Similar mixtures are also available in non-dusty dry pellet form, which horses may or may not like. Because the companies must maintain steady nutrient levels and because grains may vary in quality over a period of time, manufacturers may not always give exactly the same proportion (or weight) of grains in these prepared products. Therefore, a new bag should be opened before the old bag is empty and incorporated into the ration gradually rather than presented all at once. Feeding instructions accompanying these products can be very useful indeed. For horse owners who prefer to mix their own feed, the following general suggested rations are offered.

~~~~~~~~~~~~~~~~~~~~~~~~~~~~~~~~
Horses and poets should be fed, not overfed.
Charles II of England
~~~~~~~~~~~~~~~~~~~~~~~~~~~~~~~~

Caution should be taken in feeding grains, straight or in combination. Whole grains, especially if they are bolted by a hungry or greedy horse, can pass undigested through the system; crushing, rolling, and crimping will make grains more readily digestible, though ground grain is not always palatable because it tends to be dusty. Some people go so far as to cook or steam ground grain into mashes, although experts feel that if water is readily accessible, mashes are neither practical nor particularly desirable, since the grains lose nutritional and even digestive value. Nevertheless, as we pointed out earlier, wet bran is somewhat more effective than dry bran as a laxative and has been the traditional late supper for a hardworking horse facing a day of rest. Those who cook mashes do so to try to avoid azoturia, or Monday-morning sickness, once common among workhorses and not uncommon among high-performance animals today. It results when a heavily worked and heavily grained horse is allowed to be idle for a day and is then put back to work. The overproduction of lactic acid causes legs and hindquarter muscles to tie up and become rigid; the horse sweats profusely, and death can be the unhappy result if the animal is not treated immediately with complete rest, warmth, and the elimination of grain from the diet. Most cases can be prevented by good management—avoiding overworking a horse that is not in top form, not overfeeding grain, and exercising on a daily basis.

Several of the major feed companies have prepared booklets and brochures on equine nutrition and management. They are available at tack shops and feed stores or by mail from the companies. Among them are four that we recommend:
"Horse Nutrition And Management," published by Agway/Cooperative Research Farms.
"Horses—A Complete Feeding and Management Program," published by Carnation-Albers.
"Know Practical Horse Feeding," published by Farnam Horse Library ($1.50).
"The Purina Horse Book," published by Ralston Purina.
Although manufacturers would be pleased to have you use their products, none of the above literature takes a terribly hard-sell approach.

A lot of horsemen find it easier to use a volume measure—usually a 2-pound coffee can—than to weigh out grain for their animals. This method is fine for oats, of which about 2 pounds will fill the 2-pound can. Some grains are heavier than oats, however, and unless one takes this fact into account, you may end up giving Dobbin a serious overdose without realizing it. Corn, for instance, has a reputation for causing horses to get fat, hot, or colicky, but if it were measured out properly, by weight, problems resulting from overfeeding would not occur. Grains even of the same variety don't always weigh the same from bag to bag, and crimping and rolling will affect weight considerably. Weigh each bag of grain as it is delivered, and adjust your feeding measure accordingly. Be sure too that you get a full measure when you dip the can into your grain bin.

A 2-pound (or 1-quart) coffee can will hold approximately:
2 pounds of oats
2 pounds of some sweet feeds
2¾ pounds of pellets
3⅖ pounds of corn
1 pound of wheat bran
2⅕ pounds of linseed meal
3 pounds of barley
3⅖ pounds of sorghum grain
6 pounds of molasses
3⅗ pounds of whole wheat

POISONOUS PLANTS

Because treatment for plant poisoning is not usually effective, prevention is the best, if not the only, way to control this problem. Although few poisonous plants taste good to horses, animals will eat them when very hungry, when the plants or seeds are mixed in with grain or hay, or when plant clippings are placed where horses normally eat. If certain plants in a pasture look at all suspicious, either dig them up, kill them with chemicals (and be careful of that stuff, too!), mow them down before they go to seed, or move the animals out of the pasture at the time when the poisonous plants are particularly toxic. Some plants with a salty taste may be palatable to a hungry or young horse that may not be particularly discriminating. Occasionally such plants as oleander, which in large amounts can cause poisoning, are mixed in with hay; horse owners should therefore check new shipments of hay carefully.

Three different kinds of plants cause similar symptoms, each producing cirrhosis of the liver: *Amsinckia intermedia* (fiddleneck, tarweed, fireweed, buckthorn, and yellow burr weed), found in the West, where it is a common weed of wheat and other grain crops; *Senecio jacobaea* (ragwort, groundsel, and "stinking Willie"), found in the West and Midwest; and *Crotalaria spectabilis* and *C. sagittalis* (rattlebox, rattleweed, and wild pea), common in the Southeast. The *Senecio* species causes walking disease (also called hard liver disease or Walla Walla walking disease). All of these plants affect the liver, causing a dysfunction of the central nervous system with symptoms including staggering, aimless walking, incoordination, mania, or delirium, often accompanied by severe intestinal irritation along with diarrhea and signs of colic. When the liver has been sufficiently damaged, loss of condition and death result, and there is no cure or treatment once the liver has been damaged. Since other causes for these symptoms, however, are rabies, abscesses, brain tumor, encephalitis, and meningitis, don't assume poisoning unless you are convinced the animal had access to any of these plants.

Ricinus communis (called the castor bean, castor oil plant, and palma christi), common in the Southeast and Southwest, is the source of castor oil (which, if we remember our childhoods correctly, tastes bad but is terribly good for you). Actually, the plant is beneficial, but the seeds, if ingested, are highly toxic, causing both humans and horses severe irritation in the intestinal tract. In addition to the plants' use in commercial production of castor oil, they are sometimes grown for ornamental effect around barns or corrals where horses—young, inquisitive ones for the most part, since the older ones are sensible enough to know that what tastes bad *is* bad—can eat them. As few as 7 grams of the seeds may be fatal to a horse. Severe enteritis is the characteristic sign; at first the horse is rather dull, then uncoordinated, and then very sweaty. Spasms may be apparent, and watery diarrhea, plus other colicky symptoms, will appear. Eventually the horse goes into convulsions and dies.

Nerium oleander is also grown as an ornament in the South and in California, where it has been known to poison people who used the sticks of the

Feed Supplements. Nutritional requirements for horses are discussed on pages 43–45, and in the best of all possible worlds, these can be met by adequate daily rations of forage, hay, and/or grain concentrates. If these are not sufficiently rich in vitamins, minerals, proteins, or fats—especially for horses that are used for heavy work or breeding and for growing animals—supplements of one sort or another may be necessary on a daily basis. Vitamin supplements may feature one or a combination of ingredients, including minerals. Mineral supplements are also available separately, sometimes in the form of blocks as well as in powders. Protein and fat supplements may consist simply of soybean or cottonseed meal, wheat-germ oils, and other health-food-store specialties, or they may be more or less concentrated special preparations including vitamins and minerals as well. Feed supplements come in liquid or powder form for mixing with feed or water, and one's choice will depend on the individual horse's requirements and its willingness to eat the stuff.

General feed supplements are usually combinations of all four nutrients and are recommended for horses needing more than normal nourishment because of age, use, or condition. The most popular all-purpose powdered supplements are Cinch Horse Conditioner (Franklin Laboratories), Spectrum-4 (Equitron Co., Burbank, California), Drive (Diagnostic Data, Mountain View, California), Shell Horse Conditioner (Shell Chemical Co.), Tipp 333 Horse Feed Additive (Agri-Products, Cleveland, Ohio), Top Form Concentrated Vitamins and Minerals (Merck), Vionate (Squibb, Princeton, New Jersey), and Vita-Plus (Farnam).

Liquid tonics are usually rich in B vitamins, iron, and minerals for building blood and bone; these include Redglo (Thoroughbred Remedy Corp.), Roberts' Pacer, Super Tone (Farnam), Horse Health (Western Laboratories), and Stamin-Atom (Zirin Laboratories). These tonics are not to be confused with Gilkey's Veterinary Tonic, which contains, among other things, strychnine—an old-time horse conditioner.

Some special-purpose supplements are Albion Iron Supplement (Albion Labs, Clearfield, Utah); Ayerst's Adaquets Syrup (B vitamins); Borden's Mirra-Coat (a fat supplement); Formula 707 (John Ewing Co., La Salle, Colorado), for growing and breeding animals; Ayerst's Hemad Solution (minerals for nutritional anemia); Traileze Stress Formula (from Lee Drug Co.), for growing and breeding animals; Hoof-Gro (International Stock Food Corp., Waverly, New York), with special proteins for hooves; and Ayerst's Cyfumate for bone growth. For addresses not given here, see pages 72–73.

plant for food skewers. Lawn clippings or bales of hay containing oleander leaves are the usual source of the poisoning in horses, since they will rarely eat the shrub itself. It can be lethal; 40 to 50 grams of the green or dried leaves will kill a 1,000-

pound horse. Profuse diarrhea, abnormal heartbeat, and chilled extremities are progressive signs of the poisoning, with the pulse eventually becoming imperceptible and death following shortly thereafter. If the dose was small and nonfatal, treatment must involve removal of the contents of the intestinal tract and maintenance of general good nursing care.

Bracken, or brake fern, is common in woodland areas all over the United States, and some species of the genus *Pteridium* can poison cattle and horses, with different reactions—the latter suffering disorders of the central nervous system. Since bracken stays green into the fall, animals may begin to eat it after pasture grass has browned, even cultivating a taste for it, and bracken sometimes shows up in hay. Animals must eat bracken over a period of time (one or two months) before showing such symptoms of toxicity as loss of weight, unsteadiness, swaying, and staggering. If the animal falls, it may not be able to get up.

"Chewing disease" is the colloquial term for yellow star thistle poisoning, from the plant *Centaurea solstitialis,* which grows throughout the West and is often found along roadsides and dumps. It is an attractive, yellow-flowered annual, a member of the sunflower family. As with bracken, this thistle must be consumed over a long period before signs of poisoning appear, but once they do, death is probable. A victim will have difficulty in swallowing, and food may be spat out or become lodged in the mouth; the horse will probably be unable to drink and may develop a wooden facial expression as muscles around the mouth and tongue become paralyzed. If not helped, it will die of starvation, but in any case functional recovery is unlikely even if the animal responds to treatment.

The short, sharp prickles of yellow bristle grass (*Steraia glauca* and *S. lutescens*) cause ulcers in the stomach and irritation in the tongue and lips. Once the source is removed, healing is rapid. Many other plants, such as thistles, cacti, and thorny shrubs, will cause puncture wounds or cuts.

Some lupines are toxic, some not, and it is difficult to tell the two types apart. Poisoning occurs usually in the fall or winter in the form of gastric irritation and diarrhea, and acute poisoning will cause depression, weakness, and coma. Locoweed disease, which is caused by some species of the genus *Astragalus,* causes horses to stagger, wander in circles, act depressed, and then fall into convulsions. Some species of the same genus (woody aster, prince's plum, and "golden weed") will cause selenium poisoning, which affects the central nervous system; it also causes feces to become dark and fluid and an occasional fever to flare. The horse may die within a few hours or may linger for a few days. Other plants absorb selenium to a toxic level, causing chronic poisoning, sometimes called alkali disease. Losses of hair and hooves are characteristic, and victims become emaciated and lame. Oats, barley, and wheat grown in selenium-rich soil may be the villains here, but treatment involves simply removing the animal from the area or the feed from the animal.

There is no treatment or cure for nicotine poisoning, but you needn't keep the animal from smoking, only from eating plants of the wild tobacco family. Normally paralysis precedes the death. *Lathyrus* is another genus of poisonous plants; they are now rare, but there was an outbreak in 1969 affecting horses. Signs involve stiff hindquarters, unbalanced walking, and difficulty in rising. Removal of the plant (in the 1969 epidemic it was in baled hay) will relieve the symptoms.

Avocados are a delicacy for humans, but their stalks, leaves, and bark can be just the opposite. Severe mastitis and lack of milk production in mares result. Other plants, rarely eaten by horses but poisonous to them, include oak, ergot (a fungus), *Datura*, poison hemlock, and perhaps water hemlock.

~~~~~~~~~~~~~~~~~~~~~~~~~~~~~~~~~~

A horse shut in a stall for hours at a time can develop bad habits. Try some of the following to keep the horse interested and alert:
- *Exercise it regularly.*
- *Allow horse to watch other horses.*
- *Provide a window with a view.*
- *Keep a radio tuned to soothing music.*
- *Get the horse a pet; donkeys, goats, chickens, ducks, dogs, and cats (even mice) are acceptable.*
- *Provide toys in the stall; a rubber tire, hanging tether balls, or a large plastic bottle (a Clorox bottle is good) suspended from the ceiling makes an excellent punching bag.*

~~~~~~~~~~~~~~~~~~~~~~~~~~~~~~~~~~

EXERCISING

There are many ways to ensure that the horse gets a good daily dose of exercise. The most common method is to turn the animal out into a pen or a paddock where it can run, kick, buck, and generally provide a wonderfully picturesque show. Sometimes, however, this is not sufficient. Certain horses, like some people, are lazy. They may not want to move about, and the longer they go without proper exercise, the more their muscles will atrophy and the harder they will be to recondition. Mares in the later months of pregnancy are sometimes loath to move about and may need encouragement in the form of a rider, a lead rope, an automatic walker, or a lunge line. Obviously, the best way to exercise saddle horses is to work them under saddle. Twenty minutes of concentrated effort at all the gaits (or even at only the walk or trot) will do wonders to exercise the animal, building and developing its muscles, wind, balance, and general conditioning. We know of one pastured horse that developed its own program of daily exercise. About eleven o'clock each morning the family dog arrived in the pasture, where it began to bark at the horse. The two friends took off across the field, the horse in the lead and the dog following at its heels. When this odd couple reached the opposite fence, they turned and reversed the order of the chase, with the dog in the lead and the horse, head low to the ground, close behind. The scheduled chase always began on time, ended about fifteen minutes after starting time, and occurred every day—winter and summer.

HOT-WALKERS

Large breeding and training stables are finding hot-walkers a most useful device for cooling out, exercising, or conditioning their stock, since the apparatus frees the often overworked staff for other necessary chores. They're also good for showing a horse "who's boss." One arrogant horse used to getting its own way changed its attitude after finding that its antics could not alter the patience and persistence of the hot-walker.

The hot-walker may be housed in a separate shed or under a tent, or in the center of a paddock. The arms of the hot-walker extend about 16 feet, thus requiring an area that is about 40 feet in diameter when it is in use. When not in use, many models feature arms that fold up out of the way.

The standard hot-walker is powered by a ½- to 1-horsepower electric motor that uses normal household 110/115 AC current. For many stables, a hot-walker is an essential part of their management. But it is occasionally abused by its users, and it does have certain inherent disadvantages. Horses hooked up to a hot-walker tend to become easily bored; they may be asked to trot or even canter in circles too tight for their abilities; the machines that work in only one direction can badly overdevelop a horse's muscles on one side while the other side remains sadly underdeveloped. An automatic hot-walker will walk either two, four, or six horses at one time. Most machines have four forward and four reverse speeds. Four-speed walkers allow adjustment to approximate a slow and a fast walk and a slow and a fast trot. Some of the more expensive models permit adjustment of the speed to match the horse's natural gait instead of demanding that the animal adjust its stride to the predetermined speed of the machine.

BEDDING

In their natural state, horses will rarely lie down to sleep; when they do, they will find a soft, dry area clean of any excrement and protected from direct winds. Stalled horses haven't such choice, nor, obviously, are their needs the same as those of the horse running free. However, the addition of good bedding is necessary to make most stall flooring (discussed in Chapter 2) more comfortable for the

Hot-Walker. This four-horse model has a ¾-hp motor and a clutching system which provides a constant amount of pull, while a heavy-duty slip clutch prevents accidents. All wiring on this walker is conduit. You can order a quick-release lead attachment in case the horse should go down, and in some models the arms can be raised up out of the way. This manufacturer's models also feature a speed-control knob which can be turned to provide a range of 101 speeds in forward and reverse that go from zero to a fast trot (0–15 rpm). About $1,150. Hot-to-Trot, 5476 Lake Court, Cleveland, Ohio 44114.

horse. Indeed, there are a number of reasons why a thick layer of bedding is important. Clean bedding keeps the horse cleaner and drier (a clean coat is less prone to skin infections); it encourages the horse to lie down (resting the muscles and tendons in delicate legs); it makes it easier to muck out the manure; it cushions the horse's legs against a solid, unyielding floor (eliminating such problems as capped hock or elbow); it absorbs moisture; it cuts down the smell of fresh manure and urine; it helps to prevent reinfestation with parasites; and it cuts down the chance for disease bacteria to multiply and spread.

The average 12×12-foot box stall requires anywhere from two to four bales of fresh bedding per week. The quantity depends upon the type of material used, the weight of the horse, and the time of year. If your horse is heavier than most, you will need more bedding to settle it comfortably; if the weather is cold, you will need additional bedding to bank around the sides of the stall, preventing drafts and insulating the bottom of the stall walls as well as the floor.

There are a number of kinds of bedding that are perfectly acceptable and will do a decent job. The kind you choose most likely will depend on its availability in your area, the cost, and the season. A discussion follows of the different types of bedding, with their good points and bad. Do keep in mind that if you live in an area of the country where your horses are plagued with a very wet pasture, then a bedding that tends to dry out horse's hooves may be preferable. If, on the other hand, your pasture is extremely dry, you should avoid using any of the materials that will promote further drying of the hoof.

Straw (wheat, rye or oat) is a light, absorbent, generally available material for bedding that is preferred by most horsemen. It does not dry horse's hooves, and it fluffs dry quickly. Straw manure is highly prized by gardeners and mushroom growers, so much so that you may be able to sell used bedding for a small profit or, better still, prove yourself a generous neighbor. Unfortunately, straw is also appetizing for many horses, which will often eat it even when fresh hay is available. The best way to break your horse of that habit is to change the kind of bedding used.

Wood shavings are usually easily accessible, and few horses find them particularly appetizing. They provide a comfortable, springy surface and act as a good deodorant. Wood shavings may be drying on a horse's hooves, and we recommend you avoid using oak shavings, since the tannic acid in that wood tends to heat the hooves and cause discomfort.

Sawdust, like wood shavings, is usually easily available and is nonedible, but it does have some disadvantages that should be acknowledged. For instance, it may be dusty and, when inhaled, cause respiratory problems; it can sift into areas such as drains where it will clog the pipes; and it tends to cake into the feet, where it can cause irritation or simply draw out all moisture from the hoof.

Peat moss is a highly absorbent bedding that can be expensive and hard to find in certain areas. However, its public relations potential is great in suburban areas especially, and we recommend it highly. Peat moss is terrific for gardens, and you will find your neighbors begging to be the next to haul away your manure pile, especially during the spring and fall. Peat moss also has a pleasant deodorant effect and is not drying on hooves.

Stazdry (or Stae Dri or Scravell or Bagass) is a specially prepared bedding made from dried sugar cane. Usually available in bales, it is easy to store and to handle. Horses won't eat Stazdry, making it easier to keep under the animal than straw.

Peanut hulls are probably difficult to find in many parts of the country, but where they are readily available they are worth considering. However, they have disadvantages. You'll need a lot of peanut hulls to make a comfortable bed. They tend to pile up in one part of the stall, making it difficult to keep a uniform bedding under the horse. Hulls are small and difficult to handle and will fall through the tines of a manure fork (an advantage when you are simply cleaning out the previous night's droppings, but disadvantageous when you are cleaning out the entire stall).

MUCKING OUT

Novices, in their concern for keeping the horse

clean, usually remove too much dry bedding, while their only slightly more experienced and perhaps soured counterparts may delay the mucking-out process longer than is healthy for the horse. Removing too much bedding is uneconomical and exhausting; failing to remove the wet manure is courting such problems as thrushy hooves, skin infections, and parasite infestation.

As with many procedures, there is a secret to good mucking. First, either turn the horse out into a paddock or pasture or tie it on cross ties. Take a six- or eight-tined manure fork that will balance comfortably in one hand when held near the center of the handle. Begin mucking by scooping up the top of any obvious pile of manure and loading it into the manure wagon. Then dig down into the bedding and thoroughly shake it out. The heavier wet bedding and manure will fall to the bottom of the pile, while the lighter, cleaner bedding will be on top. Scoop off the top layer and pile it to one side of the stall. Scoop up the bottom layer of wet muck and remove. Continue doing this throughout the stall until the wettest (usually the center) part of the stall is bare. Scrape the floors clean with a shovel and disinfect regularly with lime. Spread the clean bedding, now piled in one corner, throughout the stall, adding fresh bedding to replace the amount removed where the horse normally faces.

THE ART OF MAKING A MUCKHEAP

A British-style muckheap is neat, tidy, compact, fast-rotting, less odorous, inhibiting to the growth of flies and parasites—almost a thing of beauty. It is slightly more time-consuming to build than an ordinary manure pile (but so is any artistic creation). Start by choosing a site that is a little way from the horses' stalls. Mark out a square about 6 feet by 6 feet. Fill the square area with dirty straw and manure until it covers the entire area to a depth of about 1 foot. Pound it down flat with a heavy shovel, or turn the kids loose to stomp it down with their feet. Pile another layer and pound that one down. Continue piling and pounding, making sure each layer covers the square area and is flat. To trim and finish the muckheap, use a pitchfork. With the tines pointed down, begin combing the sides of the heap, starting from the top. This will take out lumps while flattening and straightening the sides. Work on all sides until the heap is perfectly square. Remove the excess loose material that has accumulated around the base and place it around the top of the heap to form a ledge about one foot wide. You are now ready to take photographs of your work of art before calling in someone to remove it.

A dismounted New York City policeman grooming his horse.

GROOMING

Proper grooming may take only ten minutes per day per horse, it may take one hour per day per horse, or it may take eight hours a day per horse—it all depends on what you want from your horse and the conditions under which the animal is kept. To realize why grooming is important for all horses, it is necessary to understand what hides under that hair coat. The horse has two layers of "skin," known as the dermis, that layer which is not immediately visible, and the epidermis, which is actually the outer "skin" we would call by such names as hair or hoof. The dermis is porous and eliminates sweat, which is water and waste matter (much the same as urine) excreted through the pores of the skin. This waste matter is normally absorbed by the dandruff in the epidermis (hair), where it remains unless brushed or washed out. If excess sweat is permitted to remain in the hair, it can eventually clog the pores, causing skin infections, or even block the excretion of the sweat, allowing toxic waste matter to accumulate in the horse's system. A horse that is stabled, clipped, and blanketed needs daily grooming, and removal of the dust is an essential part of the grooming reason and ritual. Pastured horses permitted to retain long, woolly coats should not be heavily groomed, however—at least, not in winter. Instead, they should receive a light brushing that removes obvious clumps of dirt from the coat. This should be done to keep the hair free of lice, to prevent

mud fever from developing, and to clean the saddle-pad and girth areas. The "grease" and dust in the coat, however, should be left as a natural insulation and protection; this scruff and dust forms a layer which effectively keeps the horse warm and dry. Pastured horses will usually roll and scratch themselves on branches, rocks, or brush, a motion that stimulates the skin and keeps the pores open and functioning. They will also roll in mud,* writhing in pleasure; and like the famous mud facials Victorian ladies paid great prices to secure, the mud hardens to absorb and draw out the sweat and impurities from the skin, cleansing the pores while stimulating the circulation of blood.

For stabled and blanketed horses, grooming not only makes them look better; it actually keeps them healthy. The massaging motion of the grooming tools, like the good hearty roll on firm ground, stimulates the glands that lie just beneath the skin to secrete a fluid that can keep hair soft and glossy. At the same time, the massaging motion helps to tone muscles and to stimulate blood circulation, increasing the quantity of blood carried to the coat and bringing with it additional nutrients that make a horse's coat shine.

Stabled horses need more grooming attention and plain hard rubbing than their pastured brothers, and horses about to enter the show ring need still more care, with conscientious attention given to every small detail that can turn a turkey into a triumphant trophy collector.

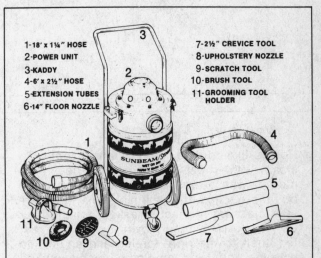

1-18' x 1¼" HOSE
2-POWER UNIT
3-KADDY
4-6' x 2½" HOSE
5-EXTENSION TUBES
6-14" FLOOR NOZZLE
7-2½" CREVICE TOOL
8-UPHOLSTERY NOZZLE
9-SCRATCH TOOL
10-BRUSH TOOL
11-GROOMING TOOL HOLDER

Grooming goes faster with a horse vacuum cleaner. The model shown here is excellent for wet or dry grooming and, when you're done, for cleaning up the barn as well. Its all-purpose features will cost about $180. Sunbeam, Stewart Products Division, 2001 South York Road, Oak Brook, Illinois 60521.

Following is a list of tools needed to do a good, basic grooming for any horse.

* Some Western horsemen claim that the horse is worth a $100 bill for each full roll.

Grooming Equipment

Tool	What It Is	Used for	How to Use It
Currycomb	hard rubber, plastic, or metal with serrated edges and a hand strap	to remove excess mud and to loosen matted dirt; to groom horses that have long, thick coats; to clean body brush	use gently in circular strokes; don't use on fine-skinned horses, or horses just clipped, or below knees or hocks
Dandy Brush or Mud Brush	wood block with strong, stiff fibers usually 2 inches long	to remove mud, caked-on dirt and sweat, and sweat marks; to brush mane and tail	vigorous brushing at caked-on dirt; brush in circular motion
Body Brush	usually made of wooden block with nylon, rice-root, or natural bristle	used from head to tail to reach through the skin, massaging and removing dirt and loose hair	brush firmly and vigorously in circular motion
All-Purpose Brush	medium-firm fibers	for removing stable dirt when a thorough cleaning is not needed; for bathing	brush all over in the direction in which the hair lies
Finishing Brush	soft bristles	to lay the horse's coat after grooming and take up dust	brush gently with the lie of the hairs
Sponge	natural or synthetic	to wipe horse's eyes, inside of ears, and nostrils; clean under tail; wipe sheath or udders	dampen sponge and wipe gently

HOW TO CLEAN A HORSE'S FEET

Horses like routine, even when it comes to cleaning their feet. If the horse has been handled by one person, then watch to see how he approaches the animal. Most handlers start cleaning the feet by asking for the near (or left) foreleg, then moving to the left rear leg, then to the right foreleg and ending up with the right hind leg. Some horses couldn't care less on which leg you start, while high-strung types may insist you follow procedure to the letter. So after you've determined how to start off on the right foot, here is the method to follow.

Facing the horse's rear, place your shoulder against the horse's shoulder and run your hand nearest the horse gently down the shoulder to the fetlock. Say "feet," or "lift," or "give," or even "come on" and a well-trained horse should lift its foot. If you do not get a response, gently pinch the tendons with your thumb and fingers just above the fetlock and at the same time press your shoulder more firmly against the horse's shoulder. Again give the voice command. Be firm and patient, and eventually even the less well-educated horse will respond to the pressure. When the horse lifts its foot, hold the front of the hoof in the palm of the hand closest to the horse and take the hoof pick in the other hand. Starting from the heel of the foot, pick around the inside of the shoe or, if the horse is unshod, along the rim of the foot. Remove all mud and other matter from the sole of the foot. Then find the two valleys formed by the frog and, always working from the heel toward the toe, clean out these valleys, making certain that no stones remain. By stroking away from you toward the toe you avoid accidentally pushing any foreign matter into the heel of the frog, where it might become embedded. When the frog grooves are clean, gently run the flat edge of the hoof pick over

Grooming Equipment

Tool	What It Is	Used for	How to Use It
Stable Rubber	soft rag of tightly woven linen or silk	for a final polish to bring out the shine and catch any remaining dust	wipe in direction in which the hair lies
Sweat Scraper	a long metal scoop	to remove excess sweat or water after bathing the horse	hold the side against the horse and slide downward, forcing the water to slide off
Hoof Pick	a hooked implement best made from a stout metal; comes in plastic	to clean out the feet and remove stones and caked-in dirt from the frog	see "How to Clean a Horse's Feet"
Mane Comb	aluminum, hard rubber, or plastic	for combing mane and tail for silky, flowing look	don't use on heavily matted or tangled hairs; tends to break hairs, causing frizzles
Cactus-Cloth Wisp or Burlap	hand-woven tough fiber; woven straw or feed sack	use for hearty massaging; to absorb sweat or rain; to stimulate circulation of blood to skin	apply with elbow grease in circular motion
Hand Clippers or Shears	scissor-action clipper with narrow head; scissor with curved blades	use for trimming and clipping horse's fetlock, mane, and head	clip against the lie of the hair
Power Clippers	electric or battery-powered; various blades	use for trimming or for full clipping of body hairs	for full clip, start with head, work against lie of hair; maintain even pressure to avoid lawn-mower stripes

the frog to check for lodged stones, cuts, or bruises and to remove excess mud. Lightly tap the frog with the side of the hoof pick, and if the horse flinches or reacts, check carefully for reasons why. If the frog looks soft and somewhat mushy in texture, lean down and sniff. If what you smell is acidic and foul, you are probably smelling the distinctive odor of thrush, and you must take measures to cure it and to prevent its recurrence. (A discussion of thrush and how to cure it can be found in Chapter 4.) Before putting the foot down, check the shoe to be sure it is firmly attached to the wall of the hoof and that there are no loose or missing nails. If a nail has worked its way loose, pull it free before it snaps off, leaving a small piece of metal that could work its way from the wall of the hoof into the bone and cause severe damage. Finally, look at the hoof wall. It should be solid, free of cracks, splits, chips,

or rings, the last indicating founder or fever. If the hoof walls are dry, apply a hoof conditioner, and if they continue to worsen, consult your farrier.

The entire process of cleaning a horse's feet should take just minutes. During those minutes, however, experienced horsemen will not only use their hands for picking; they will use all of their senses for observing the condition of the horse's feet and anticipating problems before they occur.

White Socks. A spray whitener to spray on horse's legs, face, or anywhere white markings should be whiter. Although it is used primarily for show, its antiseptic properties help heal cuts and scrapes. About $3.50.

Farnam Hoof Black. This fast-drying hoof blackener and polish gives the hoof a rich black gloss that catches the judge's eye. It also conditions the hoof at the same time, and Farnam says it "absolutely will not dry the hoof." Eight-ounce can treats 500 hooves. About $1.50.

MANE AND TAIL STYLING*

In one of the books on horses there are two drawings, the first showing a girl clad in clean jeans and blouse confronting a dirt-encrusted horse, the second drawing depicting a clean, shiny, well-groomed show horse standing beside a dirt-encrusted girl. The real joke of the drawings is, it's true! For many horsemen, a quick shower, a brush to their teeth, and a comb through their hair are usually adequate grooming to spend the rest of the day brushing, massaging, combing, clipping, pulling, and wiping horses.

Actually, for most horses, a brush or comb through the mane and tail is all that is necessary to remove caked-in dirt and keep it free of tangles and burrs. In fact, horses pastured even for a few hours during the summer depend on their long, natural manes and tails to swat away the irritating and ever-present flies. Often a herd of horses will line up side to side facing head to tail to head to

tail and so on, swatting their neighbor's face in mutual cooperation.

The shape and length of natural manes and tails vary quite a bit with each breed or type. Morgans, for instance, grow manes that reach to the bottom of their thick necks, with a forelock that can touch the tip of their nose and a tail that dusts the ground as they move. Quarter Horses, on the other hand, have naturally thin, short manes and tails that rarely reach the hock. Clydesdales, which do everything in a big way, not only grow abundant manes and tails; they also have long, thick "feathers" on their fetlocks, which are simply brushed and left unclipped.

Natural manes and tails suit the majority of horses that hack along trails. But for some owners who have the time and energy to spend grooming their horses, there are a number of reasons to trim, or pull, or braid. Thinning and shortening the mane and tail, for instance, make them easier to clean, since they are less likely to tangle in brush

Tail styles

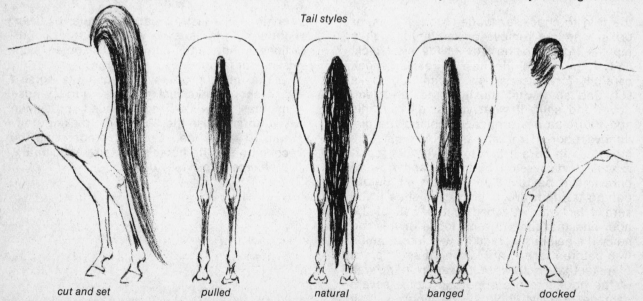

cut and set   pulled   natural   banged   docked

* This section was written with the assistance of Jamye Peters.

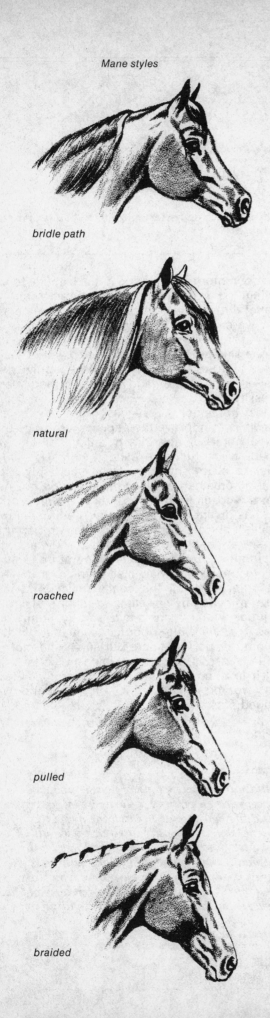

Mane styles

bridle path

natural

roached

pulled

braided

or brier, burrs being particularly difficult to remove and capable of causing skin irritations if ignored. We know of one luxuriantly maned horse that returned to the stable each day with a forelock so full of burrs it looked like a 1940s high pompadour hairstyle. Many horsemen pull the hairs near the dock for a neater tail appearance that will not look raggedy even when the horse rubs against a tree, fence, or manger. Other horsemen shear a "bridle path" along the upper portion of the mane to prevent the bridle from becoming entangled in hairs. Roaching or hogging the mane is a sure way to prevent hairs from catching in a wrangler's rope or polo player's mallet. Sometimes specialized grooming greatly enhances the horse's conformation; for example, a horse with a thick neck often looks better in a hogged mane because it makes the neck appear less deep; a thin-necked animal looks better wearing a full mane. Of course, certain breeds have a "look" that can be further exaggerated by grooming, as in the case of the Arabian, normally groomed with a bridle path that emphasizes the graceful arch of the neck and clean throatlatch while at the same time displaying the full, flowing mane that is one of the trademarks of the breed. Finally, in showing a horse there are often rules or perhaps only recommendations for specialized grooming, and before entering a horse into competition it is a good idea to check the regulations set forth by the horse show or as stated in the *Rule Book* of the American Horse Show Association.

Following are some of the ways in which the mane and tail can be worn:

Natural: The style worn by most backyard horses and trail horses. Usually the mane grows or is trained to be carried on the right side of the neck, although stock horses will wear their mane on the left side, out of the rope's way. The horse wearing its hair natural should always appear well groomed with the hairs brushed clean, free of tangles, lying flat, smooth, and silky.

Pulled (plucking): The grooming technique preferred for Quarter Horses, among others. It is accomplished by pulling a few hairs at a time along the edges of the upper tail to give the tail a neat, slim appearance; pulling longer, wispy hairs from the bottom of the tail so that the hair hangs just above the hock; and pulling long hairs from the mane so that the finished mane is about 4 to 6 inches long.

Banged: The banged tail (never mane) worn by hunter types is the only kind of trimming that requires scissors. The long hair of the tail is chopped straight across the bottom in a blunt cut so that the end falls even with the hock.

Roaching (hogging): This term applies to the mane only. It is normally found on stock horses but required on Three-Gaited Saddle Horses (but not on Five-Gaited ones, which must wear their manes long). Actually, the terms hogging and roaching have slightly different meanings, although they are often used interchangeably. Hogging means that the mane is clipped flat to the neck, while roaching means that the center mane hairs are left slightly longer, forming a herringbone pattern. Whether hogged or roached, a handhold (a wisp of hair at the withers) and the forelock are usually left unclipped.

Bridle Path: This style of mane, commonly worn by certain breeds such as Arabians and Morgans, is becoming popular on other breeds as well. The bridle-path area, from the poll down to about one-third of the mane, is hogged to prevent hairs from tangling in the bridle and to show off the animal's wide, arching neck. The remainder of the mane is worn at its natural length.

Braiding: This specialized hairstyle is used on both the manes and tails of hunters. It is also useful for training any horse's mane to lie flat. A braided mane is normally accompanied by a braided tail and may be required for certain shows. The number of braids tied is sometimes dictated by tradition. In England, for example, no more than eleven braids are acceptable. In some parts of our country mares are shown in an odd number of braids and geldings in even numbers, while in other regions mares are required to wear even and geldings odd numbers. More often, the number of braids tied into a mane or tail is determined by the horses' conformation. Many small braids make a short neck appear longer, while fewer braids make a long neck appear shorter; and fine tail braids can make a large, heavy rear end look slimmer, while fewer, thicker braids make a thin rear end look wider. Hunters' braids are usually tucked under and finished in a heavy thread of the same color as the horse's coat. Braids on ponies' manes and tails are normally sewn with a bright-colored yarn. Five-Gaited Saddle Horses, Tennessee Walking Horses, harness horses and some ponies are always shown in a braided forelock and three fine, long braids (all with a ribbon in the stable colors woven in) at the beginning of a loose, flowing mane. A utilitarian rather than decorative braid is a style called a "mud tail"—basically a single, thick tail braid that is tucked under and held in place by elastic. This style is used on hunters for wet, muddy days.

Cut and Set: Found only on fine Harness Horses, Three-, and Five-Gaited Saddle Horses, and Hackney Ponies. These animals' tails are surgically cut and then put into a tail set to heal in an artificially upright position. Often the surgical procedure must be repeated several times before the ideal set is attained. Hackneys wear their tails clipped short, about a foot from the root, and Three- and Five-Gaited Saddle Horses wear their tails full and long. Owners of these horses will often set the tail in curlers for a fluffed effect, or they may even add a switch (or chignon) for extra fullness.

CLIPPING

Clipping of a horse's winter coat should be considered when the natural protective quality of the

Braid Aid. For better, more even braids. About $1.95.

long coat interferes with the horse's ability to work efficiently. For those animals pastured throughout most of the year, a long coat is just that—a coat to keep warm. For within the coat's long hairs is a thick layer of grease and dust which helps to insulate the skin against rain, snow, and winds. But for horses that are stabled and worked regularly, that coat is a liability and clipping becomes a necessity.

Most horsemen's first reason for clipping their animals is to improve the appearance, since those with a horse of any quality enjoy riding a well-turned-out mount. The clipped horse is also far easier to clean and keep clean—certainly a plus for any horseman eager to tack up and go. Aside from the cosmetic reasons, taking a clipper to the coat has distinct advantages for the horse. For instance, a shorter coat cools out faster, permitting the sweat to evaporate more quickly and thus keeping the horse's internal temperature level. Removing the excess hair also eliminates dry ends that otherwise dull the coat's finish. And if the horse is to be shown, clipping is essential, since no judge would consider a scruffy, long-haired horse for the blue ribbon, no matter what its breeding or performance. But surely the most important reasons to clip a stabled horse is to prevent it from sweating quickly and profusely when being worked, to prevent it from becoming overly fatigued faster, and to quicken the cooling-out process, thereby preventing a propensity to chilling.

~~~~~~~~~~~~~~~~~~~~~~~~~~~~

"In India the practice among native grooms is to hold an earthen pot under the horse or gelding, and behind the mare, so as to catch the urine the moment they see the animal stretch itself out. The same custom is observed in some places on the Continent, where a pot with a long handle is used. I do not like this plan, because horses which are accustomed to it are apt, if the groom does not hold the vessel for them, to abstain from staling for a long time."

M. Horace Hayes, F.R.C.V.S.
Stable Management and Exercise, *1900*
Sixth edition revised by
Colonel Sir Andrew Horsbrugh-Porter
Arco Publishing Co., Inc., *1969*

~~~~~~~~~~~~~~~~~~~~~~~~~~~~

Trace clip   Hunter clip

Most owners of hot-blooded horses need to clip their animals only twice a year, usually in late October and again in January. Cold-blooded horses (those with draft breeding in their ancestry) need to be clipped more often; Shetland ponies sometimes need to be clipped as often as twice a month during the winter. How often to clip the horse depends on why you are clipping. If the horse will be traveling on the show circuit and judged on appearance, then regular and frequent clipping will be necessary. On the other hand, hunting or hacking horses may need only the minimum number of clippings. It is a good idea to cease clipping as the horse begins to shed late in the winter, since the clipper is likely not only to remove the dead winter coat but to clip off the tops of the fine summer coat growing in underneath. Trimming that coat may cause it to grow in with bristled ends, which can make the summer coat shaggy rather than sleek and smooth.

Three basic styles of clips are used on most horses today: the full cut, the hunter clip, and the trace cut. Certainly the full cut is the most attractive and therefore the most popular, although it may take several hours to accomplish. The full clip is easy to describe: all the long hairs except for the mane and tail are cut as close to the skin as possible. Horses that are fully clipped must be blanketed during cool weather, with at least one blanket when indoors and sometimes as many as three blankets when outdoors. In the hunter clip, preferred by many horsemen who hunt or hack, the legs are left unclipped for protection against rough and briered terrain. The rest of the coat is clipped clean, except, occasionally, that the saddle-pad area is left long. When not being used, hunter-clipped horses must be blanketed in cool weather. The trace clip is less frequently seen, since it is unacceptable for show animals and not especially attractive, but a horse clipped in such a way need not be blanketed—a decided advantage, saving both labor and clothing. In the trace clip, hair is removed from the areas of the body where the horse sweats most profusely: from under the neck, under the chest and belly, across the arm and stifle, along the buttock, and up around the dock. The trace clip is fine for horses that are hunted or hacked during the winter, and it is preferable to not clipping at all when you're trying to groom those areas where mud and manure tend to cling most tenaciously.

Before electric clippers were available, horsemen would clip their animals with razors (a time-consuming job), singe the long hairs with a candle or gas lamp (both time-consuming and dangerous), or use hand-cranked clippers. Today, wide head clippers are available in electric, battery-powered, and manual styles with a variety of blades, each designed to best handle a particular part of the horse's anatomy.

Ear Clipper. A quiet, smooth-running clipper excellent for trimming around ears. Small and lightweight, yet powerful. About $21. Oster Corp., 5055 North Lydell Avenue, Milwaukee, Wisconsin 53217.

The U.S. Department of Agriculture publishes a 50-page booklet called "Horsemanship and Horse Care," available for 35 cents. A second booklet (80 pages), called "Breeding and Raising Horses," offers information about stable construction and management for a cost of $1. Write to Superintendent of Documents, U.S. Government Printing Office, Washington, D.C. 20102.

HORSESHOEING
by Jerry Trapani

All horse owners and riders know—or should know—why horses need shoes. The primary reason is to protect their feet. Hooves are hard and strong, but not strong enough to withstand the wear and tear of rough, unyielding terrain and the work demanded by riding or driving. Another reason for shoeing is corrective. Many hoof and foot problems can be ameliorated, if not cured, by blacksmiths.

The word "blacksmith," by the way, means a worker in iron, one of the "black" metals (tin, on the other hand, is a "white" metal). Another name for my profession is "farrier," from *fer,* the French word for iron. Iron horseshoes, however, were not always used. The first shoes were made of leather, strapped like boots over the feet. They didn't last very long. Egyptians were the first to nail shoes to hooves: first wooden footware, then shoes made of iron.

What, then, does a blacksmith do when he pays his periodic call? After removing worn-down shoes, he must make sure the horse's foot is properly trimmed and balanced. Yes, balanced, just as a car's tires are. A horse that isn't standing straight and square will be subject to strains all the way up its leg. Sometimes imbalance can so affect a horse's stride that it will appear to be lame or interfere in its action.

As I trim a hoof, I cut away the dead sole and clean the frog. Only a small amount of frog is trimmed, since that fleshy part of the foot is very important to the animal's performance. The frog pumps blood throughout the foot and acts as both a shock absorber and a lever to cushion and spread the foot at each stride. In that regard, a foot should never be allowed to dry out and lose this important flexibility.

As I go about this process, I remove loose tissue and overlaps to prevent dirt and manure from being trapped in the foot. Then the wall is cut down until it is level, to eliminate hills and valleys so that the foot rests flush on the ground. The surface is smoothed with a rasp.

I ask myself several questions during this process. How should the horse stand on the ground? Is its toe too long? Are its heels too high? Are the forefeet and the hind feet matched? A well-trimmed foot needs to be symmetrical and level, and balance is determined by the angle of the foot. A straight line drawn from the point of the shoulder through the knee to the center of the foot is what a well-conformed horse should show. When a heel is too low, a horse will stand "in front of itself." Heels too high and toes too short force an animal to stand "under itself." These conformations will also affect the foot in action. A low-heeled foot tends to move close to the ground, inviting stumbling, while a high-heeled foot makes for short, choppy strides.

A horse's foot must also be balanced laterally. As viewed from the front or rear, the animal should stand straight, neither toed in nor toed out. I recommend starting early to prevent these problems. A foal's feet grow incredibly fast and need to be trimmed at least every three weeks. If a foal's feet present problems, it's fairly easy to correct them at this stage, since bones and joints are not fully developed.

A warning sign of a poorly shod horse is contracted heels. Chronic contracted heels are a conformation fault, but in the majority of cases, the condition is created by humans. Shoes that are too tight won't allow feet to expand. A foot trimmed too low at the toes, with heels left too high, will prevent weight from being carried on the frog. The result will be contracted heels.

Now comes the matter of the kind of shoes your horse should wear. Human activities call for a variety of footgear, from boots and dress shoes to sneakers and bedroom slippers. Depending on what your horse will be asked to do, durability and comfort are equally important criteria. Shoes won't turn a loser into a winner, but they will enable a horse to give its best possible performance. For example, imagine two horses in a hunter class that are equal in performance, manners, and conformation. As the judge asks them to jog in hand, he sees that one is a superb mover, while the other lacks the first's brilliance. Perhaps there's too little knee action—the horse not reaching out as it should. Perhaps it might be a wrong combination of horseshoes. The owner should know that there's a wide range from which to choose.

An open jumper needs a special shoe for its job, which includes quick turns, fast checks, and the impact of jumping. Shoes must be heavy enough to prevent slipping or twisting, yet light enough not to restrict or tire the animal. Most jumpers wear either steel or aluminum wide-webbed shoes with a runner or calk to reduce the chance of slipping. Hind shoes are heavier, with a squared-off toe or a special calk (called a "jar calk"). This item prevents a horse from overreaching.

Shoeing a show hunter aims at affording graceful movement. Wide aluminum shoes without calks are most usual. Hind shoes are flat so that the horse will move as naturally as possible.

A field hunter needs more substantial shoes, since its work includes a variety of terrain ranging from mud to unyielding roads. Field-hunter shoes need welded-on borium studs. Borium is an extremely hard metal; when applied, the studs form small crystals that act like snow tires for grip. These horses are often fitted with pads under their front shoes to protect against stones and other cross-country hazards.

Aluminum shoes used by jumpers and hunters should not be confused with the racing plates worn by racehorses. Those are much more fragile and have a toe grab to enable the horse to dig into a track's surface. If such spikes were used on jumping horses, landing on them would produce leg injuries. Jumpers and hunters wear aluminum shoes that are more substantial—⅜ inch thick and 1¼ inches wide at a bare minimum. Aluminum is useful because it absorbs concussion better than steel.

Polo and barrel-racing horses wear shoes similar to those of field hunters. The shoes are rimmed and weigh relatively little. When the rim fills with dirt, the friction of dirt against dirt provides an excellent grip.

Gaited and Walking horses, with their very long toes, have pads inserted to increase their high-stepping action. The shoes are heavy, with lead added to encourage action.

Draft horses are able to carry weight both behind and below, so their shoes are relatively heavy and resilient.

Horses that are used for trail riding or in distance and endurance competitions should wear shoes with small heel and toe calks. The calks provide better footing and somewhat more durability to the shoe.

On the other hand (or foot), these calks are not good for cutting and roping horses. They cause "drag" during sliding stops, and that drag can lead to serious foot and leg problems. The plane shoe, or plate, is therefore preferable.

Now I'd like to add a few words about the care and treatment of blacksmiths. We're a rare breed, in the sense that there are more horse owners than farriers, so we can afford to be influenced by how you people treat us. We're busy, so make appointments well in advance. Set up a schedule, whether every six weeks or two months, and we'll be there on time. Since our job shouldn't include racing around a field to help you catch a recalcitrant horse, please be sure our client (equine variety) is ready to be treated. Have a clean, dry area for us to work in; there's nothing worse than having to shoe a horse under pouring rain or freezing to death. We'd like your assistance to hold the animal and keep it calm. Blacksmiths regard with favor a horse that submits to being handled, an attitude you can facilitate by examining its hooves before and after riding and by using a hoof pick to remove small rocks and other foreign matter.

Although I don't recommend that anyone but the most experienced horseman try to shoe his own horses, there are a few steps you can take in the event your horse has a loose shoe. Remove the shoe if it's still attached to the hoof, using a pair of shoe pullers. First file the remaining clinch smooth with a farrier's rasp; then carefully pull off the

shoe. Start at the heel and work forward. Always pull toward the center of the foot; pulling toward the outside may rip the hoof's walls. Then rasp the edges of the hoof to prevent the chance of its splitting. If your horse has torn its foot, apply a poultice and wrap the foot in a burlap bag, leaving it on until professional assistance is available. It goes without saying—but I'll say it anyway—that a shoeless horse shouldn't be worked.

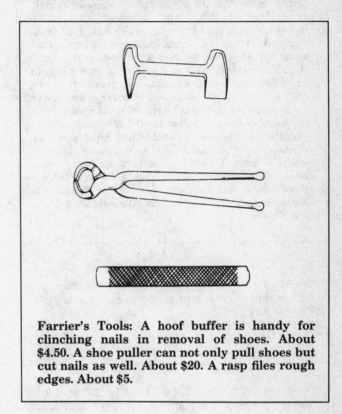

Farrier's Tools: A hoof buffer is handy for clinching nails in removal of shoes. About $4.50. A shoe puller can not only pull shoes but cut nails as well. About $20. A rasp files rough edges. About $5.

1892

Ice Creepers for Horses,

Easyboots are something every horseman should know about. Made of urethane, they slip on the foot (even over metal shoes) and are useful for parades, shipping, medication, and riding. With Easyboots, the horse can go barefoot in pasture and shod under tack. The boot gives protection, traction, and cushioning on hard pavement and rocks; it prevents the horse from sliding on slippery streets; it prevents "snowballing" and provides traction on snow and ice; and it protects the sole and frog. Easyboots, so the manufacturer claims, "outwear metal shoes by over a three-to-one ratio." And the claims go on: Easyboots can prevent or alleviate hoof cracks, contracted heels, corns, navicular disease, thrush, excessive hoof wear, and impact-caused hoof and leg injuries, and they are also useful for treating nail punctures, abscesses, and other hoof wounds. Available in natural, black, red, and blue in widths from 4 to 5¼ inches, with pony sizes and extra-large sizes available by special order. About $16.95 each, $64 set of four. Les-Kare, Inc., P.O. Box 96, Los Alamos, New Mexico 87544.

Oats—A grain which in England is generally given to horses, but in Scotland supports the people.
Samuel Johnson, LL.D.
Dictionary of the English Language

The following public and private schools offer a course of instruction in the art and craft of the farrier. Schools are listed alphabetically and while the listing was obtained from the American Farriers Association, it is not intended to imply the association's endorsement. For full particulars about each school's program, write directly to the school. Questions about any other phase of the farrier's trade may be directed to the American Farriers Association, P. O. Box 695, Albuquerque, New Mexico 87103.

Agriservices Foundation
Stockmen's School
3699 East Sierra Ave.
Clovis, California 93612

Albuquerque Horseshoeing School
Box 433
Los Lunas, New Mexico 87031

American Horseshoers Institute
Box 137
South Lyon, Michigan 48178

California State Polytechnic University
3801 West Temple Ave.
Pomona, California 91768

SO YOU WANT TO BE A BLACKSMITH
by Jerry Trapani

A lot of people—young boys, usually—tell me, when they see me working, that they would like to be farriers too. I always ask them why. Is it for the money? Is it because you can be your own boss? Or is it because you care about craftsmanship and take pleasure in a job well done? I always hope it is for the last reason, although I have to admit that there are many people in the horseshoeing trade because they can make a decent living without the hassle of getting a license or permit and without laying out tremendous amounts of capital.

Horseshoeing is one of the few businesses in which you can get started for only a few hundred dollars. Some people shoe on a part-time basis while holding other jobs. In several states, including New York, there is no regulatory agency governing farriers. Anyone who wants to can read a book or two, buy some tools, and go out and try to shoe horses.

However, if you are serious about a career in this field, there is much more to it than that. Many schools in this country offer courses in shoeing or even specialize in it. Check through horse publications; write the Veterans Administration (if you qualify), or your county extension office. (Most schools

California State Polytechnic University
San Luis Obispo, California 93401

Canadian School of Horseshoeing
Stouffville, Ontario
Canada

Central Wyoming College
Dean of Special Services
Riverton, Wyoming 82501

Colorado Northwestern Community College
School of Horseshoeing
Box 9010
Steamboat Springs, Colorado 80477

Cornell University
Extension Veterinarian
Ithaca, New York 14850

Eastern States Farrier School
R. D. 1, Box 49
Phoenix, New York 13135

Golden Leaf Farrier College
P. O. Box 195
Sturgis, South Dakota 57785

Harold Musselman Horseshoeing School
R.D. 1
Dillsburg, Pennsylvania 17019

today are accredited, but the Veterans Administration schools are usually the most reliable ones.) Compile a list of likely-looking schools, then check into them. Write to see if any of their graduates work in your area; either write to or visit a few of them. If possible, go to the school yourself.

The old apprentice tradition has pretty much disappeared now, mainly because the horseshoer has taken to the road to call on his customers rather than running a forge in town where people bring their horses. In the old shops, there were always tasks to be done, so that boys could get jobs and work their way up the ladder. Occasionally, you can find a farrier now who does hire a regular helper. Many states have organizations or associations of professional farriers, and you may get a lead on a job through one of those groups.

Although many tack shops carry some equipment for farriers, most professionals buy their tools from wholesale farrier suppliers. Aside from a truck, a forge, and an anvil—the most expensive items—a farrier will need in his basic bag of tricks at least the following: a set of shoe pullers, a set of hoof nippers, two knives (wide-blade and narrow-blade), two rasps (one for the foot and one for finishing), a driving hammer, a clinch block, a clinching tool, a farrier's apron, fire tongs, a ball-peen hammer, and a rounding hammer, as well as assorted shoes and nails.

The work itself is hard, but very rewarding. You can take a great deal of pride in the craft, but there are many problems you will be called upon to solve, not all of them having to do with horses' feet. In some cases you may be the closest thing to a veterinarian the horses will ever see. In the very old days, veterinary medicine began in blacksmith shops, since sick and lame animals were often taken there for complete tune-ups. Today life is somewhat easier, especially now that most shoes come ready-made and one needs only to trim the foot properly, adjust the shoe, and then nail it on. That sounds easy enough, and it looks easy when a professional does the job. But many inexperienced people who buy the equipment and go into business do not realize until they have been at it for a short while that shoeing horses is hardly a simple matter. Even though shoes are ready-made, there is a real art to choosing the right one and to trimming the foot in the best way. Time is the best teacher, but it helps to start out on the right foot and get as much knowledge as you can at the outset.

Hillcraft School of Horseshoeing
10890 Deer Cr. Canyon Rd.
Littleton, Colorado 80120

Horses A to Z, Inc.
Leelaunau Schools
Glen Arbor, Michigan 49636

Horses A to Z, Inc.
Middle Tennessee State University
College of Agriculture
Murfreesboro, Tennessee 37130

Horses A to Z, Inc.
State University of New York
Cobleskill, New York 12043

Kirkwood Community College
Agribusiness & Natural Resources
Box 2068
Cedar Rapids, Iowa 52406

Kansas Horseshoeing School
Route 1, Box 33
Girard, Kansas 66743

Mac's Horseshoeing Engineers
Farrier's School
Box 31
Bridgeton, Indiana 47836

Martinsville School of Farriery
P. O. Box 1341
Martinsville, Virginia 24112

Maryland-Virginia Farriers School
P. O. Box 132
Olney, Maryland 20832

Merced Community College
Department of Agriculture
Merced, California 95430

Michigan School of Horseshoeing
Box 423
Belleville, Michigan 48111

Mid-South School of Horseshoeing
4039 Brompton
Memphis, Tennessee 38118

Midwest Farrier School
P. O. Box 201
Xenia, Ohio 45385

Midwest Horseshoeing School
Maple Lane Road
Rural Route 3
Macomb, Illinois 61455

Misty Oaks Farrier School
3603 Leland Road
Sunny Valley, Oregon 97478

Montana State University
Departments of Animal & Range Science
and Continuing Education
Bozeman, Montana 59715

Nebraska Farrier School, Inc.
R.R. No. 1
Denton, Nebraska 68339

New England Farrier's School
Raymond, Maine 04071

New Mexico State University
P. O. Box 3501
Las Cruces, New Mexico 88003

North Texas Farriers School
P. O. Box 666
Mineral Wells, Texas 76067

North Texas Horseshoeing Institute, Inc.
821 East Southlake Blvd.
Grapevine, Texas 76051

Oklahoma Horseshoeing School
Route 1, Box U-26
Stillwater, Oklahoma 74074

Oklahoma Farriers College
Route 1, Box 13
Sperry, Oklahoma 74073

Oklahoma State Horseshoeing School
Route 1, Box 28-B
Admore, Oklahoma 73401

Olds Regional College
Olds, Alberta
Canada

Olympia Vocational Technical Institute
2011 Mottman Road S. W.
Olympia, Washington 98501

Oregon State University
Corvallis, Oregon 97331

Pennsylvania State University
College of Agriculture
University Park, Pennsylvania 16802

Pierce College
Animal Science Department
Woodland Hills, California 91364

Pitt Technical Institute
P. O. Drawer 7007
Greenville, North Carolina 27834

Porterville Horseshoeing School
810 North Jaye Street
Porterville, California 93257

Rogue Community College
3345 Redwood Pass Highway
Grants Pass, Oregon 97526

**South Central Missouri School of
Horseshoeing**
Route 2, Box 292
West Plains, Missouri 65775

South Jersey School of Horseshoeing
R.D. Box 126 W.H.
Mullica Hill, New Jersey 08062

T-Bone Horseshoeing School
Calabasas, California 91302

Technical Education Center
Anoka, Minnesota 55303

Texoma Horseshoeing School
Route 1
Pottsboro, Texas 75076

The Smithy
Thornton Hough
Wirral, Cheshire
England

Tri-State Farriers' School
26 Claremoor
Sibley, Iowa 51249

University of Maine
Extension Livestock Specialist
332 Hitchner Hall
Orono, Maine 04473

University of Wisconsin—River Falls
College of Agriculture
River Falls, Wisconsin 54022

Utah State University
Conference and Institute Division
Logan, Utah 84322

Valley Vocational Center
15359 Proctor Ave.
City of Industry, California 91744

Warrington's School of Horseshoeing
Townsend, Delaware 19734

Western's School of Horseshoeing, Inc.
2801 W. Maryland Ave.
Phoenix, Arizona 85017

Wolverine Farrier School
7690 Wiggins Road
Howell, Michigan 48843

4 HORSE HEALTH

No one would dispute the statement that the best horse is the sound horse, yet it is surprising how little is known by the average horse owner about equine health. Too often we rely on the once-a-year visit of the veterinarian, or his help in emergencies, to keep our horses in working order, but the old saying "An ounce of prevention is worth a pound of cure" is as true for horses as it is for people. We cannot stress enough the importance of good management, sensible nutrition, and regular veterinary care in preventing illness. We must also emphasize the necessity for each horse owner to learn as much as possible about equine health to catch trouble before it becomes serious and to know about the handling of animals in distress before the veterinarian arrives. This chapter will deal not only with aspects of good management as they apply specifically to health, but also with various preventive measures that the owner can and should take on a regular basis. Your veterinarian will be of invaluable help in establishing good programs and assisting in serious problems, but it is up to the individual to be sure that he is fully equipped with information, in the form of good references and well-kept records, and with various items that can be used in examining, restraining, and medicating animals at home. See the sample chart on page 66 and adapt a similar record for each horse you own.

SOUNDNESS IN HORSES

The first step in learning about equine health is to determine what are the normal signs in a healthy horse. The following section will act as a guide, but keep in mind that each horse can vary a bit from the norm, depending on its conformation, the way in which it is used, and its general condition. Therefore, it is always best to examine your own horse on a regular basis, daily if possible during the grooming session, and make notes of its individual peculiarities—temperature and other vital signs, appetite, and behavior. Pick a time when the horse has been at rest (exercise can increase the normal rates of respiration and pulse) and set up a routine. The veterinarian will benefit from your records and from the way in which the horse accepts the examination procedure. And you will be able to tell at a glance when something is amiss and take steps to prevent anything serious from developing. (See page 84 for first-aid remedies.)

HOW TO EXAMINE A HORSE

RESPIRATION

Using a clock with a second hand, count how many times the horse's flanks rise and fall in 30 seconds. Double the number to find the respiration rate per minute. Note whether the breathing is regular or not. In a horse at rest, the frequency should be between 8 and 16 breaths a minute; the younger the horse, the greater the rate (up to 30 a minute for foals). If the horse is lying down, the rate will be higher than normal. Increased rates may also be caused by exercise, stress, excitement, high temperature, or a health problem.

TEMPERATURE

Coat a rectal thermometer with a lubricant such as petroleum jelly and shake it down to below 96 degrees; insert it into the horse's rectum, rotating it gently, and leave it in place for about two minutes. To avoid losing the thermometer, either in the horse or in the bedding, tie a string to it with a clip that may be attached to the horse's tail. Normal temperature for an adult horse can range from 99 degrees to 100.5 degrees; a foal's normal temperature is 99.5 to 101.5 degrees. Temperatures may vary according to time of day (the highest is in late afternoon), sex (mares are usually lower than horses except when in heat, when the temperature may be 2 degrees above normal), age (young and old horses may be 1 degree higher than others), exercise, stress, environmental temperature, and disease. Thoroughbreds have higher temperatures than most other breeds, and violent exercise in hot weather can increase temperature 4 or 5 degrees. Well-fed horses have higher temperatures than poorly fed ones.

This heavy-duty thermometer is 5 inches long, with a stubby tip and a ring top to which a string may be attached. It is used rectally to determine body temperature. Thermometers of this type are usually made of glass and come equipped with a hard-rubber or plastic case, although more expensive metal ones are also available. Prices range from $2 to $3. (Available through most tack shops, agricultural catalogs, and veterinarians.) Special skin thermometers are also made for diagnosing tendinitis and areas of inflammation. The stainless steel back is placed in contact with the skin and the dial top registers the temperature (between 70 and 110 degrees F.), regardless of air temperature. Equipped with a tough plastic case and a protected dial. About $10. (Available through the Nasco catalog.)

Sample Health Chart

Animal's name:	Sire:
Birthdate and place:	Dam:
Breeder (or previous owner):	Date purchased:
Color and markings:	
Height at the withers:	
Normal weight:	
Normal respiration (at rest):	
Normal pulse (at rest):	
Normal estrous cycle (for mares):	
Ration in hay:	Pasture (number of months):
Ration in grain:	Feed supplier:
Vitamin/mineral/protein supplements:	
Blacksmith (name, address, dates of visits, and notes about unusual hoof problems, corrective shoeing, and/or treatments)	
Worming Program (dates and medication used; how dosed):	
Medical history: (illnesses, accidents, treatments, and dates; medications used and dosages; special notes about behavioral peculiarities and whether tranquilizers are necessary for examination)	
Inoculations: (dates and vaccinations used)	
Coggins Test: (dates)	
Breeding history: (gelded when; bred when, with names of mates and get)	
Name and telephone number of veterinarian:	
Emergency vets: (names and telephone numbers)	

PULSE

Using a watch with the second hand, feel for the horse's pulse at one of the major arteries—either in the girth area behind the elbow or underneath the lower jaw, a little in front of the fleshy region of the cheek. Normal pulse for an adult horse at rest is 30 to 40 beats a minute, though variations may be normal depending on the horse's age, sex, and size (the smaller and younger, the higher the rate—foals having a range of 50 to 70 beats a minute), and the climate and stress mentioned above. Note any irregularities in the beat and mention them to the veterinarian when he visits next, unless the abnormality is accompanied by other abnormal signs, in which case a special call might be in order.

EYES AND NOSE

Although a small amount of clear discharge from either eyes or nose is perfectly normal, any sign of pus, heavy mucus, or blood should be considered an indicator of possible trouble. The mucous membranes inside the nostrils and the eyelid lining should be pink, the same color as the gums (nostril lining will be bright red after exercise), and the third eyelid (inside corner of the eye) should be white to pink with visible blood vessels. Using a penlight, examine the pupils of the eyes, which should constrict within 1 to 2 seconds. Note any abnormal conditions such as cloudiness or discoloration in the cornea, which overlies the iris and pupil, or spots that may be in the center of the pupil—all of which are abnormal.

EARS

Check for any swelling or heat at the base of the ears. Look for any irritation or growth inside the ear if the horse is unusually sensitive in that area.

Ear mites are not uncommon and may give rise to secondary infections without treatment. Using your penlight, check for unusual reddening, bleeding, or other abnormalities.

TEETH

Familiarize yourself with the tooth structure of horses (see section on aging horses by teeth on page 3), and periodically check the horse's mouth for any problems, such as broken teeth, irregular growth, or sharp edges and points that may need filing. Gums should be pink, not whitish or yellow, and the horse's breath should smell sweet.

NECK AND BACK

As you groom, check for any swelling or tenderness, sores, or scars that may be signs of old sores caused by saddles or harness. Swollen glands and lymph nodes can be detected by feeling in the throatlatch region for signs of heat or sensitivity when pressure is applied. Look also for any signs of external parasites, such as ringworm, botfly eggs, and skin disorders, as well as abscesses, ulcerations, scaliness, loss of hair, and other abnormalities. The coat (except in winter) should be fine, smooth, and glossy, and the skin relatively soft and resilient. A dry coat or a hard skin may indicate nutritional deficiency, the presence of internal parasites, or disease. Check under the tail for swellings or lumps in the anal and vulvar region; if the animal has been rubbing its tail, indicating possible parasites, the hair in this area will be worn. Check the overall condition of the horse's barrel area; if ribs, backbone, and hip bones are at all prominent, the animal may not be getting sufficient rations.

ABDOMEN

If the horse is particularly sensitive in its nether region and is not calmed by regular handling or soothing noises, be alert for swellings, lesions, or sores of any sort. A horse suffering from abdominal pain will often look around at its sides or kick up. Any continued behavior like this (more than an hour) should be reported immediately to the vet.

LEGS

Run your hands carefully over all parts of the legs and feet, watching for any excessive heat, pulse, or swelling. If you find some irregularity in one leg, check the other side for symmetrical similarities. Become familiar with common ailments, such as splints, bog spavin, and capped hocks, and ask the vet to recommend suitable treatment. (See page 90 for detailed information about these conditions.) Flex the horse's legs at each joint to check for any sensitivity or restricted movement—signs of developing lameness; then note the feet for cracks, wounds, and thrush (which can also be detected by smell). See that the feet are cleanly and evenly trimmed and that the shoes are in place and evenly worn.

STOOL AND URINE

When you clean the horse's stall, note the condition of the bedding for any unusual coloration or texture. Urine is light yellow in color and a bit cloudy; a horse normally excretes between 4 and 7 quarts of urine a day, five or more times. A horse moves its bowels, or makes manure as some like to put it, anywhere from four to eight times daily. Normal droppings are brown, mucus-free, and firm in texture. Whole grains visible in manure will indicate a digestive problem. Sometimes you may notice a looser, somewhat green stool after a horse has been turned out to graze for the first time in the spring. This is not necessarily serious, but if diarrhea continues, call the vet. Incontinence or retention of urine or droppings may indicate the presence of a disease process. If the vet wishes to examine a stool or urine sample, or if you feel that an examination is indicated (by other symptoms of internal parasites), place samples in clean plastic containers with tight lids and deliver them fresh to his office, or store temporarily in the refrigerator. Mark the containers carefully with the name of the horse and the date to avoid confusion to the vet and unpleasant surprises for the rest of the family. While you are checking the stall, look at the salt block and note whether the wood of the stall has been chewed. If so, the horse may be overly nervous or bored, evidenced by wind sucking or cribbing.

BEHAVIOR

Since each horse has its own personality, every owner should become aware of normal behavior so that irregular activity can be noted as a sign of something amiss. A sudden display of bad temper may be the result of pain, not vice, and any change in normal eating habits may indicate a serious problem. When you are using the horse, keep an eye out for any signs of unusual movement—shying, lameness, or uneven gaits. Have someone else ride or lead the horse at the trot so that you can inspect its movement. Any deviation from symmetrical motion or an irregular gait should be sufficient reason for further investigation. (See page 90 for a detailed explanation of lameness diagnosis.) Heaving, or heavy breathing, after exercise is not normal in the conditioned horse, and coughing fits may indicate respiratory disease. If a horse's shoes have been unevenly worn, keep a watch for interfering hooves or cross firing when the animal is moving, and report it to your blacksmith when he next visits.

ROUTINE PREVENTIVE CARE

Once you know what is normal for your horse and have set down records for your veterinarian to check, you can begin to establish regular routines for care, based on good management, sound nutrition, and regular veterinary attention. Horses are creatures of habit, and any dramatic change in routine can cause stress and even illness, so one should take care to see that routines, once set up, are adhered to with great consistency.

STABLE MANAGEMENT

One of the most effective ways to prevent trouble is to see that the stable in which a horse or horses are kept is run efficiently. The chapter on stable management contains the basic information about routines and equipment that make up any good stable-management program, but we would like to make special note here of routines that should be developed for good health care.

~~~~~~~~~~~~~~~~~~~~~~~~~~~~~~

"Horses should be washed with warm water which has been laced with some sort of body wash containing a little oil and only when they are hot. A horse should be sweating before you wash him. If a horse comes in and he's just a little sticky under a saddle or at the girth, wipe him with a damp sponge but don't automatically wash him. It's the surest way to kill a coat I know."

From *"J. Arthur Reynolds: Showing on the Line"*
Practical Horseman, *June 1976*

~~~~~~~~~~~~~~~~~~~~~~~~~~~~~~

CLEANING

We have already mentioned the advisability of regular examinations during the usual grooming and stall-cleaning sessions. Any knowledgeable owner is already aware of the beneficial effects of a good cleaning program for both horse and surroundings—not only for appearance but also for the sake of health. Skin and coat will be kept healthy and glossy by strong, vigorous grooming, which helps stimulate circulation of the blood and removes excess dirt and oils that may attract flies, lice, and other external parasites. Special coat and hoof dressings improve appearance, though their regular use is not recommended without a vet's supervision, since poor coat and dry hooves may be symptomatic of ill health; the dressings may serve cosmetically, but they do not cure the underlying problem. Hoof dressings, for instance, help to retain moisture in the hoof, but they will not provide it; horses bedded on dry wood chips, sawdust, or shavings must be given extra moisture through the use of soaking swabs, or their hooves will become dried out. Poor skin or coat condition may be caused by internal parasites (worms) or a nutritional deficiency, and no amount of cleaning or special dressing can improve the situation on any permanent basis. Regular cleaning of the stall and pasture area is also essential to health, not just to improve the pleasantness of the environment but also to help eliminate parasites and the possibility of diseases, such as thrush, caused by the presence in the cleft of the frog of moist, decomposing organic material. Fresh bedding and daily hoof cleaning should prevent this condition; in fact, we will even go so far as to say that thrush should never be present in any self-respecting horse owner's stable.

FEEDING

A good feeding program should be established with the help of the veterinarian, who will know the nutritional requirements of the individual horse, based on weight, age, general condition, and use. (See pages 42–49 for detailed information about nutrition in horses.) The selection, purchase, and feeding of hay and grains are an integral part of preventive medicine. Check all supplies as they are delivered, and again before feeding, to be sure that weight and quality are controlled. See that feed is given under hygienic circumstances: grain and water should be fed in clean containers, and hay should—if possible—be presented away from soiled bedding, to avoid recycling parasites. Many people believe that hay should be placed on the floor of the stall. This enables the horse to eat in a more natural way and reduces the risk of irritation from dust. Nevertheless, ingestion of bedding materials and the parasites present in manure is always a risk with this kind of feeding, and good hay, properly cured and stored, should be free of dust and other foreign particles. If horses are allowed to graze, the pasture should be kept clean, with regular removal of feces, although pasture rotation (at least every two months) is more practical. Harrowing and liming pastureland after rotation are also beneficial, especially if the ground is naturally moist. (Research has shown that wet pastureland is far more likely to harbor parasites than dry land, and that warmer regions are worse than cold ones.) Poisonous plants should be avoided (see page 48) or removed from pastureland, and good, nutritious grass should be available, with fertilization and replanting programs undertaken on a regular basis. Naturally grazing horses will nibble as they move around, getting exercise and keeping busy as they take in nourishment. Horses that are confined to the stall are obviously members of the same species and deserve special attention to keep them fit and occupied. Several feedings a day are superior to one or two feedings, and constant access to hay and water will prevent the animal's developing nervous habits out of boredom. Overfeeding is as dangerous as underfeeding, however, so be sure to keep close track of the amount of food an animal takes in, and see that the horse is worked accordingly. Heavily worked animals deserve days of rest like everyone else, but azoturia (or Monday-morning sickness), in which a horse ties up (its muscles become rigid) and, if not treated, may die, should be prevented by special feedings the night before a day off. Bran mashes are traditional, and their use is recommended (see page 47). Other special feeds—such as those designed for broodmares, growing foals, and animals in need of supplements—are discussed in Chapter 3 and should be fed only under a veterinarian's supervision.

EXERCISE

Wild horses get natural exercise while grazing, as they wander from one feeding area to another. Do-

Hoof Dressings and Conditioners. Polishes and brighteners are discussed in the stable-management chapter, since they are primarily cosmetic in use, bringing out a high gloss on the hoof wall. Special dressings have more therapeutic uses, however, since they are richer in lanolin and other oils, which will help prevent or treat dry hooves. They often contain antiseptic and fungicidal ingredients as well.

Liquid conditioners are designed to penetrate the hoof wall and to moisturize the hoof without clogging pores; they will also give a glossy appearance to the wall like a brightener. Prices range from $3 to $5 a quart. Paste or ointment conditioners do not penetrate as well, but they afford an outer protective coating to keep moisture in the hoof, and they are usually preferred for use on the sole, frog, heel, and coronet. These run about twice as much in price as the liquids.

The most popular liquid conditioners are:

Absorbine Liquid Hooflex (W. F. Young), which will not congeal in cold weather, available in a pint squeeze bottle (see Hooflex below)

Farnam's Superhoof, which contains pine oil, lanolin, castor oil and linseed oil, alcohol, and iodine in a turpentine base and is available in a 28-ounce spray bottle

Fiebing's Hoof Dressing, which contains soy oil, liquid petrolatum, tar acid, and gilsonite and comes in quart and gallon cans.

Merck's Top Form Hoof Shield

The most popular paste hoof conditioners are:

Absorbine Hooflex, which is a mixture of petrolatum, neat's-foot oil, lanolin, turpentine, soya oil, pine tar, and rosin and comes in quart or gallon cans

Hoolfoilin (Thoroughbred Remedy Corp.), which contains cod-liver oil, neat's-foot oil, beeswax, oils of turpentine, cedarwood, and pine, and pine tar

Mollimentum Hoof Dressing (Troy Chemical Co., Mt. Kisco, N.Y.), which contains cottonseed oil, rosin, beeswax, paraffin, and turpentine and comes in quart, half-gallon, and gallon pails, with brush

Straight Arrow's Hoofmaker, which contains special proteins, linoleic acid, iodine, vitamins, and salicylic acid and comes in a 2-pound jar.

Hoof packing is generally prescribed for specific ailments of the sole and frog, and it may be applied with or without the use of shoe pads to keep it in place when the horse is shod. Pine tar is the traditional material, but commercial medicated packings are available, such as Fiebing's Hoof Packing in 5-pound packages and Forshner's Hoof Packing (Forshner's, Foxboro, Massachusetts) in 9½- and 24-pound packages.

Other special hoof medications are designed to treat thrush, foot rot, ringworm, and superficial wounds of the sole and frog. In addition to the usual oils, these generally contain aromatics (such as camphor) and iodine and turpentine, which will act on bacteria and fungus and afford a moistureproof coating to protect the affected foot. The best-known brands are Foulex from Troy Chemical Co., Kopertox from Ayerst, Linite Antiseptic from Naylor, Thrush-X from Farnam, Thrush Medication from Western Laboratories, and Absorbine Thrush Remedy from W. F. Young. Prices range from about $2 to $3.50 for 8 to 12 ounces.

mestic horses need the same, whether it is the exercise they get on their own in a pasture or the work they are made to do carrying riders or pulling plows, carts, or large coaches. Ideally, all horses should get a minimum of exercise a day; without it, their systems may go awry—not only the muscular but also the digestive, cardiovascular, and respiratory—and their psychological makeup may be affected as well. Bored horses with little to oc-

cupy them often take to bad habits, such as cribbing, digging into the floors of their stalls, and weaving. Common sense applies here, as in most other aspects of horse keeping. A horse that is fed lightly should not be overexercised unless its diet is increased proportionately; a horse that has not been exercised heavily should not be expected to undertake a long, strenuous siege of work without proper conditioning. Even a heavily worked horse that suddenly faces a day of rest should get some light, laxative bran mash the night before to adjust its system to inactivity. If one is unable to ride or drive, the animal should at least be lunged.

When horses are conditioned to moderate work (from one to three hours a day), they should be walked for the first few minutes and walked home for the last ten or fifteen. This will cool them out, and one should take note of their condition before putting them back into the barn or pasture. If the coat is wet, the horse should be walked until it has dried off. If work has been strenuous, water should be withheld until the animal is thoroughly cool.

While riding or driving, take care to avoid gaits faster than the walk on hard surfaces, such as tarred roads and frozen ground, or on areas with sharp stones or other objects that may injure the feet. Any horse unaccustomed to trail riding shouldn't be expected to pick its way sensibly through woods and streams, and riders should be careful to avoid allowing the animal to get itself into trouble. Leaning forward while riding up and down hills will help the horse maintain balance and increase its traction.

STABLE CONSTRUCTION

Chapter 2 covers most of the potential dangers that can lead to illness or accident, but it doesn't hurt to repeat the cautions here. Stalls should be large and free of any protuberances that a horse could run or get into—loose wiring, unprotected light bulbs, rough edges of wood or metal, uncovered windows, low ceilings, narrow doorways, badly stored hay and grain, high sills, and partitions that are not sufficiently solid. Even stall latches and bolts that are not flush with the wall can cause tears as nasty as those caused by protruding nails, and buckets and tubs should be attached to the wall so that the horse can't get its feet tangled. Many injuries have been caused by the tops of Dutch doors that swing inward or that are not latched securely whether open or shut. The bottom part of a double stall door should be at least four feet high to discourage escape and, like the top, should be secured whether open or not. Pastures and corrals must also be free of dangerous elements, and fencing should be as safe as it is sound. Barbed wire can injure highstrung or inquisitive horses, and bales of loose wire should be removed to prevent horses from getting caught.

ISOLATION OF NEWCOMERS OR SICK HORSES

If you have a stableful of healthy horses, it behooves you to be careful when any new horse arrives on the scene or when one of the residents becomes ill. Coggins tests and fecal examinations may clear your conscience about swamp fever and parasites in a newcomer, but many horses can carry infectious diseases that may not become evident for a matter of days. Although inoculating the residents will help prevent the spread of a disease, the least expensive and most sensible arrange-

"You hear of the city feller who wanted to board his horse and he asked his friends what he ought to pay and they said, 'The price ranges from one dollar a month to fifty cents to two-bits, but whatever you pay, you're entitled to the manure.' So this city feller goes to the first farmer, and the farmer says, 'One dollar,' and the city feller says 'But I get the manure?' The farmer nods, and at the next place it's fifty cents, and the city feller says, 'But I get the manure?' and the farmer nods. At the third farm two-bits and the same story, so the city feller says, 'Maybe I can find a place that's real cheap,' and he goes to a broken-down farm and the man says, 'Ten cents a month,' and the city feller says, 'But I get the manure?' and the farmer says, 'Son, at ten cents a month there ain't gonna be any manure.'"
James Michener
CENTENNIAL
Fawcett World, 1976

ment is simply to isolate a new horse in a stall or paddock away from the others. (Such an area is also useful for an injured or diseased animal, for purposes of treatment.) The newcomer should remain in quarantine for at least two weeks until your veterinarian gives it a clean bill of health. During this period, be sure that manure and horsehair are not transferred from one horse to another—whether by pitchfork, wheelbarrow, or grooming tools or by your own shoes or clothing. If a newcomer (or a horse undergoing rest and recuperation) can be kept in sight of the other horses, so that they are aware of its presence, introduction (or reintroduction) into the herd may cause fewer problems. It is fascinating to observe horses pastured together, trying to figure out the pecking order or the relative dominance of the animals. But the arrival of a newcomer may throw the order out of whack for a while, until the head horse establishes its dominance, and equine fisticuffs may result. A gradual introduction will keep disaster to a minimum, although it might also be practical to remove hind shoes from any horse you suspect of hostile behavior.

STABLE MEDICINE CHEST

Any kind of stable, whether it is a one-horse shed or a twenty-horse barn, should not be without a cabinet or box containing medical supplies for use in emergencies or in treatments of problematical situations. The container should be kept within easy reach, but locked or otherwise inaccessible to children. Items to be kept in the chest at all times—and promptly replaced as they are used—are suggested below. Keep a list of the contents in the chest and check periodically to see that none is missing. Include on that list the names and telephone numbers of at least two veterinarians for handy reference, as well as the name of the local farrier. Familiarize yourself, under a veterinarian's guidance, with the use of each of these items and with proper first-aid procedures. Be sure to leave some extra space in the chest for medications that the veterinarian may leave with you, such as worming medicines. And remember to keep a separate medicine chest in the horse van or in your tack trunk for use on the road, at horse shows, or at stables where your horse may be boarding. Do not rely on other owners or grooms to have these things on hand, but see that you do. The methods of applying internal and external medications are described later on in this chapter.

Antibiotic powder (as your veterinarian recommends) for treating superficial wounds to prevent infection

Antibiotic ointment (prescribed by the vet) for covering open wounds

Balling gun, for dosing medication

Bandaging materials: 1 large roll cotton; 1 roll 2-inch gauze; 1 roll 2-inch adhesive tape; 1 elastic bandage; 1 set leg bandages and pads; 1 package sterile gauze sponges

Boric acid, for use in solution for treating eyes

Cold pack (or soaking tub and access to hose), to reduce swelling

Dosing syringes, 12-cc and 35-cc sizes

Fly repellent, stick or spray form, for use around eyes and wounds (as well as for general use)

Hoof dressing, to keep walls pliable

Laxative and diuretics (prescribed by the vet)

Liniment, for soothing sore muscles after heavy exercise

Measuring cup and spoons

Mineral oil, for use in treating colic (prescribed by the vet)

Ophthalmic ointment, for use in the eyes

Penlight, for examining eyes and ears

Petroleum jelly (Vaseline)

Poultice—hot pack for relief of swelling

Rasp (for feet)

Rubbing alcohol

Salt, to make a saline solution for flushing out wounds and for treating colic

Scissors

Shoe remover

Tincture of iodine (or another disinfectant recommended by the vet)

Twitch, for restraint

Veterinary thermometer

Witch hazel

Wound dressing, for minor abrasions

Zinc oxide (powder or ointment)

HEALTH PRODUCTS

If your horse is sick or injured, your first step, of course, is to call the veterinarian rather than apply some home remedies, especially if you don't have much experience. The vet will have drugs, procedures, and equipment on hand to deal with most problems, and there are a number of equine centers that can handle more complicated cases requiring surgery and advanced techniques for treatment. Then why are there so many over-the-counter medications available for horses with old-fashioned names like liniment, poultice, blister,

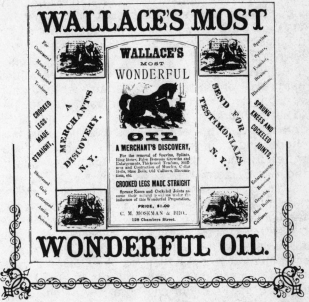

and such? Those methods went out of use years ago in human medicine along with bleeding and leeching. But look at your average drugstore—full of remedies for minor human ailments, such as coughs, colds, and stomachaches. None of these is particularly powerful, but some are sufficiently effective to bring relief unless the problem is serious enough to demand a physician's attention. And so it is with horses. Years ago, before there were veterinarians, horsemen kept their own animals reasonably healthy, sometimes relying on the farrier for help and sometimes on their own ingenuity in concocting preparations that seemed to work pretty well. Even when veterinarians did come along, there weren't very many of them that specialized in equine practice once the automobile became our major form of transportation. Nowadays, of course, there are perhaps ten million horses in the country, thanks to the boom in pleasure riding, and the number of veterinarians has also increased, if not at quite the same rate. Nevertheless, experienced horsemen who have learned to count on their own remedies still do so, and the products that are available to the public today are based in large part on those tried-and-true medications. Witch hazel, pine tar, glycerine, alcohol, and other ingredients that sound as though they came right out of a medieval herbal-medicine book are still used, along with more modern substances.

Most tack shops and feed suppliers carry a few of these products in stock or can order them from their wholesalers, although some products—such as prescription drugs—can be obtained only through a licensed veterinarian. Unless you know just what you are doing, the kind of medication you need and the way to apply it, you should probably check with your vet before investing in any for your first-aid chest. Over-the-counter products tend to be safe enough if used according to directions, but the size, age, and condition of any horse may require a slightly different product or application, and it pays to be sure. And speaking of paying, the prices given in this chapter are only approximate and only for general information; do not assume that a cheaper product is necessarily of a lower quality, or that a high price ensures greater effectiveness. Some suppliers charge very different prices for the same item (since overhead costs vary considerably), and in some cases it does pay to shop around.

In addition to checking the horse catalogs, tack shops, and your veterinarian, you might also subscribe to one of the agricultural catalogs such as those of Sears or Nasco. Not only are their prices usually more reasonable, but they also tend to carry a wider range of equipment for breeders and farm animals.

A number of companies specialize in horse products and have entire lines of medications and equipment. If you find that you like a certain product from one manufacturer and are unable to get others in its line, you can always write the company directly for a descriptive brochure and for a list of its retail distributors. Because of space limitations, we cannot list all of these companies (nor can we illustrate or describe all of the health products available), but we have attempted to select the most comprehensive well-established firms that exist in all parts of the country. Where special items are mentioned and the manufacturer is not listed below, we have included the address in the description of the product.

Anchor Laboratories, Inc. P.O. Box 999, St. Joseph, Missouri 64502
(biologicals, hoof-care products, insecticides, liniment, vitamins, wormers, wound dressings)

Ayerst Laboratories, 685 Third Avenue, New York, N.Y. 10017
(cough medications, hoof-care products, mineral and food supplements)

Bickmore, Inc. 34 Tower Street, Hudson, Massachusetts 01749
(body wash, coat dressing, cough medicine, hoof-care products, liniment, medications, ointments, wound dressings)

Bio Vet, 24201 Frampton Avenue, Harbor City, California 90701
(biologicals, coat and hoof dressings, cough medications, cribbing preventives, disinfectants, eye-care products, feed supplements, liniments, wound dressings)

Cadco, Inc., 10100 Douglas Avenue, Des Moines, Iowa 50322
(body wash, coat dressing, cough medication, cribbing preventive, disinfectant, eye-care products, feed supplements, insecticides, leg paint, liniment, medications, ointments, vitamins, wound dressings)

Carter-Luff Chemical Co., 738 Warren Street, Hudson, New York 12534
(body wash, hoof-care products, liniment, shampoo, wound dressings)

The Farnam Companies, Inc. 2230 East Magnolia, P.O. Box 21447, Phoenix, Arizona 85036
(coat and hoof dressings, cough medication, cribbing preventive, eye-care products, disinfectant, insecticides, liniment, ointments, vitamins, wormers)

Franklin Laboratories (Cinch Products), a division of American Home Products, P.O. Box 22335, 1776 Bellaire Street South, Denver, Colorado 80222
(body wash, coat dressing, feed supplements, hoof-care products, liniment, ointments, vitamins)

Horse Health Products, P.O. Box 311, 810 Park Avenue, S.E., Aiken, South Carolina 29801
(biologicals, cough medication, ointments, protein supplements, vitamins, wound dressings)

J-Ro Industries (Mean Green Products), P.O. Box 596, Mercer Island, Washington 98040
(feed supplements, hoof-care products, leg bandages, ointments, repellents, wormers)

Lee Drug Co., 5203 Leavenworth Street, Omaha, Nebraska 68106
(cough medication, hoof-care products, leg paints, liniments, vitamins)

Legear Laboratories, Inc., 1304 Ashby Road, P.O. Box 12650, St. Louis, Missouri 63132
(hoof-care products, liniment, medications, vitamins, wormers, wound dressings)

McTarnahans Pharmaceuticals (Winners Circle Products), 145 North Santa Anita Avenue, Arcadia, California 91006
(body wash, feed supplement, hoof-care products, leg bandages, leg paints, medications, skin ointments)

Merck & Co., Inc. (Top Form Products), P.O. Box M, Rahway, New Jersey 07065
(coat dressings and supplements, cribbing preventive, feed supplements, hoof-care products, insecticides, liniment, medications, repellents, shampoo, vitamins, wormers)

H. W. Naylor Co., Inc., Main Street, Morris, New York 13808
(hoof-care products, liniment, skin medications, ointments, wound dressings)

Roberts' Horse Products, Rockford, Illinois 61101
(feed supplements, hoof-care products, insecticides, liniment, laxatives, wound dressings)

Shell Chemical Co. (Animal Health Division), 2401 Crow Canyon Road, San Ramon, California 94583
(insecticides, medications, wormers)

Straight-Arrow, Inc., a division of American Equine Health Products, P.O. Box 270, Phillipsburg, New Jersey 08865

(coat dressings, cribbing preventive, hoof-care products, leg bandages, repellents)

Thoroughbred Remedy Corp., 251 Hempstead Turnpike, Elmont, N.Y. 11003
(biologicals, body wash, cough medication, disinfectant, feed supplements, hoof-care products, leg bandages and paints, liniment, skin medications, vitamins, wormers, wound dressings)

Turf Champion Products, R.D. 1, Monmouth Road, Mt. Holly, New Jersey 08060
(body wash, disinfectant, hoof-care products, liniment, medications, vitamins)

Turf Laboratories, P.O. Box 425, Tustin, California 92680
(hoof-care products, liniments, medications, vitamins, wound dressings)

Western Laboratories, 7230 North Dershing Drive, P.O. Box 594, Omaha, Nebraska 68101
(body wash, coat dressings, cough medications, feed supplements, hoof-care products, insecticides, liniment, medications, protein supplements, shampoo, vitamins, wormers, wound dressings)

Whitmoyer Laboratories, Inc., 19 North Railroad Street, Myerstown, Pennsylvania 17067
(biologicals, cough medication, disinfectant, eye-care products, feed supplements, insecticides, liniment, skin medication, vitamins, wound dressings)

W. F. Young, Inc. (Absorbine Products), 111 Lyman Street, Springfield, Massachusetts 01101
(hoof-care products, liniments, insecticides)

Zirin Laboratories International, Inc., 199 West 24th Street, Hialeah, Florida 33010
(biologicals, body wash, cough medication, disinfectant, feed supplements, leg paints, medications, shampoo, vitamins)

Once you have selected the item you want and determined the manufacturer and/or distributor, the next step is to figure out how much to buy and in what sort of container. Many medications, liniments, and such are available in giant economy sizes, just like soap, but until you know how often you will use something (which may not be much at all if the animal doesn't respond well), stick to the smaller, easier-to-store sizes, even though they may be more expensive on a unit-cost basis. Keep in mind, too, the fact that some liquids may be less economical than ointments because of the loss caused by pouring or brushing the material onto the horse. We tend to disapprove of aerosols for atmospheric reasons, and horses often react badly as well, just because they hate the sound of the spray; this supposedly efficient method of applying a substance may not be so effective after all.

Except for mentioning the names of some worming medicines and a few drugs in the text, we have not gone into much detail about the products sold by ethical-drug companies, since they can be purchased only through a licensed veterinarian—who should also be the only person to use them or

supervise their use. Only when a vet leaves medication with you and specific instructions should you attempt to give a horse any of these prescription products.

Some of the many products available over the counter should be part of each stable first-aid kit and some are to be considered optional, depending on the horse. We have been highly selective because of the limitation of space, choosing to mention and illustrate only the most popular or readily available or particularly effective brands.

Gentlemen don't fall off their horses; they are thrown.
Anonymous

A VETERINARIAN SPEAKS OUT

Somehow, when some people buy a horse they fail to consider that they will have to spend quite a bit of money for routine medical care. They forget that food is not the only thing that is important to a horse. A horse needs foot care. It needs routine dewormings. It needs help against the "dangers" that sometimes mark its outdoor life: Give me a horse and give me a small nail in a pasture fence and I will make an even bet that nail and horse will find each other—even if the pasture covers three acres.

More important, some people are seldom prepared for the "catastrophic" medical problems that can afflict horses. Thus, when faced by a four-hundred-dollar operation to save a colicky horse, some owners, forced by financial considerations, choose to put the animal to sleep.

For many race-horse owners, the animal is no more than a living racing machine. Often, when the horse breaks down, it is just patched up—even if the patchwork will enable the horse to run no more than one additional race. If a horse suffers a minor injury—to the knee, for example—it often should be laid up for a month. But to retrain a horse after a month's lay-off can cost thirty dollars per day or more for still another month. Many race-horse owners are not willing to spend that much more time and money on a minor knee injury. Instead, they ask the attending veterinarian to inject cortisone in the affected joint and keep the horse running until it finally can no longer compete and must be put out to pasture or put down.

I just like horses too much to find real pleasure practicing a medicine dictated by economic necessity.

Lucas Younker, D.V.M.
Animal Doctor (New York: Dutton, 1976)

VETERINARIANS

Although you may see the veterinarian only once or twice a year, he or she can be your best friend when you are in need—not just during emergencies but on a steady basis, helping you establish good management and feeding programs and giving your animal regular examinations, inoculations, and worming medications as preventive measures. Every horse owner should use a vet who is familiar with the horse in its normal condition and who specializes in equine work. Because small-animal practitioners will not often handle them, horses in suburban areas may not have the advantages of their country cousins, who can benefit from the presence of a large-animal vet who routinely cares for farm animals. Nevertheless, in areas where horses are kept in any number, veterinarians can usually be found without too much difficulty, even if they have more clients than they can fit into a 9-to-5 working day. Because they must go to their patients rather than work out of a clinic or hospital setup, they are not always easy to reach, but many now have effective telephone, beeper, or CB radio systems in their vehicles and can be contacted within an hour or less. There are also equine centers, sometimes connected with racetracks or veterinary colleges, where information about practitioners in certain areas can be obtained or where horses needing specialist care can be shipped for treatment or diagnosis. New owners can usually find a veterinarian through the animal's previous owner, while newcomers to an area can check the Yellow Pages or call local breeding farms or stables for recommendations. Because the veterinarian you select may not always be available when emergencies arise, or because you may want to get a second opinion on a particular question, it is always a good idea to have one or two names in reserve.

Before we talk about what you can expect of a veterinarian, let's discuss what a vet will require of you. In addition to fees, which vary widely from one part of the country to another depending on many factors, he will expect that you keep good records in addition to the one he keeps for himself. He will also want you to establish and implement on a routine basis a good management program. He will expect you to keep careful watch on your horse's general condition and behavior, to catch signs of trouble as early as possible to make effective treatment possible. Sensible observation and notation of irregularities in feeding, elimination, action, and the condition of feet, coat, eyes, and so on will be valuable bits of information in diagnosis; and, of course, good follow-up care is only common sense. If you have questions about anything that a vet says or recommends, be sure you ask them. Experienced horsemen are familiar with various ways of dosing an animal or bandaging or treating its feet, for instance, but the neophyte shouldn't be expected to do so without expert instruction. Don't rely entirely on friends who claim superior knowledge. Although they may know what they are talking about, chances are that the vet has more up-to-date and certainly more professional information at his command. It bears repeating that it is unwise to take chances when it comes to equine health. Don't count on your feed store or supplier to give you good advice about patent medicines, worming dosages, or food supplements. Always check with your horse doctor first.

In addition to giving you advice about your horse's daily care—feed ration, capability for work, and other aspects of management—the veterinarian can be expected to perform any number of other services. When you are considering the purchase of a new animal, ask your vet to join you and comment about the horse's conformation, state of health, and general condition. Later, he can help you break the animal into a new regime of feeding and exercise, if necessary, as well as providing medical attention.

A thorough examination by a veterinarian once if not twice a year is the least you owe any horse in your care. A careful look at the animal's eyes, teeth, nose, ears, feet, legs, back, coat, and general appearance will give him a good idea of the animal's condition as well as whether it needs supplementary food, corrective shoeing, or any other special care on a regular basis.

At the same time, the doctor will inoculate the animal for any diseases that may be prevalent in your area and take a fecal sample to examine for the presence of internal parasites. (Some vets will do this on the spot; others will take the specimen back to their office for microscopic examination and call you—or ask you to call them—about the results and recommended treatment.) Since few horses are free of parasites, the question is not usually whether you will need to have your animal wormed, but what kind of medication will take care of the problem and how and when it should be administered.

A yearly Coggins test to determine the absence (we hope) of equine infectious anemia (swamp fever) will be necessary in most areas; this involves the taking of a blood sample for analysis in an authorized laboratory. If the horse is to be shipped out of state, federal law says that you must have proof that the animal was free of the disease within no more than a year of the shipping date. Some states have made it illegal to trailer a horse off your own property without a negative Coggins test within the year, but laws aside, if you plan to move your horse into any location where other horses are to be present, a Coggins test is a good idea. (Also determine, if you are moving your horse to another stable, that the horses there have been tested.) For a discussion of EIA and the Coggins test, see pages 82–84.

As to specific problems the vet might encounter, broken teeth or teeth that are unevenly worn will need to be filed down with a dental float, with a speculum used to hold the horse's mouth open.

(Some brave men just pull the tongue to the side between the animal's teeth so that it is unlikely to bite, but high-strung horses aren't easy to handle, and floating isn't an easy job anyhow.) Keeping the teeth in good working order, and extracting any that may need it (such as the small wolf teeth, which are premolar vestiges and may interfere with bitting), is an important routine, especially since horses with dental problems also tend to have digestive problems if they aren't able to eat properly. Although some horsemen are experienced enough to float their own horses' teeth, it is a tricky procedure. Unless you have received instruction and done the job in the presence of your vet, it isn't recommended for beginners.

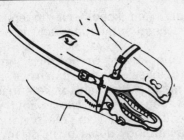

Dental Equipment. The McPherson-type speculum pictured contains two sets of plates for use on incisors or molars and is made of polished forged steel with leather straps. About $50. (Available through some large tack shops and most agricultural catalogs.)

The dental float is a simple device, consisting of one handle to which is screwed a head that holds a rasp or file (or combination) attached to the head with two screws. Most floats are equipped with two heads, one straight and one angular. The complete set ranges in price from $13 to $15; extra files and rasps from $2 to $3.

Lameness is one of the most troublesome problems that can face the owner of a working horse, and vets pay particular attention to feet and legs. (See page 90 for specific ailments and their symptoms.) An animal showing early signs of lameness, such as swelling, tenderness, heat, or irregular growth, will require an appropriate kind of treatment which you may be able to administer yourself. Hosing, soaking, and applying liniments, poultices, or other counterirritants to a horse's legs are all effective in reducing inflammation, and the vet will tell you what he thinks is the best route to follow and which are the best medications to buy. (Blistering, firing, and surgical procedures are rigorous forms of treatment and must be left to

professionals.) Ask the vet whether he recommends special leg boots or bandages, or whether hooves need special attention from the farrier on his next visit.

If any other ailments are visible—saddle sores, bruises, cuts, and so on—ask the vet for his recommended methods of treatment and types of medication to stock in your medicine chest. If because of either conformation or past history, an animal seems prone to any problems such as thrush, colic, lameness, or whatever, the vet will tell you if you should keep certain medications on hand in case of emergency.

Whatever the diagnosis and recommendations, for heaven's sake follow the advice you get. Don't assume the doctor is being too conservative, especially when you have your heart set on entering some kind of competition. If you feel you have good reason to disagree with or to disregard the vet's counsel, seek a responsible second opinion from another veterinarian. But don't take matters into your own hands unless you feel like risking your horse's health and perhaps causing the animal (and your pocketbook) a good deal of damage.

Before the vet leaves, write down everything he recommends in your record book or on the horse's chart. Make a note of his next visit, or a reminder to yourself to call him at a suggested future date. And while we are thinking about the next visit, ask the vet if you should take any special precautions for the next examination. One should always make sure that the horse is in its stall or somehow conveniently confined when you expect the vet to call. (There's nothing more annoying or frustrating for both owner and vet than to have to recapture a loose animal that has somehow become aware of the fact that the doctor has arrived.) A difficult horse might have to be tranquilized ahead of time with some promazine obtained from the vet and sneaked into the morning feed on the day of the exam. Or you might have to learn how to use a twitch to keep the animal under control. If possible, have one or two other people on hand to help you hold the horse if it should get out of hand. And of course, be there yourself to calm the animal by steady chatter and whatever other sorts of soothing noises it might need. Most horses eventually become accustomed to regular handling during shoeing, veterinary examinations, and conformation classes at horse shows, but this kind of training takes time and practice. Those periodic checkups by the owner, as well as regular grooming, will help ensure a horse's good manners during these routines, as well as keep the owner alert to the animal's condition.

WORMING

Unless a horse lives alone at the North Pole or in the middle of the Sahara, it is a fact of life that it will have internal parasites of one form or another. Though they are all usually just referred to as

worms, because it is the larval form of these parasites that uses the intestinal tract of the horse as a path toward maturity, there are actually many different species and stages of growth, some of which are more dangerous than others in terms of a horse's health. All can be controlled through medication and good management, but never completely eliminated. A horseman must always be on guard, especially when the animal is showing any of the following signs that can't be ascribed to any other ailment:
• poor hair coat
• failure to gain weight in spite of increased rations
• listlessness

• ribs showing with a big belly
• tail rubbing against the stall, trees, or fencing

Before the animal reaches that state, however, take some preventive measures: have the vet test the feces for the presence of parasites, and establish a regular program of preventive care. Some good health procedures include keeping the horse's manure away from the feeding area (or vice versa), cleaning out the pasture or paddock at least once a week, and not letting the horse out to graze in areas recently fertilized with horse manure. Lime stalls and grazing areas periodically, and rotate pastures every two months. (You can put cows and sheep into unused or "resting," horse pastures, since they are not affected by

SO YOU WANT TO BE A VETERINARIAN
by Emil P. Dolensek, D.V.M.

Like all veterinarians, I get many letters every year from young people asking me about the veterinary profession—what does it involve, how does one get into it, and may they work for me during their next vacation period. Needless to say, I can't hire all (or even a few) of them, and I have trouble finding time to answer all their questions, but it is possible to give some general advice to those who may be interested in a veterinary career. Many people do not realize that a veterinarian is a licensed medical professional with an extensive background in the field, including two to four years of undergraduate training in biology, chemistry, physics, and so on and four years of graduate study at an accredited veterinary school, followed by the completion of a state veterinary examination. All of that sounds difficult enough, but it is even more difficult in practice, for there are only twenty-four veterinary schools in the United States and Canada now, with two more in the planning stages (see list below), and these can accept only one of every ten students who apply.

My advice to young people, then, is to prepare yourself as well as possible, taking as many science courses as possible, even in high school, and making the best possible grade averages in all courses. During college, try to spend summers working with animals, at least one of them with a veterinarian, and work with both large and small animals. Remember that even if you plan to specialize in equine work, you must be equally proficient with all sorts of animals to become a vet—cats, dogs, sheep, cows, and others as well as horses. Then, after two or three years of college, apply to the veterinary school in your state. If there isn't one, write to the Board of Higher Education to ask whether your state partially supports a veterinary school in any other state; if it does not, apply to a number

of schools. And keep your fingers crossed while you keep your hopes and your grades up.

Many people who do not have the time or money to invest in this extensive program choose instead the field of veterinary technology, which requires two to four years of undergraduate work in the veterinary or animal-technology department of any of several state universities. This field is also demanding, and requires proficiency in science and mathematics, but a certificate can open the door to becoming a veterinarian's assistant.

SCHOOLS/COLLEGES OF VETERINARY MEDICINE ACCREDITED BY THE AMERICAN VETERINARY MEDICAL ASSOCIATION

Dr. J. E. Greene, Dean
School of Veterinary Medicine
Auburn University
Auburn, Alabama 36030

Dr. Walter C. Bowie, Dean
School of Veterinary Medicine
Tuskegee Institute
Tuskegee, Alabama 36088

Dr. W. R. Pritchard, Dean
School of Veterinary Medicine
University of California, Davis
Davis, California 95616

Dr. W. J. Tietz, Dean
College of Veterinary Medicine and
    Biomedical Sciences
Colorado State University
Ft. Collins, Colorado 80523

Dr. C. E. Cornelius, Dean
College of Veterinary Medicine
University of Florida
Gainesville, Florida 32601

Dr. David P. Anderson, Dean
College of Veterinary Medicine
University of Georgia
Athens, Georgia 30601

equine parasites.) Mowing and harrowing pasture-land frequently will diffuse droppings and kill the eggs by exposing them to sunlight.

Familiarize yourself with the various kinds of parasites that affect horses, the way they work to cause damage, and the means by which they may be controlled (see below).

The major endeavor in worming horses successfully is to set up an effective program and to be sure that the horse receives its medication properly. Most of the effective medications are available only through veterinarians, and the best method of getting them into the horse—tubing directly into the stomach—is best handled by a professional. Accordingly, your vet, who has diag-

nosed the particular types of worms in your horse, is the first person to talk with about medicating the animal. Actually, any experienced horseman should know how to tube a horse, for purposes of relieving gastric distress as well as for worming. The principal danger in inserting the long tube is that one may run it down the trachea instead of the esophagus, thus causing the animal to develop pneumonia. The esophagus is on the left side of the horse's neck—but knowing this isn't enough, so be sure to get an expert to show you how it's done before you take any risks in doing-it-yourself. (See page 98.)

Tubings should be done at least twice a year, but intermediate wormings every second month

Dr. Richard C. Dierks, Dean
College of Veterinary Medicine
University of Illinois
Urbana, Illinois 61801

Dr. Jack Stockton, Dean
School of Veterinary Medicine
Purdue University
West Lafayette, Indiana 47907

Dr. Phillip T. Pearson, Dean
College of Veterinary Medicine
2508 Veterinary Administration Building
Iowa State University, South Campus
Ames, Iowa 50011

Dr. D. M. Trotter, Dean
College of Veterinary Medicine
Kansas State University
Manhattan, Kansas 66502

Dr. Everett Besch, Dean
College of Veterinary Medicine
Louisiana State University
Baton Rouge, Louisiana 70803

Dr. John R. Welser, Dean
College of Veterinary Medicine
Michigan State University
East Lansing, Michigan 48824

Dr. S. A. Ewing, Dean
College of Veterinary Medicine
University of Minnesota
St. Paul, Minnesota 55108

Dr. Kenneth D. Weide, Dean
College of Veterinary Medicine
University of Missouri
Columbia, Missouri 65201

Dr. Edward C. Melby, Dean
New York State College of Veterinary
   Medicine
Cornell University
Ithaca, New York 14853

Dr. C. Roger Smith, Dean
College of Veterinary Medicine
Ohio State University
Columbus, Ohio 43210

Dr. W. E. Brock, Dean
College of Veterinary Medicine
Oklahoma State University
Stillwater, Oklahoma 74074

Dr. Dennis G. Howell, Dean
Ontario Veterinary College
University of Guelph
Guelph, Ontario, Canada

Dr. Robert R. Marshak, Dean
School of Veterinary Medicine
University of Pennsylvania
Philadelphia, Pennsylvania 19174

Dr. Ephrem Jacques, Dean
Faculté de Médecine Vétérinaire
Université de Montréal
St. Hyacinthe, Québec, Canada

Dr. N. Ole Nielsen, Dean
Western College of Veterinary Medicine
University of Saskatchewan
Saskatoon, Saskatchewan, Canada

Dr. W. W. Armistead, Dean
College of Veterinary Medicine
University of Tennessee
Knoxville, Tennessee 37901

Dr. George C. Shelton, Dean
College of Veterinary Medicine
Texas A&M University
College Station, Texas 77843

Dr. Leo K. Bustad, Dean
College of Veterinary Medicine
Washington State University
Pullman, Washington 99163

SCHOOLS/COLLEGES IN PLANNING

Dr. James G. Miller, Dean
College of Veterinary Medicine
Mississippi State University
Mississippi State, Mississippi 39762

Dr. Richard B. Talbot, Dean
College of Veterinary Medicine
Virginia Polytechnic Institute
Blacksburg, Virginia 24061

can be done by the owner, who can insert medication into a horse's mouth by use of a syringe, into the throat by means of a balling gun, or into the animal's feed. Any or all of these can be effective if—and this is a big if—the horse swallows the medication. Syringe doses often end up on the outside of the horse; balling—like tubing—is a tricky business; and putting worming medicine into feed often makes it unpalatable so that the animal won't eat. Some worming pellets (Equizole, for one) are coated and relatively tasteless, but some are not.

Whichever compound you use, be sure to check it out with your vet to make sure you are using the correct one in the correct amount. Because over-the-counter medications must meet safety requirements, they may not be particularly effective in small quantities. And some medications may be worse for your horse than for its worms; dichlorvos, for instance, should never be used in a horse with heaves, for it may cause further respiratory damage.

The following descriptions of equine internal parasites also include information about medications that have proved effective. After the descriptions is a list of these drugs giving their brand names and manufacturers.

TYPES OF INTERNAL PARASITES

BOTS: Botflies are unlike other internal parasites in that the insect, when mature, lives outside the horse's body; it is a parasite only during the larval stage. There are three species of bot that affect horses in the United States: *Gastrophilus intestinalis* (the common bot), *G. haemorrhoidales* (the nose, or red-tailed, bot); and *G. nasalis* (the throat, or chin, bot): All three have similar life cycles and can be controlled in similar ways. The common botfly female, during a life span of a week or less in late summer, lays up to five hundred yellow eggs on a horse's forelegs, flanks, or forequarters, where they will remain for as long as two weeks. If the horse licks or bites them off, the eggs will stick to the tongue, hatch in the mouth, and eventually be ingested. After a month or so they arrive in the stomach, where they attach themselves to the wall and remain for nearly a year. Then they change from larvae into pupae and pass through the intestines, to be eliminated in the manure. After a dormant period of one or two months underground, the pupae become flies which will start the cycle all over again.

The nose botfly deposits her black eggs in the hairs of a horse's lips, where they hatch in two to four days into larvae that work their way into the inner membranes of the lip. After five or six weeks they migrate to the stomach, where they live the rest of their pesty lives much as the common bot does.

The eggs of the throat, or chin, bot, also yellow, are laid under the horse's jaw. They hatch by themselves, crawling eventually into the mouth, where they get into the gum tissue and continue the rest of the bot route into the stomach, where

the damage they—like the other bots—can do may be considerable. Intestinal problems, including blockages that may result in colic and can be fatal, are inevitable if bots are allowed to multiply uncontrolled.

One way of eliminating the bot problem is to try to prevent their getting into the horse's system. Bot eggs are difficult to remove, but research into the curiously stubborn glue they possess has made possible the development of new products that will dissolve the substance that causes them to stick to the horse's coat. A traditional method has been to rub warm water into the area and scrape off the eggs in the hope that the heat, moisture, and friction will stimulate the eggs to hatch prematurely. This tiresome procedure is not one that most people would care to perform every day during the season. A more effective means of controlling bots is to kill them in the horse's stomach; trichlorfon, dichlorvos, and carbon disulfide alone or in combination with piperazine are the drugs that will do the job. One of them should be used about a month after the last frost and again two months later to catch any larvae that may not have reached the stomach in time for the earlier worming. Foals should receive medication during the egg-laying season as well as afterward.

LARGE STRONGYLES (pronounced stron-jiles) This group of bloodworms includes the most dangerous of all equine parasites: *Strongylus vulgaris,* also known as the red worm, as well as *S. edentatus* and *S. equinus,* which are to be taken seriously as well. Recent studies have indicated that strongyles are the culprit in about 90 percent of all cases of colic; every horse owner must therefore do his utmost to control the problem as effectively as possible. Unlike bots, strongyle adults are suckers that attach themselves to the walls or contents of the large intestines, where they lay their eggs, which pass out of the body with droppings. When the eggs hatch (after a day or so), the larvae attach themselves to blades of grass over the period of a week, and the horse can pick up thousands of them in a few bites. Once ingested, the larvae migrate throughout the body for at least six months, causing inflammatory arterial lesions, which may lead to thrombosis. (When a thrombus, or blood clot, is formed and dislodges, it can block the blood flow and cause sudden death.) Migrating strongyles have even been known to veer off into the brain and cause severe damage there. When the adult worms eventually arrive in the intestine, they feed on the intestinal lining, causing local irritation, tissue damage, and blood loss or even intestinal stoppage. These conditions can lead to colic, hemorrhagic enteritis, anemia, and general unthriftiness. After six to eight weeks, when permanent damage has been done, the female worms lay their eggs to begin the vicious cycle anew. Symptoms of strongyle infestation are constipation, loss of appetite, high fever, depression, and diarrhea as well as colic and anemia. The situation can best be prevented by stopping strongyles before they start—eliminating the adult population in the intestines before eggs can be laid. Because the larvae have already caused their part of the damage by this stage, a horse's condition, except its appearance, may not greatly improve, but one must start somewhere. Strongyles have become resistant to several of the medications that have been effective in the past—phenothiazine, piperazine, and thiabendazole—but when these are used in combination, they can be highly effective, as are the drugs pyrantel, cambendazole, tetramisole, diethylcarbamazine, and mebendazol. Since the migrating larvae will mature when they reach the intestine, in about six to eight weeks, worming every two months is recommended for at least a year, using different drugs each time, before a heavily infected herd and pasture can be considered under control.

SMALL STRONGYLES

There are many different genera and species in this group, of which *Strongyloides* (usually present only in foals), *Poteriostomum, Cylicobrachytus, Craterostomum, Oesophagodontus,* and *Cyathostomum* are the significant members. They all begin their cycles in the same manner as the large strongyles, but they don't migrate beyond the intestinal tract. There they may produce ulcers, but rarely blood loss in the small intestine. They aren't as harmful as the large strongyles, although they may accumulate in large numbers in the cecum and colon as well as in the small intestine, and they can cause diarrhea as a result. Young foals are particular susceptible to small strongyles (getting them in mother's milk), which may result in weakness, emaciation, and anemia as well as digestive upset. Small strongyles have become resistant to thiabendazole, but for the most part they can be controlled, if not eliminated, by treatment with the same drugs as those used for the large strongyles.

ASCARIDS

The large roundworm *Parascaris equorum* can become as thick as a pencil and has been known to reach a length of fifteen inches. Mature roundworms breed in the horse's intestine, where thousands of eggs are laid, and then pass out with manure. After about two weeks on the ground they become infective, and horses will swallow them with grass, hay, or water that has become contaminated. The eggs hatch in the intestine and penetrate the wall, where they enter small blood vessels, traveling for a week or more through the circulatory system to the lungs. There they work or are coughed out into the trachea (windpipe), to be swallowed into the stomach. The larvae then move to the intestines and grow for a couple of months into breeding adults. The greatest danger caused by ascarids is usually in horses of up to two years (older horses develop a natural immunity), in which they can cause circulatory blockage; dam-

age to liver, heart, and lung tissue; and most important, intestinal blockage, which may result in rupture and a fatal case of peritonitis. Particular care should be taken to eliminate the pest in fillies destined to become broodmares, since ascarids can penetrate the muscles of young horses and later migrate through the placenta to infect foals. Effective medication includes piperazine, pyrantel, mebendazole, dichlorvos, trichloron, and piperazine with phenothiazine, or diathiazine iodide. These drugs will eliminate the adult worms in the intestine and should reach them before they begin to lay their eggs. Because the total cycle is about ten weeks, worming for two months in succession should greatly reduce the damage they can cause.

PINWORMS

The two types of pinworms that affect horses to any degree are *Oxyuris equi* and *Probstmayria vivipara* (the minute pinworm), the latter of which is thought to be harmless. *Oxyuris equi* eggs are swallowed with contaminated grass, water, or dry food. The larvae hatch and mature in about seven weeks as they travel to the intestines. They breed in the colon, and both females and eggs are eliminated with manure, though some females may lay their eggs on the skin near the rectum, where they may be rubbed or drop off to the ground. One of the signs of pinworms is a horse rubbing itself against posts or other objects to relieve the intense itching, thereby causing hair loss, secondary infections, and further discomfort. This symptom is the best way to detect the presence of pinworms, which cannot be seen in usual fecal examinations (although they may be found in fresh feces). They do not require specific treatment, since nearly all the compounds effectively used on strongyles and ascarids will be effective against pinworms.

STOMACH WORMS

Three species of spirurids are found in the stomachs of horses, and the larvae may also invade skin wounds or abrasions, causing a condition referred to as "summer sores." Flies are the intermediate hosts for stomach worms, which can cause conjunctivitis in the eyes and pulmonary abscesses in the lungs. In the stomach one species, *Draschia megastoma,* lives in colonies, causing abscesses in the stomach wall. The two species of *Habronema* live in glandular areas of the stomach. The former can be treated with trichlorfon but resist carbon disulfide and dichlorvos, which are effective against the *Habronema.* The minute stomach worm (*Trichostrongylus axei*) primarily affects cattle, sheep, and goats, and is usually light in horses, although heavy infections can cause gastritis. They can be controlled by the drugs that are effective against strongyles.

TAPEWORMS

One of the two tapeworm species found frequently

in horses, *Anoplocephala perfoliata,* may result in severe ulcerations in the lining of the cecum. (Little research has been done toward eliminating them in horses, since heavy infestations are not common.). They are carried by orbatid mites which can live in pastures in some areas. When they are ingested, they reach maturity in about two months. Fecal examination will make detection possible. It has been found that dichlorophen and bithionol are effective in controlling them.

WORMING MEDICATIONS

In the good old days, horsemen used a number of tried (and perhaps not so true) methods of ridding their animals of parasites. One of them involved a monthly "feeding" of wood ash and tobacco, and it was supposed to be pretty effective. Nevertheless, modern medicine has come up with some superior products, and your veterinarian will be familiar with their use. Some are more effective than others on certain types of parasites; some were once effective but no longer are so in areas where parasites have developed resistant strains; and some should not be used in animals that have particular respiratory disorders. Over-the-counter worming medications may be obtained from tack shops or feed suppliers, while prescription wormers (usually stronger and involving tube dosage) are available only through a veterinarian. Since only a vet can accurately diagnose the types of parasites in your animal, it is best to follow his advice and use what he prescribes or nonprescription drugs that he recommends. Advertisements for worming medicines are often misleading, since some companies will claim that their products are superior to others in their effectiveness. This may be true, for some products include a combination of drugs where others don't, but not all horses are affected by all parasites, and it is a needless expense to attack worms that are not present. The important thing to know is that the medication you select has the proper amount of the proper drug. Some drugs are nonexclusive and are referred to below by their generic names; others have been developed by individual companies, and their brand names are included in the following list.

A few horse-worming medications are available over the counter; some are available only through your veterinarian. Some of the brand names are listed below according to the generic names of the drugs they contain.

Cambendazole: effective on strongyles
Camvet, by Merck, is tubed or fed (prescription only).

Dichlorvos: effective on bots, strongyles, ascarids, and pinworms
Shell Horse Wormer and Equigard are both made by the Shell Chemical Co. and are both given in feed.

Mebendazole: effective on ascarids
Telmin, by Pitman-Moore, is given in feed or water.

Phenoziathine: effective on strongyles where no resistance has developed
Pheno-Sweet, made by Farnam, and Mean Green, from J-Ro Industries, are both given in small daily doses in feed.

Piperazine: effective on strongyles where no resistance has developed and on ascarids
Wonder Wormer and Foal Wormer, by Farnam, Purina Horse and Colt Wormer, and Hy-Tone, by Legear, are all given in feed.

Piperazine with carbon disulfide and phenoziathine: effective on strongyles
Parvex Plus, by Upjohn, is given by tubing (prescription only).

Piperazine with thiabendazole: effective on strongyles and ascarids
Equizole-A, by Merck, tubed or given in feed (prescription only).

Pyrantel: effective on strongyles and ascarids
Banminth and Strongid-T, by Pfizer (prescription only), are fed and tubed, respectively; Ban-Wormer, by Purina, is given in feed.

Tetramisole: effective on strongyles
Levamisole, made by American Cyanamid (prescription only).

Thiabendazole: effective on strongyles where no resistance has developed
Equizole and Performance Wormer are both made by Merck (prescription only), the former given by feed or worming and the latter only in feed; Purina Horse Wormer Medication is given in feed.

Trichlorfon: effective on bots and ascarids
Anthon and Combot, made by Haver-Lockhart (prescription only), are fed and tubed, respectively; Bot Control, by Purina is given in feed.

Trichlorfon, phenoziathine, and piperazine: effective on strongyles and pinworms
Dyrex-T.F., made by Fort Dodge Laboratories (prescription only), is tubed.

For external treatment of bot eggs, one may use D*Bot, made by Four-in-Hand, or Bot Blocks, by Bot Blocks, Inc. Bot knives are also available at some tack shops, but kitchen knives or sweat scrapers will work just as well.

VACCINATIONS

Unhappily, the three most troublesome equine ailments—colic, lameness, and swamp fever (equine infectious anemia)—cannot be prevented except by good management practices. Happily, however, there are a number of diseases that can be avoided by a regular program of vaccination. As more and more horses are shipped around the country to compete in races, shows, rodeos, trail rides, and other competitions, horse owners should take special precautions to prevent the following highly contagious diseases from affecting their own animals as well as causing widespread epidemics that have been known to break out in the not-so-recent past. Some of these ailments are more common in some parts of the country than others, so be sure to ask your veterinarian for advice not only about your own area but about other locations to which your horse might be shipped. Since some vaccinations take weeks to become effective, don't wait until the last moment to get the shots.

EQUINE INFLUENZA

This viral disease is not particularly serious, but it is becoming increasingly prevalent each year, affecting horses of any age, at any time, and in any area. Proper treatment involves complete rest and confinement for at least three weeks, so anyone with a horse on a rigorous training or competitive schedule should take the precaution of having the vaccine administered. Horses that are rarely in contact with other animals, or those for which a three-week rest would not be a serious interruption, need not have the inoculation, though owners should keep an eye out for symptoms. The first sign is a dry cough, which usually lasts for only two or three days but may continue for three weeks even with complete rest. Nasal discharge is watery at first, later developing into a thick mucuslike substance. Lymph nodes may be sensitive, and laryngitis may be present. Muscular weakness, soreness, and lack of appetite are other general signs, though in very young, old, or weak horses, there may be complications in the form of heart or liver damage, secondary infections, anemia, and such respiratory illnesses as bronchitis and emphysema. An effective drug, developed in 1964 to combat both types of influenza after a nationwide epidemic in the previous year is Fluvan, made by the Fort Dodge Laboratories. The vaccine is administered intramuscularly, two injections four to twelve weeks apart. In foals, the first injection should be given at three months and the second three months later. Also recommended are booster shots when the horse is a yearling, and once a year thereafter throughout the animals' racing or performing career. Broodmares need not be vaccinated, but stallions serving mares from various locations should have the vaccine to avoid interruptions in the breeding program.

EQUINE ENCEPHALITIS

This group of diseases is far more serious than the relatively mild, nonfatal equine influenza, and vaccinations on an annual basis against the three significant types of the disease known in this country are definitely recommended. Because encephalitis was first isolated in horses during the 1930s, when hundreds of thousands of animals were lost, it was described as an equine disease. However, horses do not cause it but are victims, like many other species (including humans). The actual cause is a group of viruses carried by certain species of mosquitoes. The three types known here are Eastern equine encephalitis (also known as sleeping sickness or blind staggers), Western equine encephalitis (or Kansas horse plague), and Venezuelan EE, once known only in Central and South America but recognized in Mexico and the United States since 1971. In some Southern states, both EEE and WEE have occurred in the same horses, so vets recommend that all horses receive vaccines to prevent all three. This involves a series of two injections, the interval between depending on the type of drug, before the peak of the mosquito season. There is no known cure, and although treatment has been successful with victims of WEE, the prognosis is very poor (only half of the WEE horses survive, and almost all EEE and VEE animals die). The most obvious signs are marked depression and high fever. Drooping of the lower lip, a reluctance to move, and incoordination are also characteristic, and in the final stages, the horse is unable to stand up. The course of the disease is short, with death usually occurring in no longer than two or three days. Treatment involves trying to keep fluid and electrolyte levels in balance, to reduce fever, and to keep the animal on its feet using slings, boards, or racks.

There is a similar disease in the Far East, known as Japanese encephalitis, which is also spread by mosquitoes and results in symptoms very like the American versions of the disease. Although the mortality rate is much lower—less than 5 percent—any imported animal suspected of the disease should be reported to local, state, or federal authorities.

RABIES

Although this well-known disease is not particularly common in horses (there were 60 cases in 1968 and 40 in 1970), animals kept out in the open in localities where rabies has been prevalent among wild or farm animals should receive an annual preventive vaccination. Dogs are no longer the threat they once were (there were 185 canine cases in 1970, as opposed to 697 in 1960), but skunks and other wild mammals have been found to be rabid in recent years, and there were over 700 known cases in farm animals during 1970. Since there is no treatment for horses bitten by rabid animals, they should either be destroyed immediately or isolated and reported to public health authorities. The animal should not be shot through the head, so that the brain may be kept intact for an official laboratory diagnosis. Symptoms are similar to those in other animals: aggressiveness, self-inflicted wounds, and eating of wood, straw, or other similar materials.

RHINOPNEUMONITIS

This viral disease is an acute infection best known for causing abortion in pregnant mares. In young horses, it also creates upper-respiratory infections, once thought to be brought on by equine influenza. The disease, found throughout the world, is most prevalent in central Kentucky, where many farms have outbreaks in the fall or early winter when young animals are weaned and brought together into winter quarters. Rhino spreads rapidly and can be carried by mature horses that show no overt signs. After a two- to ten-day incubation period, the first symptoms are high fever and nasal discharge, along with (but not always accompanied by) loss of appetite, depression, diarrhea, swellings in the legs, and mild congestion. All of these symptoms are exacerbated by exercise. Recovery is complete within two weeks if the animal is treated with complete rest, which is the only effective treatment known. Because the disease does induce abortion in mares—anywhere from three weeks to four months after the mare is infected—broodmares should be inoculated at least twice a year: the first time after sixty days of pregnancy, with a booster in the fifth to seventh month. After that time, a single yearly booster given after sixty days of pregnancy should be sufficient. Other animals should receive their first immunization in two injections four to eight weeks apart, with single yearly boosters thereafter, more if necessary. Although a recovered horse is temporarily immune, animals may become reinfected after three to six months, though the disease is usually not then accompanied by the symptoms listed above.

STRANGLES

This bacterial disease is caused by *Streptococcus equi,* which is transmitted through purulent discharges of infected horses. Infection can come about through direct contact or through contact with food, water, or objects that have been contaminated. Contaminated surfaces may remain a source of infection for a year or more. After infection, a horse will show signs of the disease within three to six days: a failure to drink, a high temperature (102 to 106 degrees Fahrenheit), and a nasal discharge. The bacteria induce abscesses in the lymph tissue of the pharynx, which cause the animal pain so that it becomes reluctant to swallow. The abscesses mature and drain quickly, and healing may occur in two weeks or so, but secondary infections are possible and complications may arise. Mortality is low, except among newborn foals, which may develop septicemia and die. Animals that recover are immune to the disease, and although they may become reinfected, the disease

is then relatively mild and quick to disappear. Nevertheless, because strangles, once established among a group of horses, can last for years, it should be treated preventively by vaccination wherever it is known to exist. The vaccine, given in three doses at weekly intervals, is effective only in animals older than ten to twelve weeks; vaccination should be maintained on a yearly basis, with a single booster shot for all previously vaccinated horses. Only healthy horses should be vaccinated.

TETANUS

Also known as lockjaw, this serious disease has been a major problem in horses for centuries. The bacterium *Clostridium tetani* exists worldwide, so every unvaccinated horse is susceptible. There is no known cure, although recovery is possible (if not likely) with the use of antibiotics and supportive therapy to keep the animal quiet and comfortable and protected from injury. Particular care should be given to adequate nourishment and fluid balance. There is, luckily, a highly effective preventive—tetanus toxoid—which is given in two doses four to eight weeks apart following by a booster nine to twelve months later. Annual boosters thereafter are not necessary; an injection every four to five years should be adequate, with additional inoculations when the animal has suffered an injury. Broodmares should be inoculated four to eight weeks before foaling to enable them to produce high antibody levels in their milk. Tetanus antitoxin is effective for immediate protection in foals or horses that have not received previous immunization. But its effect is of only short duration.

VIRAL ARTERITIS

Similar to rhinopneumonitis, this infectious disease will also cause abortion in mares, and there is no proved cure except for complete rest. A vaccine has been developed to prevent it, but it is not available at the time of this writing. VA is uncommon in the United States, but there have been sporadic outbreaks in the Midwest since the 1950s.

There are a number of other health problems caused in horses by Staphylococcus, Streptococcus, equine *coli,* and *Pasteurella* organisms, such as mastitis, navel ill, colitis, septicemia, and metritis. If you have heard that any are prevalent in your area, your veterinarian will be able to reassure you or inoculate your horse accordingly.

EIA AND THE COGGINS TEST CONTROVERSY

You will note that we recommend the Coggins test for equine infectious anemia (swamp fever) on a regular basis for every horse—whether or not the animal leaves home. The majority of states require proof of a negative Coggins test within six months or a year before the animal may be shipped interstate. This recommendation, however, is made not

DISEASES TRANSMITTED FROM HORSES TO HUMANS

Because horses live less among people now than they did when we used them for transportation on a regular basis, the threat presented by diseases that can infect both horse and man is not now very great. Research and good management among horse owners have made it possible for us to prevent or control contagious diseases that affect both our species, and instances of horses causing human disease are quite rare. Nevertheless, it is interesting to learn what these conditions are, on the assumption that ignorance is not bliss and a little knowledge is not necessarily a dangerous thing. Horses are subject to various viral diseases, of which the best-known in terms of human illness is encephalitis, or sleeping sickness—the Eastern, Western, and Venezuelan varieties. In humans, symptoms can be fever, headache, drowsiness, gastric upset, lethargy, convulsions, and others. Eastern encephalitis is more serious for humans than the others, with a higher rate of fatality and permanent aftereffects for survivors. Though vaccination will build up antibody levels and prevent the disease in horses, epidemics can still occur in areas where vaccines are not used regularly, or where the disease has infected other animals from which the mosquitoes can carry the virus into humans. The other viral diseases common to man and horse are rabies (rare in horses now), vesicular stomatitis (common to many other animals as well, especially cattle, and not particularly serious), and equine infectious anemia. Human symptoms of the last-named disease, also called swamp fever, include fever, anemia, and diarrhea. Only a few human cases, however, have been reported and so swamp fever should not be considered serious except in horses.

Bacterial diseases affecting horses that man can catch are anthrax, brucellosis, glanders (now nearly extinct), hemorrhagic septicemia, listeriosis, meliodosis, tetanus, tuberculosis (the bovine type), and tularemia, but all of these could be considered of minor importance so far as horses are concerned. Cattle, cats, rabbits, and several other species are usually the source when these diseases infect humans. Leptospirosis is occasionally transmitted by both the horse and the donkey. Horses can carry both the bacteria that cause endemic relapsing fever and the ticks that transmit it, although the usual villains are wild rodents and birds.

There are several fungus diseases shared by man and horse, including a few kinds of ringworm, histoplasmosis, actinomycosis, and coccidiomycosis, among others. Equine parasites that may be significant for humans are rare in this country: sarcocystitis is rare in man, African trypanosomiasis is known only on that continent, and *Schistosoma japonicum* only in the Orient. The mite that causes sarcoptic mange is carried by the horse, as is the ox botfly, by which man may be infected.

---

just to comply with applicable federal and state laws, but because the test is one of the only means now available to help control and eradicate this terrible disease. No vaccine has yet been developed to prevent EIA, which is caused by a virus and is transmitted by biting flies, mosquitoes, and contaminated needles or pieces of equipment that come into contact with the blood of a healthy horse. (The heavy use of needles around racetracks is undoubtedly the cause of the various outbreaks around the United States.) For years, there was not even an accurate way of detecting the disease, since the virus could not until recently be grown in the laboratory. Clinical signs are obvious in horses in an acute stage of EIA: high fever, weakness, anemia, depression, swelling of the abdomen and extremities (except in ponies), and death in 80 percent of the cases. But these signs may also indicate another disease process, and to complicate matters, not all horses with EIA show signs all the time. In chronic cases, horses may be symptomatic only intermittently and otherwise appear relatively normal; as the fever recurs, however, the horse's condition worsens, and death is probable. Latent EIA horses show no symptoms but are presumed to be carriers, since there are antibodies against the virus in their blood, which shows up positive on the Coggins test. In the early '70s, Dr. Leroy Coggins of Cornell perfected a test, that had first been tried in 1960, and he was able to report 95-percent accuracy for detecting EIA antibodies in horses. It is called an AGID test (agar-gel immunodiffusion) and involves the analysis of a blood sample taken from a horse. In March 1972 the U.S. Department of Agriculture initiated an EIA control program that includes the AGID test, which was declared the official USDA test in August of that year and can be performed by various official labs throughout the country. Horses that show positive reactions must be identified (with a brand) on the neck or a tattoo on the lip, and they cannot be moved across state lines except for purposes of slaughter or research. Owners have two choices: either to euthanize the positive horse or to quarantine him for life to prevent transmission of the disease. It is hoped, of course, that elimination of all diseased horses will eventually result in the eradication of the disease, but not all horsemen believe that the "Coggins Test and Slaughter" procedure, as they call it, is the most effective way to proceed.

They feel, with well-argued reasons, that money spent on Coggins tests ($12 or more) should be used instead for research into developing a vaccine to be used in inoculating animals like those used to control equine encephalitis. Research is indeed now going on, but it is costly, and money is scarce; obviously the scientists could use the thousands of dollars spent every year on Coggins tests, but how many horse owners would voluntarily donate that money if the government did not require them to do so? Another serious argument is that not all Coggins-positive horses may in fact be carriers of the disease. Antibodies form to combat an attacking virus, and although their presence in the blood usually indicates the presence of that virus, the antibodies will often remain in the system as a defense mechanism long after the virus has been overcome. Antibodies from another horse may be transmitted (without virus) to a healthy horse (a foal may receive them from nursing), and such a healthy horse or foal will come up positive in the AGID test. There is also a great deal of evidence indicating that horses with latent EIA (showing no symptoms but coming up positive because they contain antibodies) are not necessarily carriers of the disease—although legally they are considered carriers and must be destroyed or quarantined. Foals that have picked up antibodies from their mothers may show up positive early in life but then eventually become negative after they are weaned. This situation came into prominence through the successful results with the famous Assateague ponies in Virginia. Members of this wild herd have been found positive and isolated on the northern half of the island. Their foals, however, are testing mostly negative and are being returned to the healthy part of the herd.

There are other problems with the Coggins test. Because few antibodies are present during the incubation of the disease, a horse actually developing EIA may test negative. Likewise there may be so much virus present in the acute stage that antibodies do not show, and a severely ill horse may also test negative. These various issues have convinced many experts that drastic measures taken on positive horses are premature and unwarranted. It would be impractical, if not impossible, to test every horse in the country, so the disease might always be present no matter how many carriers were destroyed. It might in fact worsen, since little or no immunity would be present and horses might become even more susceptible.

One area of agreement is that owners as well as veterinarians must learn to recognize the signs of the disease in its acute and subacute stages, immediately testing for confirming diagnosis and isolating or destroying the animals that are in fact ill to prevent transmission of the disease. In 1975 nearly 10,000 horses were destroyed or rendered useless because they tested positive, but before the Coggins test came into use, the largest number of horses in the United States known to have EIA was 440 cases, in 1967. Perhaps the government has gone overboard (as it probably did with cyclamates some years ago), but each owner should nevertheless be aware of the danger posed by the disease and recognize the need for research to come up with a better way to control it. The magazine *Horse of Course!,* edited by Dr. R. A. Greene (published by the Derbyshire Publishing Company, Temple, New Hampshire 03084), devoted its June 1976 issue to the controversy surrounding EIA and the Coggins test. Although Dr. Greene is plainly against the "Test and Slaughter" procedure, he allowed a number of experts in the field, including Dr. Coggins himself, to speak out on the subject. The issue is well worth studying in detail.

THE HORSE IN TROUBLE: PROBLEMS AND TREATMENTS

So many books are available on the subject of equine health, some good and some not so good (see page 111), that there isn't much point in listing every disease and injury to which horses are susceptible. (There also isn't enough space, since that is a book in itself.) Nevertheless, the horse owner should be familiar with the obvious, serious symptoms that require veterinary attention, as well as some of the minor ailments or injuries and the measures to take until the veterinarian arrives.

If you are familiar with your horse's appearance and behavior during normal periods, any irregularity should attract your attention. Often there may be nothing to worry about, but try to find out the reason, if only because irregularity may be an early sign of something more serious in the offing. Some disease processes arrive suddenly and without apparent warning, while others come on gradually. The earlier you can see that there is a problem and the more detailed the information you can give the vet, the better your chances are for a quick and successful recovery.

Some problems, such as lameness and digestive ailments, may be chronic, requiring special preventive care or regular treatment. Since these are often congenital—caused by conformation defects—or brought about by poor care, anyone in the process of selecting a horse should take special precautions and get a veterinarian's opinion of the animal's condition. Even if an undesirable condition cannot be cured, there may be ways of treating it and allowing a horse to live a full, useful life.

SYMPTOMS AND FIRST-AID PROCEDURES

The following symptoms should be considered deserving of a call to the veterinarian:

- refusal to eat or drink for twenty-four hours
- repeated coughing (more than twenty-four hours)

- high temperature (over 103 degrees Fahrenheit)
- shivering or excessive sweating for no obvious reason
- diarrhea or constipation for more than twelve hours
- frequent lying down or rolling, with or without moaning
- severe injury with obvious damage to skin, bone, or muscle
- persistent lameness

Any or all of these—in combination or singly—may indicate the presence of a serious disease or injury. Although many mild ailments or injuries can be diagnosed and treated at home without veterinary supervision, the inexperienced horse owner should not be encouraged to do more than exercise common sense, by calling the vet and applying some first-aid measures until he arrives or is able to give advice over the telephone. It is important to understand, however, why these symptoms—and less severe signs—are significant and what kinds of first aid are appropriate.

REFUSAL TO EAT OR DRINK

Horses are creatures of habit, as we have said, and one of their fondest habits is eating. Refusal to do so should therefore be taken seriously. Before panicking, however, do make sure that there are no extenuating circumstances. Does the horse seem interested in food but unable to eat? There may be a mechanical blockage of some sort, not a disease process, and you might be able to deal with the situation yourself. Gentle massaging upward along the esophagus (left side of the neck) may bring up an object that is blocking the passage. Does the horse eat some but not all of its ration? You might be overfeeding or giving a new kind of feed that the animal hasn't grown accustomed to. See whether the horse will accept its usual ration instead. The problem may also be a dental one; taking great care, look inside the horse's mouth (holding its tongue between its teeth at the side of the jaw to keep your exploring hand from being bitten) for any broken or protruding teeth that may be causing the animal pain. If the mouth smells putrid, an abscess may be present. Chances are, however, that if the refusal to eat or drink is accompanied by other symptoms—sweating, lying down and rolling, high temperature, or diarrhea—a disease or colicky condition is causing the trouble, and immediate professional attention is required.

REPEATED COUGHING

This might be caused by a blockage (in which case the cough is really a choke); you can determine this by feeling the esophagus and massaging upward, as described above. If accompanied by heavy breathing, coughing may indicate emphysema (or heaves), which will require a vet's treatment. Rest the horse for a day, and if a bit of exercise brings on coughing or heaving again, call the vet. In addition to antihistamines, antibiotics, and rest (or occasionally, light work), the horse may be

given a ration of special feed (with no hay), to eliminate irritating dust particles. Coughing may also indicate an upper-respiratory infection (the equine common cold), which will also involve some nasal dripping; keep the animal warm and isolated from others, put it on a soft diet (bran mash, for intance), and try a cough remedy recommended by your veterinarian. If the condition doesn't clear up within a day, call him again. Roaring—not coughing—is usually caused by paralysis of a vocal cord due to disease or a chronic condition that may be hereditary and is considered a fault.

None of these over-the-counter cough medicines contains narcotics or antihistamines, and they are safe to add to a horse's food or water, requiring no special techniques for dosing. They are expectorants, which liquefy mucus and soothe respiratory tissues, making breathing easier. Liquid formulas include Farnam's Cough Control (in a licorice base), Thoroughbred Remedy's Expectorine, and Zev Cough Remedy (W. K. Buckley, Cleveland, Ohio), which is to be mixed with honey or corn syrup and contains a conditioner to stimulate appetite. Powdered cough medications include Gay's Cough and Fever Medication (Bickmore), Western Laboratories' Cough and Heave Medication, Magic H Respiratory Preparation (Magic H Co., Hampton, New Hampshire), and Ayerst's Sedaspec, a bronchial sedative containing sodium bicarbonate, among other ingredients. Prices range from $3.50 to $7 for a pint.

HIGH TEMPERATURE

This can be caused by a variety of problems and need not be serious unless it continues for a day or more, accompanied by sweating and excited behavior. Heat in the legs or feet indicates inflammation, which may be treated with anti-inflammatory treatments that will reduce the swelling. (See page 94.) These include hosing with cold water and application of liniment or the various medications designed to cool the affected spot, so that healing may begin. If the condition persists and is accompanied by lameness, check the vet before taking more drastic measures. To treat high body temperature (over 103 degrees), keep the animal as quiet as possible, isolate it from other horses, and cover it with a blanket. Remove the usual ration, but provide plenty of cool water. If its temperature doesn't return to normal within 24 hours, call the vet.

A hunter recuperating from bronchitis with the help of an inhalator developed by the Delaware Equine Center, Cochranville, Pennsylvania.

SHIVERING OR EXCESSIVE SWEATING

Extreme cold, heat, and overexercise are obvious causes for these conditions. If none applies, you probably have trouble on your hands. Blanket the animal, isolate it, and keep it as quiet as possible. If the horse's muscles seem tight or hard, try feeding a bran mash. And go for the telephone.

PERSISTENT DIARRHEA OR CONSTIPATION

Loose stool is not uncommon when an animal has had a sudden change of diet (grazing on young green grass is a common cause), but a distinctly liquid stool is a reason to alert a vet. Constipation may be treated with a laxative medication or bran mash, but if relief is not evident within a few hours, call the expert, in. Note whether the horse has been nibbling at its bedding and tell the vet. He may recommend that the animal be placed on wood chips rather than straw or whatever it is that is so appealing.

FREQUENT LYING DOWN AND ROLLING

This most obvious sign of colic, or intestinal trouble, requires immediate medical attention if the animal is to recover. There are many different kinds of colic—among them intestinal blockage, impaction, and torsion—and treatments vary. The first rule of first aid is to keep the animal on its feet and moving. Whether the activity actually helps to alleviate the problem or simply manages to distract the animal from its considerable pain is questionable. Keeping the horse from rolling, however, does help prevent injury and may keep the intestines from twisting and making matters worse. Ask the vet over the telephone if you should try to get some laxative into the horse. Mineral oil (through a syringe or stomach tube) is a possibility, or a mixture of bran (1 quart), mineral oil (½ cup), salt (2 tablespoons), and enough water to make a mash may be effective if the horse will ingest it. Your primary task, however, will be to keep the animal on its feet until the vet arrives. Horses cannot vomit as we do, so don't try any of your own remedies to make yours do so. The vet will probably give a muscle relaxant to promote defecation, or perhaps an enema, but that decision is best left to him.

> **Colic Remedies.** There are a few commercial colic medications available (Thoroughbred Remedy's Colic Anodyne; B.E.L.L. Drops by Dr. A. C. Daniels, Webster, Mass.), but we recommend that you ask your veterinarian's advice about products to keep on hand if your horse is prone to colic. These remedies contain such ingredients as chloroform, salicylic acid (aspirin), ammonium salicylate, and alcohol, which may tend to relax muscles, but the vet's attention and drugs will be more effective.

OPEN WOUNDS

There are four general types of open wounds: abrasions (in which only surface layers of the skin are destroyed); incisions (produced by sharp instruments); puncture wounds (penetration of the superficial tissues); and lacerations (irregularly torn tissue). Wounds heal in one of two ways; either the sides of the wound, absent of infection, are kept close together (with or without suturing) so that cells grow quickly to bridge the gap, or granulation, the most common kind of healing in horses, takes place. Granulation involves the construction of new tissue growing upward from the depth of the wound and gradually filling in the gap from within until the wound closes. The presence of foreign bodies or contaminants in the wound will delay the healing process or even prevent it; the only way to avoid this problem is to remove the material. Irritation of a wound can also be caused by excessive movement of the affected area. Bandages may serve to immobilize the region of the wound, and horses may be restrained from bothering it through the use of cradles, side sticks, cross ties, or even a bit of red cayenne pepper on the bandage (not on the open wound, please!). The most common deterrent to healing is, surprisingly, the use of disinfectants, which may destroy surface cells and cause the granulating tissues to die and slough off rather than heal up. Instead of applying disinfectants, therefore, simply wash a wound with a mild salt solution (one teaspoon of salt in a pint of water) applied with cotton swabs. (The washing process will make it possible to see and remove any foreign bodies.)

If the wound is a superficial abrasion, it should heal quickly, without requiring veterinary attention. Wash the sore periodically with lukewarm water or a saline solution. Be sure that the stall and the horse are kept free of biting insects, and see that bedding is clean. Tack should be supple, soft, and well fitting, which should prevent saddle or girth sores to begin with—but if an abrasion exists, keep it free of all pressure from tack. (A piece of soft cloth or foam rubber may be used to pad the saddle.) Saddle and girth galls may develop if pressure on sore areas is allowed to continue for a long time, but if the owner is alert to the animal's condition, there is little possibility of things going that far. The skin of horses is very sensitive, especially during the shedding season, but sores need not be serious if treated properly. Witch hazel or zinc oxide can be applied lightly to soothe the irritation, but medication should not be necessary. If a sore does not heal quickly—within a few days—something is wrong, and the veterinarian should be consulted.

Skin eruptions may be caused by nervousness, allergies, dietary problems, or infection, but these too are rarely serious. Keep the horse calm and well groomed, and put it on a light diet of bran mash and hay. Again, if the situation doesn't clear up promptly, get expert advice before applying any medication.

If the horse suffers an injury of anything more than a superficial sort, remove it to a quiet spot, calm it down, and call the vet. You may clean the area with a mild salt solution, removing any foreign material as you go, but the horse may well need a tetanus shot and an antibiotic to prevent infection. Several effective antibiotic ointments are available to keep wounds covered and free of infection during the healing process, but these should not be used without supervision. Puncture wounds may heal superficially, but infections are all too likely to occur beneath the surface, causing abscesses. Incisions and most lacerations will probably require suturing to establish skin contact and promote healing, but punctures should never be sutured; drainage must be permitted to take place. Leg injuries may be treated with pressure bandages or casts, under which wounds will heal readily. Don't be disturbed by nasty-looking discharges from the top and bottom of the bandage; this is simply the sloughed-off tissue from the surface, under which the healthy granulating tissue is forming. Exposed joints require special care, flushing regularly with antibiotics as well as the use of bandages to inhibit movement and injected antibiotics as the veterinarian recommends. Some light exercise may be prescribed, since wounds will heal rapidly with complete rest but the scars that form are likely to break down and develop adhesions once the animal is allowed to move about.

If a wound is bleeding a great deal, you should

Wound Dressings. Many kinds of ointments, gels, liquid dressings, and powders are available for treating minor open wounds and abrasions, serving as disinfectants, antiseptics, and proud-flesh (or scar-tissue) deterrents. They can be brushed, rubbed, sprayed, or poured on wounds, and we recommend that you follow your veterinarian's advice as to their use. Many of them are excellent and will be necessary for certain situations, but in many cases no medication at all will be required for prompt healing as long as the wound is kept clean. Disinfectants may, in fact, deter healing by damaging tissue, and some ointments may have the same effect by keeping the wound covered when it should remain open. Preparations that prevent infection and the growth of scar tissue are useful, because abscesses and overgrown scabs may have to be removed surgically. A few of the most popular wound dressings, which range from $1.50 for 4 ounces to $6 for 3 pounds, are listed below:

Liquids: Red-Kote (N. H. Naylor), a nondrying preparation that minimizes scar formation, keeps tissue soft and pliable, and helps prevent infection; available in 6-ounce nonaerosol spray can or 4-ounce dauber bottle.
Blu-Kote (Naylor), a quick-drying liquid that penetrates deep to protect tissues; fights bacteria and fungus infection; 6-ounce non-aerosol spray can or 4-ounce dauber bottle.

Victor Gall Remedy containing gentian violet, in 6- and 14-ounce bottles.
Powders: Magic H Antiseptic Powder (Magic H, Hampton, New Hampshire), which can be used dry or as a poultice paste; 14-ounce jar. Wonder Dust (Farnam) to prevent scar-tissue formation on superficial cuts and abrasions; 4-ounce bottle.
Ointments: Fura-Ointment (Farnam) contains nitrofurazone to fight infection, also useful for cracked heels and accelerate healing; 8-ounce and 1-lb jars.
Corona Ointment (Corona Manufacturing Co., Atlanta, Georgia), antiseptic and lubricating, with lanolin and beeswax, to relieve pain and induce new hair growth; 8-ounce and 1½-pound tins.
Magic H Antiseptic Preparation, to treat heat, inflammation of legs, sores, as well as wounds; 3-pound jar.

try to stop the flow before the vet arrives by applying a pressure bandage (any piece of clean cloth will do) directly over the wound. Bright red blood spurting from the wound will indicate a severed artery, and no time should be lost in getting the bleeding to stop. Do not apply any medication yourself even after the bleeding stops unless you have instructions to do so; tranquilizers may only exacerbate the problem, especially if the animal is in pain.

STRAINS AND SPRAINS

These words are often used interchangeably to refer to injuries that are neither bruises nor fractures, but some experts like to distinguish between damage to muscle alone (strain) and injury to the structures of the joint and its tendons or ligaments (sprain). Strenuous exercise will often cause mild strain, and most horsemen routinely treat their animals to a liniment or alcohol rub after work and put them in rest bandages, which will increase circulation. More severe strains and sprains, which may involve tendons and ligaments as well as muscles, deserve a great deal of care, however, and a call to the vet is usually in order. The affected area will be swollen or hot to the touch and must be cooled off before healing may take place. Once the spot has cooled and the swelling limited, heat treatments—or anti-inflammatory agents—will serve to restore circulation so that healing may take place. Since too much heat will slow down circulation and too little will have no effect at all, this process should be carried out with the utmost care. (See pages 94–98 for further information about medications and treatments for lameness.)

BRUISES AND FRACTURES

If a horse has suffered an injury—a kick or a fall or some other trauma—and there appears to be damage to muscle or bone, even though the skin has not been broken, your first task is to call the vet. Then move the animal to a place free of distraction and keep it as calm as possible under the circum-

---

Liniments. There are many kinds of liniments available, some more effective than others, and few of them as strong as the counterirritants or blisters that contain caustic ingredients. Most liniments can be used safely on a regular basis after heavy exercise for their soothing astringent value and to reduce any muscle soreness, stiffness, or minor swelling that may be apparent. (If a horse is lame, however, call the vet.) Diluted in water, witch hazel, or alcohol, liniments make good body washes; undiluted or in a strong solution they are often called braces or tighteners. Each horseman has his own favorite, and many people use homemade recipes which they get their local druggist to make up for them, for reasons of economy. The founder of Thoroughbred Remedy Corp. on Long Island was originally a pharmacist, but when he found that many horsemen from local racetracks came to him with requests for medications, he decided to specialize in his own line of them. Whichever you choose, don't abuse it. Painting on liniment without rubbing or covering it with a bandage may have a blistering effect (we know a cowboy who lost a girlfriend with a sprained wrist that way). Any preparation that contains iodine should be used with special care. Prices range from 20 cents to 50 cents an ounce.

Absorbine Veterinary Liniment (W. F. Young) contains wormwood, acetone, menthol, thymol, potassium iodide, iodine; 12-ounce bottle, gallon can.

B.A.L. (Brace Antiseptic Liniment, from Zirin); 32-ounce bottle, gallon can.

Braceoil (Thoroughbred Remedy) contains menthol, camphor, methyl salicylate, and no iodine; quart, half-gallon, gallon bottles.

Bigeloil (Bigelow-Clark, Elmont, New York) is similar in ingredients to Braceoil, no iodine; 16- and 32-ounce bottles.

M-R (Radiol Chemicals Ltd., Essex, England) contains no iodine.

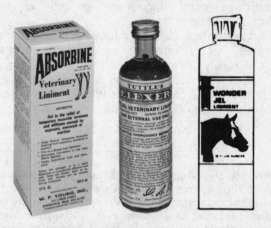

Dr. E. E. Kincade's Anodyne #1 (Lee Drug) contains, along with camphor, such exotics as myrrh, gambir, and Barbados aloes.

Ten Sol (Zirin) contains, among other ingredients, oils of wormwood and peppermint, potassium iodide, and iodine.

Top Form Liniment (Merck) contains camphor, menthol, methyl salicylate, and alcohols.

Tuttle's Elexer (Tuttle's Elixir, Mt. Kisco, New York) is made in Canada and contains oil of hemlock, ox gall, ammonia, and turpentine, along with alcohol; 4½ ounce bottle.

Vetrolin Green Liniment (Thoroughbred Remedy) contains, along with camphor and methyl salicylate, such aromatics as oils of cedarwood, sassafras, and rosemary and castile soap; quart and gallon cans.

Western Laboratories Horse Liniment; pint bottle.

Wilcoxson's Perfection Liniment (Valentine Co., Springfield, Ohio) contains camphor along with iodine, potassium iodide, and oil of turpentine.

Wonder Jel (Farnam); 12-ounce and quart squeeze bottles.

stances, while you try to determine the location and source of the injury (if you didn't witness it yourself). A bad fracture may be obvious, but many times broken bones can be determined only by x-ray, so don't assume anything, especially if the injury is in the leg.

If you are, by some unhappy chance, out on the trail and the animal cannot or will not move on its own, you can try tying up the injured limb (if it's a leg that's affected) with a belt and getting it to move on three legs. If that does not work, your only path may be out of the woods to the nearest telephone. When you are riding with someone else, make sure one of you stays with the injured animal to keep it as calm as possible. Should you be several hours (or days) from help and the animal in great pain, you may find yourself in the unfortunate position of deciding whether it should be put out of its misery right there and then. Decisions about euthanasia are, of course, best left to a veterinarian—many advanced surgical procedures have been developed for saving badly injured horses—but if you feel that the situation is truly hopeless and the animal is suffering with a severe fracture, you may have to take matters into your own hands. There are several ways of putting a horse down, but the recommended method for nonexperts is a rifle or handgun, pointed directly between the eyes into the brain, taking care to avoid the possibility of ricochet. (Cutting the jugular vein or striking the head with a heavy club or stick is far too risky and will probably cause more pain and suffering than you would care to witness.) It goes without saying that anyone who rides out on the trail so far that help is unobtainable should carry a rifle or a so-called humane killer (which is a pistol that shoots a retractable bolt rather than a bullet and is recommended where the carrying of standard firearms is illegal).

Minor bruises or contusions, caused by a direct blow to bone or muscle, may clear up completely without even being noticed. If any blood vessels have been ruptured, however, and swelling takes place, the affected area should be hosed down or cooled until the hemorrhaging stops. Because bruises can be serious, a veterinarian should be called in.

LAMENESS

Almost any sensitive, observant person can tell when a horse is lame, whether the cause is pain or some mechanical defect, such as a congenital or acquired imperfection in the construction of the leg or foot. Painful lameness is the most common problem facing the owner of an otherwise sound horse, and in the pages that follow we will discuss many ailments that affect the equine foot and leg. Bruises, fractures, strains, and sprains may cause lameness, of course, but since it is not always easy to diagnose, sudden lameness should be treated as follows. Check each hoof to be sure that no foreign body has worked its way into the sole or frog. If the object is easily removed and seems to

have caused no puncture, trot the horse for a few steps and be sure that no lameness persists. If there has been a puncture, check with the vet, who will examine the hoof and may wish to give a tetanus shot. If there is nothing visible in the hoof, run your hands over each leg for signs of heat, sores, or any other irregular condition. If after a few minutes of rest the animal still limps, call the veterinarian. The cause may be nothing more than a mild strain, which you can treat at home with applications of cold and heat (in that order, and not without reading up on treatments for inflammation), but any obvious lameness deserves professional attention, for without good care it may very well become a serious problem.

Eyewash. Many of the manufacturers of eyewashes recommend daily use of drops to prevent eye trouble, but we don't think that this should be necessary in a healthy animal. If a horse's eyes are not clear or are consistently red, with any unusual discharge, the veterinarian will undoubtedly prescribe an ophthalmic ointment. For those who think otherwise, two eye-drop solutions that are available for about $2.50 per 4-ounce bottle are Clear Eyes from Farnam and Eye Wash from Western Laboratories. A boric acid solution is perfectly safe and probably just as effective.

EYES AND EARS

Red, watery eyes may be flushed out with a warm solution of boric acid or treated with an ophthalmic ointment. Be sure that the stall is free of dust, pollen, or other foreign matter that may be affecting the eyes. If the wateriness is accompanied by swelling and accumulation of pus, the animal may be suffering from an infection—specifically, leptospirosis, of which this "moon blindness," as it is called, is a symptom. This will require veterinary treatment with antibiotics or corticosteroids. The ears are delicate instruments, and a horse suffering with an infection, an injury, or the presence of ear mites or a fungus growth will show sensitivity whenever its ears are touched. If you notice any sores, growths, or discharge, be sure to ask for veterinary advice. The condition may not be serious or require emergency attention, but if it is allowed to persist the animal may become difficult to handle during grooming or bridling or even at work.

FOOT AND LEG PROBLEMS

Because many horsemen would agree that at least 90 percent of a horse's problems are in the feet, it is worth devoting a whole section to describe some of them briefly. Several disorders have common names, indicating that they are relatively common; others may be unfamiliar and not readily diagnosed by a nonexpert. All the more reason why any continued lameness should have the attention of a veterinarian—preferably sooner rather than later. Some lamenesses are caused by injury, and if this is the case, the horse may have to be given an injection of tetanus toxoid. Some may be caused simply by conformation defects, and oth-

ers by bad care. Various ailments are curable, but others may be chronic and require regular attention and/or treatment.

PROBLEMS

Cracks in the horny wall of the hoof may start at the bottom and work up, or they may begin at the coronary band and work down. The latter are the result of an injury to the coronet which may result in permanent disruption of the hoof's growth. (A normal hoof grows ¾ to 1 inch a month.) When the crack begins at the bottom, the cause is usually drying of the wall or improper trimming. A hoof must be somewhat flexible and elastic, and this is controlled by moisture in the foot. (The wall contains about 25 percent water, the sole 33 percent, the frog 50 percent.) Cracks are identified by their location—toe, quarter, or heel, of which the last two are most serious. Sometimes treatment involves rasping a groove across the end of a crack to prevent its extending farther; toe clips may be

---

DIAGNOSING LAMENESS AT HOME

Have someone trot the animal back and forth in front of you over a level area about 200 feet long, while you watch the motion of the horse's head, neck, and hindquarters. Most lamenesses affect only one foot, thus throwing the horse's symmetry off balance; the trot is the fastest of the symmetrical gaits and thus the easiest gait at which one can detect abnormal motion. (Of course, we are assuming that you know what normal motion is; if not, observe at least a dozen sound horses moving at the trot over the same ground, so that you will recognize irregular action when it occurs.) A sound horse will carry its head and neck relatively motionless at the trot, while the croup will move up and down in a regular way as the animal springs off one diagonal and onto the other. If the head and neck movement is exaggerated during the trot, the lame leg is a foreleg. If the head and neck remain steady but the croup (or the hocks) rises and falls in an irregular pattern, a hind leg is the source of the problem.

In order to determine which of the two forelegs is lame, watch the position of the trot as the horse moves toward you. If the head lifts high above the normal level, the horse is supported at that point by the painful leg; the head will drop back to its normal position later in the stride, as the weight is borne by the healthy leg. If the head drops below normal during the stride, the pain may be caused during the break-over part of the gait, as the horse tries to transfer its weight as quickly as possible.

If the lameness appears to be in the hind legs, watch the horse trot away from you and observe the motion of the croup. One side will move perceptibly higher or lower than

the other side. If one side regularly rises higher than the other, the pain is occurring as the horse shifts quickly from the bad leg to the good one or "hitches behind." If the croup on one side never rises to a normal height, the horse is delaying the break-over phase of the stride because that leg is painful. Another sign of hind-leg lameness is that the muscles on the painful side will tend to go slack within two or three days; this may not be noticeable at rest but will be so in motion. (For a more complete explanation of this procedure, see the excellent article by Matthew Mackay-Smith, D.V.M., "Recognizing Lameness" in *Practical Horseman,* May 1976.)

This diagnosis should take only a few minutes for a horseman with a practiced eye. If you still can't be sure which leg is the bothersome one, make a careful examination of all four, feeling for heated areas which indicate inflammation, and for irregular structure, obvious sores, or foreign bodies and lesions in the hoof. Another way of detecting areas is to tap lightly around the hoof with a small hammer. Flaky sole areas should be removed with a paring knife and all black spots or lines followed through to their depths. It is best to remove the shoe or shoes at this point (see page 61); if you expect to exercise the horse as described above to help in the diagnosis, remove both shoes front or back to maintain symmetry. The veterinarian can employ a number of devices to help in diagnosis: hoof testers, which are used to compress the foot to determine pain; wedges, to accentuate lameness by applying pressure to a limited area of the foot; and nerve blocks, which anesthetize separate parts of the foot and leg.

applied to toe cracks, or proper trimming and shoeing may be enough to solve the problem. If the cracks are deep enough to reach the sensitive laminae beneath, it may be necessary to pare away the crack and fill it with plastic; this procedure often involves delicate dovetailing of the hoof wall and suturing with steel. Heel cracks are sometimes caused by injury; pressure bandages should be applied to stop any bleeding, and treatment may involve antibiotic ointments, bandaging, paring of the wall, and special bar shoes to protect the heel. Drainage of abscesses is essential, and a poultice may be required to reduce inflammation. The foot should be bandaged until the draining has stopped and the wound is dry.

Keratoma is a tumorlike growth in the wall that causes lameness as it puts pressure on the sensitive laminae. The only treatment is surgical removal of the affected area.

A *bruised sole* may be caused by stones or an improperly fitting shoe, in acute cases producing inflammation and lameness. Cold packs or anti-inflammatory drugs (such as phenylbutazone) may be applied to reduce the swelling and a leather pad inserted between the shoe and the foot, to remain in place until the horse recovers from its lameness.

Bruised heels may develop lesions generally called corns, most commonly caused by incorrect shoeing. The shoes must be removed and the feet trimmed; the horse cannot be reshod until the bruise heals. If an abscess has developed, the sole must be pared away and the foot bandaged. A proper bar shoe and full leather pad over a packing of pine tar and oakum will help the horse recover once the infection has been controlled.

Puncture wounds in the sole may be caused by stepping on sharp objects, and lameness will result, but perhaps not immediately. A black dot or line in the sole will indicate a puncture, and the object may often be found embedded. If it is not found, pare away the sole and explore all black areas. Pain will stop once the abscess, if there is one, has drained. A tetanus shot should be given, and treatment for inflammation is indicated. Because complications are common, the vet should definitely be consulted. The frog may also be affected by puncture wounds similar to those of the sole, and they require the same sort of attention.

Thrush is usually caused by poor sanitation and improper trimming of the feet and, with some rare exceptions, should not be found in any horse kept, for whatever reason. It is a condition of the frog characterized by a fetid, blackish discharge in the sulci of the frog, caused by an infection by the organism *Spherophorus necrophorus*. The horse's feet will be tender and may even come up lame if the disease is allowed to progress. The condition can be prevented if the stable is kept clean and the horse's feet cleaned and trimmed regularly. A horse with thrush should be kept on a dry surface and the affected frogs trimmed to permit drainage. Drying agents, such as formalin or Kopertox, may be applied in the early stages of the disease; an advanced case must involve soaking in a magnesium sulfate solution. A tetanus shot is also indicated.

Canker is a chronic kind of dermatitis, which also gives off an offensive odor, as thrush does. It begins with the frog and extends to the sole and wall; it is most often seen in draft horses and commonly involves the hind feet. This too is caused by poor sanitation and neglect, but unlike thrush it will affect the whole foot. The diseased tissue must be removed entirely, and the foot treated with antibiotics and bandages until it has healed. Care must be intensive, and the recovery period is very slow.

Pedal osteitis is an inflammation of the bone, caused by repeated concussion of a thin sole on a rough surface and resultant decalcification. It may be bilateral and thus difficult to diagnose, unless there has been an obvious bruise. The feet must be protected with a full leather pad and the horse given a long period of rest. When the condition becomes chronic, response to therapy is unlikely.

Contracted heels usually affect the forefeet and not just the heels. They result from improper pressure on the frog, due to neglect or a pathological condition, such as thrush or navicular disease. Contracted heels are seen often in Tennessee Walking Horses and American Saddlebreds whose feet have been allowed to grow too long for show purposes. Heel contraction is a secondary condition, and the initial lesion or cause should be identified before treatment is given. Along with treatment, therapy for the heels should be provided to reestablish normal frog pressure by correct trimming, application of a hoof softener, or the use of corrective shoes.

Navicular disease (or podotrochleosis) describes a number of disease conditions affecting the distal sesamoid or navicular bone. The cause is not clearly defined; it may involve injury or conformation defects, but nutritional and hormonal influences may also contribute. In any event, it is a serious disease and an incurable one, although its effects may be alleviated by rest, corrective shoeing and trimming, and drugs, such as steroids, anti-inflammatory agents, and so on. The navicular bone is a tiny bone in the coffin joint, which rests on the deep flexor tendon; between bone and tendon is the navicular bursa, which contains a smooth lubricating substance. As weight is placed on the horse's foot, there is a certain amount of pressure of the bone on the tendon. Excessive friction will cause cartilage and tendon damage, and the bursa will become inflamed (bursitis). Eventually the bone itself will become deformed, and pain will result when the tendon moves over it. Horses with straight pasterns and shoulders or weak navicular bones may develop this disease, although horses of all ages and types may be affected, especially if they have been worked frequently on hard surfaces. Initially, the rider may notice a slight irregularity in gait, a stumbling or sloppy stride, which will disappear after rest and then recur. Eventually the lameness will become continuous, and secondary bursitis in the shoulder may result. Overworn toes of shoes, extended forelegs at rest, and short, square development of toes on barefoot horses are other signs, and an attempt at diagnosis should be made as soon as possible so that corrective measures may be taken, if the disease has not progressed too far, to relieve pain and lameness.

Laminitis (or founder) is an inflammation of the laminae of the feet, usually the front feet, and it appears in both acute and chronic phases. The acute stage involves extreme pain, warm feet, and a rapid pulse, while chronic laminitis (which may occur after an acute case) is indicated by intermittent lameness and a diverging ring around the hoof wall. Although many different causes have been listed, most cases originate from enterotoxemia—which results from overeating of grain or from a postpartum infection in broodmares—that causes the connective tissue in the coffin joint to break down. The signs of laminitis develop quickly; feet will become hot because of increased circulation, and the pulse in the area will be very rapid. If only the forelegs are affected, the horse will try to support itself on the hind feet; if all four feet are affected, the animal may refuse to stand, and if forced to move it will make a shuffling, stumbling motion. Diagnosis is not difficult; lameness and a dropped (or flat, rather than concave) sole are common. In an advanced case, the coffin bone will rotate until it comes through the sole. There are many forms of treatment, the first one being to control the diet. Mineral oil can be used for laxative purposes and to prevent further absorption of the toxins. Nerve blocks, drugs, hormones, vitamin therapy, and soaking in warm water are other treatments, as are limited exercise, corrective shoeing, and the application of acrylic to affect the rotation of the coffin bone.

Sidebones is the common term for premature ossification of the lateral cartilages. This occurs primarily in the front feet, because of either conformation, concussion, or direct injury. As a horse ages, cartilage may normally ossify, or turn to bone, but the reason why this process may be hastened is not clear. Lameness is not common, but the foot cannot grow properly, and other disorders, such as corns, may result. If there is no pain or lameness, nothing need be done, unless one wishes to remove the calcified cartilage surgically for cosmetic reasons, since the affected foot may appear deformed.

Quittor is the common name for lateral cartilage necrosis, which is the destruction of tissue usually caused by deep puncture wounds above the coronary band, although punctures of the sole and an interfering gait may also result in necrosis. A painful swelling above the hoof is the first sign, with resulting lameness, which ceases when the lesion ruptures and drains. This draining does not cure the problem, which may require surgical removal of the affected cartilage. The long-term outlook is not good, because treatment and surgery are not always successful.

Pyramidal disease, or buttress foot, involves the tearing of fibers of the digital extensor tendon. In early stages, heat, tenderness, and swelling occur at the coronary band, and the horse will be lamed when worked. Eventually a bulge will develop and the foot will contract. The prognosis is unfavorable, although pressure may be decreased by filing of the wall below the coronet. Blistering and the use of counterirritants are not usually successful.

Ringbone is a term that refers generally to any bony enlargement below the fetlock, although there are different causes and types of affliction. True articular ringbone is a kind of arthritis or arthrosis affecting the pastern (high) or coffin (low) joint of the foot, usually caused by a sudden or chronic strain. A horse's conformation may make it susceptible to injury; a horse that toes in or out may be rotating the joint in such a way as to tear the ligaments. Forelegs are most commonly afflicted, and lameness may develop slowly or rapidly. Acute lameness accompanied by swelling in the affected joint is the usual sign; flexing of the limb to an extreme position may accentuate the tenderness. There is no cure, but the usefulness of a horse can be extended by good shoeing (or removal of shoes), trimming, and complete rest. Blistering, firing, x-ray treatment, and the use of anti-inflammatory drugs, such as bute, have been tried, with inconsistent success, for short-term relief, but none is reliable and some may even cause further destruction of the joint. Nonarticular ringbone, which looks like articular ringbone externally, does not affect the joints directly and may appear only as a blemish without accompanying tenderness; it is not as serious as articular ringbone, but it is not curable. False ringbone, which can be diagnosed by x-ray, looks like ringbone but does not usually cause lameness; this is an enlargement of the pastern joint caused by torn ligaments but not affecting the bone. It may be acute or chronic and can be treated with injection of steroids or radiation therapy, coupled with rest.

Osselets can be bony (true osselets) or they can involve no bony protuberance and be called "green." Either way, the condition involves a lesion affecting the fetlock joint, usually caused by a racing or training injury in which the fibrous joint capsule has been torn. The joint will be warm and swollen as a result, and lameness may occur. Rest with limited exercise is indicated until the inflammation has decreased; the traditional remedies are blistering, thermal cautery, and radiation therapy.

Osteoarthritis in the fetlock joint may be caused by excessive wear and tear (the condition is seen most often in racehorses), although many other causes have been described. Diet and general conformation should be evaluated and corrected; corrective shoeing, anti-inflammatory drugs, and other forms of therapy may bring only temporary relief.

Wind-puffs, or windgalls, are swellings of the joint capsule in the fetlock. There is no lameness, and treatment will vary according to the cause.

Sometimes a horse that has been in heavy training will develop a wind-puff if it is suddenly not exercised; inadequate nutrition may also be the cause. An elastic wrap over a sweat, such as equal parts of glycerine and alcohol, will reduce the swelling temporarily; draining the joint capsule and injection of a corticosteroid may also improve the condition. Permanent correction may be impossible, but since performance is not affected, this is not necessary in any case.

Sesamoiditis is inflammation of the sesamoid bones, caused by a strain of the sesamoid ligaments during racing or jumping. The area around the fetlock joint may become enlarged or not, but there is sensitivity and in some cases acute lameness, in which case the joint must be immobilized in a cast or support bandage and treatment given to reduce inflammation. In chronic cases, the treatments described above for wind-puffs may be indicated. If there is a fracture, surgery may be performed, and the prognosis depends on the degree of the ligament tearing and the progress of the condition.

Bucked, or *sore, shins* means inflammation of the cannon bone (third metacarpal), seen most often in young animals trained for racing and rare in horses over three years old. Rest, reduction of inflammation, and other forms of therapy are recommended, after which time the animal may be returned to training.

Splints refers to the same condition in the splint bones (second and fourth metacarpals), usually caused by trauma and seen most often in horses with poor conformation with badly aligned knees so that the splint bones support more weight than they are designed to do. Lameness will result, along with inflammation, heat, and tenderness. After the acute phase, lameness will end, although the leg may be blemished. Rest and counterirritants are usually recommended to arrest the progress of the disorder, though surgery may be indicated in case of fracture.

Horses confined for a long time may come up lame with *ruptured knee tendons.* At extended paces the lameness will disappear, although the leg will be somewhat less efficient than a normal one. Surgery to reunite the ends of the tendon may be considered as treatment. Other tendons may become ruptured, where surgery is not possible; rest, reduction or control of inflammation, and support of the limb are all one can do.

Contracted tendons in either forelegs or hind legs may be congenital or acquired, caused either by nutritional deficiency or injury. In foals, the leg may be splinted from foot to elbow as early in life as possible, so that tendons will relax enough to permit the leg to bear weight. In later life, the hooves should be trimmed and diet should be adjusted; at this point, prognosis is poor.

Tendinitis (bowed tendons) is most often seen in horses that have been driven or ridden at a fast pace. The flexor tendon is strained or torn when exceptional stress is put on the leg, and when it is acute, the horse will feel extreme pain and come up very lame. The leg will be hot and swollen as a result of hemorrhage, and only the toe will rest on the ground when the animal is standing. Treatment of acute tendinitis requires controlling inflammation (cold-water packs do well) and supporting the leg with a cast or bandage. Steroids can be injected, and complete rest—for as long as a year—may be recommended. Chronic tendinitis, visible as a bulge behind the cannon bone, has been treated in many ways, but blistering and firing are not usually successful. Drugs and surgery are more effective, but general good care, involving applications of hot and cold (poultices and cold hosing), rest, and supporting bandages or massage, will help relieve symptoms.

Capped knee refers to hygroma of the carpus (or knee), which is a swelling resulting from injury. (The knee joint in a horse's foreleg is comparable to the wrist joint in humans; both are referred to as the carpus.) The accumulated serum is removed and corticosteroids injected into the area, but most important is the use of an elastic bandage (for at least a week) to keep the swelling from recurring.

Carpitis is frequently seen in racehorses and is indicated by acute lameness (in the swinging phase of the gait). It is caused by injury, and fracture is often present as well. When there is no fracture, treatment may include rest, corticosteroids, or even surgery. If new bone growth takes place, the prognosis is poor, although pain can be relieved by the use of bute or other drugs.

Epiphysitis, or "big knee," is caused by compression of the epiphysis of the radial bone. It can occur in young horses, especially those that are overweight or toed in, as a result of too much exercise. Lameness does not always result, and the condition can be diagnosed only by x-ray. The area will be hot to the touch, however, and sensitive to strong pressure. Rest and diet adjustment are the best forms of treatment.

Capped elbow and shoe boil refer to olecranon bursitis, an enlargement of the elbow following an injury, often by the horse's own shoes. The condition may require surgery, but usually the injection of corticosteroids will relieve the problem. If the condition persists, a round roll or sausage boot below the fetlock should be used to limit flexion of the damaging foot or an elbow.

Osteoarthritis of the shoulder joint is not common, but it should be taken into consideration when a horse comes up lame. Usually caused by some injury, it is often accompanied by a fracture. The horse will refuse to extend its foreleg fully, and flexing the shoulder and extending the elbow will cause pain. Treatment can be only temporary, through the use of a local anesthetic or an anti-inflammatory drug.

Trochanteric bursitis, often called "whirlbone" lameness, involves inflammation of the region between the greater trochanter and the middle gluteal-muscle tendon. It is usually secondary to other conditions, but is seen in show horses or racehorses (Standardbreds especially) that are turned frequently or forced to work often in a circle. The animal becomes lame behind and sore when palpated in the region of the swelling. Rest, heat, and massage of the muscles will help, as will corticosteroids and counterirritants.

Occasionally, accidents, falls, or other injuries may cause paralysis of various leg muscles and eventual atrophy (called "shoulder sweeney" when the shoulder muscles are affected). Good nursing care, including anti-inflammatory drugs, hosing the leg, and rest, will improve the situation, though complete recovery is not always possible.

Upward fixation of the patella, when the leg is locked in an extended position, is not uncommon in young horses and is most common in the Shetland pony, in which it is probably hereditary. It is quite painful, especially if both legs are affected, and may be confused with stringhalt (see below), since it involves a sudden upward jerk in motion. The first time it is noticed, an attempt may be made to reposition the patella (you can do this by pulling the leg forward and pushing the patella upward and to the side, or by causing the animal to make a sudden movement). If it recurs, surgery may be necessary, for arthritis may follow.

Gonitis is the inflammation of the stifle joint, and it can be either very painful or a chronic problem with slowly developing lameness. Causes are numerous; the most common are strain and infection in the stifle following a wound. If infection is present, it must be identified so that it can be properly treated; drainage of the area is usually indicated, and rest and painkillers will help relieve symptoms.

Stringhalt (or springhalt) is a spasmodic flexion of one or both hind legs, seen more often in draft horses than in pleasure horses. The cause is not known, although the symptoms resemble those of other ailments—notably dermatitis, mange, and even thrush. Surgery will probably be required if a true case of stringhalt is diagnosed.

Spavin is lameness in the hock, and there are various different kinds; included are fractures and osteoarthritis, with new bone formation or with bone destruction. *Bone spavin* refers to bone destruction on the medial aspect of the hock, and it is not easy to diagnose. Lameness is most visible when a horse first gets up; at rest it will hold its hind leg slightly flexed, and in motion the lame leg moves with a jerky, stabbing movement. Pain occurs when the limb hits the ground, and the horse will try to lift it as quickly as possible. Because the degenerated tissue cannot be removed, treatment involves making the horse more comfortable through corrective shoeing in which the toe is shortened and rolled and the heel elevated. Firing and blistering have been traditional treatments, but there are more effective treatments now available, involving the destruction of cartilage in the affected joint.

Bog spavin usually results in a poorly conformed hock from strain on the tarsal joint. The horse is not usually lame unless the condition is complicated by arthritis or fracture. The blemish

may remain, but if no pain exists, treatment may not be necessary. Blisters and liniments are not too effective; prolonged massage two or three times a day may bring down the swelling, and pressure bandages, if the horse will tolerate them, are also useful. The horse's diet should be reduced somewhat, especially in terms of grain.

Thoroughpin is a distention of the sheath of the deep flexor tendon at the hock, visible on the outside of the leg; the animal is not usually lame, but it is possible to reduce the swelling by removing the fluid from the area and applying a well-padded pressure bandage. Blisters and leg paints are not effective at all.

The above are the most common ailments affecting equine feet and legs; there are others, and there are many different ways in which the rest of the musculoskeletal system may be put out of commission. Readers are referred to any number of good medical books on the subject, most particularly *Equine Medicine and Surgery* (second edition), edited by E. J. Catcott, D.V.M. and J. F. Smithcors, D.V.M., Ph.D.; Wheaton, Illinois: American Veterinary Publications, 1972. See especially Chapter 18, by J. R. Rooney, J. L. Shupe, J. H. Johnson, and J. E. Bartels.

TREATMENTS FOR LAMENESS

Special types of treatment are mentioned in the discussion of specific ailments and injuries, but we would like to give some attention to the methods and products involved in these treatments, so that nonprofessionals will be familiar with the procedures when their own horses are treated. Many over-the-counter products are available at tack and feed stores, as well as through catalogs, but because these are nonprescription agents, their effectiveness is relatively limited. Nevertheless, they should be used with care and—preferably—with a veterinarian's blessing, and they should not be substituted for a veterinarian's attention. Any injury deserves good care, and any prolonged condition involving lameness should not be allowed to go untreated by a professional.

The most effective treatment for lameness is complete rest, but because many trainers cannot afford to let their animals go unworked, they have devised many methods for treating mild injuries and other disorders. Some of these are today considered old-fashioned and not particularly effective, but you will see them still in use, as any tour around a racetrack stable will show.

Painful lameness in a horse is usually accompanied by heat and swelling in the affected area. This is usually caused by internal hemorrhage and inflammation, which must be arrested before healing can begin. The simplest way to do this is to cool the spot; hosing with cold water, soaking in a tub or whirlpool bath, and applying an ice pack or a bandage soaked in a cooling lotion are the most common methods. If you use a hose, make sure the flow of water is slow and the hose is laid against the affected part so that the water flows down in a sheet. Astringent lotions and cooling liniments are often used for rubbing on a horse's legs after strenuous exercise, but they are less effective than cold water for more serious inflammation, since for any long-lasting effect the lotion or liniment must be used to soak a cotton bandage, which is then wrapped on the leg, and when the liquid dries out the bandage will become hot and do more harm than good. It is probably the rubbing in any case rather than the liniment itself that has a therapeutic effect on the swelling.

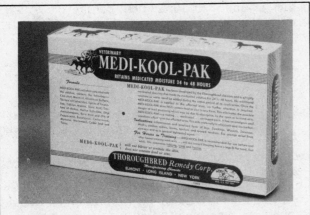

Cold Packs. Cold water and ice are the cheapest ingredients for cold packs, but easy-to-use commercial preparations are also available for immediate relief of swellings caused by injury. Thoroughbred Remedy's Medi-Kool-Pak is a powder-soaked pad to be moistened with water for a wet dressing; its Medi-Kool Titener is a liquid containing menthol, gum camphor, eucalyptus oil, and turpentine and can be rubbed on an area for temporary relief. Zirin's Deep-Freeze is a similar liquid preparation which has a soothing, cooling effect, as is Mineral Ice (by Black Hawk). Ice-O-Gel Freeze (Sioux City, Iowa) is a gel formula that produces the same kind of effect. (Keep in mind that if bandages are placed over the medicated area, heat—which you will not want—may result.) If no ice is available, an instant cold compress that stores without refrigeration is Quick Ice (by Medi, Inc., Holbrook, Massachusetts), which comes in a flexible bag that can be wrapped around the leg; once the inner bag is squeezed, the compress will keep a 45-degree temperature for about twenty minutes. Three pouches cost about $3.50. If ice is available, you may find ice boots, made of canvas with leather soles, useful for about $65 a pair; rubber ankle or knee boots are cheaper ($17 to $30 a pair) and can be used for applying hot poultices (or wet dressings) as well as cold packs.

Whirlpool Therapy Boots. These are useful for high-strung horses that cannot be made to stand in a tub. In addition to reducing swelling by applying cold water, these boots also have a therapeutic massaging action and can be used on one or two legs at a time. The portable unit is equipped with a compressor motor, two boots and suspenders, and tubes, for about $120. Made by Empire Manufacturing Co., 1021 Troy Road, Latham, New York.

The most effective anti-inflammatory agents are drugs that the veterinarian can provide. One of the most effective of these is phenylbutazone (Butazolidin, or "bute"), which has painkilling effects as well; it may be injected or applied directly to the affected joint or tissue. Because bute works so well to kill the pain, the temptation is to use this instead of proceeding with a treatment to eliminate the cause of the trouble. This is risky, of course, because the absence of pain (and subsequent lameness) does not mean that the condition no longer exists, and it may in fact be getting worse. A horse that feels no pain may injure itself again and the owner or trainer may not even notice. Also, recent research has shown that bute may not be such a miracle drug if used over an extended period of time; it is thought by some to affect bone marrow and the production of blood cells. Therefore, it is not recommended for use without expert veterinary guidance.

Corticosteroids are also effective anti-inflammatory drugs, but they too should not be overused, for horses treated with them have a lower general resistance to infection. Azium (which is dexamethasone) is the most common of these drugs; it may be injected or administered in food. Depomedrol is a useful and longer-acting steroid. Other treatments include the use of aspirin (which can also be administered for influenza, strangles, and pleurisy) and Vitamin E. Equiproxen, a new drug from Diamond Laboratories, is neither aspirin nor steroid but is an effective anti-inflammatory agent.

Once the inflammation has been reduced, circulation must be encouraged so that healing can take place. The application of heat or counterirritants of various kinds is the usual form of treatment at this stage. Some methods are relatively simple and some are drastic, the choice of method depending on the seriousness of the injury, the type of wound, the amount of time required for healing, the individual animal, its future use, and the availability of good nursing care. Counterirritants must not be used on acute injuries, since they may cause further damage to the tissue. The whole process of reducing inflammation must take place before heat or other circulation-stimulating methods may proceed.

One old-time means of promoting healing is the application of a poultice, which is a soft, moist dressing packed against the affected area, usually by a bandage of some sort to keep the material in place. This wet dressing is often an antiphlogistic—composed of glycerine, kaolin, and aromatics—and because it brings a certain amount of heat to the skin and muscles beneath, it may help in stimulating circulation. Therapy with hot water (about 120 degrees Fahrenheit) applied to the area for three or four minutes, alternating with a minute of cold water, may have the same effect if repeated three or four times—the whole procedure being performed several times a day. Obviously, this is not a very practical method for people without a lot of time on their hands. Gentle massage in the direction of the venous flow, radiation therapy, electrical stimulation, surgery, blistering, and firing are other counterirritant methods, but the use of these should, of course, be left to a vet's discretion.

Poultices. Like many other kinds of equine medication, a poultice is an old-fashioned and only partially effective remedy for inflammation and lameness. (When was the last time your own physician prescribed one for your sore shoulder?) Many old-time horsemen prefer them to drugs or heated boots, because they are cheaper and time-honored (if not veterinarian-honored). There are a number of commercial poultice preparations available if you don't have your own supply of glycerine, kaolin, and aromatics on hand. Prices vary considerably.

Antiphlogistine (Denver Chemical Co., Stamford, Connecticut, imports this from Canada, in 5-pound sacks); it contains boric acid, glycerine, salicylic acid, kaolin, methyl salicylate, and oils of peppermint and eucalyptus.

Phlogo (Thoroughbred Remedy) contains similar ingredients and is available already mixed or in powder form.

Numotizine Cataplasm (Hobart Laboratories, Chicago, Illinois), contains beechwood, creosote, guaiacol, and methyl salicylate, among other ingredients.

Because a poultice must stay in place if it is to work at all, one must cover the treated area with a bandage of some sort. If the injury is in the hoof area, however, bandaging will not hold up very well, and special poultice boots are available (for between \$22 and \$27) through large tack shops. It is not difficult to make your own, using a corner of a burlap bag with long flaps (see illustration on page 97) to tie around the ankle.

Blistering, which many horsemen believe in, is a controversial method. A caustic agent is applied directly to the skin in paste or liquid form, either once or in several consecutive treatments. Active ingredients may be iodine, red iodide of mercury, muriatic acid, and coal oil, each requiring a different type of application and bandaging. The effect is the same, however: vesicles form, serum oozes, and the skin dries, becomes crusted, and eventually sloughs off. The procedure is painful, so that sedatives and twitches are often necessary, as well

as some device to keep the animal from chewing on the blistered area. The acute pain may last from six to twenty-four hours, followed by a wet phase that can last up to four days. After a month or so, the dried material is shed and the limb begins to look normal. If reblistering is indicated, one must wait a week or so after this last stage. Aside from the painful and unattractive aspects of this practice, blistering is questionable for other reasons. For one thing, there is no way of stopping the blistering action once it has been applied. Soap and water or bandaging may help soothe the irritated tissues, but it is very difficult to control the results of the blister. Obviously, mild blisters applied in succession are to be preferred to one or two severe blisters, but many experts believe that the procedure shouldn't be used at all.

Leg painting is a more conservative method of applying the same principle. Leg paints—iodine in a glycerine or vegetable-oil base, turpentine with iodine and croton oil, kerosene and pine tar, red iodide of mercury with petroleum jelly, or some commercial preparations—are milder than blisters and less effective, but they don't necessarily involve the animal's stopping work entirely. Caustic agents may also be injected, with more immediate results and a shorter recovery time, but otherwise the risks are the same.

Firing is probably the most controversial form of equine veterinary surgery, and some people consider it unnecessary and cruel mutilation, while others still feel it is the most reliable treatment available for many common leg ailments. Briefly, firing involves the burning of the skin over an injured area—deeply or superficially—so that hardened scar tissue is formed and circulation is increased. Pin, or point, firing is the most common form, involving the application of individual puncture marks around the joints or over tendons. Line, or bar, firing means that lines are burned into the skin surrounding the flexor tendons, continuing at intervals for the length of the cannon bone. All types of objects have been used for firing: heated nails, pitchfork tines, and converted soldering irons; but rather more sophisticated tools have been developed, such as ether irons and electric cautery units, which are probably most commonly used today. Surgical conditions must be maintained during firing, including anesthesia, sterile cleansing of the area being fired, and postsurgical care, involving rest (sometimes for a long period) and painting or even blistering with counterirritants. Firing leaves a permanent scar, which may have the advantage of constantly reminding the trainer that too much work can cause the injury to recur, though it will make resale of the animal difficult and certain types of showing impossible (as in conformation or breed classes where soundness is essential). Now available from Schering is a new preparation, called Osteum, which is sodium oleate, a drug that stimulates the fibrous and fibrocartilaginous tissue in much the same way as firing does to produce scar tissue. It is recommended for use on bucked shins and splints and is

Counterirritants and Blisters. These are designed for use after injury, to stimulate the flow of blood to muscles, tendons, and joints in order to speed the healing process. While their use is often effective in certain cases, most veterinarians prefer the use of anti-inflammatory drugs or electric heat therapy, which are more easily controlled and far less cruel. Strong counterirritants have a blistering effect and take a long time to heal, requiring the animal to be taken out of work. Mild blisters, or rubifacients (blood stimulators), or leg paints, or reducines, or whatever you want to call them needn't be painful or disfiguring, and the animal may be worked lightly during treatment, but their use should be carefully controlled, since one can't stop their action once it starts. Because these preparations are more concentrated than liniments, they cost considerably more—up to $3 an ounce. Several are imported from England or Ireland, which also adds to the cost. They are designed for external use only and can be poisonous if ingested, and most require the application of bandages (which help keep the animal from licking the wound) and an application of lard or ointment for a period of time.

Bone Radiol (Radiol Chemicals, Ltd., Essex, England) contains creosote, among other things; 7-ounce bottle.

Elliman's Royal Embrocation (Elliman, Slough, England) contains acetic acid and turpentine.

Harvey's Embrocation (Harvey & Co., Dublin) contains iodine; 3½- and 10½-ounce bottles.

Lambert's Irish Reducine (Lambert's, Dublin) contains iodine along with pine tar and vegetable oils; 14-ounce can.

M.A.C. Counter-Irritant (Carter-Luff Chemical, Hudson, New York) contains turpentine oil, mercuric iodine, silver iodide, mercuric chloride, and camphor); 2-ounce bottle.

McTarnahan's Original Ball Solution contains, among other ingredients, iodine, methyl salicylate, boric acid, and menthol.

Savoss Liniment (Troy Chemical) contains iodine, camphor, and various aromatics; 7½-ounce bottle with brush.

Titen-Zem (Zirin) contains chloroform and ether; 16-ounce bottle.

Workalin (Epsom Remedies, Epsom, England, distributed by Miller Harness Co.) contains iodine, potassium iodide, and mercuric chloride; 10-ounce bottle.

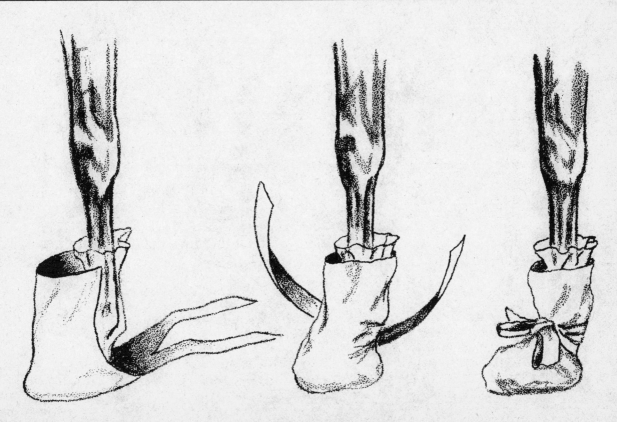

Poultice bandage

considered a more permanent solution to these injuries than blistering or firing.

The subject of bandages for horses is one on which grooms invariably know more than veterinarians. There are many different kinds of bandages for many different purposes, but some of the most common types are these. The standing bandage, a piece of flannel or other cloth about 7 inches wide and 10 feet long, can be used as a preventive bandage in shipping as well as for therapeutic purposes. Five layers of sheet cotton are folded to the desired width and wrapped around the leg and are covered with a quilted pad and then with the bandage material, which is secured with pins or tape. A cold-water bandage, to which a hose is applied, is made of a knitted type of bandage about four inches wide. A 4-inch Ace bandage can be used as a running bandage, supporting the tendons yet allowing for flexibility. (Clasps must be covered with tape for reinforcement.) Spider bandages, or a special wrapping technique that does not involve a bandage covering the whole leg, are also used for certain cases in which a great deal of pressure is not desirable. Where more support is needed, a cast bandage may be necessary. This involves the painting of a 4-inch gauze bandage with an adhesive solution (latex or plaster), or the use of a special type of bandage which has plaster worked into the material itself. This may be left in position for a week or more while the horse is training, but as with the running bandage, the pressure must be even and the animal must suffer no discomfort. Various kinds of medicated bandages are also available, as are special orthopedic bandages of moleskin or adhesive materials that may be applied over sheet-cotton bandages for extra support or immobilization after surgery.

Great care must be used in wrapping leg bandages, to avoid providing too much pressure, insufficient support, or uneven pressure which may cause further damage, especially in the case of a bowed tendon. Since careful wrapping is an art requiring great skill, the procedure should not be attempted by anyone without careful supervision.

GIVING MEDICINE INTERNALLY

Whether it be worming medication or an antibiotic that the veterinarian has left with you, keep these two things in mind as you try to get whatever-it-is into the animal: a deft, confident approach on your part and a quiet, familiar environment for the horse. If you are inexperienced in giving medication, your vet can show you how or recommend the most effective method. Most important, be sure that the horse is not likely to become excited by too much restraint, nervousness on your part, or unnatural, unfamiliar conditions if you want the medication to be beneficial rather than harmful.

Theoretically, the easiest way to dose a horse is to put medication into its water or food and let the animal treat itself. That's theory. In practice, however, horses tend to be pretty fussy about their

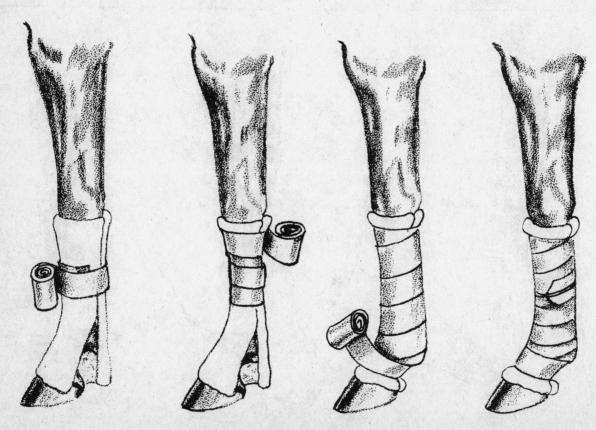

Standing bandage

food's smell and texture, and whatever isn't familiar will make them suspicious. Some medications are made to be palatable, but even these goodies will be rejected by some horses just because they are new and different. It is possible, however, to fool some of those horses some of the time. Try putting molasses into the feed to disguise the taste; horses love the sweet flavor and will usually lick the bucket clean. But untrusting animals will require the addition of molasses for a day or two before you put the medication in. An easy way of disguising scent is to rub a bit of Vicks VapoRub on the horse's nose before mealtime—the fumes should distract it from any medical aroma. Powdered medicine can be made into a sweet paste with corn syrup, honey, or molasses; liquid medications can be mixed with sugar. The paste can then be put on the tongue, teeth, or lips, and it should disappear pretty quickly. Nevertheless, one is never entirely sure just how much of the medication a horse takes, unless you watch the animal eat every bite. And not all medicines come in edible form, so the horse owner will have to become familiar with other methods of dosing.

Drenching is a means of getting liquid medication into the animal's mouth by placing a syringe or a bottle into the interdental space in front of the first cheek tooth, pouring, and allowing the animal to swallow. This is not recommmended for beginners, for the amount of medicine actually ingested is never accurate, and the risk of inhalation through the trachea is great.

Balls, pills, or capsules can be given either by hand or with a balling gun, though again great caution is required to avoid injuring the pharynx or lodging medicine in the esophagus. The smaller the horse, the greater the risk. To give a pill by hand, pull the tongue to one side between the upper and lower cheek teeth and place the pill, lubricated with mineral oil or glycerine, as far back on the tongue as possible. Hold the mouth closed until the horse swallows, and stroke the underside of the neck toward the stomach to encourage its passage into the stomach. The head should be held in a normal position. To use a balling gun, hold the tongue aside, insert the gun between the incisor teeth, and discharge it onto the base of the tongue. If it is "shot" too far back, the ball or pill may cause the horse to gag or cough it out. Care should be taken that the animal doesn't bite the end of the balling gun.

Stomach tubing is tricky for amateurs, but it is a good procedure to learn in case of emergency and vetlessness. The tube should not be too large (¾ inch in diameter for an adult horse; ⅜ inch for ponies and foals) or too flexible, for it will curl or kink. (Tubes that seem too stiff, as in cold weather, may be softened by brief soaking in warm water.) The tube should have smooth edges at both ends and should be marked at intervals to indicate the distance from the nostril (where the tube enters) to the opening of the esophagus (about 16 inches) and then again for the beginning of the stomach, about 5½ feet. Lubricate the tube's passage either

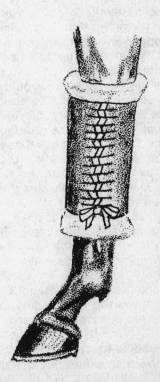

Spider bandage

by feeding the horse a little grain to stimulate saliva flow (if the horse will eat) or by rubbing the tube with petroleum jelly. Back the animal into a corner of the stall and have someone hold its head firmly with a halter lead and perhaps with a twitch as well. Violent movement of the head may cause the tube to damage the lining of the esophagus, so great care should be taken to prevent this from happening. The horse's head should be flexed, so that it will be easier for it to swallow when the tube touches the pharynx (the entry to the esophagus).

Holding the tube in your right hand, insert it into the animal's right nostril, placing your left thumb in the nostril so that you can feel the tube and keep it on the floor of the nasal passage. Work it into the nostril until it hits the pharynx, at which point the animal should swallow and admit it into the esophagus. Do not by any means try to force it at this point; just hold it firmly until it is passed into the esophagus. You can both see and feel it as it passes through, and if you are in doubt as to its exact location, withdraw the tube a few inches until you can do so. If it moves very easily, you may have inserted the tube into the trachea, which you can tell by hearing the tube rattle as you shake the animal's throat. Withdraw it and try again. Do not in any event put any medication into the tube until you are sure you have reached the stomach. One way of checking this is to blow into the tube; your assistant can hear bubbling noises in the horse's stomach. Once you are absolutely sure that the tube end is in the stomach (you can cause your horse to aspirate and choke to death if it isn't), pour in the liquid medication, using a funnel if necessary. To be sure that the tube is thoroughly drained before you withdraw it, blow through it or hold a finger over the end as you pull it out. Again, exercise tremendous caution and manipulate the tube gently rather than forcefully.

Although we don't recommend that anyone without experience try to inject any medication into a horse, or that anyone do so at all without a veterinarian's advice, we would like to point out several basic warnings. The abuse of needles and syringes has caused trouble in the past, both to individual horses and to groups, as in the spread of EIA and other infectious diseases. *Always* use a sterile syringe and needle. (Disposable syringes are not expensive and always safe; if you reuse a syringe, make absolutely sure that it has been sterilized before use and kept in a sterile condition.) A needle that breaks under the skin or in a muscle, unless removed immediately, will travel and do damage internally. If the needle is too deep to remove by hand, the vet should be called right away for surgery or perhaps an x ray. Don't bother to rub a horse's skin with alcohol before injecting the needle unless the spot is dirty. In any case, don't clip the area, for loose hairs may get into the skin. And be sure not to inject a needle where the harness or saddle touches the skin.

There are several kinds of injections: subcutaneous (usually into a fold of skin in the middle of the side of the neck), intravenous (into a vein,

Bandages. Standing bandages (used for shipping as well as to immobilize an injured leg) may be made in several ways, but in essence the idea is to give a thick cushion to the leg and to secure it with a snug bandage (not too snug or circulation may be stopped). Sheet cotton ($2.50 to $3.50 for a dozen double-sized sheets) is the traditional padding, but also available now are washable self-adhering cotton wraps ($4 to $5.50 for four), washable quilted cotton wraps ($5 to $5.50 for four), or gauze-covered cotton sheeting (about $10 for four). Bandages may be cotton web, flannel, nylon or acrylic; some are equipped with sewn-on tie tapes or Velcro self-sticking tapes, while others require the separate purchase of pins, masking tape, or Velcro tapes. Prices for the bandages vary from $5 for a knitted or flannel set of four to $10 for a set of Velcro bandages. Pins can be as cheap as the safety pins at your local dime store; a dozen Velcro tapes can run as much as $16 or more. A one-piece standing bandage is also available, made of durable knit material, 6 inches wide and 3 yards long, with Velcro fastenings, for about $11 for a set of four (less without fastenings). Shipping boots are also available for shipping purposes, but they do not afford sufficient support for injured legs. (See page 153.)

Racing bandages, to be used on an animal recovering from injury or suffering from a deformity (such as a bowed tendon), are elasticized for flexibility and are worn without any padding. These can be as simple as Ace bandages, or as elaborate as Vetrap Elastic Bandages (about $5 for four), Miller's Rubber-Reinforced Elastic Bandages (about $10 for four), Sealtex Latex Bandages (about $18 for four), or Velcro Legband Bandages (made of nylon and acrylic pile with Velcro closings, at $21 for four).

Tendon, fetlock, and hock support socks are also available—made of elasticized material to cover specific parts of the leg ($7 to $10 a pair).

Shoe Boil Boots—or sausage boots—which

are made of lightweight chrome leather with canvas sides and which buckle around the horse's fetlock to prevent damage to kicked elbows, are available through large tack shops for about $11 to $14 apiece.

which is tricky unless you know exactly where the vein is), intradermal, intra-articular (into a joint), and intramuscular. For any number of good reasons, one should not attempt any of these without first receiving instruction from the veterinarian.

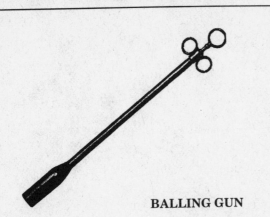

BALLING GUN

Made of nickel-plated brass or plastic, curved or straight, with or without springs to hold the capsule, about 17½ inches long, these range in price from $1 to $8.50. Available from most tack shops.

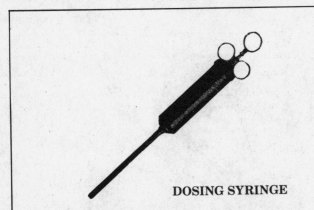

DOSING SYRINGE

Made of nickel-plated brass (which is less likely to serrate than aluminum), with 6-inch pipes and a three-ring handle for easy handling, these have a capacity of 2 or 4 ounces. $8 to $9.50. (Disposable syringes made of plastic for injections may be obtained from your vet.)

RESTRAINT PROCEDURES

It comes as no great suprise that the average horse is a fairly large animal with a great deal more muscle, weight, and power than the average human being. (Even ponies count here, especially when the owner is relatively small.) Happily, the human brain is somewhat superior to equine gray matter, so we have been able to develop various means of keeping the horse under control most of the time. Training—anything from gentle, constant handling to the finer points of equitation—is probably the most obvious, but even before halter breaking begins, humans have affected equine be-

ACUPUNCTURE

In his book *Animal Doctor*, Lucas Younker, a veterinarian living in Southern California, tells of his experiences treating animals by using the method of acupuncture. He began by working with a Korean M.D. on a mare with severe emphysema, which quite suddenly started breathing normally after Dr. Choe palpated the animal and then treated three points on each side for a minute apiece. Dr. Younker followed up with a similar treatment the following day, and the effects lasted for nearly two weeks. After that, the mare relapsed and was sent to a breeding farm. The initial success of the experiment, however, so impressed the vet that he decided to try the method on other horses to find out how many diseases were treatable, how many treatments were necessary, and how long the effect of each treatment would last. Eventually, he started up a clinic—for dogs and other animals as well—and some Hollywood stars began sending him their pets for treatment. To avoid accusations of unethical publicity-seeking, he set up a non-profit clinic with connections to the University of California at Davis to ensure academic supervision. As of this writing, there are several such organizations exploring the possibilities of acupuncture in veterinary medicine, translating Chinese literature on the subject, working with Oriental physicians, and performing successful treatments on animals throughout the country. The art of acupuncture has not yet reached the status of a science in this country, as it has in China, but it is well worth keeping an eye on. For further information, write to the veterinary school at the University of California–Davis or to the National School of Veterinary Acupuncture in Anaheim, California, or to the International Veterinary Acupuncture Society at the University of Georgia.

havior by breeding in good temperament and breeding out the bad. Domestication of the horse has been a centuries-long process, during which the natural fears of the wild horse have been eliminated and a relative docility introduced. The horse's instinct to flee (or in mules and donkeys, to stop) or, when cornered or challenged, to attack is no longer "natural" in the domesticated breeds that we know today, except in those we call "feral"—horses returned, like the American mustang, to a wild state. Even the most highly strung, badly behaved horse—whether it has been ill bred or badly treated—does not show the same characteristics as the zebra, for instance, or the Przewalski wild horse, neither of which can be successfully trained, no matter how effective gentle taming may be in reducing their fears.

The closest that the normal domestic horse comes temperamentally to the wild one is in times of extreme stress—not just when being cruelly treated, but when ill or injured. Pain creates panic along with discomfort, and even the mildest-mannered of creatures may become difficult, if not downright impossible, to handle even with more than one person present.

Several methods are available for handling an animal in trouble, both to make treatment possible and to prevent further damage. The best choice depends, of course, on the individual animal and its condition, available equipment and personnel, and general circumstances. We all remember Ruffian, that beautiful filly who was such a "bad patient" when she reacted violently to recovery from anesthesia, eventually making it necessary for the doctors to destroy her. Yet we also remember an unbeautiful grade gelding named Copperhead, who had the good sense when he sank up to his neck in a soft spot in the ground (a cesspool, if you must know) to keep his head and resist the impulse to struggle, thus managing to avoid slipping entirely out of sight. Horses differ, obviously, and the better you know your horse and what it is capable of doing in a bad situation, the better equipped you will be in dealing with it when trouble arises. The more highly trained an animal is, the more predictable its behavior. A green horse, although usually free enough of bad habits, may act unpredictably out of ignorance and be uncontrollable because it does not know enough to respond to certain commands or signals. A spoiled horse with bad habits is most difficult to handle, having undoubtedly learned too much with regard to outwitting people or pieces of equipment.

Certain kinds of equipment must always be on hand for use in emergencies: several yards of good, sturdy rope, a second halter and lead rope, and a twitch of some sort, as well as a good assistant. Other devices designed to deal with specific situations should also be considered if your horse is at all likely to require them. Most important is some self-restraint on your own part, to control the temper that an unruly horse can provoke. It is also essential that you become experienced in the correct use of the various restraint methods, since misuse of them can result in an angry horse and perhaps even further injury.

PHYSICAL RESTRAINT

The most important first step in restraining a horse for whatever reason is to gain control of the head. A halter alone is not enough; a lead rope will give the handler greater control. If the horse refuses to move, a rope may be dropped around the hindquarters, crossed over the back, and passed up through the halter to encourage the animal to advance. (If this fails, the animal should be blindfolded.) The handler must remain alert at all times to the horse's behavior, standing on the same side of the horse that the vet (or whoever) is working on. His primary function, aside from keeping the animal from escaping, is to distract him from

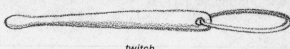

Methods of restraint

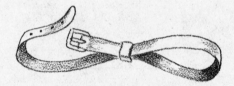

twitch

knee strap

emergency rope bridle

whatever is being done elsewhere. Reassuring noises often do the trick, but when the horse is still anxious, stronger measures will be necessary. One effective way of holding a horse's head is to keep one hand on the muzzle and the other on the nape of the neck, behind the ears. To keep the horse's head up, slip a thumb through the nose-band of the halter; to keep it down, put pressure (not enough to compress the nostrils and prevent breathing) on the muzzle. The other hand will be free to grab the mane or an ear if necessary. Twisting the ear is often effective, but care should be taken to prevent the permanent condition of a fallen ear or a head-shy horse.

For especially spirited horses, a chain shank may be attached to the halter to slip over the muzzle, under the jaw, through the mouth, or over the upper gum. Never tie a horse with such a halter, however, or use it abusively. Other special halters include those used for holding a horse to an operating table and dental halters with a rigid loop of steel in the noseband, which provides space to open the jaws without affecting the cheeks. A war bridle, of which there are several variations, is a rope gag that is used in conjunction with a halter and lead to keep a horse from rearing.

One of the oldest and most common restraint devices is the twitch, which provides restraint by distracting the horse's attention. A simple twitching method, to grasp the upper lip between thumb and fingers and hold on, usually works for only a moment or so, but long enough to get a twitch device in place. This loop of small-linked chain or rope is attached to the end of a wooden stick about a yard long. The loop is applied to the lip (which is folded so that the mucosal tissue does not show), and the handle is twisted to tighten it. It is most effective at the beginning and loses effect as the lip becomes numb, so one should alternate the pressure, applying the maximum only when necessary. (One can also resort to the lower lip.) Some horses resent the use of a twitch and will fight it by pulling back, striking out with a foreleg, or rearing. The handler should be careful to keep a good hold on the end of the handle if this happens and to stand clear. A nose clamp, a type of twitch that can be attached to the halter to free the assistant's hand, takes time to apply and remove, and it may be impossible for a spirited horse. Humane twitches, ring twitches, and blanket clamps are other variations on the same theme.

Most of us know (or should know) how to pick up and hold a horse's feet for examination or cleaning. Restraining a horse by holding one or more legs is somewhat trickier, especially if the animal is not accustomed to frequent handling. The point is to keep the horse off balance to prevent kicking or striking. Therefore, in holding or tying a leg, be sure not to let the horse persuade you to carry part of its weight. If the vet or someone is working on a hind leg, lift the foreleg on the same side, tying it if necessary so that the rope or strap can be released quickly. Tying a hind leg will not permit close examination, but should discour-

CHAIN TWITCH

There are many different designs, most of them called humane and all of them painful to the horse. (They are probably called humane because they do not shut off circulation.) There are three common varieties: the nose or chain twitch, with a wooden handle and a nickel-plated brass nose chain; the screw twitch, made of polished aluminum; and the nutcracker style, which fastens to the halter. The first of these needs constant attention on the part of the handler, but the other two can be left in place and are thus called "one-man" twitches. Prices range from $4 to $6.

SCREW TWITCH

If your horse will not tolerate a twitch, you may find a chain halter effective. Made by the Johnson Ideal Halter Company (Aurora, Illinois), this is a control halter, because the hackamore effect of the cotton rope noseband is reinforced by a chain that runs under the jaw. Available in three sizes, with or without a covered noseband, $7 to $8.50.

age kicking. Rope burns can be prevented by the use of hobbles or bandages around the leg to be tied. Discourage a horse likely to strike with its forelegs, by grasping a roll of skin over the shoulders with two hands.

Tying the tail will also help prevent kicking and facilitate a rectal examination or treatment, although one may also simply hold the tail over the animal's back. Ponies or young animals are often restrained by a handler's holding both halter and tail. If the horse is relatively large or strong, it is a good precaution to stand the animal alongside a wall and lean against it. A young foal should be handled with special care. It is not a good idea to remove it from its dam, since it will probably become very much excited when left alone. If the foal is not broken to a halter, don't try to apply one now, but cradle it gently in your arms, one around the neck and the other around the rump.

Some barns are equipped with permanent stocks made of heavy wooden timbers or pipes, while temporary stocks may be made from rope. This type of restraint can be very useful for examining and treating standing horses; it can be dangerous, however, if a horse becomes unruly, and excitable horses should be tranquilized or sedated before being so confined. A heavy kickboard is a useful attachment (made to swing like a door at the back of the stock), and any surface that the horse may hit should be padded in some way. The horse's head should be cross-tied, and the ropes in front of and behind the horse should be secured in such a way that they can be released if the animal gets on top of one of them. A rope caught underneath a horse's tail will usually provoke a kicking fit, as most experienced horsemen know.

An effective rope stock—also called a hippoharness or Sigler's method—can be made with a single length of rope 30 to 40 feet long. Pass the center of the rope over the withers, making a half-hitch around each foreleg; pass the rope back to the hind legs, make another half-hitch, and cross the ends of the rope over the loins, pulling them tight and tying them (for quick release) or having them held by two assistants. (See illustration on page 109.)

A drastic method of restraint—and one now virtually superseded by the use of tranquilizing drugs—is casting, or forcing a horse to fall and lie immobile, either by flexing the hind legs and setting the horse down before it is put on its side or by pulling all four legs until the animal falls over. Both can be dangerous, since the animal can become injured during the fall. You can cast a small horse or pony simply by pulling the halter to force the head around and pulling the animal's tail through its legs and out the opposite side; then, using the animal's body as a fulcrum, lift up and back until the horse can be lowered to the ground. Harnesses have been designed in various styles for larger horses, but are rarely used now without tranquilizers. Now most horses are cast by the use of drugs alone, harnesses being used merely for restraint or for holding certain limbs in position once the animal is down.

All of these methods are temporary, requiring the constant presence of a handler in addition to the vet or expert treating the horse, as well as being designed for use on standing animals. Slings can be very useful in helping a horse to its feet and then in keeping it in a standing position—either temporarily or over a period of time. A sling can be useful only if an animal can support its own weight, at least partially. (When a horse hangs in a sling, death is certain. Animals that can't support themselves are better off lying in a deep bed of straw or clean bedding and being turned from one side to the other at regular intervals.) Slings must be sturdy and custom-fitted to each animal. A sling is made up of a wide belly band, a breast collar (to prevent the horse from slipping forward), breeching (to prevent it from slipping back), a singletree (to keep the straps separated over the back and attached to the point of suspension), and a chain hoist firmly anchored in the ceiling of the stall. The hoist should be adjusted so that the animal can support itself without putting undue pressure on its belly, and feeding and watering containers must be placed conveniently nearby. A horse should be fully conscious when put into a sling, although tranquilizers may be necessary to prevent rearing or plunging. Once the horse has become accustomed to the confinement, a halter with a lead attached to the side of the stall should be used to keep the animal from swinging around in circles.

Many other devices have been developed to use on horses undergoing treatment. Protective hoods to prevent head injury, blindfolds to facilitate moving or recovery from anesthesia, and neck cradles to prevent the animal from licking a wound or dressing are just a few. Some horses learn to circumvent the cradle by raising a foreleg and propping it on the side of the stall until it can be reached with the mouth—in which case a leather bib under the halter will prevent chewing or licking. When a hind leg is involved, a stick made be attached from a side ring in a surcingle to the halter ring. Cross tying may also be used, or a swivel tie, consisting of a rope dropped from the ceiling and attached to the noseband of the halter. Either method will discourage the animal from interfering with a wound or dressing.

CHEMICAL RESTRAINT

The drugs described below should be used only by a veterinarian or under his supervision. Although research has made the development of various effective drugs possible, their use is nonetheless a risky business. Some horses may react in different ways from others, and highly dangerous or even fatal side effects may result if medications are not administered with utmost care and skill. Drugs used for restraint fall into three general categories: sedatives, narcotics, and tranquilizers. Used for quieting excitable animals for examination or as a preliminary step before surgery, they differ considerably from one another in effect.

Sedatives, administered most commonly to horses to quiet them before surgery in which a local anesthetic is used, allow for rapid recovery, so that the patient may walk immediately after the operation is over. They are also useful in procedures that require momentary pain, such as injection or certain kinds of treatment. Because most sedatives interfere with swallowing, horses should not be fed or watered for several hours after use. Chloral hydrate alone or in combination with other drugs reduces a horse's response to pain and makes it less likely to kick, strike, or try to escape. This drug may be given intravenously or orally in water in capsules. Injection is usually the method, for horses will not readily drink a chloral solution unless very thirsty. Drenching (by pouring down the throat) is not usually recommended for fear of irritating gums or inflaming alimentary or respiratory tracts. Oral doses, in any case, do not take effect for twenty to thirty minutes, and the degree of sedation is far more variable than it is with intravenous injection. Pentobarbital sodium in large doses may cause a horse to become overly excited, so slow, intravenous injection is preferred. Rompun (xylazine) is a sedative with analgesic (painkilling) properties; it is a potent, quick-acting sedative that can be administered intravenously, intramuscularly, or subcutaneously. Because it is efficient and relatively safe, Rompun is commonly used for loading horses prior to shipping; for clipping, shoeing, examination, or minor surgery; and as a preanesthetic drug. Horses will lower their heads and seem deeply drowsy, but they will remain steady on their feet and can even deliver a swift kick if so inclined. Recovery is generally smooth and quiet.

Narcotics are not widely used by veterinarians for horses except in severe cases of trauma or in combination with tranquilizers. Meperidine hydrochloride is the one most commonly used with horses, although most practitioners feel there is not sufficient need for narcotics to recommend their use. Methadone hydrochloride tends to cause excitement and is not recommended, nor is heroin, in spite of its former widespread use at the racetrack, which gave it the nickname "horse" and inspired the introduction of the saliva test.

Tranquilizers are good for controlling excitable animals when painful procedures are not intended. Although tranquilized horses seem to become sleepy and unresponsive, they may react more violently to pain than they would without the tranquilizer, which must not be used when an animal is in danger of shock. Unlike sedatives, tranquilizers may be fed orally as well as by injection; their effect is longer-lasting; and horses can eat and drink following their administration. Nevertheless, they are slower to work, and they may not work at all when an animal is excited; they also vary in their effect on horses, depending on breed, age, size, and temperament. The most dependable and safest tranquilizers are promazine and acepromazine, which have similar effects. Succinylcholine hydrochloride, a paralyzing drug, has been widely used in immobilizing horses, but it is risky, especially in animals that are malnourished, exhausted, excited, old, or suffering from cardiac or liver disease. Serpasil (reserpine) has also been widely used in horses because it produces a delayed reaction and may be effective up to seventy-two hours after administration (and undetectable by racing and show officials). But since it slows down the metabolic rate and the digestive process, colic and serious diarrhea may result, and

since its effects on horses—as on humans—are quite unpredictable, it is not recommended by veterinarians if the horse's health is of any value.

Many of these sedatives and tranquilizers are used in combination for anesthetic purposes during surgical procedures, so that the animal does not perceive pain or respond reflexively to painful stimuli. Although it was once common to use only one drug for anesthesia, several drugs are now used in order to shorten recovery time and to widen the margin of safety. Intravenous drugs are generally used to induce anesthesia, usually after the administration of a tranquilizer and often accompanied by the use of a casting harness after the tranquilizer has taken effect. The safest way of maintaining anesthesia is then to use inhalation methods, with drugs such as halothane, methoxyfluorane, nitrous oxide, chloroform, ether, and cycloprone (these last three are seldom used now). There are many risks involved in the use of anesthetics in horses, such as respiratory obstructions, surgical shock, and cardiac arrest—one reason that local anesthetics are used whenever possible. These are applied as topical or surface agents, in the eyes and on the mucous membranes, as infiltration anesthetics (for suturing wounds or minor surgery), field blocks (somewhat deeper than infiltration), nerve blocks, and epidural blocks (in which the nerve roots from the vertebral canal are blocked). These can be used alone or in conjunction with a sedative, with the animal either standing or lying down.

SPECIAL MEDICAL PROBLEMS

So far we have talked about care, treatment, and ailments that can apply to any horse, regardless of breed, color, or sex; but obviously there are situations in which a particular horse may require more than what we would consider routine medical attention. A bad fracture or other injury that might have meant certain death for a horse some years ago does not always mean the end nowadays. Valuable performing or breeding stock, or animals owned by people who care enough to spend the very best, can often be saved, thanks to advanced procedures that specialists in equine practice have developed. If your own veterinarian does not have the equipment or the know-how to deal with a problem, he will readily refer you to someone who does. Equine centers exist throughout the country—usually connected with veterinary schools or racetracks or in areas where horses are kept in substantial numbers—and these are equipped with specialized x-ray equipment, surgical apparatus, and specialist veterinarians to diagnose and treat difficult medical problems.

GELDING

Many minor forms of surgery may be done at home (or, rather, in your stable), since horses can be sedated and given local anesthesia from which they will recover rapidly. In most of these cases, horses can even remain standing throughout the

HORSE DOPING

The first saliva test for racehorses was introduced in 1933 at Gulfstream Park, Florida, to curb the widespread use of heroin and the fraudulent use of local anesthetics. At that time, racehorse doping was so common that the Thoroughbred breed in this country was in danger of being ruined, and federal narcotics agents began a campaign to eliminate the practice. Urine tests were then developed to supplement the saliva test, and strict regulations were adopted and enforced by the Thoroughbred Racing and Protective Bureau. Although it has never been possible to control the practice of doping entirely—Man O'War was known as the greatest hophead horse of all time—the campaign against it continues unabated. State racing associations have different rules pertaining to the use of drugs, but it is usually the first three horses in a race and the unexpected losers that are tested. Stimulants, depressants, and local anesthetics or painkillers are the primary targets for these tests, which now include the analysis of blood samples as well as of urine and saliva, but most racing associations also frown on antibiotics or anything else they consider "medicine."

Because racehorses must perform under particularly stressful conditions—hard tracks, daily exercise, and heavy racing schedules—unsoundness is a common occurrence among these young animals, whose musculature and skeletons are still in the process of growing. Veterinarians must therefore use drugs and other medical techniques to keep their patients as sound as possible under unnatural conditions. Therefore, in 1963, the American Association of Equine Practitioners offered suggested guidelines relating to the medication of racehorses in order to regulate the use of drugs and to encourage a more tolerant attitude toward their use. Most states have adopted these recommendations, which include the prohibition of stimulants, depressants, or local anesthetics if they may affect racing performance, or any drug that might screen or mask the use of a prohibited drug. No medications may be given on the day of a race without permission from officials (the "day" to be determined by those officials, according to the lasting effects of any drug). Accurate veterinary records must be made available to any official, and the use of any controversial medications must be reported so that it may be evaluated. Many states have gone so far as to allow the use of phenylbutazone ("bute"), since it is so effective in the treatment of lameness and since racing asso-

procedure. One example of this kind of surgery is gelding, or castrating, which is performed in most male horses before the age of two. In Europe, where breeding in many areas is strictly controlled, the decision whether or not to geld a horse is usually made by the organization or association supervising the improvement or continuance of certain breeds. In this country, the owner of the horse has the choice, both as to the surgery itself and as to the time when it is to take place. Most owners, unless they plan to embark on a breeding program—which can be expensive, time-consuming, and full of potential problems—prefer to keep geldings (or mares, of course) rather than stallions, since geldings are far easier to control. If a horse has particularly fine qualities that deserve to be passed along to future generations, there may be good reason to keep him whole, but even stallions with relatively quiet temperaments may not always behave calmly, regardless of how well trained they may be, especially if a mare in heat is anywhere nearby. Kelso, the famous money-winning racehorse, was gelded at two because his temperament was too much for the disciplines of racing. When he turned out to be a fantastic performer, his owners undoubtedly regretted the fact that he had been gelded (an apocryphal story circulates to the effect that the owner said to the vet who did the deed: "I paid you fifty bucks to take 'em off; I'll pay you a million to put 'em back!").

Naturally, Kelso might very well not have been able to race at all if he had not been gelded, and his career certainly would not have been so spectacular if he had been retired to stud at four. And of course, it is always possible that he might not have been a good stud; many fine horses are not good breeders (though some can be trained) and their own traits and characteristics often fail to get passed along as planned by the owners. All of which simply goes to explain why breeding is such a risky and unpredictable business.

So, assuming that you have a young colt that shows promise as a riding or driving horse but isn't anything particularly special (and here's where sentiment must be firmly controlled), gelding is the usual course as the animal matures. This is a relatively simple surgical task, and the veterinarian may decide to do the surgery on the spot with the animal standing. Shetland ponies (for some reason), breeding stallions, and intractable horses should not be gelded this way, for their surgery is more complicated and the risk to the veterinarian even greater than usual. (And no horse should be gelded at all if suffering from an infectious disease, anemia, or generally poor condition caused by parasites or malnutrition; the animal must be healthy before it is put through the stress that even minor surgery will bring on.)

If your horse is tractable, well trained (or readily handled), and young, the vet may very well decide ciations are as eager as anyone to increase the number of competitors, although this is still a highly controversial issue.

The American Horse Show Association also forbids the use of stimulants, depressants, tranquilizers, and local anesthetics that might affect a horse's performance, as well as any masking drugs, although it does permit "full use of modern therapeutic measures for the improvement and protection of the health of the horse including phenylbutazone," unless a drug might serve to stimulate or depress the circulatory, respiratory, or central nervous system. Dr. Joseph O'Dea, veterinarian for the U.S. Equestrian Team, believes that bute or comparable medications should not be permitted in any class in which intrinsic physical soundness or conformation is a specification. He believes that it should be permitted, however, for working-hunter, jumper, and eventing competitions and racing, for it is safe and efficient when properly used, and its prohibition might bring on the use of more dangerous drugs that are less easily detected and controlled than bute.

But in spite of regulations, regular testing, and veterinary recommendations, doping will undoubtedly continue as long as new drugs are developed and new techniques for escaping detection are invented. Although it is not difficult to detect about forty of the traditional substances—amphetamines, cocaine, strychnine, heroin, promazine, and various other drugs—it is not always practical to search for the hundreds of others that might be used. This is unfortunate—and not just for the bettor or the honest competitor. The abuse of drugs, as we all know from their application in humans, can lead to dangerous and in some cases fatal situations. The effects of some drugs are unpredictable, and overdoses are highly possible; side effects can be damaging; and even the injection itself can be harmful. (A nonveterinarian might easily hit an artery instead of a vein, which may result in convulsions and death, and the use of unsterilized needles can spread infection.) Some trainers will always be able to come up with a new way of subverting the rules, but they always do so at the expense of their horses, to say nothing of the notion of good sportsmanship.

For a fascinating discussion of the use of drugs in racing, read Chapter 4 ("In: Taking the Surest Shot") of *The Track* by Bill Surface (New York: Macmillan, 1976).

to take the simplest route. This involves dosing with a sedative and applying a local anesthetic, cleansing the genital area, and removing the testicles with an emasculator. Procedures vary depending on the surgeon performing the task, but the effect is the same, and the animal can be put back to very light work the day after. Exercise for about twenty minutes twice a day is the usual prescription, with the time gradually increased over a period of a week until healing is completed. The wound should be kept clean and free of flies and other biting insects to avoid infection.

If you do not want to have your young stallion gelded and are willing to undertake the considerable responsibilities of dealing with him, and with the business of breeding, you should take the trouble to consult with experts, such as veterinarians and other breeders, and with good texts on the subject in order to determine whether your venture has a chance of success. This book is directed toward amateurs rather than professionals, and once you decide to get into breeding on any scale (which ownership of a stallion usually entails), you should be looking at other books than this one.

BREEDING A MARE

One way in which nonprofessionals get into the breeding business, without making it a business, is to own a mare and decide to have her bred. Some people we know have done so in order to get another horse without spending a whole lot of money, and all we can say to others considering the same route is: keep in mind the potential expenses of veterinarians, stud fees, and special feeds, to say nothing of the fact that the mare will be unable to work for a period of time and that the foal will require a great deal of handling, training, food, and time to grow up before it will be of any use. A good-looking, well-mannered mare of any quality might very well make a good mother, but she might not. The foal might be a disappointment, the mare might be physically or temperamentally unfit for the task, and there is, of course, the risk that the pregnancy and birth will do her irreparable harm, even cause her death. Raising a foal can be a wonderful experience for humans as well as horses, but it entails a lot of work and tender loving care, even at times when it does not seem to be convenient or even possible.

If you decide to have your mare bred anyway, be sure that you read the following bits of advice. Some friends of ours recently spent more than $1,500 to have their mare bred, and they ended up with no foal at all. First, if you don't know a stud in your area, check with several local experts (trainers, dealers, or stable managers) and sift their advice carefully. Go to see any stud who sounds promising, and be sure that your veterinarian goes with you. There is hardly any point in breeding your mare to an animal whose traits—temperamental or physical—are not compatible with hers. This does not mean that the stud should be the same; many successful foals have been combinations of complementary rather than similar genes. If your mare is short and you want a tall offspring, a tall stallion might be the best choice; if color is important to you, you might do well to check the relative dominance of certain colors in the breed. (Chestnut is dominant in Thoroughbreds, for instance; gray in Arabs, and so on.) Keep in mind, however, that old story about George Bernard Shaw, who was approached by a beautiful woman with the suggestion that they "breed." He smiled and responded, "But my dear, what if the child has *your* brains and *my* looks?" Not all genetic mixes are successful, as any professional breeder (or racetrack tout) will tell you.

Once you find a stud who pleases you, and you are willing to take your chances, make certain that the financial arrangements are satisfactory, if not entirely in your favor. If your mare has not been bred before and if the stud is not proved, do not agree to pay a stud fee unless a live foal is guaranteed. Stud fees vary considerably, of course, depending on the area, the breed, the availability of local studs, and the stud itself; but anything over $100 should be considered an investment and must be taken seriously. (Unfortunately, the owners of mares cannot do what dog breeders do and offer the pick of the litter in lieu of a fee, since twins occur only once or twice per thousand foalings.)

Make sure that your agreement is in writing, and get a statement from your veterinarian about the state of health, general condition, and conformation of the stud. (The owner of the stud may very well demand the same information in the form of vet certificates about your mare, so be prepared to offer that too, along with any papers you have relating to her own family tree.) If the breeding, as it often does, involves the mare's being shipped to the stud, have your vet check into any infectious diseases that may be present in the stud's part of the world and have her inoculated, in addition to having a Coggins test performed. If at all possible, make a check yourself ahead of time into the conditions of the stable where she will be kept, and be sure that a veterinarian (with whom your own vet will have talked) will be on hand for the breeding. We have heard altogether too many unhappy tales of undecipherable invoices for examinations, inoculations, and so on that were not anticipated by the eager foal-owners-to-be.

If your mare is being shipped away from home for the purpose of breeding, you may have to expect her to be gone for two or three months, especially if she is untried. Many mares are not always receptive to stallions, although they may be in heat (and even this is not always easy to detect). There have been drugs developed to determine (or to encourage) ovulation at any particular time during the estrous cycle, but even these are not foolproof,

and it may take several breedings before a mare is actually impregnated. Most mares will show obvious signs in the presence of other horses when they are in estrus (arching the tail, moving it aside to display the vulva, and other generally flirtatious types of behavior); but some won't, and whether or not a single breeding will be effective is not easy to determine until long after the fact (at least 30 days by rectal palpation; 45 to 150 days for a urine test). Mares have a regular 21-day estrous cycle throughout the year, but cannot be bred successfully except perhaps three or four times of the year.

Estrus can take three different forms: the dormant phase (usually during fall and winter); the adjustment phase (late summer, early spring); and the true breeding period (March through July or August in Northern states). During the breeding period, estrous cycles may last five to seven days, with ovulation occurring during the second half of the cycle. The season for Thoroughbreds and most commercially important breeds can extend from mid-February until mid-June. The earlier in the year the better as far as Thoroughbreds being raised for the track are concerned, since each foal is given an official birth date of January 1 regardless of actual foaling. A well-developed two-year-old born in February, say, obviously has a distinct advantage over a two-year-old born in July or later. Gestation is normally eleven months (315 to 350 days, with 340 the average for Thoroughbreds). The deviation of a few days is not necessarily significant, but foaling two weeks or more before the calculated due date must be considered premature; a foal that is three weeks early will need special intensive care to remain alive, and one born earlier than that will probably not survive. If it does, it will always be weaker than average.

If breeding is so chancy—with barrenness, pregnancy, and potency so difficult to determine at the breeding time—why don't horsemen employ artificial insemination regularly, as cattle breeders and even human physicians seem willing to do? They do, but because horse-breeding associations regulate against it, artificially inseminated horses cannot usually be registered. The Jockey Club, for example, limits the use of artificial insemination to the period immediately following natural breeding. Other organizations allow the practice but not the transport of semen, so that the stallion and mare must be on the same premises when the mare is inseminated. There are obvious advantages to the practice: it decreases the possibility of infection transmission, and it avoids the problems caused by animals that cannot physically perform for one reason or another. But according to the breed associations, it removes as well certain means by which breeding can be controlled and increases the possibilities for fraud and deception.

However you manage to get your mare bred, be sure that you get a breeder's certificate from the owner of the stallion at the time the mare is serviced.

Diseases may affect the pregnant mare, and in

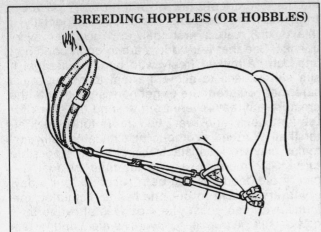

BREEDING HOPPLES (OR HOBBLES)

These are used to keep the mare from kicking the stallion and can be made of nylon or cotton rope or leather, with or without pulleys, quick-release straps, and copper rivets. The cheapest kind (about $40) is made of cotton rope with hock straps and no pulley; the most expensive—and most durable—type (as much as $95) is made of double-stitched leather straps with copper rivets, latigo-lined hock straps, and a pulley for control.

Artificial-Insemination Equipment. The Nasco catalog offers everything the artificial inseminator would want to have except for breeding papers and the stallion's contribution: artificial equine vaginas with plastic collection tubes, devices for storing semen, and insemination tubes.

A general introduction to breeding is Handbook No. 394, "Breeding and Raising Horses," by M. E. Ensminger, published by the U.S. Department of Agriculture. In addition to information about breeds, care, and other aspects of horsemanship, the booklet contains a valuable sample breeding certificate. Write to the Superintendent of Documents, U.S. Government Printing Office, Washington, D.C. 20102.

areas where these diseases are present, inoculations, if available, should be administered. Rhinopneumonitis or other viral diseases (see page 82) may be prevented in this way; other causes of abortion—bacterial infection, nutritional deficiency, bad condition generally, and genetic faults—may be avoided through good care and a sensible breeding program. Mares that seem likely to abort may be treated with hormones and the abortion prevented, but evidence indicates that the resulting foals are not particularly healthy, since they did not develop at a normal rate. Other inoculations may be indicated for the pregnant mare in order to immunize the foal against various diseases, such as tetanus, and of course, other good stable-management practices, including parasite control, are of the utmost importance.

Nutrition is another all-important consideration. Obviously, no broodmare should be too fat or too thin, since either condition can cause complications during pregnancy and foaling. During the first two-thirds of pregnancy, the mare needs no special diet, or any increase in her feed, since fetal development is slow at this stage. During the last four months, however, her protein and energy requirements will be greater, and special attention must also be given to vitamins A and D, calcium, phosphorus, and iodine. High-protein feeds, such as legume hay or protein supplements, should be fed (see chart on page 44). People living in areas where fescue grass (in pasture or as hay) is available should take note that this must not be fed during the last three months of pregnancy. Once the mare has foaled, she will need dietary supplements as long as she is nursing her offspring.

A heavily pregnant mare should be separated from other horses which might injure her or cause her stress and be given a place that will be suitable for foaling. A clean, small pasture free of steep hills, muddy areas, or piles of brush is ideal, as is a larger-than-average stall (16 feet square), in which bedding (straw rather than dusty chips) is kept clean and deep. The mare may be worked until the last couple of months, if the veterinarian approves, but should not be put under much stress at this time. Mares that are exercised regularly during pregnancy will probably have a much easier time foaling than unconditioned mares, but strenuous or risky exercise (such as jumping or cross-country work) should be avoided. Irregular exercise is probably worse, however, than none at all.

Most mares will foal in the dead of night without any trouble at all—and without giving their owners the thrill of seeing the foal's first few steps. Nevertheless, most owners will want to do everything they can to ensure the delivery of a healthy foal, and we recommend that one remain as alert as possible to the impending signs of delivery. The first sign is usually the development of the mare's udder, which can happen as early as eight weeks before delivery or as late as the day after. Most mares, however, "bag down" two to six weeks ahead of time, with a tight udder showing a day or two before foaling. Hair will drop from the udder, and teats will fill out—probably four to six days ahead—and "wax," or show a tiny drop of the yellowish colostrum, within forty-eight hours before foaling. Not all mares do wax or drip milk, however, so don't count on having a guaranteed signal. Other signs include a flabbiness around the root of the tail, which will be higher than normal with the tissues on either side relatively sunken in appearance, indicating that the pelvic canal is relaxing. The mare herself may become restless and move away from other animals she may be pastured with, eating little and perhaps even becoming somewhat unfriendly. At this point, a bran mash should be offered.

Labor has three stages, the first of which is signaled by uterine contractions and perhaps—but not always—the rupture of the water bag in which the fetus is contained. The mare may become more restless, getting up and down, twitching her tail, and becoming sweaty. Once the fetus begins to move into the birth canal, the second stage begins; at this point the mare may be lying down with her legs stretched, straining and pushing with each contraction. The foal's feet and nose should appear quickly (if they do not and the vet is not present, run for the telephone). After this point, labor—during which the foal will emerge entirely—should take no more than ten minutes to a half hour. Any deviation in this process should be considered an abnormality deserving of emergency treatment.

After foaling, the mare may lie quietly for a few minutes. Leave her alone, and do not under any circumstances assume the role of Mother Nature and cut the cord yourself (valuable nutrients and blood are still passing through the umbilical cord). Only if the foal's head is covered with membrane and it is unable to breathe should you attempt to interfere. The placenta and fetal wastes (or afterbirth) should be expelled within half an hour to three hours after birth, and if the material has not emerged by this time, the vet should be consulted. In any event, you should have on hand for the foaling at least two buckets of hot, clean water, soap, and some mineral oil, disinfectant, tail bandages, iodine (for the foal's navel), and a rubber tube or douche syringe in case the vet needs to give the foal an enema or a laxative. In most cases, and all normal ones, the foal should be on its feet and nursing within an hour or two. If it is weak and unable to stand, the vet should be called if he is not already on hand; artificial respiration (by clearing the tracheal passage, stimulating breath by rubbing and thumping the rib cage, mouth-to-mouth resuscitation, or an injection) may be required but should not be attempted by an inexperienced person.

Most foalings, happily, are uneventful and, less happily, unobserved. The foaling mare will obviously prefer to conduct her serious business when activity and stress are least apparent, and the eager owner is usually connected—in her mind, at least—with both. Nevertheless, every owner should be alert to the various signs and be ready with the telephone should anything seem out of the ordinary.

RAISING A FOAL

In the best of all worlds (and, luckily, in most cases), the mare will turn out to be an ideal mother, trying to get her offspring up as soon as she rises to her feet and urging it to nurse right away. If a foal is not nursing within two hours, the vet should be alerted to give it and the mare an examination. If the foal is not nursing at the end of three hours, hand rearing is probably indicated. This involves milking the mare and placing the colostrum into a bottle that can be fitted with a small nipple. Once the foal has managed to nurse from the bottle, it should be allowed to try nursing from its mother, but if this doesn't work (and restraint devices on an intractable mare that seems unwill-

ing have no effect), the job will probably be yours from then on. Be patient, however, especially if this is the mare's first foal, and give her every chance. See that her udders are in good condition and can be milked freely with gentle massage. If she still refuses to allow the foal to nurse, make sure that you are there to get nourishment into the creature—at least every hour around the clock for the first week, and every two hours for a week after that. Warmed synthetic or simulated milk formulas may work satisfactorily, but if it is possible to milk the mare, do so. By the time the foal is a month old, feedings can be reduced to four a day. If you are unable to get one of the simulated formulas, you can substitute 4 ounces of evaporated cow's milk, 4 ounces of warm water, and 1 teaspoon of corn syrup; the foal may consume as much as 8 ounces every hour. If diarrhea results, substitute limewater for the corn syrup. Orphaned or abandoned foals will probably require some antibiotic treatment for the first week, as well as a lot of company, human or otherwise. Warmth is important, of course, but most important is the mare's milk, which contains antibodies, and sufficient vitamins and other nutrients to ensure the foal's health.

Borden's, the manufacturer of Foal-Lac, a simulated mare's milk, has produced an excellent booklet: "The Care and Feeding of Orphan Foals and Early Weaned Foals." Write to Borden, Inc., P.O. Box 419, Norfolk, Virginia 23501.

By the time a foal reaches a month in age, solids—hay, grain, or a pelleted ration—may be introduced into its diet, which is called a "creep ration" since it is usually presented in a "creep," or a container to which only the foal has access. Ten to 12 percent of the ration may be devoted to a supplement of some sort, such as Calf Manna, a pelleted high-energy, easily digestible feed developed by Carnation for feeding to slowly developing calves. Nutrition is extremely important during these crucial months if the foal is to develop into a healthy weanling.

Whether or not the foal is hand-reared, one should always be sure to give a baby horse the most gentle and attentive of care—even if it involves only occasional (daily) handling. This will relax the mare and make the foal generally friendly toward humans, an invaluable first step toward successful training later on. Do not be overattentive—so that the mare becomes worried or nervous—and do not subject the foal to the stress of more than a few minutes of handling at a time while it is very young. But do make it aware of your existence and let it be sure from the start that you are a friend, someone that can be trusted. Some trainers like to halter a foal the moment it is born, to accustom the animal to the feel of a piece of equipment, but the first haltering can usually wait for a couple of months at least, even if you plan to show the baby or begin its training before it is weaned at about six months. Whatever you do, don't spoil the animal by presenting a treat each time you present yourself; a foal is not a pet in the usual sense, and bad habits—such as nipping and jumping up—can begin at any time during these first few months.

1892

PEAT MOSS HOOF STUFFING

ALL GOODS UNDER THIS BRAND ARE GUARANTEED. USE INTERNALLY AND EXTERNALLY

VETERINARY

EXTRACT OF WITCH HAZEL FOR MAN OR BEAST. FOR SALE BY ALL HORSE GOODS DEALERS

Emollic CAMPBELL'S IODOFORM GALL CURE MANUFACTURED BY THE JAMES B. CAMPBELL CO. LABORATORY CHICAGO. Price 25 Cents

VET BOOKS

There are many veterinary books around, some good, some not so good. The second edition of *Equine Medicine and Surgery* (1970) is probably the most thorough, but since it is aimed at veterinarians, it may tell the average horse owner more than he wants to know. Nevertheless, it is more accurate and up-to-date in its information than many other volumes addressed to a general audience. *Veterinary Notes for Horse Owners* was originally published in England in 1877 and is full of information, but for the most part it is dated; the latest edition, the sixteenth, was published in 1968. *The Horse's Health from A to Z,* by Peter Rossdale and Susan Wreford, also originated in London, although there is an American edition distributed by Arco; it was published in 1974 and is relatively up-to-date, although English rather than American in language and terminology, and its dictionary format leaves a good deal to be desired in terms of full information about treatments and diseases. It has a useful list of drug manufacturers in both countries, however, and a good bibliography. Joseph B. Davidson's *Horsemen's Veterinary Adviser* (Arco, New York) is written in a more useful narrative form, but it contains some erroneous information. James L. Naviaux's *Horses—in Health and Disease* (Arco) is much better and more up-to-date. *Merck's Veterinary Manual* is a useful reference on equine diseases (Merck; third edition, 1967), but the best works are those written for veterinarians—O. R. Adams's *Lameness in Horses* (Lee and Febiger, Philadelphia, second edition, 1966); J. T. Bryans' and H. Gerber's *Equine Infectious Diseases,* Volume II (S. Karger, White Plains, New York; 1970), originally from Basel, Switzerland; G. Lepage's *Veterinary Parasitology* (Oliver & Boyd, Edinburgh and London, second edition, 1968); Septimus Sisson's *The Anatomy of the Domestic Animals* (W. B. Saunders, Philadelphia; fourth edition, revised by James D. Grossman, 1953).

5 TACK

The making and selling of tack, or virtually anything a horse wears, has developed into a multi-million-dollar industry. While saddle making may not be the world's oldest profession, it has certainly been around for a number of centuries, changing slowly as new concepts of riding, new materials, and specialized breeding demanded. The American Plains Indian is known to have tied a strip of rawhide around the lower jaw of a horse, jumped on its bare back, and ridden off. Whether Plains Indians were in fact, the precise horsemen that movies have made them out to be is something better left to historians. One can only speculate that without a saddle to help maintain a stable seat, control of the mount was often haphazard. Actually, the Indian rawhide bit was predated by the more sophisticated hand-forged bits found in the Bronze Age. The Greeks and Romans are known to have used both the snaffle and the curb. The Romans, along with the invention of gluttonous feasts, are credited with producing the first saddle, a high-peaked affair that most likely developed from the addition of rolls of padding to the basic saddle-cloth. Later, medieval and Oriental saddles were developed with high backs to support the warrior as he charged with his lance. These chairlike saddles did not last long, however, for when the warrior was on the receiving end of the lance, he often discovered the high back might support him so well his spine would break before the saddle did. Jousting saddles without a back support followed, although by present-day standards the pommel and cantle were certainly high. The lady's sidesaddle dates from approximately the twelfth century, and the Spanish saddles ridden by the Conquistadores, obvious ancestors of our Western saddle, date from about then as well.

The biggest revolution in tack came with the invention of the stirrup, a truly ingenious device believed to have been used first by the Huns. Superb equestrians and fierce fighters, the Huns no doubt owe their reputation as horsemen to their ability to turn in the saddle and shift their weight and balance.

Tack has changed relatively little over the centuries. Probably the newest revolution in horse equipment can be found in the last fifty years with the introduction of such new materials as nylon, stainless steel, plastic, fiber glass, aluminum, and plywood. One could speculate that the single thing future historians may find most interesting about our tack is its wide variety. That variety, of course, reflects the varied and specialized work we ask our horses to perform, such as dressage, cutting, jumping, flat racing, barrel racing, steeplechasing, endurance, driving, trotting, and bronc, park, pleasure, trail, and trick riding.

For each horseman there is a catalog that sells the equipment he needs. What we hope to do is describe what all of those items are, how they are used, how one item varies from another, and lastly, where hard-to-come-by items can be found. Despite protests from the committed, we strongly feel that all styles of riding are directly related and equipment used by one horseman may be the perfect solution for another. Therefore, we have not divided this section into the traditional "English" and "Western" categories. Instead, we hope the reader will find interest in all tack and attempt to understand the "how" and "why" of its use. The English rider may discover, for example, that the Western bosal used with a snaffle can be as effective as the English double bridle and under some conditions may have advantages the other does not. In other words, tack normally associated with one style of riding may be suitable for a horse being trained to another style. Many items of tack are based on tradition, often with good reason. Some, however, are adaptable and should be considered wherever they fit an individual horse's or rider's needs.

BITS

It has been noted that one half of good riding is in the employment of the seat; the other half is in the employment of the legs. If that statement seems an odd way to begin a discussion of bits, we suggest you read on.

When you take reins and thus a bit into your hands, you are helping your seat and legs to achieve the head set basic to a well-balanced and well-trained animal. And if the head is set correctly (the "correct" head set will depend on the breed, the work you are asking the horse to do, and to some degree the horse's natural way of going),

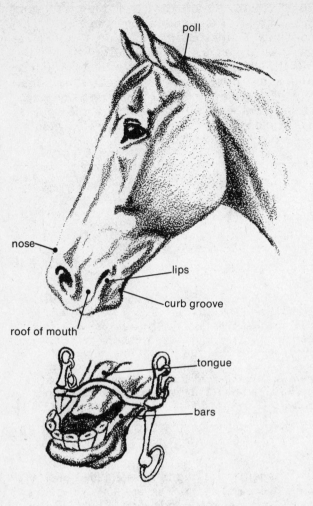

Pressure points

then such problems as evasion of the bit, improper turning, lack of suppleness, and difficulty of gait transitions can be avoided before they begin.

Bits can be grouped as follows: the snaffle, the gag, the curb, the Weymouth, the Pelham, the hackamore, and the spade. Within each of these groupings are many items, each having different emphasis.

To understand the action of various bits, it is necessary to understand that there are seven basic areas on the horse where the bridle is capable of applying pressure. These are the tongue, the bars (that area of the gum between the incisors and molars), the roof of the mouth, the lips, the chin (or curb groove), the nose, and the poll. Some bits exert pressure on only one or two of these points, while others bring pressure to bear simultaneously on a number of them. Nearly all bits work on the principle that a horse will move away from pressure or pain. For example, pressure on the poll will encourage a horse to lower its head, while an upward pressure on the lips will encourage the horse to raise its head. Therefore, in choosing the proper bit for your horse (and learning how to use it), it is necessary to know what you will be asking the horse to do and then selecting the bit that best communicates that command.

In order for your horse to remain sensitive to the pressure of the bit, and therefore responsive to your commands, it is imperative that the mouth remain moist. A wet mouth stimulates and lubricates nerve endings near the surface, while a dry mouth has the opposite effect. Many bits encourage the horse to "play" with the mouthpiece, rolling the metal against its tongue and the roof of its mouth. Some training bits include "keys" (small pieces of metal that dangle from the center of the bit) for the young horse to tongue. Horsemen with access to older, hand-forged steel bits swear by them, claiming that the metal used has a sweeter taste and a more salutary effect on the horse. Others find that copper mouthpieces have an appealing taste which encourages the horse to salivate freely (some horses, however, reject the copper as strange and unpleasant).

Most bits are made of stainless steel, which is rustproof and practically nonbreakable; many bits come with stainless steel cheeks and copper mouthpieces or copper wire wrapped around the steel mouth. Also available, however, are chrome-plated or nickel-plated bits, many of them made from malleable iron. These are far stronger than the now-outmoded solid-nickel bit, which bends or breaks easily. Aluminum, which is marvelously lightweight when every ounce counts, is used on almost all racing bits and on many Western curb bits. Finally, you can also buy stainless steel bits with hard or soft rubber or nylon mouthpieces, materials often preferred for training a young, sensitive mouth.

SNAFFLE

Although the snaffle bit is associated with English-style riding, it is becoming more and more commonly used for Western training as well. The snaffle, by applying pressure to the tongue, bars, and lips, causes the horse to raise its head. Many horsemen use it along with a curb bit or with an auxiliary to the bit (such as a dropped noseband or a martingale) to obtain a flexion of the poll or tucking of the chin which a snaffle alone cannot produce.

Snaffle bits come in various shapes and forms. The mouthpiece may be either two short arms that are joined in the middle (the jointed snaffle) or one piece that may be either straight or half-mooned in shape (the mullen mouthpiece). The jointed mouthpiece causes a nutcracker effect on the tongue as the two arms are pulled back against the horse's lips, while the mullen mouthpiece has none of this effect.

The snaffle is generally considered one of the gentlest bits now available, but it can also be quite severe (severity often meaning the amount of pain inflicted upon the animal), with misuse resulting in an overflexed, cold-jawed, mean animal with no trust or respect for its rider. In fact, few bits are severe in themselves; but when combined with heavy, jerking, pulling hands, any bit can become pure torture for the horse. However, there are several factors which can influence the amount of pressure a bit produces:

- thickness—a thin, slight-looking bit will cut into the mouth more sharply than a stout bit.
- the shape of the arms—a twisted mouthpiece has an effect much like that of a rough-toothed saw (the use of the twisted mouthpiece is banned in Maryland), and a chain-link mouthpiece can pinch the tongue and rub the bars raw.
- the flexibility of the joint—the looser the joint, the more pronounced its nutcracker effect upon the tongue; the tighter the joint, the less sharp the action. There is a variation on the jointed mouthpiece known as a "Y" or "W" mouth snaffle, made of two sets of arms, jointed off-center to opposite sides of the mouth. When pulled back, the two arms hinge and pinch a wider surface of the tongue than the single-jointed mouthpiece, and its more severe action should be used only by experienced hands. For horses with sensitive mouths there is a jointed snaffle with the two arms linked by a small ring or connecting piece of metal. This added piece actually reduces the leverage of the joint and lessens the nutcracker effect.
- the shape and size of the rings—the larger the rings, the less likely the bit is to pull around and through the mouth. Many horsemen prefer loose-fitting rings which encourage the horse to play with the bit. Rings fixed onto the mouthpiece give greater pressure to the lips and bars, as well as giving the rider extra leverage to activate the nutcracker pressure on the tongue. While a loose-ring bit sits flat along the horse's cheek and produces a straighter and therefore less severe pull, particularly large or long bit cheeks may rub the sides of the horse's cheek.

Some bits (or bit aids) feature an abrasive surface on one cheek to discourage the animal that continually runs out to that side. There is a nasty bit called a Scorrier, or Cornish, snaffle with bridle cheek rings fixed in slots within a twisted mouthpiece while an outside set of rings attaches to the reins. The bridle rings produce an inward squeezing action against the horse's lips, which in tandem with the twisted mouthpiece produces a sharp action.

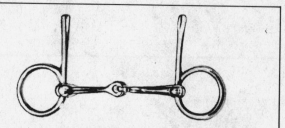

Driving Bit. This model has a 5-inch mouthpiece, but this and other styles are also available in smaller sizes for ponies. Driving bits come with a mullen or twisted-wire mouthpiece and, with a few exceptions, have cheekpieces that extend below the horse's lips, preventing the bit from slipping through its mouth while it is being driven into a turn. About $8.95.

GAG

Like the snaffle, the gag bit, essentially raises the horse's head, but its more severe action should be used by experienced hands only. You can easily spot a gag bit; the bridle cheekpieces, made of rounded leather or rope, pass through holes in the top and bottom of the bit cheeks, and the reins attach to the bridle cheekpieces below the bit. It was originally developed for polo players and was used only recently on jumpers.

How does a gag bit work? As the reins pull back on the bridle, the bit slides upward along the rounded cheekpieces. The additional upward leverage brings pressure to bear on the lips and bars of the mouth. In theory, to escape this strong pressure, the horse immediately raises its head. But some horsemen dispute the gag's ability to raise the head pointing out that pressure is also applied to the poll. The hard-mouthed horse, therefore, will lower its head to avoid that downward pull.

Some horsemen will use two sets of reins with the gag bit, one set attached to the bridle rings and one set attached to the bit rings. Therefore, depending on the reining, the bit can work either as a plain snaffle or as a gag bit. A gag bit is sometimes used to replace the bradoon in a double bridle, and some riders use a gag bit with a martingale. (The action of the martingale, basically a downward-bearing one, is discussed on page 125.) However, a martingale used along with a gag bit can be a severe means of control when you consider that the strong upward action of the gag is applied to a mouth held stationary by the martingale.

CURB

The American Plains Indians knew some of the principles of the curb when they tied rawhide around their mounts' lower jaw, and certainly heavy, high-ported curb bits were used in the Bronze Age. Like the Spaniards and knights before them, cowboys regarded their horses as beasts for work, and for the cow horse quick turns and sliding stops were essential for survival. So bitting for Western use quickly became more sophisticated, incorporating a large number of the basic pressure points as more specialized control was needed. While many people associate the curb primarily with Western reining, this bit is also an important element in English and dressage riding, and it is the basic bit for the high-strutting gaited show animals.

The curb is capable of applying pressure to as many as five of the seven basic pressure points: to the curb groove through the curb strap; to the poll via the bridle (the amount of pressure depending on the length between the mouthpiece and the bridle rings); to the bars; to the tongue; and, with the use of a bit such as the Half-Breed (a high-ported bit), to the roof of the mouth. All these pressure points ask the horse to lower its head and tuck its chin into its chest. By so doing, the animal is forced to arch its neck and flex at the poll. This reaction is ideal for the loose-reined cutting horse or calf roper required to perform sliding stops and rollbacks while balanced on its haunches and for the highly collected Walking Horse. Such a head carriage, however, would be less than ideal for the English rider about to attempt a jump or for the advanced-level dressage horse required to perform various exercises in collection and extension. These last two horses, therefore, would carry the curb along with a snaffle (the double bridle).

The curb bit comes with either a fixed or a sliding mouthpiece (either the fixed, or stiff-jaw, mouthpiece is bolted to the cheeks or the bit is molded all in one piece, while the sliding, or loose-jaw, mouthpiece can slide vertically when leverage is applied to the cheeks). The shape of the curb mouthpiece varies from the straight-mouth through numerous kinds of ports to a combination high-port and roller (either the Salinas or the Half-Breed bit).

The cheeks, or shanks, of the curb also vary greatly in overall length, from the Western reining bit, averaging approximately 7½ inches long, to the Walking Horse bit, from 8 to as much as 11½ inches long. The cheeks of the curb are either straight (as in the Weymouth, the Walking Horse, and numerous Western curbs) or curved back (as in the popular Grazing bit commonly used on cutting horses) or even curved back farther still to meet under the chin (as in the Roping bit, designed to eliminate the chance of the rope's catching in the bit).

The curb strap attaches to the bit either at the bridle rings or through special curb loops. Curb straps are available in single and double-linked chain (the single is usually thinner and therefore sharper in action, while the double-linked chain lies flat and covers a wider surface); in a leather strap with adjustable buckles (often used on Weymouth bridles); in a combination of leather strap and chain link, with or without a rubber curb guard; in an elastic strap; or in a chain that features an oval metal centerpiece designed to fit in between the jaw bones (called a "Jodhpur," it is rarely seen nowadays).

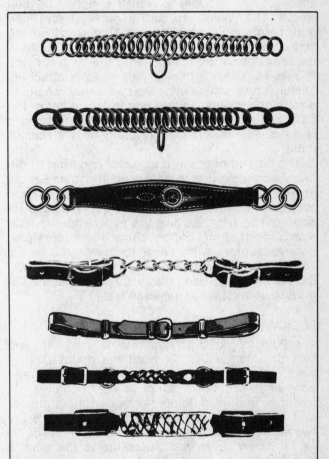

English-style curb chains range in price from about $1.95 for the medium-weight double-link style to about $6.95 for a leather curb with chain ends, and a hand-sewn leather strap will run about $3.70. Western curb chains with latigo straps start at about 70 cents, but can also be had with nickel-silver horseshoe buckle, loop, and tip for $9.75 and upward. A double-link flat chain with ⅝-inch nylon connecting straps is about $3.50. The rawhide-center curb straps are ⅝ inches wide and cost between $2.50 and $4.

BIT AND BRADOON

The double bridle, also known as a Weymouth or bit and bradoon (bridoon), is used exclusively by English-style riders. It consists of a thin snaffle (the bradoon) and a curb bit. Each bit is attached to its own headstall and its own set of reins. The bradoon reins are slightly wider than the curb reins and are normally held on the outside of the pinky fingers, while the curb reins are held between the third and fourth fingers. Both reins then pass over the palm of the hands, where they are layered over the index fingers and held in place by the thumbs.

The bradoon, which can be jointed or mullenmouth, is always finer than the snaffle, and its action is thus sharper. The mouthpiece of the curb (about 5½ inches wide) is often the same as or only slightly shorter than the total length of the cheek. A mild bit known as a Tom Thumb has cheeks which seldom exceed 3½ inches in total length. The Weymouth curb generally has a low-port mouth and straight cheeks. Unlike its Western counterparts, however, it has small loops halfway between the mouthpiece and the end of the cheeks to which a thin leather strap is attached. This lip strap, which attaches to the curb chain by means of a fly link, a small ring in the center of the curb chain, keeps the chain in the curb groove and prevents the bit from reversing in the horse's mouth.

The bit and bradoon is an advanced form of bitting combining the snaffle's ability to raise the horse's head with the curb's capacity to lower it and tuck the nose into the chest. The separate actions of the two bits give the experienced horseman additional means for control and a more precise vocabulary with which to communicate his commands. It is certainly easy to understand why the Weymouth is compulsory for horses shown at third-level and higher dressage tests.

PELHAM

The Pelham, like the Weymouth, is used with two sets of reins; unlike those of the double bridle, however, each set of reins is meant to be activated only when the other is not in use. Pelhams are available in mullen, jointed or ported mouthpieces and in curb cheeks of varying length. There are two sets of cheek rings on the Pelham—the snaffle rings, which apply direct pressure to the horse's lips, bars, and tongue, and the curb rings, which apply their leverage to the curb strap. Some Pelhams, such as the "Show Hack" or "Globe Cheek" bits, are used with only one set of reins and in the cases just mentioned function essentially as mild curb bits. The "Kimblewick" Pelham, a popular and well-designed bit, has a single set of reins that attach to the large D rings which begin a short distance above the mouthpiece and end at the bottom of the horse's cheek. When this bit is properly used, the rider can work the snaffle by keeping his hands slightly higher than normal and then switch to the curb by simply lowering his hands.

Many experienced horsemen are highly critical of the Pelham, claiming that it attempts to do too much and in fact succeeds in doing very little and even that not well. However, the bit is most effective when each set of reins is used separately for horses that go well in a snaffle most of the time but need the action of the curb to remind them to behave.

Bits

Pelham

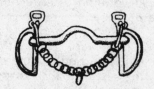

Kimblewicke

jointed snaffle

French egg-butt snaffle

Duncan cheek gag

training snaffle with keys

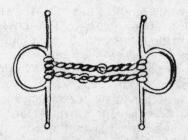

W or double-twisted mouth Fulmer snaffle

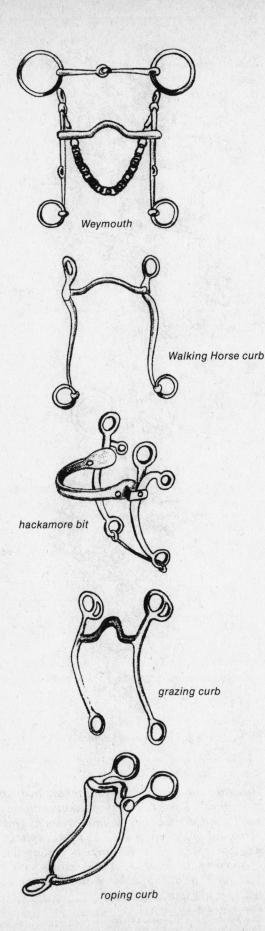

Weymouth

Walking Horse curb

hackamore bit

grazing curb

roping curb

MECHANICAL HACKAMORE

Since it has no mouthpiece, the hackamore, or mechanical bit, is not literally a bit at all. Rather than applying pressure to the horse's lips, bars, or tongue, it instead affects the nose through the pressure of a covered metal noseband and the curb groove by the leverage of the long (usually 8 or 9 inches) free-swinging metal shanks. The curb strap is attached to a short metal shank that curves back from the end of the noseband toward the chin. To complete the hackamore, a metal chin, bar, or leather strap usually joins the two cheek bottoms to prevent the bit from swinging forward and up where it would be ineffective.

Hackamore bits are used for the particularly rough riding often required in rodeo roping, steer-wrestling, and barrel-racing events, and since there is no bit in the horse's mouth, it is impossible to injure that area with quick jerking motions. Hackamores are also an excellent—and sometimes the only—solution for riding an animal with a sore or spoiled mouth.

SPADE

There are many for whom simply the mention of a spade bit causes eyes to narrow and lips to tighten in automatic signs of disapproval. In the hands of anyone but the most skilled equestrian, we must agree. But the spade bit, in highly competent hands and on an animal that has been slowly and painstakingly brought along to accept it, is capable of firmly setting the head and allowing the rider to communicate with only the lightest of touch. There is a wonderful Mexican performer named Antonio Aguilar who travels throughout North America singing and gesturing with gusto while his mount performs *haute école* dressage movements with equal enthusiasm and skill. The horse carries a spade bit, and Señor Aguilar cues for each movement. But watching them work together one feels that the rider needs simply think a cue and the horse, reading his mind, performs.

The spade was brought to this country by Spaniards and was later refined by the California Mission Indians, who were schooled in the art by the Franciscan Fathers. The Mission Indians, highly skilled craftsmen, created many beautifully engraved bits inlaid with silver and gold.

The spade bit comes in several traditional styles, but certain parts are basic to each. The mouthpiece is a straight bar with a port rising from its center. At the top of the port is a flat, shaped piece of metal (the spade), and within the port's arch there is often a "cricket" (a roller). "Keepers," two pieces of wire covered with copper wire or copper rollers, are attached to the bottom of the spade piece and to each cheekpiece. The entire length of the mouthpiece, from the tip of the spade to the bar, is between 3 and 5 inches. The mouthpiece is joined to the cheeks either by hinging (in which case the bit is known as a loose-jaw, or soft, bit), or by welding (a solid-jaw, or hard, bit).

The cheeks of the spade may be plain but are more often intricately carved with beautiful traditional designs. The cheeks of the spade are usually between 6 and 8 inches long and can be straight or curved back. Usually these cheekpieces are joined at the bottom by a solid bar or "slobber chains," which are important to the balance of the bit. The reins attach to weighted chains, normally about 8 inches long, which hang from the end of the cheekpiece, and these too play an important part in balancing the bit.

Spade bits are identified by their cheekpieces, which come in several classic patterns and shapes. Some of the best-known styles include the Santa Barbara, a straight cheek on which can usually be found a pattern of a star or a large concho; the Las Cruces, usually a solid-jaw bit with a large concho on its straight cheeks; the Santa Paula, a loose-jaw bit with a large concho and narrow cheekpieces that sweep back toward the rider; and the Santa Susanna, sometimes called a "layback," which features a "D" shape on top of a concho and a cheek that curves back.

The mouthpiece of the spade is a large and imposing thing, and its action works primarily upon the roof of a horse's mouth. However, when the spade is carried by a wise, well-schooled horse, it rarely touches the top of its mouth at all. Instead, the horse is alert and sensitive to the other pressure points and responds to a warning action from the slightest rein movement. In fact, some spade-trained horses will work only off the cheekpieces.

The spade mouth is weighted and balanced to lie flat on the tongue when the horse holds its head properly. The bit's wide mouthpiece offers a large bearing surface, while the copper rollers—"crickets"—keep the mouth moist and produce a sound most horses find soothing. For the first several months and sometimes years of training, the horse carries the bit without reins. Initial training on a hackamore and then with the spade bit balanced in its mouth teaches a horse to tuck its head and flex at the poll, a position that when maintained prevents the spade from rising to hit the roof of the mouth. While playing with the bit the horse learns to keep the spade flat against its tongue at all gaits. Only when the hackamore control is discarded can the animal be considered a "straight-up spade horse."

The height of a spade mouthpiece has less to do with its effectiveness than the balance of the mouthpiece and the shape and leverage of the cheeks. The most demanding spade is a solid-jaw Santa Barbara cheek with a vertically balanced mouthpiece, which should be used only on a show horse required to perform with an exaggerated tucked head and arched neck. Such a bit is balanced to lie flat against the tongue when the horse holds its head directly perpendicular to the ground. A cutting horse that works with a low head and extended nose will more likely be found in a Santa Susanna or Santa Paula bit with a spade balanced for a more extended head carriage.

loose-jaw

solid-jaw

Two spade bits that balance differently in the horse's mouth

"I regard the spade bit as an archaic instrument that should be seen only in museums along with such similar relics of semibarbarism as chastity belts and brain squeezers. . . . I do maintain that any horseman whose firmness of seat and delicacy of touch enable him to get fair results with a spade bit should be able to achieve excellent results without the spade."

Richard Young,
The Schooling of the Western Horse
University of Oklahoma Press, 1954

A spade bit, despite its torture-chamber reputation, is severe only in ignorant or evil hands (a razor in the hands of a monkey, as the saying goes). The sensitive rider will never tie a spade-bitted horse by the reins, nor will he ever pull back or jerk the reins. When teaching the art of light hands, some spade-bit trainers will replace a portion of the reins with a light, easily breakable twine that will snap as soon as the student pulls back too hard. For above all else, the spade bit requires light, quiet hands and an easy, steady temperament to match.

> Pricing bits is both difficult and confusing. Catalogs carrying less expensive items, like Shepler's, for instance, have a small selection of stainless steel curbs and hackamore bits starting for as little as $4.98, while the "better" catalogs not only have a bigger selection, they have a wider range of prices, with the similar curb starting at $35. Materials and workmanship, of course, differ in price. A soft-rubber mouth with stainless steel cheeks is relatively cheap (about $13.95), a copper mouthpiece with the same steel cheek is more (about $38), and bits made entirely of aluminum lie somewhere in between (about $27.50). Bradoons tend to be cheaper than hunt snaffles (from $5.50 and from $12.95, respectively) and snaffles cheaper than curbs ($14 and up). Most Pelhams (from about $18.95) are similar in range to most hackamore bits with none of the above close to the range of the spade bit (about $70 and up, depending upon engraving and silver or gem inlay).

BRIDLES

The ideal bridle simply reaffirms what early training should have taught: the proper head set for the type of work the horse will be doing. For, so the theory goes, if the head set is correct, then control of the horse's speed and direction comes close behind. If this sounds simple, it isn't. The debates over proper bitting continue to rage.

A bridle is designed to hold a bit in the horse's mouth. Most bridles complement the action of the bit, some supplement it, and some even replace it. All bridles share common parts, even though these parts may vary in form and in name. For example, every bridle has a headpiece, sometimes called a headstall—a piece of leather that lies across the poll. The headpiece frequently includes a throatlatch, an adjustable strap designed to prevent the bridle from slipping. When it is properly fitted, four fingers should be easily inserted between the strap and the horse's throat. Many Western headstalls feature a shaped, split, or sliding earpiece that slips over the offside ear. The shaped earpiece is usually sewn into the headstall; the crown of the split-ear headstall is divided slightly to the right of center for about 12 inches, and the sliding-ear

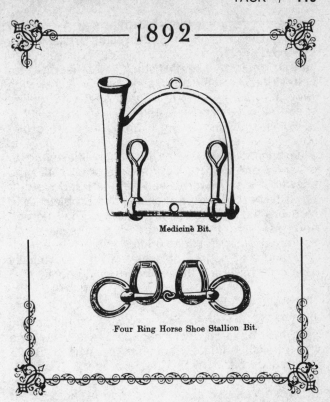

1892

Medicine Bit.

Four Ring Horse Shoe Stallion Bit.

headstall has a separate piece of leather about 6 inches long which, true to its name, forms an adjustable loop. Although some Western bridles come with a fitted earpiece, English bridles are designed instead with a browband, a piece of leather that slips onto the headpiece and wraps across the animal's forehead. Both the fitted-ear and the browband serve the same function: to hold the bridle firmly in place.

Every bridle has a cheekpiece, usually two straps which buckle on to the headpiece at one end while the other end holds the bit in place. The cheekpiece should be adjustable on both sides of the head so that the bit can be set evenly at the proper height in the mouth.

Many bridles, including all English and many modern Western types, carry a caveson, or noseband. The caveson is nothing more than an ornament for most riders, but for those who use a standing martingale or a tie-down, a caveson is an essential part of the bridle. The caveson normally buckles on the near side of the head. Many models are adjustable behind the jaw as well. (Those who are loudly harrumphing to themselves that cavesons are most useful should turn to page 124 for a discussion of the dropped, figure-8, kineton, and other nosebands and bosals—all cavesons of another color and important auxiliaries to the bit.)

If you are looking through tack catalogs, it will be readily apparent that bridles, even when labeled "English" or "Western," differ widely within each classification. And one of the major variations is the strength and weight of the materials. A hunting bridle, for example, will be a sturdy affair with the cheek about ¾ inch wide. A show bridle is usually thinner and lighter in weight than the hunt bridle, and its cheeks will average ⅝ inch or smaller. A racing exercise bridle may be equally strong, while cheeks of actual racing bridles rarely exceed ½ inch in width and will be used with lightweight rubber reins instead of leather ones for better grip. Most Western-style bridles are ⅝ inch wide, and many feature a flared cheek bottom to accommodate a screw fastening.

Unless you are having a bridle made to order, you will have to specify Pony, Cob, or Full-Size. Determining these "sizes" is much like trying to describe one clothes designer's size 8 or 42—the answer lies somewhere between him and his cutter. The best way to anticipate this problem is to measure the distance from lip to lip across the poll and then find the size that most closely corresponds. Remember that bridles should be adjustable and that degree of adjustability is especially important for fitting the young, growing horse.

SINGLE BRIDLE

As already described, this consists of a headpiece with a throatlatch, two cheekpieces, a browband (for English bridles), and often a caveson. Basic differences between the Western and English bridles can be found in the fitted-ear versus the browband and whether a caveson is included or not. Many Arabian show bridles will include a decorative browband, but they omit the caveson which would detract from that breed's beautiful dish nose.

DOUBLE, OR WEYMOUTH, BRIDLE

Designed to hold two separate bits in the horse's mouth, it is occasionally referred to as a bit and bradoon (or bridoon). The bridle has two headpieces that pass through the loops of the browband and attach to two separate sets of cheekpieces. One cheek holds the bradoon while the

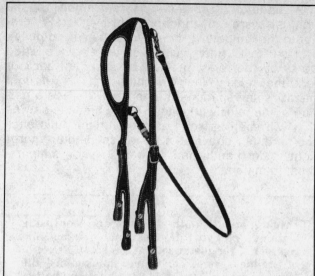

Western "Y," or forked-cheek, bridle. The longer cheek fork attaches to the bit, while the shorter cheek fork holds the tie-down at the correct height. About $20.

other cheek holds the curb (Weymouth), which lies in the mouth directly below the bradoon. The actions of the bradoon and the Weymouth are controlled through separate sets of reins, permitting the rider a large reining vocabulary for communicating with his horse.

GAG BRIDLE

Similar to the basic single bridle, this differs in one small but important way; the cheekpieces are not attached to the bit, as usual, by the bit rings. Instead, the bridle cheeks pass through small holes in the top and bottom of the bit rings (or bit cheeks), ending in a ring that attaches to the reins.

Bridles

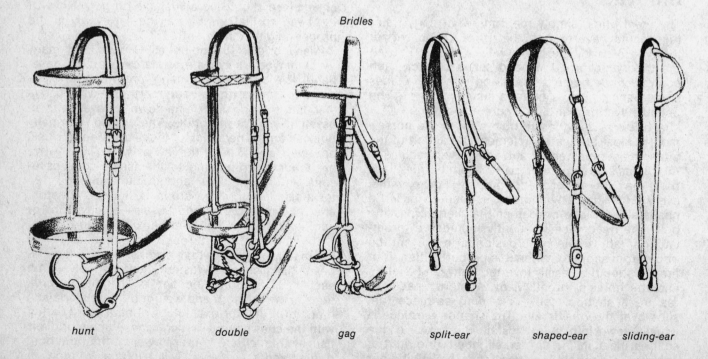

hunt   double   gag   split-ear   shaped-ear   sliding-ear

In other words, the reins and the bridle cheeks form one continuous line, with the bit strung on the bridle leather like beads on a necklace. The bridle cheekpieces are normally made of leather that has been rounded onto a piece of cord or sometimes of braided rope, in either case made thin enough to pass through the small holes in the bit and made strong enough to stand up to the constant friction as the bit slides up and down the leather.

HACKAMORE

The bitless bridle, widely used by Western and occasionally by English trainers, is a useful tool for teaching the young horse proper flexion or simply for obtaining control. In Western-style riding, Texans use a full hackamore before advancing their horses to a curb bit, and Californians use it before, during, and even after putting their horse into a spade bit.

The hackamore—the name is from the Spanish word *jáquima*—applies pressure to the horse's nose, its chin, and sometimes just below its cheeks, to teach the animal to tuck its nose, flex at the poll, and come to a halt balanced on its haunches. The basic hackamore bridle is made up of three essential parts: the bosal (bo-sal'), the fiador (Americanized to theodore), and the mecate (Americanized to McCarty). The starting bosal is a thick, heavy, rounded noseband usually made of braided rawhide and sometimes reinforced with steel. For horses that are particularly difficult to break, a braided-horsehair bosal that has been soaked in water and permitted to stiffen is used. It usually takes only one or two days in such a bosal to bring any mount to attention. If the horse responds to the stout rawhide bosal, the trainer will replace it with a lightening one, progressing to a still lighter version as training continues. All bosals meet behind the horse's jaw in a large ball called a heel butt which is weighted to hang low. A simple leather headstall holds the bosal in place, and a rawhide button on either side holds the headstall in place. (Occasionally a bosal with abrasive rawhide buttons is used. The buttons rub the area below the horse's cheeks raw—an encouragement, some horsemen feel, to take turning cues more quickly.)

The fiador is a rope that passes over the poll and around the jaw, where it is knotted to hold the heel butt. The fiador is essentially a throatlatch keeping the headstall from slipping forward and off a stubborn, head-tossing youngster. The mecate is usually a long (about 24 feet), soft, flexible cotton rope that wraps around the heel butt in a series of precise knots—part of it to loop back to the saddle as reins, the extra length to tie around the horse's neck and available for use as a lead rope. Instead of the soft rope, some horsemen prefer a stiffer mecate made from horsehair.*

* If you come across one of the old, exquisitely made horsehair ropes, you will immediately appreciate the quality of workmanship that went into its creation and understand its coarse, irritating quality when stoutly tied under the horse's jaw.

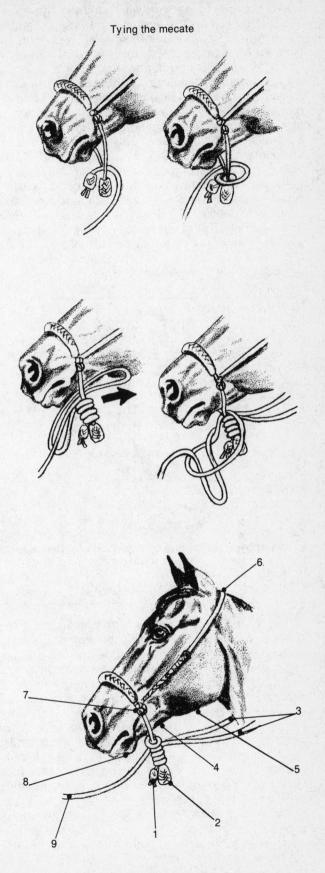

Tying the mecate

1. rope tassel 2. heel butt 3. reins 4. point of pressure 5. cheek 6. headstall 7. button 8. chin 9. lead rope

After the initial stages of hackamore training, the California horseman will introduce the spade bit. Depending on the animal's learning timetable, he eventually adds reins to the bit, replacing the training hackamore with a thinner bosal and eliminating the supporting fiador altogether. California-trained horses thus carry a lightweight bosal as an English-trained horse wears a caveson; it is no ornament, however, but a necessary means by which to tie the horse. (The spade-bitted horse is never, but never, tied by its reins, only by the thin mecate attached to the bosal.) The curb-bitted Texas horse may carry a type of bosal that is actually a tie-down noseband. This thin noseband is often made from rawhide or flexible cabled steel covered with plaited rawhide, plain leather, or vinyl. The noseband attaches to a tie-down, a strap of leather connected to either the breastplate or the girth, and it serves the same function as the standing martingale (see page 125).

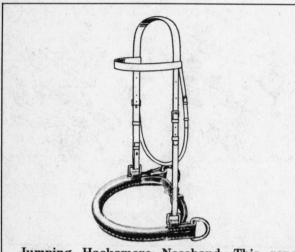

Jumping Hackamore Noseband. This rope noseband is covered with leather and ends in rings for reins. Without bridle, $20 to $22 through Smith-Worthington Saddlery Co.

The English-style bitless bridle works on the same principle as the Western hackamore. It consists of a headpiece, cheekpieces, a wide noseband, a backstrap to hold the noseband in place, and a set of reins which pass through the rings on either side of the noseband to join at a padded curb piece under the chin. Pressure is therefore applied to the curb groove and to the nose. After working a young horse in this bridle for a while, most trainers add a headpiece to which a mild snaffle is attached. For a period the horse does nothing more than carry this bit in its mouth while continuing to take its cues from the reins. Eventually, the trainer attaches a set of reins to the bit and begins to transfer the cues onto the snaffle while simultaneously lessening the use of the bridle reins.

~~~~~~~~~~~~~~~~~~~~~~~~~~~~~~~~~

Reason lies between the spur and the bridle.
George Herbert

~~~~~~~~~~~~~~~~~~~~~~~~~~~~~~~~~

For bridles, as for bits, there is no compact range of prices. Imported bridles from England or Germany are generally made by the quality saddleries, and you pay for their leathers and workmanship (Passier's round snaffle bridle is $90 less reins and bit), but they can be had less expensively and in good quality (about $35 less bit). For Western headstalls you can find cheap shaped-ear styles for as little as $6.25, but slightly better ones average around $15. A touch of silver trim on the headstall may bring the price up only $10 or put you into the $150 range and over. Weymouth bridles, although almost all imported, can range in price from $26.50 to $125. Although all prices quoted above are for bridles without bits, when the subject is gag bridles it is customary to include the bit (if only because it is so difficult to exclude). A decent leather gag bridle/stainless steel bit combination runs about $45 (headstall alone about $29.95); a nylon gag with bit is about $31.50 (headstall alone is $14.95). For training, a hackamore headstall alone can be found for around $9; a six-plait rawhide bosal and nylon fiador will cost about $21; while a preassembled hackamore with a stout starting bosal and a horsehair mecate will be about $50. The hackamore pieces can also be bought separately, with braided-rawhide bosals starting about $10 and soft cotton mecates about $14.

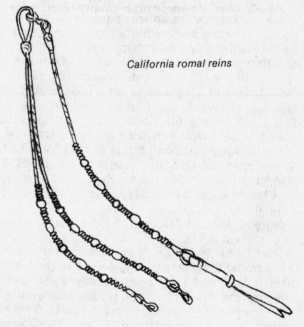

California romal reins

REINS

Reins are essentially strips of material connecting our hands to the bit. They come in leather (either plain, plaited, rolled, or laced), rubber, web, nylon, cotton, or rope. In the plaited rein the leather is split into several strips of equal length and then braided. In the laced rein a piece of thin rawhide is "sewn" through the rein in such a way that it forms a V shape down the length. Rolled reins, usually 1½ to 2 feet of rein on either side of the bit, involve leather rolled around a piece of cord and sewn closed with the remainder of the rein left flat. All of these reins give excellent grip and are commonly used on English-style bridles. The normal English rein is approximately 5 feet long and generally ½, ⅝, ¾, or 1 inch wide. Show-jumping reins may be shorter and pony reins may be shorter still, down to 4¼ feet. Each of these reins is open-style, joined at the ends by a buckle. It is customary when using a double bridle to use snaffle reins that are about ⅛ inch wider than the curb reins for easy tactile differentiation.

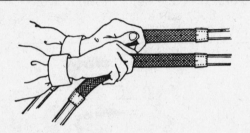

Rubber-Covered Reins. Used for hunting or jumping, these ⅝-inch reins are made of leather and covered with pimpled hand parts for sure grip. About $21.

Reins are normally sold with the bridle, and they are a great deal less expensive if bought as part of the "package." Again the English imports lead the field as the most expensive all-leather item. Passier's high-quality laced reins are about $52.50; Crosby's "Raised" plain reins are about $24.50; "School"-quality laced reins about $7.50; Borelli Web Reins about $21.50; and Plaited Linen reins about $25. Western reins, when dotted, or studded with silver, may cost over $100, but a set of roping reins can be had for as little as $7.50. Split reins tend to cost only slightly more (from $9.50), but for four-plait, hand-braided split reins better think in terms of $30 and up. California romal reins with a 4-inch popper, although you may find them cheaper, should start in the $30 price range, and for hand workmanship and/or special decorations, they can go much, much higher.

Western-style reins are split into Texas and California schools, with further variations within each style. The Texan may use an open-ended rein, between 6 and 7 feet long, or a roping rein made from one uncut piece of leather, normally between 6 and 8 feet long from end to end. A distinctive feature of the roping rein is that one or both ends are nearly always attached to the bit by swivel snaps, good for quick release when needed. Texas-style reins are single-ply, plaited, braided, or double-stitched. Weighted leather (around 1 pound more or less) open-end reins are available for training the neck-reining horse.

California reins are closed (about 8 feet long from bit end to bit end) with a romal, a 4-foot piece of leather that attaches to a ring centered in the closed reins. The romal may include a popper, which is used much like a bat or noisy crop. It is not uncommon for California-style reins to have buttons, barrels, or knots, convenient for gripping and weighted for better spade-bit balance. The reins are ⅜ or ½ inch wide, with the corresponding romals ½ and ⅝ inch.

HOLDING IT ALL TOGETHER

Fastenings, the method by which the bit is attached to the bridle and to the reins, are available in a wide range of possibilities. Sewing is a traditional, neat, strong, and non-bulky means of attaching a bit to the bridle. However, opening the stitching and resewing the leather each time the bit needs changing is inconvenient, and it is also almost impossible to clean the bit thoroughly. The stud fastening is simply a small stud or hook that slips through a slit in the leather, with the downward pull of the bit holding it tightly in place.

The basic buckle, the first fastening that might come to mind, is, in fact, rarely used directly on the bit. Buckle tongues have a tendency to corrode, bend, and eventually break; a buckle can get caught up where it shouldn't, and it usually does. A rounded buckle known as a "fiddle buckle" is less likely than its square counterpart to catch in unwanted areas, but that too is seldom used at the bit. There is a "Conway" buckle which has become popular on Western-style bridles for many good reasons: it is strong, safe, and easy to open and clean. The Conway is a curved buckle with a stationary tongue that can protrude through the holes in a piece of leather that is folded back upon itself to form a loop. The Chicago screw, which was popular for a while and then unfashionable, has regained popularity in recent years. If tightened carefully with a screwdriver, the pre-threaded screw will not loosen, and it is far less bulky than most of the previously discussed fastenings. Another common Western fastening for the bit or the tie-down is a self-locking swivel snap. Sometimes called a scissors snap (because of the action required to open it), it is strong, safe, and extremely easy to open in an emergency. Western catalogs also feature bridles with bit ends "to tie," which means that a piece of rawhide is pulled through punched holes and then tied on the outside. Although it may look authentic, and knowing how to make such a fastening in case of an emergency is useful, it has a tendency to work loose, and it is bulkier than many of the other fastenings.

Rein Snap. For roping reins, nickel-plated, self-locking, swivel trigger snap. Available in ⅜-inch, ½-inch, ⅝-inch, ¾-inch, and 1-inch eyes for rein sizes. About 95 cents.

SUPPLEMENTS TO THE BIT

A mount, as any horseman will have noticed, does not always perform to cue. The horse occasionally needs to be reminded to balance itself properly, to stay under control, and to stop such tricks as evading the bit or throwing its head. Such maneuvers are at least frightening and usually dangerous, and danger is not what horsemanship should be all about.

Before any horseman turns to additional means for controlling any of the reactions described, he must investigate the cause; more often than not the problem can be found in the bit already in use which is applying pressure the animal finds intolerable. A milder bit will often correct the problem. For those horses that go well in a particular bit most of the time but are also occasionally headstrong, something more may be necessary to maintain control consistently. Most such "extras" do not interfere with the horse when it performs well but will quickly and often forcibly come into play when the horse acts up. As with all tack, most of the adjutants to the bit are designed for a particular purpose and must be used with understanding; an incorrectly adjusted standing martingale, for instance, can be fitted so tightly that it interferes with the horse's ability to balance itself, causing it to move improperly and even to endanger the rider.

Nosebands

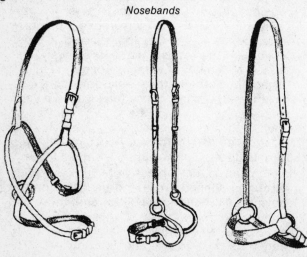

figure-8   *Kineton*   *dropped*

NOSEBANDS

One of the most commonly used adjutants to the bit is the dropped noseband, a caveson made to fit 2½ to 3 inches above the nostrils. The dropped noseband will keep the horse from opening its mouth in an attempt to evade the bit. It is also used to influence the action of a snaffle bit by applying pressure on the nose and thus causing the horse to lower its head. With the lower head carriage, the snaffle exerts a downward and inward pressure on the bars of the mouth, rather than the normal upward pressure to the lips. The combination of the snaffle and the dropped noseband can, therefore, produce some flexion of the lower jaw and the poll, something a snaffle alone cannot achieve.

Hinged Dropped Noseband. Buckles to regular caveson but does not eliminate use of standing martingale. About $5.95.

Dropped nosebands go up to $18.50, $24.50, and $29.50 for Olympic-style imports. Figure-8 nosebands start at $7.95 to about $17.50. Kineton-style nosebands are listed at $24.50. Cost-conscious English riders might do well to check out the "Western" sections of their catalogs (or write away for such catalogs), since decent-quality American-made products are almost always cheaper than the imports. For Western riders a cable noseband can be had for $2.50, a steel roping noseband for $9.95, and a leather one for $8.95; and a noseband of rawhide braided over flexible steel cable goes for about $18.75.

The bosal, the braided-rawhide noseband used in a hackamore bridle, when adjusted tightly also works like a dropped noseband and keeps the horse's mouth shut.

There is a figure-8 noseband which indeed crosses in the center like the number used to describe it. The straps intersect at the nose, with the top part of the 8 buckling beneath the rear of the bit and the bottom part buckling above the rear of the bit. More demanding and forceful than the dropped noseband, the figure-8 may be more effective against chronic bit evaders.

The kineton is also known as an "antipulling" noseband, and its action is fairly strong since it puts pressure on the nose via the bit. A piece of leather-covered reinforced metal fits into the center of the nosepiece which is attached to two slanting U-shaped loops. The U sidepiece fits inside the rings of the bit and around the mouthpiece. The consequence of pressure on the bit forces the noseband down, occasioning the horse

Martingales

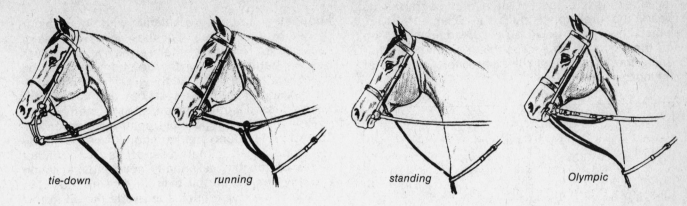

tie-down   running   standing   Olympic

to lower its head in reaction. Like most tack, the kineton is useful in the right hands, painful to the horse otherwise.

MARTINGALES AND TIE-DOWNS

Fixing a horse's head at a particular height prevents the animal from throwing its head in an attempt to evade the bit. Such restraint is also important for the rider who does not welcome the possibility of a broken nose as the horse suddenly tosses its head. For these reasons, a martingale or tie-down is a frequently necessary auxiliary to the bit. Several kinds are available, each having a slightly different emphasis.

English riders may use a standing martingale, basically a strap that fits around the horse's neck with a second strap crossing the first at chest center. This chest strap loops around the girth strap under the belly and attaches to the back of the caveson at the other end. Buckles permit proper adjustment. The Western-style tie-down is a strap that hooks onto the rear of a thin rawhide or cable bosal at one end and whose other end snaps or hooks either onto the center ring on a breastplate or directly onto the cinch. When properly fitted, both the martingale and the tie-down restrain the horse from tossing its head or "stargazing."

Many Western as well as English horsemen prefer the running martingale for its greater versatility. It is similar to the standing type except that the upper chest strap forks for approximately 12 inches, ending in rings that slip onto each rein. These rings are held from slipping forward and into the horse's mouth by "rein stops"—pieces of leather or rubber which fit onto the reins about 10 inches above the bit. If set tightly, this martingale will also increase the leverage of the bit's action on the bars of the horse's mouth. The difference between the standing and running martingales is that as the animal attempts to raise its head, the standing martingale applies pressure to the horse's nose, while the running martingale applies a restraining pressure to the horse's mouth.

A bib martingale, as its name applies, is made from a triangular piece of leather sewn between the two forked chest straps and is occasionally needed to prevent high-strung horses from getting their feet caught in the tack; bibs are frequently worn by Thoroughbred racehorses during their morning workouts.

A Market Harborough, also known as an Olympic Martingale Rein Set, works on a principle similar to that of draw reins (reins attached to the girth which pass up and through the bit rings and into the rider's hands) but has replaced draw reins in popularity. A strip of rounded leather snaps onto each running-martingale ring, passes through the bit rings, and attaches to the rein about 10 inches beyond the bit. Its action is simple. If the horse carries its head properly, then the round straps are slack and inactive. When the horse throws its head, then the straps become taut, exerting a downward pull on the bit rings and producing pressure on the horse's lips, bars, tongue, and even poll.

Several types of martingales designed to teach the horse to lower its head carriage work their influence on the top of the horse's head or even combine poll pressure with nose pressure for added emphasis. Western catalogs offer a "training headstall" used primarily on cutting horses, who must carry their heads low. The headstall presses against the sensitive nerve endings around the ears, encouraging the horse to put its head down. To produce the same reaction, English-style trainers use Continental or Chambon martingales. In the Continental, one end of a strap attaches to the noseband in the normal way; the other end passes down through a single ring at the center of the breastplate and then up to another strap that crosses the poll to buckle firmly at the throatlatch. Simultaneous pressure on the nose and poll will provide a strong inducement to quickly lower the head. The Chambon martingale, on the other hand, applies concurrent pressure to the poll and to the lips. The ends of a strap attached at its center to a breastplate run up along both sides of the head to the poll, through the rings on either end of the pollpiece (a small strap which sits directly behind the ears), and then down to hook onto the bit rings. Therefore, a pulley effect is created; when the horse raises its head, the breastplate pulls the Chambon strap, which then pulls down on the headpiece and up on the bit rings. To escape this martingale's influence, the horse usually learns to hold its head at the correct level.

Training Headstall. Made from two thin vinyl-covered wire cables, approximately ³⁄₁₆ inch in diameter, held together by adjustable Tiller clamps. The cables form a bonnet which fits along the front and back of the horse's ears, and the ends come together behind the jaw to attach to a tie-down strap. About $2.75.

We should mention a sidecheck here, although it is not actually an auxiliary to the bit. Rather, it is a support for weak hands, most often found on the bridles of ponies. The singular purpose of the sidecheck is to prevent the horse from lowering its head to chomp grass. Called an "Antigrazing Sidecheck," it is simply a strap that attaches to the pommel and to the top of the cheekpiece on the bridle.

We did not list the Irish martingale directly under the other martingales because it does not affect the horse's head carriage, as the others do. Basically, it is a short strap with loops at either end that slip onto the reins to keep them from flopping apart and may add enough weight to keep the bit properly balanced in the mouth.

~~~~~~~~~~~~~~~~~~~~~~~~~~~~~~~~~

"As soon as the little fellow can be handled calmly, a light halter can be slipped on. Most colts are so constructed that when their heads are raised, the crownpiece of the halter slips back on the neck so far that when the head is put down to the ground the nosepiece and the crownpiece pull uncomfortably. To avoid this, a brow band must be added to the halter. I usually use a double strip of muslin."
Louis Taylor
Ride Western
Wilshire Book Co., 1968, 1973 ed.

~~~~~~~~~~~~~~~~~~~~~~~~~~~~~~~~~

MISCELLANEOUS SUPPLEMENTS

Fortunately, horses are animals with some minor degree of intelligence. But they do have a major capacity for asserting themselves (which leaves one wondering whether the first horse wrote it all down in what can only be the greatest horse-training manual of all time, even now being surreptitiously passed along from one stall to another).

Probably the single most common evasion occurs when the horse get its tongue over the bit. By so doing, the animal disengages the contact points of the bit, essentially nullifying its action and any control the bit may have given the rider. As soon as a horse begins to evade the bit in this way, the trainer must first determine the cause. There are three reasons: the bit is too large and hangs too low in the horse's mouth; the bit pinches or is in some way uncomfortable to the tongue; and the horse is experiencing discomfort because of sores or tooth problems. Once you discover the cause of the problem, the cure may be easy. But there are horses for which this evasion has become a routine part of their repertoire. There may be no easy solution for these chronic evaders, and perhaps the trainer must use an alternative such as a bitless bridle. For other than the confirmed offender, there are several devices that have been found to work more often than not.

If the problem stems from a bit too large and too low-hanging, then replacement of this bit is required. The trainer may also want to add a rubber tongue port to his existing bit or turn to a "Nagbut" snaffle. The rubber tongue port is designed to slip over the mouthpiece of any bit and lie flat on the horse's tongue, facing toward the rear; the arms of the "Nagbut" snaffle are jointed onto a center tongue port which acts the same as the rubber tongue port. Both effectively present the horse with too large an object to lift its tongue over.

A stout leather standing martingale normally used by polo players runs about $24.50, but hunt-weight standing martingales start at $11.50, going to $13.50, to $49.50, and to $55.00 for elastic imports. Running martingales in leather start about $14.95 (nylon ones for $6.50) and a German round one is $69.95. A hunt breastplate with a choice of running or standing martingale starts at $16.50 and goes to about $37.50 for the English import. We found only two prices for the Olympic Rein Set, a nylon one for $22.95 and a leather import for $59.00. A nylon Chambon will set you back about $19.95 and a leather one about $39.95. Martingale attachments cost: for running, about $4.95 to $8.95; for standing, about $3.95 to $6.50; for rubbers, 50 cents. A bib fork is about $14.95; an Irish martingale about $3.50; and an Antigrazing Sidecheek from $14.95 for nylon to $19.50 for leather. A Western tie-down that is ¾ inch wide and 5 feet long will range in price from $4.50 to $9.95.

A bit that hangs too low needs a rubber bit holder, particularly effective for horses that hang or lug. It prevents the horse from getting its tongue over the bit. About $6.95.

Racehorses that habitually get their tongue over the bit are often put into an "Australian cheeker," or as one catalog calls it, a "Sure-Win" bit holder worn by Seattle Slew when he won the Triple Crown. It is basically a flat leather or rubber strap that comes down from the crown of the bridle between the horse's eyes to fork above the nose into two doughnut-shaped pieces that attach to the mouth of the bit. Some racing trainers also make use of a device known as a tongue tie. A seemingly barbaric implement, it serves the double function of keeping the horse from getting its tongue over the bit and from swallowing its tongue, a not uncommon occurrence during a race. Although a tongue tie is certainly effective, it was designed for usage over short periods of time (such as during a race) and is not recommended for other types of riding.

~~~~~~~~~~~~~~~~~~~~~~~~~~~~~

About Bits
direct from the horse's mouth

"Those who have never had a bit in their mouths cannot think how bad it feels; a great piece of cold hard steel as thick as a man's finger to be pushed into one's mouth, between one's teeth, and over one's tongue, with the ends coming out at the corner of your mouth, and held fast there by straps over your head, under your throat, round your nose, and under your chin; so that in no way in the world can you get rid of the nasty hard thing; it is very bad!"
Anna Sewell
Black Beauty
~~~~~~~~~~~~~~~~~~~~~~~~~~~~~

For horses that evade the bit because it pinches the lips, there is a rubber bit guard—simply a doughnut-shaped piece of rubber or soft leather that fits around the mouthpiece.

Another problem not uncommon to racehorses and occasionally to jumpers is a tendency to pull to one side. The problem does not normally stem from the bit, but several bitting aids are available to help deal with this fault. There is a "brush picker" or "bit burr," a bristled piece of leather or rubber which attaches to the mouthpiece on the side to which the horse swings out. Because the problem is expensive for racehorses to have, there is also a whole line of racing bits designed to cope

with it. Few of them are, however, of value to other than racehorse trainers. Sometimes something as simple as blinders—half-moon-shaped covers for horses' eyes—effectively correct the horse that lugs in or bears out by directing its attention straight ahead and eliminating many distracting sights.

Bit burr—about $2.95.
Rubber bit port—about $2.50.
Rubber bit guards—about $1.

SADDLES

The purpose of a saddle is to protect the horse's back and to aid the rider in maintaining a balanced seat, permitting him to shift his weight as needed. Most saddles allow the rider to remain in balance over the horse's center of gravity. Since the center of gravity varies according to the type of horse, the work it does, its gait, and its way of going, a large variety of saddles have been developed over the centuries.

The foundation of every saddle is the tree, usually made of beechwood for lightness, with metal (often steel) for reinforcement. Many trees today are made entirely of fiber glass or laminated Ply-Bond. The tree must be strong enough to withstand pressure, high enough to clear the horse's withers and backbone, and wide enough to rest on the muscle pads on either side of the backbone. The tree is often padded, usually with foam rubber, and then covered with leather. The kinds and quality of leather vary according to the type of saddle and the parts of which it is constructed. (For example, a soft, stretchable leather would be useless for billet or stirrup straps.) The quality of the leather is one of the major factors affecting the price of a saddle; other factors are the quality of materials used in making the tree and the overall workmanship in putting it all together. After that, the price varies with brand names and extra details.

SADDLE LEATHER

Most saddles produced in England and in most parts of Europe are made from top-quality cowhide, with pigskin often used for saddle seats and occasionally for flaps as well. Western saddles are normally made of bullhide- or rawhide-covered trees which are then covered with cowhide, either smooth-finished (later stamped or hand-tooled) or rough-out, with suede commonly used on the seat.

The leather in English- and European-made saddles (and many of the English-style saddles sold in the United States are either imported from those areas or made there for American companies) is normally tanned by one of two methods: bark tanning, which is preferable because it takes oiling and absorbs grease easily, and chrome tanning, a fairly recent process using chemicals, which does not have quite the grease-absorbing capability of the bark-tanning process. Chrome tanning is recognizable by a gray-cream or greenish color, and sometimes a light tan to brown dye is applied to make it appear bark-tanned. Rawhide is nothing more than cowhide that has been tanned by a vegetable process. It is recognizable along the edge by a light-colored untanned center layer.

In piecing a saddle together, leather is culled from different parts of the animal hide; for instance, the butt (the section from the shoulder to the tail) is the most durable and least stretchable section and therefore preferred by saddlemakers. Stirrup leather especially should come from this section of the hide and not from more stretchable areas such as the belly. Before buying a stirrup leather, test the stretch by pulling it as hard as possible. If it gives more than a quarter of an inch, shop further. The shoulder section of the hide, while strong, tends to also be wrinkled and therefore visually less appealing. Shank or leg leather should be avoided, since it is hard and will crack easily.

Leather, like the meat we eat, is graded. And as you would prefer prime-cut steaks on the table, grade A leather is most desirable in your saddle. Obviously, though, such steak and leather are available only at a price. Grade A and B leathers most often come from the United States, England, and Germany, and saddles manufactured in those countries are normally made from these quality leathers, but not necessarily. And since there are no regulations requiring the leather be graded for the consumer, no guarantees are available. Most leather that comes from South America would be graded C. It is usually a harder leather than German leather, for example, and is susceptible to grub holes, but it is a tough, long-wearing leather and perfectly fine for most weekend riders. Moving east and down on the grading scale, leather from Japan is less satisfactory, because it has poor tensile strength, meaning it rips and stretches easily. Not many saddles from Japan are sold in this country yet. However, you will find saddles from India on sale here, and few experts give them a passing grade. The weakness is not necessarily inherent in the leather as such but in the tanning process used; Indian saddle leather is tanned in clay vats, and as anyone who has worked with clay knows, the substance has a severe drying effect. Leather tanned this way will not absorb grease even when it is heavily applied, so that besides failing to "wear-in" and become soft and supple, such saddles will begin to crack and break within a short time.

ENGLISH SADDLES

"English saddle" has become a broad term of reference for a number of highly specialized saddles, each of which is as distinctive as the style it is meant to complement: jumping, show ring, racing, dressage, polo, or hacking. Despite its name, the "English saddle" has been used by the Italians, the Germans, the French, the Poles, and the Russians for over a century. The forward-seat saddle, the most popular type in use today, was developed in the late 1800's by Captain Federico Caprilli, an Italian born in 1868 who, to much ridicule and controversy, abolished the classical seat then in fashion. After continued success with his new technique, the "Caprilli system" was adopted by the Italian cavalry in the early 1900's. Soon after-

Parts of the English saddle

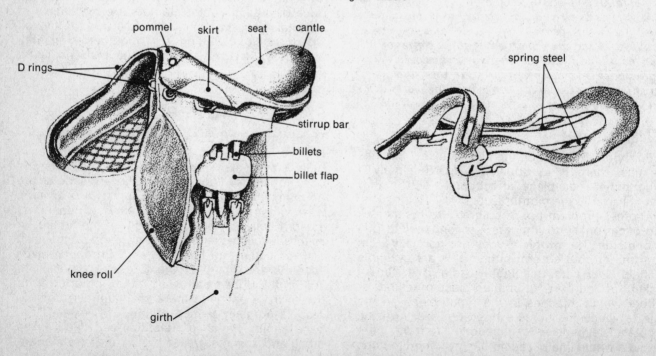

pommel skirt seat cantle

D rings

spring steel

stirrup bar

billets

billet flap

knee roll

girth

ward, English saddlemakers were making forward-seat saddles for home use and export, followed only slightly later by the Germans, who began making a heavier, more stoutly padded version. The forward-seat saddle was such a remarkable success that it is now what most horsemen think of as the standard "English" saddle. Our contemporary "all-purpose" saddle is based on the forward-seat design and should not be confused with older, straight-flapped "general-purpose" saddles.

PARTS OF THE ENGLISH SADDLE

If the tree is of poor construction, then the saddle is worthless, no matter how rich the leather or how fine the fittings. At one time all English-saddle trees were made of solid wood, but now laminated plywood and fiber glass seem to have become equally popular. What these materials have to offer makes infinite good sense—they are lightweight and they will not warp.

There are two basic types of tree construction: the rigid tree and the spring tree. Both are usually reinforced with steel arches over the head and around the cantle. In the spring tree, two strips of steel extend from the head to the rear of the tree directly under the seat where they function as springs (hence the name), and the stirrup bars are inset into the tree just below the head. Since the head of the forward-seat tree is set at a 45-degree angle to the horse's back, the stirrup bars are farther forward than those on the straighter tree. The rigid tree is normally constructed either with a straight head for normal use or with a cut-back head for use in saddle-seat saddles and for wideback mounts such as Arabians and Morgans.

Whether spring or rigid type, the tree is next fitted with webbing and padded with such materials as felt, foam rubber, wool, or leather, and that padding is then covered with a saddle leather. (Pigskin, a soft, beautiful, but not particularly strong leather, is often used to cover seats. However, it should not be used on other parts of the saddle if it is expected to be long-wearing.)

All saddles of any value will have well-padded panels under the tree. These panels act as cushions for the horse's back and are divided by a channel above the backbone, ensuring that the weight of the saddle will rest on the muscle pads on either side of the spine. Usually covered in leather, either plain or quilted, the panels are padded with felt, foam rubber, hair, or wool, and if they are well constructed a saddle pad is often necessary. Panels can be found in different styles, from a full one which provides padding under the seat and the flaps of the saddle to a short one which pads only the seat. Most forward-seat and all-purpose saddles feature narrow-waisted panels that extend forward to support the knee and include padding in the rear to hold the girth securely.

FORWARD-SEAT SADDLE

This was designed to eliminate interference with

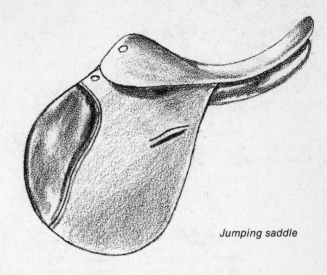

Jumping saddle

Racing saddle

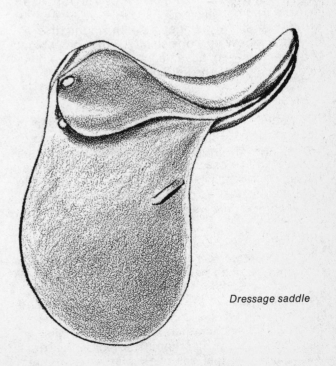

Dressage saddle

the horse and give the rider added security in jumping. Adaptable for both the two-point seat (rider's weight on legs and heels) and the three-point seat (rider's weight on legs, heels, and seat), it allows the horseman to lean forward in relation to the horse's speed and gait. The spring tree contributes to the rider's driving seat, and because of the 45-degree angle of the head, the stirrup bars are automatically farther forward. The panel or flap has a padded knee roll to support the thigh and brace the rider as he comes off a jump. The seat dips, supporting the rider in a centered position, and the narrow waist allows the rider a closer grip without stretching his thighs uncomfortably wide. Ideal for jumping, this saddle may be less comfortable on long trail rides.

JOCKEY SADDLE, OR RACING SADDLE

This is a radical extension of the Forward Seat saddle. It was first developed in America for racing and then adopted in England during the late nineteenth century. British riders traditionally sat way back on the horse's loins, as one can see in old English racing prints. The "new" American style was picked up by the conservative English only after American jockeys, riding far forward with shortened stirrups and hands only inches from the horse's mouth, won so consistently that their innovative technique could no longer be ignored. Racing saddles are light in weight, averaging 1½ pounds without stirrups. Their seat is relatively unimportant in racing, since the jockey makes almost no use of it, and the stirrups hang far forward so that the jockey is actually doubled over onto his calves when the horse is walking, balancing atop the animal's neck when galloping, and standing up in the stirrups during a canter or trot. American jockeys traditionally ride "acey-deucy" with the left stirrup slightly longer than the right; this allows the jockey to consistently throw his weight into the turn—an advantage since all American racetracks turn to the left only.

EXERCISE SADDLE

For training young horses for racing, it is used in place of the racing saddle, which can, because of minimal padding, hurt the animal's back when used daily. The exercise saddle is a slightly larger and somewhat heavier version of the racing saddle and includes stuffed panels for better cushioning. Usually this saddle weighs upward of 5 pounds.

SADDLE-SEAT SADDLE

This is designed to show off the animated action and highly arched head carriage of the Three- or Five-Gaited Saddle Horse and the Tennessee Walker. Because of the way in which the head and neck are carried, the center of gravity of a gaited horse is farther back than in either the English or the Western way of going. Therefore, the rider uses a flat seat that will allow his weight to shift back toward the cantle. This saddle features a cut-back pommel and straight flaps. Long stirrups permit the rider's heels to drop almost directly below his center of gravity. The saddle is placed 2 or 3 inches to the rear of the all-purpose saddle, and it is normally designed with a short, lightly padded panel.

DRESSAGE SADDLE

This could be described as a felicitous cross between the jumping saddle and the saddle-seat saddle. Surprisingly, the dressage saddle as we know it today is a relatively new discovery. Before World War Two, all dressage riders used a straight-seat show saddle; after the war a new saddle came into use that was better adapted to this specialized type of riding. Since the dressage horse is trained to collect and move effortlessly off its haunches with its center of balance more to the rear than that of, say, the jumper, the modern dressage saddle needed to have a deeper, shorter seat than the show saddle which would allow the rider to sit with his seat bones well under him. While it has straighter flaps than the jumping saddle it does include the useful knee roll commonly associated with that saddle. The stirrup bars are centered directly under the rider's thighs to help him maintain a straight leg and longer stirrups. All these features enable the rider to keep his weight to the rear, brace his back, and use leg pressure either ahead of or behind the girth to activate the horse's hindquarters.

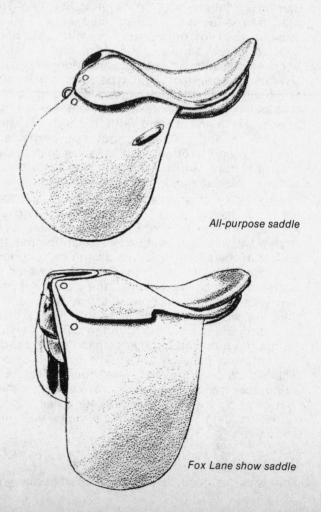

All-purpose saddle

Fox Lane show saddle

ALL-PURPOSE AND POLO SADDLE

This is designed to encourage a modified forward seat and allow the rider to rest in the middle of the saddle, supported chiefly by the seat bones. It features a deeper seat and straighter flaps than the forward-seat saddle, and it may have padded knee rolls for additional support. While the forward-seat saddle is intended primarily for jumping, this saddle is more versatile—ideal for trail riding, excellent for use in elementary jumping and dressage work, and especially adaptable to the rigorous demands of polo.

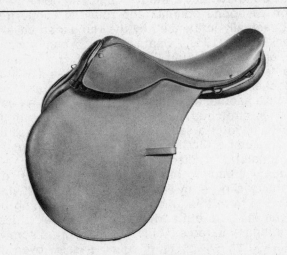

Smith-Worthington Custom Forward Seat Saddle. This is one of the very few English saddles made here. The tree, of hand-forged steel and birch, is guaranteed for the life of the original owner. The seat is pigskin (imported from England), and the panel leather is first chrome-tanned and then glove-tanned, a combination that makes the panels sweat-resistant, strong, soft, and less prone to drying. The all-wool stuffed panels have a high tallow content that wards off moisture. Smith-Worthington will make the saddle in either a forward-seat or hunt-seat style with adjustable length of center for somewhere between $698 and $780; it can be ordered through local tack shops.

If you are out to buy an English saddle, you can spend either $100 or $1,000. Obviously, most of the prices lie somewhere in between. Imports from England, Germany, and Italy run high, and some, such as Pariani, Stubben, Crosby, Kieffer, Hartley, and others, have a variety of saddles within each style. For example, among the Stubben Forward Seat Saddles are three models, the Siegfried, the Parsival, and the Imperator, priced at $350, $475, and $525, respectively. If such quotes do not provide an average, there is at least some sort of mean price for an import, which is actually around $325. Argentine saddles are generally direct copies of the British and European styles, but are priced more felicitously, from around $140 to as much as $350, with the average price around $185. Fox Lane Show Saddles also run the same gamut as the jumping saddles, about $172 for Argentine-made and $375 for a Crosby & Co. model.

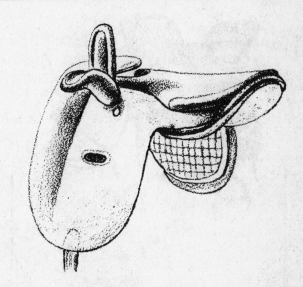

SIDESADDLE

The sidesaddle, although it seems an oddity today, was popular in the East and later in the West for a longer period than is generally recognized. Brought to our country from England, it was still being used as late as the 1920's, when proper women did not fork a horse. Reported to have been made popular by Queen Elizabeth I, who, it was said, wanted to hide her deformed legs, the sidesaddle is still most useful for physically handicapped people who cannot sit astride.

Sidesaddles evolved through the centuries from a pad that included a platform on which to rest the left foot to a two- and later three-horned saddle with a single stirrup. (The third horn is also called a "knee rest," depending upon its height.) Most of the sidesaddles available today are antiques, many of them imported from England. The English sidesaddle has three girths: a regulation wide web girth, a thin leather girth which goes over the first one, and a balance strap that runs around the girth and attaches to the rear off side of the seat. It is a small, dainty saddle, and the seat of those made before the 1800's is frequently covered in velvet or fabric.

In the 1890's, Colonel Charles Goodnight of Texas designed a sidesaddle for his wife which became the standard for the Western sidesaddle. It was longer, wider, and heavier than its English counterpart, and the balance strap was replaced with a rear cinch. The Goodnight saddle had two leg horns (one a knee rest) and a padded leaping horn. The Goodnight design also included a carpetbag strap and heavily tooled leather skirts.

The proper way to sit a sidesaddle is facing straight forward, so balanced that the impression is given that the rider has only one leg. A whip carried on the right side is necessary to replace the cueing function of the leg.

Double Seat Chair Saddle.

"Side-Saddle News" is the official publication of The International Side-Saddle Organization and the only publication of its kind in the United States. The monthly 16-page magazine is edited and published by Charlotte Brailey Kneeland, a woman who has done more than anyone else to reestablish the sidesaddle in this country. She is also the single largest source of imported antique sidesaddles and an authority on restuffing and restoring such antiques. Ms. Kneeland also runs sidesaddle clinics, usually Saturday-afternoon affairs costing about $25. For information about anything having to do with the sidesaddle or to become a member of The International Side-Saddle Organization ($15 annually) and receive a copy of "Side-Saddle News," write Ms. Charlotte Brailey Kneeland, R.D. 2, Box 2096, Mount Holly, New Jersey 08060.

Kauffman's imports a sidesaddle "comparable in detail and quality to the finest of the classic Mayhew, Martin and Martin, and Champion and Wiltons of old." Available in limited quantities and sold complete with fittings, it is available in small, medium, and large ladies' sizes. Prices quoted on request.

MILITARY SADDLE

The American military saddle, or McClellan saddle, that we know today, the two long bars joined by a high wishbone pommel and rounded cantle tree, was actually influenced by the Hungarian cavalry. Back in the 1850's Captain (later a commanding general of the Union Army) George B. McClellan was serving a tour of duty in Europe as a military attaché. There he observed the Hungarians' distinctive saddle, a hammocklike affair with a heavy leather stretched between the pommel and the cantle to form a seat above an open slit over the horse's spine. McClellan, a horseman of an inquisitive nature, studied the Hungarian design and brought it back to the States, where he married it to the existing Army Ringgold tree. The saddle that resulted from this union retained the opening between the bars but added a high pommel, a deep seat, and squared skirts fastened by brass screws. Heavy girth straps (surcingles) passed over the pommel and cantle and joined on each side in a ring much like our present-day stock saddle's "on-the-tree rigging." However, unlike our stock saddle, the McClellan was a single-cinch, center-fire-rigged saddle.

By today's standards, the McClellan was anything but comfortable; the hard wood tree was simply covered with wet rawhide, which shrank to an iron-hard finish. The rawhide, a seemingly indestructible substance, eventually would crack and erupt into hard, knifelike edges, making the long hours in the saddle often more intolerable than the battles into which it was ridden. After the Civil War, a smooth black leather enveloped the rawhide-girdled tree.

The McClellan stirrup leathers included a separate sweat leather, or fender, whose wide triangular shape helped to protect the rider's legs. The stirrups were heavy, usually made of oak or hickory, and were covered in front by leather hoods which a cowboy would call tapaderos but the Army called leather hoods and stamped U.S. Regulation McClellans always had four brass rings—two affixed to the pommel, two to the cantle—to which had to be attached such necessities as the saber, the canteen, the crupper, the breastplate, and the martingale. The breastplate, used primarily by officers in full-dress outfit, usually carried a brass tack which displayed a picture of the American bald eagle.

Compulsory equipment with the McClellan was a blue wool blanket, 67×75 inches, that was normally folded into six thicknesses. The blanket was finished in an orange border and carried an or-

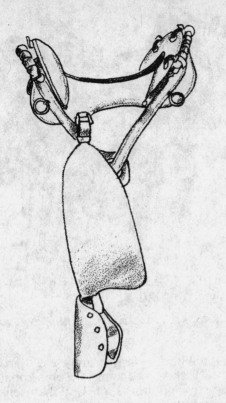

McClellan saddle

ange U.S. in the center. Officers might have a saddle cloth that either went over the blanket or could cover the entire saddle to shield the rider from leather stains.

The McClellan, used by the Remount Division of the U.S. Army until the beginnings of World War Two, when tanks replaced the horse in warfare, is still used for ceremonial purposes and by mounted police today.

WESTERN SADDLES

These came from Spain via Mexico and entered this country probably by way of Texas. At least one source tells of Juan de Oñate, who, in 1598, crossed the Rio Grande with eighty wagons and thousands of head of livestock including about one hundred head of breeding horses. This early rancher also brought new techniques of herding along with him. The Mexican style of the *vaquero* (cowboy) had taken much from Spanish ancestors, but the open country of Mexico demanded something more than the Spaniard's long prod poles then used to move cattle, and the long *reata* (lariat) was devised for roping. One end of the rope was attached at first to the horse's tail, later to the rear of the saddle; after much trial and error, it ended up on the horn, a squat rounded shape on the top of the fork. From these beginnings the modern horn evolved into a higher, stronger, and essential part of the saddle. The Californians

Western saddle

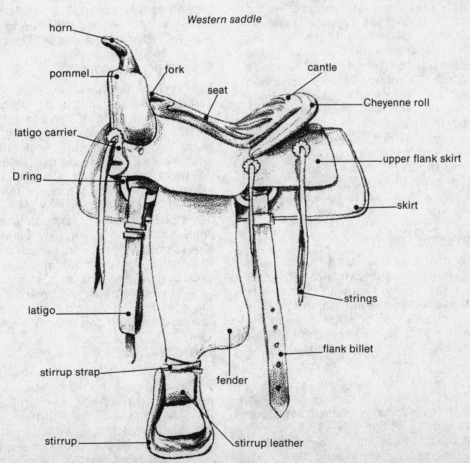

horn

pommel

fork

seat

cantle

Cheyenne roll

latigo carrier

D ring

upper flank skirt

skirt

strings

latigo

flank billet

stirrup strap

fender

stirrup

stirrup leather

quickly adopted the lariat for their ranches, while the Texans turned to a shorter rope which performed better in the heavy brush country where a quick, accurate throw was essential.

"Western" is, in fact, a broad term for several styles of riding. The type of country where cattle ranged determined the kind of work the horse had to do and, therefore, the kind of tack the wrangler needed. Styles in each region and even in each town varied greatly, and the smallest detail could pinpoint a cowboy's origins and his skills. In California where the country was open, the cowhorse was trained to line the rider up for a clean throw of the long lariat. Californians were dally men (from the Spanish *dar la vuelta,* "to give a turn"), which meant that they wrapped the end of the rope around the saddle horn, allowing it play instead of tying it fast. This style spared the horse the sudden jolt as the calf's weight reached the end of a slack rope. The heavy brush country of Texas, however, called for a horse with quick responses as it routed out the cattle. This was the country where the cutting horse developed, and a good one was a much-appreciated treasure. Bred to anticipate its quarry's every move, the cutting horse could maneuver the calf, thereby giving its rider a clean throw of the rope. Here the tie-fast horseman reigned, tying his rope firmly to the saddle horn and letting it rip.

Working the Texas range also required that the horse be able to perform sliding stops, quick turns, and rollbacks (because reining was generally rough, the curb was preferred over the spade bit). And because Texas ropers trained a horse to keep up the slack between itself and the calf, the impact of several hundred pounds on the front of the saddle was too great for the Mexican's single-cinch saddle. Therefore, Texans developed a rear cinch that was worn loose but would keep the saddle from slipping over when they dismounted to approach a calf.

The Western saddle is continuing to evolve today as horsemen are participating in ever-wider varieties of riding events. Western saddles, if you don't count such specialty saddles as the bronc-riding or trick-riding types, may be categorized into three basic styles.

GENERAL-PURPOSE SADDLE

This is the most common one, ideal for pleasure and trail riding. It weighs approximately 30 to 35 pounds and features a deep seat with high swells and cantle. The padded seat is built up in front for extra comfort. Since the horn is not needed for roping, it is smaller than the one found on a Roping Saddle—usually 2 inches high with a 2½- to 3-inch cap.

ROPING SADDLE

The heavy-duty stock saddle is made from stout leather, and everything about this saddle is intended to hold up to stress and hard work. The roping saddle weighs anywhere from 38 to 55

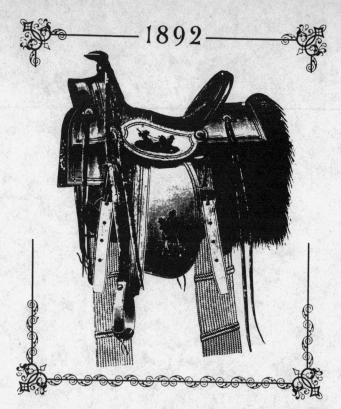

1892

pounds; the horn is large, rarely less than 3 inches high or 3 inches in diameter. Some ropers prefer rawhide-covered horns or will themselves wrap cotton rope or strips of rubber around the horn to prevent the rope from slipping and to ease the friction as it is dallied. The swells and cantle of the roping saddle are usually low and will not interfere with the rider as he speedily dismounts.

EQUITATION SADDLE

This is designed for show, either in the ring or in parades, and is usually elaborately decorated with intricate embossed or hand-tooled designs on the panels and fenders. These, in turn, may be finished with contrasting buck stitching. Nickel plate or silver wire often laces the perimeter of the cantle and Cheyenne roll. Other potential areas for heavy ornamentation include the conchas, horn cap, skirt corners, cantle plate, stirrups, and breastplate. The horn is small and low and sometimes inlaid with silver. The padded seat, almost always covered in suede, is built up in front toward swells that are of medium height. The cantle is usually high˙ and the dish of the seat deep. The basic measurement to consider when buying a show saddle is the dollar measurement. And, needless to say, it can go very high.

BRONC SADDLE

Totally Western in origin, this specialty saddle was designed to give the rider the best ride on a bucking horse. In rodeo competition, points are given not only for lasting the full time but for skill and control as well. Judges look to see if the cowboy's spurs are hitting the points of the shoulders when the horse's front feet hit the ground and that the rider's feet are dragged back ready to swing forward when the horse kicks. It is essential, therefore, that the bars of the bronc saddle allow the rider such freedom. The size of the undercut of the swells determines the rider's leg action, and the Rodeo Cowboy Association specifies that the swells may not be undercut more than 1 inch on each side. Most bronc riders prefer a saddle with a low cantle and stirrup leathers that will not accordion. The bronc saddle is always three-quarters double-rigged, with the front rigging ring directly below the center of the swells.

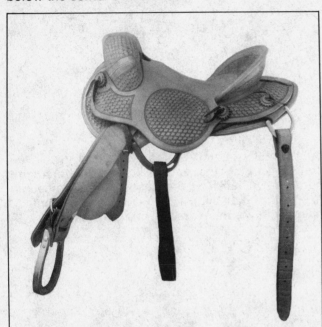

Bronc Saddle. This saddle conforms to RCA specifications. It is built on a bullhide-covered tree with a 16-inch seat, 14-inch-deep undercut swells, and a 4½-inch cantle, and the stirrups are hung up front through the rigging. The narrow oxbow stirrups are uncovered, and the rigging is three-quarters double. Available from Potts Longhorn Leather Saddlery, 3141 Oak Grove, Dallas, Texas 75219. Price on request.

Some bronc-riding contests require a bareback rig instead of a saddle. It is always made of heavy saddle leather and features a "handhold"—a sturdy piece of leather, often three-ply, which loops back to lace in either a center, right, or left position. Some of these rigs also add a soft padding to the area directly under the handhold to protect both the hand and the horse. The "skirt" of the rig is extremely short and ends in heavy rings to which 2-inch latigo straps and a contest-type cinch are attached. The bronc rider sits directly behind the rig with his legs forward over the skirt and the handhold between his legs.

PARTS OF A WESTERN SADDLE

The tree of the basic Western saddle was commonly made from beechwood covered with bullhide or rawhide. Now, with modern materials

RCA CONTEST SADDLE SPECIFICATIONS

Rigging: ¾ double—front edge of D ring must pull not farther back than directly below center of point of swell. Standard E-Z or ring type saddle D must be used and may not exceed 5¾-inch outside-width measurement.

Swell Undercut: not more than 2 inches—1 inch on each side.

Gullet: not less than 4 inches wide at center of fork of covered saddle.

Tree: Saddles must be built on standard tree.
　Specifications:
　Fork—14 inches wide
　Height—9 inches maximum
　Gullet—5¾ inches wide
　Cantle—5 inches maximum height, 14 inches maximum width
　Stirrup leathers must be hung over bars.
　Saddle should conform to the above measurements with a reasonable added thickness for leather covering.
　No freaks allowed.
　Front cinch on bronc saddles shall be Mohair and shall be at least 5 inches wide.

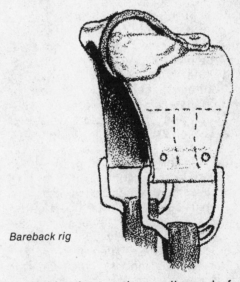

Bareback rig

available, the tree is usually made from laminated wood, often white ponderosa pine fitted together with the grain pointing in different directions and then glued under high pressure. This technique, which is also used by most of the European saddlers, is warp-resistant and less likely to break through stress to certain joints. Trees are also available in aluminum and in fiber glass. Both of these materials are lightweight and strong, and the fiber-glass tree is quickly becoming popular for children's saddles. However, horsemen often have a "prove it" attitude about most new materials, and until all the results are in, wood will remain the most called-for material. Certainly this is not true of plied wood, which has replaced solid wood in repute.)

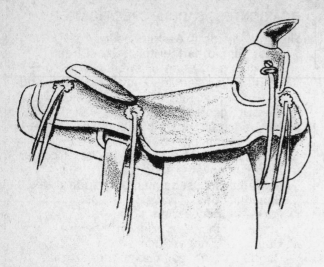

Flat seat

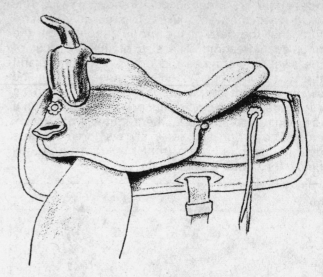

Built-up seat

The tree of the Western saddle is made up of a fork, horn, bars, and cantle. The fork includes the gullet (that space formed by the shaping of the fork) and the swells (the area on either side of the horn mount). The height and width of the gullet may vary, depending on the use for which the saddle is designed, from an average of 5¾ inches wide, 6¾ inches high to an average of 6¼ inches wide, 8 inches high. Measured from swell to swell, the width of the fork averages 10½ to 14 inches. A saddle horn can be made of wood, brass, steel, or iron covered in either bullhide, saddle leather, or rawhide and is either laminated onto the fork or mounted on with bolts and screws. Horns are usually available in a range of shapes, cap widths, and heights (from a low of 2½ inches to a high of 4 inches), with these measurements depending on whether it is intended for actual roping, for either tie-fast or dally men, or for grabbing onto for balance during barrel-racing or pleasure events.

The bars are a particularly important part of the tree, and skilled craftsmanship is necessary to angle them for good fit on a horse's back and proper balance for the rider. Bars are categorized as follows: regular (about 5½ inches), semi–Quarter Horse (about 6 inches), Quarter Horse (about 6½ inches), and Arabian or Morgan (about 6¾ inches). If wider-spaced bars are desired they must be specially ordered. Many saddletrees come with steel-reinforced bars, and a number of models feature bar slots for stirrup leathers. For those styles with built-up seats, a riser is often added on the bars directly behind the fork.

The cantle, basic to any Western saddletree, helps the rider maintain a deep seat. Western cantles are often between 2¾ and 4½ inches high, average 12½ to 14 inches wide, and dish approximately ⅞ inch to over 1¼ inches deep.

Within this century the seat of the Western saddle has been padded with foam rubber and covered with suede, quilted or plain, and has included such extras as the ''Cheyenne roll,'' that extra pad-

ding directly behind the cantle that is most welcome if you ever get caught behind the horse and come down hard on the cantle. Many horsemen are finding that this kind of seat is more comfortable and gives them greater grip and security.

Saddletrees can be bought precovered with rawhide or bullhide. The one illustrated is "Arizona Roper" from Tex Tan Western Leather Co. The company's catalog offers eight pages of trees with four different bar widths and various styles of horns, forks, and cantles. Hand-sewn wet rawhide or bullhide covers a laminated fork made of ponderosa pine and a ductile-iron horn that is bolted into the fork. Tex Tan trees come with one of the following types of horn: regular, egg-shaped pelican, pelican, two-rope, high dally, and double dally. Average price is about $75.

The best type of seat for the Western saddle is a subject of raging controversy that this book will attempt simply to describe but not enter. Early Western saddles—those brought here from Mexico, for instance—put nothing between the tree and the rider's seat bones. Shortly thereafter, the tree was covered first with bullhide, then with a layer of saddle leather, and that was the standard method for a long, long time. Today, the majority of Western saddles have a quilted and foam-rubber-padded built-up seat which slopes downward toward the rear, forcing the rider to sit deep into the cantle. Monte Foreman, a man who is gradually influencing many a Western horseman's way of riding, designed a "Balanced Ride" seat that eliminates the built-up front. Instead, the flatter seat allows the rider to move with the horse, sitting well into the saddle when it walks and getting forward when it travels at a faster gait or goes up and down hills. Stirrups on Monte Foreman saddles also hang farther forward than do those on the conventional saddles.

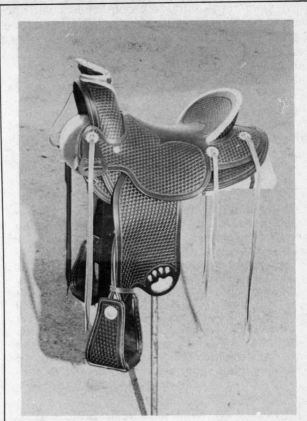

A three-quarter-rigged saddle similar to the one used on a 6,400-mile ride by Mary Ellen Eckelberg. From Carroll Saddle Co. About $600.

The seat size of any saddle depends a great deal on the type of tree selected and whether there is padding. The average size is from 14¾ to 15¾ inches long. Seat size is occasionally misunderstood by the novice saddle buyer. Essentially, what the experienced Western horseman is looking for is a seat large enough to allow him freedom of movement, especially to swing his stirrup fenders forward; short enough, on the other hand, so that he doesn't find himself "riding the cantle," and not so wide that it causes him to stretch uncomfortably.

To measure the seat, place a ruler at the center base of the fork and measure the distance between that point and the center of the top of the cantle. Most manufacturers publish charts which give approximate size ranges, taking into consideration the rider's height and weight. The novice should ask the advice of his local tack shop. Most shops will allow the buyer to sit on the saddle perched atop a rack designed for this purpose. Testing the feel of the saddle in this way is obviously inadequate, but the buyer may have no choice. There are some neighborly tack shops that will throw the saddle being considered onto a horse pastured out back. Short of saddling up the horse for which the saddle is intended, this is the best way to get the feel and the proper fit.

RIGGING

How a saddle is rigged indicates how it is balanced on the horse's back and how the girth attaches to the saddle. All English saddles are "center-fire" rigged, and so was the rigging brought into this country by the Mexicans. Their center-fire rigging consisted of two stout straps, one which passed around the front of the fork and the second which ran over the rear of the tree behind the cantle. The ends of the two straps joined to a large ring centered on either side of the tree. When the rear strap was considerably longer than the front strap, the ring to which they were joined was then balanced further forward and it was known as three-quarter rigging. The early Texas ropers found that neither the center-fire rigging of the Mexicans and Californians nor the three-quarter rigging could adequately hold the saddle in place when they were roping a large animal. For when several hundreds of pounds of calf hit the horn, the impact would jerk the saddle forward and badly bruise the horse. Ropers needed a solution, and since necessity is the mother of invention, they quickly found one. They shortened the two straps and finished each in a large ring, so that two rings instead of one appeared on either side of the tree. This was known as "rim-fire" rigging, a name which has since evolved into "full rigging," "double rigging" or "full double."

The full-double rigging was particularly successful, and the design traveled throughout the Southwest and into the Northwest. Today, of course, the full-double is found in every state. But it is also beginning to lose some of its popularity. Many nonroping horsemen find that the full-double saddle is too heavy for everyday use and that the forward cinch tends to chafe a horse directly behind the elbow, a problem particularly apparent in steep-shouldered animals. Many horsemen are turning to a seven-eighths double-rigged saddle with the girth to the rear of the full-double but forward from a center-fire rigging. Instead of the usual "on-the-tree" rigging, the rigging rings on other than roping saddles are often sewn into the skirt. This "in-skirt" rigging, while obviously inadequate for calf roping, is excellent for pleasure riding since it is less bulky and allows the rider closer contact with the horse.

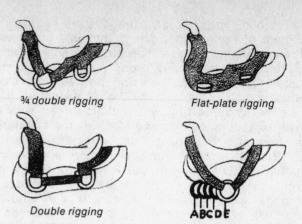

¾ double rigging   Flat-plate rigging

Double rigging   ABCDE

A. Spanish B. ⅞ C. ¾ D. ⅝ E. Center-fire

If you look hard enough, you can find a Western pleasure saddle for under $100 (with no guarantees about comfort or quality), and for $10,000 you can get a custom-made silver-and-gem-decorated parade saddle. Obviously, for most horsemen the latter price is unnecessarily high and the former price too cheap. A good-quality saddle will more likely range from $350 to $750. Custom-made saddles usually cost more than ready-made ones (but not as much more as one might expect). What changes the price is whether you want hand tooling instead of stamping, buck stitching, silver, built-up seat, a different horn shape, or other details that require special attention.

BAREBACK PAD

For those who enjoy closer contact with the horse but want some covering to protect the animal's back, the bareback pad is a useful piece of equipment. It comes with either leather, cotton duck, or canvas outer covering and is lightly padded with felt or sponge rubber or fiber hair. Bareback pads are available in English style with a web surcingle and handhold sewn onto the pad and metal D rings for attaching leathers and irons. Western-style bareback pads are practically identical, with a slight difference found in the girth, which ends in a metal D to which a latigo holds a string girth, and in the stirrups, which are usually made of bent wood.

Because these pads are frequently used by less than experienced riders who may, when feeling insecure in their seat, rely on the reins for balance (a habit that encourages heavy hands and a hard mouth to match), we recommend pads with the handhold rather than those without. Neck straps are also useful in this regard.

PACKSADDLE

For those who want to travel away from the well-worn trails and plan to go where McDonald's and Pizza King aren't—at least, not yet—a pack horse or mule may be necessary. Most people think that these animals are much stronger than in fact they are, so you should not expect the horse to carry more than 175 pounds. That may sound like a lot

of gear, but remember to count the weight of the feed and the weight of the pack itself. Of course, the feed weight will lighten considerably as each day goes by.

The most common packsaddle is the "sawbuck" type, which is made of two sets of sturdy wooden pieces joined to form a high-slung X. The bottom part of the X is attached on either side to bars which rest on the muscle pads on either side of the horse's backbone—much like the bars on most saddletrees. The bars are usually rounded on each end, tapered to fit the animal's back and then lined with sheepskin or another type of soft padding. Two leather rigging straps pass up the inside of the X frames to crisscross around the bucks and down the opposite side. The two rigging rings on each side are joined by a cross strap, and two latigos hold the front and rear cinches. A breast collar and breeching are important parts of the packsaddle; a breast collar eases the strain to the girths when the horse is going uphill, and breeching, held in place by a back strap and a strap to the rear X frame, eases the strain when it is going downhill.

Canvas covered English bareback pad—from about $11.50 to $19; with stirrups from $20.
Duck-covered Western padded back with cord cinch and adjustable stirrups—from $19 to $37.

Saddle pack bags can be made of canvas, leather, plywood, or any lightweight but sturdy material. They are usually longer than they are deep (approximately 24 inches long and 22 inches high) and are hung on either side of the saddle. Usually the entire pack is then covered with a tarp and secured in place with a diamond or squaw hitch.

Humane Packsaddle with breastplate and breeching—about $110.
Pack Bags, heavy-duty duck reinforced with leather—$73 to $167.

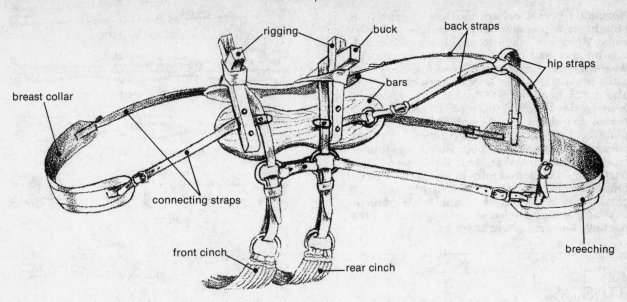

Sawbuck pack saddle

rigging

buck

back straps

hip straps

bars

breast collar

connecting straps

front cinch

rear cinch

breeching

SUPPLEMENTS TO THE SADDLE

BREASTPLATES

The Western-style breastplate is most often used to hold the saddle from slipping backward for riding in hilly country. Now, however, it is also used as a place to attach a tie-down strap or a running martingale, and parade riders find it ideal for showing off elaborate tooling or silverwork. The Western breastplate comes in two styles: the standard and the ring type. The former is simply a strap of leather that loops on either end through the cinch rings to buckle back upon itself. A second strap loops around the horse's neck just above the withers. Some breastplates have a third strap which attaches on one end to a small D in the center of the breaststrap and, at the other end, between the horse's front legs to a small D on the cinch. The ring breastplate is made of two pieces of leather (sometimes of cord to match the cinch) joined in the center by a large ring. This permits the straps on either side of the shoulder to move independently of each other and conform to the horse's anatomy as it moves. The center ring is often preferred by those who use a tie-down or martingale.

The English breastplates serve a number of the same purposes as their Western counterparts, although they are rarely decorated. English breastplates also come in two different styles: the hunt breastplate and the racing, or polo, breastplate. The former consists of a chest strap attached to the girth which ends in a metal ring near the center of the horse's chest. Two straps connected to this ring pass each on one side of the neck, where they are joined by another strap that crosses the mane just above the withers. Two additional straps, one on each side of the withers, buckle to the metal eyes of the saddle and hold the breastplate firmly in place. A running or standing martingale is commonly attached to the center chest ring. The racing, or polo, breastplate is similar to the standard Western breast collar; however, it is usually lighter in weight and padded with less bulky material, and the neck strap is adjustable.

Breastplates

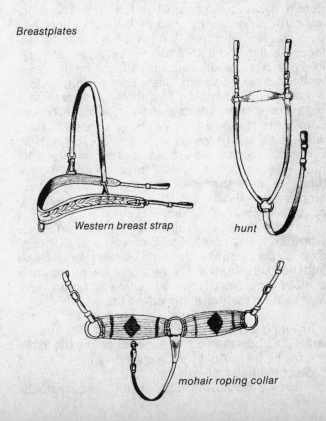

Western breast strap

hunt

mohair roping collar

Normally, breast collars are less expensive if bought in a package with a saddle and stirrups. Many are made to match a specific saddle, but you can certainly buy one separately. Western center ring straps are often sold with a tie-down strap. The leather ones range from about $25 to about $45 (unless you choose a heavily decorated one); mohair cord breastplates are about $17. The single-strap breastplate sold without a tie-down strap is usually cheaper, from about $15 up. Polo breastplates tend to be cheaper than their Western counterparts (about $20), and hunt breastplates can be found for under $16, but most of them are closer to $28. Often, the hunt breastplate is sold only with a choice of martingales, and the package can cost about $38.

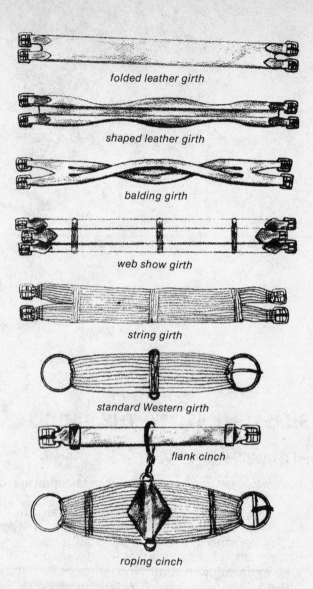

folded leather girth

shaped leather girth

balding girth

web show girth

string girth

standard Western girth

flank cinch

roping cinch

GIRTHS

There is at least one girth to match every saddle, Western or English. Girths, or cinches, are available in leather, vinyl, web, nylon, cord, linen, elastic, and cotton, rayon or mohair strands. For English hunt-seat riding the girth is usually made of leather or vinyl and may be shaped on the three-fold design—a straight piece of leather or vinyl folded over to form three layers about 3 inches wide—or may be the chafeless girth, slightly tapered behind the elbow to prevent chafing, or the Balding girth, in which the center of the leather strap is split into three equal pieces and then twisted in two places. The chafeless girth often has elastic at one or both ends for easier saddling and, more important, to give the horse more freedom to expand its chest when jumping. The Balding girth is frequently used by hunt members and polo players, who find that the three separate surfaces lie flat under the horse's belly and are less likely to slip. Saddle-seat riders traditionally use a white canvas, web, or linen show girth usually 5 inches wide. Jumping and dressage riders use a girth made from either mohair, nylon, or Trevira cord. This string girth is normally sixteen strands wide, with eight strands woven into each buckle. Girths for racehorses are similar to those used by hunt riders but are usually much thinner, sometimes no more than two inches wide. Elastic webbing is often used, since it allows the horse to expand its chest freely when working.

Several accessories used on English girths are worth knowing about. For instance, a girth extension, a small double strap with buckles on one end and holes to buckle on the other, is particularly useful for horses that have become so fat on summer pasture their girth no longer fits.

A buckle guard, simply a small piece of medium-weight leather with three sets of slits spaced evenly across the top to accommodate the billet straps, helps to hold the billets firmly in place and protect the flap from scarring.

Fleece girth covers made of machine-washable acrylic are tubular-shaped to slip over a leather or elastic girth. Because these covers are particularly soft, they help prevent chafing to the horse's belly.

Racehorses and jumpers, especially those used for open jumping, sometimes carry an Olympic overgirth, or surcingle, to prevent the saddle from flopping forward as the horse comes off the jump. Usually it is used in addition to the saddle's own girth and wraps around over the center of the seat and under the horse's belly.

In talking about Western girths, it is necessary to distinguish between front and rear. Almost all front girths are made of cincha cord of pure mohair, pure cotton, or a combination of mohair and rayon—a particularly strong and soft blend. The standard front cinch is generally 30 inches long and made from an average of seventeen braided cords with cords of a different color woven in perpendicularly in anywhere from three to seven places. The cinchas are attached to flat metal rings that often have a tongue to buckle. This type of girth also comes with two small D's woven into the center crossbar, the forward D for snapping on a tie-down or a breastplate and the rear D for attaching the connecting strap to the flank girth. A roping cinch is a wider version of the standard one, often made from twenty-four strands of braided cord with a diamond-shaped center made out of either woven cord, a webbing strap, or a leather patch.

Western girth accessories include girth covers with the tops of the ends scooped out to accommodate the latigo knot and the cinch, D's, good for preventing galling and rubbing along the animal's belly. They are available in woolskin or synthetic fleece. There is also a ring chafe made from woolskin or fleece which slips over the back of the ring to cushion the horse against rubbing.

While the front girth on a Western saddle is normally made of cord, the flank cinch is usually made of leather, often about 3 inches wide. The flank cinch should never be drawn up tight but rather left hanging with about 2 inches of space between it and the largest part of the horse's belly. A connecting strap holds the flank cinch to the front girth and prevents it from swinging and interfering with the horse. Most flank cinches are about 36 inches long, and roping cinches are sometimes as wide as 4 inches.

English-style girths are almost always sold separately from the saddle, while Western saddles nearly always come with both front and rear cinches. But all tack catalogs sell girths separately. English girths come in numerous shapes, sizes, and materials, so it is difficult to generalize a price range. More specifically, chafeless, three-fold leather, and Balding styles cost from about $25; white web about $4.50; tubular linen show girths from $22; overgirths from $13; nylon cord about $7; mohair cord from $9. Western cord girths come in cotton (about $2 for 13-strand), rayon (about $5.00 for 15-strand) and mohair (about $7 for 15-strand). The number of strands also make a small price difference; mohair 17-strand runs about $11 and 27-strand mohair roping girths are $13 and up. Flank cinches, including the connector strap, start about $8, and a heavy-duty roping flank cinch is about $21.

Girth extension straps for English saddles are about $5.50, and synthetic-fleece girth covers are around $4. Real sheepskin Western girth covers are about $16 and synthetic ones near $5.

BILLETS

For the Western saddle there are three different styles of billet straps, and all three are used on the same saddle. The front girth is attached on the off (right) side to an "off billet," a strong piece of leather approximately 1½ to 2 inches wide and 33 inches to 8 feet long that is folded in half, with the cinch tongue buckling through matched holes in the double layer. The longer off billet is known as a half-breed off strap, and it wraps through the cinch rings twice for extra strength.

The near (left) side of the front girth is attached

"The dressage seat, the stock saddle seat, the jumping seat and the racing seat, apparently so different, are all basically the same. The only real differences are the lengths of the stirrup leathers and the forward inclination of the rider's torso to enable him to keep his weight as close as possible over his mount's center of gravity. For between a state of balance and a state of unbalance there is no intermediate point, no half of one and half of the other. Either a rider is in balance with his horse (not merely in balance on the horse) or he is off balance."

John Richard Young
"The JRY: A Forward Seat Stock Saddle"
American Horseman, *October 1973*

---

to the saddle by a latigo, or tie strap, a long (approximately 5 to 7 feet), pliable "latigo" leather. One end is folded and tied to the rigging ring on the saddle. The other end is looped down through the cinch buckle, up through the rigging D, and back through the cinch buckle, to be secured either by the cinch tongue or more often by a tie knot which loops around the rigging D. The extra length of strap is slipped into the tie-strap holder which can be found directly in front of the fork.

Both rear billets are the same on either side of the saddle. Each is tied into the rear rigging D's and fastens to the flank billet by buckles.

Billets on English saddles extend directly from the tree and are made of stout nonstretchable leather which is tapered into either two or three straps with holes to accommodate the girth buckles. Often the off side of the saddle will have two straps while the near side, which must take the most stress each time the saddle is used, will have three straps. Some riders buckle the girth alternately to any two of the three billets, thereby lessening the wear to one particular strap.

If you have an English saddle, you can't go into most tack shops and buy extra billets. If you need them, you'll have to find a saddle-repair shop that can replace the old ones. Western billet straps, on the other hand, are easily replaceable. An off strap of 2-inch skirting leather is about $5.50, and a half-breed off strap is about $9. Latigo tie straps start at about $5 and go up to about $10 (depending on the width and length). Flank billets are usually sold in a package with the flank cinch but can be had separately for about $4 each.

STIRRUP LEATHERS

Stirrup leathers attach the stirrup to the bars of the saddle and allow for a degree of length adjustment. In the Western saddle most stirrup leathers also include a fender, necessary to keep the rider's legs from rubbing raw. The outside of the fender, though it may be left plain, is usually decorated with embossing or hand tooling. Fenders average approximately 17 inches long and 8 inches wide, with the ends quickly tapering to form stirrup leathers about 2½ inches wide.

There are several methods for fastening the ends of the leathers together, and all of them are strong and dependable. One technique, called the "quick-change buckle," is not really a buckle at all. Rather, it consists of two rectangular pieces of metal, one with prongs, that attach one beneath the other to the same end of the strap so that they are free to slide up and down the leather. It works when the opposite end of the leather, with its sets of punched holes, slips under both loops of metal until the prongs grab into the desired holes and the first loop is lowered over the pronged end to hold it fast. The "Blevins buckle" is similar in theory to the former fastening but slightly different in form. It works this way: the pronged piece of metal is affixed to one end of the stirrup leather; the other end has punched holes and a sliding metal loop. The pronged end grabs into the holes and the sliding loop is brought down over the prongs to hold them securely in place.

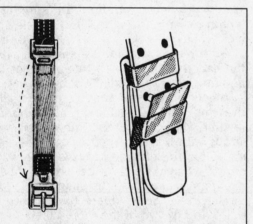

For horsemen who have difficulty mounting 16-hand-plus horses, there is a most useful gadget called the extension leather. The near (mounting) leather is fitted with a slot off of which extends an extra piece of material, usually made of web. The end of the web contains a buckle and a hook; the hook rests in the slot when the leathers are normal length and can be quickly unhooked when the rider mounts. From $21.95 to $25.95.

Quick-Change Buckle. Used on Western stirrup leathers for fast adjustment. About $2.

There is a third method of holding the stirrup ends together, and this too is not actually a buckle. For this fastening, matching sets of holes are punched through both ends of the stirrup leathers. Two stout metal pins with holes drilled into their ends are inserted through the two layers of leathers until only the ends protrude. A metal clasp (something like a safety pin) is passed through the holes and then closed.

On some Western saddles metal is not used at all; instead, matching holes are punched through

the ends of the leathers and a thin piece of rawhide is laced through to tie. This last method, often seen on older saddles, is less commonly used today, probably because it is so time-consuming to undo and retie each time you want to change the length of the stirrups.

An important part of any Western-style stirrup leather is the "hobble strap," a thin strip of leather with either a straight or a shaped body that measures about 12 inches long and ½ to ⅞ inch wide. Hobble straps wrap around the stirrup leathers just above the stirrup and prevent the stirrup from slipping out of position.

English-style stirrup leathers for hunt and pleasure saddles are often ⅞ to 1⅛ inches wide, with polo leathers often a bit wider and racing leathers narrower, available in ½, ⅝, and ¾ inch and up. Sewn-in, heavy-duty buckles fasten through punched and often numbered holes on the other end.

Stirrup leathers for English saddles are readily available and are often bought separately from the saddle. Sturdy utility leathers (1⅛-inch width) are about $6, butt-leather hunt leathers are about $18 and up depending on the quality of the leather and the tanning process, and extra-long leathers usually start at about $25. Western saddles, on the other hand, always have fenders which are stamped or tooled to match the rest of the saddle. Replacing a fender is, therefore, not so simple. The best way is to contact the dealer (probably through your tack shop) and have them send fenders to match. Most saddle manufacturers make plain fenders and stirrup leathers and Simco has one for about $46.

STIRRUPS

It wasn't until after the discovery of the stirrup that horsemanship began to develop from its early inexpertness into a highly polished art. While it was the Huns who were credited with introducing the stirrup into Europe, it was actually adopted in what is now Hungary and didn't come into common use there until as late as the 9th century and in Britain still later.

The English-style stirrup is always made of metal—either nickel-plated steel or stainless steel—and it comes in two basic types, regular and offset. The regular stirrup is designed with the eye centered so that when resting on a flat surface it is perfectly symmetrical, while the eye of an offset stirrup is set to one side so that when the iron is placed on a flat surface it leans appreciably to that side. These irons are keyed to the right or left foot, since it is the tilt that encourages the rider to keep his ankles cocked, his heels down with the force of his weight on the inside ball of his foot. Highly desirable for hunt-seat riding, the offset stirrup would not be acceptable for such riding styles as dressage.

English stirrups

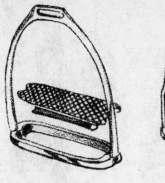

fillis

hunt

peacock

offset

cradle

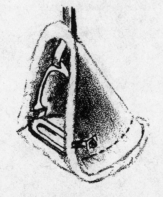

foot-warmer

To determine the correct stirrup length for any style of riding, sit in the saddle with legs relaxed and hanging down straight. The bottom of the stirrup should be:

- Forward hunt seat—just above the anklebone
- Balanced English seat—at anklebone or just below
- Saddle seat—just above sole of boot
- Western—1 to 1½ inches above sole of boot

The center-balanced stirrup is still the more frequently used, and there are many shapes and weight available within this style. There is a safety iron known as the Peacock pattern, a three-sided stirrup open on one side and held together by a heavy rubber band. If the rider falls, the rubber band releases to prevent him from being dragged. A lightweight cradle pattern, which may be described as a squat rounded iron, is most popular with jockeys and is available in aluminum and in small sizes.

Bottoms of irons either are finished with a rough tread or accommodate stirrup pads for better grip. These pads are made from either rough-textured metal or, more commonly, rubber.

When buying stirrups, you should consider the weight—normally the heavier the iron, the easier a stirrup is to regain when lost—and the width: in case of a fall, a too-narrow stirrup can grip the foot too firmly and a too-wide stirrup makes it an easy matter for the entire foot to slip through.

The Western stirrup is made from a wooden form that is covered either with a strap of metal bound along the side or, more commonly, entirely in leather. Some leather-covered stirrups also have a second layer of leather wrapped around the bot-

Your basic nonrustable stirrups can start around $7 for 4-inch width and go up to $26 for 5½-inch-wide Eldonian stainless steel irons. The Peacock safety stirrup style runs about $23, and the Fillis style with rubber stirrup pad is about $28. Offset irons range from about $14 to $25. All the prices vary depending on the quality of the metal, how they are finished, and the size. Fleece foot warmers, sold to fit any size iron, can be found for around $18.

Western stirrups start for as little as $4 for the metal-bound wood Visalia style. The standard rawhide-covered Visalia-style stirrup with 1-inch tread and 3-inch neck is about $21. Laced, leather-covered oxbow stirrups are in the same range. Bell-bottom stirrups start at about $25 and go up from there depending on embossing or other decoration along the side. Deep leather-covered roper stirrups start just a bit higher, about $28. Hooded stirrups are available for around $15, but wing taps are around $40 and up depending on decoration.

tom of the stirrup for better wear and grip.

Western stirrups come in several basic styles: the Visalia, the bell-bottom, the roper, and the oxbow. The last one is a particularly narrow, rounded-bottom stirrup designed to support the arch rather than the ball of the foot; used by horsemen who wear their stirrups driven home, it is frequently found on rodeo and bronc saddles.

Tapaderos, or stirrup hoods, originated with the early Mexican saddle. Called "taps" by Texans, they were tooled, stamped, or decoratively carved but an important protection against the thorny brush. "Taps" were sometimes enclosed and lined with fleece, almost a winter overshoe, certainly most welcome during cold weather. Californians preferred a larger type called a wing tap that extended below the toe and was indeed shaped like one half of an angel's wing. For parades, elaborately tooled, silver-inlaid tapaderos were used, and these designs are visible today during, for instance, the Rose Bowl parade in Pasadena.

While we're on the subject of tapaderos, English-style riders have a small version which they call cups or hoods. Lined with fleece or wool, these cups slip over the front of the stirrup to enclose the toe and provide warmth on freezing days.

HALTERS

From its first day of life, the single item of tack any domestic horse requires is a halter—a simplified bridle without bit or reins. There are any number of good, serviceable all-purpose halters sold through tack shops, and there are also several specialized types as well. Most stables use one of the following materials and styles for general needs: cotton rope or nylon rope (often identical in style, they are normally held together by tiller clamps or may even be of one-piece construction with no hardware); nylon web (usually has a friction buckle; it should be double-stitched at stress points); leather (extremely attractive when properly cared for, it should be stout, with plenty of stitching, and have quality hardware that won't crack the leather). For animals in shipment, there is a jute-fiber shipping halter, a wide, stout halter that includes a thin browband and throatlatch. The halter has little hardware and the lead often cannot be removed. Shipping halters are made to slip off the horse easily when this is needed. On the other end of the halter spectrum is the show halter. More like a bridle, it is often thinner than the other halters, may be rolled or buck-stitched, and is too lightweight to use for anything other than show. Instead of a bit, it has a chain chin strap whose ends slip through the two cheek rings and join under the chin to attach to the lead rope.

When purchasing a halter you should look for one that is not skimpy, with stress points double or even triple and sewn together with small stitches (about ten to the inch); made carefully, with no rough edges and with strap ends that are either beveled or tapered; more heavily stitched

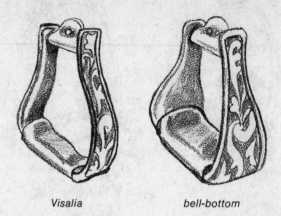

Western stirrups

Visalia   *bell-bottom*

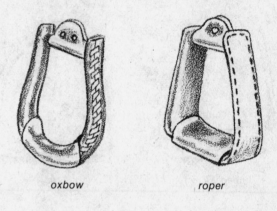

oxbow   *roper*

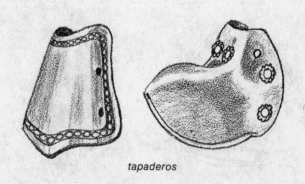

tapaderos

Halters

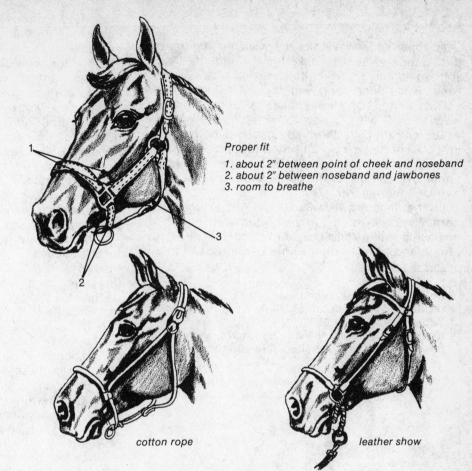

Proper fit

1. *about 2" between point of cheek and noseband*
2. *about 2" between noseband and jawbones*
3. *room to breathe*

nylon web　　　　*cotton rope*　　　　*leather show*

than riveted (an abundance of rivets usually indicating cheap manufacturing); and of good-quality materials. Nylon should feel soft and supple, leather smooth; hardware should be rustproof, smooth and shaped so that it does not cause undue wear on the halter.

Rope halters—about $4.
Nylon stable halters—about $5.50.
Leather utility halter—$15 and up.
Round leather show halter—from $30.
Quarter Horse show halter and lead—around $75 and up.
Arabian show halters—around $75 and up.

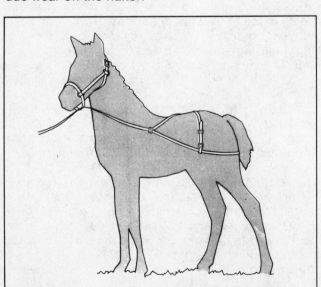

Colt Come-Along. Encourages the foal to lead. Made of heavy white webbing, it is adjustable to fit ponies and foals up to yearlings. About $4.95 (halter not included) from Ryon's Saddle & Ranch Supplies, Inc.

"Every one may not know what breaking in is, therefore I will describe it. It means to teach a horse to wear a saddle and bridle, and to carry on his back a man, woman, or child; to go just the way they wish, and to go quietly. Besides this, he has to learn to wear a collar, a crupper, and a breeching, and to stand still while they are on; then to have a cart or a chaise fixed behind, so that he cannot walk or trot without dragging it after him; and he must go fast or slow, just as his driver wishes. He must never start at what he sees, nor speak to other horses, nor bite nor kick, nor have any will of his own, but always do his master's will, even though he may be very tired or hungry; but the worst of all is, when this harness is once on, he may neither jump for joy nor lie down for weariness. So this breaking in is a great thing."

Anna Sewell
Black Beauty

LEADS

Lead ropes or lead shanks are available in most of the materials used to make halters and are often sold to match show halters. Leads average between 6 and 8 feet long, with the 1½ to 2 feet nearest the halter sometimes made of chain, and always hook with a swivel snap. For young, exuberant animals, the lead snap can be hooked to the right halter ring and then passed under the lip and up through the left halter ring; the additional leverage under the chin usually gives a handler a bit more control.

Lunge lines are usually about 25 feet long and normally made of nylon or cotton web about 1 inch wide with a swivel trigger or spring-style snap at one end. Some come with a sewn-in handhold.

Cotton-rope leads—about $3.
Nylon-web lead—about $3.50.
Latigo lead—about $10.
English bridle-leather lead—about $13.
Show leads to match halter—$13 and up.

Adjustable Neck Rope. A combination lead and neck rope with a thimble adjusted near the center and a trigger snap at one end of the rope. To secure the rope, the thimble is set so that it joins the snap at the base of the horse's throat where the trigger snap clips into the eye of the thimble. About $4.

HARNESS

In A.D. 800 the Arabs, returning from such territories as Bokhara and Samarkand, brought the hame collar into northwestern Europe. An invention of the Turkic peoples, it radically affected the harness then in use and with the addition of shafts permitted one horse to pull carts that could previously be drawn only by two bullocks. On the other hand, the breast collar entered Europe from the North, where it was probably adapted from reindeer harness. These two discoveries were far more efficient than the yoke-and-pole technique then in use and, in combination with improved wagons, changed the course of European travel and development.

Today, horses are driven in harness for many purposes, the least of which is transportation.

There is a variety of types of driving done in all parts of the country, and clubs gather to encourage and promote their own brand. (See pages 211–217 for more on the subject.)

Huge draft horses are still used by the Amish people in Pennsylvania to plow and cultivate their prosperous farms. In all sections of the country you can find individuals who continue to rely on horses for working the land and pulling heavy wagons. Work harness is made of stout leather, and everything about it is heavy-duty. Special clubs and fairs include draft-horse pulling or plowing contests, and many of the contestants will invest in silver-inlaid patent leather–covered harness for these competitions.

Trotters, as anyone who has bet $2 knows, are bred for speed. Racing harness is designed to help the horse move easily and maintain its gait. Unlike flat-racing tack, a trotter's harness needn't be exceptionally light; it must, however, be strong and may include such specialized tack as a pool cue (a pole to discourage the horse from turning its head to the side) or any of the other pieces of equipment special to the racing trotter.

Show harness or light-carriage harness is designed for one horse to pull a small carriage or cart, and it is the harness used by the majority of horsemen. Light harness is often used in training a young horse, in showing gaited horses, Arabs, and Morgans, and for pulling a buggy or sleigh down the road.*

Harness is specialized tack designed to allow the horse to pull either a vehicle or a plow while under the driver's control. With only slight variations, almost all harness is made up of a bridle, a saddle, traces, a collar, and breeching or thimbles that slip over the fills.

The bridle is similar to a basic English-style headstall with the addition of blinders attached to the cheekpiece and to the browband. Blinders were made in traditional patterns, with coachmen-driven horses in square or D-shaped blinders, light-carriage-driven horses in hatchet-shaped or round blinders, and racing trotters in any variety that will work, including half-moon-shaped blinders. Trotters and occasionally light-harness carriage horses will also carry an overcheck—a strap of leather that attaches to each of the bit rings, joins in the center of the horse's face, runs up between the eyes through a loop in the crownpiece of the bridle, and follows the crest of the neck where it hooks onto the saddle. The overcheck is used to dictate the proper extension of the head as the horse moves along at a fast pace.

The single-harness saddle fits around the horse's girth and has padded panels which rest on either side of the horse's backbone. On top of these panels two ring terrets serve as guides for

* Probably the least-known type of driving today was one of the most widely practiced sports about one hundred years ago. We are talking about coaching, a sport that requires great skill and elaborate equipment. Coaching and even tandem driving now boast a small, highly dedicated group of experts, all of whom know each other and where to find coaching equipment. We will not attempt to describe coaching further except to recommend that those interested in learning more see the section on Driving, pp. 211–217.

Single harness

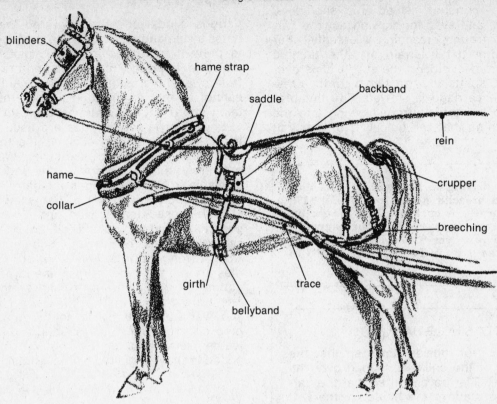

blinders
hame strap
saddle
backband
rein
hame
crupper
collar
breeching
girth
trace
bellyband

the reins. The saddle head usually has a brass hook to which to attach the overcheck. The belly-band includes tugs—loops, which hang from either side of the saddle, to hold the shaft—and is loosely buckled over the girth. To prevent the saddle from slipping forward, a crupper, a piece of padded leather which encircles the base of the tail, is connected to the saddle by an adjustable backband.

Horses trained to pull may be fitted in either a neck collar or a breast collar, depending on traditional styles and the type of work expected. The neck collar is pear-shaped, designed to lie closely around the base of the horse's neck along the shoulder line. It is heavily padded. Usually the top of the collar is closed by a strap or a special snap fastening. The hames fit in the groove that lines the outer part of the collar and are joined together at the top and bottom. These two gracefully shaped pieces of metal or wood reinforced with metal help to distribute the pulling pressure across the horse's shoulders. The breast collar is a wide band of stout leather that fits around the horse's chest and is held in place by a strap which passes over the neck just above the withers. Traces, two thick leather straps, attach at one end directly onto the hames or onto the breast collar at the point of the shoulder and, at the other end, onto the carriage or plow.

For most types of use the harness is now complete. However, for single harness used on a cart or carriage, breeching is often a necessity. Con-

sisting of a strap that passes along the horse's hindquarters, it is held in place by a second strap which passes over the croup and across the back-band, with the ends of the breeching hooking onto each of the shafts. Breeching should be thought of as a counterpart to the breast collar; when the

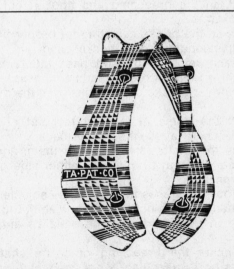

Collar Pads. Quilted awning-stripe drill with composite stuffing and four hooks. Sizes 16 to 30 inches, and it is suggested you order two sizes larger than the collar. About $8.40 from Smith Worthington and slightly more or less (depending on size needed) from Cumberland General Store.

horse is going downhill, the weight of the carriage is borne by its haunches instead of its shoulders. In hilly country and even for slowing down a carriage on level ground breeching is essential. For horses worked on flatter terrain, a leather thimble extending from each side of the saddle slips over the front of the shafts and bears some of the pressure when the carriage is slowed. The thimbles can also keep the vehicle from plowing into the animal, something that can quickly sour a willing horse.

> Single-horse driving harness with breast collar or plate and breeching runs from about $175 up. Pony harness is cheaper, from $75 for an economy harness to over $115. Stout teamwork harness will run over $350 with replacement parts, such as a set of breeching from $60 to about $130.

PUTTING ON A SINGLE HARNESS

1. Put collar on upside down so that the widest part of the collar is slipped over the horse's eyes. Then reverse it so that the narrow part rests above the horse's withers. If the collar does not slip on easily, remove the hames and undo the collar.

2. Set saddle on horse's back, slightly farther back than normal.

3. Put tail through the crupper and attach the crupper to the saddle by the backstrap.

4. Place saddle in proper position, tighten the girth so that it fits the horse snugly, and buckle the bellyband so that it hangs loosely under the belly.

5. Put on the breeching and hook it onto the backstrap.

6. Put on the bridle, adjusting for proper fit, and adjust length of overcheck if used.

7. Attach reins to bit and pass the reins through the terrets on the saddle. It is usual for the driver to take up the reins from the off side.

8. Put the horse in front of the cart and raise the shafts above the horse's back.

9. Pull the shafts forward, lower them, and run them through the tugs on either side of the harness.

10. Hook the traces to the cart, so adjusted that when they are pulled tight, the shaft tugs will be in the middle of the saddle's side panels.

11. Buckle the breeching onto the shaft leathers or, if breeching is not used, slip the thimble over the front of the shaft.

12. Attach overcheck, if used, and hook it to the top of the saddle.

13. Pick up the reins.

14. Calmly get into the cart and enjoy the ride.

SADDLE PADS

Various kinds of fabric layered between the horse's skin and the saddle are used by horsemen to prevent rubbing that causes galls, to absorb moisture, to protect the saddle and the rider's legs from sweat, and as ornamentation. Although pads cannot correct an ill-fitting saddle, they can certainly improve the fit of almost any saddle.

English-style saddle pads are usually designed to fit specific saddles, such as the forward-seat, saddle-seat, and all-purpose styles. Western pads are rarely cut to conform to the saddle, but are available in rounded edges for barrel racing and with a cut-back head for a high-withered animal. Materials used for English and Western saddle pads and blankets include felt, cotton, sheepskin, synthetic fleece, hair, foam rubber, nylon, duck, wool, rayon, and jute. Pads used for English saddles are normally made from one layer of wool or cotton felt or sheepskin or from synthetic fleece. There are often sewn-in leather strap loops which slip over a billet strap and hold the pad from slipping out from under the saddle. A piece of wear leather sewn into the neck of the pad is often added to prevent galling a high-withered animal.

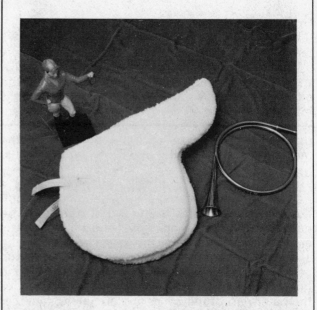

Wash-a-Pads. Machine-washable synthetic-fleece saddle pads used by leading show riders and the USET are available in white and yellow (the latter color to resemble old-fashioned sheepskin used by fox hunters). The pad comes in stock 16-, 17-, and 18-inch forward-seat saddle sizes, in a Hermès-style pad that fits all saddles cut along the Hermès lines, and in Western styles. If you want a custom-made pad, submit a saddle pattern indicating where the billets are to go. Delivery on custom-made pads takes about two weeks. About $30 from M. L. White, Jr., 406 East Main Street, Dalton, Pennsylvania 18414.

Western saddle blankets were traditionally made by Indian weavers. Such patterns as the Navajo, Mojave, and Chimayo were greatly prized and are still valuable today. A number of factories copy their designs in wool or synthetics. Californians used *tirutas,* heavy woven black-and-white blankets made by the Sonora Indians. These blankets normally included tassels extended along the rim of the saddle and are most decorative. Western saddle blankets are usually 30×60 inches and folded in half so that the fold crosses the horse's withers. Many horsemen preferred to use two blankets under the saddle; the bottom layer made of cotton, the top blanket of wool. By layering the two blankets sweat was more efficiently absorbed and chafing from the saddle was therefore reduced.

Many of the excellent synthetic fibers on the market are becoming popular with good reason; they are usually available in pads about 30 inches square. Each of the synthetics reacts differently to use, and a few are such good absorbent agents that we heard one horseman complain that his drew out all the moisture from the horse's skin. Other horsemen have found that foam rubber tends to heat up and irritate the skin. Some of the Western blankets come with two pieces of leather sewn-in along opposite edges. When folded and placed on the horse's back, the leather strips fall directly under the front billet straps and the fender, minimizing chafing from these parts of the saddle.

HORSE BLANKETS

One thing that has become apparent in the consideration of tack is that nothing is simple and there is no single answer to any question. So you may well expect that if the question is "What kind of blanket should I use?" the answer will be "That depends on the type of animal, the facility in which it is kept, and the work you expect it to perform."

There are blankets to keep a horse from the effects of a cold, drafty stable; there are blankets to keep the horse's heavy winter coat from growing in too quickly; there are blankets to absorb moisture; to repel moisture (rain), and to insulate; and there are blankets to protect the animal's fine skin from flies and mosquitoes.

Horse blankets for warmth are usually made with an outer layer of canvas or duck lined with either wool, flannel, or any number of excellent synthetics. Blanket liners are sold separately, and there are a number of good reasons for acquiring one. Many are made of materials that are easy to wash (an important consideration), and such liners, while necessary for cold nights, can be removed when the day warms.

Cooling sheets are simply blankets designed to be used in warm weather. Usually made of washable cotton and occasionally duck or even lightweight wool, they are used to absorb moisture and

A Cushy New Pad. Taking a cue from foam ski boots and astronauts' lift-off chairs, the "Flow Free" saddle pad incorporates two featherweight sections of urethane inserted into pockets on either side of the pad to rest beneath the saddle's bars. The pliable urethane "cells," expanding to fill gaps between saddle and horse, act as a nonirritating self-contouring cushion. The pad's top is made of rough-out leather which is the functional equivalent of billet straps—the leather's high-friction surface prevents the pad from slipping. Although somewhat thicker than conventional pads, the "Flow Free" is made of an absorbent wool felt that "breathes" to permit air to circulate. There are models for standard-size English and Western saddles. The components are sold separately: $50 for the pad, $30 for a pair of "cells," and an underblanket (to keep sweat and dirt from the pad) for $10. Available only through Crafters, P.O. Box 7671, Colorado Springs, Colorado 80933.

Western saddle blankets are wide-ranging in price. A solid-felt pad can be had for about $6, a hair-felt pad for about $11, hair sandwiched between two layers of wool-nylon fabric for about $15, multimaterial "Navajo"-type blankets for about $13 (30×30 inches) and about $25 (30×60 inches). A pure-wool authentic Navajo blanket is $35 and up for the 30×60-inch size. Polyester saddle pads are about $25 for a 30×30-inch-square pattern, and foam-rubber-padded pads are about $14.

English-style saddle pads are usually made to fit the contour of the saddle. Felt pads start at about $9. Synthetic-fleece pads are about $10; fitted to the saddle with a rolled edge, about $30. Although not machine-washable, real sheepskin can be had for about $33.

to protect the horse against becoming chilled after heavy exercise.

Blankets normally rest over the horse from its withers to the base of its tail. The sides hang to the bottom of the horse's belly, where they are held in place by surcingles (usually two), front and rear straps that wrap around the animal's barrel in either a straight or a crisscross pattern to fasten on the left side. The front part of the blanket wraps around the horse's chest to buckle close. Some blankets also include a full tail flap (or a tail strap with snaps for attaching a tail guard) and front D's for connecting a hood. Some coolers are long, square pieces of material that wrap the animal from the poll to the base of the tail. These coolers sometimes come with browbands and strings to tie in the front.

Surcingles are usually sewn onto blankets, but they may be ordered separately.

Some show and race horses require additional stable clothing in the form of a full hood. Such hoods are made in almost all of the blanket materials and are used for the same reasons you would use a blanket. A jowl hood, or sometimes simply a jowl neck strap, is intended to be worn, winter or

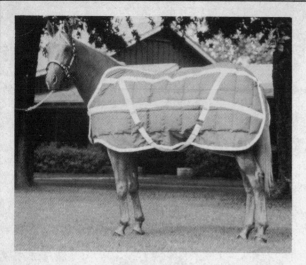

The Classic. A down-filled blanket-and-hood set that has a comfort range of −15 degrees to 60 degrees. Its superior nylon shell and flannel lining are thickly down-filled for insulation. The blanket has a cut-back neck and shaped tail and is available in sizes 68, 72, 74, 76, 78, 80, 84, and 60 and 64 by special order. The hood comes in small, medium, large, and colt by special order. Available in ocean blue only from Ryon Saddle & Ranch Supplies for $600.

summer, on those show horses which must keep a trim throatlatch. The jowl strap, made of either wool, rubber, or vinyl-lined duck or a blend of wool and nylon, will cause the horse to sweat off fat before it ever accumulates. Jowl sweat straps are frequently used on Morgans and Arabians that are shown in conformation classes.

Stable sheets—range around $25.
Coolers—from about $20 to over $40 for pure wool.
Blanket liners—about $15.
Warm blankets—about $50.
Fly sheets—about $15.
Hoods—from $12 for sheeting hood, about $22 for wool, about $38 for Baker hood to match blanket.
Jowl sweat strap—about $15.

You can make your own "poor man's cooler" by opening the stitching on two large burlap feed sacks and sewing them together along one side of their length. Slip over the horse's back with the seam along the withers and push some baling twine through the weave of the burlap where the two sidepieces meet at the chest. Tie to close. This cooler absorbs moisture as the horse is being cooled out; but don't leave it on when you're not nearby, since it will easily slip off the horse's back and hang down the front of its neck.

TACK FOR SPECIALIZED TRAINING

Before any horse is "finished" there are a number of training phases the young animal must successfully pass through, as a child must complete the first grade before he may enter the second grade and certainly before he receives his graduation diploma. To continue with the school analogy, the young, green horse that has been taught to accept a halter and lead can be said to be ready to start the first grade of training. For some people, a horse is "finished" when it has received just enough training to accept a saddle and bridle and carry a rider (passenger); for others, training continues until the animal qualifies for the equivalent of a Ph.D. in a specialty such as dressage, eventing, or cutting.

No matter what the type of work the horse is being prepared to do, the trainer must begin by teaching the animal to be attentive to cues and to learn to balance itself properly for its physique, its way of going, and ultimately, the work it will eventually be asked to do. An entire wardrobe of training equipment exists, and while the amateur trainer may be able to improvise in making some of the tack necessary to advance his horse from one grade to another, he should have an understanding of how such tack works. Following is a description of some of the equipment available.

LUNGING EQUIPMENT

Especially useful for initial training, the lunging caveson is essentially a halter with a ring in the center of a reinforced and padded noseband. The most versatile type will have three rings, one on each side of the noseband and the third one in the center. For the individual who needs to lunge his horse only occasionally, a bridle or halter, plus a saddle, is sufficient. For the trained horse, usually clipping the lunge line to the halter's D ring under the jaw will permit you to reverse the direction without readjusting the setting. It is used with a lunging rein—simply a long (usually about 25 feet) length of lightweight material (webbing, cotton, or nylon) with a swivel snap at one end and perhaps a handhold loop on the other end.

SURCINGLE AND BODY ROLLER

There are a number of practical uses for this piece of equipment, which, to define it simply, is either a girth strap that goes around the horse's middle or a saddle without seat or stirrups. Web, cotton, and nylon surcingles are used to hold blankets and fly sheets in place. A body roller is a surcingle with two pads that rest on either side of the horse's backbone. Its most common use is as part of a bitting or training harness.

Passier Vaulting Surcingle. Used in most European riding clubs for gymnastic performances. Leather-padded with two fixed handles. About $170.

BITTING HARNESS

This flexion-producing device is a common training aid for most English-trained horses, and it has become popular with Western trainers as well. The harness consists of a roller, made of a rubber-based webbing or leather, that has a number of sets of D rings (as many as five sets on the top and two sets at the girth) for adjusting to the bit and such tack as the sidecheek, the overcheck, the crupper, the breastplate, the driving reins, and, for gaited animals, to shackles and the tail set. Most bitting rigs come with elastic side reins and a stout leather bridle. There is a Western equivalent of the bitting rig, basically a running martingale on two side reins which are attached to the curb bit on one end and to the horn of the saddle. It can be used both while the horse is being ridden and while it is standing in its stall. When the horse's head is out of position, the running martingale pulls back on the curb until the animal learns to hold its head properly to stop the action of the bitting rig.

SHACKLES

Developed primarily for use with Three- and Five-Gaited animals, it is made of two often weighted front boots that fit over the shoe and are held in

Lexington Bitting Harness. Made of sewn leather lined with felt under the saddle. Complete with bridle, side reins, checkreins, crupper, and body roller. Fully adjustable. About $75 for horse size and $65 for pony size.

place by elastic or latigo leather that either attaches to a riding saddle or a roller or, like a suspender, encircles the horse over the withers.

ANKLE RATTLERS AND ACTION CHAINS

These specialized pieces of equipment are used primarily on horses trained for park riding and on Three- and Five-Gaited horses. Rattlers are ankle bracelets loosely strung with rubber or heavy aluminum beads, and as the horse moves, it learns to work its feet so that the anklet rattles. These come in varying weights, from under 10 ounces to over 34 ounces, with additional weight requiring extra muscle to lift the leg up high. Chains, either plain or soft-rubber-covered, are used to provide weight only and are relatively noiseless. Ankle-chain rattlers are usually made of heavy leather lined with a softer leather. Dangling from the anklet are eight sets of three 1-inch links of chain which swing freely and are designed to hit the horse's pastern as it moves.

TAIL SET

This item will only be found in the wardrobe of a gaited horse such as American Saddle Horse, the Tennessee Walking Horse, or the Hackney pony. It is designed to be worn by the young horse to ''set'' the healing surgically treated tail. For those breeders who use this equipment, we do not need to describe it further or indicate where it can be found.

HOBBLES

To the Eastern horseman, hobbles are used solely for breeding mares and for special grooming or medicating needs. For the Western horseman, however, hobbles are an everyday fact of horse care and often the only way to keep a saddle horse from wandering off. Although horses have only four legs, horsemen have managed to invent more than four types of hobbles. They include the breeding hobble (made of either reinforced leather or nylon, it fits around the mare's hocks, with a strap coming off each hobble to pass under the belly and attach to a neck strap); the chain hobble; the Utah hobble; the figure-8; the four-way hobble; extra-long hobbles (can be used to sideline or cross-hobble); pacing hobbles; pawing hobbles (a hanging chain hits the coronet when the horse paws); and kicking chains (usually ½-inch heavy chain links that hit the horse's leg when it kicks).

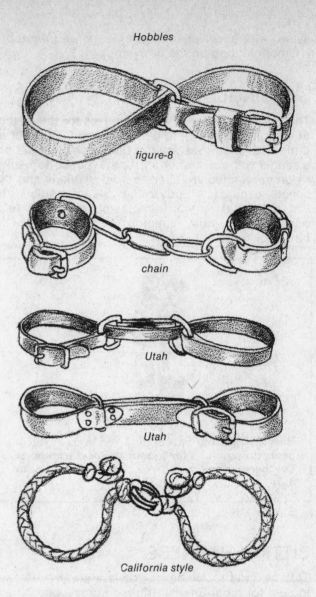

Hobbles

figure-8

chain

Utah

Utah

California style

The price and quality of lunge cavesons vary greatly. A nylon caveson is about $13, while a leather one can be found for about $20 (made in India) or for about $50 (made in England) or for about $85 (made in Germany). Nylon lunge lines are about $5 to $12, while cotton web lines start at about $8 and a tubular web line imported from England can be had for $25.

Surcingles used primarily to hold blankets in place are about $7. A cotton-web and nylon all-purpose surcingle useful for training, driving, or lunging costs about $30, while an imported German leather body roller goes for around $85.

Bitting harness is available in a mostly nylon version for about $70 and in leather with elastic sidelines for not too much more, about $90. The bitting harness made of rubber-based webbing is slightly higher, about $100. A Western bitting rig made of rubber tubing is about $30.

Shackle boots cost about $30, shackles that hook onto the saddle are about $40, and shackles attached to a surcingle are priced about $45.

Ankle-action chains for gaited horses start at about $3 for a pair and climb quickly depending on the leather and the number and weight of the chains. A Tennessee-style tail set ranges from about $105 to about $135.

Hobbles vary almost as much in price as they do in kind. Breeding hobbles are probably the most expensive, with a set of nylon ones costing about $35 and leather hobbles about $60. Chain hobbles range from about $9 to $15; Utah hobbles are about $7 for nylon and $8 for leather; leather extra-long hobbles are about $9.50; rawhide hobbles (eight-plait) run around $13; pawing hobbles made of skirting leather with felt lining are near $14; and kicking chains made of heavy leather, sheepskin-covered, with ½-inch heavy chain, are about $13.

PROTECTIVE EQUIPMENT

Most of the protective equipment listed here is to protect the horse, some of it is intended to protect the horse's tack, and such equipment as the muzzle is intended to protect the horseman.

A neck cradle is an important item to have around a stable for horses that refuse to understand that the blanket they are wearing will keep them warm or that the bandage covering a wound is necessary for healing. The most common neck cradle is made from smooth, rounded pieces of wood held together by wooden beads that allow the cradle some flexibility. The wood cradle hangs from the horse's neck by two leather straps.

Some horsemen prefer to use a bib to prevent the horse from tearing its blanket or opening up healing sores. Most bibs are made of leather and are designed to hook onto the two side rings and the chin ring of the halter. Some also come with an adjustable noseband that permits the horse to eat and drink but restricts it from reaching around to grab with its teeth.

For those horses that can't kick the cribbing habit, a problem that can ruin an otherwise good animal, most catalogs sell "cribbing straps." The variety of devices ranges from a plain broad strap that tightly encircles the horse's neck to a French-type strap reinforced with metal to prevent the neck or windpipe from expanding. There is also a spike cribbing strap, a deterrent if we ever saw one, which, to quote the catalogs, has "proved most effective to prevent wind sucking and crib-bing." It works in response to the expansion of the neck, forcing metal spikes through holes in a neck strap that prick the horse as it sucks in air. Actually, although it looks like an instrument of torture from the Dark Ages, it doesn't deter many horses at all.

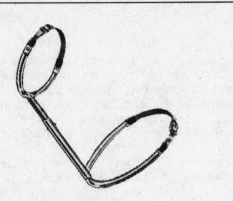

Neck cradles—about $18.
Shaped leather bib—about $13.
Flat leather bib—about $10.
Wide cribbing strap—about $19.
French cribbing strap—about $16.
Spike cribbing strap—about $30.

For the short- or long-necked horse, there is an adjustable neck cradle made of lightweight chrome-plated aluminum that adjusts to correct length. About $23.95 from Libertyville Saddle Shop.

BANDAGES AND BOOTS

When rating a horse, knowledgeable riders look at the animal's feet and legs first, and if they aren't in good shape, the rating is "worthless." When you consider that an animal as massive as the horse is supported by four relatively thin legs and tiny feet, you can see that leg and foot problems are common, with lameness a perpetual companion of most of the finer-bred animal's existence. Because it is the fine-boned, thin-legged horses that are the most valuable to racing and jumping enthusiasts, years of experience, money, and intellect have been dedicated to theories behind bandaging and booting horses.

Bandages and boots, although not the same, serve many of the same functions. Bandages, however, do have a greater variety of uses. They are obviously necessary for such health reasons as covering a deep wound, for a wrap over a heating liniment, or as a container to hold ice around the horse's legs. (See page 99 for medicinal uses of bandages.) But bandages are also used regularly on the horse in perfect health, and these bandages serve such important functions as giving support to fine tendons, preventing chafing caused by muddy tracks or rough terrain, keeping the legs warm in a cold stable, holding a tail in shape, pre-

venting a horse from harming itself should it cross-fire or interfere, and finally, protecting the animal's legs in shipment. Stable or standing bandages used for warmth are normally made of wool or flannel and cover the leg from below the knee to below the fetlock. Exercise bandages that fit snugly for support are usually available in elastic, and many catalogs feature elasticized hose that slip over the necessary area; the exercise bandage should cover the area below the knee to the top of the fetlock only. There is also a shipping bandage, similar to the stable bandage except that it is used over cotton batting and protects the animal's legs from cuts and scrapes or worse during shipment.

Ankle boots—from $16 to $22 per pair.
Shin and ankle—about $25 to about $30 per pair.
Tendon and front-shin boots—about $25 per pair.
Polo boots—about $40 per pair.
Galloping boots—about $25 per pair.
Rubber bell boots—from about $7 to $13 per pair.
Shipping boots—leather hock boots about $35, leather front-leg boots about $45; poly-foam, vinyl-covered, set of 4 about $25.
Quilted leg bandages—set of four about $6.
Elastic support bandage with Velcro closures—set of four about $20.
Cotton wrap bandage—4 inches × 4 yards, about $3.50 a dozen.

Because horses are capable of inflicting an incredible number of sores, wounds, or bruises upon themselves, horsemen have retaliated with an equally incredible number of preventives in the form of boots, and there are boots available that cover every part of a horse's legs. There are also boots for teaching or improving gaits or for simply protecting the legs from irritating mud. Catalogs feature boots made of leather that may be lined with foam rubber, with vinyl, with felt, with wool felt, with lamb's wool, or with French calfskin. These boots are designed to cover the shin, tendon, ankle, coronet, knee, and hoof (as standard protection for hunters), to protect the hock during shipping, to protect the heels during cutting and roping, and thick boots to protect the polo pony's legs during a game. Bell boots, which fit over the horse's hoofs, are used on hunters as protection against bruising their feet if they knock down a pole. Racing trotters and pacers wear quarter boots to protect them if their feet interfere with each other, and Five-Gaited Saddle Horses wear a hinged quarter boot to improve the action of the legs. Horses that develop a capped elbow will be put into a show boil roll, a padded roll, much like a rubber tire, that fits around the horse's coronet to prevent the horse from bruising its elbow with its shoe as it is lying down. Overreach boots are often necessary protection for many of the gaited horses and trotters that have a propensity toward striking heel or foreleg with the shoe tip of the hind foot. Brushing, or ankle, boots protect that area from hind legs that tend to brush against the inside of the front ankles. Horsemen can easily make a brushing "boot" by taking a piece of heavy felt, wrapping it around the horse's leg, tying it in the center with a ribbon, and then folding the top over the ribbon to form a double layer of material.

Sno-Pruf. Use on saddles and boots to soften and preserve leather while protecting it from snow and rain. Your local hardware or tack shop should carry it, or write to the company directly. About $1.36 for 3¾ ounces. The Snow-Proof Co., Livonia, New York.

HOW TO CLEAN TACK

Equipment
- saddle or glycerine soap
- sponge for applying soap
- towel for removing mud
- soft rag for drying leather
- dandy brush for serge saddle linings
- metal polish
- neat's-foot oil, castor oil, Snow-Proof or Lexol
- toothpicks for cleaning dirt out from holes
- a pail of warm water
- saddle stand and bridle hooks

Tack must be cleaned regularly to prevent drying, rotting, or breaking, and it should always be cleaned after each use. While going through the basic cleaning process, stay alert to such signs of wear as pulled or broken stitching; buckles that bend against the laws of leverage; billets, girth, or bridle parts that are cracked and dry. All tack that is not in storage should be sponged several times a week with a glycerine saddle soap, which not only cleans but leaves a waxy, protective coating for the leather. At least once or twice a week, the saddle and bridle should be taken apart completely for a thorough cleaning. To do this, disassemble the saddle entirely: remove the girth(s), the billets (on the Western saddle), the fenders and stirrup leathers, and the stirrups. Put the bit, along with the metal stirrups, in a basin of cool water to soak.

Begin cleaning by forcefully damp-sponging or brushing with a coarse towel all mud from the saddle and bridle, taking special care that the panels do not retain any cling-ing clumps of mud. If the saddle has a sheep-skin or serge lining, go over it thoroughly with a dandy brush. If the girth is made of washable fabric, brush it out and soak it in cool water with a mild soap. After the leather parts have been cleaned of mud, dry them with a soft, absorbent cloth and set them aside to dry. Don't put them in direct sunlight or near other direct sources of heat or the leather will dry out and become brittle. If the leather seems at all dry (particularly when you're checking the billets, stirrup leathers, and girth), apply a light coat of neat's-foot oil; however, do not if the leather feels soft and pliable. Overapplication of neat's-foot can make tack very tacky and unpleasant to touch or ride. Finish the saddle off with an application of saddle soap. Barely dampen a sponge or soft cloth and rub the soap onto the leather. If it lathers, that means the sponge is too wet.

Before putting the saddle and bridle aside, take a wooden toothpick and poke it through the holes in the stirrup leathers to remove any dirt or excess saddle soap. Buff the leather, if you like, for that wonderful shine that means clean tack.

Before sitting back to relax, remember to take the metal bit and stirrups out of the water in which you left them to soak. Scrub off any remaining mud or crust, dry, and then polish with a metal cleaner. Take the wash-able girth out of its water bath and if it is not satisfactorily clean, dump it into a washing machine with the saddle pad, using a cold setting and a mild detergent.

If you are interested in learning more about the subject of tack, the first reference to go to is E. Hartley Edwards, "Saddlery" (Arco Publishing Co., 1963; $6.95). Although just the slightest bit dated and a little too British at times, it offers the most complete and articulate description of bits, bridles, saddles, and accessories to be found. A useful book for further understanding of the three major groups of bits—the snaffle, double, and Pelham—is "Bit by Bit: A Guide to Equine Bits," by Diana R. Tuke (Arco, 1974; $5.95). Over 190 photographs complement the text. Ed Connell's "Hackamore Reinsman" ($4) explains how to take a green horse and trainer from the first bosal to sliding stops and whirls on the hacka-more. The accent is on making a finished hack-amore horse with an untouched mouth, California style. Ed Connell's "Reinsman of the West: Bridles & Bits," Volume II ($5.50), gives the how and why of making a spade-bit horse out of the hackamore horse. Both books published and distributed by Longhorn Press, Box 150, Cisco, Texas 76437. "The Illustrated Glossary of Horse Equipment," Arco, 1976 ($3.95), is just that: 101 photographs of English and Western equipment with clear, concise explanations of what each item is and what it does.

6 APPAREL

Most books and catalogs neatly divide riding apparel into two distinct sections—English and Western—as if little knowing or caring that the two can and do overlap in many different ways. True, there is a special "look" worn by people who favor the English style of riding, and there is certainly a familiar cowboy image shared by all those who prefer stock saddles, but curious as it may seem, these two costumes have quite a bit in common. For one thing, apparel for the horseman evolved over centuries of horsemanship, and designs were developed to fulfill specific needs and functions, which may help explain why these styles, once they reached their peak of development in nineteenth-century England and America, tended to stop right there without much concession to popular fashion thereafter. Levi's, Stetsons, hunting "pinks," and top boots still look very much the way they did around the turn of the century, and though this conservatism might bother those who like to change their fashions from one season to the next, the reaction has in fact, in recent years at least, been quite the opposite. Denim has become *de rigueur* even for the jet set, and hacking jackets and high boots are as familiar to readers of *Vogue*—even those who are likely never to set foot near a stable—as they are to readers of *The Chronicle of the Horse.*

THE HISTORY OF APPAREL FOR HORSEMEN

Actually, it is somewhat ironic that riding clothes should be considered fashionable only now, when it was the English riding outfit of the 18th-century country gentleman that set the style for all men's clothing (and some ladies' garb as well) worn throughout the Western world today. When William Coke, Duke of Norfolk, went to court to plead the cause of the American colonies to George III, he wore his riding clothes which were like those of all aristocratic English gentlemen of the day, and

Two 19th-century English gentlemen, a U.S. Cavalry officer and a Mexican vaquero

soon launched a revolution of his own. Gainsborough immortalized the costume in paint, and within a generation, everyone but everyone in England was wearing it as well. Hunting and riding for sport had developed late in the 18th century, and the French styles then ruling the world were unsuitable. Riders needed simple materials that could be easily cleaned and were sturdy enough to withstand the wear and tear of the hunting field. Coats had to be shorter and cut away at the front for freedom and comfort. Breeches replaced silk hose, plain linen rather than lace ruffles graced the neck, and high-crowned hats were devised to save the rider's head in case of a fall. Thanks to the Industrial Revolution, which made England the world's leader in the spinning and weaving of cloth goods, and to the sheep business in Australia, which produced fine merino wools for the Empire, not to mention the excellence of British tailors, suitable materials could be turned into attractive, durable, and well-fitting clothing that exactly met the needs of the sportsman. Once the style became widely popular in England, George (Beau) Brummel and his Regency dandies turned it into an art form—by refining and tightening the clothing and making it an international rage. Since materials were pretty invariable, expert tailoring became something of an art as well; Beau Brummel boasted that he had his coat, waistcoat, and breeches all made by different tailors, each one the master of his particular specialty. An example of Brummel's powerful influence: the Prince of Wales was seen to burst into tears when Brummel told him that his breeches didn't fit properly.

In spite of the overrefined nature of Regency costume—when breeches were tailored very tight (and very uncomfortable, especially in the rain) and made of doeskin and then corduroy—serious English riders came to their senses and demanded breeches that were looser above the knees and a more comfortable single-breasted coat to replace the tight, double-breasted swallowtail (although the latter is still worn in the hunt field today). Thus English riding clothes for men became fairly fixed in cut by about 1820, and the style continued to exert its considerable strength on men's wear of all kinds—from the formal cutaways and top hats proper for occasions of state and the tailcoats still worn in the ballroom (where true chivalry may be said to exist even today) to the everyday suits worn on Madison Avenue. The English were not so rigid, however, as to overlook useful styles from other parts of the world (so long as they were in the Empire). India, where polo was popular, was the source of jodhpurs and the jodhpur boot, as well as the sport itself.

Ladies were not so easily accommodated. In the early 18th century, riding clothes for women resembled masculine garb, but by mid-century, Englishwomen rarely rode astride. Few of them hunted until well into the 19th century, if only because the sidesaddle was uncomfortable, if not dangerous, for cross-country riding. When the third pommel was invented, it became safer for la-

~~~~~~~~~~~~~~~~~~~~~~~~~~~~~~~~~~~
What the Well-Dressed 18th-Century Equestrienne Wore

"A coat and a waistcoat of blue camlet trimmed and embroidered with silver, with a petticoat of the same stuff, by which alone her sex was recognized, as she wore a smartly cocked beaver hat, edged with silver and rendered more sprightly with a feather, while her hair, curled and powdered, hung to a considerable length down her shoulders, tied like that of a rakish young gentleman, with a long streaming scarlet riband."
The Spectator *(London)*
~~~~~~~~~~~~~~~~~~~~~~~~~~~~~~~~~~~

dies to hunt, but the clothing, at least from the waist down, had to be (and still is) specially designed for the saddle (and tailored, in fact, while the lady was sitting *in* her saddle). Even Queen Victoria, who wore a high hard hat, a tailored bodice, and masculine neckwear, kept her long, flowing skirts, (which made mounting and dismounting very awkward indeed without help). Tailor-made clothing became fashionable for women by about 1870, and by the end of the century, as women began to ride astride again, it became widespread. (Actually, it was still considered proper in England for women to use a sidesaddle as late as 1930, and nearly half the women equestrians still did so, but the love of cross-country riding won out. The style, which is very elegant indeed if not always practical, is currently enjoying something of a revival).

In the meantime, riding clothes were adapted throughout the rest of the world from the English styles. America was an eager recipient of English woolen goods as well as fashion. As hunting clothes became simplified for street wear, Americans developed their own versions of riding and military clothing, wearing them West as they explored, exploited, and settled the frontier and built towns where more formal garb was appropriate. Long frock coats, jackboots (or Wellingtons or Napoleons) and Southern wide-brimmed planter's hats or bowlers were the sign of a Western gentleman—not a dude, but a prosperous civilian. ("Dude," incidentally, is a sort of international put-down. It seems to come from the dialectical German word *Dudenkop,* meaning "stupid-head," and in England it indicates a fop.)

Out on the range, work clothing was rougher and more suitable for riding. Much of what eventually became the cowboy outfit was likely to have been produced at first in the East—as the Stetson hat was—or at least designed by an Easterner—as Levi's were. Nevertheless, the influence of the Spanish-American *vaquero,* whose own style derived originally from North African Moors and medieval warriors, was strong. Since Spanish riding styles were different from those in the East, Westerners made some pretty important changes in their dress for riding purposes. In the brush country of Texas, hats, like the Mexican sombrero, had to be wide enough to keep the sun off the face, and bandanas became standard neckwear to keep the neck and face free of scratches, sunburn, and dust. Pants had to be as stout and as comfortable as possible for long, hard hours in the saddle. Snugness at the knees mattered less, since the combination of the Spanish saddle with long stirrups and horses bred to lope rather than trot made posting unnecessary. Mexican aprons, or *armitas* (little arms or weapons), were refined into leather chaps, which afforded wonderful protection for the leg (against thorns and cold) and a good grip on the saddle as well. Boots were high, like the English type, because they had a protective function too, but they were narrower at the toe to get into and out of the stirrup easily. Heels were raised—not just to keep them from sliding through the stirrup or to dig into the ground for holding a wild calf, but perhaps also to give the cowboy a bit of stature on the ground as well as on a horse (though cowboys were proud, it is said, of having small feet). Spurs had an elaborate look quite different from the modest, stubby English spurs; Spanish and Mexican versions, like those worn by the knights of yore, had long steel shanks with huge rowels, and Texans took to them quickly, scorning the small brass cavalry spurs.

Western styles differed from region to region, depending on climate, strong regional snobbery (Texas vs. Mexico vs. California vs. Oregon, ad infinitum), and the differences in riding and herding techniques and equipment. Californians were more directly influenced by the Spanish than the Texans were, wearing low-heeled shoes and truly enormous spurs. Northern cowmen in the dead of winter could be seen wearing fur chaps, heavy wool shirts, warm vests, and overcoats. And Indians had their influence, too, on beaded gauntlets, horsehair hatbands, fringes for chaps (or leggings), and silver tobacco canteens, as well as many other decorative trappings that would later become important in parade dress.

It seems to be true of all styles of riding clothes, regardless of region or purpose, that a show—whether it be in the hunting field, in the show ring, at the rodeo, on the polo field, or at the racetrack—always brings out the formal, traditional costumes in which rigid conservatism plays a heavy role. For when we are preparing ourselves to perform at our best, the old adage about clothes making the man (or woman) is still true. Although we may scoff at the rules for hunting apparel, shudder at the contempt with which a Texan regards a spur-dragging Californio (or vice versa), and wonder at the amounts of money, time, and energy spent on clothing one can wear only on the back of a horse, we may as well relax, enjoy it, and join in. For all of the clothing that horsemen and horsewomen wear developed for specific purposes, and in looking over the products available today, we would do well to keep the practical as well as traditional aspects in mind.

So, starting at the bottom, which as everyone knows is the foundation of a good riding seat, we shall begin with boots and move up the body,

stopping now and then for some interesting sidelights of the historical as well as the anatomical sort. After a general discussion of the different types of apparel, we offer up complete costumes for specific equestrian events, and we will drop in along the way some information about manufacturers and distributors of ready-made items and sources for custom-made products.

~~~~~~~~~~~~~~~~~~~~~~~~~~~~~~

- *These boots are made for traveling: jodhpur and Western boots can most easily be worn in transit. Since feet tend to swell during flights, high boots are the least comfortable. Rubber boots, including Newmarkets, can safely and easily be folded in a suitcase. Leather boots toted by hand can be guarded from scratches by carrying bags. Cloth bags start at $6 a pair, while heavy vinyl and zippered carriers cost about $15. You can protect your headgear either by wearing the hat or by placing a hunt cap in a waterproof zippered vinyl case (about $11). All items are available at tack shops.*
- *Boots carried by hand provide a surprisingly large amount of packing space. If you're not using boot trees, stuff the footwear with socks, underwear, and other small foldables—you'll appreciate the additional space in your suitcases.*

~~~~~~~~~~~~~~~~~~~~~~~~~~~~~~

BOOTS

Sturdy riding boots as we know them today would certainly be unnecessary if it were not for the stirrup. (The carvings on the Parthenon and the paintings of Frederick Remington are testament to the fact that the stirrupless Greeks and Native Americans had no need for either.) The invention of the stirrup is credited to the nomadic Huns of Asia in the 5th century, but it was not used in Europe until the 9th century, after Charlemagne's wars in what is now Hungary. And it was not until the year 1000 that the stirrup arrived in Britain, thanks to the Scandinavians, who had adopted it a century earlier from the steppe peoples of Eastern Europe. Nevertheless, the development of the riding boot did take place in Western Europe, and the styles that we use today descended directly from medieval long leather boots designed to protect the legs in battle and secure the foot in the stirrup. Jackboots were worn over pants by courtiers in England in the early 17th century, and eventually they were streamlined into military boots such as the *Wellington,* and then into the *Napoleon.* (Ironically, Waterloo notwithstanding, it was Napoleon who won the boot battle, for it is from that style that the *top, or hunt, boot* derived. Wellington, however, can be said to have triumphed in the long run, for variations of his style of boot are still made today.) Fashioned of grain leather, with the inside left brown and the outside blackened with a combination of egg white and lampblack, the boot had a top high enough to cover the knee while its wearer was riding through brush or enemy lines

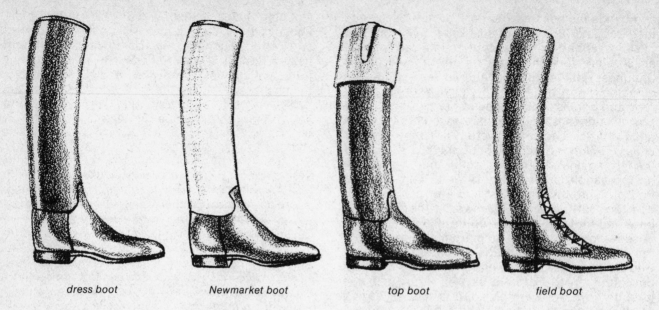

dress boot   Newmarket boot   top boot   field boot

and soft enough to be turned over to reveal a brown cuff.

As riding developed into a sport, this cuff disappeared, leaving a vestigial sewn-on brown top to contrast with the black of the boot itself. (Beau Brummel was said to have polished his boot tops with champagne and peach marmalade—or apricot jam, some say—and the boots themselves with port wine and black currant jelly.) Eventually mahogany became the fashionable color for boot tops, although to this day there is much discussion about the proper shade. In England there were strong regional differences and sets of rules determining same, but in this country, the principal rule is that colored tops may be worn only by members of the hunt and then only with white breeches. Ladies may wear black patent leather tops, presumably because patent leather needs no polish that might stain a lady's breeches. *Jockey boots,* once made with stitched-on tops, are now simply dyed in two colors to create a fake top, which would be frowned on at a formal hunt or in an appointments class. Gentleman hunters who wish to wear top boots some of the time and butcher boots (topless black hunting boots) on other occasions may buy slip-on tops, but they tend to slip around during use and leave a noticeable mark on the boot beneath.

Hunting, or dress, boots, with tops or without, should reach to the small of the knee in back, or—as tradition has it—to the spot just below the second (some say fourth) button of the breeches, or eyelet if the breeches are laced. In these days of buttonless, laceless stretch breeches, the best test of a new boot is to make sure that the back of the boot top touches the back of the upper leg when the knee is bent, for as boots are broken in they will drop, especially if only half lined. Dress boots traditionally have relatively straight tops, but these days the Spanish, or Continental, top—which rises in front and dips behind the knee—is fashionable, presumably because it gives the look of a higher

boot. Bootmakers claim that it also affords more freedom for the leg.

Whatever the style, boots must fit snugly at the knee (so that only one finger can be inserted and then with some difficulty), over the calf, and at the heel and instep, but not so tightly that they cut off circulation. People with large calves have often complained that boots were designed only for thin people, and this is generally true where ready-made boots are concerned. Gussets or zippers may be inserted at the top, and the tab that still exists as a decorative element on some boots is said to have been designed as a cover-up for the seam of an inset (though we suspect that it was for pulling on the boot, since insets would weaken the boot's structure). However, none of these measures to widen a boot is recommended; a far more satisfactory solution is a pair of custom-made boots, which will accommodate not only a wide calf but a pair of different-sized feet, or any other irregularity one's foot might have. Custom-made boots will disguise a foot's natural flaws; a double layer of leather at the top, for instance, will make the calf look narrower and more in proportion with the rest of the leg. A boot that is made to measure and then stretched, after soaking, to a proper fit is always superior to a pinching ill-fitting boot. And custom-made boots, which have many other advantages as well, will last a lifetime with good care and can be readily repaired—if necessary by the original bootmaker, who will try to preserve the boot's original shape.

Although several kinds of leather can be used to make boots, the best choice is full-grain calfskin, which is supple, easily shined, and porous so that the leg and foot may breathe. The best calfskin comes from France, where veal is a much-loved dish, but it is becoming increasingly difficult to obtain, as the French learn to love steak *à l'américaine.* Unblemished hides are also rarer now, since hedgerows are being replaced with barbed wire, which will scratch and scar the hide.

Scratches may be sanded off the leather, but this spoils the surface; as Hank Vogel, a custom bootmaker, points out, a full-grain hide with minor blemishes is much better than a corrected hide (scar tissue is stronger than normal tissue, for one thing), and we may just have to get used to them in the future. American calfskin—in spite of our enormous beef industry—is not particularly satisfactory for bootmaking; not only is it likely to be badly marked, but there are very few tanners of calfskin around these days, and many people believe that calves raised to do nothing but eat in sheltered barns cannot possibly have skins tough enough to stand up under wear. Baby calf is even finer than calfskin (which can be from an animal of an age up to one year), but it is not very durable. Jockeys, for whom every ounce counts, may order custom-made boots of baby calf, but most other riders find that in spite of its good "feel," it rarely lasts more than a season or two with hard wear. Cordovan, another popular boot leather, although increasingly difficult to obtain, is not simply a dark brown leather (all hides are colorless before being dyed brown, black, or any other shade you like) but the hide of a mature horse. Twice as heavy as calfskin, although not as strong (it will tear, rather like paper, under stress), it is warmer on the foot and won't hold a shine. Scotch grain is calf with a texture stamped on; it is heavy and stiff and doesn't take a good shine, though the stamping will cover up minor, unimportant blemishes in the leather. Patent leather is sometimes used to dress up jodhpur boots for evening saddle seat wear. Porvair is a synthetic material that has enjoyed some popularity in recent years. It is relatively inexpensive and easy to clean and care for, but it is not particularly durable and does not have the feel of genuine leather.

Many people like the look of a leather-lined boot, but an unlined boot made of heavier leather is cooler and more flexible and permits a better feel of the horse. Lined boots give more protection and hold their shape, but they don't wear as long, since the lining at the ankle—the point of greatest stress—will eventually crack and pull away from the outer leather, and for this there is no repair. A German (or three-quarter) lining is a good compromise for those who prefer the sturdiness of the lined boot, since it is fully lined except for a cutout oval area at the inner calf. One custom bootmaker with whom we spoke told us that 90 percent of his boots were ordered without linings and that the German-lined boots were preferred by dressage riders.

Soles and heels are traditionally made of leather, but synthetic material for the former is more durable, and waterproof rubber for the latter is skid-resistant (important for one's dignity on a linoleum or highly polished wooden floor if not in the stirrup). Whatever the material, soles should always be full, since half soles will interfere with the stirrup iron. Spur rests, or wedges attached to the back of the heel, are optional additions to hunting boots but are probably better left off. Spurs should fit properly without slipping down, and a knocked-off spur rest leaves an unattractive heel that will need to be repaired. *Garter straps,* which buckle around the top of the boot with the buckle on the outside, are required in formal hunting attire. They were originally designed to keep the boots themselves from slipping down (inevitable with soft, unlined leather), but their primary usefulness nowadays is a feeling of security, for they can double as pieces of bridle should any become broken in the field. Straps should match the color of the breeches if top boots are worn, although patent leather tops need patent leather garters, and plain black boots need plain black garters.

The *field boot,* usually brown and thus not appropriate for formal hunting, has laces to allow for a high instep. It is probably the best-fitting of all boots, since the ankle can be drawn to a good tight fit no matter how much room the foot may need to get into the boot. Because of this, field boots (whose style takes the name of its inventor, Blucher) are now being made in black for hunting, although some masters still frown on their use. These boots are sometimes reinforced at the toe with a toe cap for extra protection, although the stiffness may be uncomfortable for some people. This is really more decorative than useful, especially when punch marks are patterned on them, as in men's dress shoes.

Waterproof *Newmarket boots* take their name from rainy Newmarket, the famous racing center in England. They are attractive, practical, and a good deal cheaper than hunt or field boots. Traditionally made with legs of box cloth (a linen canvas) lined with leather and water-resistant leather vamps, Newmarkets are now available with more effective rubber feet and waterproof tops. (Box cloth is no longer produced, even in England.) Most Newmarket boots are shaped like dress boots, but there

jodhpur boot

gaiter boot

paddock boot

gaiter boot

are also a field boot style and a paddock boot (or high shoe) with canvas sides.

Black rubber boots are also made for wet weather in imitation of the dress hunting boot. Although they are cheap and lightweight, they don't allow the boot to break in or to breathe, and in hot weather they may cause an uncomfortable accumulation of perspiration, in spite of woven-linen liners. Plastic materials are also used, but they too are hot, and they never really fit the foot very well. Nevertheless, they are often practical for growing children, because they are inexpensive and provide a certain amount of leg support. Rubber boots with leather linings are a new compromise, but we haven't subjected them to experiment as of this writing. Spur rests are sometimes built into rubber boots, since they have a slicker surface than leather.

A variation of the field boot is the high-laced shoe, or *paddock boot.* Designed to be worn under chaps or jodhpurs, it is quite a bit less expensive than the higher boots. Like other low boots, it gives far less support to the leg and is less desirable for jumping. But paddock boots are more comfortable in cooler weather and more easily removed than high boots, and they make fine walking shoes as well. Paddock boots can be made in various designs and in various colors. *Turf boots* are similar but employ zippers instead of laces in front and elastic inserts for maximum comfort and a good fit.

Jodhpur boots, usually worn by children and saddle-seat riders, were brought to England in the 1920's from India, where they derived from polo boots. Like high shoes, they reach a few inches above the ankle and fit under pants or leggings. They have split sides rather than frontal laces and are closed with straps (one or two) or, more recently, with elastic or zippers. (This style may be referred to as a *gaiter boot* or jodgore shoe.) The elastic-sided boots are easy to remove and are often selected by nervous parents who would rather lose a boot than have their children catch a foot in the stirrup and be dragged. Because jodhpur boots are so popular, they are readily available at reasonable prices in most tack and apparel shops, though these are usually made of cowhide rather than the more desirable (and more expensive) calf.

Gaiters (leggings or puttees, as they are called in India) are rarely worn today, since the traditional material of which they are made—box cloth—is no longer manufactured. But they are a fine traditional riding garment, although it is difficult to know whether to consider them as boots or pants, and may still be seen—made of natural sail-cloth with calf heel collars and laces—on formally dressed ringmasters, coachmen, and chauffeurs. They derive from old English leggings (a kind of knee-high chap), protecting the leg like a boot and giving a better fit on the calf and more support than a pair of trousers. They are meant to be worn in lieu of boots, covering the lower leg (and trousers) when ankle-height shoes are worn. They are

snug at the calf, cover the gap between shoe and cuff, and serve to protect the ankle as well. The Newmarket boot, with its canvas (originally box-cloth) sides derived from the look of the gaitered leg.

Surprisingly, jodhpur boots are popular in the West these days as well as in the East, because they fit comfortably under long chaps and are easier to walk in than *high-heeled cowboy boots*. But the high-heeled boot is still the most distinctive feature of the Western rider (with the possible exception of the Stetson), and it is undoubtedly the most popular boot worn today anywhere. The boots are manufactured in many styles and used for everything from riding motorcycles to standing around in drugstores. But like hunting boots, they were designed originally for riding horses, and they too derive from the jack, Wellington, and Napoleon boots of the 18th and 19th centuries. (Those were, after all, what Americans wore West, whether they went as soldiers or as civilians.) Early Western boots didn't have much of a heel, but eventually cowboys added them—for various reasons, the primary one being to keep the boot from sliding through the large stirrups of the stock saddle. The first heels were slanted in under the boot and were about two inches high; later, as roping cowboys needed a good way of digging into the earth as they hung on to a struggling calf on the other end of a rope, they demanded straighter, wider *"walking"* heels. Both types of boot are made today for riders and walkers, along with the short Wellington boots, which are only 9 or 10 inches high, unlike the 12-to-13-inch-high cowboy boots. Polo boots, now increasing in fashionability out of as well as in stirrups, are very tall (19-inch) boots similar to old Western cowboy boots with underslung heels and stitched uppers.

Proper cowboys of old—like professional or serious riders anywhere today—avoided the store-bought boot, even though a pair might run only $3 or $4 a hundred years ago. The best boots, then as now, were custom-made to one's personal measurements and designed to last a good, long time. Bench-made boots were a bit less expensive, because there was less handwork in them, but because they were partially made up ahead, they never fitted exactly right, an important consideration when most of your waking hours were to be spent wearing them. Handmade boots invariably had unique, handmade decorative elements worked into the leather. These designs were used not just for looks or to cover up minor blemishes in the leather, but also to stiffen the leather and increase the amount of leg support and protective value (to leg as well as to boot). Although the old ready-made boot was fairly plain, modern ready-mades are usually dressed up with cutouts, stitched decorations, incised patterns, and inserts of colored leather. These designs go into and out of fashion very quickly (to preserve that individual, handmade look), and even the basic style of the boot seems to take some surprising turns for the sake of stylishness, especially in the shape of the heel and toe. The latter now tends to be round or pointed rather than square, as the toe always used to be. Toes still are narrow, however, an important detail for the cowboy who must find the stirrup without looking down. The traditional cowboy boot came up to the knee and was cut straight across the top, with perhaps some leather mule ears (or straps) hanging down the side for pulling-on purposes. These days, straight tops are reserved for the shorter Wellington boots, while the higher boots are scalloped front to back with shorter leather pull straps.

Most good Western boots were and still are made of calfskin, like English boots, although cowhide is more common (and less supple and less expensive) in ready-made styles. Caribou, water buffalo, and sharkskin are exotic work-boot leathers; lizard and other exotics are only for dress boots. They are usually lined with oil-resistant soles of synthetic material or treated leather, with steel-reinforced toes for extra protection. Soles must be light and flexible, with the arch curved high; the instep may be pegged with wood for extra support.

BOOT WEAR AND CARE

The purchaser of a new pair of riding boots—regardless of style—must be sure that they are well-fitting. Well-fitting means roomy at the toe, reasonably snug at the heel and ankle, and tight over the calf. Badly fitting ready-made boots may be stretched on a machine or mold, or, if you can bear it, on your foot, but all care should be taken to avoid damaging your feet or unnaturally weakening the leather. All boots will relax a bit eventually; the softer the leather, the more they will stretch or drop. Any good rider trying to keep his heels down will cause some flexing and wrinkling at the heel; this part of the breaking-in process is to be expected and worked for. But once they are broken in, boots should be cared for properly to prevent deterioration of the leather and to preserve the original shape of the boot. Boots should be given internal support when not in use. Custom-made *wooden boot trees* are worth the investment for custom-made boots, but ready-made trees are available. Most good bootmakers do not recommend lightweight spring-type trees, which can distort the shape of the boot, but prefer the idea of stuffing boots with rolled-up newspaper or a magazine to fill the entire leg.

Before we store the boot, however, let's get back to the way it fits on the foot. A heavy sock is probably the best form of protection for both foot and boot, even in warm weather, and this should be taken into account in fitting the boot. Socks will absorb sweat, protect the foot from abrasion, and preserve the condition of the leather. As anyone who has ever ridden during the winter will know, these socks are not particularly effective for keeping the foot warm. One can try two pairs of socks—light cotton inside a woolen pair—but these, or extra-heavy long socks, may make the

mule-eared boot   *Wellington boot*

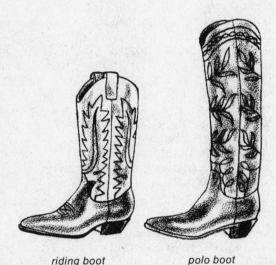

riding boot   *polo boot*

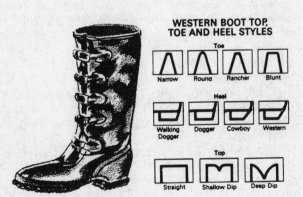

overshoe

WESTERN BOOT TOP, TOE AND HEEL STYLES

Toe
Narrow   Round   Rancher   Blunt

Heel
Walking Dogger   Dogger   Cowboy   Western

Top
Straight   Shallow Dip   Deep Dip

calf uncomfortable. Long underwear that covers the whole foot is often a good solution—and a traditional one as well, for the British were quite accustomed to wear wool or silk mixed with wool from top to toe. Whatever the material, long johns with seams at the seat or inside the leg are to be avoided if one plans to be comfortable in the saddle. Light thermal socks or short heavy socks are warm too, and they will not affect the calf (have them knitted to your specifications, or cut off and hem a long pair). Sheepskin innersoles are helpful, or you might decide to go whole hog and order boots with fleece-lined feet, available in both Western and hunting boots for an extra $15 or $20. Fleece foot warmers may also be attached to stirrups—perhaps a bit more practical for riders who confront different kinds of weather the year around.

All sorts of devices and remedies have been dreamed up to make boots easier to pull on and off. English boots are usually pulled on with jockey, or *boot, lifts* that hook into canvas or webbing loops inside the boot. (These loops, incidentally, once had a double purpose; a button hook attached to them would connect to a button on the breeches to keep them from riding up; some boots even had buttons installed inside for the purpose.) Western boots, like some English boots, have mule ears, or straps for pulling by hand. Some people sprinkle chalk or talcum powder inside the boot before sliding it on; this will also help later on, especially if the foot is wet. For removal, *boot jacks,* some simple of wood or acrylic plastic and some elaborate with iron handles for leverage—occasionally designed like beetle antennae or steer horns to fit around and grip the boot—are more efficient and dignified than struggling alone or begging help from a friend. Whatever method you use, however, be sure that your leg and foot are entirely relaxed before you start tugging.

Good leather deserves considerate care, and it will reward the wearer with years of service for the trouble. In the old days when servants were plentiful, hunt boots were waxed as they were blacked, so that scratches could be rubbed down with bone and filled with black wax to make them disappear. The wax also insulated the leather against horse sweat; boots could then be easily sponged off with warm water to eliminate any sweat marks. For cleaning, boning, and waxing, the boots had to supported by boot trees to give a firm base, and boots properly kept could last forever with no disfiguring marks. Although this kind of boot can still be made by custom bootmakers, most boots are made of unwaxed black-dyed calf, like regular black shoes. Scratch marks cannot be removed, worn areas will lighten in color, and sweat can damage the leather; but they are cheaper, and caring for them does not require a staff of servants and a supply of deer bones.

Because calfskin is more delicate than cowhide, saddle soap is too strong. If dirt cannot be brushed off or wiped off with a dry cloth, a mild soap and a cloth dampened with lukewarm water

---

HOW TO MEASURE YOURSELF FOR CUSTOM-MADE BOOTS

Sit on a chair and place your bare foot on a piece of white paper; putting no weight on your foot and holding the pencil upright but slightly in toward the foot, trace the outline. The higher your arch, the more the line should swing in under your foot. Without moving your foot, slip a tape measure under the ball of your foot and wrap it snugly around the top; note the circumference measurement and note on the paper the exact spot at which the tape was placed. Repeat this at the instep, where the bone at the outside of your foot is most prominent; mark the spot where you measured and note down the circumference of your foot. Run the tape from the instep at the same spot around the heel just where it begins to curve off the ground and back to the instep. Note this measurement. Repeat the whole process with the other foot. Next, measure the widest part of your calf (still sitting and with no socks) and the top of your leg, holding the tape as high as you can at the back of the knee. Measure the length of your leg from a little above the prominent bone below the knee straight down to the floor. Repeat these measurements for the other leg.

From "All About Boots"
The Pennsylvania Horse (Philadelphia)
December 1971

---

will remove mud and sweat marks. Water dries out the leather and soap pulls the color, so be sparing. Gasoline and isopropyl alcohol will also clean the leather (especially good for built-up polish), but—like water—they are drying agents, and a leather conditioner should be applied after use. Boots that have become soaking wet should be dried completely and naturally (not in front of a fire or radiator) after each wearing and given a leather conditioning to keep them from losing natural oils; do not use too much conditioner or the leather will become too soft, and avoid neat's-foot oil, which will inhibit the shine. Some people like to rub glycerine on the leather lining to keep it supple. Silicone or Sno-Pruf will act as a water-resistant dressing for those who like to ride in the rain; the latter is also a conditioner and will help keep the leather soft.

Once the boot has been cleaned and dried, apply a thin layer of polish—cream polish such as Meltonian cream is best, as paste-wax polishes will crack and flake off—and let it settle. Then buff it up until you can see your face in the shine. Dark polish will help darken boots, although boots that have lost their color, usually on the inner calf, are more difficult to restore, if not impossible. An alcohol-based dye will help—with some leather conditioner to prevent drying—but since the original

Most tack shops carry basic types of English and Western boots in various price ranges. Because retailers usually stock only the most salable models and sizes, you may not always be able to find what you want at first, but shops can usually order out-of-stock items from their wholesale suppliers. Ordering boots by mail is not always successful, because boots are not as easy to fit as shoes. Most shops require that you send a tracing of your stocking feet, with the desired boot height measured from the floor (still in your stocking feet); your regular shoe size in flat-heeled shoes; and your calf measurement over breeches for English boots and over socks for Western boots. Custom bootmakers usually require more information than that (see page 162); you can write to them directly (or through your tack shop, if it is the distributor for a particular firm) and ask for leather swatches and a measuring chart.

The best-known custom makers of English boots in this country from which one can order direct as well as through certain tack shops are E. Vogel (19 Howard Street, New York, New York 10013) and The Dehner Co., Inc. (2059 Farnam Street, Omaha, Nebraska 68102). These companies have retail price lists for their products, which include the standard styles of top boots, dress and field boots, steeplechase boots, Newmarket dress and field boots, Wellington boots, jodhpur boots, paddock shoes, and turf boots. Extras include special materials (such as baby calf, waxed calf, reverse calf), double or stitched soles, special straps and linings, and rush delivery.

Prices for custom-made English boots will depend, of course, on the bootmaker and the materials and extras you select, but it is safe to say that no good pair can be had for much less than $200 and that prices may go considerably higher than that. Prices for ready-made boots, however, vary quite a bit. Top boots and field boots may run about $150 a pair, but plain dress boots can be as inexpensive as $50, and rubber boots—plain black or in the Newmarket style—may range from $15 to $30. Jodhpur boots start at about $30; paddock and turf boots are higher—in the $40-to-$60 range for ready-made boots. Custom-made short boots can run from $80 to $100. Removable boot tops in patent or brown leather start at about $10.

Western boots are manufactured ready-made in an extremely wide range of materials, styles, colors, and sizes, and they vary in price accordingly. The cheapest boots are made of cowhide, rawhide, or synthetic leather; the most expensive are handmade from fine French calfskin or any number of exotic leath-ers (anteater, anaconda, ostrich, sea turtle, and so on). Most tack shops carry boots from several different manufacturers, which also advertise in the horse magazines. The quality of workmanship differs from one firm to another and from one price range to another. If you find a boot that you like and want to order another pair from the same firm, your tack dealer will be able to order it, or you can write to the firm yourself for the names of its distributors. The best-known manufacturers of Western boots are

Acme Boot Company
Clarksville, Tennessee 37040

Austin Boot Company
P.O. Box 12368-H
El Paso, Texas 79912

Champion Boot Company
P.O. Box 10717
El Paso, Texas 79997

Dan Post Boots
Clarksville, Tennessee 37040

Durango Boot Company
Franklin, Tennessee 37064

Hyer Boot Company
Box 191
Olathe, Kansas 66061

The Justin Companies, Inc.
Box 548
Fort Worth, Texas 76101

Lucchese Boots
1226 Houston Street
San Antonio, Texas 78205

Nocona Boot Company
P.O. Box 599
Nocona, Texas 76255

Sanders Bootmakers
6995 Industrial
El Paso, Texas 79905

Tony Lama Company
P.O. Drawer 9518
El Paso, Texas 79985

Most of these companies produce relatively inexpensive boots (from $25 to $75) in the basic styles—riding (with underslung heels), walking or utility (with straight heels), Wellingtons, and polo boots. But many of them will have expensive styles as well or can make boots to order; Lucchese boots, for instance, can run as high as $200 or more, and Ryon's catalog features special styles at $400 or more.

leather color is very thin and dyes will rub off quickly, the light leather color will wear through sooner or later. But take those marks as a compliment to your riding; at least it will be obvious that you are using your calves properly.

Once the boots are polished, they can be stored (or carried) in *boot bags* or simply put away with boot trees. Take care to keep the boots in a place that is neither too damp nor too dry, for mildew will discolor leather and drying will ruin it. If your boots need repair, don't wait until just before your next ride. Take them back to your dealer or bootmaker, who will make sure that a new sole will not alter the original size and that heels are replaced, not ground down, since that will distort the shape of the boot.

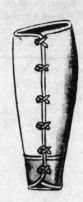

Gaiters, or English leggings, are available only custom-made; for prices and availability, write to the Deluxe Saddlery Company, 1817 Whitehead Road, Baltimore, Maryland 21207.

Boot bags can be obtained in knit fabrics with a drawstring top for about $6 a pair, in a suedelike material for about $15, and in zippered vinyl or leather double bags with handles from about $20 to $50 or more.

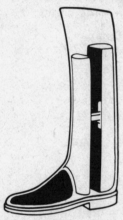

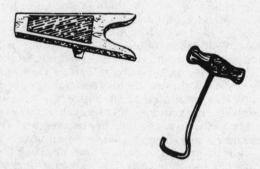

Boot accessories are available wherever boots are sold, although even here special items may be ordered by mail from specific manufacturers or distributors. Boot trees in plastic or aluminum are relatively cheap—from $13 to $20—but wooden trees, which are often preferred by custom bootmakers to preserve rather than stretch the shape of the boot, will run up to $100 a pair. Miller's Harness Company distributes English-made Equi-Trees, which are remarkably effective and inexpensive ($15 to $20, depending on whether you want a cushionlike tree for the shoe area). These are adjustable to fit any width of boot leg and exert firm even pressure while they allow for air circulation.

To get boots on and off, you may want boot hooks or lifts and boot jacks. Hooks are made of metal, usually nickel-plated, with or without wooden handles, and range from $1.50 to $2.50 a pair. Boot jacks can be made at home for the cost of the wood, but simple wooden or acrylic jacks with rubber treads and with or without leather-lined throats cost only $3 to $5 apiece. A club boot jack with a closed circular throat may run $15, and elaborate iron jacks with designs and special handles to grip the boot can cost as much or as little as you like. If you can't persuade your farrier or a local blacksmith to make you one, try looking in secondhand stores that specialize in Western antiques.

PANTS

Although Americans have still not come up with a good substitute for leather, we have managed to develop new materials for making pants and other cloth garments. No one has improved on cotton denim for Levi's, and many die-hards believe that wool and cotton have never been surpassed for feel, durability, and appearance. The good old

days of cotton breeches, whipcord, and cavalry twill, however, seem beyond recall. Cotton may sneak into some pants, but only in combination with nylon, rayon, and various polyester materials, at least as far as riding breeches and jodhpurs are concerned. But we shouldn't despair, for the stretch fabrics are creating something of a revolution in riding apparel, the first perhaps since 1820. One of the strict requirements of riding an English saddle, in which the rider is forced to post at the trot, is a tight-fitting knee, with no excess material to cause soreness to the rider or wear in the fabric. At the same time one must be able to mount, flex the leg, and dismount—which can put a lot of strain on tight-fitting pants. In addition, the fabric used must be sturdy and easily cleaned, if it is to remain in good condition over any period of time. In the days when tailors were faced with a choice of leather, corduroy, wool, or heavy cotton gabardine, expertise in designing the garment and fitting it to the individual's specifications really deserved to be called an art. Buttons or laces were used to fasten the breeches at the knee and below, leather patches (or "strappings") had to be stitched on inside the knee and at the calf to improve grip and prolong wear, and material had to be relatively loose above the knee for purposes of comfort. And there you have your *traditional breeches*—flaring at the thigh, gripping tightly at the knee, and disappearing smoothly beneath the boot. Fly fronts could be made simply with buttons or with drop fronts buttoning at the sides over a buttoned fly. (Ladies' breeches, when they were worn, had modest side buttons, of course—later replaced, as were men's buttons, by zippers.) It is believed by some experts that the flare of breeches was particularly exaggerated for women—to hide the hip's curve for the sake of modesty.

This distinctive style was practical because sturdy cotton or wool fabrics were not stretchy. Cavalry twill, one of the most popular traditional materials, was developed from a double twill during the early years of World War One (for the cavalry, of course) when it was discovered that a twill running to the left (instead of right) with the yarn twisted against the direction of the weave resulted in a remarkably strong material. In fact, it took 600 miles of woolen or worsted yarn to make a 53-yard piece of the stuff, which was heavy, solid, and attractive at the same time. Cotton or wool whipcord too was strong, even more so than gabardine, and had the advantage of not picking up animal hairs. These were definite improvements over the buckskin or doeskin that Beau Brummel and his dandy colleagues tried to put over on the world in the name of sleek fashion. Worn skin-tight, these leather breeches were terribly uncomfortable, especially in the rain (though they looked wonderful in the drawing room). Even the Prince Regent in those days tried white kidskin but only once, for it was not strong enough to contain his royal person.

Then, in the mid-20th century, thanks to the U.S. Equestrian Team's observation of ski teams at the Winter Olympics, came rayon and nylon and the other synthetics, which suddenly made it possible for breeches to stretch—two ways, four ways, and maybe someday even eight ways. Breeches could be made well-fitting without the help of a custom tailor. And for the first time since the demise of leather breeches, the garment could be designed without the customary flare (or peg)

above the knees. (Actually, as we now know, the traditional flare was a bit exaggerated in any case; and custom-made twill pants nowadays have a much slimmer look that they did a decade ago, usually because of the elimination of pockets as well as pegs.) These new fabrics are also easy to clean and they hold their shape (even if the wearer doesn't hold his). Breeches of *stretch* fabrics have become so widely popular that it is now impossible to buy them in cotton or twill short of applying to a custom tailor. Stretch breeches aren't without their problems, of course. They are not particularly flattering if your figure is imperfect, for instance, and they aren't quite as ventilating as the cotton or wool fabrics. (Modest ladies can wear panty hose to suppress the lines caused by underwear.) Also, they don't wear as well as the traditional breeches, and one should take care in buying a new pair—by sitting on a saddle—since they may tend to pinch behind the knee in a sitting position. But stretch breeches are serviceable, and they also eliminate the need for buttons or laces below the knee, since the stretchy fabrics and small zippers or Velcro self-sticking closings will keep that area snug. You can even buy elasticized waists, although zippers are commonly used, and leather (or synthetic) knee patches.

There are strict rules about the proper material and color for breeches worn in the hunt field. Synthetics are frowned upon; only white is permitted with a scarlet coat or formal black riding coat, and then only for the master, the hunt staff, and gentleman members (or entrants in an appointments class at a show). Lady members wear buff or brown breeches; the staff and gentleman members may wear buff or brown, but only if the individual hunt allows it. Other riders in the field may

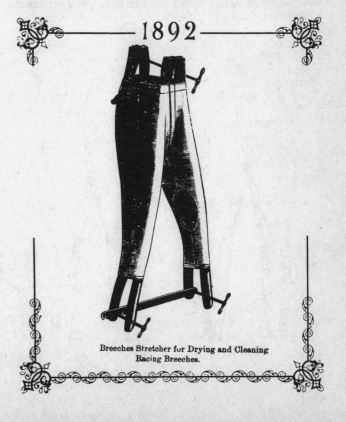

— 1892 —

Breeches Stretcher for Drying and Cleaning Racing Breeches.

wear buff, canary, or rust; gray, light green, and other colors are available, but should be worn only for cubbing and hacking. Brown and navy are popular now for informal wear—another credit to the U.S. Equestrian Team and its international experience.

Jodhpurs were brought by the English from India because of the greater comfort they afford in hot weather, as well as the ease of wearing the accompanying short boots. Like breeches, jodhpurs usually flared above the knee until recent years, when the stretch fabrics took over. They may or may not flare at the ankle, but all (except Kentucky jodhpurs) usually have cuffs and are reinforced at the knee. As with breeches, colors should be conservative—beige, brown, canary, and gray are most popular—and it is nice, although not necessary, to consider the color of your horse in selecting them. Cotton-denim and wide-wale-corduroy jodhpurs are popular variations, the former for schooling, the latter for winter wear. Pants for saddle-seat suits are sometimes still made of wool, since they must match the coats, which are usually wool worsted. However, polyesters are creeping in here too and are often preferred for warm-weather costumes. The *"Kentucky" pants* developed by Meyers of Lexington, Kentucky, and worn by saddle-seat riders are actually variations on jodhpurs, reinforced at the knee and flared cuffless over the boot. (They were once shorter, to reveal rather than cover the boot.) Some are made of black or dark brown material with satin stripes down the sides, like tuxedo trousers, for formal evening classes on gaited horses. Riding pants of tweed or other materials to match riding jackets are also popular nowadays for informal hacking or afternoon saddle-seat riding. Pants clips can be worn with flared legs to prevent complications with stirrups.

Happily for traditionalists, denim is still made of cotton, and Levi's (or Lees or Wranglers, or the other kinds of dungarees) are still made of denim. Levi Strauss was a New York tailor who went West to find gold in 1849—and instead he found miners wearing the wrong kind of clothes. He panned his own gold by selling them pants made of the cloth that he had expected to sell for tents and quickly ordered as much additional duck and denim as he could get from New York. (Duck, incidentally—from the Dutch word *doek,* meaning cloth or, particularly, canvas—is a closely woven cotton twill, originally a linen canvas; denim is a firm twilled cotton made with a colored warp and white filling threads, the name coming from the French *de Nîmes,* referring to the town in France famous for its manufacture of serge cloth. And if you're interested, "dungaree" is from the Hindi word *dūgrī,* meaning pants made of twill, and "jeans" originally stems from the French name for Genoa, the town in Italy known for its production of cloth.)

The pants that Levi Strauss designed were intended for heavy wear and comfort in the mines, and cowboys all over the West quickly found them suitable for riding as well. At first they were made in brown or natural canvas color, but Strauss happened on an indigo-blue dye as the most distinctive and stain-camouflaging color he could find, and he had it woven into the denim that we see today all over the world. As he continued to refine the pants, which became known as Levi's, he used copper rivets for the pockets and strain points, and a great American tradition was born. Cowboys resisted the rivets at first as a low-caste innovation, but by the 1890's they had caught on. At that point, complete with heavy-duty orange thread and an oilcloth ticket identifying the garment, *Levi's* as we know them now were worn everywhere in the West. The patent on the design lasted

stretch breeches

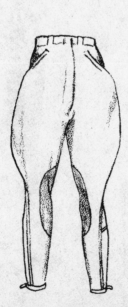

traditional breeches

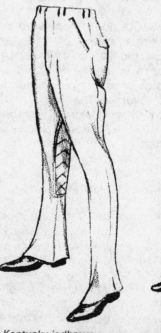

Kentucky jodhpurs

jodhpurs with cuffs

until 1908, when many other manufacturers got into the act.

Because the stock saddle and the Western cow pony do not require posting at the trot, Western riding pants don't have to be snug at the knee, but legs must be narrow and tapered to fit into boots, and comfort demands close-fitting hips and a low waist. Long hours in the saddle demand the utmost in durability. As they wear and are washed, blue jeans, or dungarees, become a faded blue, soft, and especially well fitting. Because it took time and heavy work to make them so, the faded look was a desirable sign of achievement. Nowadays, of course, one can buy Levi's or other denim pants already softened and faded; where else but in America can you pay someone to do so much work for you, even wearing your own pants! Jeans are also decorated these days with various unnecessary but often attractive designs and features. Flared pants are no good for riders—at least, not without pants clips—and decorations don't matter so much, as long as the material is sturdy; and the rider is fortunate in that for jeans, special catalogs and custom tailors are hardly necessary today. Care should be taken, however, to avoid badly placed or sewn seams at the seat and inseam, which can cause considerable discomfort. Suspenders and belts were not common in the old West, although sashes were occasionally worn, as well as holsters and belts (or whangs) for chaps. In the new West, belts—preferably with a large silver buckle incised with elaborate designs—are an integral part of the costume.

CHAPS

Leggings made of calfskin or pigskin were and are a traditional part of informal British garb. These developed from the "start-ups" worn by peasants in the 16th century—woolen or linen leg wrappings held by a string at the ankle. Because they were not tailored to fit or made from expensive materials, start-ups were practical only as protection, but as they became more sophisticated, leather was used to improve the grip on the saddle. It was more durable and better-fitting as well. Leggings are still available in England today, but in this country, *schooling and polo chaps* are relatively common, usually custom-tailored with a tapered zipper leg (often improved with elastic) and an adjustable buckle front or back or both. Made of full-grain natural cowhide with the rough (suede) side out, chaps are long-lasting and comfortable, and make for a wonderfully secure seat. They are also warm in cold weather (and in warm weather too, which may be a disadvantage in some areas). When appearances don't matter, chaps are often preferred to breeches, and certainly to any pants not designed for riding in an English saddle. They are long—to the ankle; and as any Westerner would point out they are plain old shotgun, or wingless, chaps, which are a far cry from English leggings.

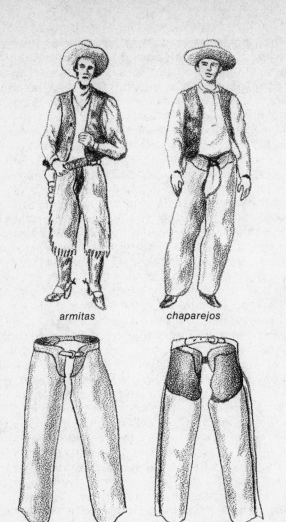

armitas   chaparejos

shotgun chaps (front and back)

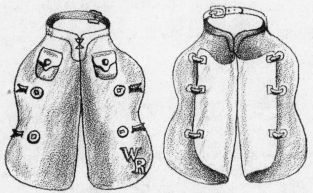

batwing chaps (front and back)

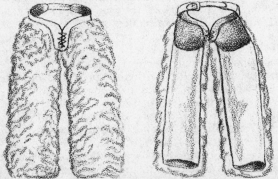

woollies (front and back)

Chaps are certainly a more familiar sight in the West, where they have a good long history. In Mexico, riders wore big flaps of leather called *armas* that fastened over the front of the saddle and hung down on each side, tucking over the legs like a robe. These were designed to protect the rider against cactus or mesquite and were extremely useful, except when one dismounted and left them in the saddle. Eventually, *armas* were made to fit the man rather than the saddle and became known as *armitas,* which were leather shields that hung from a belt around the waist and came down to the boot tops, attaching around the leg with leather thongs. These too were relatively clumsy, and gradual refinement resulted in chaps as we know them. (This word is pronounced "shaps," incidentally. It is short for the Spanish word *chaparejos* or *chaparreras,* meaning leather breeches. This word derives from the root word *chaparro,* or evergreen oak, which referred to the oak thickets that were so abundant in Southern Texas.) These early chaps were closed around the legs, permanently sewn, often with fringe down the outer seam, and resembled Indian leggings except that they had no seat. Just after the Civil War, Texans usually referred to them as leggins, if only to avoid using a Mexican word, but chaps they became in any case, especially as their use spread over the whole West. This type was the *shotgun variety,* since the legs resembled the twin barrels of a shotgun. Because they were hot and difficult to get on and off, wraparound open-leg chaps were devised in the Southern states. Nevertheless, cowboys in the North hung on to their shotguns for the warmth, and that style became associated with mountain men, who called them Texas legs. Lone Star cowboys, in the meantime, refined the open-leg chap into what became known as a *Texas*

wing. In this style, a wing, or outer flap, was attached to the inside part of the chap (the part between the leg and the horse) with leather thongs held by conchas or rosettes, the flap being left loose to extend back over the leg for additional protection. Some cowboys favored chaps with wide, flaring wings, called *batwing chaps* for obvious reasons, which they could easily pull on and off over boots and spurs simply by unsnapping the conchas, loosing the whang around the waist, and backing away. Later on, chap makers cut away the lower part of the inside leg and curved it so that it could not catch on the stirrup (this was the Cheyenne leg). Originally the chap was fastened all the way down to the boot, but now it is generally left open from the knee strap down. In some areas, where brush was not thick, half chaps, or chinks, were preferred, because they were cooler. Like the shotguns, chinks derived from *armitas* and came down just to the boot tops. They attached with thongs rather than being sewed together like shotguns.

In most places chaps were made of cowhide, but in cold, brush-free prairies, where chaps were worn for protection against the cold rather than thorns, they were often made of sheepskin or angora goat hide, with fur intact. *Woollies,* or angoras, were usually worn in the North, although they—like most other chaps—were manufactured in Texas. Like boots and spurs, chaps were usually plain for everyday wear, but cowboys with money and a fancy taste could dress them up as much as they pleased. Conchas of silver or nickel were elaborately patterned or engraved; initials could be spelled out in nailhead brads on the wings; and pockets (in front of the leg) could be made of a different-colored leather. Sometimes the material of the chaps itself could be gussied up; one King

---

As with other items of apparel, tack shops usually carry a wide range of styles and sizes in pants for English and Western riding, either from name manufacturers or under the name of the shop. In buying pants by mail, order your usual pants size only if that size always fits you well. For greater accuracy, enclose with your order your overall height in stocking feet, your weight, and exact taped measurements of your waist, hips (over the buttocks), outseam (from natural waistline to the floor in stocking feet), inseam (from crotch to floor), and calf at the widest point. Most catalogs feature measurement charts along with their order blanks.

Ready-made breeches and jodhpurs—whether imported or of American manufacture—are available these days only in stretch materials, although styles vary considerably. The usual range in price is $25 to $60, depending on special features and material. In ordering pants, be sure to note whether cuffs, belt loops, and pockets (if you want them) are included and that side zippers are used for

women's pants (if you want those), and specify otherwise if you wish otherwise. Breeches and jodhpurs can be made to order in almost any material you desire—from cotton to heavy twill to special worsteds—and costs range from $100 to $250 (for breeches). If your tack shop does not have a tailor and your usual sources do not offer custom-made breeches or jodhpurs, write to M. J. Knoud (716 Madison Avenue, New York, New York 10021) for prices and swatches of material. For breeches made entirely of leather, write to the Silver Bit, Mount Kisco, New York, and for stretch breeches with suede inseams and seats, write to Sportco, Inc., Wilton, Maine. Jodhpur garters, a stylish accessory worn below the knee to prevent riding up, can be ordered from DeLuxe Saddlery Co., 1817 Whitehead Road, Baltimore, Maryland 21207, for about $7 a pair. Elastic pants clips or bottom straps cost around $1.50.

Western pants can usually be found ready-made without much difficulty; denims with no flare, the traditional button-front fly, and shrunk to fit can be had for $10 to $20, while

Fisher of South Texas even went so far as to "borrow" the hide of a visiting circus tiger. The hides of equally unfortunate wolves, cougars, and horses were pressed into similar service, though cowhide remained the most practical material for the working cowhand. In addition to their normal function, chaps, or leggins, had a special use: "to give a leggin" meant to punish a cowboy by beating him with a pair of chaps.

SHIRTS

Although there doesn't seem to be much in common among blue work shirts, polo shirts, and body shirts, they were all originally designed for the same purpose: to be worn by riders. Regardless of style, the most important requirements of a riding shirt are that it be absorbent (horses may sweat, but gentlemen perspire too, and even, as the old expression has it, ladies glow); easily cleaned; warm when necessary and cool when not; shaped at the waist to prevent riding up; and free of restriction at the shoulder. Since English and Western riding shirts were usually worn beneath a vest and/or a coat, appearance was less important than comfort. In England, shirts could be woolen or cotton or silk. In the hunting field they were invariably white, with a soft collar to which a stock could be attached. For informal hunting or hacking, a shirt could be colored or checked, and like the informal tweed riding jacket, it was dubbed *ratcatcher*—implying, no doubt, that the nonformal hunter was no better than a hunter of rodents, one who traveled on foot accompanied by a ferret or dog.

Riding shirts originally had a high cravat, proba-

bly borrowed from the court, but the detachable white stock, or hunting cravat, has been in common use since the second half of the 19th century. Polo shirts, originating in India for the sport and designed to be comfortable in warm weather, had an open collar and buttoned down to midbreast. Shirts were shaped at the waist for a good fit. Fishtail shirts were particularly effective, since their long tails came between the legs to button onto the front of the shirt, making them remain in place no matter how strenuous the ride. The body shirts fashionable today for women are modern versions of these practical garments.

Western shirts in the 19th century were almost always *pullovers*, usually of wool or flannel (or linsey-woolsey, a combination of linen and wool), with buttons to mid-chest (or none at all) and an open collar. Military shirts were made of gray flannel until 1881, when the Army borrowed blue wool from miners and lumbermen and cowboys, who generally didn't bother about a collar unless they were dressing up. Fancy civilian shirts (or boiled shirts) were usually linen pullovers of the same style, with or without ruffles at the neck and with detachable collars. Montgomery Ward, the famous early mail-order house, advertised around 1870 five boxes of paper collars (with suspenders thrown in) for a dollar, or five linen shirtfronts (or dickeys) for the same price. But cowboys preferred hickory (sturdy cotton) flannel, or wool pullovers with no collar at all but a bandana to protect the neck. The fancy decorated frontier shirts so familiar today (on country-and-Western singers more than on riders) were adapted from the old pullover shirts. The only similarity in style is the tapered waist and the construction of the shoulder, which allowed for free movement of the shoulders and arms.

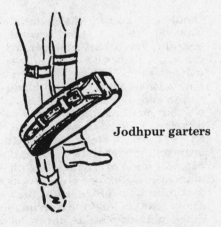

Jodhpur garters

all-wool cavalry twill "ranch pants" may run to $60 or more. In buying pants for riding, be sure that the seams at the seat and the inseam are properly made so that they won't cause rubbing in the saddle.

Chaps are available ready-made in three or more standard sizes, depending on the manu-

facturer, and are usually much cheaper than custom-made chaps, sometimes as low as $25. The best chaps are, of course, cut to measure from a single piece of top-grain cowhide, and since these will last a long time, they are well worth the investment, which can be as little as $55 (for children) or as much as $120 (or more if you want special features). Schooling or polo chaps (shotguns) are usually made suede side out with zippers running down to the ankle; batwing chaps, fringed shotguns, and show chaps can be made in various colors (blue, purple, rust, red, brown, and so on), grain or suede side out, with many different stitching designs and colors and ornaments, depending on what you want. In ordering chaps, specify your waist size (below the belt at the hipbone), inseam and outseam length (with boots on), length from knee to floor, your height, your weight, and the measurements of upper thigh, mid-thigh, one inch above the knee, and the calf at the widest point, with boots on. Most tack shops and catalogs offer custom-made chaps.

NECKWEAR

Stocks, which to some may seem an unnecessary frill, actually have a purpose for the rider beyond covering up the neck. Made traditionally of white piqué linen or silk, *stocks* could be made in various widths to be used in case of accident as a bandage or sling for the rider or as a tourniquet or pressure bandage for the horse. Although ready-tied stocks that fasten behind the neck are much easier to put on, they are not allowed in formal hunting or appointments classes. The *stock pin*, usually of gold and measuring 2½ to 3½ inches long, is essentially a plain safety pin, which also can be pressed into service in emergencies, although its primary purpose is to keep the stock from bulging in front. The pin should always be worn horizontally, to avoid lacerating the chin. Informal riders in English saddles often prefer simple *button-on chokers* or ties worn with plain or checked shirts; hacking scarves—worn like ascots—are popular in England, where polka dots are the fashionable design, although Hermès scarves would certainly be appropriate anywhere today.

Because Western pullover shirts had terrible collars or none at all and because riders didn't need or want to bother with detachable collars, *bandanas* were the traditional form of neckwear. These were ordinary farm handkerchiefs made of printed cotton in colorful red or blue designs, although silk was preferred if one could afford it, since it was cooler in summer and warmer in winter. Bandanas (from the Hindi word *bāndhnū*) are usually folded in a triangle to tie at the front or back in lieu of a collar, though they can also be worn inside the shirt to make an open collar look dressier, or tucked into a pocket. On the range, they are still worn close-wrapped around the neck

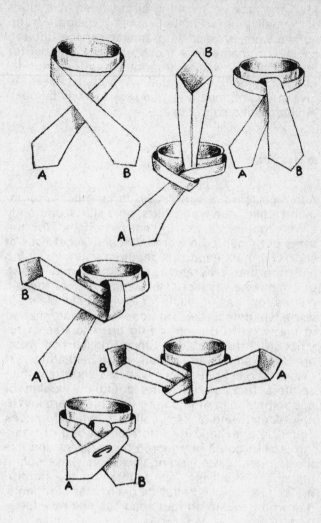

RATCATCHER SHIRT WITH CHOKER

HOW TO BUY RIDING SHIRTS AND NECKWEAR

Most riding shirts—English or Western—come in regular shirt sizes, but care must be taken to be sure that they are not constricting at the shoulders and that the material can be easily cleaned. Durability and warmth (or coolness) are other important considerations, depending on your particular riding style. Simple ratcatcher shirts with or without straight collars and button-on ties will cost about $10 to $15 for cotton and slightly more for knit fabrics. Chokers that can be buttoned onto shirts are made in velveteen, cotton, or silk and will run from $2 to $4. White stock shirts without the stock are usually in the $10-to-$15 range, and stocks can cost up to $10, depending on material. Permanent-press oxford-cloth stocks start at $3.50, and silk four-fold stocks start at about $9. These can be obtained ready-tied or plain. Stock pins can be as cheap as $1 (these are really overgrown safety pins) or as expensive as you like.

Western shirts are widely available in any number of styles and prices, in muslin, wool challis, or even velour with sequins, but the usual range is $10 to $35. Cotton bandanas can be as cheap as $1 or less, and bolo ties with special designs can run from $2 to $10.

(or tied down over hat brims) to protect the rider from cold, the sun, or brambles. In dust storms, too, the bandana can be pulled up over the face to keep nose and mouth from getting filled up. (It offered another sort of protection to the stagecoach bandit who preferred to remain anonymous.) Like the stock, the bandana can also double as a tourniquet or bandage in an emergency. It can be used as well to strain unclean water, and not surprisingly, it will perform the numerous other services traditionally associated with handkerchiefs. In town, one could wrap a length of black ribbon around the neck under a paper or celluloid collar (the latter only if you didn't smoke, for it was highly flammable) and tie it around your neck in a bow, but the bandana was very much more convenient.

VESTS

Although most people think of the vest—or waist-coat, or weskit—as a rather unnecessary part of a three-piece suit, it is actually one of the oldest and most useful articles of clothing for the rider. During medieval times, horsemen often wore vests, usually in the form of short, sleeveless leather jerkins. Knights wore them as padding under coats of mail; lesser soldiers wore them as the armor itself. Wool-lined leather vests were worn in the U.S. Army as recently as World War One. Furnished with pockets, made of stout warm material (for protection against weather, slings, arrows, and even musket fire), and sleeveless to allow the rider freedom of arm movement, vests have been equally important in the horseman's apparel in both England and America.

In the hunting field, the *vest* was refined for the sake of appearance and is traditionally made of plain wool melton cloth in yellow or white or buff, with four pockets (each with flaps) and five buttons. Long enough in the back to cover the kid-

English vests for hacking can be made of corduroy or wool in various colors and patterns. Solid colors include camel, rust, brown, black, or the traditional canary yellow required for hunting; patterns include plaid or tattersall check, usually in red or white with black, yellow, or red. Sizes are small, medium, or large for both men and women, and prices range from $30 to $40. Western vests can be made of leather, denim, or sheepskin; unlined leather vests run about $35 and sheepskin can be as much as $75. Quilted trail vests with Dacron fiberfill insulation will cost from $15 to $30.

neys, often with satin insets (now nylon) rather than wool, and seamed at the waist for comfort in the saddle, vests are still practical garments for the sake of warmth and extra pockets. Informal riders often prefer knitted or tattersall-checked vests, named for the famous London horse market.

Western vests are usually sturdier affairs, made of buckskin or stiff duck cloth. They probably derive from the waistcoat of colonial times—really a sleeveless coat with lapels and pockets to be worn under a heavier topcoat. In the old West, yellowish buckskin vests were widely available—conveniently sleeveless for the rider, warm enough when buttoned for a hardy life out-of-doors, and soft for comfort. Lined with fleece, they could be made warmer, and so they are today. Although fancier vests were and still are made, decorated with porcupine-quill beads, elaborate stitching, buckskin fringes or black braid edging, or cloth inlays, most hardworking riders prefer the plain version.

The informal rider, east or west, tends to use the same cold-weather garment—the down-filled nylon *trail vest* that looks like a ski jacket without sleeves. This vest can be worn over a sweater or

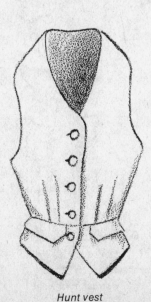

Hunt vest

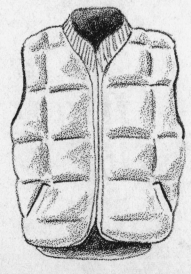

Trail vest

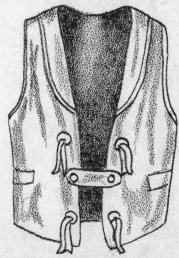

Western vest

shirt or under an outercoat. With a roll collar at the neck and throat and 2 inches of extra length at the back, it is wonderfully warm and even more comfortable than a full jacket for riding.

COATS

As we noted earlier, the ordinary suit coats that we know and wear today owe their basic design to the riding coat of the English country gentleman of the 18th century. So does the formal swallowtail coat, which closely resembles the formal riding coat still worn in the hunt field. Rules for proper garb at the hunt are strictly observed in most areas where fox hunting is taken seriously (see the end of this chapter for those rules), although to the casual observer these may seem overly fussy. There are reasons for these rules, one of which is indeed formality for the sake of tradition. More

practical, however, are the differences in clothing worn by the master of foxhounds, the huntsmen, the whippers-in, the gentleman and lady members, juniors, guests, farmers, and servants. Obviously, these differences exist to enable everyone in the field to distinguish one category of rider from another and to tell hunters of one locale from another. These variations may be as subtle as the number or design of buttons or as obvious as the color or cut of the riding coat. Before we get into these distinctions, however, let's look at the basic requirements for the riding coat itself.

For comfort in the saddle and a trim appearance, the coat should be narrow at the waist with the skirts allowed to cut away toward the back to allow for freedom of the leg. Lapels should be short (so that the wind won't flap them around) and equipped with a throat tab (so that the coat may be buttoned at the neck). Side pockets with flaps to keep the contents inside have obvious practical purposes, as do the long center slit at the back—or double slit with a fuller skirt—to allow

Saddle-seat suit   *Hacking outfit*   *Formal hunt wear*

the skirts to cover the saddle (and not to be sat upon) and a waterproof lining to protect the coat's fabric from the sweat of the horse and saddle-soap stains. Other pockets may also be part of the garment—a breast pocket, a ticket or whistle pocket (on the upper right side), and at least one inside pocket, called a poacher's pocket and made large enough to hold a hare. The material should be sturdy and easily cleaned for long wear. Several traditional cloths are still used today. Melton cloth is a densely woven wool, which is soft and warm and yet keeps its shape. The name comes from the town of Melton Mowbray in England, where it first became popular. Boncloth is like melton but even smoother. Twill is made of wool or worsted yarn, which is twisted to make the fabric more durable. Variations of this include Bedford cord, in which the wool or cotton is given a rounded cord effect in the weaving; covert, or Venetian twill, which is lightweight and has a flecked appearance; and whipcord, which is very strong with a noticeable rib and a resistance to animal hair. Melton and twill are still used these days, although they are very expensive (melton is $60 a yard or more). Polyesters are cheaper and lighter in weight but not so long-lasting; they are often used in combination with wool or cotton. Dacron, silk, rayon, and madras are other materials worn often in warm climates.

Formal hunting—whether in the field or in appointments classes—requires the use of certain traditional cuts for the riding coat. The *frock coat* has long skirts, with square corners and buttons to the waist for the master and rounded skirts for gentlemen members. The *swallowtail* (or shadbelly) coat is a double-breasted garment that cuts straight across at the waist and has long tails extending down the back. This cut is usually preferred by lady members, although others may wear it, and other cuts are also acceptable. *Weasel-belly coats,* which are also called cutaways or Dublingtons, are a variation of the shadbelly. All of these formal cuts must be custom-made, but many kinds of simpler riding coats are available ready-made. Olympic jackets are variations of the frock coat, except that the skirts are shorter and the materials usually lighter in weight. These are what one usually sees on riders in open-jumper classes; unlike most riding clothes, they may be quite bright in color—scarlet, green, or blue as well as black. For informal riding and for equitation hunter and jumper classes that do not require appointments, brown or gray tweed or conservatively solid-color riding coats are ideal. *Traditional-length coats* have a single vent in back, with no pleats or belt, and usually (but not always) a seamed waist. Length depends on the build of the rider; the bottom of the coat generally comes as far down the thigh as the rider's wrist can reach. The more recent and more stylish *continental length* is shorter (if less flattering for wider, less-than-expert riders), because it has a double vent in back, which cannot extend as far up the back as the single vent

and thus necessitates a shorter skirt. In the days when breeches and jodhpurs were flared at the thigh, the skirts of the coat were ample to allow for them; nowadays coats are much trimmer, although a long look—especially in saddle-seat suits—is flattering and desirable. Riding coats generally have three or four buttons to the waist (buttons on some old coats came below the waist), a high front, narrow notched lapels, and at least two pockets with flaps.

There is always a good deal of concern about buttons and collars when formal hunting apparel is discussed, mainly because these are the ways in which one hunt distinguishes itself from the others. Hunt colors (on the detachable collar) and insignia (on the buttons) may be worn by members of the hunt only by invitation, and "earning one's colors" is a great honor. (In appointments classes, entrants are required to carry a copy of the letter authorizing the use of colors by the master.) Until one reaches this stage, collars and buttons must match the coat instead of the hunt livery. The number of buttons also varies, depending on one's rank. Six-buttoned coats (four in front and two over the back vent) are traditionally reserved for the master and hunt staff; three or four buttons are worn by everyone else. Gentlemen wear hunt buttons on the front of their coats; ladies wear them on the vest or on the back of the hat to hold the hat guard. The hunt staff may also wear buttons on their sleeves—either a relic of the days when sleeves buttoned closed or a handy way of carrying extra buttons.

The coats of *saddle-seat suits,* unlike hunting coats, must match the pants in color and material. These coats are quite long—about halfway (or more) down the thigh—with rounded flared skirts that may have a center vent or long double inverted pleats, usually embroidered with silk arrowheads. Made of fine wool worsted or double-stretch worsteds, saddle-seat suits are generally black, navy blue, or brown—sometimes with pinstripes or faint patterns—and silk or nylon linings that may be plain, colored, or handsomely patterned. For evening wear, coats may be designed like tuxedos with satin, nylon, or silk lapels in the same color as the coat. Silk brocades were popular during the 1960's but matte-finish, lighter-colored monotone coats are currently in vogue. Accessories or jacket color are occasionally designed to match the browband and ribbons worn by the horse.

Informal gaited classes are somewhat less rigid about color, and gray, green, beige, and white—in season—are allowed, with plain matching lapels. Saddle-seat coats usually have two buttons and semipeak lapels for a stylish appearance.

Fit is very important in a riding coat, especially in the shoulders, which should be restricted as little as possible. This is perhaps the most important reason why a rider should steer clear of the hacking jackets designed and sold for street wear. These fashionable garments often omit pockets and insulated linings for the sake of a trim look, and the material used is generally less sturdy, since nonriders rarely encounter athletic situations or mud splattered up by the hooves of galloping animals. These jackets for nonriders are usually more expensive as well, for the sake of the designer, and it behooves the serious rider to investigate the clothing specially designed for riding. If a ready-made garment is not suitable, then one should consider a coat made to order by a tailor familiar with the requirements of riders. With good care, the coat will last for a long time and be well worth the investment.

A COAT OF A DIFFERENT COLOR

It's about time we debunked a few old myths. For one thing, 19th-century hunting prints aside, scarlet coats were not and are not worn by everyone in the field, but are restricted to the master, the huntsmen, the whippers-in, and invited gentlemen members. (Ladies, juniors, and guests must all wear black.) Even then, scarlet is often replaced by the hunt livery, or whatever is traditional for a particular hunt (which can be almost any color but green, which is reserved for hunt servants). For another thing, scarlet—not pink—is the accurate name for the color. Many believe that the word pink derived from the name of a London tailor who obviously made a fortune while reddening the English countryside, but no evidence has been found that such a tailor ever existed. It is far more likely that the word pink was first applied to the scarlet riding coat as a journalistic slur. It was used as early as 1828 in an Oxford newspaper, perhaps coming from the old expression "Fight in scarlet, hunt in red, dance in pink"—which refers to the fading color of an old field coat whose brilliance would disappear through years of cleaning. The coloring agent used to make the old coats was cochineal dye—made from a paste in which the blood of Mexican cactus beetles was mixed in a solution of tin.

In any event, scarlet undoubtedly became the traditional color for hunting for political reasons. Fox hunting was a Tory sport, and red was the Tory color, having derived from the royal livery worn for deer hunting (all deer in England having belonged to the throne). And even then, the use of scarlet was not simply traditional but practical as well, for it is visible from a great distance, so that fallen or missing persons were less likely to be overlooked in the excitement of the chase. Scarlet is now used as well by Olympic and equestrian-team riders from countries where teams are not dressed in military garb, and this is the only occasion on which women are allowed to wear red.

Happily, good care of the woolen riding coat need not involve the expense of professional attention. Dry cleaning is not necessary and may even cause damage by removing dye from the buttons. Steam pressing will make good cloth brittle, for it extracts natural oils, and the fabric may be damaged by the pressure. Allow a wet and muddy coat to dry naturally (not in front of a fire) and then brush it with a stiff brush (not on a hanger, or the shoulders and collar may stretch out of shape). If dirt still remains, sponge the area with lukewarm water and a detergent until the surface becomes damp but not soaked. Do not rub, and don't use soap, but use that stiff brush again and allow the material to dry slowly. To remove a shine on the surface, rub gently with a warm damp cloth. During periods when a coat is not being used, do not simply hang it in a closet. Lay it flat in layers of newspaper and surround it with Epsom salts (not camphor balls), which are cheap, are odorless, and will not affect the color of the garment.

Although Western riders often prefer a vest to a coat, *short denim jackets* cut at the waist and often adorned with a brown corduroy collar have been as traditional for years as they are popular now. Made like Levi's with metal rivets and orange thread, they match the pants nicely and made up what was probably the first leisure suit. *Chaquetas* were heavy cloth or leather jackets worn in the Texas–Mexico brush country. As with English riding coats, there are certain features that these short jackets must include for the sake of the rider: full sleeves, at least two button-flap pockets, a waist tab to make the jacket snug around the waist, and—for cold weather—a lining of blanket material or soft fleece, for additional protection, with a collar that buttons across the throat.

FOUL-WEATHER GEAR

Although cowboys in the Far West may have to contend more with weather than the English rider who can always simply turn around and go home, horsemen should always be prepared to deal with the elements wherever they ride. In 1823, Charles MacIntosh of Glasgow received a patent for a solution of naphtha and crude rubber cemented together, and this waterproof material quickly became popular throughout the British Isles. In 1825, the Duke of York wore a blue cape of the stuff, but before long special riding macintosh coats and aprons were designed specifically for the rider. *Riding aprons* were simple affairs that dropped 8 inches below the knee and fastened on the right side with a belt at the waist; a leg strap made certain that breeches were covered. They could be folded easily into a large pocket for carrying, but were somewhat less effective than the *macintosh coat*. With taped and sealed seams, a belt and buckles of a soft finish that would not cause friction, ventilated underarms, a long back vented with a fan of the same material to cover the saddle, knee flaps, and a pommel strap to keep the whole rig in position, this very useful garment still

riding raincoat

slicker

English riding coats come in all types of material (like prizefighters, in lightweight, middleweight, and heavyweight divisions); in synthetics, wool, and corduroy; and in conservative solid colors, gaudy patterns, and tweeds. The selection of material and the quality of tailoring are what make the difference in price, since cuts tend to be traditional. Correct hunting coats, even ready-made items, are usually more expensive than hacking jackets; frock coats made of polyester or double knit will run $100 to $125, of medium melton or cavalry twill from $125 to $150, and custom-made in heavy melton up to $500. Formal cuts, such as the swallowtail or weasel-belly styles, are available custom-made only, for up to $400, and melton hunt coats can cost from $80 to $400 depending on material and tailor. Hacking jackets or riding coats in frock, Continental (double vent), and traditional (single-vent) styles will run from $60 to $140 ready-made, depending on material.

Saddle-seat suits are available ready-made in double knit, wool worsted, or gabardine from $150 to $250, although a custom-made suit may cost up to $500. Saddle-seat show coats in tropical weights will range from $85 to $100. Standard coat sizes are used (with long, regular, and short lengths), although if you are ordering by mail, include tape measurements of chest or bust, natural waistline, and the largest part of your seat, as well as your height in stocking feet and your weight. In trying on any coat, make sure that it allows for freedom of movement at the shoulders, is well fitting at the waist, and is sturdily built for long wear.

If you plan to order a custom-made garment, write or ask for samples of material and price ranges before you order. The tailor may have a special measuring chart or instructions as well. If your tack shop does not have its own tailor, look for specialists in your particular field. Meyers of Lexington, Kentucky, who invented the Kentucky jodhpur, will be your best source for saddle-seat suits and coats. Lord Geoffrey apparel by Tailored Sportsman (275 Seventh Avenue, New York, New York 10001) includes custom-made saddle suits and formal-cut hunt coats as well as stock sizes in breeches and jodhpurs and stockman pants. M. J. Knoud of New York specializes in custom hunting apparel and will also make sidesaddle habits. Grey's of Westbury, Long Island, New York, is a polo supplier.

exists today. Now made of rubber, rubberized nylon or cotton, or clear plastic, raincoats of this type are lightweight and easily packed. The three-quarter length is preferred, with generous pleats at the back for easy mounting, raglan sleeves for freedom of movement, elastic or snap closings at the wrist, and straps for the cantle, legs, and pommel.

In the West, *slickers,* or fishskins, voluminous enough to cover the whole saddle as well as the rider, were made of canvas duck treated with oil or paint to keep the rain out. Designed like coats, slickers had sleeves and pockets furnished with slits for easy access to pants pockets. Like the foul-weather gear worn by sailors, slickers are traditionally yellow for good visibility, but the material from which they are made nowadays is usually rubberized cloth or plastic, more durable than oilcloth. Mexican *ponchos,* worn in the South, are like blankets made of finely woven wool or wool and linen with a slit in the middle to accommodate the head. Although they fit less snugly than a coat, ponchos are effective protection, since the material sheds water and is very warm. Both slickers and ponchos are rolled and tied behind the saddle and are used for making bedrolls or covering packs or slapped in the face of cattle to turn them. The slicker could even stop a horse from bucking when tied behind the saddle with its ends hanging down the animal's sides.

GLOVES

Like foul-weather gear, gloves have always been worn by riders for protection against weather, but they also serve to prevent rubbing and blisters caused by leather reins. Not only must the material be strong enough to afford such protection, but it

must also be supple enough for the rider to maintain a good grip even in the rain and a sensitive feel on the reins or rope. Leather has always been the preferred material and pigskin the preferred leather, for it is sturdy, supple, and soft. Many other materials have also been and are still used. In the West, buckskin, horse or steer hide, and even kangaroo leather are used, and in the East, *string gloves,* knitted in one piece from white cotton yarn, are very popular, because they give a good grip, are cheap, and are easily cleaned. *Rain gloves* for the hunting field, made of white or col-

If you don't want to pay the high prices that special tailors require and are clever at the sewing machine yourself, you should explore the possibility of making your own riding clothes. Jean Hardy Patterns (2151 La Cuesta Drive, Santa Ana, California 92705) and Country Carriage Originals (Box 1182, Grand Forks, North Dakota 58201) have a wide range of patterns for English-style and Western riding clothes for women and children. The patterns themselves are cheap (from $1.50 to $5), but the materials can (and should) be relatively expensive. There really isn't much point in spending a lot of time making a riding coat or a pair of pants out of a poor fabric.

Western jackets are widely available in cotton, denim, or suede leather, and prices vary accordingly. An unlined jacket may cost as little as $15; a fleece-lined denim may run $25 to $30. Custom-made leather jackets can, of course, cost as much as you are willing to spend.

Outerwear or foul-weather gear designed for riding can be made of clear, light plastic or specially treated fabric, with or without linings. A plastic jacket may cost as little as $7.50; in nylon, around $20. A rain slicker will run about $25, and an imported Irish MacIntosh riding coat will cost as much as $75.

ored cotton, are carried under the girth, with each glove on its proper side of the saddle, thumb against the palm of the glove and against the saddle, the fingers toward the front.

In recent years, leather-like vinyls have been developed for *riding gloves.* In addition to being cheaper than leather, these gloves are elasticized for perfect fit and reinforced at the palm for long wear, and yet they are thin enough for maximum sensitivity. Variations on the theme include crochet-back gloves with leather palms and mesh gloves with durable nylon palms and rubber strips

for a good grip. (Leather gloves in England were once made with knitted string inserts for the same reason and to protect the leather from wear.)

Gloves worn for *bull riding,* in which the cowboy's life (or at least the skin on his palm) can depend on the sturdiness of the material, are usually made of strong leather with long sleeves to protect the wrists. These gloves resemble the traditional Western gauntlets—now relatively rare, but very effective in preventing rope burns and in keeping cold wind from blowing up the sleeve. The flaring cuffs were often six inches long or longer and decorated in some way, more or less elaborately depending on taste. Fringed leather, Indian beadwork, nailheads worked into the leather, and colored stitching could be made in a variety of designs, many of them created by Indians and sold at trading posts. In spite of their usefulness, however, gauntlets were cumbersome to handle when not in use—they couldn't be fitted into a pocket, for one thing—and this may be the reason they went out of style. Elaborately decorated leather cuffs or bands of leather to fit over shirt cuffs at the wrist would help protect bare wrists against weather and preserve the cuffs of the shirt or coat from wear.

Polo gloves, traditionally worn on the left hand only (the one that gripped the reins), were usually ventilated like golf gloves, but polo players now often wear light full-leather gloves on both hands to avoid blisters.

Whatever gloves you select, their usefulness will be extended by good care. Leather gloves may be cleaned with a solvent, but be sure to rinse off any substance, including soap, with a cloth moistened in lukewarm water, and to dry them naturally. Cotton gloves may be washed in mild soap and water; don't wring them out but dry them slowly—on your hands or a form if possible to keep them from shrinking or losing their shape.

STRING GLOVES

The least expensive riding gloves are made of cotton string, wool, or stretch vinyl ($4 to $10); leather gloves or lined string gloves may cost $12 to $15; wool-lined leather and special thermal gloves may run $25 or more. Heavy steer-hide bull-rider gloves with long sleeves will cost about $6 apiece; if you want them for riding horses, you'll want a pair, of course. Gloves may be available in standard sizes (4 to 10 for men, women, and children) or simply in small, medium, and large; stretch fabrics may be available in one size only.

LEATHER RIDING GLOVES

HATS

Hats, like gloves, are considered a fashionable accessory in most areas, except when needed for protective purposes. Easter bonnets, straw boaters, and silk top hats hardly have a place in everyday contemporary dress, any more than white cotton or pigskin gloves do. However, hats should be considered an integral part of the complete riding outfit, and not just an additional expense for the sake of style. Tricorn hats with elaborate feathers have disappeared, but top hats are still used in the hunting field—not the tall silk stovepipes but specially made protective hats designed to keep the rider's head intact should he take a tumble. *Riding top hats* are about ⅝ inch lower in the crown than the formal silk hat (ladies' hats are lower still). They were once made of laminated twill and calico impregnated with shellac and ironed on a form in layers. The covering was beaver until silk became widely available in England after import duties were lifted many years ago. The brim was shaped and trimmed with a wide leather band. All riders wore adjustable draw cords at the chin and hat guards in back to keep the hat in place; ladies also wore hunting veils to protect their delicate complexions from the ravages of weather and mud. *Hat guards* are still required in formal hunting; they are loops that attach to a ring sewn inside the back of the coat collar, a little to the side.

Because William Coke, Duke of Norfolk (the one who started the revolution in men's clothing, you'll recall), had the unfortunate experience of losing his silk hat in mid-stride, he employed the hatmaking Bowler family of Southwark to design him a smaller, more wind-resistant hat with a rounded crown. First called the Coke hat or Billycock after its original wearer, it eventually took on the name of its maker. Off the hunting field and on the heads of racing enthusiasts, it became known as the *derby,* but for riding purposes it retained the shellacked crown for protective reasons.

In 1780 another design, the *hunt cap,* was introduced. When George III wore one in Windsor Park, it became quite fashionable, and it is still worn today by the hunt master and staff (and no one else in the field except for juniors). The term "capping fee"—the sum paid by nonmembers—evolved because the hunt secretary, who collected the fees, wore a hunt cap. This type of helmet was made in the same way as the top hat—with layers of laminated, shellacked material fashioned over a wooden block. The foundation material was felt, and the covering was velvet or velveteen; only the lining was silk, and that was quilted and padded with felt for further protection. Because the hat was close-fitting, a ventilation hole was necessary; this was placed on the top of the crown, covered with a screw-on button. The ribbon attached to the back of the cap is used to distinguish the hunt staff from juniors (as if that were difficult to begin with) and paid wearers from unpaid wearers. Children's caps have one bow with two tails pointing

Hunt cap

Derby

Top hat

down. The master and the staff boast two bows and two tails, pointing up if paid, pointing down if not.

These styles have remained unchanged (except that top hats have lower crowns for hunt, dressage, and saddle-horse classes), but materials are now virtually indestructible heavy plastic or fiber glass, which is light as well as strong. Caps give better protection against superficial scalp wounds, and they don't interfere with hearing. Bowlers are better protection against more serious injuries, and they also prevent rain from dripping down the neck and protect ears and cheeks from brush. Collapsible visors, hammock chin straps, or harnesses, with or without protective chin cups, are a good deal more secure than the usual elastic cords that replaced the original adjustable drawcords. Velvet is still traditional for hunt caps, as silk is for top hats and derbies, but for everyday informal wear riders often prefer plain *schooling helmets,* which derive from polo and racing helmets designed more for protection than for looks.

Polo helmets were once made of three-ply natural cork, employing at least thirty pieces of cork laminated over rubber padding and crossed tapes within the crown. As with racing helmets, these were designed to cover the ears and were furnished with sturdy chin straps for additional protection, holes for ventilation, and even face shields like those worn by football players. Nowadays, heavy plastic or fiber glass has replaced cork, and inner cushions to prevent concussion and absorb shock are made of rubber or felt.

Needless to say, helmets do little good unless they are worn, and even then they're not much good if they don't fit snugly. Newspaper may be used as padding in an emergency—as for the casual rider who must borrow someone else's hat. Because head protection is of extreme importance, especially for children and for beginners, no expense should be spared in acquiring this particular piece of gear.

In the hunting field, ladies who wear their hair in long, flowing tresses (our 18th-century equestrienne to the contrary notwithstanding) have always been frowned upon. The reasons for this may have something to do with the conservative attitude of fox hunters, who frown as well upon perfume and heavy makeup, which are equally incongruous with a hard day's cross-country ride. But the more practical aspects of cleanliness also apply, which is why the manes and tails of hunters are so painstakingly braided. Although hairnets are not always necessary if one can pin one's hair under a hat or wear braids, anyone with a lengthy head of hair—and this goes for ladies, women, girls, men, and boys alike—should make some effort to keep it under control on the hunt field and in the show ring, for the sake of general appearance as well as for the sake of the rule.

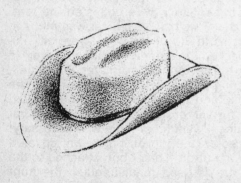

Stetson

Schooling helmet

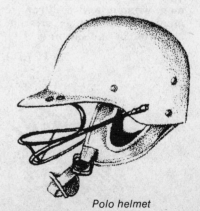

Polo helmet

Riding caps of tweed, fine wool, or felt have no protective function in falls, but they are good for keeping sun or rain out of the eyes. They must be designed with a snug crown and moderate wings to prevent their flying off at a gallop; in training gallops at the track, it is customary to turn the hat around front to back just to avoid this sort of problem. Men in informal saddle-horse classes nowadays prefer snap-brim felt or straw hats over derbies or top hats.

Like tweed caps, Western hats are no help in an accident, but they are one of the most distinctive features of a cowboy's gear, worn as much for style as for their usefulness in keeping the elements off one's head and out of one's eyes. They can also double as water buckets and as pillows during a night out on the range, and they come in handy for slapping ornery horses or fanning ornery fires. Western horsemen have always taken a good deal of pride in selecting the best available. There have been many different types of Western hats, not all of them of the ten-gallon variety. Soft felt slouch hats, wide-brimmed *planter's hats,* bowlers, and wool or wool-felt hats were all commonly worn in the 19th century, each acting as an index to the identity and status of the wearer. Rich men in town tended toward high hats and bowlers—as did gamblers and gunfighters, though one could easily get into trouble for being "duded up" if one ventured out of town. (Butch Cassidy and his famous gang got into a different kind of trouble for wearing bowlers, but only because they were unwise enough to have their photographs taken while wearing them.) Wool hats were worn by poor men, and to be called one of the "wool-hat bunch" was to be soundly insulted.

The most familiar Western hat is undoubtedly the Stetson—a name that like Colt or Winchester has become one of the great institutions of the West. Yet this hat, like the rifles, has an Eastern origin. John Batterson Stetson was a Philadelphian who traveled to the West for his health during the Civil War. He noticed en route that no one was making hats that suited the practical needs of the cowboy. Texans wore *Mexican sombreros,* which had very wide brims with high curved edges, a high-peaked crown, and a loose dangling strap (or *barbiquejo*) under the chin. But these were a bit impractical for hard riding, since the wind could pull them off and the chin strap could strangle the rider if the hat got caught in the brush. When Stetson got back to Philadelphia in 1865, he started to manufacture hats of his own design. They became popular immediately and have been called *Stetsons* (or John B's) ever since. Quality was the Stetson trademark from the beginning, and the hats have never been cheap, costing as much as $10 or $20 even before the turn of the century when a cowboy's pay might be only slightly more for a month's work. But they were made to last, and a good hat would be considered a lifetime investment. Cowboys swore they could dance on their hats, soak them, and shoot holes in them without destroying the shape. Stetsons now start at about $30 and come in a wide variety of styles and materials. The original "Boss of the Plains" and the "Carlsbad" are no longer standard items, but one can still feel the old West in names like "Revenger" and "Rider"—to say nothing of the new West in the "Marlboro."

Like the sombrero, the Stetson had a wide brim and a peaked crown, but it was designed to give a better fit and made soft enough to be creased. Hat creasing in the old days was something of a regional specialty and identification; the four-finger Montana peak was a style that affected even the Army, with its traditional fore-and-aft-creased campaign hats. Fancy hats made of beaver-fur felt and standard hats of wool or fur felt are available now, along with synthetic felt and straw for summer wear. Brims vary in width, but they have always been made wide enough so that in cold weather they could be tied down over the ears with a bandana, while in warm weather they were wide enough to keep sun off the neck.

"Ten-gallon," incidentally, doesn't refer to the

Sombrero

Planter's hat

capacity of the hat but was a slang expression. Cowboys would use the brims—not the crowns—for scooping up water to drink. Hat decoration was another area in which cowboys could show their individuality and region. Hatbands were and are still made of leather rawhide, tooled leather, feathers, and braided horsehair, often of Indian design and manufacture.

In spite of the claims about a hunt derby's strength or the durability of a Stetson, there isn't much point in deliberately damaging these valuable items of apparel. Obviously, good care and occasional cleaning (usually a brushing is sufficient) will keep the hat looking its best. Some people like to carry or store their hats in hat bags; special hat racks, from which Stetsons can hang by the brim, are often installed in the closets of affluent cowboys. For rain, clear-plastic hat covers are available for both English and Western styles.

Now that we have dressed the rider for various styles of riding and in all kinds of weather, let's consider those other items that help to complete the equestrian outfit. They are not clothing exactly but important pieces of equipment that enable a person to become a real horseman, not just someone wearing riding clothes. They do not count as accessories but are real aids to riding—sticks and spurs, specifically—which emphasize and strengthen the effect of natural aids such as the legs and hands.

STICKS

Contrary to popular notions, riding sticks and whips are not instruments of torture but effective and invaluable aids, to be used in conjunction with other aids (such as the legs in riding and the reins in driving). A stick is used to reinforce the others, either by giving additional pressure or by creating a noise to attract a horse's attention. A stick should be applied firmly and immediately after disobedience or a failure to respond; otherwise its use is likely to confuse the animal and may have the opposite effect from the one intended.

Crops are sticks between 2 and 3 feet long with a handle at one end, usually with a wrist loop attached, and a leather tab at the other. Many riders, especially beginners, find the wrist loops handy, but they make switching hands more difficult, and some instructors advise against them (a razor blade will make a neat job of removing the strap). The least expensive crops (around $2 or more) are made of fiber glass or plastic covered with woven thread, vinyl, or braided leather. More expensive models are leather throughout or steel with a covering of braided flax or tooled leather. Some come equipped with silver handle caps, suitable for engraving. Tradition dictates that the crop's color match the rider's boots: black with black footwear and brown with brown.

Jumping bats are sturdy, short (about 19 inches) but very flexible sticks. They are usually

Traditional silk top hats for hunting and dressage, with crowns ranging from 4 to 5 inches in sizes from 6½ to 7½, will cost between $60 and $75 and are available at most tack shops that specialize in hunting gear. Saddle and hunt derbies will run from $20 to $40. Hat cords or guards in black or red range from $7 to $9.

Hunt caps with black velveteen covering start at about $15, although caps of different colors (brown, navy, and so on) and with special chin guards, sponge-rubber head cushions, safety harnesses, and so on can run up to $40. Schooling helmets are usually white (or other solid colors) plastic or fiber glass with elastic chin straps; these start at about $18, but special leather chin straps and back webbing may bring the price up to $25 or more. Caliente protective helmets, distributed exclusively by Miller's and mandatory at most racetracks in this country, have a special inner harness and cushion and cost $32.50 as of this writing. Polo helmets with face shields and a leather safety harness cost about $50. Nylon or plastic covers for caps will run from $1 to $15; plastic derby covers cost about $1.50. Carrying cases start at about $10. Nonprotective (but attractive) riding caps in tweed or plaid or checked wool start at around $13.

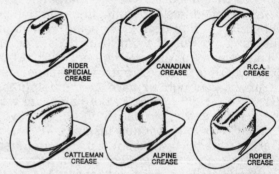

In Western hats, safety is not an important consideration but style and material are what make the difference. Style can mean width of brim, height of crown, or type of hatband, but more important is the type of crease. Hats made by Gary's, Inc. (312 Louisiana Street, Houston, Texas 77002) and Stetson (St. Joseph, Missouri 64502) are individually hand-creased in various styles. Tack shops that carry the hats of these manufacturers may have several crease styles in stock, but if you are particular, write directly to the manufacturer. Materials, rather than style, are usually what determine price. Straw hats may cost as little as $7; beaver-fur (or mink) felt can run $100 or more. Linings may be nylon or silk; sweatbands, of synthetic or real leather. Hats in the moderate range—from $25 to $60—are usually of felt made from wool or fur, although synthetic felts (available from Stetson and from the Moore Hat Company, Lawton, Oklahoma 73501) may be had for less than $20. Western-hat covers vary in price from $1.50 to $3.50; carrying cases may be $20 to $80 depending on the number of hats you want to carry; and metal hat racks that attach to the ceiling (of room, car, or truck) cost about $3.50.

Riding Sticks

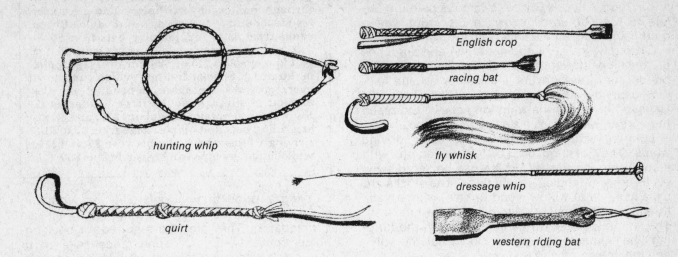

hunting whip

English crop

racing bat

fly whisk

dressage whip

quirt

western riding bat

made of rawhide with a braided leather cover, a leather handle, and leather "feathers" which may be arranged in various patterns. Variations include fiber-glass centers, tape or rubber handles, and braided-thread covers. Popular in England are bats made of twisted willow wood with leather handles. Bats do not have wrist loops, and the tabs at the business end are wider than those on crops. These shorter sticks are more suitable for jumping, because of the forward seat and shorter stirrup used by the rider, who needs only to reach the area of the flank just behind the girth. Feathered bats are less likely to hurt a horse and are often recommended for children or adult beginners with bad tempers.

Jockey bats are heavy sticks, made of plastic or fiber glass coated with leather or thread and furnished with leather, tape, or rubber handles. Like jumping bats, these have wide leather "poppers," or flaps, to make a noise when slapped against the horse's flank.

Dressage whips are longer and thinner than crops or bats, long enough (about 3 feet) so that only the rider's wrist need move to apply it. These do not have wrist loops but have leather or steel button heads at the end of the handle to prevent slipping. The other end of the whip, which is usually made of fiber glass covered with braided flax, is a thin tip or lash rather than a noise-producing tab.

Gaited-Horse whips, slightly shorter than dressage whips, have the same general shape and features. They are made of fiber glass with a white leather (or black rubber) handle and a black linen-thread covering.

Polo whips are similar to crops in shape, complete with wrist loop, but generally with a larger tip (or "mushroom") on the handle to ensure a firm grip. Once traditionally made of whalebone (now illegal, of course), braided gut, or flax, covered with pigskin and with a rubber handle, they are now usually fiber glass with a waterproof thread cover.

Hunting whips, which are properly carried in the hunt field or in an appointments class, have a crook handle (18 to 19 inches long) for opening gates and a long lash to keep hounds in line. The old-fashioned hunting whip was fashioned of whalebone covered with plaited kangaroo hide, calfskin, or pigskin with a staghorn hook, serrated to prevent slipping when one was pushing the bar of the gate. Nowadays the hook is still serrated but is usually made of ash, while the whip itself is made of fiber glass. There are usually a silver or nickle collar on the handle and a plaited leather thong or lash with a silken tip, the thong attached by a leather keeper to the whip itself. The master's thong is usually longer—about 1½ yards—than that of the other riders—usually 1¼ yards—but never long enough to interfere with horses' legs. The whip is held two-thirds up the stick and carried with the hook up, facing the rider, and the thong is looped (not wrapped around the whip) several times and held next to the whip.

Fly whisks are sticks furnished with long horsehair brushes. They double as riding sticks and as a useful means of keeping flies away from the horse during riding. They can be made of Malacca with horsehair braided over it as a cover, although fiber glass is more common.

Western riding bats are heavier than English crops, with leather flaps and a large loop for wrist or saddle horn. These bats may be made of braided calfskin or rawhide.

Quirts are used like bats; the name comes from Mexican Spanish word *cuarta,* meaning a horsewhip. They are made of plaited flexible rawhide with no stiff central core—just a leaded butt from which a lash (or several lashes) or slender leather extends for anywhere from a foot to 3 feet. The handle is short and there is always a wrist loop. Quirts used to be made of woven horsehair or stitched buckskin (doubling as a slingshot in a fight). Quirt making was sometimes a prison activity. Indians were expert quirt braiders. Since they wore no spurs (because they wore no boots), Indians would use these in a simple version with a wooden handle and several rawhide lashes about a foot long. Charles Russell's famous painting *Salute to the Fur Trade* shows a Blackfoot with a quirt made from an elk antler.

Driving whips are 4 to 5 feet long and are made of rawhide (traditionally of holly wood) with braided or thread covers and leather or tape handles capped with silver or nickel. They have silk lashes at the tip of the whip long enough to reach the horse's withers from a sulky or carriage.

Lunging whips are even longer than driving whips. They can be 6 or 7 feet in length, with eight-to ten-foot lashes, which can be set in swivels to prevent tangles as one turns. The stocks are usually made of willow wood or steel with a black thread cover, a leather handle, and a rawhide lash. The whips are used in conjunction with the lunging line, reinforcing from behind what the voice and the line command up front.

SPURS

Spurs, like sticks, are usually considered by non-equestrian types to be a cruel means of forcing the horse to obey; but—again like sticks—they are relatively simple aids used to reinforce leg pressure or apply leg aids more precisely, to attract a horse's attention, and to punish disobedience gently but firmly. They are a time-honored accessory to the art of equitation, having been worn since the Middle Ages when boots were invented to deal with the stirrup. Spurs can be overused or abused, and horses that have been mistreated may resent them, even going so far as to move away from active heel with or without a spur on it. Because they are practical, however, every rider should learn to wear them at some point, and any rider wearing them should take care to avoid

Sticks are available at most tack shops or through mail-order distributors, and price varies depending on material and style. Crops range from $3 to $12, jumping bats from $7 to $15, and whips may cost anywhere from $6 (for gaited horses) to $15 or $20 (for dressage, polo, or hunting). Special hunting whips can, however, cost $60 or more depending on the amount of silver, bone, horn, or leather used. Fly whisks generally cost about $10, and Western riding bats and quirts range from $7 to $10. Driving whips are usually between $7 and $15, while lunging whips can be as much as $30.

carrying a good thing too far. In some hunting classes and on the formal hunting field, their use is mandatory. They are also required for bucking-horse contests—not for appearance sake or to stay on, but to goad the animal into action; they are called grappling irons. Western spurs certainly look cruel with their long shanks and sizable rowels, but the construction of the stock saddle requires a larger spur simply to reach the horse's flanks (misused English spurs with single spikes can be far more painful). The basic difference between the English and Western spurs, however, and there are many variations even within these two categories, is in origin as much as in practical application.

ENGLISH SPURS

Because all spurs were originally European, we can't call these European spurs, although they are made in Germany as well as in England; however, since they came to this country via England—and in the West, at least, are referred to as Anglo spurs—we shall call them English anyhow. The most common type is a simple steel (usually stain-

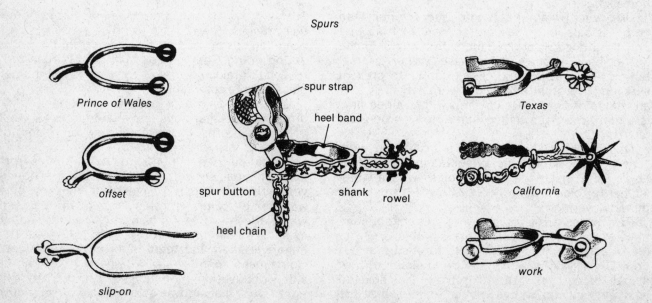

Spurs

Prince of Wales

offset

slip-on

spur strap

heel band

spur button

shank

rowel

heel chain

Texas

California

work

less or chrome-coated) spur, curved around just above the heel of the boot, with necks to which leather straps attach for fastening around the boot foot and short, blunt, slightly downward-curving shanks. These are *Prince-of-Wales spurs,* and they are preferred for beginners and for riders in the hunt field where unroweled spurs must be worn. *Hammerhead hunt spurs* are usually worn by the hunt staff and gentlemen riders; they are heavier, and their shank has a head at its tip. Ladies' show spurs have flat-sided shanks with a small head on the tip and are somewhat more severe than the simple Prince-of-Wales design. Rowels (or small wheels) are not uncommon on these English (or German) spurs, but they are quite fine and hardly resemble their Western counterparts. *Dressage spurs,* with horizontal rowels, are delicate, to be used for this most delicate of riding styles, in which the rider's motion must be virtually imperceptible. *Side rowels,* or angled shanks (toward the horse, of course), offer unusual control, but these are not to be worn by any but the most experienced riders. Spur straps are russet or black leather, matching the color of the boots. Chains are sometimes used instead of leather, but these are not allowed in some hunting circles or classes. Most spurs have loop ends to which straps are attached; others are designed with buckle ends and require four straps rather than a pair. "Anglo" spurs are what Westerners called the military type, usually made of brass with a shank curving slightly upward, a small rowel, and straps attaching them firmly to the lower part of the heel. These were worn West by cavalry men, but no cowboy worth his salt would be seen dead in them.

WESTERN SPURS

Horsemen out West got their spurs from Mexico, where they were known as "chihuahuas" and featured large rowels and long shanks. *Texan spurs* were and are usually hand-forged of steel with rowels between 2 and 3 inches in diameter (or smaller) and a heel band about an inch wide. The shank is about 2 inches long and straight, while the rowel wheel is blunt-pointed with anywhere from five to eighteen points. A chap-guard barrel or thumb keeps the chaps from getting entangled in the rowels. The leathers attach to buttons at the front ends of the heel band; swinging buttons are attached to a staple, but buttons are often forged directly on the band itself. The leather strap is made in two pieces, with the long piece acting as tongue and the short piece carrying the buckle. The buckle is usually worn on the inside of the leg to avoid catching on brush, and a decorative concho may be applied to the spot where the tongue piece connects with the spur button on the outside. To hold the spurs down (they are worn higher than Anglo spurs), tie-down straps or chains are worn around the arch just in front of the heel, though the weight of the spur is often enough to hold it in place. Bell clappers or jingle bobs are sometimes added to clink against the rowels as one rides or walks, which one can actually do in these huge contraptions because they ride high above the heel.

California spurs were actually closer to the Mexican spur in design, with even larger rowels, or cartwheels—up to 6 or 7 inches in diameter—which were often equipped with sharp spikes. These were designed to be worn on low-heeled shoes rather than high boots, but even after Californians adopted the cowboy boot they preferred their own spurs, even though they could not walk with them on. These highly decorated spurs were usually, unlike Mexican spurs, worn loose, with chains under the instep. This, and the fact that shanks curved downward in quarter, half, or full curves, were what gave the Californians so much trouble when dismounted.

Slip-on spurs have no straps or chains at all and are designed with blunt-end rowels.

English-style spurs, whether they are imported from England or Germany or made in this country, range in price from $5 to $30. Prince-of-Wales spurs, the most common style, come with ¾-inch or 1-inch necks, straps, and loop ends or buckles. Hammerhead and walking-horse spurs cost about $7, but special roweled dressage spurs or offside schooling spurs can cost up to $15. Extra spur straps run about $1 to $3.

Western spurs, however, range much more widely in price, since they tend to be elaborate. Slip-on or strapped spurs with simple rowels can start at $7 or $8, but fancy rowels, engraved designs, and silver or platinum spurs can cost as much as $150.

MISCELLANEOUS ACCESSORIES

Most catalogs featuring riding apparel and equipment include, along with the workaday breeches, pants, boots, hats, spurs, and such, a bright array of attractive horse-related items that don't fall into any of the categories discussed so far. Some of these things are gift-shop goodies—key chains, handbags, change purses, scatter pins, and other kinds of jewelry—but others are downright useful for the horseman and deserve attention here.

GOGGLES

Drivers of sulkies and carriages use specially designed goggles to protect their eyes from kicked-up turf, mud, or stones, as well as from wind, rain, or horse tails. Although these may be considered specialties for specialists, riders who wear contact lenses on horseback might find them very useful indeed. Wraparound goggles, available with clear or tinted shatterproof plastic lenses, have close-fitting strong plastic frames and are relatively inexpensive. Some styles have cutout pieces over the nose to reduce pressure, and some are equipped with chrome-wire frames, a hinged nose, and adjustable earpieces. To keep eyeglasses in place during a strenuous ride, the adjustable elastic straps worn by runners or tennis players are handy. They clip onto the eyeglass frames and fit tightly around the back of the head.

1892

GROOMING APRONS

Unlike the macintosh aprons worn during rainstorms in England, the sidesaddle aprons worn by ladies in the 19th century (and some even today), or the early version of the Western chaps, these aprons are somewhat less elegant but equally useful. Equipped with two roomy pockets, these sturdy hide garments wear forever and give good protection to clothing. The blacksmith's apron is similar in that it is made of hide, but it ties at the waist instead of wrapping around the neck and is chrome-tanned to keep the farrier cool as he works at his forge.

HUNTING HORNS

Expensive copper horns with nickel mouthpieces in fine bridle-leather cases can hardly be considered useful or even necessary equipment for anyone but the professional huntsman in the field, but the idea of a horn—or a whistle—isn't a bad one for riders who do a good deal of cross-country

or trail riding. Westerners use highly polished hollow steerhorn, although whistles are more convenient and a good deal easier to blow. If one gets into trouble—because of an accident or getting lost—the high, piercing sound of a horn or powerful whistle might just bring help in a hurry.

ROPES

Although trail riders might find it helpful in an emergency to have a rope in hand (on the saddle, most likely), a belt could serve the same purpose—to repair a piece of broken tack or tie a horse (or its front leg, say, if the animal becomes hurt and is unable to use the limb). Ropes of very specific types are necessary equipment, however, for cowboys, who use them to catch horses, rope and tie calves, drive cattle, make temporary corrals, drag cows to safety, haul firewood, rescue drovers at streams, kill snakes, make hackamores, and hang their enemies. Ropes have in the past been made of different materials, each with its own defenders: the reata (meaning to tie again) is made of rawhide, or cowhide dried in the sun; grass ropes were made of twisted, not braided, hemp, sisal, and later cotton and were stronger than reatas but didn't last as long; and hair ropes, or *mecates,* were made of horsehair (soft), cow tails (stiff), and mohair (silky). A lariat (from *la reata*) or lasso (from *lazo,* meaning noose) was a rope of any sort with a running noose (through a honda or slip ring) used for throwing to catch and bring down animals. It might be 40 to 50 feet long—or even 70 feet in open country; shorter in brush country. There are two basic styles of roping: hard-and-fast tying and dally roping. The former involves a shorter rope (usually grass) attached to the horn of the saddle with a horn string or thong, and the latter used a longer rope (60 to 100 feet, depending on the kind of country) which was held free in the hands until the target was caught and then turned around the horn. (One could always recognize a dally roper by the missing thumb on his roping hand.) The best ropes used for lariats today are made of nylon $3/8$ to $7/16$ inch thick and 30 to 35 feet long. Shorter strings (all ropes are called strings) of cotton or nylon are used for hog-tying animals, usually calves, by the two hind legs and one foreleg. Hitches are many and varied, their names reflecting their uses or shapes: barrel hitch, basket hitch, bed hitch, double-diamond hitch, half hitch, hex-diamond hitch, pack hitch, prospector's hitch, and stirrup hitch.

WIRE CUTTERS

Like ropes, these useful pieces of equipment are necessary gear for the cowboy and the fox hunter, and like knives they should be considered necessary for any trail rider who expects to be out for more than just an hour or two. Not designed for cutting into someone's pastureland, wire cutters can get a horse or a rider out of a sticky and perhaps dangerous situation, one not to be taken lightly. These can be purchased together with leather cases that can be strapped to the saddle. They are traditional (and required) gear for whippers-in in the hunt field.

> Accessories for the horseman can be very cheap or very expensive depending on your taste, your needs, and the prices charged by your tack shop. Goggles may run as little as $4; holders for glasses may be even cheaper. Hunting accessories, such as horns and wire cutters, made of brass or steel with leather cases, can cost as much as $50 an item or more.

SPECIAL NOTES ON BUYING RIDING APPAREL

The charts that follow these notes include dress regulations (or firm suggestions) that apply to specific equestrian events or activities—in the hunt field, in the show ring, on the polo field, and at the racetrack, as well as in the schooling ring, on the trail, and in the backyard. Except where competitions are being judged by a rigid set of rules (such as those listed in the *Rule Book* of the American Horse Shows Association), these charts need not be followed strictly by the beginning rider. But as one acquires experience and develops an interest in competitive events, one should keep them in mind, since riding clothes are not cheap and any significant purchase should take future use into account. Obviously, one can wear whatever one likes around the stable—and the less fancy the better, since mucking out has never been a particularly dainty job—but even here sturdiness of fabric and comfort should be considered. The moment one gets on a horse, however, appropriate riding clothes become important, not for the sake of appearance so much as for practical reasons. Ill-fitting pants and boots will soon take a toll of the rider, and tight-shouldered, too-long jackets may restrict one's freedom in the saddle. Gloves, hats, warm vests, and rain gear may not be necessary if the weather is always perfect, but even California can't guarantee that sort of climate throughout the year, and one should therefore be sure to get accessories that are designed to stay on, stand up under wear, and avoid interference with one's contact with the horse, as well as protect the rider from the elements.

Even for growing children, a sensible outlay of money is recommended, not necessarily for custom-made apparel, but at least for reasonably well-fitting clothes that are designed to do their job. When one is learning to ride, one needs all the confidence and support one can get, and a good pair of shoes or boots and a protective hat of some sort will be a big help—to both rider and parent. Children's clothing is widely available ready-made in relatively low price ranges, but the wise purchaser may get some real bargains by reading bulletin boards at stables or tack shops, where secondhand clothing is often announced at bargain rates. In the good old days before the population explosion caused a threatening situation, large families often made the purchase of good children's wear a practical investment, for one could hand down boots, pants, and other pieces of garb from one growing child to the next. These days, apparel often has to leave the family to be handed down, but one should not fail to take advantage of the occasional "slightly used" advertisement. And speaking of hand-me-downs, don't scorn a good old pair of breeches or a riding coat because it is out of fashion. Exaggerated "pegs" or flares and wide skirts can be altered, usually at a reasonable cost, by any tack shop with access to a tailor, and the original garment, because of its fine fabric, may be worth its weight in melton for many years longer.

Even if one rides only occasionally and not in competitive events, one should try to perform well—if not for one's own sake, then at least for the horse's—and comfortable, practical riding clothes will help keep one's mind on one's work by eliminating potential distractions caused by blisters, flapping pieces of material, restricted arm movements, or concern about one's cleaning bills.

Although riding clothes come in many shapes and colors, one would do well to heed the following words of George Morris in his book *Hunter Seat Equitation* (Garden City: Doubleday, 1971).

> All in all, a rider entering a show ring should appear elegant in an understated, conventional way. No part of his riding attire should draw attention to itself and under no circumstances should there be any flashiness. Imagination can enter in subtly tailoring clothing to the rider's build and in coordinating colors with the horse.

Although he certainly wasn't concerned here with parade classes, Morris brings up two important points that most riders—Eastern or Western, in the show ring or out—must think about in selecting clothing: well-fitting coats or shirts and pants to display the rider's figure to best advantage and to hide flaws; and overall appearance in terms of the horse-and-rider combination. Short, dumpy riders, for instance, may compensate for their unhorsemanlike build by choosing clothes that emphasize height and slenderness. There is nothing less attractive than a baggy coat, which may affect the rider's posture in the saddle, to say nothing of the impression that a judge may receive. High-heeled boots designed for fashionable street wear may look wonderful but may be just the wrong thing to put into a stirrup. Boot heels for Western stock saddles shouldn't be more than 2 inches high, if that, and on an English saddle, 1 inch is really quite sufficient.

If one cannot find well-fitting ready-made clothing or boots, one should always consider the fact that custom-made equipment can be far more practical in the long run than badly made, cheaper apparel. This may be especially true for people whose individual conformation requires careful tailoring and for those who want specific types of traditional wear for the sake of the rule book or for the love of history and excellent materials.

Now that you have decided to spend some money and have a pretty good idea of what to spend it on, the next step is to find the items you want. The simplest solution—though not always the most satisfactory—is to visit your local tack shop. Most parts of the country in which there is a certain amount of equestrian activity can support a tack shop of some sort (check the Yellow Pages under Riding Equipment and Apparel)—or at least a department in a sporting-goods, hardware, or farm-supply store. If you have trouble locating such a store, check with your feed supplier, your farrier, or a neighboring horse owner. Tack shops usually have a number of ready-made items on hand or can easily order out-of-stock items from their suppliers. Many shops will also have custom tailors or bootmakers on call or even on their staffs to make new apparel or to repair old or damaged equipment.

Some manufacturers—here and abroad—restrict their distribution exclusively to a certain retailer or group of retailers, and if you have your heart set on something that your own tack shop cannot obtain, write to the manufacturer directly—either for a catalog and prices or for the name of the dealer nearest you.

People who live in areas where tack shops are small or nonexistent should get their names on the mailing lists of the big mail-order shops described at the end of this *Catalog.*

Custom tailors and bootmakers, like manufacturers and retail shops, frequently advertise in the horse magazines and will supply catalogs or price lists on request if they deal direct with customers; when they work through distributors, they will give the name of the shop or dealer in your area.

DRESS REQUIREMENTS

HUNTING
(in the field, on hunt teams, and in appointments classes)

The master of foxhounds wears a square-cornered single-breasted frock coat of melton or heavy twill in either scarlet or hunt-livery color with one flap pocket on each side, a whistle pocket (optional), a collar of the hunt's adopted colors, and four buttons ending at the waist seam, two on the back above the vent, and two or three on each cuff. Vests should be plain white, buff, or yellow, and brass buttons on vest and coat must conform to hunt livery, engraved with the insignia of the hunt. Breeches must be white unless otherwise specified, with no more than four small buttons showing at the knee (cotton or silk breeches not permit-

ted). The stock should be plain white with a gold stock pin. The hunt cap must be black; heavy leather gloves are worn, with rain gloves carried under the saddle. Boots must be of black calf with sewn-on brown or colored tops and sewn-on but not sewn-down tabs, and white (or colored) boot garters to match the breeches are to button on the outside of the leg between the two lowest buttons. Heavy spurs with a short neck and no rowel are worn high on the heel, and a regulation hunt whip must be carried (with a hunting horn, sandwich case, and flask attached to the saddle).

Huntsmen and whippers-in wear the same as the master but must carry a pocketknife and wire cutters. Whippers-in can forget the horn but must have a poaching pocket inside the coat and no outer pockets, carrying an extra pair of stirrup leathers (or hound couples), one across the upper body (from right shoulder down to waist) and the other on the off side of the saddle.

Gentlemen members who have been so permitted by the master may wear three-button scarlet coats, the hunt livery, or black in one of the accepted formal cuts (shadbelly, cutaway, or weaselbelly or frock coat with rounded, not square, skirts), and white breeches. (Buff or brown breeches may be worn with black coats, but white is preferred.) With the following exceptions, the gentleman member dresses like the hunt staff: vest buttons may be brass or bone, black bone to be worn with a black coat; high silk hats with hat guards are worn except that a black derby must be worn with a black coat, in which case boots must not have tops and garters must be black.

Riding sidesaddle to hounds

Lady members riding astride may not wear scarlet but must wear a black or dark-colored hunting coat, or a shadbelly or cutaway cut, with buff or brown (not white) breeches and a black derby or silk hat (required with shadbelly or cutaway) with a hat guard and no veil. Boots must be black, with or without tabs or tops; patent leather tops are permissible for ladies (and for no one else), and garters must be black or made of patent leather if patent leather tops are worn. A lady will carry a light hunting whip (its color the same as the girth), and except for her stock pin, a wristwatch, and finger rings, no jewelry is permitted.

Lady members riding sidesaddle wear habits of black, dark gray, or navy blue, which include a formal one-button jacket, breeches or a full skirt, and an apron over breeches that rides parallel to the ground slightly above the ankle of the left boot and is held by a strap at the waist. Hats may be black derbies or silk hats, and hat guards must be worn (except when a veil is worn). Boots without tops, gloves, a hunt whip, and rain gloves on the off side of the saddle complete this elegant outfit.

Ladies and gentlemen who have not "earned their colors" are considered guests, and they are to wear the same costume as the members except that scarlet is not worn, collars must be of the same color and material as the coat, and buttons are to be plain. Juniors under 18 wear the same except that a hunt cap is permitted.

~~~~~~~~~~~~~~~~~~~~~~~~~~~~~

"The seat on a horse makes gentlemen of some and grooms of others."
Cervantes

~~~~~~~~~~~~~~~~~~~~~~~~~~~~~

HUNTER-SEAT EQUITATION (ratcatcher, cubbing, jumper classes)

Any plain-colored (not scarlet) or tweed riding coat or jacket, with (or without) a vest of a solid color or tattersall checks, over breeches or cuffed jodhpurs of any color except white. Ratcatcher or plain shirt with stock, choker, or tie; turtleneck sweaters may be permitted. A glove of leather or string in any color, and any kind of appropriate riding boot or shoe, without a colored top. Dark blue, brown, or black hunt caps or black or brown derbies are required in hunter-seat classes, and spurs must be unroweled. Ratcatching hats may be of soft felt, porkpie, or tweed, although hunt caps are preferred in case of falls. Equestrian teams wear their regulation team uniforms.

ENGLISH PLEASURE

Coats of any tweed or solid material suitable for hunting in solid conservative colors (black, blue, gray, beige, or brown) with matching breeches or jodhpurs and boots. Dark blue, black, or brown hunting cap or derby. (Conservative wash jackets in season.)

SADDLE-SEAT (formal evening classes for gaited horses and park horses)

Dark gray, dark brown, dark blue, or black tuxedo-type coats with collars and lapels of same color worn over jodhpurs and vests to match, with a top hat and gloves. Unroweled spurs, whips, and crops are optional. Boots may be of black patent leather or calfskin; elastic-sided jodhpur boots are permitted.

SADDLE-SEAT (informal gaited classes)

Conservative solid-colored (black, blue, gray, green, beige, brown) jacket with matching jodhpurs. (White jackets permitted in season.) A derby or soft hat must be worn, along with jodhpur boots of black or brown. Unroweled spurs, whips, crops are optional.

DRESSAGE (formal, third level and up)

Formal-cut black riding coat (shadbelly, cutaway, frock coat with rounded sides) over white breeches, with white stock and gold pin. High silk hats and leather gloves, with unroweled spurs on topless black boots, complete the outfit.

INFORMAL DRESSAGE (up to third level)

Black or dark-colored hunting coat over breeches or jodhpurs of matching color with black boots. A stock must be worn, as must gloves, and a black derby or a dark blue or black hunt cap. Unroweled spurs are optional, as are whips.

RACING (flat or steeplechase)

Racing silks, appropriately colored to identify the owner of the horse, are recommended, the lighter the material the better (silk is not required). Jockey boots are usually black with mahogany tops, sewn on or dyed. Goggles are recommended for rainy days; no spurs are allowed in flat racing, but sticks are essential, and jock (as in jockey) straps are basic equipment for males.

POLO

A lightweight, short-sleeved shirt in appropriate team colors, open at the neck, with a white polo cap or helmet and brown polo boots with brown leather garters. Leather gloves (on one or both hands), a polo whip or stick, and a polo belt made of wide ribbed canvas for support are recommended. Spurs must be blunted, and ribbed knee guards must be as sturdy as possible. In the old days, when these things mattered, polo players were allowed to wear camel-hair coats between chukkers.

WESTERN PLEASURE

Western hat, Western trousers, and a long-sleeved shirt are required. Boots are necessary, too, but rope, reata, and chaps may also be requested in some classes, such as those for working cow horses. Spurs are optional.

ARABIAN COSTUME CLASSES

Native-type costume including flowing cape or coat, pantaloons, headdress, scarf or sash. Nothing must be in either hand other than reins, a portion of the sash, and a riding crop.

PALOMINO SPANISH FIESTA CLASS

Spanish costume is required, with special tack.

APPALOOSA AND PINTO COSTUME CLASSES

These require authentic Indian warrior costumes.

DRIVING (single sulky or buggy)

A dark tailored costume for men and women with leather gloves and a soft felt hat with plain dark band for men. In evening classes, ladies are permitted an evening dress with a neutral-colored lap rug; men should wear a black lounge suit, black shoes, and a gray top hat.

DRIVING (road coach)

Male drivers should wear black top hats and morning coats in the show ring; ladies may wear dark tailored suits with skirts and with small hats that will not catch the wind. The coach guard must wear a scarlet coat with gold braid and gaiters. Aprons and gloves may also be required, along with a whole battery of equipment for the coach (an extra collar, reins, brake shoe, blankets, lap robes, tool kit, and so on and on).

COMBINED TRAINING AND THREE-DAY EVENT

The clothing recommended for dressage, polo (or cross-country), and hunter-seat equitation are used in the three phases of this activity. The higher the level, the more formal the apparel in dressage and stadium jumping, especially when one reaches Prix St.-Georges and Olympic competition.

TRAIL RIDING (Distance and Cross-Country)

Comfort and protection are the only real rules here, but anyone who plans to ride for more than just a couple of hours should take along some practical items: a knife, a pair of wire cutters, a map, a canteen filled with water, a piercing whistle, a raincoat or blanket rolled behind the saddle, and—in any remote area where help cannot be summoned by yelling or blowing the whistle—a rifle, handgun, or humane killer. This last item, which can be fitted into a special holder for the saddle, is not simply for protection against wild animals or madmen loose in the woods, or even for food gathering, but also for the awful—yet possible—event that a horse should become so badly injured that it must be put out of its misery before help can be expected to turn up.

BOOKS ON RIDING APPAREL

With the single exception of an excellent English book entitled *Clothes and the Horse* by Sydney D. Barney (London: Vinton, 1953), there are no books devoted entirely to clothing for the horseman, and the subject is usually given rather short shrift in general books about horses and horsemanship. Margaret Cabell Self in *The Horseman's Companion* (New York: Barnes, 1949) and M. A. Stoneridge in *A Horse of Your Own* (Garden City, New York: Doubleday, 1968) give the subject more than passing attention, but the best sources by far (except for the treatment given here, of course) are the major tack-shop catalogs which illustrate and describe (but do not explain the use of) as wide a variety of riding apparel as the nonspecialist is likely to want to know about. As for Western wear, two books stand out: Peter Watt's *Dictionary of the American West 1850–1900* (New York: Knopf, 1977) and *The Look of the Old West* by Foster-Harris (New York: Viking, 1955). Miller's Western Wear catalog is also a good source for illustrations as well as for the equipment itself. Magazine articles of particular interest are described in the sections where their content is discussed.

"There are only two classes of good society in England; the equestrian classes and the neurotic classes. It isn't mere convention; everybody can see that the people who hunt are the right people and the people who don't are the wrong ones."
G. B. Shaw
Heartbreak House

7 EQUESTRIAN ACTIVITIES

Now that your horse is (1) yours, (2) in its stable, (3) well fed and cared-for, (4) in good health, (5) dressed properly, and (6) ridden or driven by an equally well-turned-out person, let's consider activities. Pleasure riding and hunting are great fun, and at some point the lure of trying to compare your horse's abilities or your own against others' will become irresistible. After all, riding is a sport, and sports involve competition.

But what if you don't own your own horse? There are ways, as you'll see, to borrow or rent one so that you can compete. You don't even have to be a rider or driver to appreciate equestrian competition. Competition calls for spectators, and you can spend many happy hours watching good horseflesh and riding. Maybe your interest will grow to expertise and you can become an official. The possibilities are limitless.

This chapter is intended as a panorama of activities. Obviously, to discuss horse shows, rodeos, dressage and combined-training trials, endurance riding, or any of the myriad activities that fit under the chapter's heading with any degree of thoroughness would require the bookshelf space of an *Encyclopaedia Britannica* as well as the size and expertise of such a project's staff and consultants. Instead, you'll discover the wide variety of competition, some of which may kindle your interest about using your horse or yourself to see how you'll do against the world. This chapter will also contain selected "insider" views of what goes on in the show world. We're grateful to participants who have shared their expertise and experiences with us—and you.

HORSE SHOWS

What is a "horse show"? To most people living in the East it is a place where hunters, jumpers, and equitation riders can win ribbons. In the South, it's for gaited and fine harness horses. Westerners think of shows primarily in terms of stock-seat equitation and classes. Breed devotees consider shows as places to exhibit specific breeds.

The answer is that all these people are correct. A horse show is a competition in which many (or few) activities take place. Perhaps the best way to

Outdoor show at Coto de Caza, California

focus on exactly what takes place is by saying a few words about the variety of classes (a class is a group of competitors competing under the same criteria and rules against one another) found at horse shows.

EQUITATION DIVISION

Here only the rider, not the horse, is being judged, for horsemanship form and ability. Hunt-seat equitation is based on the skills needed to negotiate a fox-hunting situation. Saddle-seat equitation calls on skills involved in riding gaited horses. Stock-seat equitation is based on Western-style riding.

HUNTER DIVISION

These classes judge the horse against certain requirements needed by fox-hunting animals. Conformation classes take an animal's build into consideration; judges look for the kind of build that will carry a rider comfortably and handily across country. Working hunters will be required to perform either on the flat or over fences. Courses approximate the obstacles found in the hunting field, such as brush fences, post-and-rails, and oxers (see pages 191–92 for definitions of jumps). Way of going is an important consideration, taking into account a horse's style, smoothness of pace, and manners. Hunter horses are divided according to experience, from preliminary and novice to first- and second-year green and open. Appointment hunter classes come even closer to hunt-field requirements. Riders must wear or carry appropriate gear, as must their mounts, down to an edible item in the sandwich box and a letter from a master of foxhounds authorizing the rider to wear his hunt's colors. Corinthian classes are open only to members of a recognized hunt, and hunt-team classes are for two or three members of such recognized packs.

JUMPER DIVISION

Jumping classes are open to horses of any breed, size, or gender. Preliminary jumpers are animals that have won less than $1,000 in AHSA competitions; Intermediate, $1,000 to $2,000; and Open, in excess of $2,000. Another category is Amateur-Owner, whose owners show their own horses (and may keep any prize money without jeopardizing their amateur status). The height and spread of fences are smaller for horses just starting out in the Jumper Division. Courses are also accordingly less demanding.

The object of jumping is to clear obstacles cleanly; style and grace over fences are irrelevant. Scoring is done in terms of penalty points called faults. In classes where touches (coming into contact with the obstacle without dislodging it) are penalized, one-half fault is incurred when the horse's body behind the stifle touches a fence,

Michel Vaillancourt of the Canadian Equestrian Team on Branch County, winners of the Individual Silver Medal at the Olympic Games at Bromont, Canada

and one fault if in front of the stifle. Touches don't count under FEI rules (the Fédération Équestre Internationale is the worldwide ruling body of equestrian sports). Knockdowns (dislodging any element of an obstacle) and refusals do. Each knockdown counts as four faults. A refusal, stopping in front of a fence, is three faults. Three cumulative refusals requires elimination, as do starting a course before the judge's signal, failing to begin within one minute after a warning signal, and jumping obstacles in the wrong order.

Some classes include liability for time penalties. One-quarter fault is assessed for each second or portion thereof in excess of the stated time limit.

A round is concluded after all entrants have performed. In the event of an equality of faults by two or more entrants, another round called a "jump-off" may be called for. One that results in yet another equality of faults may require a second jump-off. In that case, if two or more entrants are still tied in jumping faults, the fastest time around the course will determine the winner. Fences are raised and widened and the course shortened for each jump-off to make the round more demanding.

Two jumping classes never fail to enthrall spectators. In a "Gambler's Choice" (or "Take Your Own Line"), each obstacle is allotted a point value according to its difficulty. Competitors may jump all the obstacles they choose in any order or direction. If a fence is jumped cleanly, the competitor will receive its value. The highest score amassed within a time limit (usually 60 or 90 seconds) will win.

"Puissance" means power, and a Puissance class may end with finalists attempting a "great wall" standing in excess of 7 feet.

Open and International jumping are always the feature attractions of important shows. Sometimes, as in the case of Gambler's Choice and Puissance classes, civilian (including professional) riders will compete against Olympians.

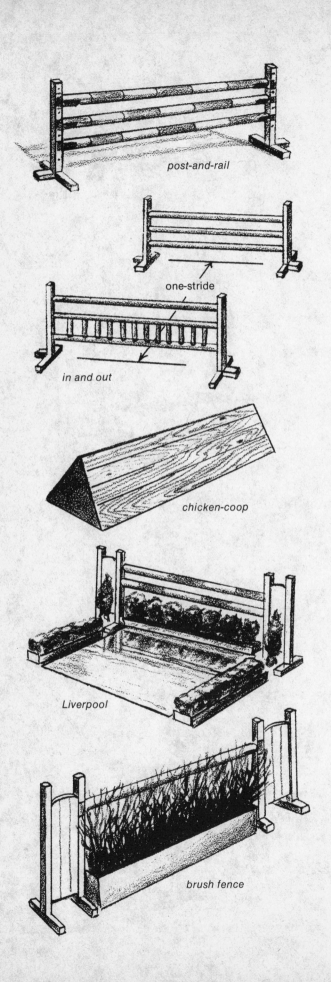

post-and-rail

one-stride

in and out

chicken-coop

Liverpool

brush fence

JUMPS

The types of jumps used in hunter classes are representative of natural obstacles found in the hunt field. These include the post-and-rails, stone wall, Aiken, chicken coop, brush, plank, and white gate. The Aiken, a split rail over bushes, is named for a famous hunt in South Carolina. An "in-and-out" duplicates the type of fencing found along either side of country lanes, and the two elements should be separated by the width of a lane. This combination is generally meant to be jumped in one stride and is so arranged at horse shows.

The post-and-rails is a natural rail fence, usually of three cross rails. The chicken coop is a triangular wooden obstacle ranging from perhaps 2 feet 6 inches to 4 feet. It's not that hunters jump real chicken coops in the field; panels in fences are shaped that way because cattle won't jump widths. The Liverpool jump is named after a famed jump at the Grand National Steeplechase in Liverpool, England. This water jump may have a rail or brush element as well. Wings are added to narrow fences to channel the horse to prevent runouts.

It should be noted that whatever the shape or composition of the jump, the obstacle should be constructed to collapse easily to prevent injury to a falling horse or rider. Much of the breakaway characteristic depends upon the type of cups that hold the rail to the jump standards. A shallow cup will permit the rail to roll out with ease. A deep cup and narrow rail will not be dislodged with less than a full crash. The inside dimensions of a cup for a 4-inch pole must be a minimum 1½ inches deep and 5 inches across; the maximum depth must not exceed one-half the diameter of the pole. Metal pins are required to hold the cups (friction or tension devices are banned). While the AHSA prefers metal cups, plastic ones may be used. They are obtainable from Helvetia Diversified, 11490 Julianne Avenue North, Stillwater, Minnesota 55082, at $3.50 per cup, complete with metal pin attached with nylon string. Metal cups can be made by your local blacksmith.

Jumps may cost thousands of dollars for a sufficient supply to run a Grand Prix—the reason why many shows rent or lease jumps rather than make or buy their own. One source of custom jumps is Walker's, 3929 Louisville Road, Finksburg, Maryland 21048. Tarli Fences, R.D. 1, Cooperstown, New York 13326, will sell a complete set of two 4×4-inch standards (adjustable from 18 inches to 6 feet), two octagonal 10-foot-long by 4×4-inch bars, and four steel cups with pins for $50 per set. The company also builds obstacles to order. Other sources of show and practice jumps are: Horse Head Jumps, 334A Foreston Road, Parktown, Maryland 21120, and Jumps by Fuzzy, 1224 Otter Creek Road, Nashville, Tennessee 37215.

Many shows use 12-foot, 14-foot, or, rarely, 16-foot lengths. Obviously the longer the pole, the greater the weight and the less the tendency to pop out of the cups when hit.

The jumper-competition fences are not representative of hunt-field conditions, but are really special fences constructed to test a horse's jumping abilities. Jump testing for height are straight rails or poles, stone walls, and series of straight fences used in *barrien-springer* events.

Fences designed to test for horizontal distances are called spread fences. They may include the oxer, double oxer, hogback, and triple bar. While these obstacles are of different configurations, they can all be raised and lengthened, as for jump-offs.

The formidable-looking puissance walls are generally constructed of light plywood, and the upper elements slide off easily. The solid appearance is only paint-deep.

Paint is employed to create illusions which the horse may find difficult to handle. There are traditional patterns used such as stripes to simulate railroad crossing gates. Bull's-eye are often painted on panels. No "Gambler's Choice" class would be complete without one fence painted to represent the joker in a deck of cards.

The paints used are standard outdoor waterproof formulas. Colors are pretty much left to choice. Very popular are poles painted red and white, with all-white or other variations used at will.

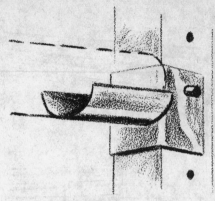

deep cup

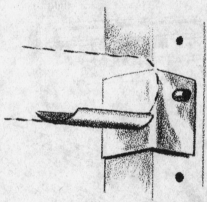

shallow cup

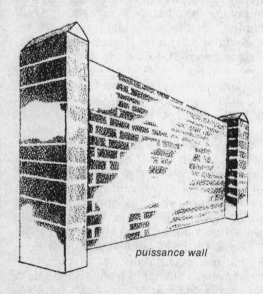

puissance wall

oxer

SADDLE-HORSE DIVISION

American Saddle Horses are the "peacocks" of the show ring. They enter in a flurry, then try to attract the judge's attention as being the flashiest in the class. Three-Gaited Horses perform at the walk, trot, and canter, their roached manes setting them off from Five-Gaited Horses. This latter group, with flowing manes and full tails, are judged at the walk, trot, canter, and two artificial paces called the slow gait (or singlefoot) and the rack. Both gaits, natural to the breed and developed through training, hark back to antebellum days when Saddle Horses provided comfortable and hardy mounts for Southern plantation owners as the men inspected their vast holdings. Classes within this category are for amateur and professional riders, women, and, with regard to horses, stallions and geldings and mares.

Tennessee Walking Horses are also Southern-derived flashy movers. Their gaits are a smooth running walk, trot, and what has been described as a "rocking chair" canter. Walkers most commonly perform in Southern shows, especially in Kentucky and in the state whose name they bear.

HARNESS DIVISION

Animals featured in these events pull light vehicles and display a flashy, high-actioned pace akin to that of gaited horses. Indeed, fine harness horses are American Saddlebreds—shown, however, at just the walk and trot (or park gait). Manners as well as action are a criterion; since ladies drive the rigs, their horses must be the kind that they could take for a spin through traffic and other distractions.

Hackneys are another breed used for harness classes. These high-stepping ponies are shown either singly or in pairs. Here too judges look for brilliance in way of going as well as manners.

WESTERN DIVISION

This division is composed of three sections. A Stock-Horse class requires competitors to perform something of a cowboy dressage test, executing figure-8's, changes of lead, spins, and rollbacks. Sometimes horse and rider will be asked to work a calf, moving the animal according to the judge's instructions.

The Trail-Horse section duplicates a cross-country ride. Horses are shown at the walk, jog, and lope on a reasonably loose rein. Obstacles are also involved: the rider must open, pass through, and close a gate, then cross a bridge or ride through water. Other movements include carrying objects, backing over obstacles, and the rider's dismounting and mounting from either side.

Horses in the Pleasure-Horse section are judged at the walk, jog, and lope as well as backing in a straight line. Classes may be divided according to horses' weight, age, and gender. As in the other sections of the Western Division, performance is given greatest consideration in the judging of entrants. Conformation, manners, and appointments are also taken into account in varying degrees.

BREED DIVISIONS

So far, except for the Saddle-Horse Division, we have been talking about events open to more than one breed or type of horse. Quarter Horses compete as jumpers, crossbreds as hunters, and any number of breeds appear in the Western Section. The American Horse Shows Association recognizes other divisions which are limited to specific breeds: Appaloosa, Arabian, Morgan, Paint, Palomino, Pony of the Americas, Shetland, and Welsh (as well as the previously mentioned Saddle Horse, Hackney, and Tennessee Walking Horse). Within each division is a variety of sections and classes all stressing the breed's versatility.

The Morgan Division emphasizes this point. Morgans are shown as harness horses, as English and Western pleasure mounts, and as Western working and English jumping horses. And speaking of versatility, the Justin Morgan class requires its entrants first to trot ½ mile in harness, then run the same distance under saddle, show as an equitation horse, and finally pull at least 500 pounds a distance of 6 feet.

Anyone who wants to participate in a horse show will need to know the rules, and spectators will better enjoy watching a show by understanding qualification, performance, and judging criteria. Members of the American Horse Shows Association, Inc., receive a copy of the current "Rule Book" and "Horse Show" magazine. Annual membership for juniors (under 18 years of age) costs $10 and Seniors $20; A Contributing Membership is $50; a Life Membership is $350. For further information, write to the AHSA at 598 Madison Avenue, New York, New York 10022, or telephone (212) 759-3070.

Trick or Streak?

A few years back, in 1975 to be exact, Halloween night was celebrated in an unusual way at the Washington International Horse Show. Between jumping classes, a young man wearing only a painted plaster pumpkin head and a pair of boots cantered his mount around a jumper course, took all the fences, and raced out of the ring, much to the amusement of the crowd. Questioned later, the president of the show was heard to reply, "I haven't a clue who it was, but he sure was one hell of a rider!"

WHERE TO FIND A SHOW

The ASHA lists almost 1,100 of its recognized shows in its *Rule Book*. There must be at least double that number of unrecognized, informal backyard or school events around the country, to which must be added shows put on by riding academies, dude ranches and riding resorts, and scholastic and collegiate clubs.

To give some idea of the geographic diversity of shows we include this general calendar of events.

	Arabian	
January	Southern Arizona Arabian Charity	Tucson, Arizona
	Whittier Lions Club All Arabian	Pomona, California
February	Tropical All Arabian	Miami, Florida
March	Austin Livestock (Arabian Division)	Austin, Texas
April	Wadi Arabian Horse Association	Turlock, California
	Waterloo All Arab	Waterloo, Iowa
May	Maryland Arabian	Bel Air, Maryland
	South Dakota Arabian	Sioux Falls, South Dakota
	Louisiana Spring All Arab	Baton Rouge, Louisiana
June	Maine All Arabian	Bangor, Maine
	Trails End All Arabian	Pueblo, Colorado
	Finger Lakes Arabian	Syracuse, New York
July	Ahane All Arabian	West Springfield, Massachusetts
August	Eastern Arabian	Devon, Pennsylvania
September	Canadian National Arabian	Edmonton, Alberta, Canada
October	San Joaquin Valley Arab	Bakersfield, California
December	Fullerton Recreational Riders All Arabian	Fullerton, California

	Combined Training	
May	Concord Mount Diablo Spring	Concord, California
	Loudoun Hunt Horse Trials	Leesburg, Virginia
	U. of New Hampshire Spring Trials	Durham, New Hampshire
June	California National Horse Trials	Fresno, California
	Blue Ridge Hunt Pony Horse Trials	Boyce, Virginia
	Ontario Three Day Event Championship	Maple, Ontario, Canada
	Flying Horse Three Day Event	South Hamilton, Massachusetts
	Chaddwynn Farm Horse Trials	Chadds Ford, Pennsylvania
August	Pebble Beach Three Day Event	Pebble Beach, California
	Delaware Valley Combined Training	Devon, Pennsylvania
	Equestrian's Institute Three Day Event	Stanwood, Washington
	Lake Placid	Lake Placid, New York
	Windfield Manor Horse Trials	Fargo, North Dakota
	Rojan Farms	Pine Plains, New York

	Dressage	
January	Lake Erie College	Mentor, Ohio
April	Arizona Dressage Association	Phoenix, Arizona
May	Bloomfield Open Hunt Dressage	Bloomfield Hills, Michigan
	Cornhuskers Dressage Classic	Lincoln, Nebraska
	Los Alamos Spring Dressage	Baptistown, New Jersey
	Virginia Dressage Association	Middleburg, Virginia
June	Long Island Dressage	Westbury, New York
	International Equestrian Organization All Dressage	York, Pennsylvania
August	Thistledown Dressage	Verona, Wisconsin
	Pebble Beach Dressage	Pebble Beach, California
	Wisconsin Dressage Association	Milwaukee, Wisconsin
September	Illinois Dressage Fall	New Lenox, Illinois
	Tennessean's Dressage Trials	Nashville, Tennessee
October	Eastern States Dressage	East Freehold, New Jersey
	Oregon Dressage Society	Oswego, Oregon
November	Suburban Essex Dressage	West Orange, New Jersey

Hunter-Jumper

January	Central Florida Hunter and Jumper	Brookville, Florida
February	Coach House Stables	Rye, New York
	Alamo Pony Club	San Antonio, Texas
	A to Z National	Phoenix, Arizona
	Blue Ribbon Winter	Northbrook, Illinois
March	Palm Beach International	West Palm Beach, Florida
	Coto de Caza Hunter and Jumper	Trabuco Canyon, California
April	Memphis Hunter and Jumper Classic	Germantown, Tennessee
May	Bridlespur Charity	St. Louis, Missouri
	Big D Charity	Dallas, Texas
	Devon	Devon, Pennsylvania
June	Pin Oak Charity	Houston, Texas
	Ox Ridge Hunt Club	Darien, Connecticut
July	Lake Placid Horse Show	Lake Placid, New York
	Youngstown Charity	Youngstown, Ohio
	Chagrin Valley Professional Horseman's Association	Chagrin Falls, Ohio
August	Sussex County	Augusta, New Jersey
	Post Time	Lexington, Kentucky
September	American Gold Cup	Philadelphia, Pennsylvania
October	Houston Hunter and Jumper	Houston, Texas
	Penn National	Harrisburg, Pennsylvania
	Washington International	Washington, D.C.
November	National Horse Show	New York, New York
	Royal Winter Fair	Toronto, Ontario, Canada
December	The Hill	North Salem, New York

Morgan

May	Uvada Morgan	Las Vegas, Nevada
	Morgan Classic Royale	Santa Rosa, California
June	Wheat State Morgan	Salinas, Kansas
	Morgan Gold Cup National	Columbus, Ohio
	Granite State Morgan	Deerfield, New Hampshire
	Vermont Morgan	South Woodstock, Vermont
July	Golden West Regional Championship	Monterey, California
August	Key Classic All Morgan	Spanaway, Washington
	Massachusetts Morgan	Northampton, Massachusetts
September	Continental Divide Morgan	Loveland, Colorado
	New York International Morgan	Syracuse, New York
October	Grand National Morgan	Oklahoma City, Oklahoma

Western

January	National Western Stock	Denver, Colorado
	Sioux Empire Farm	Sioux Falls, South Dakota
March	Houston Livestock Show and Rodeo	Houston, Texas
	Coto de Caza Western	Trabuco Canyon, California
June	All American Horse World Exposition	Oklahoma City, Oklahoma
	Silver Birch Saddle Club	Fairbanks, Alaska
	Box 21 Rodeo and Horse Show	Dayton, Ohio
July	Nevada Quarter Horse Association	Carson City, Nevada
August	Missouri State Fair	Sedalia, Missouri
	Trail Dusters of Hamel	Hamel, Montana
	Colorado State Fair	Pueblo, Colorado
September	Yavapai County Fair	Prescott, Arizona
October	Florida All Breed	Pompano Beach, Florida
November	SPCA Charity	Tucson, Arizona
	Nevada State Horse Association	Las Vegas, Nevada

Other Interesting Events

January	Pacific Coast Buckskin Horse Association National	Diamond Bar, California
March	Arizona Appaloosa Association	Scottsdale, Arizona
April	Mission Valley Pony Club	Kansas City, Missouri
May	American Walking Horse Association	Quentin, Pennsylvania
June	Silver State Paint Horse Club	Las Vegas, Nevada
	Greater Cincinnati Charity Saddle and Walking	Lebanon, Ohio
July	International Champion Pinto	Tulsa, Oklahoma
August	New York Pony	North Salem, New York
September	San Francisco Sheriff's Mounted Posse's	San Francisco, California
October	Stony Brook Driving Competition	Stony Brook, New York

For specific dates and locations, check local and regional newspapers' sports pages, advertisements in equestrian magazines, and for smaller shows, notices at tack shops and feed stores. The Sporting Calendar pages of *The Chronicle of the Horse* are an extraordinarily good source. AHSA-recognized shows are listed in that organization's *Rule Book*.

OFFICIALS OF THE SHOW

Horse shows are not spontaneous or haphazard events. Those sanctioned by the American Horse Shows Association must be run according to the rules and procedures of that governing body, while to coordinate hundreds of horses exhibited in dozens of classes over several days requires attention to other kinds of rules and procedures. Throughout the year and the country, thousands of people are involved in making shows of all sizes work. Most are unpaid volunteers who donate their services. The AHSA prescribes the number and types of officials used at its rated shows, but fixtures will often employ even more people for even smoother operation.

A show's president, vice-president(s), treasurer, and secretary assume ultimate responsibility for its success or failure. The president is spokesman for the show, since actions are taken in his name. He may also be the final arbiter, depending on the table of organization. The president is assisted by vice-presidents who are assigned specific tasks such as publicity, press relations, stabling, and ground crew.

The treasurer's role is clearly defined. He collects fees from exhibitors and through ticket sales, and he issues checks for expenses and prizes. At the end of the show he must render a clear accounting of all financial matters.

The secretary, who bears the brunt of the work, is in closest contact with the exhibitors. His first task is to prepare the official prize list, a detailed presentation of what the show offers in the way of classes and awards. Exhibitors' response determines the size of classes and the amount of stabling space required (if the show is longer than one day). The secretary also corresponds with offi-

RIBBONS, TROPHIES, AND PRIZES

Ribbons and trophies are badges of triumph, proclaiming to the world successes of horses, riders, and teams. Usually only the first six places are awarded ribbons, although eight is the number in horsemanship and stakes classes. Each place is given a different color, and this order is uniform through the United States and Canada:

First place	Blue
Second place	Red
Third place	Yellow
Fourth place	White
Fifth place	Pink
Sixth place	Green
Seventh place	Purple
Eighth place	Brown

The Grand Championship ribbon is a large rosette composed of blue, red, yellow, and white ribbons, while the Reserve (or runner-up) Championship is made of red, yellow, white, and pink.

A point system is used to determine the champion and reserve recipients. It is based on cumulative points for position in each class within a division during the entire show. First place counts for five points, second is three points, third is two points, and fourth is one point. Equal points are given in case of a tie.

cials selected to help run the show in coordination with the AHSA. He can usually be found during the show at a paper-strewn table surrounded on one side by ribbons and trophies and on the other by exhibitors who range from questioning to querulous.

Larger shows frequently employ a show manager, who is not an ASHA official. He coordinates the efforts of various committees and resolves disputes whenever they arise (much as a president would). In addition he acts as referee in such matters as arguments over stall space or jumping order.

The veterinarian is a licensed medical man whose presence, either actual or on call, is re-

Four companies that manufacture not only ribbons but badges, rider numbers, score cards, and other such show paraphernalia are:

Stineman Ribbon & Trophy Manufacturing Co.
Lambs Bridge,
South Fork, Pennsylvania 15956

Imperial Badge Co.
P.O. Box 109
Everett, Massachusetts 02149

Garden Spot Badge Co.
P.O. Box 254
Lititz, Pennsylvania 17543

Dalton Awards and Badges Co.
35 Bodwell Street
Avon, Massachusetts 02322

If any prize money is offered, it is prorated according to position. In a $1,000 stake class, for example, the division might be first place, $500; second, $250; third, $125; fourth, $75; and fifth, $25. Some state championships are determined simply by a totaling of all the money won by each horse throughout the year at the state association's recognized shows. Each dollar represents one point, and at the end of the year an official audit discloses the order of finish.

Trophies are substantial, at least more so than ribbons, and often quite imposing. The winner of an important class or all winners at important shows may receive, in addition to a blue ribbon, anything from a simple plated goblet or plate to a sterling tray, bowl, or statuette. In challenge classes, the same trophy is awarded year after year until the same rider, horse, or owner wins three "legs" on it, resulting in permanent possession. Other challenge trophies are lent to the winning exhibitor during the year and must be returned prior to the next year's show. Some shows have given up on the involved work of trying to regain trophies; they keep the original and issue a replica or plaque which the winner may keep. On the other hand, some exhibitors do not wish to be burdened with actual possession of a cup or trophy that must be returned suitably engraved and in good condition a year later. Frequent winners find it difficult to keep track of which trophy belongs to which show, and perhaps they don't plan to campaign on a particular circuit the following year. These are people who therefore graciously decline physical possession after the ceremonial presentation.

Popular and frequent prizes at Western shows (including rodeos) and distance rides are silver or bronze belt buckles. Like ribbons, plates, and cups, buckles are engraved or stamped with the show's name and date and often with the winner's name.

Lest equine participants be neglected, horse blankets bearing the name and date of the show, as well as sometimes the horse's name, are given to champions and reserve winners.

Whether sterling or plated, silver trophies require a fair amount of elbow grease to stay shiny. One way to cut down on polishing time is to keep silver in an airtight cabinet, where tarnishing is much slower. This method is particularly good for cheaper plate, which will wear down to the base metal after a few polishings.

Prize money is distributed in one of three ways. Most common is a check handed to the winner along with the ribbon and/or trophy. Some shows keep running records of winnings, paying the total at the end of the fixture or offsetting the amount against stabling and entry fees. Least satisfactory is mailing checks after the show has ended, since resolving any conflicts or disputes is quite difficult.

With regard to money, international shows are beginning to offer considerable prizes, especially where corporate and television sponsorship is involved. The International Grand Prix of Ireland at the Dublin Horse Show, for example, has a first prize of approximately $4,000.

Ribbons, trophies, and prizes, along with fading photos and newspaper clippings, attest to the transitory glory of the show ring. But since they represent past recognition, they really never lose their luster.

quired by recognized shows. When requested, he rules on animals' soundness and fitness, and he takes urine samples to test for the presence of drugs. His decisions are "nonprotestable."

Many shows also have blacksmiths on hand to replace loose or lost shoes.

Other officials include gatekeepers, who handle In and Out gates and supervise the jumping order. Some shows have "official" photographers or tack-shop displays. They are "official" only in that they have been so designated, frequently after payment of a fee for that exclusivity.

These officials are more or less permanently attached to a particular show. Others, those licensed by the AHSA, rotate from fixture to fixture. They do not work as a team, but are assigned individually after being nominated by a show committee.

More than 2,000 Registered or Recorded judges are on the AHSA roster. The Registered judge has had more experience, having passed rigid testing procedures to demonstrate his (or her) expertise to judge one or more divisions. A Recorded, or junior, judge must work under a Registered, or senior, judge for ten shows, then be highly recommended before he can advance his rating. How many judges of either category a show will have depends on its duration and the types of classes it offers. For example, there may be one for hunter-jumper classes, one for saddle seat, and a third for Western division events. Many, if not most, judges are qualified in more than one division, but where more than one ring will be in use, there must be more than one to assess the class.

Also either Registered or Recorded, a steward is

paid as a member of a show's official staff. As the official representative of the AHSA on the show grounds, he makes sure that events are run as specified, oversees the performance and conduct of exhibitors and other officials, is responsible for drug testing and regulations, supervises weigh-ins where minimum weights are required, and makes sure small and large ponies are accurately measured for appropriate classes. Within three days after the show, the steward files a detailed report with the AHSA commenting on the show, its facilities, and any irregularities or complaints.

The announcer has a dual role. To the public he is the "voice" of the show, informing spectators about which entrant is performing. His official function involves introducing specific horses to the judges, informing exhibitors with regard to which gait and direction to take, and outlining various tests to riders in certain classes.

A ringmaster, usually resplendent in a scarlet coat and carrying a coaching horn, keeps events moving. He sounds his horn to "call" each class, escorts those who present awards to the center of the arena, and also assists in pinning winners.

One or more timekeepers will be required in classes where excessive time is penalized. They will use stopwatches or supervise the deployment and use of electronic chronometers.

DRESSAGE

by Catherine McWilliams

Dressage has been described as "the gradual harmonious development of the horse's physical and mental condition with the aim of achieving the improvement of its natural gaits under the rider and a perfect understanding with its rider." Basic dressage training is the best preparation of a horse for any number of tasks, notably jumping, hunting, and pleasure riding.

Aside from its value in training the riding horse, dressage as an end in itself is increasing in popularity as a competitive sport. Horse shows offering competition in dressage are being held all over the United States. Local dressage organizations in many areas sponsor shows, clinics with expert instructors, and educational meetings. Since dressage is an Olympic sport, the USET has a dressage squad which has made a respectable showing in recent international competitions.

The goal of elementary dressage is to produce a horse that is calm, is obedient to the rider, and moves freely and easily at the walk, trot, and canter. Trained on a simple snaffle bit, it is expected to accept the rider's contact while maintaining a quiet, low head carriage with a certain degree of flexion at the poll. The horse's balance and suppleness are developed so that it is able to make smooth transitions between the gaits, halt on command, lengthen and shorten strides at the trot and canter, and bend its neck and body to follow the curves of simple turns and circles.

Harry Boldt of West Germany on Lido, winners of the Individual Silver Medal in dressage at the 1976 Olympics.

Dressage training is the systematic method of producing these desired goals. To be most effective, a rider should be trained in the fundamentals of the dressage seat, sometimes called the "classical," "full," or "normal" seat. Its principal characteristics are a fairly long stirrup, facilitating close leg contact; a deep seat, with all the rider's weight in the middle of the saddle; and an erect upper body, supporting quiet hands that maintain a steady contact with the horse's mouth. Except in the earliest stages of training for a young horse, the dressage rider sits in the saddle at all times, absorbing the motion of the horse's slow and fast paces alike by the suppleness of his body, rather than by knee grip or rising forward out of the saddle.

The purpose of this deep seat is the great control afforded over the horse. The rider can use his legs and weight aids most effectively from this position. (For jumping or cross-country riding, of course, the dressage rider would assume the forward seat.)

A major requirement of dressage training not stressed in most other types of schooling is the way in which the horse accepts the rider's hands through the bit and the reins. Contact in dressage means much more than the horse's merely tolerating a certain amount of pressure on its mouth. A horse correctly in contact, or "on the bit," not only accepts the pressure of the rider's hands but seeks to maintain it. The horse must be relaxed in both its jaw and its poll and be willing to yield at these points if the pressure is slightly increased. If the pressure is gently decreased, the horse should stretch its neck in an attempt to maintain contact. There should be no leaning against or pulling on the bit, nor should the animal try to tuck its chin away. The correct type of contact is not easy to achieve and requires skilled hands and legs to develop.

Because contact is not a characteristic of the

OVER 25 AND SHOWING!
(A TEST OF SANITY)
By Sarijane Stanton

Is there logic when an intelligent, healthy "middle-aged" person wants to embark on a difficult, hazardous, and expensive hobby? Throughout your life, things have fitted into your plan; you have organized your efforts and achieved goals. Possibly you have a family and/or business with their multiple responsibilities. Into this confusion you set out to take up horse showing as a hobby.

The first mistaken idea is that horse showing is not a hobby, but another business. This connotes complete faith that horse showing will be workable and attainable as are other accomplishments. Little do you know at the outset the multiple problems you will be faced with as an amateur.

Here are some of the various obstacles to showing:

1. How liberated can a woman feel while traveling cross country and getting a flat tire on her trailer or truck—hoping at any moment that a gallant knight will stop and help?

2. Traveling cross country via airlines and rental cars hoping to find a show in some obscure town. You finally arrive to find that your horse injured himself an hour earlier and can't compete.

3. How the expense of showing is always more than you allotted; will your family eat a lot of rice, or will you do without that special piece of furniture for your home?

4. Baby-sitters who call at 11 P.M. to cancel when you were leaving for the show at 4 o'clock the following morning.

5. Family crises: A schooling show is running overtime, you are in the last class, and you are entertaining business associates that evening.

6. You fall and feel as if you had been run over. You return home to little sympathy and much abuse.

7. "Setting up house" in a motel room with all the luxury of coffeepot, ironing board, clothes you did not have time to press, and beverages and food for several days. Also one Suburban filled to the top with enough clothes for months and enough equipment to stock a tack shop.

8. The bitter disappointment of realizing you won't be chosen for the Team (you started too late for this particular goal).

9. The new attitude toward "bookkeeping" as you try to figure out show expenses—did you or not? Which classes? Hauling? Farrier???

10. Your children tell their friends that their mother is a "fireman" because she wears black boots.

11. The awareness of how many divorces occur over horses.

12. What is the equine mystique that you can't outgrow? When you ride you become captivated with the total beauty and excitement of the horse; often this takes precedence over other responsibilities. As an adult you would think you could control this lust. Somehow you can't and you return daily for that "moment." That's what showing is all about, and that's why you will never become "overage" in this sport.

horse's mouth alone but is a product of the carefully fostered desire to go forward, impulsion must be painstakingly developed by the rider. The forward impulse originates in the energetic stepping forward of the hind legs, then is transmitted through the horse's relaxed back to a stretching of the neck and a "reaching" for the bit. The most skillful hands can never produce good contact from a horse that does not go forward energetically. Thus the energy of the gaits, contact, and head carriage are inextricably related.

Dressage competition is available at all levels of training. In fact, the requirements of the dressage tests themselves, as written by the AHSA, provide an outline for the correct sequence of schooling. The simplest way to describe the degree of training of any horse is to name the dressage test it is capable of performing well. Saying that an animal is a "second-level horse" or a "Prix St.-Georges" horse produces quite an accurate picture in the mind of anyone familiar with these tests.

A dressage test is a written pattern of exercises which is carried out in a special dressage arena. In competition, each horse performs the pattern individually, while the judge (or judges) assigns a numerical score and makes comments on each individual movement.

There are two or three different tests at each level. Test 1 is always less difficult than Test 2 at any one level.

The simplest test is Training Level, Test 1. At the Training Level, a horse performs clockwise and counterclockwise on the correct leads at all three gaits. The animal should accept contact with the bit, keeping its head quiet and mouth closed. In addition to the walk, it is shown at the "working" trot and canter. The working paces are gaits "in which an individual horse presents himself in the best balance and is most easily influenced and worked" (AHSA). A good working trot or canter involves a regular rhythm, a good length of stride, and a generous degree of energy, or impulsion resulting from lively action of the hind legs. The Training Level horse should be able to bend easily on large (width of arena, or 20-meter-diameter) circles while changing direction. The horse must pick up the correct lead from the trot in both directions, as well as making transitions between halt and walk, walk and trot, and trot and canter.

While an experienced rider with a suitable mature horse that has not been specifically trained in dressage might be able to produce a good Training Level test in a few weeks, a young or difficult horse may require a year or more to attain this standard.

First Level tests require, in addition to the exercises in training level a lengthening of stride in the trot and canter. In this exercise the horse is expected to maintain the rhythm of the working gait while covering more ground with each stride. Circles of 10-meter diameter are performed at the trot, and the transitions and changes of direction are more numerous.

At Second Level, the horse is expected to perform the shoulder-in at the walk and trot. This is one of several lateral, or two-track, movements in which the horse travels simultaneously forward and to the side. Ten-meter circles at the canter and a turn on the haunches from the halt are also required.

While many of the movements in Training, First, and Second levels are similar, the standard of proficiency at which they are judged increases with the level of the test. The same change of rein at the working trot that earns a score of 6 or 7 in Training might barely receive a score of 5 if done during a Second Level test.

Third Level tests are considerably more difficult than Second Level in that they introduce the collected gaits. A correctly schooled horse usually requires at least 2 years of training to produce them. Collection is the ability of the horse to shift its balance toward its hind legs. The results are gaits that are springy, light, and graceful. Although the strides of the collected paces are shorter than those of working gaits, the horse uses even more energy, which is channeled into upward as well as forward motion. This produces the elevation of good collected gaits.

A Third Level horse must also show the extended paces. Extension is developed from lengthening the stride, but is also characterized by a maximum of energy directed forward. The extended trot is one of the most spectacular dressage movements, in which the horse produces so much push with its hindquarters that the front legs "snap" straight forward at each stride.

Other Third Level exercises are the haunches-in and two-track movements, the simple change of lead at the canter, the rein-back, and the counter-canter. Circles of 6 meters (at the trot) and 8 meters (at the canter) are also required.

Fourth Level tests add flying changes of lead at the canter; pirouettes, or turns on the haunches, at the walk and canter; and two-track and 6 meter circles (volte) at the canter.

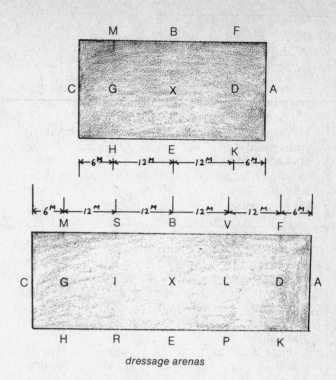

dressage arenas

Prix St.-Georges and Intermédiaire call for essentially the same exercises as Fourth Level, but in progressively more difficult sequences. For example, repeated flying changes are required after four, three, and two canter strides. Also, the standard against which the horse is judged becomes increasingly high.

The Grand Prix de Dressage is an Olympic test. In addition to all the difficult paces, figures, and transitions of the lower-level tests, it includes three exceptional exercises. These are the flying change of lead at every stride (informally called "onesy"), the piaffe (trotting in place), and the passage (a highly collected trot). The Grand Prix de Dressage is truly an acme of the horse world.

Perhaps the most spectacular form of dressage is noncompetitive. *Haute école* ("high school") dressage is done by such troupes as the Spanish Riding School of Vienna, the Cadre Noir of Saumur, France, and the Andalusian Riding School of Jérez de la Frontera, Spain. There you will see the "airs above the ground"—breathtaking rearing and leaping movements as the horses are guided by riders in the saddle or on the ground.

Dressage is one phase of combined training, taking place on the initial day of a three-day event. Tests range from Training to Third Level, depending on the level of the event.

Additional information can be obtained from the U.S. Dressage Federation, Box 80668, Lincoln, Nebraska 68501. The magazine *Dressage & Combined Training* (P.O. Box 2460, Cleveland, Ohio 44112) covers the sport's activities and lists dates and locations of dressage events throughout the United States and Canada.

Further Reading
"Dressage" by Henry Wynmalen (Arco) explores training techniques up to the most advanced levels. "The Complete Training of Horse and Rider" and "The Art of Dressage" (both published by Doubleday) were written by Alois Podhajsky, former director of the Spanish Riding School. An excellent introduction is "Dressage for Beginners" by R. L. V. Ffrench Blake (Houghton Mifflin). For dressage combined-training style, see "Eventing in Focus" by Jeremy Beale and Alix Coleman (Lippincott). Olympic riders and trainers share some of their experiences and techniques in "The U.S. Equestrian Team Book of Riding" (Simon and Schuster).

RODEOS

The word *rodeo* is Spanish for "roundup," and this truly American sport had its origins in that cowboy activity. Not during roundups, but afterward, when ranch hands gathered to relax, talk turned to who could rope a steer the fastest or ride the meanest bronco. The only way to find out was by trying, and the resulting informal contests became popular throughout the West. In the latter decades of the last century cities began to sponsor events, prize money was offered, and the sport was formally established.

There are now more than five hundred professional rodeos sanctioned by the Rodeo Cowboys Association, ranging from local events to giant pageants. Add to these fixtures unsanctioned rodeos and others conducted on the scholastic and intercollegiate level, and the total swells to more than two thousand every year. Some even take place in penitentiaries, the most famous of which is the Huntsville (Texas) Prison Rodeo.

Five events constitute the most traditional and widely seen activities. Bareback bronc riding requires a combination of brute strength and fine balance. The rider is perched on the horse's back holding only a grip cinched around the animal's belly. He must stay on board for 8 seconds. Scoring ranges from none to 100 points; each of two judges awards up to 25 points for the rider and a like number for the horse. The man is judged on his technique, while the horse earns high points for ferocity. Disqualification results from failing to spur the horse at the first jump out of the chute, changing hands on the girth, touching the horse with the rider's free hand, and being bucked off.

Saddle bronc riding is similarly scored, but the equipment differs. The saddle is much smaller than a regular stock saddle and lacks a horn, while the rein is merely a length of braided hemp tied to the horse's halter. Ten seconds is the required time.

Bull riding places entrants on Brahma bulls. Riders may use both hands to stay on board, and spurring isn't called for while cowboys are spinned and bucked around the arena. Eight seconds is the time limit.

Taurine belligerence is also a factor in steer wrestling, also known as bulldogging. An entrant gallops after a longhorn, then jumps from his saddle, plants his feet while grabbing the bull by the horns, and twists the animal to the ground. The fastest time wins.

The fastest time also wins in calf roping. The animal receives a head start; the rider gallops after in hot pursuit and with a flick of the wrist lassoes the calf. He wraps the rope around the saddle horn and dismounts. Then, while the horse backs up to keep a firm tension on the rope, the rider flips the calf to the ground and ties three legs together with a short length of rope known as a piggin' string. A judge signals when the animal is immobilized, at which point the time is measured.

Several other events are part of a large-scale

Barrel racing

Calf roping

rodeo. Barrel racing is for the ladies, as each rider traces a cloverleaf pattern around a triangular course marked by three barrels. Chuck-wagon and chariot races are hair-raising affairs. Exhibitions may consist of trick riding or trick roping. And of course, every rodeo includes grand-entry and finale parades.

Professional rodeo riders refer to the country-wide route they take over the year as the "suicide circuit." There are easier ways to make a living. Bruises, sprains, and more serious injuries are accepted as a matter of course. A few turns of adhesive tape, a couple of painkilling aspirins, and the cowboys are ready for the next event. Fatigue also takes its toll, since few rodeo participants can afford to own or charter airplanes as transportation between far-flung shows. More often they'll pack their tack and horses into a trailer, then drive all night to the next competition. To stabling expenses must be added entry fees, and the financial aspect can prove as much a killer as bone-crushing rides and falls on horses and bulls. Why, then, do rodeo riders go through such agony? Part of the answer is the glory, bolstered by amounts of money a successful person can win. Contenders for title of the National All-Around Champion, based on prize money earned over the year, may average in excess of $50,000. Those who are in the public limelight can also receive bonus money for television commercials and product endorsement.

As in other equestrian sports, rodeo riders can start out early in life. There are small-fry events—rodeos for high schoolers and collegians. Further education, rider style, is available from rodeo schools run by former and present stars (many teachers have lost to their pupils who learned their lessons too well).

Rodeoing isn't only for riders and ropers. Stock dealers who own strings of bucking horses and bulls lease them to rodeos. Clowns do more important jobs than perform amusing stunts; they rescue fallen riders from horses' hooves and bulls' horns. Hazers gallop alongside steer-wrestling quarries to keep the bulls on a straight course.

Further Information
The Professional Rodeo Cowboys Association publishes a biweekly tabloid, "Rodeo Sports News." Information about membership and subscription is available by a letter to 2929 West 19th Avenue, Denver, Colorado 80204. A monthly magazine, "Rodeo News," is available from P.O. Box 8160, Nashville, Tennessee 37207. Another organization is the International Rodeo Association, P.O. Box 615, Pauls Valley, Oklahoma 73075.

Undergraduates who want information about their set will find it from the National Little Britches Rodeo Association, 2160 South Holly, Suite 105, Denver, Colorado 80222; the National High School Rodeo Association, P.O. Box 35, Edgar, Montana 59026; or National Intercollegiate Rodeo Association, Sam Houston State University, Box 2088, Huntsville, Texas 77340.

Dates and locations of rodeos are available from all the above organizations and also from listings in "Western Horseman" and other Western-oriented magazines.

Action during a match at the Ox Ridge Polo Club, Darien, Connecticut

POLO
by Christine and W. Reid Graham

At midfield, eight horses and riders line up, two abreast. All eyes are on the mounted referee in front of them. The horses are silent, ears forward; the players hold mallets outstretched. The crowd is silent in the bleachers.

"Play!"

The ball is tossed into the middle, and suddenly the horses spring to life. Mallets crack together as the two teams fight for the ball. A horse and rider spring free from the melee, heading toward the goal, and the crowd roars its encouragement.

The game they are watching is in many ways one of the most challenging of all team sports. It demands not only the concentration, timing, and teamwork of the individual player, but also the stamina and handiness of the horse. The polo player must be in complete harmony with both his mount and his teammates if they are to be effective in outscoring their opponents.

The word *polo* comes from the Tibetan word *pulu*, which means "root" or "ball." It was played in Persia as early as 600 B.C. From there it became popular in India and Tibet, where it was played with as many players as the field could accommodate. Paintings depict early polo players as both men and women.

In the 19th century, British Army officers in India took up the sport, and in 1869 polo was first played in England, with more players and at a much slower speed than we know it today.

However, the sport was an instant success, and its popularity quickly spread to the Americas. In the late 1880's the first United States polo clubs were formed in New York City and on Long Island, and the United States Polo Association was organized to sponsor tournaments, publish the rules of the game, and assign ratings, or "handicaps," to the individual players.

The handicap system was a great step forward for the sport. Its purpose is to equalize the competition so that the two teams in a match can start out on the same footing. Each player is assigned a rating (usually between −1 and 10 goals), based on his ability in relation to other players. Obviously, ability on the playing field is determined partially by the quality and number of one's horses, so this factor is also taken into account. In a polo match, the ratings of the individual team members are added to get a total for the team. The team with the lower handicap is allowed to assume the difference between its total and that of the higher-rated team. For example, a 5-goal team playing an 8-goal team would start the game with 3 points already on the scoreboard.

In formulating and publishing the rules, the United States Polo Association provides set standards for the safety of the sport. The game is often divided into four or five periods, or "chukkers," of seven and one-half minutes each. Teams consist of four players in an outdoor game, which is played on a field measuring 300 yards by 150 yards. The outdoor ball is made of wood and is about the size of a baseball, thus allowing players to hit shots ranging over 100 yards. Indoor polo is played by teams consisting of three to a side in an arena measuring 100 yards by 50 yards. The indoor ball resembles a miniature soccer ball and lends itself well to the fast-paced arena game (which is much like ice hockey).

Right of way on the field is determined by the "line of the ball," or the direction in which it is traveling after it is last hit. If a player is riding on the line, for example, and taking a shot on his right-hand, or "off," side, he has the right of way. Any infringement of the rules is a foul. A player crossing the line in front of one having the right of way is causing danger to that player and thus must be penalized. Crossing the line is perhaps the most common foul. Some other examples of riding that endanger others on the field are bumping another player at a dangerous angle, reaching with a mallet in front of a horse's legs, unnecessarily rough bumping, or high hooking of an opponent's mallet. Penalties are assigned a number from 4 to 1, depending upon their severity. A Number 1 penalty, the most serious, is committed when a player knowingly and dangerously fouls in front of the goal he is defending in order to prevent his opponent's shot from entering the goal. In this case, a free goal is automatically awarded to the other team. The other penalties result in a free shot awarded to the team that has been fouled, ranging from a free shot of a set distance at a defended goal to a free shot of a much shorter distance at an undefended goal. Fouls seem to occur much less frequently among experienced players, who can anticipate the moves of the ball and place

themselves and their mounts in the right place at the right time. Those who have taken the time and effort to train a polo pony correctly realize that the safety of their mounts is too important to risk.

The ability to anticipate the play and a good working relationship with horse and teammates are the most important characteristics of an accomplished polo player. Aggressiveness, also important, must be tempered with an ability to sense when and where your presence is most beneficial. It is almost impossible for one player to beat another team singlehandedly. A team can work far more efficiently if responsibilities and strategies are designated in advance. This is why each team member wears a number on his jersey. A Number One is basically responsible for receiving passes and scoring goals and for covering the actions of the opposing team's "back," or Number Four, player. This involves "riding off" in such a way as to divert him from interfering with the shots of your teammates.

The Number Two player is more important offensively and is responsible primarily for scoring goals or passing to his Number One. He must be versatile and a strong and accurate hitter, as he often alternates positions with both the Number One and Number Three players if they are not otherwise occupied. He must be able to play both offense and defense.

The Number Three player must also play both offense and defense. Many polo players feel the Number Three must be the strongest member on the team. He not only must stop the attack of his opponents, but also must change the direction of the ball by passing it up to the offensive territory covered by his Number One and Two men.

The Number Four, or "back," primarily defends the goal and attempts to turn the play when his goal is under attack. As any good player knows, these are not rigid guidelines corresponding to the number of his jersey. Positions are interchangeable when circumstance calls for it. Ideally, all players should be capable of assuming any one of these responsibilities when necessary. All players are also required to guard against the activities of their opponents by riding them off the play or by hooking an opponent's mallet when he is in possession of the ball.

Great physical strength is not always a necessary qualification for a good polo player; a sense of timing is by far more important. If you are sufficiently in tune with the rhythm of your horse to sense the instant in which his foreleg pushes off and lifts from the ground, you can time your mallet to meet the ball at precisely that instant, thereby using the power of the horse rather than relying on your own strength. Many women polo players have used this principle quite successfully.

One does not necessarily have to be an accomplished equestrian to play polo, in fact, many beginners are taught polo and riding simultaneously. Polo represents a unique style of riding. In order to lean over to take a shot, you must be willing and able to lift yourself entirely out of the saddle. The game demands full concentration; little or no thought is given to posture or placement of the legs and hands. The reins are held loosely in the left hand.

However, a sound knowledge of the basic principles of equitation is essential in a sport where so much depends on achieving the best possible performance from your horse. Leg pressure alone must often be enough to stop and turn, or to jump from a standstill into a gallop. These spontaneous responses require a mutual understanding between horse and rider, and patient training of both can usually eliminate the need for anything more severe than a snaffle bit.

Most polo players agree that 75 percent of the game depends upon the horse. As the old polo adage tells us, "It doesn't matter how good a player you are if you can't get to the ball first." Although a horse does not have to be of any particular breed, Thoroughbreds or horses with some Thoroughbred blood seem to excel in the sport because of their speed and stamina. There is constant pressure on the horse to stop, turn, and gallop, and very few breeds can sustain this pressure for too long. Many polo ponies are ex-racehorses, and Arabians and Quarter Horses are often used successfully in arena games, where the length of the playing field is much shorter than it is outdoors.

A good polo pony must also be well balanced and surefooted. In South America, ponies are often taught to execute a 180-degree turn on their forelegs. This takes a great deal of coordination and training and is believed to save time. However, many players in the United States feel that this movement puts undue strain on their ponies' legs. Instead, the horse is trained to wheel on its haunches. The hindquarters can absorb the shock and at the same time provide the drive to start a horse again at a full gallop. Proper balance involves a great deal of schooling as well.

Balance and stamina are to a large degree qualities that good training can provide. Any player who can't afford the luxury of a full-time trainer must be prepared to spend many hours galloping his mount to develop its wind, trotting to develop muscles and tone, and executing figure-8's and circles for balance and turning ability.

But no matter how much time and patience is spent, a potential polo pony must have an innate sense of aggressiveness and courage. Many horses truly enjoy competition and will keep abreast of the ball without flinching from the mallet or from the physical contact with another horse.

A horse that was donated to the University of Virginia polo team was a magnificent example of this courage and love of competition. To see him in the fields, one would have doubted that he ever could or would play polo. He was a huge animal and stood pigeon-toed when he was not crossing his legs. It seemed that he didn't even have the strength to raise his ears from their usual horizontal position. But when he was tacked up for a game, he would raise his long, thin neck; his ears would come up; and those huge, ungainly hooves became sure and quick. Many inexperienced players were totally unprepared for his speed, his adroit split-second turning, and his deliberate pleasure in riding off another horse. Often he anticipated the movement of the ball more accurately than did his rider; if it took a sudden change of direction, he wheeled on his haunches so quickly that for a few seconds it would seem as though he were actually galloping backward. At the age of 18 he could—and did—show many $5,000 ponies the backs of his heels.

Although it requires much time, as well as financial commitment, on the part of the player, polo in the United States today is a growing sport that offers a great deal of enjoyment to those persons who love horses and competition. There are numerous polo clubs throughout the United States, and the expense and quality of polo vary commensurately. However, anyone who really wants to play the game will undoubtedly be able to do so. If one cannot afford the cost of a "made" polo pony, he can always train his own. The U.S. Polo Association runs a strong schedule of both high-goal and low-goal tournaments for players of all abilities. Local clubs often hold their own tournaments to determine regional championships.

Perhaps the most important and certainly the fastest-growing polo forum is at the collegiate level. College polo offers the student an opportunity to learn all facets of the game, ranging from basic riding skills and horse care all the way to playing in the National Intercollegiate Polo Tournament. The cost to the student of college polo is kept very low because older players donate horses, time, and money to support the teams. Another significant side of college polo has been the emergence of women's teams at the varsity and junior-varsity levels. At present there are at least eight colleges and universities which sponsor women's teams and provide full-season schedules culminating in a national tournament.

Polo is one of man's oldest sports, and the reasons behind its longevity are numerous. It is a sport that offers something to everyone. To the fan it is a high-risk, fast-paced game full of contact, skill and action, often ending in a breathless sudden-death overtime. To the player, man or woman, it offers the excitement of competition, the camaraderie of teammates, and the overwhelming satisfaction when player and pony merge into one dynamic being intent on only one objective: the Game.

~~~~~~~~~~~~~~~~~~~~~~~~~~~~~

A canter is a cure for any evil.
Benjamin Disraeli
The Young Duke

~~~~~~~~~~~~~~~~~~~~~~~~~~~~~

Further Information: The sport's governing body is the U.S. Polo Association, 1301 West 22nd Street, Suite 706, Oak Brook, Illinois 60521. Queries on national, regional, and intercollegiate activities will be either answered or referred to appropriate sources.

Nineteen colleges, universities, and secondary schools are members of the U.S. Polo Association, and you can watch games between them at matches and tournaments over the academic year.

Cornell University, Ithaca, New York
Culver Military Academy, Culver, Indiana
Harvard University, Cambridge, Massachusetts
Menlo College, Menlo Park, California
Midland Lee High School, Midland, Texas
New Mexico Military Institute, Roswell, New Mexico

Norwich University, Norwich, Vermont
Robert Louis Stevenson School, Pebble Beach, California
St. Andrews College, Aurora, Ontario
Skidmore College, Saratoga Springs, New York
Texas A&M, College Station, Texas
University of California–Davis, Davis, California
University of Connecticut, Storrs, Connecticut
University of Texas, Austin, Texas
University of Virginia, Charlottesville, Virginia
Valley Forge Military Academy, Wayne, Pennsylvania
Washington and Lee University, Lexington, Virginia
Xavier University, Cincinnati, Ohio
Yale University, New Haven, Connecticut

Three-day eventing: Tad Coffin of the U.S. Equestrian Team on Bally Cor, winners of the Individual Gold Medal at the 1976 Olympic Games, during the cross-country phase.

COMBINED TRAINING

by Catherine McWilliams

Combined training is a competition that tests the all-around training and ability of horse and rider. (The French call it "*concours complet,*" or "complete competition.") At advanced levels in this sport, competitors take part in a Three-Day Event which requires speed, endurance, jumping ability, soundness, courage, obedience, suppleness, and handiness. Three separate tests—a dressage ride, a cross-country ride over obstacles, and stadium jumping—make up the Three-Day Event. At lower levels of competition, these three phases may be offered over one or two days, and the competition called a horse trials, one-day event, combined training, or three-phase event. Some shows offer only dressage and either cross-country or jumping. The rules governing all these competitions are

promulgated by the United States Combined Training Association, which publishes a schedule of events held throughout this country, gives a number of year-end awards, and maintains a rating system for horses.

An important characteristic of combined-training events is the great variety of the courses. Unlike ordinary hunter of jumper competitions, where one finds essentially the same types of fences in similar arrangements at every show, each fence on a cross-country course is unique. In addition to the wide variety of materials used (e.g., telephone poles, stone walls, natural hedges, earth banks, streams, ditches, tractor tires, beer barrels, hay bales, log piles, and farm wagons), the positioning of the fences creates both interest and degree of difficulty.

Obstacles may be placed at the top or bottom of steep hills, before or after sharp turns, at the edge of dark woods, and on slopes. The simplest type of jump, which any horse could hop over in the ring, thus becomes a real challenge because of its placement on the terrain. An increasingly popular type of obstacle is the puzzle fence, where the rider has a choice of several routes over a complex obstacle. Usually the puzzle is arranged so that the shortest route over it requires the greatest jumping ability or effort, while the safer or easier routes involve a loss of time.

The most arduous type of combined-training competition is the international-, or open-, level three-day event. A breakdown of the requirements for each phase shows what is required in this demanding competition.

First Day: The dressage phase consists of a special FEI test approximately equivalent to AHSA Third Level. Working, medium, and extended paces are required, as well as countercanter and two-tracks. The test calls for a great degree of impulsion and suppleness, as well as considerable collection to perform well, even though the true collected paces are not required. The dressage score, converted into penalty points and weighted to give the correct ratio of 3:12:1 (dressage, cross-country, stadium jumping, respectively), is added to the penalties for the other two phases to determine final placings. Elimination in this or any other phase is elimination from the entire competition, since no separate awards are given for the three phases.

Second Day: The cross-country day is by far the most-important of the three. It consists of four phases:

Phase A: Roads and Tracks   The distance is usually 2 to 4 miles, taken at a speed of 240 meters per minute, (about 9 miles per hour), or the equivalent of a fast trot. It is done over a marked trail that includes all types of terrain, but without jumps. Phase A serves as a warm-up for the remainder of the course.

Phase B: Steeplechase   This begins with a standing start immediately following Phase A. The course is about 2 miles long at 550 meters per minute (or 20 miles per hour). Bonus points are given for faster times. The course consists of about ten typical steeplechase jumps up to 3 feet 3 inches in their solid parts, but up to 4 feet 7 inches to the top of the brush portion.

Phase C: Roads and Tracks   A route 8 to 10 miles long at 9 miles per hour, run over varied terrain, almost always includes long up and down slopes. No scored obstacles (where jumping-fault penalties are counted) are included, but this phase takes great skill to negotiate while saving the horse as much as possible for the real test to come.

Ten-minute compulsory halt and veterinarian check   After Phase C, riders dismount, adjust saddlery, and sponge off sweaty horses. A veterinarian inspects each horse and eliminates any that are tired or unfit.

Phase D: Cross-Country   This course is about 5 miles long at 45 meters per minute (or 17 miles per hour), over about thirty obstacles. The maximum height of the jumps, 3 feet 11 inches, is low by show-jumping standards, but their breadth, construction, and siting make them formidable. They may be 6 feet 7 inches wide at the *top* (!) and 9 feet 10 inches wide at the base. Jumps with a 6- to 7-foot drop on landing are common. Most events feature nearly vertical slides 20 to 30 feet high, often with fences at the top or bottom. Obstacles commonly involve streams or ponds. Each course includes a few multiple obstacles with up to four or five jumping efforts required at each one.

Scoring: Since all the cross-country obstacles are solid, the only jumping faults are refusals, run-outs, and falls. A horse may refuse twice at *each* fence on the course (thereby earning an awesome penalty score) without being eliminated. However, the third refusal at any of the obstacles constitutes elimination, as in the second fall in steeplechase and the third fall in cross-country.

All four phases are timed with stopwatches. Penalties are assessed for going too slowly. In the steeplechase and cross-country, bonus points are given for faster times, up to a stated maximum.

Third Day: The stadium-jumping competition is a test of the horse's ability to recover from the rigors of the second day. First, a veterinary inspection eliminates any unsound horse. Then each remaining competitor negotiates a stadium-jumping course, in which the obstacles are of the same height as in the cross-country phase. The course should be "irregular and winding" and usually includes several combinations and a water jump. This course is not intended to test jumping ability as much as the horse's obedience and suppleness. It rewards handiness and precision, as all the fences can be knocked down easily in contrast to the solid obstacles of the day before. As in horse shows' stadium-jumping competition, refusals, falls, knockdowns, and exceeding the time allowed are all penalized.

The Three-Day Event tests more facets of a horse's training and abilities than any other single type of competition. Preparing for an event gives the rider a very clear picture of the horse's capabilities in many areas and is an excellent basis for future training. Many good event horses later go on to further success as show jumpers or dressage horses.

Competition in combined training is not limited to grueling advanced events as described above. There are smaller events where the phases are all ridden on the same day, available with intermediate levels of difficulty. A prospective eventer can begin by participating in "Pre-Training"-Level events.

These competitions involve a dressage test of the Training Level variety, a 1- or 2-mile cross-country phase taken at slow speeds over obstacles no higher than 3 feet 3 inches (often much lower), and accordingly lower fences during the stadium-jumping round.

Thanks to the attention drawn to Princess Anne and the success our U.S. Olympic squad achieved in Montreal, eventing is becoming both a rapidly growing spectator and participant sport. The magazines "Dressage & Combined Training" and "The Chronicle of the Horse" list dates and locations of events; another source is the U.S. Combined Training Association, One Winthrop Square, Boston, Massachusetts 02110.

Further reading: "Give Your Horse a Chance" by A. L. D'Endrody (British Book Centre) is the classic work on combined-training schooling. More recently, "Eventing in Focus" by Jeremy Beale and Alix Coleman (Lippincott) shows the activity in words and photos. There is a nice section on eventing in "The U.S. Equestrian Team Book of Riding" (Simon and Schuster).

A meet of foxhounds in front of an 18th-century Virginia mansion.

FOX HUNTING

Although man has hunted from horseback for thousands of years, the sport of fox hunting is a relative newcomer. Its catalyst was the Enclosure Acts passed by the British Parliament beginning in the early 18th century. That legislation required landowners to separate private property from common land, and the fences, walls, hedges, and banks and ditches were inviting obstacles for the squirarchy's sporting set to jump. More serious hunters enjoyed watching packs of hounds finding and following a fox, while farmers were pleased to see the countryside rid of predators on their chicken coops. British colonists brought fox hunting to North America, where it became especially popular in the Middle Atlantic states. Important packs were later established in New England and the South. There are now 146 hunts in the United States and Canada. Most pursue live foxes; some, however, are "drag" hunts (following a scent which has been previously dragged across the countryside); and a few Western hunts chase coyotes.

We asked several fox hunters to list and answer some of the most frequently asked questions put to them about the sport. Their responses provide a nice overview of hunting:

—Q. Why do people still hunt when there are more effective and efficient ways to eliminate foxes?

A. The primary purpose is not to kill. Hunting is also known as "riding to hounds," and the canines are the stars. Hunting should be considered a spectator sport, the chance to watch hounds in action. That's why people continue to wake up before sunrise, travel many miles to where hounds meet (that is, the starting place of that day's hunt), and disregard inclement weather. Many have hunted for years without ever seeing a fox killed, especially if they hunt with a drag pack. Indeed, most American and Canadian hunts try to avoid killing a fox, so that it can provide a merry chase on future days.

—Q. When does hunting take place?

A. The season is divided into two segments. Cubbing, so-called because young foxes are encouraged to run across country, begins in September. The formal season extends from late October or early November until February or March. Climate determines a season's duration—the warmer the longer, at least until vixens start to whelp and farmers begin to till their land.

Most packs hunt two or three days a week, one of which is usually a Saturday. The time when hounds meet varies from hunt to hunt, from 7 ot 10 o'clock in the morning. A hunt may last for only a few hours or all day, depending on the weather, scent, and enthusiasm of the participants.

—Q. Is hunting one long gallop?

A. Not at all. There's a fair amount of standing around while hounds explore likely spots to pick up a scent. Even during a chase, you may have to stop and wait your turn to jump a fence.

It should be added that going out hunting is not a license to gallop in all directions or jump everything in sight. Trampling crops, traumatizing livestock, or trespassing on posted property will lead to owners' denying the hunt permission to ride across that land (and there isn't all that much acreage still available for hunting in most places). "Larking," or jumping unnecessarily, is the mark of an ignorant hunter. Jumping dangerously or trying to clear a fence that's too big for your abilities is plain dumb. There's no shame in taking an alternative route or waiting for a gate to be opened—just be sensible, and you won't need to pack your Blue Cross card in your sandwich case.

—Q. What does a day's hunting cost?

A. Hiring and transporting a horse averages at least $50. Some hunts charge a "capping" fee (the cash is deposited in a hunt official's outstretched cap) for a day's cubbing, while others do not. All, however, require a capping fee during the formal session, from $15 to $35 per outing.

In addition, you'll need special apparel during the formal season (see Chapter 6, pages 186–87, for chapter-and-verse about what to wear). Cubbing is less formal sartorially; some hunts encourage wearing "ratcatcher" (hacking) clothes, while others permit jeans, chaps, and just about anything else.

—Q. Then who is permitted to wear those red coats?

A. Only people so invited by a hunt, and hunt officials. Speaking of officials, the master of foxhounds is in charge of the entire operation. The huntsman (some MFHs assume that function) supervises hounds, assisted by whippers-in, or "whips," who help keep hounds in line. The honorary secretary takes care of finances and paperwork. The field master determines what route members of the field (those following hounds) will take.

—Q. As a newcomer, where should I place myself?

A. There is a scrupulously adhered-to order in the hunt field. The master, huntsman, and whips stay in the front with the hounds. Members of the hunt lead the field, with juniors and guests behind them. One advantage of being back is that fences may have been lowered by the time you reach them, and stone walls turned into Kitty Litter by preceding horses' hooves.

—Q. Should I use my own horse?

A. Only if it's mannerly and in good condition. You don't want to be mounted on a horse that kicks or is difficult to control (hunt-field activity has been known to turn usually manageable horses into maniacs). Stamina is equally essential, since hunting horses must be able to negotiate trappy (uneven and difficult) terrain for many miles and hours.

—Q. What is the most important thing a novice fox hunter should do?

A. Be familiar with hunting etiquette and protocol and adhere to it. Most rules all boil down to "Don't interfere with the hounds or the people who are working them."

—Q. Where can I learn these rules?

A. *Riding to Hounds in America* by William Wadsworth, published by *The Chronicle of the Horse,* is something of a Bible on the subject. *Invitation to Riding* by Sheila Wall Hundt (Simon and Schuster) contains several good chapters on hunting. The best way to be introduced to the sport is in the company of a member of the hunt, and it's also reassuring to be in the company of someone who knows the territory.

If you're not sure that you're quite up to riding to hounds or you'd merely like to watch the proceedings, you can follow the hunt by car or on foot. It's known as "hilltopping," and regular hilltoppers can indicate the best routes and spots to follow and view the action.

The Chronicle of the Horse, published in Middleburg, Virginia, is among other things the official organ of the Masters of Foxhounds Association. *The Chronicle*'s annual Hunt Roster issue provides names and addresses of whom to contact about participating in specific hunts. Most of the following hunts accept guests and visitors, and in some instances a hunt may be able to help you hire a horse.

Alabama:
Mooreland Hunt, Huntsville
Arizona:
Grass Ridge Hounds, Sonoita
California:
Los Altos Hunt, Woodside
Pine Valley Hounds, Los Angeles
Sante Fe Hunt, Rancho Santa Fe
Santa Ynez Valley Hunt, Solvang
Colorado:
Arapahoe Hunt, Littleton
Roaring Fork Hounds, Aspen
Connecticut:
Fairfield County Hounds, Westport
Mr. Haight Jr.'s Litchfield County Hounds,
   Litchfield
Middlebury Hunt, Middlebury

Delaware:
Vicmead Hunt, Wilmington
Florida:
Two Rivers Hunt, Tampa
Georgia:
Belle Meade Hunt, Thompson
Live Oak Hounds, Thomasville
Midland Fox Hounds
Shakerag Hounds, Atlanta
Tri-County Hounds, Griffin
Illinois:
Fox River Valley Hunt, Barrington
Mill Creek Hunt, Wadsworth
Oak Brook Hounds, Naperville
Old Stonington Hounds, Taylorville
Southern Illinois Open Hunt, Herrin
Wayne-DuPage Hunt, Wayne
Wolf Creek Hounds, Goreville
Indiana:
Hound and Horn Hunt Club, Schereville
New Britton Hunt, Spencer
Romwell Fox Hounds, Romney
Traders Point Hunt, Zionsville
Kansas:
Fort Leavenworth Hunt, Fort Leavenworth
Mission Valley Hunt, Stanley
Kentucky:
Iroquois Hunt, Lexington
Licking River Hounds, Carlisle
Long Run Hounds, Louisville
Maryland:
Antietam Hunt, Hagerstown
De La Brooke Foxhounds, Mount Victoria
Elkridge-Harford Hunt, Monkton
Foxcatcher Hounds, Elkton
Goshen Hunt, Olney
Green Spring Valley Hounds, Glyndon
Howard County Hunt, Glenelg (Ellicott City)
Mr. Hubbard's Kent County Hounds, Chestertown
Marlborough Hunt, Upper Marlboro
Middletown Valley Hunt, Middletown
New Market Hounds, New Market
Potomac Hunt, Potomac
Wicomico Hunt, Salisbury
Wye River Hounds, Easton
Massachusetts:
Myopia Hunt, South Hamilton
Nashoba Valley Hunt, Pepperell
Norfolk Hunt, Dover
Old North Bridge Hounds, Concord
Michigan:
Battle Creek Hunt, Augusta
Metamora Hunt, Metamora
Waterloo Hunt, Grass Lake
Minnesota:
Long Lake Hounds, Long Lake
Mississippi:
Austin Hunt, Lake Cormorant
Missouri:
Bridlespur Hunt, Ellisville
Nebraska:
North Hills Hunt, Omaha
New Jersey:
Amwell Valley Hounds, Ringoes

Essex Fox Hounds, Peapack
Monmouth County Hunt, Moorestown
Spring Valley Hounds, Green Village
New Mexico:
Juan Tomas Hounds, Sandia Park
New York:
Genesee Valley Hunt, Geneseo
Golden's Bridge Hounds, North Salem
Hopper Hills Hunt, Victor
Limestone Creek Hunt, Manlius
Millbrook Hunt, Millbrook
Old Chatham Hunt, Old Chatham
Rombout Hunt, Salt Point
Smithtown Hunt, Stony Brook
Windy Hollow Hunt, Florida
North Carolina:
Mecklenburg Hounds, Matthews
Moore County Hounds, Southern Pines
Sedgefield Hunt, Greensboro
Triangle Hunt, Durham
Tryon Hounds, Tryon
Ohio:
Camargo Hunt, Cincinnati
Chagrin Valley Hunt, Gates Mills
Lauray Hunt, Bath
Miami Valley Hunt, Dayton
Rocky Fork–Headley Hunt, Columbus
Oklahoma:
Lost Hound Hunt, Edmond
Pennsylvania:
Beaufort Hunt, Middletown
Brandywine Hounds, West Chester
Chestnut Ridge Hunt, New Geneva
Dutch Fork Hunt, West Alexander
Eagle Farms Hunt, West Chester
Harts Run Hunt, Allison Park
Huntington Valley Hunt, Philadelphia
Mr. Jeffords' Andrews Bridge Hounds, Christiana
Limekiln Hunt, Reading
Pickering Hunt, Phoenixville
Radnor Hunt, White Horse (Malvern)
Rolling Rock–Westmoreland Hunt, Ligonier
Rose Tree Fox Hunting Club, York
Sewickley Hunt, Sewickley
Mr. Stewart's Cheshire Foxhounds, Unionville
Westmorland Hunt, Greensburg
Rhode Island:
Bradbury Fox Hounds, Warwick
South Carolina:
Aiken Hounds, Aiken
Camden Hunt, Camden
Greenfield County Hounds, Landrum
Middleton Place Hounds, Charleston
Woodside Hounds, Aiken
Tennessee:
Cedar Grove Foxhounds, Cornersville
Early Grove Hunt, Moscow
Hillsboro Hounds, Nashville
Long Green Foxhounds, Collierville
Mells Fox Hounds, Lynnville
Oak Grove Hunt, Germantown
Texas:
Hickory Creek Hunt, Dallas

Vermont:
Green Mountain Hounds, Stowe
Winsor County Hounds, Woodstock
Virginia:
Bedford County Hunt, Bedford
Blue Ridge Hunt, Boyce
Bull Run Hunt, Manassas
Casanova Hunt, Casanova
Deep Run Hunt, Manakin
Fairfax Hunt, Sunset Hills
Farmington Hunt, Charlottesville
Glenmore Hunt, Staunton
Keswick Hunt, Keswick
Loudon Hunt, Leesburg
Middleburg Hunt, Middleburg
Old Dominion Hounds, Warrenton
Piedmont Fox Hounds, Upperville
Princess Anne Hunt, Virginia Beach
Rapidan Hunt, Rapidan
Rappahannock Hunt, Sperryville
Rockbridge Hunt, Lexington

Warrenton Hunt, Warrenton
Washington:
Woodbrook Hunt, Tacoma
Canada.
British Columbia:
Fraser Valley Hunt, Surrey
Ontario:
Bethany Hills Hunt, Bethany
Eglinton and Caledon Hunt, Terra Cotta
Frontenac Hunt, Kingston
Hamilton Hunt, Hamilton
London Hunt, London
Ottawa Valley Hunt, Stittsville
Toronto and North York Hunt, Toronto
Wellington-Waterloo Hunt, Hespeler
Quebec:
Belle-Rivière Hunt, Montreal
Lake of Two Mountains Hunt, Como, Vaudreuil
County
Montreal Hunt, Bromont

The Blue Ridge Hunt point-to-point races, Berryville, Virginia.

Most hunts sponsor related activities in which spectators are as welcome as participants. Hunter paces require teams of riders to complete a course in as close to a predetermined optimum time as possible. Hunter-trial participants are judged according to how well they emulate the pace, handiness, and manners of a perfect field hunter. Hound shows focus on canines, with individuals and groups assessed in terms of foxhound conformation. Dates and locations are available from individual hunts, "The Chronicle of the Horse"'s Sporting Calendar pages, and, in the case of hound shows, the American Foxhound Club, 120 Delaware Trust Building, Wilmington, Delaware 19801.

Steeplechase racing originated as an adjunct to hunting when riders with excess energy raced each other home (the most visible finish line was usually a church's steeple, hence the name). Many hunts sponsor hunt races, which feature events for professional and amateur riders, many of whom ride horses they ride to hounds. Hunt races tend to be informal affairs for spectators, who enjoy tailgate picnics and watch jumping and flat races from hillsides overlooking the course. For dates and locations, check local newspapers, look in "The Chronicle of the Horse," or write to the National Steeplechase and Hunt Association, Box 308, Elmont, New York 11003.

GYMKHANAS

Gymkhana is a Hindu word rhyming with "Ghana" and meaning "field day." The event originated among British cavalrymen stationed in India, and it now describes a morning or afternoon of games for horses and riders.

A typical event is "Musical Tires," adapted from that old parlor favorite "Musical Chairs." One fewer automobile tire than contestants is all the equipment that's required, along with a portable tape recorder, radio, or phonograph. The tires are placed around the field or ring in a circular pattern, spaced about 25 feet apart. When the music starts, riders canter their horses in a counterclockwise direction. As soon as the music is stopped, they dismount and, leading their horses, run to the nearest unoccupied tire. A rider "occupies" a tire by standing (with both feet) inside it. Contestants are required always to move forward; even if they are only several feet in front of a tire, they may not move clockwise. When the dust settles, one rider will be "un-tired," and that person is eliminated. One tire is removed before the next round begins, and rounds continue until all but one contestant—the winner—are eliminated.

Gymkhana events may be included in horse shows or rodeos, or they can be combined in a separate activity. More than fifty competitions for individuals and teams are described in the book *Gymkhana Games* by Natlee Kenoyer, published by The Stephen Greene Press (hardcover, $5.95).

Since riding to hounds can be an all-day activity, a spot of sustenance along the way will be welcome. A sandwich case (or box) and a flask are traditionally carried attached to the saddle (although jacket pockets are often pressed into service). Stainless steel cases and flasks in leather coverings cost from $50 to $150 apiece. Less expensive are lunch kits or canteens with room for both liquid and solid refreshment. Plastic and synthetic-leather models start at $15, and more de luxe stainless steel and real-leather items will run about $100.

Ham or beef sandwiches are traditional fare, and tidbits of cheese and raisins are excellent quick-energy snacks. Go easy on complicated victuals, because holding the pickles and the lettuce will be hard to do when the field is preparing to gallop away. Flasks traditionally contain brandy or port, and remember what alcohol's effect on a less-than-full stomach can do to you.

One hunting definition of "music" is the sound of a hound's voice. There's also music in the lyrics and tunes that celebrate fox hunting. You'll ken "John Peel" and lap up "Drink Puppy Drink" and other songs through "The Songs of Foxhunting" by Alexander Mackay-Smith, published by the American Foxhound Club, Millwood, Virginia. There is an accompanying long-play record performed by the John Peel Singers, distributed by Milton Heath International, 1230 Nepperhan Avenue, Yonkers, New York 10703.

DRIVING

by Robert G. Heath

For 3,000 years horses have served as driving animals in agriculture, transportation, battle, and sport. While the other uses have all but died away, the sport of driving flourishes. In fact, interest in pleasure driving is so strong that as recently as 1975 a need was recognized for an organization that would bind together, inform, and aid persons interested in this fascinating aspect of the equine sports, and the American Driving Society was formed.

Driving calls for a refined style of horsemanship, with the horses moving quietly and under complete control of the driver, called the whip. In the show ring, the judges like to see a touch of flair and brilliance in movement, and these skills accrue to the whip and his horse, as in any other activity, as experience is gained and potential fulfilled.

In modern driving, several combinations of horses or ponies may be put to a variety of carriages.

One horse, or a single, can comfortably convey four people in a four-wheel surrey, but more commonly a single horse is put to a two-wheel vehicle such as a Meadowbrook or Road cart, or if you're going "fancy," a Stanhope gig. Two horses can be driven side by side, a pair, or one in front of the other, a tandem. Except when utilizing a rather unusual two-wheel vehicle called a curricle, or a Cape cart, a pair is driven to a four-wheel vehicle. The tandem, which is almost always driven to a two-wheel carriage, is considered the most sporting of the driving turnouts and perhaps the most difficult to drive.

The lead horse in the tandem does not have shafts at its side to restrain it, and it must share the confidence of its driver to stay out there on its own and not waver. It is not unusual for a tandem's lead horse, whether from lack of training or because it shied at a strange object, to turn completely around and face the driver! At this point, the groom, who is essential to the safe driving of a tandem, has to jump down and correct the situation.

Three horses can be hitched in any one of three ways. Most commonly they are put together as a unicorn, a pair in the wheel and one out front on his own. The same problems faced by the tandem driver come into play here. Three horses hitched abreast are called a trandem, and though this is seldom seen, three in line, one in front of another, are called a randem.

The epitome of driving thrills comes in handling

Robert Heath driving his Thoroughbred horse to a Norfolk cart.

the four-in-hand. Two pairs of horses, one in front of the other, make up this turnout. It is particularly suited to pulling a road coach, which was both a commercial and a private means of transport from 1874 until the railroads eclipsed its commercial use in the early 1900's.

The early training of a driving horse is essentially the same as that for any other horse. Assuming the animal is entirely unbroken, he must first be handled and made to feel at ease around the stable. He must lead into and out of the barn without resisting. Then a progressive program, using quiet voice aids, is instituted. Lunging is done first with a caveson or halter; then with a roller pad around the girth; then with a crupper under the tail. An open bridle with a light bit is put on in the stall and is worn while the horse is on the lunge, though the line still goes to the caveson and not the bit. Next, "long lines" are attached to each side of the caveson and our young driving horse has his first experience at being driven from behind. All of the work thus far should be done in a ring, so that if there is a problem the horse has the confidence that the ring imposes on him. Once the horse moves freely and comfortably, the "long lines" are attached to the bit, and the trainer moves nimbly behind the animal at the walk and trot, maintaining a light contact with the mouth.

A five- to ten-pound object, such as a five-foot piece of two-by-four, is attached by way of two lines that go through the roller pad to a breastplate. And now, for the first time, our pupil learns what it is like to have something dragging behind it. A blinker bridle replaces the open bridle, and for a while the horse will be unsure of itself because its vision is restricted. I want to stress here that all of these formative training stages must be gone through easily and quietly; progress is to come only when the horse is entirely comfortable at each stage of the training.

The conclusion of the preliminary training is almost complete. The horse stands quietly, responds to the voice, and moves away without diving into the collar or breastplate, and the entire picture is one of ease and unhurried activity. We can now put the horse to a two-wheel jogger, or breaking cart.

The trainer, still on the ground, asks the horse to move off, and here it is desirable to have an assistant on either side of the animal, with lead shanks attached to a halter over the bridle. The assistants may have to help the animal around corners, since the shafts and the restrictions caused by them are new to it. In a short time, the trainer may quietly get into the cart, and at this point we should have the makings of a good driving horse.

It is strongly advisable to have any driving horse go well in single harness before it is asked to drive in pairs or tandem.

Subtlety of aids is the goal of almost all equestrian pursuits, and so the accomplished whip uses the voice aids as quietly as he can and makes his adjustments smooth and unobtrusive. The right hand, which should at all times carry the whip, must be ready to use it to enforce a voice aid. Adjustment of the reins, if slight, may be done by backward and forward turning of the left hand. To shorten the reins, to go downhill, for example, the right hand pushes them back through the left hand; likewise, the reins should be drawn through the left hand for lengthening. The whip must become completely familiar with the position of the reins so that by using the right hand he can make any single adjustment or multiple adjustments without looking down. Not only does this manner of handling the reins convey the appearance of complete ease on the part of the driver, but it also maintains an even contact with the horse.

Four-in-hand or tandem driving brings with it a real challenge. Now four reins must be handled in the left hand, in this order: between the thumb and first finger, the rein of the near-leader; between the first and second fingers, the off-leader and near-wheeler; and between second and third fingers the off-wheeler—quite a handful, especially in the case of a "four" if they lean on their bits.

Two further techniques must be mastered. The use of the brake, particularly on heavy carriages, is important to overall driving skill. The driver puts on the brake with the right hand and, if it is properly adjusted, can release it by knocking it off with the right elbow. The application of the whip is another facet of driving that takes a measure of skill, particularly when it is to be used on the front of the leaders in a "four" or tandem who are almost 15 feet away from the driver. It is necessary, of course, that the whip be that long, and it requires considerable practice to be able to use it neatly at this distance and flick it back onto the stick out of the way.

The groom's role in driving should not be overlooked; it requires a great deal of knowledge. He must first of all be a good horseman; he must know how to fit a harness to various combinations of horses; and he must be aware of the simple yet profound mechanics of a carriage. In addition to these responsibilities, he must be of sharp personal appearance so that he will dress appropriately for the vehicle that is being used.

Were it not for the important contribution that horse-drawn carriages made to commercial transportation in the mid-1800's, we might not enjoy such a varied sport today.

The Concord coach was developed in the 1820's by an enterprising New Hampshire firm led by Lewis Downing, who was joined by an expert coach builder, Stephen Abbot. The Concord was a popular long-distance vehicle, which eventually achieved worldwide renown, and such was the de-

Philip Hofmann driving his team of Holsteins.

mand for it that the men worked 14-hour days and produced coaches with scrupulous attention to detail. This stagecoach was pulled by four or six horses and was designed to carry up to nine passengers within, plus the same number on top, at an average speed of 10 miles an hour. Luggage and mail completed the load, and directly under the driver's seat—or box, as it is still called—was a compartment in which was placed the "treasure box."

Most of the trips covered about 100 miles, but imagine the coordination and organization, not to mention the durability of vehicle and harness, that made the longest stagecoach route in history a reality. In 1858, the famous Overland Stage carried the mail from Missouri to California—a distance of 2,795 miles. It took 24 days and 165 changeovers to complete, and the fare was $150 per person. Despite enormous difficulties, the Overland's Concord coaches, so expertly built, so skillfully driven, and with the trips so completely organized, made a significant contribution to the conquest of the West.

At the same time in England, the Royal Mail was already running 1,500 coaches a day out of London. Road coaches made their appearance as early as 1784, but evolved into much finer and lighter vehicles than the Concord coach because of the invention of the paved road by Messrs. Telford and Macadam. The government leased various mail routes to enterprising individuals; the operators supplied coaches, horses, and coachmen, while the government provided a uniformed guard for each coach. He was responsible for the coach's keeping its schedule and for the safety of its cargo. The Royal Mail, which ran with near split-second timing, primarily carried postal matter, although when the mail bags constituted less than a full load passengers were permitted aboard—as many as five on top and six inside the vehicle. So intense was the competition among the various operators of these coaches that, with the sound of the coach horn (blown by the guard) as forewarning, the changeover of teams at a relay point was accomplished in less than thirty seconds from the time a coach stopped until it was on its way again. Punctuality was a source of pride to these operators, whose precision was such that coaches at a full gallop passed each other going in opposite directions at exactly the same place on the road day after day after day. One might wish the same could be said of our present-day public transportation!

This exceedingly professional commercial operation took on an aspect of sport in England when "dandies"—dashing young men who were always looking for excitement—would pay the coachmen to be allowed to sit on the box and take the reins. In the late 1800's private coaches became fashionable to own and drive, though the only persons able to equip themselves with a stable of horses and a carriage house full of vehicles were the very wealthy. As the railroads came into prominence in the United States and in England, so the number of commercial coaches declined, though the gentry continued to drive these and smaller vehicles for pleasure.

In the early 1900's, the sport of coaching really took hold, along with the pleasure driving of smaller two- and four-wheel carriages of all sizes and shapes. A typical Sunday afternoon in New York's Central Park and along Fifth Avenue would see a parade of elegant barouches with grooms in formal livery riding on the back, ladies driving fine horses to George IV phaetons, and gentlemen driving single horses to Stanhope gigs.

The National Horse Show in New York's Madison Square Garden in the early 1900's was dominated by Hackney-horse and pony-driving classes. On several occasions no fewer than twenty park drags—a relatively light and formal road coach—entered the ring to be judged. Great whips such as Alfred Vanderbilt and his famous coach Venture, horsed by four grays, were known across the country. He took his team to England to compete and won the championship at the world-famous Olympia horse show, the only American ever to win this top coaching prize.

World War One interrupted the growth of driving, but the sport rebounded strongly during the 1920's, only to go into a steady—and understandable—decline after the stock-market crash of 1929 and the Depression that followed on its heels. The economic recovery from the Depression coincided with World War Two, and the driving sports continued to be dormant. In fact, no recovery came about until well after the war, in the 1960's. But once it began, it grew in quantum leaps. The Devon (Pennsylvania) Marathon for driving turnouts started in 1965 and drew twelve entries; in 1975 ninety-six entries from all over the Eastern Seaboard came to compete.

The American Driving Society was formed in 1975 to encourage all those persons interested in driving, regardless of the breed of horse they drove. However, various breed clubs, particularly the Morgan, Arabian, Hackney and American Saddlebred organizations, have encouraged driving for a long time. The emphasis that the breed societies place on their driving animals is more toward performance in the show ring and, therefore, often requires a professional trainer. The American Driving Society, on the other hand, places its emphasis more on the complete turnout and the pleasure of driving a horse or pony to various vehicles, most of which date back to the early 1900's.

A typical driving show has pleasure-driving classes wherein the judges take into account the complete picture presented by the driver, his whip, his horse, and his vehicle. The judge observes the way the animal moves at the walk, trot, and extended trot, or trot-on, and whether it stands quietly and backs under control. Then the judge will turn his attention to the harness and vehicle, looking for safety, cleanliness, and appropriateness. This last consideration allows a hunter type of horse driven to a sporting two-wheel natural-wood meadowbrook cart with russet harness to compete

1892

against a well-bred Hackney driven to a two-wheel Stanhope gig complete with patent leather harness and a groom in full livery. Each turnout is equally appropriate if presented properly, and therefore the competition is open to many more persons than might be the case if a different set of requirements were applied.

Tests of a driver's skill are always popular, and two types of show-ring classes measure whips' competence—those judged primarily on the basis of time and those requiring the driver to execute a number of difficult maneuvers.

Time classes can be extremely exciting; cantering is allowed, although it requires a real expert to move through the obstacles that are placed only 8 to 12 inches wider than the widest part of the vehicle. Plastic traffic cones often serve as obstacles so that even if the vehicle dislodges one, no damage will result. The usual obstacle class consists of a course through twenty or so sets of cones.

Gambler's Choice classes are great fun, as much for the spectators as for the participants. Eight or so obstacles are each given a point value of 20 to 100, dependent on their degree of difficulty. Obstacles take such forms as bridges, farmyards, a water splash, a serpentine and a T—perhaps the most difficult. Here the whip is required to drive into the top portion of the T from its side, back up into the vertical portion of the letter, and drive out the same way he came in—not much room for error. A supple, well-schooled horse and a skilled whip are required to accomplish this quickly, since time is also a factor. Each competitor is normally given 2 minutes in which to complete as many obstacles in a Gambler's Choice class as he can in whatever order he chooses, the winner being the entry that accumulates the most points during this time period.

In classes not judged against the clock, obstacle courses are also driven. Here the whip is asked to execute movements similar to those in the timed classes, but a qualitative judgment is made on the basis of the ease of the horse's maneuvers and the ability of the whip to drive through the obstacles without apparent effort. Judges look for smooth performance, subtle aids, and no resistance from the horse—in fact, for the sort of animal we would all like to own and drive.

In 1968, a group of driving enthusiasts in Europe, under the leadership of H.R.H. Prince Philip, president of the Fédération Équestre Internationale, world governing body of equestrian competitions, put forth the idea of holding a competition based on a format similar to the ridden three-day event. Although originally developed for teams of four horses, the idea expanded so that most of the competitions other than the International ones have sections for singles and pairs, both horses and ponies, and now even tandems.

The first day of a driven three-day event covers presentation and dressage. Presentation consists of a thorough check by the judges of the harness and vehicle. As in pleasure-driving classes, the judges scrutinize the turnout for cleanliness and correctness—in fact, everything that makes the turnout safe and attractive.

The dressage phase takes place in an arena that measures 40 × 100 meters (36.56 × 91.40 yards). Each horse and carriage is required to perform a series of movements at the walk, trot, and trot-on, following a prescribed sequence and changing pace at specific marks. The judges grade for accuracy, fluency, and brilliance.

The cross-country phase of the competition takes place on the second day—the day of excitement, many thrills, and sometimes spills. The horse and vehicle have to drive a course across country, from 5 miles at elementary events to 26 miles in International competitions. Five sections are driven at varying paces, and they must be completed in specific times; penalties are given for going too fast or too slowly. In the fast-trot section, hazards are often introduced to add to the difficulty—water crossing, various obstacles through trees, and so on—so that the skill of the whip is tested to the full. Of course, the demands of any part of this competition are increased by the number of horses put to the vehicle, with the tandems and four-in-hands being the most difficult. Although the dangers inherent in driving cannot be compared with those in, say, steeplechasing, suffice it to say that in top-level competition vehicles not infrequently turn over.

The third and final day of the event calls for an obstacle driving test; again, time is a crucial factor, and a 10-second penalty is added to the entry's score for each of the twenty or so cones it can knock over while completing the course.

The results of the three days of driving are now added together, and the winner can justly be called an "expert whip."

For many persons, the long hours of preparation that are demanded of competitors and the rigors of the show ring are too much to contemplate; the simple pleasure of driving behind a horse is reward enough. In addition to the fun of driving, many enthusiasts enjoy restoring carriages during the long winter evenings and then putting their horses to the finished vehicles in the spring. Sleighing is a winter sport still enjoyed, of course, by drivers who don't mind the cold, and the sound of jingling bells has a magic of its own.

The Sunday drive through the country reminds one of the unhurried way of life of years gone by, whether you're driving a "horse and buggy" or a carriage to a pair of high-stepping Hackney horses. The joy is timeless!

Anyone attracted to the sport of driving should seek the advice of a knowledgeable person when selecting a suitably trained horse or pony, a vehicle, and a harness that is safe and fits well. (Safety is a factor that should never be underestimated in any aspect of the driving sports. A broken strap can partially separate the horse from the vehicle and may frighten the animal sufficiently to cause it to run away—with most unpleasant consequences. Anybody who takes up driving should beware of "Grandpa's old harness." It may look all right, but almost certainly it is rotting at crucial points.) With proper guidance, a whip will quickly become familiar with the techniques that have been mastered by the experienced International competitor

Major Events In U.S. Driving Calendar

May	First Weekend	Combined Driving Competition (three days, FEI Rules) Shone's Driving Establishment Nine Partners Lane Millbrook, New York (914-677-6332)
	Last weekend (Sunday before Memorial Day)	Devon Marathon & Four-in-Hand Coaching (seven days) Contact: John G. Burkholder Devon Show Devon, Pennsylvania
June	Last week	Myopia Three-Day Driving Event (FEI Rules) Contact: Deidre Pirie Aquilla Farm Hamilton, Mass. (617-468-2788)
July	Last week	Fairfield Driving Show (three days) (Dressage, Pleasure Driving, Obstacle Classes) Contact: Marie Frost Fairfield County Hunt Club Westport, Connecticut
August	Third weekend	Walnut Hill Farm Driving Competition (three days) Contact: William Remley (716-385-2555) Walnut Hill Farm Pittsford, New York (Nr. Rochester)
September	Last weekend	A.D.S. "Driving for Fun Weekend" (three days) Noncompetitive Mohonk Mountain House New Paltz, New York (914-478-4045)
November		Toronto Winter Fair (ten days) Four-in-Hand Classes, Full Hackney Division Toronto, Ontario, Canada

Rules for the above events are to be found in the AHSA/ADS Rules & Regulations for Driving Shows, obtainable from American Horse Shows Association, 598 Madison Avenue, New York, New York 10022 or American Driving Society, 339 Warburton Avenue, Hastings-on-Hudson, New York 10706.

Annual membership for the American Driving Society: $15 individual, $25 family. Apply to Robert Heath, Secretary, ADS, 339 Warburton Avenue, Hastings-on-Hudson, New York 10706.

driving a team of four horses or the owner driving his finely tuned show horse. But even more important, every whip, regardless of the level of skill he or she aspires to, will share equally in the thrill of driving a horse or pony to a vehicle.

~~~~~~~~~~~~~~~~~~~~~~~~~~~~~

"The New York State Police were first forming and the horses for the various troops were in White Plains, New York. As the horses were assigned into the troops they were loaded into railroad cars and taken to their various assignments. There was one particular stallion, Big Red, that was assigned to B Troop Malone. The horse refused to load in the car. They tried every trick in the book, but Big Red refused. The captain of B Troop called Trooper Harmodue and asked him to saddle and mount Big Red, which the trooper did. The captain handed the trooper a checkbook and said, "He's assigned to B Troop Malone. Ride him up there." Trooper Harmodue rode Big Red from White Plains, New York, to Malone. He put a new set of shoes on Big Red at Blue Mountain Lake. Big Red arrived in B Troop Malone in fine shape, and trooper and Big Red were friends for years; the horse would whinny each time Trooper Harmodue entered the stable. Both Big Red and Trooper Harmodue served in B Troop Malone until the trooper's retirement many years later."
William P. Brayton
~~~~~~~~~~~~~~~~~~~~~~~~~~~~~

DISTANCE RIDING

The sport of distance riding encompasses two distinct but similar activities. Competitive riding asks contestants to cover a specified span of overland country within a stipulated time; arriving too soon or too late results in penalization. An endurance ride is more of a race, in which the goal is to cover the distance under a maximum time allowance.

In addition to prizes given to those riders who finish closest to the optimum time in a competitive ride or at the head of the pack in an endurance ride, there are awards for horses that demonstrate the best physical condition.

Condition and conditioning are of utmost importance, when once considers that distances from 25 to 100 miles must be covered in three, or two days or even one day. Horses must be of breeds and types whose conformation and stamina qualities are up to the demands (Arabians, Appaloosas, and Morgans have been consistant winners). Riders build up their mounts' wind, tone, and circulation gradually through short, then longer rides. Not only must they be convinced of their horses' condition; a panel of lay judges and veterinarians assesses all equine entrants before, during, and at the conclusion of each ride. They conduct their judging in competitive rides by basing it 100 percent on condition, then deducting points for time penalties.

Distance riding takes place in all fifty states and Canada. Among the most important events are the

Matthew Mackay-Smith, D.V.M., on Vertain, winning the Old Dominion (Virginia) One Hundred Miles in Twenty-Four Hours Ride.

Woodstock 100 Mile in Three Days Ride in Vermont, a competitive ride, and two endurance fixtures, Virginia's Old Dominion 100 Mile and California's Tevis Cup.
Further information:

North American Trail Riding Conference
1995 Day Road
Gilroy, California 95020

American Endurance Ride Conference
P.O. Box 1605
Auburn, California 95603

There are two books on the subject. "Distance Riding From Start to Finish" by Virginia Weisel Johnson and Thule Johnson (Houghton Mifflin) is a fine introduction to the sport with valuable information about selecting and conditioning horses. So is "Endurance Riding" by Ann Hyland (Lippincott), another volume which also delves into how to compete in and stage a distance event.

HORSE TRANSPORTATION

If you're going to compete or fox-hunt or take your horse along on a vacation, some form of equine transportation will be necessary. Although renting a trailer or hiring a professional horse-transportation company is a possibility, chances are you'll end up owning your own trailer or van.

The primary consideration involving what kind to buy depends on the number and the size of your animal or animals. A van (a "trailer" with a built-in truck) is necessary for more than two animals; otherwise a trailer will serve for one or two. The proper length, height, and width are functions of the horse's or pony's size. Smaller breeds and types can fit into a smaller spaces, but it is never desirable to cram an animal into a small a vehicle (chafing and poor posture will result).

Regardless of size, a trailer or van needs to meet certain requirements. Proper ventilation is important, both when the vehicle is at rest and when it is in motion. Air flow should be available, but indirect; a steady blast of air on a horse's head can lead to serious medical problems.

You will also need easy access to the front of the vehicle. Horses should be led into a trailer, and front doors allow the handler to make the safest exit, as well as permitting access should the horse become unruly. The space near the front door is very useful for storing a day's supply of feed, hay, water, and tack.

A two-horse trailer requires a removable divided bar or panel, which should be heavily padded to protect against injury. The partition should be kept in when you are transporting only one horse, since it will act as a restraint to support the horse when the vehicle is in motion. The partition can be removed if you need to transport bales of hay or another bulk load.

Tail chains should also be padded so they won't rub hide or hair when horses rest against them.

Trailers with tandem axles are far more stable than the single-axle variety. The axles should be independently sprung so that they can ride at different heights. If they are not sprung, the height of the hitch is of paramount importance. Rear wheels will not ride on the ground if the towing point is too low, while the front wheels will leave the ground when a hitch is too high.

Trailers are usually fitted with an electric or hydraulic brake system, which automatically operates in conjunction with the towing vehicle's brakes.

A 2-ton trailer is a formidable load for a car, and many small models should not be expected to play Percheron. Larger cars, station wagons, and jeep-type vehicles, as well as pickup trucks, should encounter no difficulty. Whatever you use, make sure that the hitch is welded as well as bolted to the towing vehicle. This job is not for an amateur mechanic, since the safety of your horse, as well as your car or truck, depends on the solid foundation of the hitch.

Driving a trailer requires some training, and a

Devon two-horse trailer

Devon two-horse trailer, interior view

Devon eight-horse "gooseneck" trailer

bit of practice with an empty vehicle is a good idea. Avoid jackrabbit starts and quick stops; anticipate your braking needs, then apply the brakes gradually. When passing other vehicles, remember the additional length because of your load. Be especially careful at high speeds or in high wind; a trailer seesawing across a road is hazardous to both occupants and others on the highway. Backing up presents certain problems, which can be overcome by practice. Remember: to turn right, steer left and to turn left, steer right. These principles apply to a one-horse trailer or an eight-horse rig. Some larger trailers have a "fifth wheel" construction whereby the hitch is fastened to a pivot mounted on the towing pickup truck.

Driving a van is somewhat easier, since the cargo area is an integral part of the vehicle. Vans are handled like any truck, although novices will need to become familiar with the transmission's special gearing (designed to carry great weight under different road conditions).

The additional weight of a loaded trailer will also take some getting used to, and you'll want to practice locally with your horse in the back before setting out to drive a long distance.

An experienced horseman was heard to remark as he watched an animal walking quietly up a trailer ramp, "That's worth a few hundred dollars right there." Anyone who's ever struggled to load a recalcitrant horse into a trailer or van knows what he meant. A well-schooled horse should include as part of its education learning to accept vehicular transportation. It's a matter of practice, patience, and tact on your part, and the lesson should be completed well in advance of shipping. Two hours before your event is scheduled to begin several miles away is not the time.

Loading a stubborn or frightened horse is also a matter of practice, tact, and cooperation. As you entice the animal gradually with a bit of its favorite feed or a treat, have someone (or several people) push its rump with a broom or a rope behind the horse. Watch out for rearing or flying hooves. If a horse absolutely refuses, there's little to be done except wait awhile, then start over (blindfolding can sometimes help).

Before any animal is loaded, it should be outfitted in protective shipping boots or bandages. Padded head bumpers protect against injuries to the poll.

Trailers and van can be bought new or used. Among leading trailer manufacturers are

Shoop's Trailer Co.
R.D. 4, Box 226
Dillsburg, Pennsylvania 17019

Cotner Manufacturing Co.
Route 611, Box 42
Revere, Pennsylvania 18953

Hartman Trailer Manufacturing Co.
7 Walnut Street
Perkaskie, Pennsylvania 18944

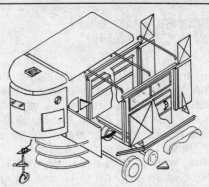

Carl-Built. All parts needed to build a horse trailer are now in stock ready for immediate shipment to any part of the United States and Canada. No plans are offered; with a little thought and care, however, almost anyone who has some mechanical and welding ability can assemble this trailer. For more information, call or write Carl-Built, Inc., Drawer 948, Chickasha, Oklahoma 73081.

Cherokee Manufacturing Co.
Industrial Park Road, Box 344
Sweetwater, Tennessee 17874

Devon Trailers
Ragged Hill
West Brookfield, Massachusetts 01585

Their vehicles, as well as those of other manufacturers, are sold through distributors. Check Yellow Pages or ask around at tack shops and horse-show parking lots.

Used trailers and vans can be bought at considerable savings, but only if the vehicle is worth the price. As in the purchase of any used auto or truck, a thorough mechanical inspection is a prerequisite. Look particularly, in addition, to see that the roof, sides, floor, electrical system, and tires are in satisfactory condition. Better still, have someone familiar with trailers do the inspecting for you.

Long-distance transportation, hundreds or thousands of miles, requires considerable preparation. If you're not going to make the trip at one clip or you have no one to spell the driving chore, arrange in advance where both you and your horse can bunk down for the night. Take along enough hay, feed, and water for your animal, and punctuate the trip every several hours by stopping and letting the horse out to stretch its legs.

Many long-distance transport vehicles now have Citizens Band radios. They're worth their weight in gold if you have an accident and need to summon assistance, or to learn about traffic and weather conditions from your fellow voyagers. Pick yourself a suitably horsey CB "handle," and "Ten-four to you, good buddy."

Few people put as many miles on their vans over a year as Billy Robertson, a former member of the U.S. Equestrian Team's stadium-jumping squad and now a successful trainer and exhibitor of hunters and jumpers. Whom better to ask to say a few words on the subject?

SOME CONSIDERATIONS IN
BUYING YOUR TRAILER
by William G. Robertson

"If you are going to haul your own horses, then the only way to go is to buy a ———!" I so often hear that statement, and it always tickles me. For when I hear the blank filled in with one noted make of trailer or another I always have the desire to reply, "That's true—they're nice; but have you ever tried to (1) drive one all day? (2) drive one on ice? (3) haul a bad shipper in one? (4) load a tough horse into one? (5) repair or sell one?—or, all too often, (6) have you ever tried to afford one?

Buying the perfect trailer as a means of transportation for your horse or horses and being happy with it is like buying the perfect horse. It takes a lot of thought and planning to acquire it, and an equal amount of hard work and "luck" to be happy with it.

With regard to forethought and planning, certain questions must be answered. Once they are, there's an endless list of manufacturers eagerly waiting to sell you your dream machine. But first beware that the dream is not a nightmare! Let me pass along certain basic misconceptions: Basic Misconception Number 1: Hauling your own horse is really fun. Basic Misconception Number 2: Hauling your own horse is a lot cheaper. Basic Misconception Number 3: Hauling a friend's horse is even more fun and can save you money. (But wait until the horse tears your equipment apart, it tears itself apart, and your "friend" hales you into court and proves that because of your negligence his valuable show animal is now a total financial loss.) Basic Misconception Number 4: Nothing beats pride of ownership.

'Nuff said. Now you must put pencil to paper and labor over the pros and cons of "To buy or not to buy," remembering that your alternatives are to ship with a friend in his van, to use your stable's van, or to go commercial. To make an intelligent decision, you'll have to answer the following questions in order:

1. What will be the cost of the original equipment, the cost of maintenance, and the cost of operation?
2. How frequently will it be used, and who will use it?
3. How many horses will I be hauling most of the time?
4. How long will the trips be, and how much loading and unloading will be involved?

With respect to Question 1, I'm always amazed how someone can justify a purchase of an $8,000 pickup truck and a $2,800 trailer just to avoid that horrible $60 shipping bill incurred every other month or so. Question 2, frequency of use and who will be using the trailer, bears on accessory equipment. When I was delivering horses for dealers, I drove trucks that lacked air conditioning, AM-FM stereos, power steering, and other amenities. They do make life more pleasant when it's my rear end behind the wheel all day, but decide whether the accessories are needed for your groom/driver.

On the third point, most people *undertruck* themselves. That is, don't buy a two-horse trailer if you'll need one for four animals, and be sure your engine is strong enough to haul the load it will be required to pull. Undertrucking is both false economy and dangerous.

Ending with Question 4, long distances require major equipment, and there's very little loading and unloading. Let me suggest a floor plan I've used for years. A van stopped at my ranch on its way from New Mexico to Florida one year, and ten polo ponies filed out of that dinky vehicle after a long 14-hour drive. I was amazed; I thought you might get away with small ponies, but not expensive competition horses. However, as I learned, "Horses don't know how much they cost," and cheap ones tend to ship the same as expensive ones—hopefully, with all four feet on the floor. And the best way to keep all four on the floor is to ship them standing at an oblique angle.

This theory is certainly not original with me. Horses were shipped for years loose in boxcars, and mares and their foals are always shipped in large boxes in vans. I just noticed how these animals always position themselves to travel at an angle (I've found that standing that way on subways or buses provides the most comfortable position for humans too). In my 24-foot-long and 6-foot-wide eight-horse trailer, I've shipped such nationally known horses as Circuit Breaker and Fur Balloon without any incident, and these are physically big animals.

Such an arrangement is clearly unsuitable for one-day shows where the trailer must also be a portable stall. That is, to remove seven other horses to get to the first one is impractical and difficult. But for cross-country shipping, to my mind nothing beats this system, and as proof, it's being copied by other shippers.

For wide-angle shots, be sure to stand far enough back to capture all the action.

Positioning yourself at the "right" spot permits capturing the horse, rider, the jump, and the spectators.

A Five-Gaited Saddle Horse taking a conformation pose at the National Horse Show.

HOW TO PHOTOGRAPH YOUR HORSE—OR SOMEONE ELSE'S

You've seen many photos of horses. Some animals have been in repose, while others were in action. Some photos were appealing, while others made you wince. When it comes time for you to snap a shot, you'll understand how difficult equestrian photography can be.

Let's start with taking a photo of a horse standing still. The best angle is a side view, especially if you want to show it to a prospective purchaser who can thereby discern all the strengths (and few, if any, of the weaknesses) of the animal's conformation. First, be certain to include the whole horse. Too many pictures crop off the animal's knees or feet. On the other hand, don't step so far back that excessive background is included to detract from the subject.

There's a real trick to posing a conformation shot. The hind leg closest to the camera should be the farthest back, and the foreleg on the same side should be farthest forward, both framing the legs on the other side. This posture provides the most balanced perspective. Alertness is equally important. Ask the person holding the animal's lead line or reins to attract the horse's attention by whistling, waving a rag, or going through any sort of contortion that forces the subject to raise its head and prick its ears forward. A simple background—a solid barn or empty field—will be least distracting from the horse. Avoid shadows, especially that of the photographer or handler.

Action photographs are more difficult, if only because you're no longer in control of the subject. If you don't want the action to pass you by, plan your shots in advance. Station yourself at a fence and, if you're not planning to shoot one of the first entrants, determine the pace and angle you'll need by watching a few of the early riders and horses. When your subject comes into view, pan the camera (following the subject's movement through the viewfinder) and shoot at preselected moments. Time your shutter release: capturing an early take-off seems to diminish a fence's height and a horse's performance, while a picture of a horse landing shows the animal in an awkward position. Although head-on pictures can often be effective, side or three-quarter head-on views are better, especially if the photographer stays low to give the illusion of a formidable fence.

Lighting is a problem, but it can be simplified through today's films with their fast emulsions. Sometimes a blur gives the effect of speed and motion. If you don't want that effect, use Kodak's Tri-X black-and-white film. Its 400 ASA rating (speed quotient) can be pushed during developing from twice to three or four times with only a moderate occurrence of graininess. Confer with your camera shop salesman and processor. The same can be done with color film, both slides and prints, although some loss of color values may occur.

Unless you have a very sophisticated camera, shooting indoors will compound the lighting problem. Flashcubes, lights, and strobe units can be distracting and dangerous if used close up. Moreover, their efficiency is reduced by the square of the distance to the subject. Physicists understand that technical talk, but we should know only that beyond 20 feet bulbs, cubes, and strobes are less than useful.

Telephoto lenses are a way to move close to the action. A fixed focal length (from 100mm to 300mm) is one choice, while a zoom lens which by a flip of a lever can be changed from 85mm to 210mm is a more useful alternative. A high shutter speed and steady hand (or tripod) are essential in this case, since magnification will translate vibrations into blurs.

You may wonder (and marvel) at how professional equestrian photographers always seem to have the right shot "in their pocket." A motor-driven camera is of great assistance. They merely point and shoot up to five frames per second, an equivalent of freezing frames through a movie camera. The gear, it should be pointed out, is expensive—up to $500 above the cost of a good 35mm single-lens-reflex camera.

At the other extreme are pocket cameras. The most important consideration is to keep both photographer and subject still while the shutter is snapped. Pocket Instamatics or their equivalents won't provide the sharpest slides or prints, but they have their advantages in portability during trail rides, hunts, and other cross-country activities.

HOW TO DO A TERRIFIC PAINTING OF YOUR HORSE IF YOU DON'T KNOW HOW TO PAINT
by Mary Dee English

The Picture For a first try, don't attempt to work from "life." Find, or take, a color photograph of your horse that you really like—one that looks especially like the animal or one that you would like to have a painting of. Keep in mind that if your horse is a dark color it will show up nicely against a light background and if your horse is a light color it will look best with dark objects in the background—trees, for example. To get the most reliable view of the animal's conformation, you might pose your horse in the "classic" style—facing to the right, with the head slightly turned toward you, the near front leg a little forward and the off front leg a little back, the near hind leg straight and the off hind leg slightly forward. Or if you can't get the horse to stand still, a photo of it bucking in a field would do just fine!

The Size You will need a *small* canvas, which you can buy already stretched, or a piece of canvas board (canvas pasted on cardboard—available at art stores). If you can't find a canvas board small enough, cut down a large one to the size you need. Believe me, doing a tiny painting is much, much easier than doing a large one. It takes less time and less skill and is quite impressive none-

theless. Do your painting the *exact* size of the photograph. I've found that 3 × 5 or 4 × 5 inches is a good size. If your photo is smaller, take the trouble to have it enlarged to fit nicely in that size.

The Next Step Take a piece of tracing paper, place it over the photo, and with a No. 2 pencil (the regular kind) trace the outline of your horse; also mark any muscle lines and any background objects you want to include in the painting. Now turn the tracing paper over and go over your lines with the same pencil. This is your basic design, so try to get it exact! Then place the tracing paper, right side up, on the canvas (you can tape it, so that it doesn't shift position) and go over your outline again, pressing down firmly, so that the pencil image ends up on the canvas. Remove the tracing paper, and don't give up hope!

The Paint and Brushes Use acrylic paints, not oil or a watercolor. Acrylics don't smell, and they dry superfast, so you can paint over mistakes without the colors getting mushy. Also, you don't have to have a special palette—any nonporous surface will do. I use an old white china dinner plate. Have a jar of water handy, to keep your brushes wet in and to use for thinning the paint. As for the brushes—use good-quality sable brushes, not nylon. You will do fine with just two brushes—a No. 2 flat and a No. 2 pointed.

Here You Go! Mix a little burnt sienna (even if it's not your horse's color, it's okay—this will be painted over) with water, and using your pointed brush, go over the outline. After it's dry, erase the pencil. Be sure to get it all off, so that it doesn't mix with your colors.

The Colors From the color chart opposite, you will notice that most horses are made up of the same colors—only the proportions change. Keep mixing and experimenting until you find the color closest to your horse. Unless your horse is black or gray, *do not* use black for the shaded areas. Use the colors indicated on the chart.

Finally Start painting! Paint the background areas first, using your flat brush. Then, also using your flat brush, paint in the basic body color of your horse. Next paint in the shaded or dark areas, and then the highlighted areas. All the while, keep a careful eye on the photograph and try to match those dark and light areas exactly. Blend areas where different tones meet while the paint is still wet. Don't expect a miracle yet! His leg is bound to look crooked, or her neck ewed because you didn't get the shadows right. Let the paint dry (it takes only a few minutes) and do it again. Always, always keep looking at your photo and then at your painting—analyzing it. Ask yourself: Is his ear really that small? Is his nose really that long? Are her pasterns at the right angle? Where are the highlights? Where are the shadows? If there's a white highlight in the photo, don't be afraid to splash it on! Be brave—if it's in the photo, it will look good in your painting and will add that "professional" touch. Use your pointed brush for the delicate areas, and save the mane and tail for the very last.

Color Chart

Color of Horse	Basic Color	Shadows	Highlights
Chestnut or sorrel	burnt sienna yellow ocher titanium white	basic color plus ultramarine blue	basic color and shadow plus titanium white
Dun and Palomino	burnt sienna yellow ocher titanium white	basic color plus ultramarine blue	basic color and shadow plus titanium white
Bay	burnt sienna yellow ocher titanium white	basic color plus ultramarine blue	basic color and shadow plus titanium white
Gray	titanium white ivory black	basic color plus yellow ocher and ultramarine blue	basic color plus titanium white
Black	ivory black titanium white burnt sienna	basic color plus ultramarine blue and ivory black	basic color plus ultramarine blue and titanium white

Final Tips
- Mix your paints with water—just a little—and always keep your brushes wet.
- To preserve your painting after it's completed and to give it an even finish, go over it with a glossy glaze (mixed with water so that it's not too shiny).

Identify the following movies that involve equestrian activities:
(1) Elizabeth Taylor and Mickey Rooney starred in this film about the world's most demanding steeplechase.
(2) Director John Huston played the role of a master of foxhounds in this cameo-studded mystery.
(3) Nautical, the U.S. Equestrian Team jumper, was the subject of this Walt Disney movie.
(4) Ronald Reagan and Alexis Smith appeared in this film about training show horses.
(5) Another Disney film, about the Spanish Riding School.
(6) The classic Will James tale starring Fred MacMurray, Anne Baxter, and Burl Ives.
(7) He helped rescue the Lipizzaner horses during World War Two.
(8) The Marx Brothers picture in which Harpo played a jockey.
(9) The character played by Vivien Leigh lost her father and daughter in separate jumping accidents in this movie.
(10) The last film made by Marilyn Monroe and Clark Gable was about rounding up wild horses.

Answers:
(1) National Velvet
(2) The List of Adrien Messenger
(3) The Horse with the Flying Tail
(4) Stallion Road
(5) The White Horses of Vienna
(6) Smoky
(7) Patton
(8) A Day at the Races
(9) Gone with the Wind
(10) The Misfits

The National Archives in Washington, D.C., promulgates four "regulations" with regard to the positions of horses and riders depicted in equestrian statues.
- A horse standing on all four legs with rider mounted designates the rider to be a "national hero."
- A horse with three legs on the ground with rider mounted indicates that the rider died as a result of wounds suffered in battle.
- A horse with two legs on the ground with rider mounted indicates that the rider died during a battle.
- With the horse in any of the above positions, the rider standing beside the horse indicates that the horse was also killed.

A good indication of how equestrian sport has grown is in the area of vacations. Like other sportsmen, riders are traveling far and wide to spend time at favorite places or to discover new and unusual facilities. And even if someone isn't able to devote an entire holiday to riding, it's quite possible to spend a few hours in the saddle or to be a spectator at a racetrack, a horse show, or a more exotic exhibition of horsemanship.

Whether at home or abroad, a horseback vacation is a nice way to meet people. Other guests at a riding resort, and the staff too, share at least one interest with you, and common experiences and *après-cheval* conversations can lead to instant camaraderie and often lasting friendships.

Will you need special equipment? That depends on what kind of riding you plan to do and where you plan to do it. Boots and breeches, jodhpurs, or riding pants are, of course, essential. Make sure new boots are well broken in before you leave, since stiff or pinching footwear can put a crimp in a vacation. New jeans also require a bit of breaking in. Boot hooks and a bootjack are relatively small items, but their absence can prove annoying. You can count on finding them at riding resorts, but if you're staying alone at a nonhorsey hotel, phoning for a bellman may be the only way to get out of your boots (in a pinch, folded wire coat hangers can become improvised boot hooks).

For riding in cold weather, several layers of light clothing are better than one heavy sweater; your body heat is retained between the layers, and you can always remove one garment if you become too warm. Feet always seem to be the greatest sufferers. Remedies include fleece-lined boots, a foot warmer for stirrups, and a pair of heavy thermal socks. Don't forget warm gloves for your other digits. Fox hunters know that long underwear isn't only for warmth; it reduces the chance of chafing and sores, especially during long hours in the saddle. Bodily comfort can also be improved by medicated talcum powder and rubbing alcohol, both items remaining in your room until you return from a day's riding.

Weekend riders contemplating an extended vacation should think about getting into shape. Ride more frequently during the month before you leave, do calisthenics, or otherwise improve your endurance and muscle tone. Your body will appreciate the effort.

THE UNITED STATES AND CANADA

PLEASURE RIDING

The simplest form of vacation riding, even if it involves only a trip across town, is to hire a horse for an hour or more of hacking. To locate public stables, look in telephone directories' Yellow Pages under "Riding Academies" or "Stables." Questions at tack shops may lead to public stables that do not advertise or some private places that will rent horses.

Telephoning in advance is always a good idea, to inquire about style of riding (English or Western), facilities (ring and/or trails), and cost. With regard to the last, an hour's hack can cost as little as $2.50 and as much as $11. If an establishment's policy doesn't permit strangers to ride on the trail alone, you may have to pay for the services of a guide. Even if you learn that a stable doesn't rent horses, consider taking a lesson; you never know

what nuggets you'll pick up from the resident instructor.

You may arrive at a place only to discover it's a dump or, worse, its conditions can be dangerous to equine health and human safety. Chances are you won't enjoy a ride at a stable where horses are kept in dirty stalls in a poorly ventilated barn. Another indication is the quality and condition of tack. Saddles don't have to be made by Hermès, but tack that's dirty or held together with baling wire is both unattractive and potentially dangerous. So is a stable owner who permits his animals to be abused by their riders. Note whether riders come galloping back to the barn, their horses dripping with sweat. Sad to say, some owners tolerate such behavior.

Although this book doesn't intend to offer advice about riding techniques, a few words might be appropriate here, starting with common sense. First, don't get carried away and overestimate your ability, or you might find yourself literally carried away. When you're asked about your riding ability, don't be embarrassed about admitting you've ridden only in rings or that you'd like a well-mannered quiet animal if that's the case. Many owners insist on observing for a few minutes how strangers ride before allowing them to leave the ring. Don't make a scene if you're remounted on a more placid horse or refused permission to go out on the trail; the decision is for the owner's—and your own—good.

If you do ride outside by yourself, be sure you're wearing a watch to keep track of time (some stables allow five or ten minutes grace at the end of an hour, while others go by a time-clock philosophy and charge accordingly). Stick to trails. Even better, go out with someone who knows the area. The other person may be glad of the company, and the stable owner won't have to worry about having to send out search parties.

The life of hack horses is no bed of roses. Different riders with varying abilities and attitudes toward horsemanship all try to get their money's worth out of them, so it's little wonder that insensitivity to rein and leg aids are the rule, not the exception. In defense, hacks have learned how to take advantage of riders. Their tricks range from bucking and rearing to stopping, with goodies like trying to rub off riders against trees thrown in. Accordingly, treat an unfamiliar horse with respect, and don't permit the animal to get you into a potentially dangerous situation (for example, moving within biting or kicking range of another horse). Of course, if you find yourself on a real problem, take it back for another horse.

One way to get the most out of an hour's hack, especially if you're riding in a ring, is to try to school your horse. Work on collection, extension, bending, and smooth transitions between gaits. Although you shouldn't expect to work miracles, every little bit will help both the horse and you.

Your attitude toward other riders is also important. Courtesies in ring riding include calling out "Rail!" before overtaking another rider along the outside track and "Heads up!" to call attention to yourself under other situations. Cutting off another person is bad manners, as is interfering with an instructor and student who may be having a lesson at the same time you're riding. The fact that you have paid a few bucks doesn't mean you own the place.

"Rules of the road" on the trail are essential. Don't gallop past others, and when passing another rider, slow down to the slower gait (if you're cantering and he's trotting, you trot too). If you stop along the way, don't tie your horse by its reins. At worst the animal may injure his mouth, and at best you risk the possibility of a long solitary walk back to the barn. If you have a serious accident, wait for help; your horse knows its way home, and someone will come looking for you. Along the same lines, don't go galloping after another rider's loose horse, for you'll only frighten the animal. The better play is to try to help the person. Finally, walk the horse for the first five minutes (longer if it's a cold day) to loosen equine and human muscles, and walk the last mile back. If your horse is sweaty, offer to walk it until it's cooled off. (Asking whether you can remove the tack is also a nice gesture.)

Thousands of national, state, and county parks and forests have riding facilities or are serviced by nearby stables. A complete listing appears in the *Rand McNally Guidebook to Campgrounds* (published by Rand McNally).

Like golf courses, bridle paths have become places where business deals are negotiated. When one advertising executive went on a business trip to Philadelphia, his host asked about his sports interests. He said he enjoyed riding. So, as it turned out, did his host. One morning, as they trotted around Fairmont Park, a substantial commercial arrangement was successfully concluded. Moral: Even captains of industry like to ride.

DUDE RANCHING AND PACK TRIPPING

Although dude ranches are associated with the Old West, such resorts may be found in all fifty states and Canada. Some are rather primitive, perhaps run by a family that takes in a few guests who share their hosts' house and meals. Others are posh, with deluxe accommodations and gourmet food. Some cater to a sedate family crowd, while others attract swinging singles. All, however, offer Western-style riding and other activities to satisfy fantasies of playing cowboy.

A typical day might begin after breakfast with a three-hour jaunt around the countryside for experienced riders (beginners can receive instruction in a corral). If the weather is warm, you might want to spend time after lunch relaxing around the ol' watering hole (nowadays a swimming pool), followed by another ride. Many ranches have tennis courts as an athletic alternative or arrange trips to nearby sight-seeing spots. Dinner may be a barbecue, and evening entertainment can be a hayride, square dancing, or just sitting around a roaring television set. Some ranches stage weekly rodeos in which staff members (and selected guests) compete in calf roping, bronc riding, and such other events as trying to balance an egg on a spoon while riding around a ring or chasing after a greased pig.

The cost of a week's vacation ranges between $100 and $400 per person, depending on facilities and season. Transportation to and from the ranch must be taken into account, especially if it involves jetting across the country.

There was once a dude-ranch association to which a letter of inquiry would result in an avalanche of brochures from its members. It's no longer in existence, so you'll have to check equestrian magazines and newspaper travel sections for advertisements. If you know to what part of the country you'd like to travel, write to the state (or in Canada, provincial) tourist agencies listed in this chapter for information, as well as referral to individual ranches. Their brochures will fill you in on cost, formality, and activities, so you'll know what clothes (and cash) to take.

Pack tripping, often included as a dude-ranch activity, is also available separately through organizations which arrange horseback excursions through backcountry. There are trips to satisfy all desires for ruggedness, from no contact with civilization and looking after your horse's and your own creature comforts to meals and lodging at posh places along the way.

Like dude ranches, pack-trip organizations advertise in equestrian magazines and newspaper travel sections; you can also learn of them through state and provincial tourist agencies. An initial inquiry should concern the trip's duration, which can range from a few days to several weeks. All the organizations supply horses. Some provide sleeping bags, tarps, and other necessary gear, while others require participants to furnish their own. Depending on the trip's length and who provides what, a pack trip will cost between $100 and $400 per week.

If the idea of a do-it-yourself pack trip is appealing, people who have tried it strongly suggest preparing well in advance. Plan your route thoroughly, especially with regard to where your horse can be fed. Although you may be able to live on roots and berries, your horse will still require its feed. Farms, ranches, and riding stables along the way should be contacted about this aspect. You'll also want to work on endurance, building up the requisite amount of muscle tone and bone for many human and equine hours on the trail.

Also prepare for the dark side of such a trip. Let the police know what route you'll take and check in with them daily; if anything happens along the trip, you'll welcome assistance in the form of a rescue party. (Better still, say those who have done it, find someone to take the trip with you.) Be sure to include a medical kit and extra rations in your pack. You should also carry a pistol or rifle, the most effective and humane way to euthanize your horse if it breaks a leg along the way. If all this advice sounds discouraging, and your experience with the great outdoors is just sleeping with a window opened a crack, leave your good horse at home and join a pack-trip organization's expedition.

RIDING RESORTS

Riding resorts are the English-style equivalent of dude ranches, offering hours of instruction and hacking every day. One highly recommended establishment, Meadowbrook Riding Farm in East Stroudsburg, Pennsylvania, is typical.

After breakfast, lessons begin at 10 o'clock and last for two hours. Instruction in equitation, dressage, or jumping (based on guests' experience and interest) takes place in two outdoor and one indoor ring or over a hunt course. The afternoon session, another two hours, begins at 2:30, spent on cross-country rides or working in one of the

rings. During the rest of the day, there's tennis, swimming, Ping-Pong, shuffleboard, or just loafing.

A feature at many riding resorts is special-event clinics conducted by internationally known instructors and riders. Name-dropping that "Colonel So-and-So believes that . . ." back at your own stable is hardly the reason to attend; your technique will improve considerably under the watchful eye of such people.

Riding resort prices range from about $35 a day for dormitory accommodations up to a double room with bath at $100. Most places have weekend packages, which like the daily rate include meals and riding.

Check for advertisements in equestrian magazines and local newspapers.

SUMMER CAMPS

Riders under the age of 18 may want to spend their summers at camp. Although many general-interest establishments include riding as part of the curriculum, some camps emphasize the sport. Campers there can ride every day, can compete in shows, and may even be assigned one horse which they will look after all summer.

Riding camps (some riding resorts become camps during July and August) advertise in equestrian magazines and in local and national newspapers (the back pages of *The New York Times Magazine* are a fertile spot in which to look). The American Camping Association, 225 Park Avenue South, New York, New York 10003, will refer inquiries to its members. Indicate the state or part of the country in which you're interested, as well as whether you prefer an all-girl, all-boy, or coed camp.

Tuition runs between $1,000 and $2,000 for a two-month stay exclusive of such extras as uniforms, laundry, and "canteen" purchases. Parents should also take into account the expense of visiting their children on Parents' Weekend. Some camps accept children for two- or four-week seasons at proportionately lower fees.

Don't despair if you're over 18. If you have the necessary time, interest, and ability, you may be able to spend a summer as a riding counselor. Depending on the size of a camp's equestrian program, there may be only one counselor or perhaps a large staff, sometimes assisted by grooms. An instructor should be prepared to teach at least five hours every day and perhaps take a group for an occasional all-day trek or an overnight camping expedition. One day off a week is par for the course, and a rainy morning, afternoon, or entire day means even more leisure (of course, you may have to make up the schedule by extra sessions).

To find such a job, contact the American Camping Association, 225 Park Avenue South, New York, New York 10003; check newspaper classified or equestrian-magazine advertisements; or inquire at riding academies (many provide horses to camps and also furnish counselors). A letter of recommendation from someone who can attest to your riding skill and sense of responsibility is helpful. Start making inquiries in autumn or early winter, since camp owners or directors like to hire their staffs as early as possible.

See *Teaching Riding at Summer Camp* by Steven D. Price (The Stephen Greene Press).

FURTHER INFORMATION

The following state and provincial agencies will supply information and answer questions about equestrian tourism:

Alabama Bureau of Publicity and Information
Room 403, State Highway Building
Montgomery, Alabama 36104
(205) 269-6835

Alaska Travel Division
Pouch E
Juneau, Alaska 99811
(907) 465-2010

Arizona Office of Economic Planning and
    Development
1645 West Jefferson Street
Phoenix, Arizona 85007
(602) 271-5638

Arkansas Department of Parks and Tourism
149 State Capitol
Little Rock, Arkansas 72201
(501) 371-1087

California Division of Tourism
1400 10th Street
Sacramento, California 95814
(916) 445-2008

Colorado Division of Commerce and Development
602 State Capitol Annex
Denver, Colorado 80203
(303) 892-3045

Connecticut Department of Commerce
Division of Tourism
210 Washington Street
Hartford, Connecticut 06106
(203) 566-3977

Delaware Division of Economic Development
45 The Green
Dover, Delaware 19901
(302) 678-4254

District of Columbia Convention and Visitors
    Bureau
1129 20th Street, N.W.
Washington, D.C. 20036
(202) 659-6460

Florida Department of Commerce
Development Division
107 West Golines Street
Tallahassee, Florida 32304
(904) 488-5606

Georgia Department of Community Development
P.O. Box 38097
Atlanta, Georgia 30334
(404) 656-3590

Hawaii Visitors Bureau
Suite 801, 2270 Kalakaua Avenue
Honolulu, Hawaii 96815
(808) 923-1811

Idaho Division of Tourism and Industrial
    Development
Room 108, Capitol Building
Boise, Idaho 83702
(208) 384-2470

Illinois Department of Business and Economic
    Development
222 South College Street
Springfield, Illinois 62704
(217) 782-7500

Indiana Division of Tourism
336 State House
Indianapolis, Indiana 46204
(317) 633-5423

Iowa Development Commission
250 Jewett Building
Des Moines, Iowa 50309
(515) 281-3401

Kansas Department of Economic Development
Room 122-S, State Office Building
Topeka, Kansas 66612
(913) 296-3481

Kentucky Department of Public Information
Capitol Annex
Frankfort, Kentucky 40601
(502) 564-4930

Louisiana Tourist Development Commission
P.O. Box 44291
Baton Rouge, Louisiana 70804
(504) 389-5981

Maine Department of Commerce and Industry
State House
Augusta, Maine 04330
(207) 289-3276

Maryland Division of Tourist Development
2525 Riva Road
Annapolis, Maryland 21401
(301) 267-5517

Massachusetts Department of Commerce and
    Development
100 Cambridge Street
Boston, Massachusetts 02202
(617) 727-2305

Michigan Tourist Council
300 South Capitol Avenue
Lansing, Michigan 48933
(517) 373-0670

Minnesota Department of Economic Development
480 Cedar Street
St. Paul, Minnesota 55101
(612) 296-3981

Mississippi Agricultural and Industrial Board
1504 State Office Building, P.O. Box 849
Jackson, Mississippi 39205
(601) 345-6715

Missouri Department of Consumer Affairs and
    Regulations Licensing
P.O. Box 1055
Jefferson City, Missouri 65101
(314) 751-4133

Montana Travel Promotion Unit
Department of Highways
Helena, Montana 59601
(406) 449-2654

Nebraska Department of Economic Development
State Capitol, Box 94666
Lincoln, Nebraska 68509
(402) 477-8984

Nevada Department of Economic Development
State Capitol
Carson City, Nevada 89701
(702) 885-4322

New Hampshire Division of Economic
    Development
Box 856
Concord, New Hampshire 03301
(603) 271-2666

New Jersey Department of Labor and Industry
P.O. Box 2766
Trenton, New Jersey 08690
(609) 292-7757

New Mexico Department of Development
Travel Bureau
113 Washington Avenue
Santa Fe, New Mexico 87501
(505) 827-3101

New York State Department of Commerce
99 Washington Avenue
Albany, New York 12210
(518) 474-4116

North Carolina Department of Natural and
    Economic Resources
P.O. Box 27685
Raleigh, North Carolina 27611
(919) 829-4171

North Dakota Highway Department
Capitol Grounds
Bismarck, North Dakota 58501
(701) 224-2500

Ohio Department of Economic and Community
    Development
30 East Broad Street
Columbus, Ohio 43215
(614) 466-8844

Oklahoma Tourism and Recreation
    Department
500 Will Rogers Building
Oklahoma City, Oklahoma 73105
(405) 521-2468

Oregon State Highway Division
Travel Information Section
101 State Highway Building
Salem, Oregon 97310
(503) 378-6546

Pennsylvania Department of Commerce
Travel Development Bureau
South Office Building
Harrisburg, Pennsylvania 17120
(717) 787-5453

Rhode Island Department of Economic
    Development
One Weybosset Hill
Providence, Rhode Island 02903
(410) 277-2614

South Carolina Department of Parks, Recreation
    and Tourism
Box 113, 1205 Pendleton Street
Columbia, South Carolina 29201
(803) 758-2536

South Dakota Department of Economic and
    Tourist Development
Pierre, South Dakota 57501
(605) 224-3301

Tennessee State Tourism Development
1028 Andrew Jackson State Office Building
Nashville, Tennessee 37219
(615)741-2158

Texas Tourist Development Agency
Box 12008, Capitol Station
Austin, Texas 78711
(512) 475-4326

Utah Travel Council
Council Hall, Capitol Hill
Salt Lake City, Utah 84114
(801) 328-5681

Vermont Agency of Development and Community
    Affairs
61 Elm Street
Montpelier, Vermont 05602
(802) 828-3236

Virginia State Travel Service
6 North 6th Street
Richmond, Virginia 23219
(804) 770-2051

Washington Department of Commerce and
    Economic Development
General Administration Building
Olympia, Washington 98504
(206) 753-5610

West Virginia Department of Commerce
Travel Division
1900 Washington Street, East State Capitol
Charleston, West Virginia 25305
(304) 348-2286

Wisconsin Department of Natural Resources,
 Vacation and Travel Service
P.O. Box 450
Madison, Wisconsin 53701
(608) 266-2147

Wyoming Travel Commission
2320 Capitol Avenue
Cheyenne, Wyoming 82001
(307) 777-7777

Canada

Travel Alberta
10255 104 Street
Edmonton T5J 1B1, Alberta
(403) 424-0474

Department of Travel Industry
1019 Wharf Street
Victoria V8W 2Z2, British Columbia
(604) 387-3464

Tourist Branch
Department of Tourism, Recreation, and Cultural
 Affairs
Norquay Building
401 York Avenue
Winnipeg, Manitoba
(204) 946-7455

Tourism New Brunswick
P.O. Box 1030
Fredericton E3B 5C3, New Brunswick
(506) 453-2170

Tourist Services Division
Department of Tourism
Confederation Building
St. John's, Newfoundland
(709) 722-0711

Travel Arctic
Division of Tourism
Yellowknife, Northwest Territories
(403) 873-2611

Travel Division,
Department of Tourism
Hollis Building
Hollis Street, P.O. Box 456
Halifax, Nova Scotia
(902) 424-7657

Tourism Division,
Ministry of Industry and Tourism
900 Hearst Street, Hearst Block
Toronto, Ontario
(416) 365-4026

Department of Tourism
Cité Parlementaire
Quebec City, Province of Quebec
(418) 643-2237

Department of Environment and Tourism
Provincial Administration Building
P.O. Box 2000
Charlestown, Prince Edward Island
(902) 892-7411

Information Division, Extension Services
Department of Tourism and Renewable Resources
Box 7105
Regina, Saskatchewan
(306) 522-1691

Tourism and Information Branch
Box 2703
Whitehorse, Yukon Territory
(403) 677-5435

INTERNATIONAL

A world of equestrian activities awaits beyond our borders for both participants and spectators. Some countries have a wealth of things to see and do, while others are admittedly short on horsey goings-on.

For detailed information, contact government tourist offices and local equestrian associations, or work through a travel agent. Once you arrive in a foreign country, check equestrian magazines for participant and spectator activities, and read newspapers' sports pages for racing, shows, and other fixtures.

United Kingdom. Equestrian activities in Great Britain are a movable feast. Riding opportunities range from a sedate canter around London's Hyde Park to trekking through the moors and mountains of Wales, Scotland, and the north of England. Many fox hunts welcome visitors. Spectators will enjoy racing, horse shows and trials, and polo.

Moss Brothers, a noted tack and apparel shop located in Covent Garden in London and at several other cities throughout England, publishes an annual list of horse shows and trials.
further information:

British Tourist Authority
680 Fifth Avenue
New York, New York 10019

British Horse Society
Stoneleigh, Kennilworth, Warwickshire

magazines: *Riding, Horse and Hound, Country Life.*

REPUBLIC OF IRELAND

As horsey a country as any in the world, Ireland has pleasure riding, trekking, hunting, and horse-drawn caravans. The Dublin Horse Show, held in late August, leads the country's shows and trials, and there are also racing and polo to watch.
further information:

Irish Tourist Board
590 Fifth Avenue
New York, New York 10036

Irish Horse Board/Bord nagCapall
St. Maelruan's, Tallaght,
County Dublin

Hunting in Ireland, with the Rock of Cashel (County Tipperary) in the background.

SCANDINAVIA

Trekking is a lovely way to view fiords, glacier fields, and mountain greenery. There is hacking at riding academies, and spectators will find racing and horse shows and trials.
further information:

Denmark:

Danish National Tourist Office
75 Rockefeller Plaza
New York, New York 10020

Dansk Rideforbund
Vestre Paradisvej 51,
Holt.

Finland:

Finland National Tourist Office
75 Rockefeller Plaza
New York, New York 10020

Suomen Ratsastjainlitto
Paasitie 9B2
Helsinki 83

Iceland:

Iceland National Tourist Office
505 Fifth Avenue
New York, New York 10017

Norway:

Norwegian National Tourist Office
75 Rockefeller Plaza
New York, New York 10020

Norges Rytterforbund
Postboks 204L
Oslo

Sweden:

Swedish National Tourist Office
505 Fifth Avenue
New York, New York 10017

Svenska Ridsportens Centralförbund
Ostermalmsgatan 80
Stockholm

BENELUX

Belgium, the Netherlands, and Luxembourg have manège and cross-country riding at and from private and public stables, as well as horse shows and trials.
further information:

Belgium:

Belgian National Tourist Office
720 Fifth Avenue
New York, New York 10017

Fédération Royale Belge des Sports Équestres
Avenue Hanoir 38
1180 Brussels

Netherlands:

Netherlands National Tourist Office
576 Fifth Avenue
New York, New York 10017

Nederlandse Hippische Sportbond
Waalsdorperlaan 29a
Waasenaar (Post Den Haag)

Luxembourg:

Luxembourg Tourist Information Office
One Dag Hammarskjold Plaza
New York, New York 10017

Fédération Luxembourgeoise des Sports Équestres
Route de Thionville 90
Luxembourg

FRANCE

Although most riding in France is done on a private basis, visitors can arrange to use club facilities. With regard to noted establishments, the Club Méditerranée has an equestrian village at Pompadour, near Limoges. It combines excellent riding facilities with typical Club Med ambience. Contact: Club Méditerranée, 40 West 57th Street, New York, New York 10019, or through travel agents.

The P-L-M Hotel chain features riding at several of its hotels, especially in the east and south of France. Contact: P-L-M Hotels of France, 14 East 60th Street, New York, New York 10022.

The National Riding School at Saumur, in the Loire Valley, is the home of the Cadre Noir, France's *haute école* dressage troupe. Tickets for exhibitions must be secured in advance.

Spectator sports include racing around Paris at Longchamps, Auteil, Vincennes, and Saint-Cloud. During summer months, racing moves to Deauville in Normandy. There are polo and horse shows and trials throughout the country.
further information:

French Government Tourist Office
75 Rockefeller Plaza
New York, New York 10020

Fédération Française des Sports Équestres
Faubourg St.-Honoré 164
75 Paris

magazine: *L'Année Hippique.*

The French Cavalry School at Saumur.

SPAIN AND PORTUGAL

Pleasure riding and trekking on the Iberian penin-
sula are done on a rather formal basis and, accordingly, must be planned in advance. Spectator
events include horse shows, polo, and *rejoneo*
(bullfighting from horseback).

The Andalusian Riding School in Jérez de la
Frontera, Spain, combines classical dressage with
native folklore elements. It presents monthly exhibitions, for which tickets must be arranged in
advance.
further information:

Spain:

Spanish National Tourist Office
665 Fifth Avenue
New York, New York 10022

Federación Nacional Hípica
Montesquinza 8
Madrid 4

The international dressage master Nuno Oliveira has a school
outside Lisbon where he teaches advanced-level students.

Portugal:

Portuguese National Tourist Office
570 Fifth Avenue
New York, New York 10036

Federacão Equestre Portuguesa
Rua de San Pedro de Alcantara 29
Lisbon 2

ITALY

Relatively few public stables and private clubs afford the chance to ride in Italy, although there are
several near Rome and other large cities. The
Rome Horse Show is the country's premier fixture,
and there are other horse shows and trials and
racing.
further information:

Italian Government Tourist Office
630 Fifth Avenue
New York, New York 10020

Federazione Italiana Sport Equestri
Palazzo della Federazione
Viale Tiziano 70
Rome

SWITZERLAND

There are many riding stables, schools, and clubs
in Switzerland for hacking and *manège* work, as
well as horse shows and trials for spectators.
further information:

Swiss National Tourist Office
608 Fifth Avenue
New York, New York 10020

*Alvarito Domecq performing at the Andalusian Riding School,
Jérez de la Frontera, Spain.*

Fédération Suisse des Sports Équestres
Comité Central: Bahnhofstrasse 36, Zurich

Section Concours Hippiques: Blankweg 70
3072 Ostermundigen

WEST GERMANY

Riding stables and clubs throughout West Germany permit both school and cross-country riding.
Horse shows are popular and plentiful, and there
are Thoroughbred and trotting tracks near several
large cities.
further information:

German National Tourist Office
630 Fifth Avenue
New York, New York 10020

Deutsche Reiterliche Vereinigung
Adenauerallee 174, 53 Bonn

magazines: *Reiter*

EASTERN EUROPE

Cross-country trekking is a popular and pleasant
way to see this part of the world.

One of the world's most famous riding establishments, the Spanish Riding School in Vienna,
Austria, is certainly worth a visit. Tickets to performances must be secured well in advance, although there are daily tours of the stables. The
School is closed during summer months.

Poland's native breeds may be viewed at state-
run breeding studs at Vielkapolska and Byali Bor.
further information:

German Democratic Republic (East Germany)
Deutsche Pferdesport Verband der
Deutschen Demokratischen Republik
Nationale Reiterliche Vereinigung
Storkowerstrasse 118, Berlin 1055

Polish Travel Bureau, Inc.
500 Fifth Avenue
New York New York 10036

Polski Zwiazek Jezdziecki
Sienkiewicza 12, Warsaw

Austrian National Tourist Office
545 Fifth Avenue
New York, New York 10017

Österreichische Campagnereiter Gesellschaft
Haus des Sports, Prinz Eugenstrasse 12
Vienna IV

Danube Countries Promotion Groups
380 Madison Avenue
New York, New York 10017

Hungary
Fédération Hongroise d'Équitation
Holda Utca 1, Budapest V

Czechoslovak Travel Bureau
10 East 40th Street
New York, New York 10016

Fédération Équestre Tchécoslovaque
Na Porici 12, Prague 11

Bulgarian Tourist Office
50 East 42nd Street
New York, New York 10017

Comité Suprème de Culture Physique et des Sports
Boulevard Tolbukhin 18, Sofia

Yugoslavia Travel Agency (Centrotourist)
509 Madison Avenue
New York, New York 10022

Fédération Équestre Yougoslave
27 General Zdanov Street, Belgrade

Greek National Tourist Office
601 Fifth Avenue
New York, New York 10017

Association Hellénique d'Athlétisme Amateur
Avenue Panepistimioy 25, Athens

Romanian National Tourist Office
500 Fifth Avenue
New York, New York 10036

Federatia Romina de Calarie
Vasile Conta 16, Bucharest

SOVIET UNION

Russia has some trekking, but there is more for spectators: horse shows and trials, driving competitions, and racing. The equestrian world will focus its attention on that country when the Olympic Games take place there in 1980.
further information:

U.S.S.R.—Intourist
45 East 49th Street
New York, New York 10017

Fédération Équestre d'U.R.S.S.
Skaternyi Pereulok 4, Moscow

ASIA

The continent of Asia offers a rather limited number of participant activities, ranging from trekking in the Near East to more of the same in Japan. Spectator sports are more varied. India and Hong Kong have polo, there's racing in Japan and Hong Kong, and the Afghanistani sport of *bushkashi*, a kind of mounted rugby with a goat carcass as the ''ball,'' is a hair-raising spectacle.
further information:

Turkish Tourism and Information Office
500 Fifth Avenue
New York, New York 10036

Fédération Équestre Turque
Ucyol-Mazlak, Istanbul

Israel Government Tourist Office
488 Madison Avenue
New York, New York 10017

The Israeli Horse Society
P.O. Box 14111, Tel Aviv

Iran Information and Tourist Center
10 West 49th Street
New York, New York 10020

The Iranian Equestrian Federation
Iranian Olympic Committee
Kakke Verzesh, Teheran

Lebanon Tourist and Information Office
405 Park Avenue
New York, New York 10022

Fédération Libanaise des Sports Équestres
B.P. 5035, Beirut

Afghanistan Tourist Organization
535 Fifth Avenue
New York, New York 10017

India Government Tourist Office
19 East 49th Street
New York, New York 10017

Hong Kong Tourist Office
548 Fifth Avenue
New York, New York 10036

Japan National Tourist Office
45 Rockefeller Plaza
New York, New York 10020

Fédération Équestre Japonaise
Kanda Surugadai 4–6, Chiyoda-ku, Tokyo

Korean Tourist Corp.
460 Park Avenue
New York, New York 10022

Korean Equestrian Federation
19 Mukyo-Dong
K.A.A.A. Building, Room 611, Seoul

AUSTRALIA AND NEW ZEALAND

The combination of British tradition and ranch work makes these two countries a gold mine of equestrian activities. There are good English-style school work and hacking, as well as trekking and hunting. Stock-seat riding is also available. Spectator goings-on include racing, polo, shows, and trials, along with Down Under versions of rodeos. further information:

Australian Tourist Commission
1270 Avenue of the Americas
New York, New York 10020

The Equestrian Federation of Australia
Royal Show Grounds, Epsom Road, Ascot Vale 2

New Zealand Government Tourist Office
Suite 970
One Maritime Plaza
San Francisco, California 94111

The New Zealand Horse Society
P.O. Box 13, Hastings

AFRICA

Riding in Africa is largely informal, such as trekking across mountain trails and plains or along sandy beaches or deserts. Rhodesia, Kenya, and South Africa have hunting, polo, and racing (remnants of their British legacy).

A number of safari tours in East Africa include horseback rides through game preserves (there's no danger, according to all reports, that you or your mount will be featured on local carnivores' menus).
further information:

Egypt Government Tourist Office
630 Fifth Avenue
New York, New York 10020

Algeria
Fédération Algérienne des Sports Équestres
Rue Didouche Mourad 21, Algiers

Libya
Fédération Nationale Libyenne Équestres
Maidan Abi Setta
P.O. Box 4507, Tripoli

Tunisian National Tourist Office
630 Fifth Avenue
New York, New York 10020

Fédération Tunisienne de Tir et d'Équitation
Stand National de Tir El Ouardia
Sidi Belhassen, Tunis

Morocco National Tourist Office
597 Fifth Avenue
New York, New York 10020

Fédération Royale Marocaine des Sports
Équestres
Garde Royale, Rabat

Kenya Tourist Office
15 East 51st Street
New York, New York 10022

The Rhodesian Horse Society
P.O. Box 2415, Salisbury

South Africa Tourist Corporation
610 Fifth Avenue
New York, New York 10020

South African National Equestrian Federation
17 Tulip Avenue
Sunridge Park, Port Elizabeth

CENTRAL AMERICA AND THE CARIBBEAN

South of the border, riding along beaches is a pleasant way to the enjoy Caribbean sun. There's also racing in Puerto Rico, Panama, and Jamaica. Jamaica also has polo.

The Escuela Equestre S.M.A., located in San Miguel de Allende, 175 miles northwest of Mexico City, is Mexico's most popular riding resort. Three hours of instruction each morning concentrate on dressage, jumping, and cross-country horsemanship.

The El Salvador Jockey Club is the site of the Izalco International Equestrian Center. Director Hubert Roher, who studied at Vienna's Spanish Riding School, offers instruction in dressage and provides facilities for jumping, cross-country, and general pleasure riding.
further information:

Puerto Rico Tourism Development
1290 Avenue of the Americas
New York, New York 10019

Federación Puertorriqueña de Deportes Ecuestres
Apartado de Correos 4959, San Juan

Jamaica Tourist Board
200 Park Avenue
New York, New York 10017

Haiti Government Tourist Bureau
30 Rockefeller Plaza
New York, New York 10020

Dominican Republic Tourist Office
64 West 50th Street
New York, New York 10020

Mexican National Tourist Council
677 Fifth Avenue
New York, New York 10022

Federación Ecuestre Mexicana
Insurgentes Sur no 222 Desp. 405
Mexico 7, D.F.

El Salvador Information Office
703 Market Street
San Francisco, California 94103

Panama Government Tourist Bureau
630 Fifth Avenue
New York, New York 10020

Guatemala Consulate General
1270 Avenue of the Americas
New York, New York 10020

Federación Ecuestre de Guatemala
Apartado Postal 1525, Guatemala C.A.

SOUTH AMERICA

South America evokes images of gauchos galloping across the pampas, and you'll find bolo-wielding cowboys at home on Argentine, Chilean, and Brazilian ranges. You'll also be able to ride at private clubs and watch polo, racing, and horse shows in large cities throughout the continent.
further information:

Argentine Consulate
12 West 56th Street
New York, New York 10019

Federación Ecuestre Argentina
Rodriquez Peña 1934—Planta Baja
Buenos Aires

Bolivian Consulate
10 Rockefeller Plaza
New York, New York 10020

Federación Boliviana de Deportes Ecuestres
Casilla 329, La Paz

Brazilian Consulate
630 Fifth Avenue
New York, New York 10020

Confederaçao Brasileira de Hipismo
Rua Sete de Setembre 81, Sala 302
Rio de Janeiro

Chilean Consulate
866 Second Avenue
New York, New York 10022

Federación Nacional de Deportes Ecuestres
Calle Compania 1630, Santiago de Chile

Colombia Government Tourist Office
140 East 57th Street
New York, New York 10022

Asociación Colombiana de Deportes Ecuestres
Calle 13 no 8–39—Oficina 609, Bogotá

Ecuadorian National Tourist Office
2067 Broadway
New York, New York 10023

Federación Ecuatoriana de Deportes Ecuestres
Apartado 410, Quito

Peruvian Consulate
10 Rockefeller Plaza
New York, New York 10020

Federación Peruana de Deportes Ecuestres
Estadio Nacional, Puerta 29, Lima

Uruguay
Federación Uruguaya de Deportes Ecuestres
Avenida Agraciada 1546, Montevideo

Venezuela Government Tourist Office
485 Madison Avenue
New York, New York 10022

Federación Venezolana de Deportes Ecuestres
Apartado 3588, Caracas

9 ORGANIZATIONS

Now that you have acquired your horse, your stable, your management routines, your equine health regimen, your tack, and your apparel and have become involved in one or more equestrian activities—perhaps even including a horseback vacation—you will feel ready to meet other horse people, or at least to read about them. The following chapter includes information about magazines to which you may want to subscribe, organizations you may want to join, and catalogs you may want to order and order from.

MAGAZINES

Name a breed or an activity and there's sure to be at least one national or regional magazine on the subject. Since there's no complete list of equestrian periodicals, we had to use various sources to compile this one (and no doubt we missed a few). Some sources did not include subscription rates.

Many of these magazines are sold at tack shops and large newsstands, while others are available only by membership in breed or activity organizations. (Unless otherwise indicated, publication is on a monthly basis.)

GENERAL INTEREST (NATIONAL):

American Horseman. $9.59/year.
The Chronicle of the Horse. Weekly. $18/year.
Classic. Bimonthly. $15/year.
Horse and Horseman. $6/year.
Horse & Rider. $7/year.
Horseman. $6/year.
Horse Lovers. Bimonthly. $5/year.
Horse of Course. $8.50/year.
Horse Play. $12/year.
Practical Horseman. $8/year.
Western Horseman. $6/year.

ACTIVITIES (NATIONAL):

Carriage Journal. Quarterly.
Cutter and Chariot Racing World.
Cuttin' Horse Chatter.
Dressage & Combined Training. $12.50/year.
Equestrian Trails (distance riding).
Grand Prix (stadium jumping). Quarterly.
Hoof and Horn (rodeo and ranching)
Horse Show.
Polo News. Monthly except January.
Rodeo Collegian.
Rodeo News. Monthly except January.
Rodeo Sports News. Biweekly.
Side-Saddle News.
U.S. Combined Training Association News.
   Bimonthly.
The Whip (driving). 8 issues per year.

BREEDS (NATIONAL):

(American Saddle Horses)
Horse World. Monthly except January. $12/year.
National Horseman. $12/year.
Saddle and Bridle. Monthly except January. $14/year.

Appaloosa News $7.50/year.
The Appy.
The Spot-Lighter.

The Arabian Horse.
Arabian Horse News. $12/year.
Arabian Horse Times. Weekly. $5/year.
Arabian Horse World. $10/year.

Buckskin World News. Quarterly.

Draft Horse Journal. Quarterly.

The Hackney Journal. Bimonthly.

The Morgan Horse. Monthly except January.

Mr. Longears (donkeys and mules). Quarterly.

The New Racking Review. 18 issues per year.

The Paint Horse Journal. Bimonthly.
The Pinto Horse. $6/year.

Palomino Horses. $4/year.

Percheron Notes. Annual.

Peruvian Horse Review. Quarterly. $4.50/year.
Peruvian Horse World. Quarterly.

Pony of the Americas. Monthly except January. $7.50/year.

Eastern/Western Quarter Horse Journal.
Quarter Horse Digest. $4.50/year.
Quarter Horse Journal.
Quarter Horse World. $7/year.
Quarter Horse Youth.

American Shetland Pony Journal. Monthly except January. $8/year.

Spanish Barb Quarterly.

Voice of the Tennessee Walking Horse. $10/year.
Walking Horse Report. 50 issues per year.

Welsh Pony World. Quarterly.

REGIONAL PERIODICALS:

Arizona Horseman. Bimonthly.
The Arizona Quarter Horse. Bimonthly.
California Horseman's News.
California Horse Review.
Cal-Western Appaloosa.
Canadian Appaloosa Journal.
Canadian Horse (Thoroughbreds) $8/year.
Canadian Rodeo News.
Canadian Western Rider.
Capital Horseman (Colorado).
Central Ohio Saddle Club News.
The Corral (North-central). $5/year.
Eastern Quarter Horse Journal. $6/year.
Equine Events (Midwest). $6/year.
Florida Horseman.
The News of Georgia's Horses.
Heart of America Horseman (Midwest).
Hoofbeats and Pawprints (New York). Monthly except January.
Horse Country (Oklahoma).
The Horseman's Exchange (New York Metropolitan Area).
Horseman's Gazette (Northwest).
Horseman's Guide (Midwest).
Horseman's Review (Midwest). $5/year.
Horseman's Yankee Pedlar (New England). Monthly except January.
Horses and Hoofbeats. (Midwest).
Horse News (Far West).
Horses Today (Midwest).
Illinois Equine Market. $5/year.
Indiana Quarter Horse Journal.
Intermountain Quarter Horse (Rocky Mountain states).
Iowa Saddleman.
The Larriet (Pacific Northwest). $5/month.
The Maryland Horse. $7.50/year.
Michigan Appaloosa News.
Michigan Arabians.
Mid America Rodeo News.
New Jersey Equine Industry News.
New Jersey Horseman.
New York Horse.
Northeast Horseman.
The Oregon Horseman.
Piedmont Horseman (North Carolina).
The Piggin' String (Western states). $10/year.
The Quarter Horseman (Midwest). Bimonthly.
Quarter Horse of the Pacific. $6/year.
Rocky Mountain Quarter Horse.
Sentinel Horseman (California).
Shining Mountain Sentinel (Montana).
Showday Guide (Middle Atlantic states).
Southern Horseman. $7/year.
Southwest Iowa Horsemen's News.
Spur (Virginia). Bimonthly, $6/year.
The Texas and Southwestern Horseman. $4.50/year.
Thoroughbred of California. $18/year.
Valley Horse News (Midwest).
Volunteer Horseman (Tennessee).

The Washington State Horseman Canter. 10 issues per year.
Western Tennessee Walking Horse Journal (Far West). Bimonthly.
Wisconsin Horsemen's News.

Subscriptions are easier and somewhat less expensive than buying individual copies over the year. An alternative to subscribing through the publisher is to use one of the subscription services that advertise in the magazines themselves. Not only is there no surcharge, but you can frequently receive free gifts or reduced prices on merchandise when you place your orders.

One such firm is The Book Shelf, whose free catalog lists many equestrian magazines as well as books and stationery items.
The Book Shelf
5119 Sherrill Drive
Fort Wayne, Indiana 46806

EQUINE HUMANE MOVEMENTS

Because horses are legally considered farm animals in the United States, they are ignored by the Animal Welfare Act of the U.S. Government, except under exhibition conditions or when they are transported interstate. In other words, no federal legislation exists to protect a horse that is being abused or kept in bad condition by its owner. Thanks to the hardworking members of the American Horse Protection Association, there are laws against the exhibition of any horse that has been "sored" or is forced to wear chains, boots, or other devices that affect its gait while causing pain. This Section 11.2 of the Animal Welfare Act came about because of the heavy abuses suffered by Tennessee Walking Horses, although it does, of course, apply to any and all horses exhibited in the United States. (Wild mustangs are also protected by the Federal Government—but because they are wild animals, not because they are horses.)

State laws, too, are not generally concerned with the welfare of horses, except as they are shipped into the state—and in this case the goal is not to protect the individual horse but to keep resident animals free of disease. Such regulations vary from state to state, but usually involve the presentation of a health certificate signed by a veterinarian and a negative Coggins test dated within the previous year or six months.

With the single exception of the state of Maryland, no set of state laws exists to protect horses from abuses caused by cruel handling or negligent stabling. The Maryland law concerns horses rented to the public. Although it was promoted by the Maryland Humane Association for the sake of the horses, we can't help feeling that it was passed primarily because of the potential danger that ill-used animals present to the unwary riders who rent them. Although these regulations—which involve the licensing and inspection of the stables—seem a bit overprotective, this kind of legislation is sorely needed not just in Maryland but in every state in the country. There is some humane activity going on in other states—California, Pennsylvania, and New York, for example—thanks to the efforts of local animal organizations. States also regulate against the use of unacceptable drugs in race horses—but again, we can't help suspecting that this has to do with protecting bettors and other owners rather than with keeping horses healthy. It is true, of course, that the doping of horses was originally made illegal because Thoroughbred racing (and indeed the breed) in the United States was thought to be in real danger of deterioration as a consequence of the practice. Thanks to the Thoroughbred Racing and Protective Bureau, the use of drugs has been severely curtailed. The Pennsylvania SPCA is working to put phenylbutazin on the list of unacceptable drugs, because of the number of accidents it feels the use of this painkilling anti-inflammatory drug has caused.

If you are interested in putting through legislation in your own state—or even just in reporting single instances of abuse—several avenues are open to you. Keep in mind that it will be difficult to do much about even the most obvious cases of abuse. Nevertheless, it is worth trying, even if all your efforts result only in a bit of adverse publicity for the abuser. First, be sure that you are not the only person to witness the bad conditions. Take photos if possible. Get an affidavit signed by one or more veterinarians attesting to poor conditions and—if it exists—the presence of untreated diseases or injuries. Starvation, poorly ventilated and/or filthy stables, and any other obvious wrongs should also be noted. Once you have put your dossier together, get in touch with the officials of your local humane society or a local branch of one of the national organizations (the Humane Society of the United States, the Fund for Animals, and others). If there is no such organization in your community or area, find out whether there is a state organization where you live. If not, call or write your local law-enforcement agency and be sure that the local newspapers are notified. Many times the pressure of public opinion alone will be enough to force the issue. It was in New York City, where a carriage horse had to be destroyed right in front of the Plaza Hotel. The incident aroused so much indignation that investigations were immediately undertaken into the stabling of carriage horses. Even without state or local laws to cover the abuse you are trying to correct, most newspaper editors respond to animal-interest stories, and most public stables—or private individuals (though you must take care not to bring a libel suit on yourself)—do not enjoy having their dirty laundry (or stall bedding) aired in public.

If you are concerned with legislation on a higher level—not simply the improvement of one or two situations—you may try working with others who are similarly concerned. The League for Animal Protection in New York State managed to have Peace Officers elected to investigate cruelty cases and to make arrests. It might be worth writing for advice concerning your own state to Mr. and Mrs. Warren Abrams, 147 Daly Road, East Northport, New York 11731. You can also express your interest to Mrs. William Blue of the American Horse Protection Association, Inc., 3316 N Street, N.W., Washington, D.C. 20007.

FUTURE FARMERS OF AMERICA

The Future Farmers of America includes among its activities horse proficiency awards. Sponsored by the American Morgan Horse Association, Inc., they are intended to encourage FFA members to explore careers in the horse industry, such as breeding, training, feeding, and showing.

Among recent winners are youngsters who established a successful stable, bred new strains of horses, and exhibited animals at fairs and shows. They all worked through their state programs under the supervision of local Vocational Agriculture Instructors.

For further information, contact your county extension agent or write to Future Farmers of America, National FFA Center, P.O. Box 15160, Alexandria, Virginia 22309.

PONY CLUBS
by Catherine McWilliams

The British Pony club, inaugurated in 1929, was the model for the United States Pony Clubs, Inc., which was formally incorporated in 1954. The purpose of the pony club is "to produce a thoroughly happy, comfortable horseman, riding across a natural country, with complete confidence and perfect balance on a pony equally happy and confident and free from pain or bewilderment." The term "pony" is loosely used to refer to any mount, regardless of size or breeding, of a junior rider (the latter considered by the Pony Club to be anyone under the age of 21).

The Pony Club realizes its goals through education in riding skills as well as in teaching the responsibilities and techniques of horse ownership and stable management, such as grooming, feeding, stabling, shoeing, and first aid.

Organization is through local chapters, usually centered in a town or county and often sponsored by a recognized hunt. Local officers are all volunteers, and each chapter decides on its own programs.

The unifying factors that are decided at the national level are, more importantly, the rating system for each level and competition rules. Every pony-club member is rated on a scale from D, the most elementary, to A. While local officers and instructors within a chapter assign D and C ratings, a rider must pass an extensive test conducted by a nationally sanctioned examiner before becoming a

B or an A. The requirements for becoming a Pony Club A are so demanding that only a few dozen members in the entire country each year receive this designation.

The rally is the heart of Pony-Club competition. It is available at all levels and designed to test all phases of horsemanship. Few individual awards are offered; most pony clubbers compete in teams of five, with only the group score taken into account. Rallies last over one to three days, and there is little assistance allowed from coaches and other adults.

There are five phases at every rally. First comes a written test covering all aspects of horsemanship and stable management. The second, stable management, begins when competitors arrive at the event and continues throughout the entire rally. Along with formal inspections of stabling and tack, judges continuously patrol the area to note any infractions of safe and correct procedures.

The next three phases, which all involve riding, are modeled after a Combined Training event. Each competitor rides a dressage test ranging in difficulty from a modified Training Level test for D's to the AHSA Second Level Test 1 for A's. A cross-country course is followed by a round of stadium jumping, also varying in difficulty according to riders' abilities.

Local clubs usually sponsor many other activities. Most chapters provide regular expert instruction at minimum cost, as well as horse shows, lectures, demonstrations, films, and mounted and unmounted practice sessions. In all cases, sportsmanship, teamwork, and paramount concern for a horse's welfare are always emphasized.

United States Pony Clubs, Inc.
303 South High Street
West Chester, Pennsylvania 19380

INTERCOLLEGIATE HORSE SHOW ASSOCIATION

The purpose of the Intercollegiate Horse Show Association is to provide a framework for competition on the collegiate level. Some three thousand students and alumni associated with more than one hundred colleges and universities participate, and at all levels. There are Beginner and Advanced Walk-Trot and Walk-Trot-Canter classes, Novice and Open Horsemanship on the flat and over fences, and also Hunt Team events. Graduates of member schools are eligible to compete in Alumni flat and jumping classes for as many years as they wish.

IHSA shows take place throughout the academic year. Owning one's own horse is no prerequisite, since such animals are ineligible. Host schools arrange with nearby stables to supply mounts, for which riders draw by lottery. Entry fees are kept to a minimum, and frequently the cost of transportation and lodgings is assumed by colleges and universities.

Regional finals are held toward the end of the school year, followed by a national finals at which regional high-point champions compete. Judges at local, regional, and national levels are noted riders and trainers; Mary and Frank Chapot, Gordon Wright, Victor Hugo-Vidal, George Morris, and Bertalan de Nemethy have all participated. Clinics and field trips are also part of an IHSA year.

The IHSA is growing annually, and additional regions are in the process of being formed. For further information, contact someone in the physical-education department at any of the following IHSA member schools. You can also write to the IHSA's Executive Director, Robert E. Cacchione, Suite 6L, 480 Halston Avenue, Harrison, New York 10528.

1976–77 MEMBERS OF THE INTERCOLLEGIATE HORSE SHOW ASSOCIATION

REGION I
Adelphi University—N.Y.
Briarcliff College—N.Y.
Brooklyn College—N.Y.
City College of New York—N.Y.
College of New Rochelle—N.Y.
College of St. Elizabeth—N.J.
Columbia University—N.Y.
C. W. Post College—N.Y.
Drew University—N.J.
Fairleigh Dickinson, Madison—N.J.
Fairleigh Dickinson, Rutherford—N.J.
* Fairleigh Dickinson, Teaneck—N.J.
Fordham University—N.Y.
Hofstra University—N.Y.
Jersey City State College—N.J.
Kean College—N.J.
Molloy College—N.Y.
Monmouth College—N.J.
Montclair State College—N.J.
Nassau College—N.Y.
N.Y.S. Institute of Tech.—N.Y.
New York University—N.Y.
Pace University—N.Y.
Queensborough Community—N.Y.
Ramapo College—N.Y.
St. John's University—N.Y.
Sarah Lawrence—N.Y.
Southampton College—N.Y.
S.U.N.Y., Farmingdale—N.Y.
S.U.N.Y., Stony Brook—N.Y.
**Suffolk Community College—N.Y.
U.S. Military Academy—N.Y.
Westchester Community College—N.Y.
William Paterson College—N.J.
REGION II
Alfred University—N.Y.
Bennett College—N.Y.
Broome Community—N.Y.
Cazenovia College—N.Y.
Cobleskill College—N.Y.
Cornell University—N.Y.
Delhi Agri. & Tech. College—N.Y.
Humber College—Canada

Ithaca College—N.Y.
Morrisville College—N.Y.
St. Lawrence University—N.Y.
Skidmore College—N.Y.
**S.U.C.O., Oswego—N.Y.
S.U.N.Y., Binghamton—N.Y.
S.U.N.Y., Potsdam—N.Y.
REGION III
American International College—Mass.
Babson College—Mass.
Colby-Sawyer College—N.H.
Connecticut College—Conn.
Dartmouth College—N.H.
Framingham State—Mass.
Mount Holyoke College—Mass.
Nasson College—Me.
New England College—N.H.
Smith College—Mass.
Springfield College—Mass.
Tufts University—Mass.
University of Connecticut—Conn.
University of Hartford—Conn.
University of Massachusetts—Mass.
University of New Hampshire—N.H.
**Worcester State College—Mass.
REGION IV
Averett College—Va.
Hollins College—Va.
Longwood College—Va.
Lynchburg College—Va.
Madison College—Va.
Mary Baldwin College—Va.
Mary Washington College—Va.
Radford College—Va.
Randolph Macon College—Va.
Southern Seminary College—Va.
Sweet Briar College—Va.
University of Virginia—Va.
** Virginia Intermont College—Va.
REGION V
Beaver College—Pa.
**Bucks County College—Pa.
Centenary College of Women—N.J.
Delaware Valley College—Pa.
Indiana Univ. Of Pa.—Pa.
Lafayette College—Pa.
Moravian College—Pa.

Northampton C.A. College—Pa.
Penn State University—Pa.
Princeton University—N.J.
Rider College—N.J.
Rutgers University—N.J.
Temple University—Pa.
Trenton State College—N.J.
University of Delaware—Del.
University of Maryland—Md.
Ursinus College—Pa.

*Executive Director
**President College

~~~~~~~~~~~~~~~~~~~~~~~~~~~~~~~~~~

Horse Words

Philip (or Phillip)—from the Greek words philos *and* hippos, *meaning lover and horse, respectively—means, obviously, a lover of horses, as in Philip of Macedonia or Prince Philip of England.*

Hippalectryon—a four-legged beast with the foreparts of a horse and the hind parts of a rooster

Hipparch—a cavalry commander

Hippia—referred to Athena, as the "horse goddess"

Hippiatrics—equine veterinary medicine

Hippocampus—a sea horse in classical mythology

Hippocurius—referred to Poseidon and meant "horse tending"

Hippodrome—an arena for equestrian spectacles

Hippogriff—a creature with the foreparts of a griffin and the hind parts of a horse (which should obviously be griffohip)

Hippology—the study of horses

Hippophagist—one who eats horseflesh, or practices hippophagy

Hippophile—one who loves horses

Hippopotamus—a "river horse"

~~~~~~~~~~~~~~~~~~~~~~~~~~~~~~~~~~

CATALOGS

One of the largest and finest tack shops in the heart of New Jersey hunting country, Beval Saddlery has a wide range of ready-made items—tack, apparel, and stable supplies, as well as the usual gifts. but it also has an unusually large assortment of books and an antique collection that is well worth a visit, even if you don't intend to buy. Beval imports apparel and tack from England and Europe (its Dutch breeches, even at $80, are justifiably famous) as well as jewelry from France and elsewhere. It also offers custom tailoring and bootmaking, and its Gladstone saddles—named for the nearby town that houses (or stables) the U.S. Equestrian Team's jumper and dressage horses—are particularly well designed and well made. Beval Saddlery Ltd., Inc., 67–69 Claremont Road, Bernardsville, New Jersey 07924.

Blue Ribbon Leather Co., Inc., makes a large variety of equipment for the English rider, specializing in tack for gaited and walking horses and for hunt and jumping, plus a line of Thoroughbred and Quarter Horse racing equipment. Most of its products are made in its English subsidiary manufacturing plants in Walsall, England, or in Shelbyville, Tennessee. The catalog, over 100 pages, is worth taking a look at. Blue Ribbon Leather Co., Inc., 737 Madison Street, Shelbyville, Tennessee 37160, or 7217 West Broad Street, Richmond, Virginia 23230.

For custom-made (from tree to cantle plate) Western saddles, bridles and bits, Carroll's makes gear designed by such horsemen as Ed Connell, Lee Wood, Charles Williamson, and Jack Carroll. Carroll tells us, "we are dedicated to preserving the ancient Moorish-Spanish methods of horsemanship." For $1 you can order the catalog with its emphasis on balanced-seat stock saddles and California-style reining. Carroll saddles are not offered in fixed seat sizes, since trees and covers are cut to measure. The rider can order any seat size as well as such changes as smaller swell, higher or lower cantle, more or less upsweep to seat, different horn, special carving or stamping, and so on. Carroll's asks customers to provide such measurements as height, weight, waist, hip, and inseam, as well as tracing out the pattern of the horse's back and withers and enclosing a side-view photograph of the animal. "Local riders can bring a horse to our shop." Carroll Saddle Company, McNeal, Arizona 85617.

The store puts out a catalog ($3) entitled a "Wish & Want Book," and for those who like to dip into our history, it is exactly that. Water rams, oak kegs, washpots, wood stoves, top hats, grist mills, froes and much more fill the pages and offer a delightful afternoon's thumbing. For the horseman, there is a wide variety of harness, pleasure and work, as well as parts for harness. Farrier tools and forges, driving bits for horses and for mules, leather hides, vehicles (from buggies and farm wagons to breaking carts and a Conestoga wagon costing $6,999) with replacement parts, and plows are all here even for those whose farming is only gladiolus bulbs. Cumberland General Store, Route 3, Crossville, Tennessee 38555.

Although DeLuxe carries some Western saddles and gear, the company specializes in importing tack and apparel from England. In addition to English jumping and show saddles and bridles, it also carries Stubben, Passier, and Kieffer saddles from Germany. DeLuxe handles a large assortment of imported Pytchley riding coats and Harry Hall coats and breeches. American brands include many ready-to-wear styles of hunting, saddle-seat, and hacking apparel and accessories, custom-made Dehner boots, and a wide variety of miscellaneous sportswear, jewelry, gifts, stable supplies, and books. The prices, though not low, tend to be a bit more reasonable than those in some of the other major tack catalogs. DeLuxe Saddlery Co., 1817 Whitehead Road, Baltimore, Maryland 21207.

Founded in 1906, Eiser's is one of the oldest riding-equipment institutions in the country. It makes and carries a complete line of equipment for the horse and the rider—from spurs and boots to socks and hunt caps; from Western hats and roping saddles to riding crops and imported English saddles. Saddles carried by Eiser's include Hartley, Passier, Kieffer, Stubben, Pariani, a line of Argentine forward-seat saddles, and Don West stock saddles. The catalog is large and chock-full of good-quality horse equipment. Eiser's, Inc., 1304 North Broad Street, Hillside, New Jersey 07205.

Gleckner's publishes a 160-page catalog with an emphasis on Western and some harness equipment. Its Western saddles are all Simcos, and it has a large selection of that brand's ready-made stock, show, Arabian, roping, contest, parade, Buena Vista, standard bar, and economy saddles. Most of the saddles are under $400, with some under $200. The catalog also has a wide selection of Simco saddle accessories and stable accessories, (it sells leather by the pound and sheep-wool shearling by the foot). Gleckner's also offers harness—driving (single or team), buggy (single or double) and team cutter, pony (single or double), harness accessories, and some carts. Work harness and accessories are also available. W. W. Gleckner & Sons Co., Box 175, Canton, Pennsylvania 17724.

Hamley's, Western saddlemakers since 1883, makes some of the best-looking, quality Western saddles, and all saddles are made to order. Prices range from $534 to about $773, and Hamley's says it is "impossible for us to guarantee delivery in less than four to six months following receipt of minimum deposit of 50%, or full remittance." Hamley's, Hamley Building, Pendleton, Oregon 97801.

One of the most famous tack shops in the country—perhaps the world—Kauffman's has been in business for more than one hundred years. Horsey visitors to New York City invariably trek down to East 24th Street for a look in at Kauffman's, and it is always gratifying to see that the latter has changed very little over the years. The Kauffman family still runs the shop and a large mail-order business as well, supplying tack, apparel, and equine equipment to horsemen all over America. Except for chaps, boots, and saddle suits, most Kauffman apparel is ready-made; the establishment has a particularly wide range of riding hats, and it carries Justin, Frye, and Acme Western boots and Levi's as well as English riding clothes. Kauffman's imports Stubben, Passier, Pariani, Barnsby, and various Argentine saddles as well as its own English-made "Centennial" saddle, design in honor of Kauffman's 100th birthday. Polo and racing equipment, a wide assortment of stable supplies, horse-care products, and books, gifts, and accessories for the horse lover fill out the annual catalog and the invariably busy shop.

Although Knoud does not advertise or produce a catalog, the shop is well worth visiting when one is in New York City, or writing to for information about its fine custom-tailored riding clothes and boots. It specializes in hunting apparel (it will even make sidesaddle habits) and can supply tradition-minded perfectionists with garments made in any style and in the fabulous fabrics of days gone by (as long as they are still available, of course). When box cloth was still manufactured, Knoud would make gaiters for chauffeurs, and shiny black limousines could often be found parked along the avenue as their drivers went inside for fittings. Knoud will also alter or adjust older clothing to newer fashions. It carries ready-made apparel too, though the staff is quick to point out that some new materials do not wear well. Knoud also stocks crops, sticks, spurs, gloves, hats, and gift items of many different types. The shop is small and expensive, but snug and picturesque. M. J. Knoud, 716 Madison Avenue, New York, New York 10021.

Recently appointed Official Saddler to the U.S. Equestrian Team, Miller's is one of New York City's best-known institutions—both as a shop (at 123 East 24th Street) and as a mail-order house. Many products, manufactured to Miller's specifications and distributed under its own name, are available nationwide through dealers as well as through the Miller catalog. Miller's specializes in tack, apparel, and equipment for English-style riding and offers custom-made hunt and saddle apparel and an especially wide selection of boots. It is the exclusive importer of the famous Hermès Saddle built to the specifications of Bill Steinkraus, and it carries a wide range of Crosby, Passier, Zaldi, Pariani, Argentine, and Indian saddles. Crosby and Maycraft bridles and mar-

tingales are featured, as well as Eldonian stainless steel bits and stirrups and all types of training and specialty tack and equipment. Miller's own Neo-Pro-Tek products—boots, hoods, and tail wraps—are only part of its large assortment of horse-care products, stable supplies, and other equipment. The establishment carries some Western gear—Tony Lama boots, Levi's, Lees, Stetsons, and Simca saddles. And, of course, there is the usual selection of books, gifts, and other accessories for horse people. Miller's Harness Company, 131 Varick Street, New York, New York 10013.

Nasco is one of the country's major suppliers of farm equipment. Its farm and ranch catalog has much to offer the horseman, at prices that are usually lower than those of the big tack shops. Nasco carries very little tack and no apparel, but it does supply a good deal of stable equipment, such as halters, girths, saddlebags, ropes, whips, leather-working gear, feeders, buckets, health products, farrier equipment, and ribbons and trophies. It also offers artificial-insemination equipment for horses and many general farm supplies for people who grow their own hay and grain or raise other animals as well. Nasco, 901 Janesville Avenue, Fort Atkinson, Wisconsin 53538.

Potts Longhorn makes a full line of Western saddles, specializing in bronc-riding and rodeo equipment. According to the company, Longhorn saddles have been chosen as the official saddle of the National High School Rodeo Association; there is a range of "youth" 13- to 15-inch seat saddles. One of the most popular sellers is the Martha Josey Barrel Racing Saddle which features a 14-inch foam quilted seat and weighs 30 pounds (price on request). Potts Longhorn Leather, 3141 Oak Grove, Dallas, Texas 75219.

Located in Fort Worth, Texas, Ryon's is run by Whistle Ryon, son of the late rodeoing Windy Ryon. Twice a year Ryon's mails out over seventy thousand catalogs "listing everything from saddles and spurs to hats and boots." The store keeps sixteen people busy in the mail-order section, and ten saddlemakers "ply their trade upstairs in the saddle shop where each saddle is completely handmade by one man." Whistle says he is "always ready to discuss and develop new ideas with trainers"; the establishment has developed such items as bits with Matlock Rose, Milt Bennett, Sonny Perry, and George Glasscock; the Lanhan Riley jowl sweat wrap; and saddles designed by Buster Welch, Don Nesbitt, Loyd Jenkins, Phil Lyne, Scott Stubbfield, Chuck Sheppard, Dale Wilkerson, and Wanda Harper Bush. Ryon's says it was the first store to stretch, age, and tie rope and to put buck stitching back on the saddle. The 144-page catalog is chock-full of quality Western-style equipment. Ryon's Saddle & Ranch Supplies, Inc., 2601 North Main Street, Fort Worth, Texas 76106.

Sears' Western Catalog, published by that American tradition, Sears, Roebuck and Co., offers "A complete selection of authentic western Jeans, Ranch Pants, Shirts, Outerwear, Boots and Square Dance Clothing for Men and Women. Also Saddles, Tack and Grooming Accessories plus English-style Riding Clothes and Equipment." The saddles and tack items are made for Sears, and the prices are generally high for the quality. To order a catalog, look under Sears, Roebuck and Co. in the phone book.

Shepler's, which calls itself (or themselves) the world's largest Western store (or stores), has shops in Wichita, Oklahoma City, and Denver, as well as a large catalog for its mail-order business. Many items won't interest horsemen specifically, since Shepler's caters to everyone who likes the Western look, but it does carry a wide range of good boots (including Lucchese, Durango, Dan Post, Acme, Tony Lama, Justin, Nocona, and its own brand), denims, cold-weather garments, shirts, and hats (including a special line of Stetsons made exclusively for Shepler's). It also offers custom-made chaps, a few saddles, a small number of horse supplies, bits, spurs, farrier equipment, and miscellaneous rodeo gear. Shepler's, Inc., P.O. Box 202, Wichita, Kansas 67201.

The Smith-Worthington Saddlery Co. started making saddles in 1794, and the Hartford, Connecticut, firm continues to produce products for horsemen English and Western, sold through tack shops around the country. Its 72-page catalog features a custom-made Smith-Worthington Forward Seat as well as Equitation and Dressage saddles (from $435 to $598) and its own ⅜-inch-round "Thoroughbred IV" bridle (about $88). The catalog also features Argentine Forward Seat saddles from Rossi Caruso; Pleasure, Show, and Race harness and equipment; and Western saddles and equipment. For catalog write to The Smith-Worthington Saddlery Co., Hartford, Connecticut (the catalog gives no street address or ZIP code).

In its small (47-page) but well-stocked catalog, Tanbark is especially strong on bandages, boots, and harness-racing equipment. It also carries a large selection of driving bits in addition to the usual assortment of English bits. Bartley & Lloyd Corporation, 1251 Linda Street, Rocky River, Ohio 44116.

This 156-page catalog ($1) emphasizes Western roping and barrel-racing saddles along with several Arabian Show Saddles and Monte Foreman Balanced Ride Saddles. Prices range from $350 to $550, with a few items slightly less or more. Bridles, breastplates, cinches, bits, halters, and other closely related equipment make up much of the remainder of the catalog. Tex Tan Western Leather Co., Box 711, Yoakum, Texas 77995.

Although we've not seen catalogs from the following firms (alas! some places failed to answer our inquiries), they have all been highly recommended:

Bona Allen Saddle & Leather Co.
P.O. Box 121
Sweet Home, Texas 77987

Fallis Saddlery
Star Route, Box 34
Elbert, Colorado 80106

Frost Tack and Pack Co.
Bellvue, Colorado 80512

Lehman's
111 South Flores Street
San Antonio, Texas 78214

Luskey's Western Stores
101 North Houston Street
Fort Worth, Texas 76102

Meyers Inc.
175 East Main Street
Lexington, Kentucky 40507

Miller Stockman
Box 5407
Denver, Colorado 80217

Pair's Saddlery
1008 South Loop
Stephenville, Texas 76401

Ralph Shimon
Route 1, Box 79
Brush, Colorado 80723

Visalia Stock Saddle Co.
3740 Castro Valley Boulevard
Castro Valley, California 94546

Wholesale Horse Equipment
3047 West Valley Boulevard
Alhambra, California 91802

INDEX

abdomen, examination of, 67
actinomycosis, 83
action chains, 151–52
acupuncture, 101
African trypanosomiasis, 83
age, teeth and, 3–4
AGID test, 83
Agriculture Dept., U.S., 83
Aguilar, Antonio, 117
Aiken jump, 191
Albino, 12
alfalfa, 45–46
alkali disease, 50
alleyways, in stable, 31–32
aluminum shoes, 61
American Association of Equine
    Practitioners, 106
American breeds, 10–13
American Camping Association,
    226
American Driving Society, 214
American Horse Protection
    Association, 237
American Horse Show Association,
    107, 193, 196
American Saddle Horse, 10, 151,
    193
amino acids, 43
Amsinckia intermedia, 49
Andalusian, 12
Anemia, worms and, 78
    see also Equine infectious
        anemia
Animal Welfare Act, 237
ankle-action chains, 151–52
ankle boots, 153
ankle rattlers, 151
Anoplocephala perfoliata, 80
anthrax, 83
anti-inflammatory agents, 95
Antiphlogistine, 96
Appaloosa 11
apparel, 155–88
    buying of, 185–86
    history of, 155–57
    see also boots; hats; riding
        coats, etc.
Arabian costume classes, 188
Arabians, 11
arenas, 35–36
armas, 168
arthritis, 92
ascarids, 79
asses, 15
Astragalus, 50
auctions, 4–5
Australian cheeker, 127
avocadoes, toxicity of, 50
Azium (dexamethasone), 95
azoturia, 48, 68

back, examination of, 67
bad habits, 69
balling gun, 99
bandages, 98–100, 153–54
bandanas, 157, 170–71
barbed-wire fence, 39
bareback pad, 138
barns, as stables, 22, 34–35
barrienspringer events, 192
Bartley & Lloyd Corp., 243
Bashkir, 12
Basuto, 15
bay (color designation), 13
bedding, 51–52
behavior, health and, 67
Belgian, 12
bell boots, 153
Bermuda grass, 46
Beval Saddlery, Ltd., 241
billets, 141
bishoping, 4
bit and bradoon, 115–16
bit holder, 127
bitless bridle, 121–22

bits, 112–19
    driving, 114
    pressure points in, 113
    supplements to, 124–27
    types of, 113, 116–17
bitting harness, 151
blacksmithing, 60–65
blankets, 149–50
bleeding, 87–88
blind staggers, 81
blistering, 96–97
Blue Ribbon Leather Co., Inc., 241
body roller, 151
bog spavin, 94
bonecloth, 173
bone spavin, 94
boot bags, 164
boot hooks, 164
boot jacks, 164
boots (for horses), 153–54
boots (riding), 157–64
    custom-made, 160, 162
    manufacturers of, 163
    polishing of, 163
    waterproof, 159–60
    wear and care of, 161–63
boot trees, 161, 164
boredom, 115–16
borium shoes, 60–61
bosal, of hackamore bridle, 121–22
bracken, 50
braided mane, 58
bran, 47, 68
breastplates, 139
breeches, 164–67
breeching, breast collar and, 147–
    148
breed associations, 10–15
breeders, 4
breeding, of mare, 107–11
breeds
    divisions of, 193
    magazines on, 236
bridle, 119–22
    bitless, 122
    double, 120
    prices of, 122
    single, 120
    Weymouth, 120
bridle hook, 32
bristle grass, 50
bromegrass, 46
bronc saddle, 135
broodmare, 109
brucellosis, 83
bruises and fractures, 88–91
brushes, 54
Bucephalus, 37
buckle, 123
buckle guard, 140
buckskin (color designation), 13
buckthorn, 49
buildings, types of for stables, 22–
    23
bulldogging, 201
bursitis, 91
Butazolidin (phenylbutazone or
    "bute"), 95, 106–07

cactus cloth, 55
calf roping, 201
California reins, 123
cambendazole, 80
canker, 91
capped elbow or knee, 93
Caprilli system, 128
Carleton, Martha, 39
carpitis, 93
Carroll, Jack, 241
Carroll Saddle Co., 241
catalogs, 241–43
Catcott, E. J., 94
cavalletti, 37
cavalry twill, 165

caveson, lunging, 150
Centaurea solstitialis, 50
chain-link fences, 38
chain twitch, 103
Chambon martingale, 125
chaparejos, 168
chaparro, 168
chaps, 157, 167–69
chaquetas, 174
cheekpieces, 118–19
chemical restraint, 104–05
chewing disease, 50
Chicksaw, 13
cirrhosis, from poisonous plants,
    49
Cleveland Bay, 11
clippers and clipping, 55, 58–59
Clostridium tetani, 82
clover, 45–46
Clydesdale, 12
coats, riding, 172–75
cob, 15
coccidiomycosis, 83
Coggins tests, 70, 74, 83, 108
Coke, William, 177
cold packs, 95
colic, 43, 86
colors and markings, 1–2
colt come-along, 145
combined training, 205–06
concentrated foods, 47
conformation, 6
Connell, Ed, 241
Connemara breed, 12
constipation, 47, 86
contracted heels, 91
corn silage, 46
corticosteroids, 95
coughing, 85
counterirritants, 75, 97
cowboy boots, 160
cowboy hats, 179
Craterostomum, 79
cribbing, 29
crossbred, 14
cross-country driving, 215
Crotalaria sagittalis, 49
Crotalaria spectabilis, 49
culls, 4
curb bit, 115
curb chains, 115
currycomb, 54
Cyanthostomum, 79
Cylicobrachytus, 79

dally roping, 184
Datura, 50
dealers, 5
De Luxe Saddling Co., 241
denim, for riding wear, 155, 166,
    174
dental equipment, 75
depressants, 107
Depromedrol, 95
diarrhea, 86
diathiazine iodide, 79
dichlorvos, 79–80
diet, see nutrition
diseases, 75, 83, 105–11
distance riding, 217
Dolensek, Emil P., 76–77
donkeys, 15
doping, 106–07
Draschia megastoma, 79
dressage, 198–201
    apparel for, 187
    saddle for, 130
    whip for, 181
dress requirements, 186–88
    see also apparel
driving, 211–17
    dress requirements for, 188
driving bit, 114
driving show, 214
drugs, misuse of, 106–07
duck twill, 166
"dude," origin of term, 156
dude ranching, 225–26
dungarees, 166

ear clippers, 59
ears
    care of, 89–90
    inspection of, 66–67
East Bulgarian, 15
Eastern equine encephalitis, 81, 83
easy boots, 62
Eiser's, Inc., 241
electric fences, 39
emasculator, 107
encephalitis, equine, 81
endurance ride, 217
English, Mary Dee, 222
English pleasure, dress
    requirements for, 187
English saddle, 128–31
English spurs, 182–83
English vest, 171
enteritis, 49
epiphysitis, 93
equestrian activities, 189–223
equestrian statues, rules for, 223
equestrian vacations, 224–35
equine encephalitis, 81, 83
equine humane movements, 237–
    238
equine infectious anemia, 74, 82
    Coggins test for, 82–84
equine influenza, 81
Equiproxen, 95
equitation saddle, 134
estrus, 108
examinations, 65–67
exercise, 41, 48, 68–70
extension leather, 142
eyes
    care of, 89–90
    inspection of, 66
eyewash, 89

farrier, 60–65
feeding, 42–50
    frequency of, 42
    health and, 68
    problems in, 41
feeds, pelleted, 42
    see also food
feet, see foot
fences, 37–39
fern, toxicity of, 50
fetlock, swelling of, 92
fetlock support socks, 100
fiador, 121
fiddleneck, 49
field boots, 159
field keeping, 17–18
fireweed, 49
firing, surgical, 96
Five-Gaited Saddle Horse, 58, 153,
    193
Fluvan vaccine, 81
fly whisks, 181
foal, raising of, 110–11
Foal-Lac, 110
food
    basic components of, 43
    recommended daily rations of,
        47
    refusal of, 85
    storage life of, 43
    types of, 45–48
    volume measure for, 48
    see also feeding; feeds
food concentrates, 47
food manger, 30
foot
    balancing of, 60
    cleaning of, 54–55
    picking up, 54–55, 103
foot and leg problems, 90–98, 153
foot rot, 69
forage, 45
forequarters, shape of, 6
forward-seat saddle, 129–30
foul-weather gear, 174–75
founder, 43, 45, 92
four-in-hand driving, 213
fox hunting, 174, 207–11
fractures and bruises, 88–89
frog, cleaning of, 60
Future Farmers of America, 238

gag bit, 114
gag bridle, 120
Galiceno, 13
gall cure, 111
Galvayne's groove, 3
garters, 160, 164
garter straps, 159
gelding, 105–07
girths, 140–41
glanders, 83
Gleckner, W. W. & Sons Co., 241
gloves, 175–77
goggles, 183–84
gonitis, 94
Gotland, 13
grade horses, 15
Graham, Christine, 202
Graham, W. Reid, 202
grain mix, for breeding stock, 47
grains, feeding of, 48
grasses, types of, 45–46
grazing, 42
    health and, 68
grooming, 41, 53–59
    equipment for, 54–55
grooming apron, 184
groundsel, 49
gymkhanas, 211

Habronema, 79
hackamore bit; 117
hackamore bridle, 121
hackamore noseband, 122
Hackney, 151
Haflinger, 15
hair ropes, 184
Half-Arabian Anglo-Arab, 14
half-breed bit, 115
Half Quarter Horse, 14
Half Saddlebred, 14
Half-Thoroughbred, 15
halter, 102–03, 144–45
halter hook, 32
Hamilton Travel Service Inc., 235
Hamley's, 241
harness, 146–48
harness division, 193
hats, 177–80
hay
    dusty, 43
    food content of, 43
    health and, 68
    kinds of, 46–47
"hay bellies," 46
hay fever, 33
hayloft, in stable, 32–33
hay rack, 18, 30
head
    control of, 102–03
    shape of, 6
headstall, 126, 146
health
    signs of, 8–9
    stable construction and, 70
    see also food; horse, problems
        and treatment of
health chart, 66
health products, 71–73
heels, bruised, 91
hemorrhage, lameness and, 94
hindquarters, shape of, 6
hinny, 15
hippoharness, 104
histoplasmosis, 83
hobbles, 151–52
hocks, shape of, 6–7
hock support socks, 100
hoof (hooves)
    cleaning of, 54–55
    cracks in, 90–91
    shoeing of, 60–61
hoof blackener, 56
hoof dressings and conditioners, 69
hoof packing, 69
hoof pick, 54–55
horse
    age of, 3–4
    anatomy of, 6–7
    basic needs of, 40–41
    bored, 69

colors of, 1–2
condition of, 8–9
diseases transmitted to humans
    by, 83
examination of, 65–71
exercise for, 41
experience of, 4
feed for, see feeding
healthy, 8–9, 65
ill-tempered, 41
individual assessment of, 6–9
medical problems of, 105–11
minimum nutritional
    requirements for, 43–44
overworking of, 43, 48
painting of, 222–23
pet for, 50
photographing of, 221–22
price of, 9–10
problems and treatment for, 84–
    111
purchase of, 9
refusal to eat and drink, 85
selection of, 1–15
sex of, 3
size of, 2
soundness in, 65–67
state laws for protection of, 237–
    238
testing of, 7–8
toys for, 50
tubing of, 77
tying of, 28
unhealthy, 8, 105–11
vacuum cleaner for, 53
veterinary medicine for, 105–11
water for, see water
horse blankets, 149
horse doping, 106–07
horse feeder, 18, 30
Horse of the Americas, 13
horse products, companies
    specializing in, 71–72
horseshoeing, 60–64
horseshoe stallion bit, 119
horse show(s), 189–98
    divisions of, 190–93
    list of, 194–95
    officials of, 196–98
    ribbons, trophies and prizes in,
        196
horse stalls, see stalls
horse transportation, 218–20
horse vacuum cleaner, 53
horse words, 240
hot-walkers, 51
hunt cap, 177
hunter classes, 190
hunter-seat equitation,
    dress for, 187
hunting, dress for, 186–87
hunting boots, 158
hunting coats, 173
hunting horns, 184
hunting whip, 181

ice creepers, 61
Incitatus (Caligula's horse), 37
Indian horse, 13
infectious diseases, 70, 83
inflammation, 75
    lameness and, 94–95
infrared heaters, 33
injections, 100–01
injuries, 87
insurance, 10
Intercollegiate Horse Show
    Association, 239–40
internal parasites, 77–80
    see also worms

jackass, 15
Japanese encephalitis, 81
jar calk, 60
jeans, 166–67
jenny, 15
jockey bats, 181
jockey boots, 158
Jockey Club, 108
jockey lifts, 162
jockey saddle, 130

jodhpur boots, 160
jodhpur garters, 168
jodhpurs, 166, 168
joint ownership, 10
jumping bats, 180
jumping classes, 190–91

Kauffman, H. and Sons, 242
Kelso, 106
Kentucky bluegrass, 45–46
Kentucky pants, 166
keratoma, 91
Knabstrup, 15
knee tendons, ruptured, 93
Knoud, M. J., 168, 242

lameness, 75, 89
    bursitis and, 92
    diagnosis of, 90
    hemorrhage and, 94
    treatments for, 94–98
laminitis, 43, 92
lariat or lasso, 184
lateral cartilage necrosis, 92
Lathyrus, 50
latigo, 141
lead ropes, 146
leather, care of, 162
leather boots, 158–59
leather chaps, 157
leg bandages, 98–99
leggins, 160, 164, 167–68
legs
    examination of, 67
    painting of, 96
    problems associated with, 153
    shape of, 6, 8–9
leptospirosis, 83, 89
Levi's, 166–67
liniments, 75, 88
linseed meal, 47
Lipizzaner, 13
listeriosis, 83
liver, diseases of, 49
Liverpool jump, 191
lockjaw, 82
lunging equipment, 146, 150
lupines, toxic, 50
lying down, as symptom, 86

McClellan saddle, 133
MacIntosh, Charles, 175
macintosh coat, 174
Mackay-Smith, Matthew, 90
McPherson speculum, 75
McWilliams, Catherine, 37, 205,
    238–39
magazines and periodicals, 236–37
malnutrition, 41
    see also food; nutrition
man, diseases shared with horses,
    83
mane comb, 55
mane styling, 56–58
manger, food, 30
mare
    breeding of, 107–10
    exercise for, 50
    pregnancy and foaling of, 109
Market Harborough, 125
markings, 2
martingales, 125–26
mebendazole, 79–80
mechanical bit, 117
medical problems, 105–11
medicine, kinds of, 98–100
medicine bit, 119
medicine chest, for stable, 70–71
meliodosis, 83
Melton cloth, 173
meperidine hydrochloride, 105
Miller's Harness Co., 242
mineral blocks, 18
minerals, need for, 45
Missouri Fox Trotting Horse, 13
Monday-morning sickness, 48, 68
moon blindness, 89
Morab, 15
Morgan, 11, 193
Morris, George, 185
movement, assessment of, 7–8

muckheap, "mucking out" and, 52
mud brush, 54
mules, 15
mustangs, 13–14

Napoleon boot, 157, 160
narcotics, 105
National Horse Show, 214
navicular disease, 91
neck, examination of, 67
neck ropes, 146
neckwear, 169–71
Nerium oleander, 49
New Forest, 15
Newmarket boots, 159
nicotine poisoning, 50
nose
    examination of, 66
    tubing of, 100
nosebands, 124
nutrition, 43–45
    health and, 68
    minimum requirements for, 44
    see also food

oats, 47
O'Dea, Joseph, 107
Oesophagodontus, 79
oleander leaves, toxicity
    of, 49–50
organizations and associations,
    236–240
osselets, 92
osteoarthritis, 92–93
osteum, 96
outdoor rings, 36
overfeeding, 68
overworking, 43, 48
Oxyuris equi, 79

packsaddle, 138
pack tripping, 225–26
paddock boot, 160
painkillers, 95
Palomino, 11
pants, types of, 164–67
Parascaris equorum, 79
parasites, in "newcomer," 70, 75–
    80
    see also worming; worms
part-blooded horse, 15
Paso Fino, 15
Pasteurella organisms, 83
pasture keeping, 17
pasture grass, 45
patella, upward fixation of, 94
peanut hulls, as bedding, 52
peat moss, as bedding, 52
pedal osteitis, 91
Pelham bit, 116–17
Percheron, 12
periodicals, 237
Peruvian Paso, 13, 15
pets, need for, 50
phenothiazine, 79–80
phenylbutazone, 107
Phlogo remedy, 96
pills, administration of, 99
pin firing, 97
pinworms, 79
piperazine, 79–80
planter's hats, 179
podotrochleosis, 91
poisonous plants, 48–50
pole buildings, for horse farms, 24
polo, 202–04
    dress requirements for, 187–88
polo boots, 160
polo chaps, 167
polo gloves, 177
polo helmet, 178
polo whips, 181
ponchos, 175
ponies, 14–15
pony clubs, 238–39
Pony of the Americas, 12
post-and-rail jumps, 38, 191
Poteriostomum, 79
Potts Longhorn Leather, 242
poultices, 96
prairie grass, 46

preventive care, 67–84
private sales, 5
promazine, 75
protective equipment, 152–54
proteins, 43
Pteridium, 50
puissance walls, 190–92
pullover shirts, 169
pulse, taking of, 66
puttees, 160
pyrantel, 79–80
pyramidal disease, 92

quarantine, 70
Quarter Horse, 11
quirt, 181
quittor, 92

rabies, 81–82
racehorses, saliva test for, 106–07
racing bandages, 100
rack gait, 13
radio, in stall, 50
ragwort, 49
rain gear, 175–76
rain gloves, 186
Rangerbred, 14
rattleweed, 49
reata, 184
rectal thermometer, 65
Reddick, Kate, 15
reins, types of, 123
Remington, Frederick, 157
remuda, 17
reserpine, 105
respiration, 65
restraint, methods of, 101–05
rhinopneumonitis, 82, 109
ribbons and trophies, of horse
    shows, 196
Ricinus communis, 49
riding, gaits in, 70
riding aprons, 174
riding caps, 179
riding coats, 172–73
    materials for, 175
riding gloves, 176–77
riding resorts, 226
riding shirts, 169
riding to hounds, see fox hunting
rigging, of saddles, 137–38
ringbone, 92
rings, 35–36
ringworm, 69, 83
Robertson, William G., 220
rodeo, 201–02
Rodeo Cowboys Association, 201
rolling, as symptom, 86
rope burns, 103
ropes, types of, 184
Rosa multiflora, 39
roughage, 46–47
rowels, 182–83
rubber boots, 160
Ryon's Saddle & Ranch Supplies,
    Inc., 242

saddle(s), 127–38
    all-purpose, 131
    bronc, 134–35
    dressage, 130
    English, 128–31
    equitation, 134
    forward-seat, 130
    general-purpose, 134
    jockey, 130
    military, 132–33
    polo, 131
    proper fit of, 131
    rigging of, 137–38
    roping, 134
    saddle-seat, 130
    specifications for, 135
    supplements to, 139–44
    Western, 133–38
saddle brackets, 33
saddle bronc riding, 201
saddle-horse division, 193
saddle leather, 127
saddle pack bags, 138
saddle pads, 148–49

saddle rack, 33
saddle-seat classes, 187
saddle-seat suits, 173
saddletrees, 136
sales, private, 5
saliva test, 106–07
salt blocks, 18
sarcocystitis, 83
sawdust, 52
Schistosoma japonicum, 83
screw twitch, 103
Sears, Roebuck & Co., 243
selenium poisoning, 50
Senecio jacobaea, 49
Serpasil, 105
sesamoiditis, 93
Sewell, Anna, 41, 127, 145
shackles, 151, 188
sheds and shelters, 18–19
Shepler's, Inc., 243
Shetland pony, 12, 59
shin, bucked or sore, 93
Shire, 12
shirts, 169
shivering, 86
shoeing, see horseshoeing
shoulder joint, osteoarthritis of, 93
"shoulder sweeney," 94
sick horses, isolation of, 70
    see also medical problems
sidebones, 92
sidesaddle, 131–32
Sigler's method, 104
silage, 46–47
skin, eruptions of, 87
sleeping sickness, 81
slickers, 175
Smith-Worthington Saddlery Co.,
    243
snaffle bit, 114
snowproofing, 154
sole, puncture wounds of, 91
sombreros, 179
sorghum grains, 47
soundness, indications of, 65–67
soybean meal, 47
spade bit, 117
Spanish Barb breed, 14
Spanish Mustang, 14
spavin, 94
Spherophorus necrophorus, 91
splints, 93
springhalt, 94
spurs, 157, 182–83
stable medicine chest, 70
stable rubber, 55
stables, 19–20
    alleyways in, 31–32
    builders of, 23
    cleaning of, 68
    construction of, 70
    designs for, 21
    doors of, 28–29
    electricity for, 25–26
    environment of, 24–26
    feed room of, 32
    fire prevention, checklist for, 22
    flooring of, 25
    grooming area in, 34
    hayloft for, 32–33
    large-scale, 34–35
    lighting for, 24
    management of, 40–46, 68–70
    manure disposal in, 34
    materials for, 20–22
    money-saving tips for, 42
    organizing of, 26–35
    stalls for, 27–31
    tack rooms for, 33–34
    temperature and humidity of, 24
    tool storage in, 34
    types of, 22–24
    water for, 25–26
stabling, principles of, 18–39
stagecoach route, 214
stall(s)
    bedding for, 51
    box, 27
    cleaning of, 68
    cross ties in, 31
    food manger for, 30

portable, 27
    tying horse in, 28
    water trough or bucket for, 31
    wood for, 28–30
    see also stable
stallion, gelding of, 105–06
stallion barns, 35
stall screens, 30
Standardbred, 11
Stanton, Sarijane, 199
Staphylococcus organisms, 83
Stazdry bedding, 52
Stetson hat, 179
sticks, types of, 180–82
stifle joint, inflammation of, 94
stimulants, 107
"stinking Willie" plant, 49
stirrup, 142–44, 157
stirrup leathers, 141–42
stomachache, 43, 71
stomach tubing, 99–100
stomach worms, 79
stool, examination of, 67
strains and sprains, 88
strangles, 82
straw, 47, 52
Streptococcus equi, 82
string gloves, 175
stringhalt, 94
strongyles, 78–79
Strongyloides, 79
Strongylus vulgaris, 78
Suffolk, 12
summer camps, 226–27
support socks, 100
surcingles, 149, 151
surgery, forms of, 96
swamp fever, 70
    see also equine infectious
    anemia
sweating
    clipping and, 58
    excessive, 86
sweat scraper, 55
"sweet feed," 48
swivel snap, 123
symptoms and treatment, 84–91,
    105–11
syringes, 100–01

tack, 112–54
    cleaning of, 154
    defined, 112
    for specialized training, 150–52
tack room, 33
tack trunk, 33
tail set, 151
tail styling, 56–58
tandem driving, 213
tapeworms, 79–80
tarweed, 49
Taylor, Louis, 126
teeth
    as age indicators, 3
    healthy, 67
temperature, body, 67
tendinitis, 93
tendons, contracted or ruptured,
    93
tendon support socks, 100
Tennessee Walking Horse, 11, 14,
    58, 151, 193, 237
tetanus, 82
Tetramisole, 80
Tex Tan Western Leather Co., 243
thermometer, rectal, 65
Thiabendazole, 80
Thoroughbred, 11
Thoroughbred Racing and
    Protective Bureau, 106
thoroughpin, 94
Three-Gaited Horse, 193
thrush, 69, 91
tie-downs, 125-26
timothy, 46
tongue tie, 127
top hats, 178, 180
trailers, 218–19
trail riding, dress for, 188
Trakehner, 14
tranquilizers, 9, 104–5, 107

Trapani, Jerry, 60–64
Traveller (Lee's horse), 37
Trichlorfon, 79–80
Trichostrongylus axei, 79
trochanteric bursitis, 93
Trottingbred pony, 14
troughs, 18
tuberculosis, bovine, 83
tubing, 99–100
    worming and, 77–78
tularemia, 83
twitch, 103

United States Polo Association,
    203
urine examination, 67, 106–07
utility scale, 32

vacations, equestrian, 224–35
vaccinations, 81–82
vacuum cleaner, 53
vaquero, influence of, 156
Velcro tapes, 100
vests, 171–72
veterinarian
    horse show and, 197
    need for, 4, 71, 74–75
    records for, 67
veterinary books, 111
veterinary medicine
    problems of, 105–11
    schools and colleges of, 76–77
veterinary preparations, 71–72
viral arteritis, 82
viral diseases, 83
vitamins, 44, 47, 95
Vladimir Heavy Draft, 15
Vogel, Hank, 158

walking, cooling by, 70
walking disease, 49
Walking Pony, 14
Walla Walla walking disease, 49
water
    need for, 31, 41–45
    refusal of, 85
water bucket, 31
water pump, 191
water trough, 31
water witch, 26
Wellington boot, 157, 160
Welsh Mountain Pony, 12
Western boots, 160–61
Western division, 193
Western equine encephalitis, 81,
    83
Western hats, 179–80
Western pleasure, dress for, 188
Western riding bats, 181
Western saddles, 133–38
Western shirts, 169
Western spurs, 183
Western vests, 171
Weymouth bridle, 120
wheat bran, 47
whips, 180–82
whirlbone lameness, 93
"white socks" spray, 56
wild pea, 49
Williamson, Charles, 241
windgalls, 92
windpuffs, 92
wire cutters, 184–85
wire-mesh fence, 38
wood, chewing damage to, 29
wood shavings, for bedding, 52
wool hats, 179
worming, 75, 80
worms
    symptoms of, 76
    types of, 78–80
wounds, care of, 86–88

yellow burr weed, 49
yellow star thistle, 50
Young, John Richard, 118, 141
Younker, Lucas, 73, 101